ESTHER

EVANGELICAL EXEGETICAL COMMENTARY

ESTHER

Anthony J. Tomasino

LEXHAM
ACADEMIC

Esther
Evangelical Exegetical Commentary

Lexham Academic, an imprint of Lexham Press
1313 Commercial St., Bellingham, WA 98225
LexhamPress.com

English quotations from Esther in this commentary are the author's own translation.

Unless otherwise indicated, quotations from biblical books other than Esther are from the Lexham English Bible (LEB). Copyright 2013 Lexham Press.

ISBN 9781577995739

Lexham Editorial Team: Claire Brubaker, Lynnea Fraser, Elliot Ritzema
Cover Design: Brittany Schrock
Typesetting: ProjectLuz.com

25 26 27 28 29 30 / IN / 12 11 10 9 8 7 6 5 4

To Cordelia

Contents

Commentary Editors		xiii
Acknowledgments		ix
Editors' Preface		xi
Abbreviations		xiii
Introduction		1
1:1–2	The Introduction	136
1:3–2:23	The Rise of Esther and Mordecai	144
3:1–4:17	The Threat to the Jews	210
5:1–7:10	The Plot Reversed	253
8:1–9:32	The Triumph of the Jews	304
10:1–3	The Greatness of Xerxes and Mordecai	358
List of Foreign and Technical Words		367
General Bibliography		369
Index of Biblical Verses		381

Commentary Editors

General Editor
H. Wayne House

Old Testament Editor
William D. Barrick

Assistant Old Testament Editor
JoAnna M. Hoyt

New Testament Editor
W. Hall Harris

Assistant New Testament Editor
Andrew W. Pitts

Acknowledgments

To my many friends, colleagues, and students who have undertaken to read portions of this commentary in its earlier incarnations, I wish to express my deepest gratitude. Your comments, criticisms, and encouragement have been invaluable. My fondest thoughts of appreciation go to my late colleague Dr. Gene Carpenter (of blessed memory), who was one of my first Old Testament teachers. It was he who got me involved in this project. I also would like to express my thanks to our editor, Dr. Bill Barrick, for catching many errors and patiently correcting my formatting mistakes. Any errors that remain, of course, are my own responsibility. Most of all, I must thank my wife, Cordelia, for enduring my infatuation with the beautiful Jewish Queen Esther for the last two years. It is to her that this volume is lovingly dedicated.

—Anthony J. Tomasino

Editors' Preface

We are happy to present the Evangelical Exegetical Commentary (EEC) series on the Bible. Though there are many excellent commentaries that have been produced in recent years, the EEC is a needed addition for scholars, pastors, and students of the Bible. As the title of the series indicates, the authors of this series are committed to both the evangelical faith and a careful exegesis of the biblical text. Each of the authors affirms historic, orthodox Christianity and the inspiration and inerrancy of the Holy Scriptures. In this series, the biblical books are studied with the tested tools of biblical scholarship, keeping in mind that these books, produced by human authors, come from the very mouth of God (2 Tim 3:16). The EEC reflects the important interpretative principles of the Reformation, while utilizing historical-grammatical and contextual interpretative methods.

Each part of the biblical text—as reflected in the original reading—has something to teach us about God, his world, and how we should relate to him and to others. Thus in this series, each biblical unit is analyzed and interpreted. Then recommendations for application to everyday life and biblical theology are offered. This last step will aid pastors and teachers in their ministry of God's Word.

We hope that you will have greater appreciation for the Word of God and the ability to better share it because of reading the EEC.

For us, the EEC is an offering of praise to the great Triune God, who is our Creator, Savior, and Sustainer, and who, through Jesus the Messiah and Lord, dwelled among humanity to bring us salvation and gifts of His grace.

ὅτι ἐξ αὐτοῦ καὶ δι' αὐτοῦ καὶ εἰς αὐτὸν τὰ πάντα·
αὐτῷ ἡ δόξα εἰς τοὺς αἰῶνας, ἀμήν. (Rom 11:36)

Because out of him and through him and unto him are all things; To him be the glory unto all the ages, amen. (Rom 11:36)

H. Wayne House, General Editor

William D. Barrick, Old Testament Editor

JoAnna M. Hoyt, Assistant Old Testament Editor

W. Hall Harris, New Testament Editor

Andrew W. Pitts, New Testament Editor

Abbreviations

3	third person
abs.	absolute
ACCS	Ancient Christian Commentary on Scripture
Add Esth	Additions to Esther
adj.	adjective/adjectival
adv.	adverb/adverbial
Ag. Ap.	Josephus, *Against Apion*
AJSL	*American Journal of Semitic Languages and Literature*
AJT	*Asia Journal of Theology*
ANE	Ancient Near East(ern)
ANEP	J. B. Pritchard, ed., *Ancient Near East in Pictures*
ANET	J. B. Pritchard, ed., *Ancient Near Eastern Texts Relating to the Old Testament*, 3rd ed.
Ant.	Josephus, *Antiquities of the Jews*
ASTI	*Annual of the Swedish Theological Institute*
ASV	American Standard Version
AT	Alpha Text
ATD	Das Alte Testament Deutsche
AUSS	*Andrews University Seminary Studies*
AYB	Anchor Yale Bible
AYBD	D. N. Freedman, ed., *The Anchor Yale Bible Dictionary*
BA	*Biblical Archaeologist*
BCBC	Believer's Church Bible Commentary
BDB	F. Brown, S. R. Driver, and C. A. Briggs, *Hebrew and English Lexicon of the Old Testament*
BIOSCS	*Bulletin of the International Organization for Septuagint and Cognate Studies*
BBR	*Bulletin for Biblical Research*
BHRG	Christo H. van der Merwe et al., *A Biblical Hebrew Reference Grammar*
BHS	*Biblia Hebraica Stuttgartensia*
BJRL	*Bulletin of the John Rylands University Library of Manchester*
BKAT	M. Noth and H. W. Wolff, eds., *Biblischer Kommentar, Altes Testament*

BN	*Biblische Notizen*
BR	*Biblical Research*
BRev	*Bible Review*
BSac	*Bibliotheca Sacra*
BSOAS	*Bulletin of the School of Oriental and African Studies*
BT	*The Bible Translator*
BTC	Brazos Theological Commentary
BZ	*Biblische Zeitschrift*
ca.	circa
CANE	J. Sasson, *Civilizations of the Ancient Near East*. 4 vols.
CBQ	*Catholic Biblical Quarterly*
CEB	Common English Bible
CEV	Contemporary English Version
chap(s).	chapter(s)
CH	Code of Hammurabi
CHI	I. Gershevitch, ed., *The Cambridge History of Iran*
CJB	Complete Jewish Bible
conj.	conjunction
consec.	consecutive.
const.	construct
Cyr.	Xenophon, *Cyropaedia*
DBI	*Dictionary of Biblical Imagery*
dittogr.	dittography
DSD	*Dead Sea Discoveries*
DSS	Dead Sea Scrolls
EDB	*Eerdmans Dictionary of the Bible*
Eng.	English translation
Esth. Rab.	*Esther Rabbah*
ESV	English Standard Version
EvQ	*Evangelical Quarterly*
ExpTim	*Expository Times*
fem., f.	feminine
FOTL	Forms of the Old Testament Literature
gen.	genitive
Geog.	Strabo, *Geography*
GKC	E. Kautzsch, ed., *Gesenius' Hebrew Grammar*, trans. A. E. Cowley, 2nd ed.
GNT	Good News Translation
haplogr.	haplography
HAT	Handbuch zum Alten Testament
Hist.	Herodotus, *Histories*
Hist. eccl.	Eusebius, *Ecclesiastical History*

HTR	*Harvard Theological Review*
HUCA	*Hebrew Union College Annual*
IB	*Interpreter's Bible*
IBC	Interpretation: A Bible Commentary for Teaching and Preaching
IBHS	B. K. Waltke and M. P. O'Connor, *Introduction to Biblical Hebrew Syntax*
ICC	International Critical Commentary
inf.	infinitive
ITC	International Theological Commentary
JANES	*Journal of the Ancient Near Eastern Society*
JB	Jerusalem Bible
JBL	*Journal of Biblical Literature*
JCS	*Journal of Cuneiform Studies*
JETS	*Journal of the Evangelical Theological Society*
JJS	*Journal of Jewish Studies*
JNES	*Journal of Near Eastern Studies*
JQR	*Jewish Quarterly Review*
JR	*Journal of Religion*
JRAS	*Journal of the Royal Asiatic Society*
JSOT	*Journal for the Study of the Old Testament*
JSOTSup	Journal for the Study of the Old Testament: Supplement Series
JSS	*Journal of Semitic Studies*
JTS	*Journal of Theological Studies*
juss.	jussive
KAT	Kommentar zum Alten Testament
KJV	King James Version
KJ21	21st Century King James Version
LB	*Linguistica Biblica*
lit.	literally
LXX	Septuagint
masc., m.	masculine
MH	Mishnaic Hebrew
MSS	manuscripts
MT	Masoretic Text
NAB	New American Bible
NAC	New American Commentary
NASB	New American Standard Bible
NAV	New American Version
NBD	D. R. W. Wood and I. Howard Marshall, eds., *New Bible Dictionary,* 3rd ed.

NCV	New Century Version
NIB	*The New Interpreter's Bible*
NIBC	New International Biblical Commentary
NIDOTTE	*New International Dictionary of Old Testament Theology and Exegesis*
NIV	New International Version
NIVAC	NIV Application Commentary
NJB	New Jerusalem Bible
NKJV	New King James Version
NLT	New Living Translation
NRSV	New Revised Standard Version
NT	New Testament
obj.	object
OEANE	E. Meyers, ed., *Oxford Encyclopedia of Archaeology in the Near East*
OL	Old Latin
OT	Old Testament
PAAJR	*Proceedings of the American Academy of Jewish Research*
par.	parallel(s)
pass.	passive
Phil	*Philologus*
prep.	Preposition
ptc.	participle
RB	*Revue Biblique*
ResQ	*Restoration Quarterly*
RevQ	*Revue de Qumran*
RH	*Review and Herald*
RHA	*Revue hittite et asianique*
RQ	*Römische Quartalschrift für christliche Altertumskunde und Kirchengeschichte*
RSV	Revised Standard Version
SBLDS	Society of Biblical Literature Dissertation Series
SBLSCS	Society of Biblical Literature Septuagint and Cognate Studies
SEA	*Svensk Exegetisk Arsbok*
sg.	singular
suf.	suffix
SwJT	*Southwestern Journal of Theology*
Syr.	Syriac
TDOT	*Theological Dictionary of the Old Testament*
Tg.	Targum
Tg. Esth I	*First Targum of Esther*
ThTo	*Theology Today*

TOTC	Tyndale Old Testament Commentaries
TWOT	R. L. Harris, et al., eds., *Theological Word Book of the Old Testament*
USQR	*Union Seminary Quarterly Review*
Vg.	Vulgate
VT	*Vetus Testamentum*
VTSup	Supplements to Vetus Testamentum
WBC	Word Biblical Commentary
WTJ	*Westminster Theological Journal*
WZKM	*Wiener Zeitschrift für die Kunde des Morgenlandes*
ZAW	*Zeitschrift für die alttestamentliche Wissenschaft*

Introduction

In his powerful memoir *Night*, Elie Wiesel tells of his experiences in a Nazi prison camp through the remembrances of a semi-fictional Jewish teenager named Eliezer. Wiesel's book is, in a sense, a chronicle, but it is also far more than that. It is his *Confessions*, his record of an emotional and spiritual descent into the maelstrom, precipitated by relentless, unfathomable evil. One of the most moving passages in the book appears in chapter 4, when Eliezer is forced to watch the hanging of a child. Wiesel writes,

> The SS seemed more preoccupied, more disturbed than usual. To hang a young boy in front of thousands of spectators was no light matter. The head of the camp read the verdict. All eyes were on the child. He was lividly pale, almost calm, biting his lips. The gallows threw its shadow over him. ...
>
> "Where is God? Where is He?" someone behind me asked.
>
> At a sign from the head of the camp, the three chairs tipped over. Total silence throughout the camp. On the horizon, the sun was setting.
>
> "Bare your heads!" yelled the head of the camp. His voice was raucous. We were weeping.
>
> "Cover your heads!"
>
> Then the march past began. The two adults were no longer alive. Their tongues hung swollen, blue-tinged. But the third rope was still moving; being so light, the child was still alive.
>
> For more than half an hour he stayed there, struggling between life and death, dying in slow agony under our eyes. And we had to look him full in the face. He was still alive when I passed in front of him. His tongue was still red, his eyes were not yet glazed. Behind me, I heard the same man asking:
>
> "Where is God now?"
>
> And I heard a voice within me answer him:
>
> "Where is He? Here He is—He is hanging here on this gallows."[1]

1. E. Wiesel, *Night* (New York: Bantam, 1983), 61–62.

Wiesel's character is obsessed with the idea that God seems either unwilling or unable to intervene on behalf of the concentration camp prisoners. Where is God in the midst of this suffering? How can He stand by and do nothing? Eliezer (whose name, significantly, means "God is [my] helper") struggles to come to terms with a God who seems to stand aloof in the face of the possible annihilation of his people.

It is no small irony that in this account of the most recent attempt to exterminate the Jewish people, we find a theme that echoes that of the first account of an attempted Jewish genocide. On the surface, the book of Esther and Wiesel's *Night* could hardly be more dissimilar. One is an almost comical romp; the other is almost unrelentingly dark. One ends with a joyful deliverance; the other with a deliverance, but little joy. And yet, in both accounts of dire threats to His people, God is remarkably absent. In the Heb. version of Esther, there are no overt miraculous interventions; there are no angelic messengers commissioning heroes to deliver their people; there are no references to answered prayers. Indeed, in this book, God is not mentioned at all, either by name or by allusion. For the readers of the book of Esther, like the characters in Wiesel's memoir, the compelling question inspired by the narrative is, "Where is God?" In the face of this first threat of *shoah*, why does the God of Israel hide Himself?

Like *Night,* the book of Esther also pivots on the scene of a hanging. For Wiesel, the gallows is a sign of despair, the final nail in God's coffin. But in Esther, it is not God who hangs on the gallows—it is the enemy of God's people, the wicked Haman. Though God is as invisible in this scene as in all the others of the book, Haman and all the enemies of the Jews learn that the God who may seem so distant is actually ready and able to defend His people. Though He is never seen, never apprehended by senses or even acknowledged in word, He is present and He is working. Indeed, we might see the entire book of Esther as a graphic illustration of Psa 115:2–3:

> Why do the nations say, "Where is their God?"
> But our God is in Heaven.
> Whatever pleases him, he does.[2]

In this work of remarkable literary artistry, the theme of divine providence is developed with profound erudition. As is sometimes the case in Scripture, the text's message is not conveyed explicitly through sermons or expositions, but implicitly through the remarkable coincidences and ironic reversals that can only be understood as manipulations by the hand of God.

2. Author's translation.

Synopsis

The story of Esther is familiar to many, having been popularized in Sunday school lessons, novels, and movies. It is set in the Persian city of Susa, where the Persian king Xerxes (in the Heb. text, Ahasuerus) had decided to throw a banquet for his nobles.[3] When the king was full of wine, he summoned his queen, Vashti, to come and display her beauty to his party guests. When the proud queen refused, Xerxes was nonplussed. Warned by his counselors that her example could result in a wave of insubordination among the women of his empire, Xerxes deposed the queen and issued an edict, so that all the men of the kingdom would be established as the heads of their households.

After the king's anger had abated, he recognized the need to replace Queen Vashti. Following the advice of his courtesans, Xerxes held a contest in which young maidens from throughout the empire were brought to Susa to compete for Vashti's position. Among the women brought to the court was a Jewish orphan named Esther. Advised by her cousin and guardian Mordecai not to reveal her ethnicity, she was enrolled into a yearlong program of cosmetics and purifications in preparation for her appearance before the king. Each woman was given only a night to impress Xerxes, but when Esther's turn came, she somehow beat out all her rivals and was named queen of Persia.

Mordecai was stationed at the city gates, from where he could periodically check on his cousin. It was there that he overheard of a plot by two of the king's eunuchs to assassinate the king. Mordecai told Esther, who took word of the plot to the king. When it was investigated and found true, the eunuchs were put to death. Mordecai's boon was recorded in the official annals of the empire.

Soon, however, a crisis arose. A villainous courtier named Haman noted that Mordecai refused to bow down before him when he passed through the gates. Haman felt insulted, but believed it was beneath his dignity to order the execution of a single nobody. Instead, Haman devised a scheme that would kill all the Jewish people. He approached Xerxes and informed him of the presence of an insubordinate race in the empire, a people who might incite rebellion. For the good of the empire, he recommended that the potential threat be eliminated. Almost nonchalantly, the king of Persia signed Haman's order to "destroy, kill, and annihilate" all the Jews within

---

3. In some modern commentaries, a transliteration of the Heb. is used in place of the more commonly known "Xerxes." While the Greek form Xerxes is not an especially accurate transliteration of the Persian name, it is widely accepted and recognized. Therefore, we will use the name "Xerxes" in this commentary.

his realm. Haman had cast lots (in Akkadian, *pur*) in order to determine the day on which the slaughter would occur, and concluded that it would take place on the thirteenth day of the twelfth month of the year. Couriers went throughout the empire carrying news of the fatal decree.

Mordecai, learning of the impending doom, urged Esther to speak to the king on behalf of her people. Esther summoned her courage, aware that appearing in the king's presence unbidden could result in death. But when she entered the throne room in her royal garb, the king's heart was softened toward her, and he invited her to present her request. Esther asked that the king and Haman would come to a banquet she had prepared for them. The king had Haman summoned, and they dined with the queen. Again, the king asked her to state her request. But Esther replied that she wanted the king and Haman to come to a banquet the next evening, and there she would make her petition known.

On leaving the banquet, with an invitation to dine with the king and queen the next night, Haman was filled with joy and a sense of his own importance. But when he saw Mordecai sitting in the gate, still refusing to do him obeisance, his anger burned. When Haman arrived home, he summoned his wife and friends to tell them of his good fortune. But then he added an account of Mordecai's insult, and how it galled him. Haman's wife and friends urged him to make an example of Mordecai by having a seventy-five-foot-tall pole erected in Susa and impaling the impudent Mordecai in the sight of the entire city.

That night, the king could not sleep, so he ordered the royal chronicles brought to his chamber and read to him. There, he was reminded of the incident of the foiled assassination. He inquired about what reward had been given to Mordecai. On hearing that none had been given, the king asked who was currently in the king's court. Haman had just arrived, impatient to speak to the king about the execution of Mordecai. The king ordered Haman brought inside, but before he could present his petition, the king asked his advice on what should be done for someone the king wished to honor. Haman, certain that there could be no one the king would wish to honor more than him, recommended a lavish display:

> For the man whom the king is pleased to honor, let them bring a royal robe that the king himself has worn, and a horse upon which the king has ridden, which has a royal crest placed on its head. Then let the robe and horse be placed in the charge of one of the king's most noble princes. Let them place the robe on the man whom the king is pleased to honor, and let them make him ride on the horse through the city streets, proclaiming before him, "Thus will be done for the man whom the king is pleased to honor!" (Esth 6:7–9)

The king was pleased with the counsel and ordered Haman, "Go and do all of that for Mordecai the Jew." The mortified courtier was ordered to lead his archenemy through the streets of Susa in splendor.

Haman was humiliated, and even his wife warned that it was futile for him to oppose one of the Jews. But just then, Haman was summoned to attend the queen's banquet. As they dined, the king once again asked for Esther's request. This time, she did not demur: "If I have found favor in your sight, O King, and if it seems good to the king, grant me my life at my request, and the life of my people, at my entreaty. For I and my people have been sold to be destroyed and slain and to perish." The king, unaware that his beloved queen was Jewish, demanded to know who had done such a deed. Esther revealed that it was none other than Haman. As the king rushed from the room to compose his thoughts, Haman threw himself upon the queen to beg for her life. But when the king re-entered the room and saw Haman accosting the queen, the king concluded that Haman was attacking her in his very presence. Haman's doom was assured. The king ordered him hanged on the pole he had erected for Mordecai.

Mordecai was given the office vacated by Haman, but the crisis was not yet past. According to the laws of the Medes and Persians, an official decree of the king could not be rescinded. So instead, a decree was issued allowing the Jews to assemble and arm themselves against any who would attack them. On the day when the Jews were to be destroyed, they instead rose up and attacked their enemies. Haman's sons, too, were executed and hanged. At Esther's request, the king granted the Jews yet another day of slaughter. Instead of being destroyed, the Jews ended up killing seventy-five thousand of those who opposed them.

So on the fourteenth and fifteenth of Adar, the Jews had a great celebration, which they called Purim, named after the lots cast by Haman. All the Jewish people were exhorted to keep the feast of Purim as a day of rejoicing, of gift-giving, and remembering the poor.

Historical Background

The book of Esther is set in the days of the Persian Empire, which lasted from 538 to 332 BC. These two centuries comprise one of the least-chronicled eras of Judaean history, situated as it is between the days of the Israelite monarchies and the well-documented times of the Greek states. When this era begins, the Jews had already known a generation of domination by foreign powers. In 605 BC, Judah had become a client state of the Babylonian Empire, thrall to the mighty emperor Nebuchadnezzar the Great. They still had their own king and largely ordered their own internal affairs, but they were forced to pay yearly tribute and provide service to Nebuchadnezzar. When King Jehoiakim of Judah attempted to revolt against Nebuchadnezzar in 597 BC, the emperor retaliated by carrying away many Judahites to Babylon as hostages. There, the expatriates began to form a cohesive community and soon adapted to life in what was then the world's greatest metropolis.

But in Jerusalem, the spirit of rebellion persisted. In 587 BC, King Zedekiah, ignoring the warnings of the prophet Jeremiah, again revolted against Babylon. This time, there was no restraint on the part of Nebuchadnezzar. The whole land of Judah was decimated; Jerusalem was devastated; Solomon's temple was destroyed; and many of Judah's citizens were deported in an operation that has become known as the Babylonian exile (or Babylonian captivity). Though their anger seethed at the destruction and humiliation they had suffered, these new exiles, too, soon became accustomed to their surroundings. The Babylonian authorities tolerated their religion, and their movements were unrestricted, so the Jewish exiles in Babylon took advantage of the opportunities afforded them, laying the foundations of what would be a prosperous and vibrant community for centuries to come.

The Jews were in unwilling exile for about a generation. But in 540 BC, Cyrus the Great, king of Media and Persia, conquered Babylon. Shortly after the conquest, Cyrus issued a decree allowing the Jewish captives to return to Jerusalem and rebuild their temple. Though a few thousand eventually made the trek, many chose to remain in their adopted homeland. After living there for almost half a century, the Judahites had become settled, and many were enjoying a standard of living they could not have known elsewhere. The thought of returning to the ruined and isolated land of "Yehud," as it was called in this era, had little appeal to them. In fact, the lure of economic opportunity drew many of the Jews still farther to the east, to the new seat of world power and commerce: Susa, the capital of Persia. There, they once again found that ambitious and capable individuals could attain positions of affluence and influence, regardless of their ethnic or religious background. There seemed to be no ceiling on one's possible ascent, with a Jew such as Nehemiah even becoming cupbearer for King Artaxerxes I. In such a setting, the idea that a woman like Esther could become queen of all Persia did not seem so farfetched.

The story of Esther is set in the reign of a king identified in Heb. as Ahasuerus, who has now been positively identified as Xerxes I (ruled 486–465 BC).[4] Xerxes' career was chronicled by the Greek author Herodotus,

---

4. Ahasuerus is identified as Artaxerxes, son of Xerxes, in the LXX and other ancient sources, and the mistake persisted through the centuries. The identification of the name as "Xerxes" now seems certain. See commentary on 1:1.

who wrote his *History of the Persian War* around 445 BC, a mere twenty years after the great king's death. Nonetheless, Herodotus must be read critically: the Greeks and the Persians were bitter enemies, and Herodotus was sometimes less than objective. Furthermore, he was also known to include much hearsay and even legendary elements in his accounts. Even so, aided by the twenty or so inscriptions attributed to Xerxes and information from other classical authors, it is possible to put together a fairly complete profile of the early years of his reign, during which the events of Esther are said to transpire.

Xerxes was the son of King Darius I and Queen Atossa, who was the daughter of Cyrus the Great, founder of the Persian Empire. He was the fourth ruler of Persia's "Achaemenid" Empire, which traditionally begins with Cyrus and continues until the conquest of Alexander the Great in 330 BC.[5] Before the days of Cyrus, Persia had been a vassal of the Median Empire, a sizable kingdom that had extended from India in the east to Asia Minor in the west. But around 550 BC, Cyrus revolted against his overlords and made the Median Empire subject to Persia. After securing control of the Median lands, Cyrus went on to conquer the Lydian Empire of Asia Minor, apparently in retaliation for a Lydian attack on a Persian city. Soon after, he had added the kingdom of Elam and its capital, Susa, to his empire as well. Finally, through a brilliant combination of effective propaganda and military strategy, Cyrus even managed to incorporate the Babylonian Empire into his realm. The king of Babylon, Nabonidus, had incited the ire of the priesthood and many of the people of Babylon by patronizing the moon goddess Sin instead of the traditional state god Marduk. Cyrus won the goodwill of the Babylonians by portraying himself as an agent of Marduk and a benefactor of the people. This policy of patronizing the gods of his subjects would continue to serve Cyrus well, earning him the reputation of a reformer and deliverer rather than a usurping tyrant. He himself was likely a Zoroastrian, a worshiper of Ahura Mazda, but the Achaemenid monarchs were generally very tolerant of religious diversity within the empire.[6]

5. "Achaemenid" means "descended from Achaemenes." Achaemenes was an ancestor of Darius who had ruled over the realm called Parsumash in southwest Iran. Though Darius attempts to identify Cyrus as an Achaemenid as well, scholars doubt that such a relationship existed. See M. Waters, "Cyrus and the Achaemenids," *Iran* 42 (2004): 91–102.

6. So M. Boyce, "The Religion of Cyrus the Great," in A. Kuhrt and H. Sancisi-Weerdenburg, *Achaemenid History III: Method and Theory* (Leiden: Brill, 1988), 15–31.

In 539 BC, the Persians defeated the Babylonian army at the Battle of Opis. They then went on to take the Babylonian city of Sippar without conflict, having negotiated a surrender with the commander of the army there. Nabonidus, who was in Sippar at the time, fled to Babylon. But two days later, Cyrus' troops entered Babylon, again with little conflict. According to Herodotus, Cyrus' general Gubaru diverted the waters of the Euphrates River into a canal, allowing the army access to the city by wading through the nearly empty riverbed (*Hist.* 1.191). The capital city capitulated with little resistance, and the Babylonian king Nabonidus was taken captive. A few days later, Cyrus was crowned king of Babylon. Having thus annexed the realms of the Babylonian Empire to his own kingdom, Cyrus became master of the largest empire the world had ever known.

Cyrus died in 530 BC. While the ancient sources are not in agreement about how he met his demise, it appears that he died in battle near the Syr Darya River.[7] He was succeeded by Cambyses II, his son by Cassandane, a Persian noblewoman. During his reign of seven years, Cambyses conquered Egypt and added it to the Persian Empire as well. In spite of this spectacular accomplishment, Cambyses does not seem to have enjoyed anything like the popularity Cyrus had known. Herodotus accuses him of numerous acts of cruelty. On one occasion, he arrested twelve Persian nobles on a trifling charge and had them buried alive, heads downward (*Hist.* 3.37). He flayed a judge who had taken a bribe and had his skin made into a chair for his successor as a reminder of what happens to corrupt officials (5.25). He was also reputed to have killed his brother Bardiya (called Smerdis by Herodotus) and his wife (3.30–32), as well as one of his cupbearers (3.34–35). Herodotus accuses Cambyses of rank impiety in Egypt, including the desecration of the dead (3.16, 37), the mocking of Egyptian gods (3.37), and the slaying of the Apis bull (3.27), regarded by the Egyptians as an incarnation of the god Ptah. Herodotus concludes that the only explanation for Cambyses' behavior was that he was mad (3.38). It must be noted, however, that the charge that Cambyses slew the Apis bull has been thoroughly investigated and appears to be false.[8] In fact, inscriptional evidence depicts Cambyses

---

7. Darius' account is preserved in the Behistun inscription. Herodotus (*Hist.* 1.214) and Ctesias (*Persica* 7–8) both have him fall in battle; Xenophon in his *Cyropaedia* (8.7.6–28) claims that Cyrus died peacefully in his capital.

8. On the evidence contradicting the account, see E. Bresciani, "The Persian Occupation of Egypt," in *The Cambridge History of Iran,* ed. I. Gershevitch (Cambridge: Cambridge University Press, 1985), 2:504–5; T. C. Young, "The Early History of the Medes and Persians and the Achaemenid Empire until the Death of Cambyses," in *CAH 4: Persia, Greece, and the Western Mediterranean*, ed. J. Boardman (Cambridge: Cambridge University Press, 1988), 51; P. Briant, *From Cyrus to Alexander: A History of the Persian Empire*, trans. P. T. Daniels (Winona

participating in the funerary rites for the Apis bull that died (of natural causes) in 524, while Cambyses was in Egypt.[9]

Whatever the truth behind these allegations of cruelty, that such stories could be propagated is evidence enough that Cambyses was not a popular ruler. While he was in Egypt, a revolt broke out in Persia, led by a man who claimed to be Cambyses' brother. He was actually an imposter, since Cambyses' brother Bardiya was already dead, as both Herodotus and the Behistun inscription (B.D. ¶¶ 10–11)—an important monument in which Darius the Great describes his rise to power—agree. The Behistun inscription gives the usurper's name as Gaumata, while Herodotus claims that he coincidentally had the same name as the deceased prince and even resembled him (3.61). Cambyses attempted to return to Persia, but died on the way under disputed circumstances. According to the Behistun inscription (¶11), he committed suicide. The Greek historians, however, attribute his death to an accident—divine retribution for the slaying of the Apis bull.[10] Some modern scholars believe he was assassinated, perhaps by his successor, Darius.[11]

After the death of Cambyses, Darius and six Persian noblemen formed a pact to remove the usurper and place a legitimate king on the throne. Once they had captured and killed Gaumata, they decided to hold a contest among themselves to see who would succeed Cambyses. The seven men would ride out on their horses at daybreak, and the one whose horse neighed first would be king. Darius won the contest by having his groom excite his horse with the smell of a mare, but according to Herodotus (*Hist.* 3.84–86), the sign was confirmed with an immediate peal of thunder that caused the other nobles to fall before Darius in acknowledgment of his destiny. After being proclaimed king, he married Atossa, daughter of Cyrus the Great, in an effort to further legitimize his claim to the throne.

While it seems that the procedure whereby Darius attained the throne was somewhat suspect, it all turned out well enough. Darius (reigned

---

Lake, IN: Eisenbrauns, 2002), 57. Klasens, "Cambyses en Égypte," *Ex Oriente Lux* 10 (1946): 339–49, defends Herodotus' account. L. Depuydt, "Murder in Memphis: The Story of Cambyses's Mortal Wounding of the Apis Bull (ca 523 BCE)," *JNES* 54 (1995): 119–26, argues that the evidence is ambiguous.

9. Briant, *From Cyrus to Alexander*, 57.

10. The Behistun inscription says that Cambyses "died his own death." Some have interpreted this statement to mean he died of natural causes, but given the context (the account of massive revolts breaking out in the empire), suicide seems more likely. Herodotus (*Hist.* 3.64) claims that as Cambyses was mounting his horse, his own sword pierced his thigh in the very place he had stabbed the Apis bull.

11. So, e.g., M. Van De Mieroop, *A History of the Ancient Near East: Ca. 3000–323 BC* (Hoboken, NJ: Wiley-Blackwell, 2003), 271.

522–486/5 BC) proved to be a very competent leader. He divided the empire into twenty administrative districts, each presided over by an officer called a satrap. He standardized the required tribute from each satrap and commissioned inspectors—the "eyes and ears" of the king—to be sure that his orders were being carried out. He also adopted Aramaic as the common language of the empire.[12] Darius took a number of steps to facilitate trade, including the creation of a universal coinage, the construction of roads, and the institution of a postal system. All these initiatives helped to create a much more efficient system of taxation, and the increased government revenue was used to fund building construction, irrigation projects, and a public banking system.

But not all of Darius' undertakings enjoyed unalloyed success. His efforts to expand the Persian Empire into Europe initially triumphed, as he conquered a good portion of the northern Aegean region. Darius had less luck with the Greek colonies of Asia Minor. In 499 BC, several of them, with encouragement and reinforcements from Athens and Eretria, revolted against Persian rule. It took Darius several years to quell the revolt, and he vowed to punish Athens and Eretria for their part in the uprising. In 492 BC, he sent his fleet to Macedon and Thrace. He received the submission of both realms, but his fleet was destroyed by storms before it could proceed further. Fearing that word of the disaster would embolden the Greeks against him, Darius sent envoys to the city-states, demanding they accept his sovereignty. While most of them agreed, Athens and Sparta killed the envoys instead. Darius answered by invading Greece, subjugating several islands, and destroying Eretria before suffering a humiliating defeat at the Battle of Marathon (490 BC). While Darius was preparing for a second invasion of Greece, a revolt broke out in Egypt. The uprising disrupted his plans and taxed his already failing health. In 486 BC Darius died, leaving a well-organized but unsettled empire to his son Xerxes.

As soon as Xerxes took the throne, Babylon joined Egypt in rebellion. It was a typical challenge faced by a new monarch, and Xerxes proved equal to it. Both revolts were put down efficiently, even ruthlessly, as Xerxes used the insurrection as an opportunity to demonstrate his strength. He dealt

12. In the early years of the Persian Empire, the language of the Persian court had been Elamite, since the seat of government, Susa, had formerly been the capital of the old Elamite kingdom. After the conquest of Babylon, Aramaic enjoyed wide use in the eastern empire, and Darius seems to have made its use official (but see R. Frye, "Review of G. R. Driver's 'Aramaic Documents of the Fifth Century B. C.,'" *Harvard Journal of Asiatic Studies* 18 [1955]: 456–61, who argues that no official pronouncement was ever issued). The traditional language of the Persians, Old Persian, obviously continued in wide use, but it is attested primarily in inscriptions.

with Babylon especially harshly, destroying local temples and carrying away a large statue of the god Marduk. It was a strange reversal from the policy of his grandfather Cyrus, who had attempted to show great respect toward the religious sensibilities of his subjects.

Xerxes' most famous exploit was his attempt to carry out his father's planned invasion of Greece, which was chronicled, with great bias, in Herodotus' *History*, books 7–9. Preparations were begun in 483 BC, including forging alliances with Carthage, stocking supplies, and building a bridge across the Hellespont for the transport of troops. As the Persians marched inland, several Greek city-states gave their support to the invaders. Xerxes encountered little resistance until the Battle of Thermopylae (*Hist.* 7.199–239), where (according to Herodotus) a group of three hundred Spartans held off the massive Persian army until the city of Athens could be evacuated. Eventually, however, the Spartans were overcome (according to Herodotus, through being betrayed by a Greek), and the Persians took Athens in 481 BC. Athenians and Spartans were forced into retreat.

Soon, however, the tide would turn: at the maritime Battle of Salamis (*Hist.* 7.76–96), the Persian fleet was decimated by the Greeks. This setback was not totally debilitating, since Xerxes still possessed a vast army. But for reasons that are still unclear, the king decided to withdraw from mainland Greece and return to Asia Minor, leaving only part of his army to finish off the Athenians and Spartans.[13] In 479 BC, the Greek city-states rallied against the invaders. The Persians suffered crushing defeats to their cavalry at Plataea (*Hist.* 9.41–75) and the destruction of much of what remained of their fleet at Mycale (*Hist.* 9.96–106). Emboldened by these Greek victories, some of the colonies in Asia Minor revolted against Persia. At about the same time, Babylon also rebelled. Faced with revolt on two fronts, Xerxes left Asia Minor to deal with the trouble in Babylon. He never attempted another invasion of Greece. Instead, he seems to have devoted the latter years of his reign to expanding Persepolis, a royal residence and the main religious center of Persia.

The events portrayed in the book of Esther are set in the first half of Xerxes' career. Esther 1, in which Vashti is deposed as queen, is dated to the third year of Xerxes' reign (Esth 1:3), which would have been before he left on his Greek campaign (ca. 483 BC). The next dated event in the book is Esther's elevation to the position of queen (Esth 2:16). It is dated to the tenth month of the seventh year of Xerxes' reign, which would have been a few months after his return from Greece in 479 BC. It is not impossible to reconcile the account of Esther with the most well-established details of Xerxes' reign, but it is not possible to verify it, either. Indeed, some

13. Briant, *From Cyrus to Alexander*, 531–32.

major aspects of the story cannot be reconciled with Herodotus' account of Persian history, and some key details seem to fly in the face of what we know of typical Persian court procedure. But scholars who argue that the text is a historical account of actual events contend that none of these difficulties are insurmountable.[14]

There is much debate, therefore, about whether the book of Esther should be read as a historical record or as a work of realistic fiction. In the absence of external evidence, judgments will be based in part on how one identifies the text's genre, a subject that we will consider in the next section. But for now, we should note that even those scholars who reject Esther's historicity have noted that the author seems to have had a great deal of familiarity with Persia and its customs, weaving them into his story even while subtly (and not so subtly) mocking them.[15]

Table 1: The Achaemenid Dynasty

Cyrus the Great	550–529 BC
Cambyses I	529–522 BC
Bardiya (Pseudo-Smerdis)	522 BC
Darius I (the Great)	522–486 BC
Xerxes I	486–465 BC
Artaxerxes I	465–425 BC
Xerxes II	425–424 BC
Darius II	424–405 BC
Artaxerxes II	405–359 BC
Artaxerxes III	359–338 BC
Arses	338–336 BC
Darius III	336–330 BC

14. See J. S. Wright, "The Historicity of the Book of Esther," in *New Perspectives on the Old Testament,* ed. J. B. Payne (Waco, TX: Word, 1970), 37–47; W. Shea, "Esther and History," *AUSS* 14 (1976): 227–46; E. Yamauchi, *Persia and the Bible* (Grand Rapids: Baker, 1990), 237–39.

15. So, e.g., Moore 1971, xxxv.

Textual Witnesses

The Hebrew Manuscripts

The textual criticism of the book of Esther is a fairly uncomplicated matter. The Heb. version of the MT will be most familiar to most readers, since it is the version that underlies the translation found in all Protestant Bibles. Manuscripts of this Heb. book abound: as observed by Paton (5), more manuscripts exist of the book of Esther than any other biblical book. Not only is it found in every synagogue and in many collections, but many private homes possessed manuscripts as well because of the popularity of the book and its connection with the feast of Purim. None of these texts, however, derives from earlier than the eleventh century AD. Since Esther was not found among the Dead Sea Scrolls, our sole witnesses to the Heb. text come from the Middle Ages and beyond.

The earliest manuscript for the Heb. text of Esther is the Leningrad Codex 19A, dating to AD 1009.[16] It is this text that is represented in the version of Esther found in *BHS*. Any later manuscript, however, could have served just as well, since all the existing Heb. manuscripts are virtually identical. All display the Tiberian vocalization of the Masoretes. They all preserve the same idiosyncrasies, including the abnormally large first letter in 1:6 and the arrangement of the names of Haman's ten sons (9:7–8) in columns. All include a note that the book contains 167 verses and that the middle verse of the text is 5:7. The remarkable uniformity of the manuscripts attests to the excellent preservation of the book, at least in its Heb. form. Reading the text as it stands presents only a few difficulties. Bush (278) identifies only two conjectural readings that are preferable to the MT (these will be noted in the commentary). In a handful of other cases, the *Qere** (oral tradition) presents a superior reading to the *Kethib** (consonantal text); these too will be noted in the commentary.

The Greek Versions

The Septuagint version of Esther has come down to us in numerous manuscripts, the most important including the Codex Vaticanus ("B," fourth century AD), Codex Alexandrius ("A," fifth century AD), and Codex Sinaiticus ("S," fourth century AD). It represents a very loose translation of an original Heb. (or Aramaic) text into Greek. Indeed, the translation sometimes borders on paraphrase. Moore writes, "There is scarcely a verse where the LXX^{b} does not omit a word, phrase, or clause of the MT."[17] The informality

16. For the facsimile edition of this manuscript, see D. Freedman, ed., *The Leningrad Codex: A Facsimile Edition* (Grand Rapids: Eerdmans, 1998).
17. Moore 1977, 162.

of the translation makes the LXX almost worthless for textual criticism of the Heb. text.

But what the LXX took away from the book of Esther with one hand, it more than added with another. The principal difference between the MT and the LXX is the presence of six passages in the Greek version that do not exist in the MT. These additions—labeled A, B, C, D, E, and F by scholars—are rather different in character from the rest of the text, and even in some cases from one another. The first and last (A and F) form bookends for the text: addition A recounts a symbolic dream experienced by Mordecai (along with a plot against the king), foretelling the events to transpire in Persia. In addition F, Mordecai recalls the dream and explains how it was fulfilled. Additions B and E purport to provide the text of edicts issued by Haman and Mordecai. These additions are so similar in form that they likely originate with the same author. Addition C consists of two lengthy prayers uttered by Mordecai and Esther when they hear of Haman's plot to destroy the Jews. Addition D is an expansion of the scene where Esther comes before the king to invite him to her banquet. It is widely accepted that additions B and E were composed in Greek, while the others are believed to have been composed in Heb. and translated into Greek.[18]

In addition to the LXX, there exists another Greek text, once called the "Lucianic" version, but now referred to as the Alpha Text (AT). It has proven the most controversial of the versions.[19] This text is preserved in

18. Moore 1977, 5–6, 195–99, 237–38.

19. The text may be found in A. Brooke, N. McLean, and H. Thackeray, eds., *The Old Testament in Greek* (Cambridge: Cambridge University Press, 1940), 1:32–42; and in R. Hanhart, *Septuaginta. Vetus Testamentum Graece. Auctoritate Academiae Scientiarum Gottingensis editum,* VIII, 3, *Esther*, 2nd ed. (Göttingen: Vandenhoeck und Ruprecht, 1983). D. J. A. Clines, *The Esther Scroll: The Story of the Story,* JSOTSup 30 (Sheffield, UK: JSOT Press, 1984), provides the Greek text and an English translation in an appendix. Some important studies on this text include: C. Torrey, "The Older Book of Esther," *HTR* 37 (1944): 1–40; C. Moore, "A Greek Witness to a Different Hebrew Text of Esther," *ZAW* 79 (1967): 351–58; H. Cook, "The A Text of the Greek Versions of the Book of Esther," *ZAW* 81 (1969): 369–76; E. Tov, "The 'Lucianic' Text of the Canonical and the Apocryphal Sections of Esther: A Rewritten Biblical Book," *Text* 10 (1982): 1–25, with a revised version appearing in *The Greek and Hebrew Bible—Collected Essays on the Septuagint,* VTSup 72 (Leiden: Brill, 1999), 535–48; D. Clines, *Esther Scroll*; J.-C. Haelewyck, "Le texte dit '*Lucianique*' du livre d'Esther: Son étendue et sa coherence," *Le Muséon* 98 (1985): 53–95; M. Fox, *The Redaction of the Books of Esther* (Atlanta: Scholars Press, 1991); K. Jobes, *The Alpha-text of Esther: Its Character and Relationship to the Masoretic Text,* SBLDS 153 (Atlanta: Scholars Press, 1996); A. Lacocque, "The Different Versions of Esther," *Biblical Interpretation* 7 (1999):

only four manuscripts, the oldest dating to AD 1021.[20] It contains the same six additions as the LXX, in very similar form. In other sections of the text, however, it greatly abbreviates the narrative. The story of the establishment of the Purim festival, for example, has been dramatically shortened. Furthermore, there is a tendency in this version to place more emphasis on the role of Mordecai and to reduce that of Esther. Once widely regarded as an abridgement of the LXX, the AT is now considered by many a translation of a separate Heb. (or Aramaic) version of Esther, perhaps older than that found in either the MT or the LXX *Vorlage**.[21] Others regard it as a different translation of a text very similar to the MT. It is considerably shorter than the LXX version and even shorter than the MT.

The evidence for this theory has been thoroughly recounted in a number of places, so we will provide only a brief summary here.[22] First, it is universally acknowledged that the additions in the AT are copied from those in the LXX. They are nearly the same as in the LXX, aside from some minor changes in wording, and quite different from the rest of the AT, which otherwise abbreviates the Esther story significantly. Most scholars, therefore, disregard the additions when attempting to reconstruct the origins of the AT. The remainder of the AT, while considerably shorter than the LXX, cannot be regarded merely as an abridgement of it. Not only is it shorter, but it also varies from it significantly. In some cases, the unique wording of the AT seems to be a more literal rendering of the Heb. of the MT.[23] In other cases, however, the AT renderings seem to be translations from a Semitic

301 22; K. De Troyer, *The End of the Alpha Text of Esther*, SBLSCS 48 (Atlanta: SBL, 2000); idem, "Translation or Interpretation? A Sample from the Books of Esther," in *Proceedings of the Xth Congress of the International Organization for the Septuagint and Cognate Studies, Oslo 1998*, ed. B. Taylor, SBLSCS 51 (Atlanta: Scholars Press, 2001), 343–53; idem, "The Letter of the King and the Letter of Mordecai," *Text* 21 (2002): 175–207.

20. The manuscripts are designated Manuscript 93 of the British Museum, Manuscripts 19 and 108b of the Vatican Library, and Manuscript 319 of the Vatopedi monastery on Mt. Athos (this is the oldest of the manuscripts).

21. The current interest in this position stems from the arguments of C. Moore in his 1965 Johns Hopkins dissertation, summarized in Moore, "A Greek Witness." The case for this position has been considerably expanded since, esp. by Clines, *Esther Scroll*; Fox, *Redaction*; and Jobes, *Alpha-Text*.

22. De Troyer, *Alpha-Text*, chap. 1, provides a critical summary of the history of this theory. The idea is also espoused by Talmon and others.

23. Jobes, *Alpha Text*, employs the criteria developed by R. Martin, *Syntactical Evidences of Semitic Sources in Greek Documents*, SBLSCS 3 (Missoula, MT: Scholars Press, 1974) to the analysis of the Alpha-text. Jobes determined that, when cases of insertions or deletions are excluded, there is "84% semantic agreement and

original, but not the MT. The theory that the AT derives from a separate, and perhaps earlier, Semitic *Vorlage* would account for some of these features.

But not everyone has been convinced. The "classical" theory that the AT is a revision of the LXX continues to find advocates.[24] It must be acknowledged that the AT occasionally duplicates the precise words of the LXX and sometimes even seems to have duplicated its errors. These cases, however, are relatively rare (if the additions are excepted), and the bulk of the AT bears little verbal or structural semblance to the LXX. It is difficult to understand why, if the AT were based on the LXX, it would have reproduced the additions of the LXX so precisely, while departing from the text so freely elsewhere. More likely, it is argued, is that the AT was corrected by a scribe using the LXX—including the insertion of the additions. The "proto-AT"—the Greek version without the additions—may indeed represent a witness to a variant Heb. (or Aramaic) version of Esther. But the text has been rather heavily revised, and it appears dangerous to rely on it too heavily for reconstructing the history of the Esther narrative.

In both of these texts, the additions are notable for the fact that they bring religious content to what is otherwise an ostensibly very nonreligious book. This fact makes them very easy to identify as additions rather than original features of the text; the tone of these sections is quite unlike that of the rest of the book. If we remove the additions from the LXX or the AT, we are left with a book that is just as lacking in religious content as the MT. This very important fact demonstrates that the "secularism" of Esther is not a feature of the MT alone. It was a common characteristic of the three versions and their *Vorlagen* (if, indeed, three different *Vorlagen* existed).

Along with these versions, we should not neglect the account of Esther's story found in Josephus' *Antiquities*. While it is primarily based on the LXX version, there are some key differences between them.[25] In some cases, it appears that Josephus has followed the traditions of the MT. For instance, Josephus identifies Haman as an Amalekite, whereas the LXX identifies him

---

54% formal agreement" between the AT and the MT (64). By comparison, the LXX exhibited 88 percent semantic agreement and 64 percent formal agreement.

24. The classical advocates for this position include B. Jacob, "Das Buch Esther bei den LXX," *ZAW* 10 (1890): 241–98 (esp. 261); Hanhart, *Esther*, 88. More recently, E. Tov (1982 and 1999) and K. de Troyer, *Alpha-Text* and *Rewriting the Sacred Text: What the Old Greek Texts Tell Us about the Literary History of the Bible* (Atlanta: Society of Biblical Literature; Leiden: Brill, 2003), chap. 3, have championed the idea.

25. On the use of the LXX by Josephus, see H. Bloch, *Die Quellen des Flavius Josephus in seiner Archeologie* (Leipzig: B. G. Teubner, 1879), 78–79. E. Bickerman, "Notes on the Greek Book of Esther," *PAAJR* 20 (1951): 104, argues that Josephus depended on a lxx-like Greek text used by the Jews of Rome that is now lost.

as a Macedonian and the AT as a "Bougean." Furthermore, Josephus seems to be familiar with some traditions espoused by the rabbis: with the rabbis, he identifies Esther as Mordecai's niece (*Ant.* 11.198), whereas all three of our versions identify him as her cousin. But the basic account of events is the same as that found in the MT and the Greek traditions.

Other Translations

The MT, LXX, and AT provide us all the data we possess for reconstructing the process whereby the book of Esther came into existence. The other translations are based on these versions. The Vulgate of Jerome and the Syriac text (the Peshitta) are based on the Heb. text.[26] The Coptic, the Armenian, and the Slavonic versions apparently are translations of a LXX-like text. The Old Latin, an ancient Latin translation predating Jerome's Vulgate, appears to be based on the LXX, but it sometimes differs from it substantially. It also shares some readings with the AT of Esther.[27]

There are two targums (Aramaic translations) of Esther that were in use among the Jews.[28] With regard to the first targum, Paton (18) describes its relationship with the Heb. text as "a curious compound of fidelity and freedom." Every word of the Heb. text is faithfully represented, but there are numerous glosses of a haggadic (expository) nature, making the targum twice as long as the original Heb. text. These glosses often reflect some common rabbinic understandings of the text. For example, in Esth 1:11, where Vashti is ordered to come before the king wearing the royal crown, the targum adds that she was forced to appear naked, because she used to force Israelite girls to work in the nude on the Sabbath day. The same tradition is found in *b. Meg.* 12b. The other targum, known as *Targum Sheni*, contains even more glosses and expansions, making it fully twice as long as the first targum! These texts are more important as witnesses to the Jewish interpretations of Esther in antiquity, rather than to the original text of Esther.

Author and Composition

Author

Traditionally, it was assumed that the book of Esther was the product of an eyewitness of the events it records, or at least by someone closely connected

26. On these texts, see Paton, 16–31.
27. See further K. de Troyer, "The Many Texts of the Esther Story," *Folio: Newsletter of the Ancient Biblical Manuscript Center* 19, no. 2 (2002): 3, 7–8.
28. A convenient translation of the targums is found in G. Grossfeld, *The Two Targums of Esther: Translated, with Apparatus and Notes* (Collegeville, MN: Liturgical Press, 1991).

with the events. The great medieval Jewish commentator Rashi asserted that the text was the work of Mordecai himself, based on Esth 9:20: "And Mordecai wrote these things ... " This judgment has been followed by many popular treatments of the text, though few scholars seem to hold to it today.[29] Indeed, the text itself seems to militate against this idea. In Esth 10:3, we read, "For Mordecai the Jew was second to King Xerxes, and prominent among the Jews, and held in esteem by the multitude of his fellow Jews, because he sought the good of his people and spoke up for the welfare of all his kin." Not only do these words seem to lack in modesty, but they also read like a eulogy. Similarly, Esth 10:2 seems to imply that King Xerxes was already dead when the text was written.

According to the Talmud, Esther was composed by the men of the Great Synagogue (*b. Bat.* 15a), the transmitters of tradition between the time of the prophets and the earliest rabbis. Most scholars, however, have little confidence in the literal existence of the Great Synagogue, let alone its literary undertakings.[30] No mention of such a group appears in the contemporary literature of the period (e.g., Ezra-Nehemiah, Ben Sira, the books of Maccabees, or the Dead Sea Scrolls). Furthermore, Jewish society in the Second Temple period exhibits a great deal of religious diversity, especially in the area of *halakhah* (legal interpretation), and it seems unlikely that any doctrinaire central authority such as the Great Synagogue could have existed in the period.

Some conservative scholars have argued that the book was composed by Ezra (following Augustine, *City of God*, 18.36) or Nehemiah.[31] These were individuals who would have been familiar with both the Persian court and with Jewish history and traditions. They would have possessed the knowledge of the Heb. Scriptures that the author of Esther undoubtedly possessed. This theory, however, is pure speculation, based not on evidence, but on a desire to provide the book with the authority of a known biblical figure. Surely there were many people who would have knowledge of Persian customs and Jewish Scriptures. Furthermore, the writing style

29. So, e.g., Matthew Henry in his magisterial *Commentary on the Whole Bible* (1708), who argued that since the book attributes some writing to Mordecai, "we have reason to think he was the penman of the whole book." More recently, J. Wright, "Historicity," has identified Mordecai as the author. Commentators J. McGee, *Thru the Bible Commentary* (Pasadena, CA: Thru the Bible Radio, 1982), 2:544, and Smith (215) have stated that Mordecai is a "possibility."

30. See E. Schürer, *The History of the Jewish People in the Age of Jesus Christ*, rev. and ed. G. Vermes, F. Millar, and M. Black (Edinburgh: T&T Clark, 1979), 2:358–59.

31. See Martin, 700, who notes that this position is held by some conservatives, but that there is "no evidence" for it. Nonetheless, it continues to appear in Sunday school curriculums and on numerous websites.

of Esther—its use of humor, irony, and most of all, its lack of overt religious language—is jarringly at odds with the pious and serious tones of Ezra and Nehemiah. Finally, both Ezra and Nehemiah strongly opposed the intermarriage of Jews with Gentiles (see Ezra 9; Neh 10:10; 13:23–30). How could they have written approvingly of Esther's marriage to the king of Persia? In light of these facts, it is highly unlikely that Ezra or Nehemiah wrote this book. Most conservative scholars simply state that the author of the book is "unknown," while nonetheless maintaining that he must have been intimately acquainted with Persian customs and society.[32]

Critical scholars have been even less inclined to try to identify Esther's author, except in terms of general characteristics. For those who believe that the book was written in the Persian period, it is commonly argued that the book was written by a Persian Jew—Persian, because of his familiarity with Persian society and customs, and Jewish, because of the obvious spirit of nationalism that pervades the work. Scholars who argue that the book is a product of the Greek age hold that it was written by a Palestinian Jewish author, striving to encourage Jewish resistance against the Greeks.[33] The issue is complicated, however, by the belief of most modern scholars that the book of Esther went through a long editorial process and may be composed of multiple sources. In this case, we would not be seeking a single author, but only the final redactor of source documents originating in different times, circumstances, and perhaps even different languages.

Composition

The question of how the book of Esther came into existence involves a good deal of speculation. On the surface, there is no obvious reason to doubt its literary integrity. The book is relatively short; it is written in only one language; it contains no embedded narratives that could be removed without doing serious damage to the integrity of the text. Furthermore, the book possesses a literary structure that is clear and tight. Removing a scene or episode from the text would seem to destroy the structure of the Heb. narrative.

And yet, few scholars doubt that the story consists of materials from a variety of sources. Bush (279) writes, "the book of Esther presents such striking incongruities, repetitions, and changes in literary style and diction that there has been a strong consensus of opinion among scholars that it is a composite work." The theories regarding its composition focus on three

32. See, e.g., Larson and Dahlen, 281. Likewise, Jobes, 28.

33. See, e.g., R. Stiehl, "Das Buch Esther," *WZKM* 53 (1956): 4–22; A. Morris, "The Purpose of the Book of Esther," *ExpTim* 42 (1930): 126; H. H. Rowley, *The Growth of the Old Testament* (repr., New York: Harper & Row, 1963), 155; and the studies cited under "Time and Place" below.

major issues: first, the use of earlier biblical materials as sources for the composition of Esther; second, the question of whether chaps. 9–10 are later additions to the text; and third, the sources behind the episodes in chaps. 1–8.

Biblical Sources

The issue of the use of biblical sources for the Esther narrative could only be considered controversial by those who hold that the text is a very literal rendering of historical events. Modern scholarship has become comfortably reconciled to the fact that biblical authors drew freely from the well of tradition that they inherited, framing their narratives according to the venerable ideas and images found in the Pentateuch and other texts.[34] In the case of Esther, two biblical episodes have been frequently cited as sources: the stories of the exodus and of Joseph. Gerleman (11–23) has argued that the story of Esther is simply an adaptation of the exodus. He notes a number of parallel elements between the stories: the Jewish (Israelite) orphan taken into the royal palace, the concealment of the hero's Jewish identity, the threat to the Jews' existence, the deliverance from the threat, the revenge taken on the enemies, the institution of a feast. These parallels are interesting, but they are too general to prove a conclusive case of literary dependence. Moore may be correct in his estimation that the parallel elements may be the results of "the demands of effective story-telling technique."[35]

The efforts to identify links between Esther and the Joseph story, on the other hand, have proven somewhat more successful. These parallels have long been recognized and have been the subject of several studies.[36] Like Esther, the Joseph saga is set in the court of a foreign king. The Jewish (Israelite) hero rises to a position of power and prominence. From this position, she (he) is able to effect the salvation of the Israelites. At a banquet, the heroine's (hero's) ethnic identity is revealed. Meinhold argues from such parallels as these that Esth 1–8 is an adaptation of the Joseph story for

34. This technique is often called "inner-biblical exegesis," though the term is not precise. Exegesis implies a cognitive process of interpretation, whereas the technique we are considering here is often more poetic than interpretive and may even be unconscious.

35. C. A. Moore, "Esther Revisited," 166. See also the critique of S. Berg, *Book of Esther*, 6–8.

36. Stylistic and thematic similarities between Joseph, Esther, and Daniel were identified by L. Rosenthal, "Die *Josephsgeschichte* mit den Buchern Esther und Daniel verglichen," *ZAW* 15 (1895): 278–84. The findings were confirmed and expanded by M. Gan, "מגילת אסתר באספקלריית יוסף במצרים," *Tarbiz* 31 (1961–1962): 144–49. A summary of these and several more studies can be found in Berg, *Book of Esther*, 124–42.

the Jewish Diaspora, given a new "secular outlook" that matched that of the world into which the Jews had been cast.[37] There may be some merit to this suggestion, though the notion of a "secular" Hellenistic world is highly suspect.[38] Berg has thoroughly investigated the parallels and has concluded that Esther is in some way dependent on the Joseph narrative, but that the nature of the relationship is unclear.[39] The shared linguistic and thematic elements may demonstrate that the author of Esther had the story of Joseph in mind, at least unconsciously, when composing his own story. Once again, however, the parallels between the stories seem too general to indicate that Esther is merely Joseph in a dress. Some of the most prominent elements of the Joseph narrative—the clash of brothers, the unjust suffering of the hero, his supernatural insights, his salvation of all Egypt—have no parallel in the Esther narrative. Furthermore, some central elements of Esther's story—the conflict with the wicked courtier, Esther's role as intermediary, the Jews' vengeance on their enemies—seem to lack any parallel in Joseph. Given the numerous differences between the stories, the influence of Joseph on Esther seems to have been indirect, a subtle shaping of the language and imagery, rather than a conscious effort at emulation or interpretation.

The Independence of 9–10

The earliest challenge to the unity of the book of Esther came from J. Michaelis, who argued for the independence of 9:20–10:3 in 1783.[40] The essence of the argument is that the account of the institution of Purim is not intrinsic to Esther and Mordecai's story. Rather, it has been appended to a story that is complete in itself, transforming a narrative of deliverance into an apology for the celebration of Purim.[41] Paton (57–60) expanded

37. A. Meinhold, "Die Gattung der Josephsgeschichte und des Estherbuches: Diasporanovelle I und II," *ZAW* 87 (1975): 306–24; *ZAW* 88 (1976): 72–93. The idea has been taken up by K. Butting, "Esther: A New Interpretation of The Joseph Story in the Fight against Anti-Semitism and Sexism," in *Ruth and Esther: A Feminist Companion to the Bible,* ed. A. Brenner (Sheffield: Sheffield Academic Press, 1999), 239–49.

38. There were certainly some secular "intellectuals" in the Hellenistic era, but Mediterranean society in general was permeated by religious sentiment among both Jews and pagans. See further the discussion below, under "Theology of Esther: Contemporary Approaches."

39. Berg, *Book of Esther*, 124–42.

40. J. Michaelis, *Deutsche Uebersetzung des A.T. mit Anmerkungen für Ungelehrte* (Göttingen: J. C. Dieterich, 1783).

41. It is not impossible that anti-Semitic resentment for the Purim festival played into this tendency as well. See T. Beal, *The Book of Hiding: Gender, Ethnicity, Annihilation, and Esther* (London: Psychology Press, 1997), 4–12.

this concept, assembling varied evidence to argue that this section was based on a different source from the rest of the book, perhaps the Persian chronicle mentioned in 10:2. More recently, however, this argument has been modified to include all of chaps. 9–10.[42] Numerous repetitions and "inconsistencies" between these chapters and the rest of the narrative have been noted, including:

- the duplicate accounts of Haman's conspiracy in chaps. 3–7 and 9:24–25;
- an assumed discrepancy of whether Purim was celebrated on one day or two;
- the repetition of the detail that the Gentiles became afraid of the Jews (8:17 and 9:3);
- the question of whether Haman's sons were hanged alone (9:13–14) or with Haman (9:25);
- the repeated references to days of rejoicing and gladness (8:17; 9:17–23);
- and the general change from straight narrative to repetitive emphasis on Purim beginning in 9:17.

Clines has built an elaborate case that the last two chapters represent an unnecessary expansion of the narrative.[43] He holds that all the major tensions of the story are resolved in the simple declaration that the Jews could defend themselves against their attackers: "The story reaches its resolution at the moment when permission—nothing more—is given to attempt to avert the threat!"[44] Thus, Clines concludes, the story originally ended at 8:17 (though he admits that 8:17 as currently worded would have been an unsatisfactory conclusion for the book).[45] But we would contend that the issuance of a decree allowing the Jews to defend themselves is not the same as deliverance. The sword of Damocles still hangs over their heads. Would the readers not feel cheated if there were no account of the great battle to ensue? Furthermore, 8:13 anticipates that the Jews will be able to take vengeance on their enemies—a promise that is not fulfilled until the following chapters. Unless one posits that the original text also included the king revoking the order for the massacre—as does the AT, but not the LXX or MT—then it is unlikely the story ended simply with the proclamation that the Jews could arm themselves. Finally, we must also bear in mind the structure of the MT, wherein the last chapters' two banquets form an

42. See, e.g., Paton, 57–60; Torrey, 1–40; Moore, 90–91; Clines, *Esther Scroll*, 39–63.
43. Clines, *Esther Scroll*, esp. chaps. 3–4.
44. Ibid., 27.
45. Ibid., 189n25.

inclusio* with those of the first chapter. While it is possible to imagine an earlier version of Esther that did not include chaps. 9–10, that narrative would be a rather different story from that of the MT or LXX.

Many scholars maintain that just such a narrative is found in the AT. Several scholars have argued that the extant ending of the AT version of Esther is not original to the text, but rather has been derived from the LXX.[46] In the original ending of the AT version of Esther, it is argued, much or all of the material found in chaps. 9–10 would have been wholly absent. As noted earlier, a number of scholars believe that the AT is based on a different Heb. *Vorlage** than either the LXX or the MT and in fact represents an earlier edition of the book of Esther than either extant text.[47] The AT, then, could bear witness to a tradition wherein the Esther story was not so closely bound with the holiday of Purim. It could, in fact, reveal that the association of Esther with Purim is a later addition to the original Esther tradition.

The case, however, is not airtight. Though numerous scholars have attempted to identify where proto-AT ended and the LXX addition began, there has been no consensus. According to Torrey, the AT originally ended with chapter 7. Clines puts the ending at 8:17; Fox argues that the original text included 8:18–21 and 33–38;[48] Bush (284) would add 39–40 as well. Has the original ending of the AT been lost, or has it been partially preserved in the existing ending? While we might speculate, it is impossible to know just how much of the AT's original ending has been replaced with a composition based on the ending of the LXX.

The AT's efforts to deemphasize Purim may have less to do with the original form of the Esther tradition than with scribal emendation of the story. The tendency of the emendation may well be revealed in the AT's treatment of some other troubling passages. In Esth 8:17, the MT reads, "Many of the people of the land became Jews; for the fear of the Jews fell on them." The LXX translates this section fairly literally, with a small addition, "Many of the Gentiles were circumcised, and became Jews, because of fear of the Jews."[49] The AT, however, deals with the text differently: "And many Judeans were circumcised, and no one rose up against them, because they feared them." This apparent reluctance to speak of Gentiles being circumcised and converting to Judaism might well suggest that this portion of the AT has

46. The first study to espouse this position was Cook, "A-text," 369–76.

47. See Clines, *Esther Scroll,* 71–92; Fox, *Redaction,* 10–95; Jobes, *Alpha Text, passim.*

48. *Character and Ideology,* 38–42.

49. The addition is logical, since in the Hellenistic era, circumcision became the principal criterion of Jewish identification. See, e.g., 1 Macc 1:15. Note too Paul's use of the word *circumcision* as a synonym for *Jewish* (e.g., Rom 3:1; Gal 5:11; Eph 2:11; Phil 3:3).

undergone a Christian revision. The idea is strengthened by yet another peculiarity of the AT: while the LXX (followed by *Ant.* 11.266–67) states that Xerxes ordered that Haman be "crucified" (σταυρωθήτω; 7:10), the AT states in the corresponding passage that he ordered him to be "hanged" (κρεμασθήτω; 8:13). Again, given the resentment that Christians developed over Purim being used as an opportunity for mocking the crucified Christ, it would be understandable for a Christian redactor to be sensitive about this passage as well. If the AT's ending was, in fact, emended by a Christian scribe, it would not be surprising that he would also want to deemphasize Purim, given the general unpopularity of the festival with Christians.

If the evidence of the AT is disregarded, we are left only with the stylistic issues as the basis for arguing the independence of chapters 9–10. What should not be overlooked, however, is that in the MT, these chapters have a number of important connections with the material in chapters 1–8. Fox argues that "ch. 9 does indeed have a different prehistory from most of the book. Nevertheless, the Aftermath is not incompatible with the Base Narrative, but, on the contrary, is required for its fulfillment."[50] This fact is also demonstrated by an analysis of the text's structure, as shall be seen below: the final chapters are not an appendage, but an essential component of the text. Finally, it is obvious that the closing verses of this book are patterned after similar formula found in the book of Kings.[51] The narrator has deliberately added these verses to tie his story in to the biblical greater narrative.

The Sources behind Chapters 1–8

Attempts to dissect the contents of chapters 1–8 are necessarily speculative, since there is little on which to base reconstructions. There has, however, been a good deal of agreement among scholars, who believe they can discern at least three separate stories underlying the current text: the story of a deposed queen; a tale of a conflict between Mordecai and Haman (a "tale

50. *Character and Ideology*, 110.

51. There has been much discussion regarding the "inappropriateness" of chap. 10 as an ending for the book of Esther, some of which will be addressed in the commentary. For now, let it be noted that this ending is very similar to that of the accounts of Israel's kings:

> Esth 10:2—And all his works of power and might, and the account of the greatness of Mordecai, whom the king had exalted, are they not written in the book of the chronicles of the kings of Media and Persia?
>
> 1 Kgs 11:41—Now the rest of the acts of Solomon, and all that he did, and his wisdom, are they not written in the book of the acts of Solomon?
>
> 1 Kgs 14:49—Now the rest of Jeroboam's acts, and all that he did, are they not written in the book of the chronicles of the kings of Judah?

of court intrigue"); and the story of a woman who delivers her people from destruction (a "deliverance story").

Once again, the reconstruction of Clines (*Esther Scroll*) seems to have gathered the most support. Clines argues for a five-step composition of the book of Esther. He contends that two originally independent episodes, the Mordecai court tale and the Esther deliverance story, were combined into the pre-Masoretic version of the Esther story. In the next stage, yet another independent story, the Vashti tale, was added to the Esther narrative. At this stage in its development, the Esther-Mordecai tale was not devoid of religious content, as the final MT Esther would be, but Clines does believe that it tended to emphasize the "role of the coincidental."[52] He also believes that this stage of Esther's evolution is reflected in the Heb. *Vorlage* of the AT version (without, of course, the additions or the ending, which were copied in later from the LXX). In the next stage of the book's development, the concept of the irrevocability of Persian law was introduced, along with the story of the conspiracy of the eunuchs. At this stage as well, the religious elements were removed from the text. Finally, the Masoretic version of the story came about by the addition of three appendices (9:1–19, 20–32; 10:1–3), which comprise chapters 9–10. Yet another stage of Esther's development is displayed in the LXX, with its six additions. According to Clines, the LXX Esther "represents a more thorough and substantial reworking of the story than any version we have hitherto considered."[53] While Clines does not reject the positions of Paton (44) and Moore[54] that the additions are designed to provide religious content to an otherwise secular-seeming book, he holds that their primary effect is "to assimilate the book of Esther to a scriptural norm, especially as found in Ezra, Nehemiah, and Daniel."[55]

Date and Provenance

Critical scholarship (from both evangelical and non-evangelical perspectives) has certainly conceded that the author of Esther is unknown, but this fact has not impeded efforts to identify the author's (or authors') time and place. There are some basic facts that can be gleaned from the text itself. Clearly, the text must have been composed some time after the reign of Xerxes (486–435 BC). The text seems to assume that the reign of Xerxes is long past (1:1; 10:1–2), though there is no indication that it is viewed as a distant antiquity. The *terminus ad quem** may be established by the colophon of the LXX version: these manuscripts add a postscript briefly

52. Clines, *Esther Scroll*, 151.

53. Ibid., 168.

54. Moore 1977, 8.

55. Clines, *Esther Scroll*, 169.

describing the provenance of the text and the date of its translation (more will be said of this colophon later). If it is taken as genuine, the colophon establishes the date of the LXX translation around 78–77 BC.[56] Since the LXX version of the story (without additions) is quite similar to that of the MT, we can say with some confidence that the text had reached its familiar form sometime well after 435 BC and well before 77 BC.

In the nineteenth century, the reigning critical consensus held that the book was a product of the Hellenistic era, perhaps even of the time of the Hasmoneans (164–63 BC).[57] Their reasons for this position included:

- The failure of the apocryphal book of Ben Sira (ca. 200 BC) to mention Esther and Mordecai in its list of great biblical heroes (Sir 44–51), along with the lack of notice of the Esther's events in the books of Ezra, Nehemiah, Chronicles, or Daniel.
- The unflattering portrayal of the Persian king. It was argued that a book written while the monarchy was still in existence would have been more flattering, or at least less negative in its portrayal.
- The necessity for explaining Persian customs, as in 1:13 and 8:8.
- The "late" style of the Heb.

Some of these difficulties have been largely discredited, for various reasons. Ben Sira's omission of Esther and Mordecai may have more to do with the canonical status of the book at the time rather than its composition. In any case, all would agree that "absence of evidence is not evidence of absence." Ezra does not appear in Ben Sira's list, either, and most would agree that his story had been composed long before the days of Ben Sira.

The depiction of the Persian king requires some consideration. First of all, how negative, really, is the depiction of Xerxes? He appears somewhat clueless, but he is not painted as the monster one might expect after the Jews' persecution by Antiochus Epiphanes.[58] (Even before the Antiochan persecution, Jewish relations with their Ptolemaic and Seleucid overlords were strained.) The unflattering portrait that we see is easily explained if the book was written for Jewish consumption only, as its Heb. language would

---

56. E. Bickerman, "The Colophon of the Greek Book of Esther," *JBL* 63 (1944): 347.
57. Commentators holding this view include L. Herzfeld, *Geschichte des Volkes Jisrael: von vollendung des zweiten Tempels bis zur Einsetzung des Mackabäers Schimon zum hohen Priester und Fürsten* (Leipzig: Wilfferodt, 1863), 357–66; H. Ewald, *The History of Israel* (London: Longmans, Green, 1874), 5:230–34; E. Berthau, Die Bücher *Esra, Nechamiah, und Ester* (Leipzig: Hirzel, 1862), 279–80; H. Bloch, *Hellenistische Bestandtheile im biblischen Schriftthum, eine kritische Untersuchung über Abfassung, Charakter und Tendenz, sowie die Ursachen der Kanonisirung des Buches Esther* (Magdeburg: Jüdische Literaturblatt, 1877).
58. See Bush, 296.

definitely indicate. There would be no need to flatter the overlords if one never anticipated them reading the text. Furthermore, if the book is representative of Jewish resistance literature, as we will argue below, we would surely expect the king to be depicted in a less-than-positive fashion. He is no particular friend to the Jews, but he is no active enemy to them either. It is a portrait that would have been compatible with the Jewish experience of foreign rule from the time of Cyrus until the Antiochan persecution.

As for the necessity of explaining Persian customs, how much explanation actually occurs? The lavish banquets prepared by Xerxes, for instance, are described in vivid detail, but they are taken as a matter of course. The presence of the eunuchs—very incompatible with Hellenistic practice—is also presented as status quo. Persian words are used without translation. The explanations for Persian customs that do occur—such as the reference to the immutability of Persian law or the danger of approaching the king unbidden—are for practices that are scarcely attested outside the book of Esther. They may have been literary devices invented by the author or explanations designed to enlighten Jewish readers living outside Persia.

On the other hand, there is significant evidence that would seem to place the book of Esther, or at least its sources, in the Persian period. Scholars have noted that the depiction of Persian customs, names, and even the layout of the city of Susa show remarkable accuracy.[59] It is unlikely that such features would have been familiar to a non-Persian Jew writing in the Hellenistic period. Furthermore, the linguistic evidence, taken by earlier scholars to demonstrate the late composition of Esther, has been largely discredited.[60] One of the frequently noted features of Esther is the lack of Greek loanwords in the text. Aramaic and Persian words, however, are well represented. Moore (1971, lvii) has argued that Esther's Heb. bears great similarity to that of Chronicles and Ezra-Nehemiah, rather than the Heb. of the Dead Sea Scrolls. Bergey's linguistic analysis of the text places its composition at the latter half of the fifth century BC, but the reliability of his linguistic dating methods is open to challenge.[61] An attempt to date the

---

59. These features will be discussed in detail below, under "Historicity."

60. Linguistic dating tends to be a dubious undertaking because of differences in writing styles, regional variations, "archaizing" (writing in imitation of an older style of language), and even "modernizing" (scribal updating of the orthography or linguistic features of texts to make them more readable). See further I. Young, R. Rezetko, and M. Ehrensvärd, *Linguistic Dating of Biblical Texts*, 2 vols. (London: Equinox, 2008).

61. See R. Bergey, "The Book of Esther—Its Place in the Linguistic Milieu of Post-Biblical Hebrew Prose: A Study in Late Biblical Hebrew" (diss., Dropsie College, 1983); "Late Linguistic Features in Esther," *JQR* 75 (1984): 66–78. On the problems in the method of linguistic dating used, see Young et al., *Linguistic Dating*.

book of Esther to the fifth century BC (older than Ezra-Nehemiah) based on its use of Babylonian month designations is intriguing, but it has been strongly challenged.[62]

The question of Esther's date is complicated by Esther being likely a composite document, as noted above. Archaic features in the text may originate from the sources, not from the final form of the document. The Greek texts, too, add some difficulty to the discussion. Should our quest for the earliest book of Esther focus on the MT or on the AT? All of these facts contribute to a very muddled picture. There may be little more we can say about the date of Esther's composition than to affirm that the general structure of the book was very likely established near the end of the Persian era. The MT version, which represents the product of a significant process of literary development, was almost certainly completed before the days of the Antiochan persecution, since it reflects little of the hostility toward foreign rule that we would expect from literature that took shape in that era.

Canonicity

Today, almost all Jews, Catholics, Orthodox Christians, and Protestants acknowledge the place of the book of Esther among the canonical Scriptures, but the issue has not always been so clear-cut. Its status was debated in rabbinic literature; it was rejected by some early church fathers; it has puzzled and even repulsed some Christian commentators through the centuries. Martin Luther famously wrote, "I am so hostile to this book [2 Maccabees] and to Esther that I would wish they did not exist at all; for they judaize too greatly and have much pagan impropriety."[63] Even in modern times, it sometimes garners the disdain of Bible scholars and theologians. W. M. L. De Wette, a founding father of modern biblical criticism, wrote that the book displayed a "blood thirsty spirit of revenge and persecution."[64] Paton (97), noting the inclusion of Esther in the Jewish canon, argues, "With this verdict of late Judaism [on its canonicity] modern Christians cannot agree. The Book is so conspicuously lacking in religion that it should never

62. A. Friedberg, "A New Clue to Dating the Book of Esther," *VT* 50 (2000): 561–65. See the response of G. Larsson, "Is the Book of Esther Older than Has Been Believed?," *VT* 52 (2002): 130–31. Friedberg responds to the objections in "Dating the Composition of The Book of Esther: A Response to Larsson," *VT* 53 (2003): 427–29.

63. *Table Talk*, xxiv, *Weimar Ausgabe* 22, 2080.

64. W. M. L. De Wette, *A Critical and Historical Introduction to the Canonical Scriptures of the Old Testament*, trans. T. Parker (Boston: Charles C Little and James Brown, 1850), 2:346.

have been included in the Canon of the OT, but should have been left with Judith and Tobit among the apocryphal writings." More recently, Beal has written that the book of Esther is "exotic, savage, violent, difficult to reach, difficult to map, dangerous, perhaps irredeemable."[65] Bush (39–40) has collected numerous snippets from Bible introductions and commentaries that express similar negativity toward the book.[66] But on the other hand, the book of Esther is the only text of the Heb. Bible outside the Pentateuch that is the focus of a Jewish holiday celebration—a celebration that is the most raucous of the Jewish year. Also, even among Christians, Esther has inspired devotionals, Sunday school plays, and even motion pictures. Our relationship with this book has been, we might say, conflicted.

Esther in the Jewish Canon

While most English translations of the Scriptures follow the LXX ordering of the biblical texts and place Esther with the historical books, in the Heb. Bible, Esther is found in the third division of the canon, the Writings or Hagiographa ("holy writings"). This division consists of a hodge-podge of materials, including poetic, sapiential, and more-or-less historical works such as Ezra-Nehemiah and Chronicles. In Jewish tradition, Esther is included in a subgroup of the Writings known as the Five Megilloth, or "scrolls." The grouping of these scrolls—Ruth, Song of Songs, Ecclesiastes, Lamentations, and Esther—as a unit first appears in the Midrash Rabbah, a medieval collection of commentaries on the Pentateuch and the Megilloth. Traditionally, these texts are read at prescribed festivals of the Jewish year: Esther is universally read at Purim, and Lamentations on the Ninth of Ab (the day commemorating the destruction of the temple); in some Jewish communities, the Song of Songs is read during Passover, Ruth during the Feast of Weeks (Shavuot), and Ecclesiastes during the Feast of Booths (Sukkoth). Nonetheless, when Jews speak of *Hammegillah* (*the* Scroll), they are referring to the book of Esther, preeminent among the Megilloth.

Esther has a strategic place in the Jewish canon. It is located at the end of the Megilloth, perhaps because chronologically it would represent the latest of these five texts. But in the context of the Writings as a whole, it is not in its proper chronological place, appearing as it does before the book of Daniel. Nonetheless, its placement is probably not an accident. As Howard observes, "Its appearance following Lamentations offers hope, since its

65. T. Beal, *Book of Hiding*, 5.

66. Negative assessments of the book may also be found in R. Pfeiffer, *Introduction to the Old Testament* (New York: Harper, 1941), 747; O. Eissfeldt, *The Old Testament. An Introduction* (New York: Harper & Row, 1965), 511–12; S. Sandmel, *The Enjoyment of Scripture* (New York: Oxford University Press, 1972), 44.

emphasis is upon celebrations and the turning of mourning into gladness, a sharp contrast to the gloomy situation depicted in Lamentations. It immediately precedes Daniel, another book about Jews in a foreign land who prosper."[67]

Given the threefold division of the Heb. Bible (Law, Prophets, Writings), the placement of Esther among the Writings might seem self-evident. After all, the book of Esther is obviously not one of the Mosaic books (Law), and it surely could not be considered prophetic in the usual sense of the word. The matter, however, is not quite so clear cut, since the "Prophets" includes the historical books of Joshua, Judges, and Samuel-Kings (the so-called former prophets), as well as the texts more typical of the prophetic genre. In fact, later Jewish tradition seems quite willing to ascribe prophetic inspiration to the book of Esther. Josephus, who dated the story of Esther to the time of Artaxerxes, writes in *Ag. Ap.* 1.38 that "as to the time from the death of Moses till the reign of Artaxerxes king of Persia, who reigned after Xerxes, the prophets, who were after Moses, wrote down what was done in their times in thirteen books." In the Talmud, both Mordecai (*b. Meg.* 15a) and Esther (*b. Meg.* 14b) are said to be prophets, with Mordecai even being identified as the prophet Malachi. In light of this tradition, one might well ask why Esther did not find a place among the Prophets. At first blush, its claim to such a position would seem to be at least as strong as, e.g., Joshua's.

Scholars continue to debate how the threefold division of the Heb. Bible came to be. The issues are too involved to explore in detail here, but we must give them some brief consideration if we are to understand the controversy regarding Esther's canonical status.[68] First, the three divisions of the Heb. Bible seem to represent three successive stages of canon development.[69] That is, the first division, the Law, was canonized earliest; the

67. D. Howard, "Esther, Theology of," *NIDOTTE*, 4:584.

68. There have recently been several thorough studies on the formation of the canon, several of which are noted in the bibliography. Some recent influential studies include S. Leimann, *The Canonization of the Hebrew Scripture: The Talmudic and Midrashic Evidence* (Hamden: Archon, 1976); R. Beckwith, *The Old Testament Canon of the New Testament Church* (Grand Rapids: Eerdmans, 1986); L. McDonald, *The Formation of the Christian Biblical Canon,* 2nd ed. (Peabody, MA: Hendrickson, 1995); E. Ulrich, *The Dead Sea Scrolls and the Origins of the Bible,* Studies in the Dead Sea Scrolls and Related Literature (Grand Rapids: Eerdmans, 1999); L. McDonald and J. Sanders, eds., *The Canon Debate* (Peabody, MA: Hendrickson, 2002).

69. The three-stage position on the development of the canon is widely (though by no means universally) accepted. As Chapman states, "With minimal adjustments and qualifications, this linear three-stage model of Old Testament canon formation remains the majority view today, continues to be upheld by leading scholars

Prophets were canonized next; and the Writings apparently continued to be in some confusion until well into the Greek or Roman period. Typically, it is argued that the Pentateuch took its canonical form under the hand of Ezra, or at least in his era (mid-fifth century BC). The corpus of the Prophets was apparently solidified prior to 180 BC, for in the introduction to the Wisdom of Ben Sira, the sage's grandson (who translated the book into Greek) writes of "the Law, the Prophets, and the rest of the books" (Sir 1:1–2) as if the first two divisions were well defined. We cannot say with certainty, however, how long the Prophets had existed as a group. The *terminus post quem** would be the writing of the latest prophetic materials. We can date the book of Malachi with some precision to the mid-Persian period, roughly contemporaneous with Ezra and Nehemiah, but there are sections in Zechariah that most scholars would date later still. The closing of the canon of the Prophets, then, likely occurred between 400 and 200 BC.

Although it is very likely that some form of the book of Esther already existed at that time, there was apparently still some uncertainty, at least among some Jewish groups, about whether Esther should be considered Scripture. But even if there had been no controversy, Esther would have been an unlikely candidate to be grouped with the Prophets. Each of the works in the second division of the canon, it must be acknowledged, possess a certain prophetic "ambience." Joshua stands in the tradition of Moses, prophet *par excellence*. The books of Judges and Samuel may already have been traditionally attributed to the prophet who lends his name to the latter. Since Samuel was the last in the line of judges, who would be better qualified, in the ancient Jewish mind, to record the stories of the era? Also, the books of Kings feature the exploits of prophets, especially Elijah and Elisha, to an extent far surpassing the books of Chronicles, giving these books a decidedly prophetic flavor. Finally, note that Jewish tradition attributes 1–2 Kings to the prophet Jeremiah, but we do not know when this tradition first developed.[70]

In any event, when the collection of the Prophets was completed, Esther was excluded. But when did it find its way into that group that Ben Sira's grandson called "the other writings"? A few decades ago, scholars might have confidently stated that Esther's place in the Bible was ascertained at

---

and appears in most of the current introductory handbooks and textbooks in the field." See S. Chapman, "Reclaiming Inspiration for the Bible and the Canon of the Old Testament," in Craig Bartholomew et al., *Canon and Biblical Interpretation*, Scripture and Hermeneutics Series 7 (Grand Rapids: Zondervan, 2006), 168–69.

70. See R. Friedman, *Who Wrote the Bible?* (New York: Summit, 1987), 146–49.

a council of rabbis in Jamnia in AD 90.[71] Today, this idea has all but been abandoned, as there is little evidence that the rabbis of Jamnia were responsible for anything so grand as the closing of the biblical canon. Many scholars would argue that the entire canon was set by the second century BC and that later debates concerning the canonicity of certain books were more theoretical or heuristic than records of actual disagreement. Others, however, would hold that there was widespread disagreement about the contents of at least the Hagiographa even in the second century AD. Specifically, the Song of Solomon, Ecclesiastes, and Esther seem to have been the texts most prone to controversy. While it is obvious that all of these books were eventually regarded as biblical texts, we are unsure about when their status was confirmed.

The sources that we typically consult for confirmation of canonicity are nearly silent on the book of Esther. Since the events of Esther occur near the end of the biblical period, we would not expect to see the book quoted in other texts from the Heb. Bible. Our earliest and best postbiblical source on the canon, however, also fails to mention Esther. Writing about 200 BC, Ben Sira was a world traveler and scholar whose collection of proverbs and observations was translated into Greek by his grandson and preserved in the Apocrypha. Chapters 44–50 of the Wisdom of Ben Sira (also called Ecclesiasticus) is a panoramic overview of the heroes of the Jewish faith, stretching from the time of Adam to the high priest Simon, who died in 196 BC. Except for the story of Simon, this account consists of synopses of biblical episodes. It bears witness to the existence of the corpus of the twelve minor prophets (49:10), and includes mention of several figures from the Persian period, including Zerubbabel, the high priest Joshua, and Nehemiah (49:11–13). These chapters are an important clue to the state of the canon in the late Ptolemaic/early Seleucid period, but they are silent on the work of Mordecai and Esther.

We should not draw too definitive a conclusion from this omission, since as we have already mentioned, some other prominent Jewish figures, such as Ezra, were also left out of the overview. But given the enormity of the deliverance supposedly wrought by Mordecai and Esther, one might well expect that their story would have merited at least a line or two in a survey of illustrious Jewish heroes.

---

71. This idea seems to have first been articulated by H. Graetz, *Kohelet oder der Salomonische Prediger* (Leipzig: Winter, 1871), 147–73, and popularized by such scholars as H. Ryle, *The Canon of the Old Testament* (London and New York: Macmillan, 1892), and F. Buhl, *Kanon und Text des Alten Testamentes* (Leipzig: Akademische Buchhandlung, 1891). D. Aune, "On the Origins of the 'Council of Javneh' Myth," *JBL* 110 (1991): 191–93, traces the idea to Spinoza.

The earliest allusion to the events of the book of Esther is found in 2 Macc 15:36, after the account of Judas Maccabeus' defeat of the Greek general Nicanor: "And they all declared by public decree never to let this day go unobserved, but to celebrate the thirteenth day of the twelfth month (which is called Adar in the Syrian language), the day before Mordecai's day." Second Maccabees is an abridgment of a five-volume history of the Hasmonean Revolt that was written in Greek by a certain Jason of Cyrene. The book includes two introductory letters, the latter of which can be dated to 124 BC. The book itself, it seems, was probably written some time afterward (though conceivably, the letters could have been prefaced to the book after it had been completed—though in any event, not before the defeat of Nicanor in 161 BC).[72] The text says little about the character of "Mordecai's Day" at this time, but there can be little doubt that the reference is to the feast of Purim, which was celebrated on the fourteenth of Adar. This text demonstrates that at least the events of Esther were known by ca. 100 BC, but it does not really confirm that the *book* of Esther was known at this time.

Indeed, the reference raises some questions: why is the holiday here not identified by its biblical name, Purim? Why is there no mention of the holiday in the parallel version of the story found in 1 Macc 7? Was the holiday of so little significance at this time that a celebration of a military victory could be scheduled on its eve without even a mention of a potential "conflict"? The juxtaposition of the holidays seems even more significant in light of the similar circumstances being celebrated: in both the case of Purim and Nicanor's Day, the Jews were to commemorate the downfall of a foreign monarch's regent who was bent on the extinction of the Jewish people. The reference to Mordecai's Day seems to suggest that Purim was not yet a major holiday such as one might expect of a biblically mandated celebration of a thwarted genocide.

Yet another line of evidence that must be taken into consideration is the testimony of the Dead Sea Scrolls—or rather, the lack thereof. It is often stated that the book of Esther is the only Heb. Bible text that was not found among the Dead Sea Scrolls. (This statement is somewhat misleading, since it is based on the assumption that Ezra and Nehemiah comprised a single book in this era, as in later Jewish tradition. No copy of Nehemiah has been found, but portions of Ezra were preserved among the scrolls.) What is more, not only is the book unattested, but the festival of Purim is unattested as well. In the several Dead Sea Scrolls that discuss the various Jewish

72. On the possible date of composition of 2 Maccabees and its sources, see the thorough discussion of J. Goldstein, *II Maccabees,* AYB (New York: Doubleday, 1983), 28–54.

holidays and feasts, Purim is passed over in silence.[73] While the absence of the book of Esther at Qumran could be explained as a simple accident of preservation (i.e., the book was there, but perished in antiquity), the failure to recognize the feast of Purim implies a more deliberate omission.

There are several ways to account for the absence of Esther at Qumran. One way would be to argue that the text did not exist when the Scrolls were assembled, but no scholars seem to seriously argue for this approach. Scrolls were being deposited in the Dead Sea caves well into the NT era, long after Esther had been translated into Greek.[74] Many scholars have suggested that the book was rejected because of its ostensibly secular character and its failure to mention God. There is a problem with this explanation, as well: the Greek versions of Esther are considerably more religious than the MT version. Scholars are in agreement that there existed Heb. (or Aramaic) *Vorlage* for these versions, including some of their religious sections. Could not the Qumran community have acquired the more religious versions of the book of Esther, rather than the secular version preserved by the Masoretes?

Perhaps the best explanation for the rejection of Esther among the Dead Sea Scroll covenanters is found in its story line: the deliverance of the Jewish people through marriage to a Gentile king. There can be little doubt that the Dead Sea Scrolls community was strongly opposed to miscegenation. Marriage to Gentiles is condemned explicitly in several texts, and negative attitudes toward the practice may be implied in others.[75] These texts include the "sectarian charter," designated 4QMMT, which explicitly states some of the community's most significant differences with the Jerusalem "establishment."[76] The pseudepigraphic book of Jubilees, too, which takes a very negative view of Gentiles and also condemns intermarriage (Jub 20:4, 22:20, 30:11), was apparently considered a foundational document for the sect. Fifteen copies of the text have been found among the Scrolls, and there

73. The texts include 4QMMT, 4Q320–321 (the Priestly Courses), 4Q Calendrical Document A, 4Q Calendrical Document B, 11QTemple (the Temple Scroll), and the book of Jubilees.

74. See the discussion on the composition of Esther above.

75. In addition to 4QMMT and the book of Jubilees, other texts that condemn intermarriage among the Scrolls include the Aramaic Testament of Levi and 4Q265, a text of mixed genres.

76. Studies on intermarriage in 4QMMT include C. Sharp, "Phinehan Zeal and Rhetorical Strategy in 4QMMT," *RevQ* 18 (1997): 207–22; C. Hayes, "Intermarriage and Impurity in Ancient Jewish Sources," *HTR* 92 (1999): 3–34; and W. Loader, *The Dead Sea Scrolls on Sexuality: Attitudes towards Sexuality in Sectarian and Related Literature at Qumran* (Grand Rapids: Eerdmans, 2009), 71–90.

are references to Jubilees in such texts as the *Damascus Document* (*CD*).[77] It seems very unlikely that a group with such an ethos would embrace the book of Esther, with its thematic elements of exogamy and cooperation with foreign overlords.

In 1992 Milik claimed to have discovered an Aramaic "proto-Esther" among the Scrolls.[78] Were it to be confirmed, this discovery would have little direct bearing on the question of Esther's canonicity, since the presence of an Aramaic "proto-Esther" would not confirm the acceptance of the Heb. version that later became part of the biblical canon. But in actuality, it seems unlikely that the text in question has anything to do with the canonical book of Esther. While it does appear to be a story set in the Persian court, it apparently includes no mention of Esther or Mordecai. From what little remains of the text, it seems that the text's villain is identified as a Cuthean (Samaritan), not an Agagite (as in the MT) nor Macedonian (as in the LXX). This text alone, then, is unable to tell us whether Esther in its

---

77. On intermarriage in the book of Jubilees, see M. Satlow, *Jewish Marriage in Antiquity* (Princeton, NJ: Princeton University Press, 2001), 141–43; C. Hayes, *Gentile Impurities and Jewish Identities: Intermarriage and Conversion from the Bible to the Talmud* (Oxford: Oxford University Press, 2002), 73–81. On the significance of Jubilees among the Dead Sea Scrolls, see C. Hemphill, "The Place of the Book of Jubilees at Qumran and Beyond," in *The Dead Sea Scrolls in their Historical Context,* ed. Timothy H. Lim (Edinburgh: T&T Clark, 2000), 187–96. J. VanderKam has identified Jubilees as "one of the most authoritative or 'biblical' texts at Qumran" (J. VanderKam, "The Jubilees Fragments from Qumran Cave 4," in *The Madrid Qumran Congress*, ed. J. Trebolle Barrera and L. Vegas [Montaner; Leiden: Brill, 1992], 648).

78. J. Milik, "Les Modèles Araméens du Livre d'Esther dans la Grotte 4 de Qumran," *RevQ* 15 (1992): 321–406. The text, designated by Milik 4QprEst ar (but technically designated 4Q550), had been identified many years earlier by J. Starcky, "Le travail d'édition des fragments manuscrits de Qumrān," *RB* 63 (1956): 66, as "les restes d'un texte *pseudo-historique* se situant à l'époque perse rappelent Esther ou Daniel." So Starcky, while comparing the text to Esther, did not see a direct relationship between the two. Milik's identification of the text with the Esther tradition was endorsed by S. Talmon, "Was the Book of Esther Known at Qumran?," *DSD* 2 (1995): 253–56. It was identified as a "tale from the Persian Court" in R. Eisenman and M. Wise, *The Dead Sea Scrolls Uncovered* (London and New York: Element, 1995), 99–103. The identification of the text as a "proto-Esther" or model for Esther has been adopted by F. Garcia-Martinez and E. Tigchelaar, eds., *The Dead Sea Scrolls Study Edition* (Leiden: Brill, 1998), 2:1096–103, and by H. Steggemann, *Die Essener, Qumran, Johannes der Täufer und Jesus* (Freiburg: Herder, 1993), 124. S. White-Crawford, "Has Esther Been Found at Qumran? 4QProto-Esther and the Esther Corpus," *RevQ* 17 (1996): 307–25, argues the text may have been a source document for the biblical book of Esther.

present or "proto-" form was read as sacred Scripture by the community. On the other hand, Talmon has demonstrated that there are allusions to the book of Esther among some of the Dead Sea Scrolls.[79] While some of Talmon's proposed allusions seem open to challenge, there is enough evidence to warrant the conclusion that the book of Esther was familiar to those who composed and assembled the Scrolls.[80] But Talmon's conclusion that the book of Esther was known but not considered canonical at the time of the Scrolls' composition seems to go beyond what can reasonably be deduced from the evidence. While there are no examples of the book of Esther being cited as "Scripture" among the Scrolls, it is entirely possible that it was merely the sectarian authors of the Scrolls who rejected the book and not the broader Jewish community of the time. There can be no question that the book of Esther was eventually accepted as Scripture.[81] The only issues are when, and by whom, it was accepted.

The LXX may provide some evidence that the book of Esther was considered Scripture by at least some Jews in the first century BC. A unique feature of the LXX version of Esther is that, unlike any other book of the OT, it includes a colophon, a statement of provenance. The text of the colophon is as follows:

> Ἔτους τετάρτου βασιλεύοντος Πτολεμαίου καὶ Κλεοπάτρας εἰσήνεγκεν Δωσίθεος, ὃς ἔφη εἶναι ἱερεὺς καὶ Λευίτης, καὶ Πτολεμαῖος ὁ υἱὸς αὐτοῦ τὴν προκειμένην ἐπιστολὴν τῶν Φρουραι, ἣν ἔφασαν εἶναι καὶ ἑρμηνευκέναι Λυσίμαχον Πτολεμαίου τῶν ἐν Ιερουσαλημ.
>
> In the fourth year of the reign of Ptolemy and Cleopatra, Dositheus, who said he was a priest and Levite, and Ptolemy his son, brought this epistle of Phurim, which they said was authentic, and that Lysimachus the son of Ptolemy, of those in Jerusalem, had translated it.

79. Talmon, "Was the Book of Esther Known at Qumran?," 253–56.

80. Some of Talmon's allusions depend on attributing vowel points to certain phrases in ways that are unique to the book of Esther. For example, Talmon notes the unique construction אִישׁ וָאִישׁ in Esth 1:8 and similar constructions where a definite article is used on a repeated noun with a *waw*-conjunctive to indicate inclusivity: "every man." He attributes the same vowel pointing and meaning to several phrases from Qumran texts where it appears a simple distributive meaning would be just as likely.

81. As noted by the medieval Jewish commentator B. Levin, *Oztar Hagaonim*, *b. Meg.* 7a.

Moore writes, "This is unquestionably the most important verse in the entire Greek version of Esther."[82] Bickerman demonstrated that such colophons were often appended to the ends of Greek books when they were added to royal libraries, such as the one in Alexandria, Egypt.[83] Frequently, they included grammatical notes or references to the scribes who had produced the texts. But in cases where the authenticity of a text might be in doubt, colophons could be added to assure the pedigree of the manuscript. Such colophons could, of course, be forged, and some scholars have argued against the authenticity of Esther's. Yet there seems little reason to reject these lines out of hand. The dates and personages named are not inherently improbable. Furthermore, the careful wording of the reported claims—"said he was a priest"; "they said it was authentic"—sounds like the reluctant concession of a minor official striving to maintain a position of plausible deniability.

If we accept the authenticity of the colophon, it gives us some clues into the way Esther was viewed at the time this translation was undertaken. It was considered by the priests of Jerusalem to be the authoritative statement on the celebration of Purim. It was considered of such importance that the Jewish community in Jerusalem had undertaken to translate it into Greek for the use of Jews of the Diaspora and then had sought to have it deposited in a Hellenistic library. Of course, "authoritative" does not necessarily mean "holy Scripture": 1 Maccabees was an authoritative account of the Hasmonean Revolt and inspired the establishment of Hanukkah, a feast regularly observed by the Jews, but it was nonetheless excluded from the Jewish canon.

As for the date of this colophon, there are several possible candidates. All the Macedonian rulers of Egypt bore the title "Ptolemy," and several were married to a queen called Cleopatra. But as Bickerman notes, only three of these were associated with a Cleopatra in the fourth year of their reign: Ptolemy IX Soter (reigned ca. 116–107 BC), Ptolemy XII Auletos (reigned ca. 80–58 BC), and Ptolemy XIII Theos Philopater (reigned ca. 51–47 BC).[84] Most scholars, like Bickerman, favor the second, though Moore has expressed preference for Ptolemy IX.[85] In any event, the colophon indicates that the book of Esther was recognized as authoritative, if not as "Scripture," in at least some Jewish communities before the first century AD. It is worth noting that even though this colophon places the book of Esther

82. C. A. Moore, "On the Origins of the LXX Additions to the Book of Esther," *JBL* 92 (1973): 382.

83. Bickerman, "Colophon," 342–44.

84. Bickerman, "Colophon," 346–47.

85. Moore, "Origins," though he refers to the ruler as Ptolemy VIII.

in Alexandria by the last century BC, Esther is never quoted or alluded to in the writings of prolific first-century Alexandrian Jew Philo.

Perhaps the earliest and best evidence for the canonization of Esther in early Judaism comes from the writings of Josephus. As mentioned above, Josephus summarizes the story of Esther in *Ant.* 11.184–296. We will consider his treatment of Esther from time to time below, but for now, it is not his account of the story that is significant. The inclusion of the story here does not indicate that Josephus considered the book of Esther to be canonical Scripture, since he draws accounts from a number of nonbiblical sources (e.g., 1 Maccabees) for his histories.[86] Rather, for our current purposes, the possible reference to Esther in *Ag. Ap.* 1.38 is more significant. Here, he writes of the "twenty-two" books that comprised the Jewish Scriptures. Obviously, in our modern editions, the Heb. Bible contains far more than twenty-two books. But Jewish tradition typically grouped several texts together and counted them as a single book: the twelve minor prophets were considered a single book; the two books of Kings and Chronicles were each counted as one; Ezra-Nehemiah was a single book. Also, if the tradition attributed to the Jews by the church fathers Origen, Epiphanius, and Jerome was in practice in Josephus' day, Ruth was numbered together with Judges, and Lamentations with Jeremiah (somewhat surprising, since Ruth and Lamentations appear in the Writings, while Judges and Jeremiah are in the Prophets). Using this reckoning, many scholars conclude that Esther must have been part of the twenty-two-book canon referenced by Josephus.[87]

Even more persuasive, however, is Josephus' mention in the same passage of the "thirteen books" that recorded events of "the time from the death of Moses till the reign of Artaxerxes king of Persia, who reigned after Xerxes." It is difficult to determine with certainty to which books Josephus refers here, because it is impossible to reconcile this number with the twenty-two he mentioned earlier. Apparently, he is now dividing the books of Samuel, Kings, Chronicles, and Ezra-Nehemiah into separate books, as was done in the LXX, and perhaps counting Daniel as a history. More important for our purposes, however, is his reference to Artaxerxes, son of Xerxes. The histories of Samuel-Kings and Chronicles end in the era of Cyrus the Great, more than one hundred years before the time of Artaxerxes, and so cannot exhaust the thirteen books. Josephus explicitly attributes the events of Ezra and Nehemiah to the reign of Xerxes (e.g., *Ant.* 11.183). The events of

---

86. On the sources used in Josephus' *Antiquities*, see E. Schürer, *The History of the Jewish People in the Age of Jesus Christ (175 B.C.–A.D. 135)*, trans. and rev. G. Vermes, F. Millar, and M. Goodman (Edinburgh: T&T Clark, 1987), 3:48–53.

87. Thus, e.g., S. Leiman, *The Canonization of the Hebrew Scriptures*, 153n160; Moore 1977, xxiii; Beckwith, *Old Testament Canon*, 79–80.

the book of Esther, however, he located in the reign of Artaxerxes. It seems likely, therefore, that Josephus counted Esther among his thirteen books of history and thus considered it to be Scripture.[88]

Some thirty years after Josephus, yet another source attesting to the canonical status of Esther is found in the work of Aquila, a second-century Jewish scholar who wanted to produce a Greek translation of the Heb. Bible superior to the LXX. According to Jerome (*Isaiam* 8.14), he was a pupil of the Rabbi Akiba (d. AD 135), while Epiphanius (*de Mensuris et Ponderibus* 15) remarks that his Greek translation of the Heb. Bible was produced about the twelfth year of the Emperor Hadrian, so ca. AD 128–29. From the surviving fragments of his text, it is clear that Aquila's Bible included all the "disputed" books of the Heb. Bible. A fragment of his translation of Esther has survived in the midrash *Esth Rab.* 2:7. The inclusion of Esther in this translation is a clear indication that this scholar of exceptional rabbinic pedigree considered Esther to be Scripture.

While Josephus and Aquila may have considered the matter of Esther's canonicity settled, the rabbinic sources express some ambivalence toward the book. One passage reflecting this ambivalence appears in *b. Sanh.* 100a:[89]

> Levi b. Samuel and R. Huna b. Hiyya were repairing the mantles of the Scrolls of R. Judah's college. On coming to the Scroll of Esther, they remarked, "O, this Scroll of Esther does not require a mantle." Thereupon he reproved them, "This too savours of irreverence."

The "mantles," or covers, on biblical scrolls served two functions. On the one hand, they provided extra protection to works that were considered more precious, due to their canonical status. On the other hand, they made it possible for people to handle the books without having to go through the process of ritual washing afterward. According to rabbinic tradition, the books of Scripture imparted ritual impurity to the hands, while secular books did not.[90] Even books that discussed religious ideas

88. As noted by M. Stuart, *Critical History and Defense of the Old Testament Canon* (Andover, MA: Allen, Morrill, and Wardwell, 1845), 227–28.

89. Citations of the Talmud are from I. Epstein, ed., *The Babylonian Talmud,* 18 vols. (London: Soncino, 1961).

90. Numerous explanations have been given for this seemingly counterintuitive position. R. Beckwith, *Old Testament Canon*, 279–80, summarizes and rightly rejects several of these explanations. He reasonably suggests that the procedure was designed to protect the scrolls from careless treatment: one would be disinclined to handle them unnecessarily if doing so resulted in needing to wash the hands. We might also add that the study of Scripture had displaced temple ritual as the center of Jewish worship during this period, and it is possible that customs formerly

or were highly regarded as edifying reading, such as the Wisdom of Ben Sira, were not deemed to defile the hands.[91] Blessings copied onto pieces of parchment were not considered defiling—unless they contained more than eighty-five letters of Scripture. Rabbis Levi and Huna (ca. AD 300) felt that Esther required no mantle. It did not render the hands unclean, meaning it was not holy Scripture. Rabbi Judah reproved them for denigrating the sanctity of the book.

The most extensive passage in this discussion is found in *b. Meg.* 7a, the tractate dealing with the reading of the book of Esther on Purim:

> Rab Judah said in the name of Samuel; [The scroll] of Esther does not make the hands unclean. Are we to infer from this that Samuel was of opinion that Esther was not composed under the inspiration of the holy spirit? How can this be, seeing

---

associated with the cultus—including the requirement for ritual ablutions following sacrifices—were transferred to the study of Scripture.

91. There has been some recent discussion on whether "canonical" and "inspired by the Holy Spirit" were synonymous concepts in rabbinic Judaism. Some scholars have contended that books such as Esther were already considered canonical long before the time of the rabbis, but the debate only concerned whether or not the texts were inspired. For example, Leiman writes, "Speculation on the date of the closing of the biblical canon, based upon evidence from Talmudic passages treating books defiling the hands, would appear gratuitous. The rabbis were questioning the inspired status of some of the books in the biblical canon already closed; they were neither discussing canonicity nor closing the biblical canon" (*Canonization*, 119–20). Leiman's approach (since adopted by several scholars) would introduce a category of "uninspired Scripture"—books that were considered canonical, but nonetheless regarded as products of humans rather than God. This approach prompts the question: if it were not the inspiration of the Holy Spirit that determined canonicity, what were the criteria? There are several sources that suggest that "inspired" and "holy Scripture" were considered synonymous concepts. The earliest of these is likely 2 Tim 3:16, "All Scripture is inspired by God and is profitable ... " (though admittedly, the verse could also be translated, "All Scripture which is inspired by God is profitable ... "). Josephus (*Ag. Ap.* 1.38) also seems to make an organic connection between scriptural status and prophetic inspiration, contending that the Scriptures are trustworthy precisely because they were given under divine inspiration. Finally, medieval rabbis, including Yom Toy Ashbelli (Ritva), Rav Hai Gaon, and Meiri understood the question of "defiling the hands" to be a matter of canonicity (see M. Broyde, "Defilement of the Hands, Canonization of the Bible, and the Special Status of Esther, Ecclesiastes, and Song of Songs," *Judaism* 44 [1995]: 65–79). There was almost certainly popular recognition of many of the Hebrew Bible books by the end of the second century BC, but the Dead Sea Scroll library, the rabbinic witness, the NT, and the church fathers suggest that some controversy remained. On the status of Ben Sira, see *t. Yad.* 2.13.

> that Samuel has said that Esther was composed under the inspiration of the holy spirit?—It was composed to be recited [by heart], but not to be written. The following objection was raised: "R. Meir says that [the scroll of] Koheleth does not render the hands unclean, and that about the Song of Songs there is a difference of opinion. R. Jose says that the Song of Songs renders the hands unclean, and about Koheleth there is a difference of opinion. R. Simeon says that Koheleth is one of those matters in regard to which Beth Shammai were more lenient and Beth Hillel more stringent, but Ruth and the Song of Songs and Esther [certainly] make the hands unclean"!—Samuel concurred with R. Joshua.

Apparently, Samuel (ca. AD 250) had argued that the oral version of Esther was inspired by the Holy Spirit, but the written version was not. This argument does not seem to have been seriously entertained by the other rabbis and apparently was peculiar to Rabbi Samuel. Nonetheless, the misgivings of this great Jewish sage to accept the scroll as Scripture are noteworthy.

In this same passage (*b. Meg.* 7a), we read how Esther personally appealed to the council of rabbis for her book to receive inclusion in the Bible:

> R. Samuel b. Judah said: Esther sent to the Wise Men saying, Commemorate me for future generations. They replied, You will incite the ill will of the nations against us. She sent back reply: I am already recorded in the chronicles of the kings of Media and Persia. Rab and R. Hanina and R. Johanan and R. Habiba record [the above statement in this form]: ... Esther sent to the Wise Men saying, Write an account of me for posterity. They sent back answer, Have I not written for thee three times—three times and not four?[92] [And they refused]

It is apparent from these passages that the rabbis recalled a time when the status of Esther was in dispute. We need not accept these passages as historical record of an official debate. The "Wise Men" mentioned here probably refers to the Great Synagogue, which (as noted above) is most likely fictional. If not the Great Synagogue, then the story implies that

---

92. Here, they cite Prov 22:20 as evidence that a tradition should only be recorded three times. There were already three accounts of Amalek's downfall recorded in Scripture (Exod 17:8–16; Deut 25:17–19; 1 Sam 15), so Esther's story was to be excluded. The rabbis concluded that the two citations in the Pentateuch constitute but a single instance and that the other two citations were to occur in the Prophets (1 Samuel) and the Writings (Esther).

Esther spoke from beyond the grave, perhaps to the men of Jamnia. But on the other hand, it seems likely that the suspicious attitude expressed toward the book of Esther here is a historical reality. It is especially interesting that the first reason cited for the book's rejection has to do with how its canonization would be viewed by the Gentiles: it would anger them, probably because of the ludicrous way in which the Gentiles were portrayed and/or the horrible slaughter the Jews managed to perpetrate against them.

The rabbis continue on in this tractate (*b. Meg.* 7a) to give several evidences for why the book of Esther must have been inspired by the Holy Spirit. Several of these "proofs" are concerned with the author of Esther often seeming to possess knowledge beyond that of the senses. For example, in Esth 6:6, it is written, "And Haman thought to himself … "; in 2:15, we read, "Esther was favored by all who saw her … " The rabbis were convinced that no one but the Holy Spirit could know the thoughts of the heart. They also argued that the statements in Esther that the feast of Purim would be perpetually observed by the Jews indicated divine inspiration. Who but God could know the future? These arguments would be persuasive to few today, and even some of the rabbis acknowledged their weaknesses.

The tone of the rabbinic disputes over Esther may best be characterized thus: the book of Esther was generally accepted as Scripture, but there were some who questioned its status. There could be many reasons for this ambivalence toward the book. One obvious and oft-noted feature that characterizes the three disputed Hagiographa is the lack of the divine name. Of all the books of the Heb. Bible, only these three never use the full Tetragrammaton in reference to God.[93] The book of Esther compounds the difficulty, since it has no references to God nor to any pious observance at all. Beckwith further argues that the book of Esther was questioned because of its institution of a feast not mentioned in the Pentateuch.[94] He cites *b. Meg.* 14a in support of this position: "Our Rabbis taught: 'Forty-eight prophets and seven prophetesses prophesied to Israel, and they neither took away from nor added aught to what is written in the Torah save only the reading of the Megillah.'" But in fact, this passage says nothing about the canonicity of Esther and does not even imply disapproval of the feast. It merely states that this feast was not prescribed in Torah. Similarly, Maimonides would claim that after the coming of Messiah, only the written and oral Torah and the reading of the Esther scroll would remain of the scriptural traditions.[95]

93. It is possible, however, that an abbreviated form of the Tetragrammaton appears in Song 8:6, which may be read, "Like the fire of YAH," or may simply exhibit a form of the 3 fem. sg. poss. *he* ending. See R. Murphy, *AYBD* 6:154.

94. Beckwith, *Old Testament Canon*, 290.

95. Moses Maimonides, *Laws of the Scroll* [of Esther], 2:18.

All others would be nullified, but Esther would remain: God had promised that the earlier tribulations would be forgotten (Isa 65:16), but that the celebration of Purim would endure forever (Esth 9:28).

Esther in the Christian Canon

Among Christians, the issue of Esther's canonicity was somewhat different from for Jews. For Christians, it was complicated by a matter of technology. While Jews preferred to record their texts on scrolls, Christians early adopted the use of the codex, or book, for their Scriptures. Among Jews, a scroll of a book that was deemed noncanonical was simply treated differently from a canonical text (e.g., not fitted with a mantle, or simply set aside). But in Christian tradition, a book regarded as noncanonical would not be bound together with the other texts in the Bible. This fact made the explicit delineation of biblical books more urgent in Christianity than in Jewish tradition. But as in the Jewish tradition, there were apparently some early misgivings among some church fathers regarding Esther.

The New Testament

The earliest evidence of Esther's status among Christians would be its use in the NT. Frequently both academic and popular authors state that the book of Esther was not quoted nor alluded to in the NT.[96] While it is true that the book is not cited by name, there do appear to be a few allusions, demonstrating both a familiarity with the words and (unlike the Qumran allusions) the story line. The first of these appears in Mark 6, in the story of John the Baptist's death. In this chapter, several echoes of Esther occur.[97] The setting is a banquet celebrating Herod Antipas' birthday. Herod is referred to, in accurately but significantly, as "king" (he was actually *tetrarch* of Galilee, a

96. Among the many examples, see. B. Anderson, "Place of the Book of Esther in the Christian Bible," 42: "It is significant that the Book of Esther is not once quoted in the New Testament, despite the fact of its popularity among the Jews of the first century." Also Martin, 699: "The New Testament does not quote from the Book of Esther." J. H. Hayes and E. Krentz, *New Testament: History of Interpretation* (Nashville: Abingdon, 1984), 233; I. Loken, *The Old Testament Historical Books: An Introduction* (Maitland, FL: Xulon, 2004), 315; C. Swindoll, *Esther: A Woman of Strength and Dignity* (Nashville: Thomas Nelson, 1977), 127, likewise state that Esther is not cited in the NT.

97. See R. Aus, *Water into Wine and the Beheading of John the Baptist* (Atlanta: Scholars Press/Brown Judaic Studies, 1988), 39–74; N. Duran, "Return of the Disembodied or How John the Baptist Lost His Head," in *Reading Communities Reading Texts*, ed. G. A. Phillips and N. Wilkinson Duran (Philadelphia: Trinity Press International, 2002), 277–91; B. Schildgen, "A Blind Promise: Mark's Retrieval of Esther," *Poetics Today* 15 (1994): 115–31.

governor). As ruler, he is waffling and ineffectual, subject to manipulation by evil courtiers, as was Xerxes. His wife Herodias, like Haman, schemes to kill a righteous Jew (in this case, John the Baptist). A young woman is summoned to entertain the guests, just as Vashti was (Esth 1:10–11). In Mark 6:22, 28, Herodias' daughter is called a κοράσιον (damsel), the same word used of Esther in the LXX version of Esth 2:7. Her performance "pleases" (ἀρέσκω) "king" Herod, just as Esther had pleased King Xerxes (Esth 2:4). So pleased was he, in fact, that he promised to give the damsel anything she requested, "up to half his kingdom" (Mark 6:23), using precisely the words used by Xerxes in his promise to Esther (Esth 5:6; 7:2). (This precise phrase is found nowhere else in Scripture.) Xerxes may well have been exaggerating, but Herod outdid him for bombast, since he, being a governor, actually had no kingdom to give! Instead of a literal account of Herod's promise, these words were deliberately chosen by the author to make explicit the parallelism with the book of Esther. This echo sets up an ironically opposite outcome for the two episodes: in Esther, the villain is killed and the Jewish hero is rewarded with his property; in Mark, the hero is killed and the villain is rewarded with his head.

It would take us too far afield of the subject of canonization to discuss the purposes of Mark's use of Esther. Rather, for us, these parallels suffice to demonstrate that Mark felt the Esther tradition significant enough to incorporate it into his Gospel in a way that parallels how he and the other evangelists used the Moses tradition.

Another likely echo of Esther in the NT is found in the Gospel of John. This allusion often passes unnoticed, likely because it comes not from the MT version of Esther, but rather from one of the additions. In John 21:15–17, Jesus issued His threefold challenge to Peter, restoring Peter into his office as leader of the disciples. Three times Jesus asked Peter, "Simon, do you love me?" Twice Peter responded, "Lord, you know that I love you." But after the third time, Peter became troubled, and answered, "Lord, you know all things. You know that I love you": Κύριε σὺ πάντα οἶδας σὺ γινώσκεις ὅτι φιλῶ σε. The phrase "Lord, you know all things" is about as close as the Bible ever comes to an affirmation of the idea of divine omniscience. Yet it has no parallel in the Heb. Bible.[98] There are, however, a couple of parallels in Esther LXX. In Addition C, we find the prayers that Mordecai and Esther prayed before Esther was to approach King Xerxes. In Mordecai's prayer (LXX 7:24), he uses a phrase similar to that found here in John:

98. There is a similar statement in John 16:30, where the disciples affirm, "Now we recognize that you know all things" (νῦν οἴδαμεν ὅτι οἶδας πάντα). The meaning is similar, but the grammatical construction is quite different.

> σὺ πάντα γινώσκεις σὺ οἶδας κύριε ὅτι οὐκ ἐν ὕβρει οὐδὲ ἐν ὑπερηφανίᾳ οὐδὲ ἐν φιλοδοξίᾳ ἐποίησα τοῦτο τὸ μὴ προσκυνεῖν τὸν ὑπερήφανον Αμαν
>
> You know all things. You know, Lord, that it was neither in arrogance nor in pride nor for any love of glory that I did this, not bowing down to proud Haman.

In this verse, several of the same key words occur: the pronoun σὺ, the proper noun Κύριε, and two verbs of knowing, οἶδας and γινώσκεις, appearing in the same form. But the next use of this phrase, in Esther's prayer (LXX 8:15), provides an even more interesting parallel:

> κύριε πάντων γνῶσιν ἔχεις καὶ οἶδας ὅτι ἐμίσησα δόξαν ἀνόμων καὶ βδελύσσομαι κοίτην ἀπεριτμήτων καὶ παντὸς ἀλλοτρίου
>
> O Lord,[99] you have knowledge of all things, and you know that I hate the glory of the lawless and I abhor the bed of the uncircumcised and all the foreigners.

In both of these verses from Esther, the speaker associates the Lord's omniscience with His ability to know the feelings and motives of his/her heart, just as in John 21. The parallel to Esther is particularly apropos, because Esther has been committing what appears to be apostasy by sharing the bed and table of the pagan Persian king. In her prayer, Esther, the most prominent Jew of her day, affirms that God knows her true feelings: she actually *hates* her status. The situation provides a loose parallel to Peter's in the Gospel of John: Peter, most prominent of the disciples, had recently denied knowing Jesus and had abandoned Him, apparently committing an act of apostasy. In his responses, Peter acknowledged that Jesus knew his true feelings: he *loves* Jesus. Neither Esther nor Peter admits to apostasy; though appearances would seem to say otherwise, they both claim that the Lord knows their hearts.

In these two examples, the Gospel authors have used verbal allusions to the book of Esther to draw out parallels between situations that seemed to them somehow analogous. These references seem not only to imply that the evangelists regarded the book of Esther to be Scripture, but that they were very familiar with its Greek form.

---

99. In standard versification of the Greek text, the κύριε at the beginning of this verse is found at the end of 8:14. It may, however, be read at the beginning of this verse without doing violence to the meaning of the previous verse, and it provides an appropriate address to the Divinity, which the verse as divided in the printed editions lacks.

The Church Fathers

In the writings of the church fathers, attitudes toward the book of Esther seem to have been divided along geographical lines. The Western church, for the most part, seemed generally to accord the book a place among the Scriptures, although even here references to the book are not widespread. In the Eastern church, on the other hand, opinions tended more toward the negative, with several prominent Eastern Fathers appearing to reject the book.[100] The earliest Christian allusion to Esther outside the Bible comes from the Western church father Clement of Rome (30?–99). In *1 Clem.* 55 (written ca. AD 97–98), Esther is evinced as an example of sacrificial love because of her willingness to humble herself and risk her life for the sake of her people. It is evident that Clement, like the evangelists, knew the LXX version of Esther, since he describes how, with fasting and humiliation, she entreated the everlasting God "who sees all things" for the deliverance of her people. Clement's dependence on the LXX is also apparent in the fact that he refers to the apocryphal story of Judith in the same context.

The link between Judith and Esther is substantial: in three of the earliest Western works to allude to the book (*1 Clement*, the *Stromata* 4.19 of Clement of Alexandria [ca. AD 150–215], and *Constitutions of the Holy Apostles* [AD 375–80]), it is linked with the contrasting story of Judith. And well it may be, since the stories share a common theme. Both are books about Jewish women who, through acts of heroism, deliver their people from dire threat. Both use their beauty to effect the deliverance. Judith is clearly the more orthodox in its theology, with many references to God and with the heroine refusing to compromise her integrity by sharing the bed of a pagan. But it is Judith that was excluded from the "orthodox" Heb. canon.[101]

Other church fathers who clearly regarded Esther as Scripture are so few that they can be listed in short order. They are:[102]

- Origen (185?–254), who included it in his Hexapla, a sixfold parallel edition of the OT;
- Cyril of Jerusalem (ca. 313–86), in his fourth catechetical lecture (issued 347–48), identifies Esther as the twelfth book of the OT;
- Epiphanius (315–403), the bishop of Salamis and metropolitan of Cyprus (*On Weights and Measures,* chap. 23), in explaining how

100. See Moore, "Esther," *AYBD* 6:635. Beckwith, *Old Testament Canon,* 295–97, argues that Esther was always considered Scripture in the Western church.

101. For an exploration of this mystery, see S. White-Crawford, "Esther Not Judith: Why One Made It and the Other Didn't," *BR* 18 (2002): 22–31, 45.

102. Several of these sources are conveniently reproduced in original language and translation by M. Stuart, *Critical History,* 431–52.

the Jews reckoned the books of their Bible to be twenty-two in number, equaling the number of letters in their alphabet, includes Esther in the count;
- Rufinus (ca 345–410), Italian monk and scholar, in his *Commentary on the Apostles' Creed*, places the book of Esther at the end of the historical books;
- Jerome (ca. 347–420), who lists it among the books of the Hagiographa in the introduction to his translations of the books of Samuel and Kings (indeed, the canon he endorses here is identical to the modern Protestant OT canon);
- Hilary (355–367/8), in his *Prologue to the Book of Psalms*, includes Esther among the twenty-two books of the OT (again, equaling the number of letters in the Heb. alphabet);
- Augustine (354–430) alludes to the book of Esther in his *City of God*, including it among the historical books of Scripture.

None of these writers demonstrate any great love for the book of Esther or devote much effort to its exposition. Their remarks, then, are only of interest with regard to Esther's status, not in understanding its message.

The Fathers who clearly rejected Esther form nearly as imposing a group as those who accepted it. It is difficult to prove which of the church fathers thought Esther should not be considered canonical, for the failure to mention Esther can hardly be taken as a definitive vote against the text. In this case, since there are no Fathers who actually repudiate the book, we must rely on canon lists that clearly omit it.

The earliest such list happens to be the earliest canon list ever compiled. Bishop Melito of Sardis (d. ca. 180) is reported to have traveled to Jerusalem in order to discover what books should be included in the OT canon. Church historian Eusebius (*Hist. eccl.* 4.26.14) quoted him as follows:[103]

> Accordingly when I went East and came to the place where these things were preached and done, I learned accurately the books of the Old Testament, and send them to thee as written below. Their names are as follows: Of Moses, five books: Genesis, Exodus, Numbers, Leviticus, Deuteronomy; Jesus Nave, Judges, Ruth; of Kings, four books; of Chronicles, two; the Psalms of David, the Proverbs of Solomon, Wisdom also, Ecclesiastes, Song of Songs, Job; of Prophets, Isaiah, Jeremiah; of the twelve

103. A. McGiffert, trans., *Nicene and Post-Nicene Fathers*, second series, vol. 1, ed. P. Schaff and H. Wace (Buffalo, NY: Christian Literature, 1890), 206.

> prophets, one book; Daniel, Ezekiel, Esdras. From which also I have made the extracts, dividing them into six books.

Esther is thus omitted from our earliest surviving canon list.

Another Eastern church father who rejected Esther was Athanasius (ca. 296–373), bishop of Alexandria and hero of the Nicene Council. Athanasius is often cited for his endorsement of a thirty-nine-book OT canon, and his rejection of the apocryphal writings. His thirty-nine books, however, differ significantly from the Jewish and Protestant canons in that he rejects Esther and includes Baruch. Indeed, he groups Esther with books that would be considered part of the Apocrypha:[104]

> But for greater exactness I add this also, writing of necessity; that there are other books besides these not indeed included in the Canon, but appointed by the Fathers to be read by those who newly join us, and who wish for instruction in the word of godliness. The Wisdom of Solomon, and the Wisdom of Sirach, and Esther, and Judith, and Tobit, and that which is called the Teaching of the Apostles, and the Shepherd. But the former, my brethren, are included in the Canon, the latter being [merely] read ...

Still another church father who snubbed Esther was Gregory of Nanzianzus (326–391). Near the end of his life, Gregory composed a poem about the canon entitled "Concerning the Genuine Books of Divinely Inspired Scripture." His list of historical books ends with Ezra. Finally, if the hostile report of Leontius of Byzantium is to be believed, great Antiochan scholar Theodore of Mopsuestia (350?–428) also rejected Esther.

The canonical status of Esther was ultimately decided in the church councils. The Council of Hippo (393) endorsed the book of Esther, and the final word on the matter was made by the third Council of Carthage in 397. A report on this council, issued by Dionysius Exiguus in 419, goes as follows:[105]

> It was also determined that besides the Canonical Scriptures nothing be read in the Church under the title of divine Scriptures. The Canonical Scriptures are these: Genesis, Exodus, Leviticus, Numbers, Deuteronomy, Joshua the son of Nun, Judges, Ruth, four books of Kings, two books of Paraleipomena,

104. Festal Letter 39, trans. R. Payne-Smith, *Nicene and Post-Nicene Fathers*, second series, vol. 4, ed. P. Schaff and H. Wace (Buffalo, NY: Christian Literature, 1892), 552.

105. Trans. B. F. Westcott, *A General Survey of the History of the Canon of the New Testament*, 7th ed. (London: MacMillan, 1896), 447–48.

> Job, the Psalter, five books of Solomon, the books of the twelve prophets, Isaiah, Jeremiah, Ezechiel, Daniel, Tobit, Judith, Esther, two books of Esdras, two books of the Maccabees. Of the New Testament: four books of the Gospels, one book of the Acts of the Apostles, thirteen Epistles of the Apostle Paul, one epistle of the same [writer] to the Hebrews, two Epistles of the Apostle Peter, three of John, one of James, one of Jude, one book of the Apocalypse of John. Let this be made known also to our brother and fellow-priest Boniface, or to other bishops of those parts, for the purpose of confirming that Canon, because we have received from our fathers that those books must be read in the Church.

In spite of this broad endorsement, the attitudes of the Fathers toward Esther remained less than enthusiastic. In Christianity and Judaism, Esther's fortunes took opposite trajectories. In Judaism, because of the connection of Esther with Purim, the book was kept in the public eye. It became the subject of many commentaries and popular stories. In Christianity, Esther seems to have retreated from view such that there were few homilies preached on it, and no Christian commentary was written on it before the ninth century AD.[106] It was officially part of the canon, but it seemed to have been sequestered away in a cupboard under the stairs.

Genre

Historicity

The literary genre of the book of Esther appears, on first glance, to be a historical chronicle of remarkable but by no means miraculous events that transpired during the reign of a well-known ancient monarch.[107] It contains no talking animals, eye-popping wonders, or blatant impossibilities that might make rationalists question its veracity. For many centuries, the church and synagogue unanimously accepted the book for what it appears to be: a literal account of events that occurred during that shadowy era

106. As far as we know, the earliest Christian commentary on the book of Esther was composed by Benedictine monk and archbishop of Mainz, Rabanus Maurus (780–856). It may be found in Migne's *Patrologia Latina* vol. 109.

107. Indeed, R. Gordis, "Religion, Wisdom and History in the Book of Esther—A New Solution to an Ancient Crux," *JBL* 100 (1981): 375, has designated the genre of Esther "Persian chronicle." It is a difficult case to make, since we have no ancient Persian chronicles with which to compare Esther. Even Gordis admits that "no historical chronicles, royal or otherwise, for the Achaemenid period (550–331 B.C.E.) have survived, the only records being a few Persian inscriptions and proclamations."

when the Jews were subjects of the Persian Empire. And yet, in recent times, the majority of scholars have rejected the identification of Esther as history. Over a hundred years ago, the *Jewish Encyclopedia* could state, "The vast majority of modern expositors have reached the conclusion that the book is a piece of pure fiction, although some writers qualify their criticism by an attempt to treat it as a historical romance."[108] More recently, Fox writes, "Various legendary qualities as well as several inaccuracies and implausibilities immediately throw doubt on the book's historicity and give the impression of a writer recalling vaguely remembered past."[109] And Levenson (23) states, "[T]he historical problems with Esther are so massive as to persuade anyone who is not already obligated by religious dogma to believe in the historicity of the biblical narrative to doubt the veracity of the narrative."

In this case, we cannot simply blame the verdict on a knee-jerk bias against supernaturalism, because Esther contains no overt supernatural elements. Nor is there a well-recognized form-critical marker that automatically informs the reader that the story should not be taken literally (such as the fairy tale rubric "Once upon a time ... "). Rather, there are two bodies of evidence that are most frequently cited by those who would identify this story as fiction: internal improbabilities and information from external sources that is irreconcilable with Esther's depiction of Persian history and policies.

The Internal Improbabilities

A number of these difficulties have been tersely summarized by Moore (1971, xlv–xlvi). The internal improbabilities he cites include:

- the feast given by the king for the leaders of the empire (1:1–3) lasting 180 days;
- Vashti's refusal to obey the king's command;
- the king's "ridiculous" letter ordering all the men of his empire to be masters in their own houses (1:22);
- the appointment of non-Persians to the position of prime minister within the empire;
- the letters sent out in all the languages of the empire, rather than in Aramaic and Persian, the official languages of the empire (1:22, 3:12, 8:9);

108. "Esther," *The Jewish Encyclopedia* (London & New York: Funk & Wagnalls, 1905), 5:235–36.

109. Fox, *Character and Ideology*, 131.

- the king's granting permission for an entire ethnic group of the empire to be exterminated (3:8–15) and issuing the command nearly a year in advance of the event; and
- the king's sanction of fighting through his empire, even in the royal palace (9:11–15).

To these improbabilities, we could add still others:

- selecting the queen of the world's largest and most well-administered empire based on a "beauty" pageant (2:1–4);
- the maidens' yearlong preparations for a single night with the king (2:12);
- Haman's offer to deposit ten thousand talents of silver in the royal treasury for the destruction of the Jews (about 375 tons—according to Moore [1971, 39], the equivalent of about two-thirds of the Persian Empire's annual income!);
- the seventy-five-foot-tall gallows that Haman prepared for Mordecai (5:14); and
- the slaughter of over seventy-five thousand "enemies of the Jews" (9:11–16)—in those days, about the population of a very large city. Adding to the apparent improbability is the fact that the Jews suffered no losses in the slaughter.

None of these points, as Moore admits, in itself proves that the Esther narrative is not historical. Any one of them, strange as it might seem, *could* have happened. Together, however, they would seem to present an imposing challenge to logical probability.

Many of these difficulties, however, have been addressed, with varying degrees of success, by conservative scholars. Some of the internal difficulties can be countered with the observation that improbable coincidences happen every day and that people will often act in ways that make little sense. This fact may be especially true of the Persian court, known for its extravagance and, at times, irrationality. Some other issues have been addressed specifically:

- There is nothing in Esth 1:3–4 to indicate that the banquet itself must have lasted 180 days; the text merely says that for 180 days, the king displayed the wealth of his kingdom. The text could mean that the king took his officials on a six-month tour of the kingdom, which was followed by a seven-day feast.[110]

110. Herodotus (*Hist.* 7.8) states that Xerxes gave a banquet for his "war council" before the invasion of Greece. Jobes, 60, suggests that Xerxes took his allies on a 180-day tour of the kingdom to consolidate their support before the seven-day banquet spoken of here.

- Gordis observed that Antiochus III once issued an order four months in advance of the time it was to be carried out, so the eleven-month lag between the issuing of the decree to destroy the Jews and the time it was to have been enacted is not without parallel.[111]
- Regarding the slaughter of an entire ethnic group, Gordis notes that in 88 BC, after conquering the Roman province of Asia Minor, Mithradates VI of Pontus ordered a general slaughter of "all who were of Italic race" within the newly subjugated territory.[112]
- It is also reported that eighty thousand people were killed on that day, making Esther's report of seventy-five thousand slaughtered seem less unprecedented.
- It has been argued that the seventy-five-foot-tall gallows should be understood as a more modest pole erected on a prominent hill.

Many of the more specific charges of incompatibility have been addressed as well. Some of these issues will be noted in the commentary.

The External Evidence

More convincing to many is the external evidence against the historicity of Esther. At a number of points, the narrative contradicts ancient records or Persian practices attested in other ancient literature. Many of these ancient sources are from Greek writers, the most significant of which is the *Histories* of Herodotus. As noted earlier, Herodotus writes a good deal about the early career of Xerxes and includes a number of details about Persian politics and court intrigue. Herodotus is hardly infallible, his accounts being heavily biased against his subject matter. On the other hand, he has often proven trustworthy, even when compared to ancient records and inscriptions from the Persians (e.g., his account of the usurpation of Bardiya generally agrees with that given by Darius in the Behistun inscription and even gets the names of six of the seven conspirators correct).[113] When compared to these records, several features of Esther have been identified as problematic (as noted by Paton, 71–72, and many others since):

- The book of Esther states that Xerxes reigned over 127 provinces (1:1), whereas Herodotus reports that Xerxes reigned over twenty "satrapies" (administrative districts). Inscriptions from the time

111. Gordis, "Religion, Wisdom and History," 383.
112. Ibid.
113. For an interesting discussion of Herodotus' reliability, see R. Strassler, ed., *The Landmark Herodotus: the Histories* (New York: Anchor Books, 2007), xxiv–xxxii.

of Darius put the number of satrapies between twenty-three and thirty.

- According to the book of Esther, Xerxes' queen in the early years of his reign was Vashti (1:9–12), who was later replaced by Esther. According to Herodotus, Xerxes' queen was Amestris, daughter of Otanes, one of the seven conspirators against Pseudo-Bardiya (*Hist.* 7.61, 114; 9.109–114). Furthermore, Herodotus and Ctesias of Cnidus both indicate that Amestris continued to give orders throughout Xerxes' reign. Ctesias (*Persica* 34–46) has her acting in the capacity of "queen mother" long after her husband's death.
- Herodotus states that the Persian king would only wed women from one of the seven noble Persian families (*Hist.* 3.84). Indeed, several sources indicate that the Persian monarchs tended to practice endogamy, and Cambyses even married his sister (*Hist.* 3.31, 88). According to Briant, "In these instances we can see the institution of a policy of endogamy that was applied consistently by the Achaemenids throughout their history and that permitted them to wipe out the royal ambitions of any other great aristocratic family."[114]
- The idea that the laws of the Medes and Persians were irrevocable (1:19) is attested in no ancient texts or inscriptions outside the Bible (though the same notion is invoked in Dan 6:8, 11, 15). Indeed, such a policy would seem extremely foolish and inimical to efficient government. On the other hand, this scenario does make an effective literary device, as demonstrated by several Greek myths in which the gods are trapped by their own promises (e.g., Zeus and Semele [Ovid, *Metamorphosis* 3.253–315], or Apollo and Sybil [*Metamorphosis* 14.101–153] or Cassandra [in Aeschylus' *Agamemnon*]), since the promises of gods were also irrevocable.
- Many scholars have argued that the book presents Mordecai as an exile, taken to Babylon with Jehoiachin (Esth 2:5–6). The year of this exile is usually identified as 597 BC. Even if he had been an infant when he had been taken from Jerusalem, he would have been well over one hundred when Xerxes became king in 486 BC.
- It has been noted frequently that there has been no confirmation of any of the events portrayed in the book of Esther in any ancient inscriptions, artifacts, or literary works. While lack of evidence is not persuasive in itself, the events depicted here—the deposing of a queen, the execution of a prime minister, the extermination of seventy-five thousand people—are of such magnitude that one

114. Briant, *From Cyrus to Alexander,* 93.

may well wonder how they could have left no impression in the historical records, especially given the fascination of the Greek writers with the Persians in this era.

Some of these problems can be easily addressed:

- The "127 provinces" of Esth 1:2 probably does not refer to satrapies, but to smaller administrative districts. The Heb. word used here (מְדִינוֹת) is used in Neh 1:3; 7:6 for the province of Judah, only a small subsection of the satrapy Abar-Nahara.
- Several scholars have argued that the text does not necessarily indicate that Mordecai was one of the Babylonian exiles and thus impossibly old for the events that transpire in Esther. Rather, they claim that the relative phrase, "who had been carried away to Babylon" (2:6) refers not to Mordecai, but to his great-grandfather, Kish.[115]
- Wright has demonstrated that the notion that the Persian king would only wed a member of the seven noble houses is not supported by attested practice.[116] The Persian kings had multiple wives, and not all could have been drawn from the noble families of conspirators. In fact, Xerxes' mother Atossa was a daughter of Cyrus the Great, who was certainly not one of the conspirators. Whatever the meaning of this stricture, it did not represent a principle that all Persian monarchs observed. (Of course, the question of the Persian king making a non-Persian commoner his queen is an entirely different matter.)

In spite of numerous efforts, there has still been no satisfactory explanation offered for the principal issue of incompatibility: the identification of Xerxes' wife. There have been three major approaches to this problem:

Vashti is Amestris. Wright has argued that, with a few linguistic adjustments, the name "Amestris" could be understood as a distorted Greek version of the name "Vashti."[117] Alternatively, it has been argued that Vashti may have been a title for the queen (the word *Vashti* has been identified with the Persian word meaning "beloved") rather than a proper name. The main difficulty with this theory is that the book of Esther demands that Vashti would have been deposed before Xerxes left on his Greek campaign, but in Herodotus, Amestris appears to be acting as queen after Xerxes returns

115. See, e.g., R. K. Harrison, *Introduction to the Old Testament* (Peabody, MA: Hendrickson, 2004), 1090. It is likely, however, that the name "Kish" is designed to evoke connections with the house of King Saul. See further below.

116. J. Wright, "Historicity of the Book of Esther," 38.

117. Ibid., 40–42.

(*Hist.* 9.107–109). In the story told by Herodotus, Xerxes had begun an affair with his niece (who was also his daughter-in-law) soon after his return from Greece. He attempted to keep the affair secret, because "he feared Amestris" (9.109). But Amestris learned of her husband's unfaithfulness, and she responded by demanding the king give the lover's mother into her power. Because she had put the request to him during a royal banquet, Xerxes felt compelled to agree to the demand. Amestris had the woman horribly mutilated and sent back home to her husband—Xerxes' brother. A woman who had been banished from the royal court would not have been able to carry out such a cruel vengeance on the king's sister-in-law with impunity. Shea has argued that the story indicates that Amestris was out of Xerxes' favor at this time, since she came before Xerxes as a supplicant, instead of just taking her vengeance directly.[118] This argument is not persuasive. First of all, if Amestris had already been demoted from her place as "head wife," why would she have cared about Xerxes' love affair at all? She would have been no more than a member of the royal harem, unentitled to jealousy. Also, if he had already demoted her, why would Xerxes fear his wife? Finally, the queen of Persia was not above law or custom, as the book of Esther abundantly indicates: not only was Vashti deposed simply for refusing to appear before the king's guests, but Esther trembled to come before the king unbidden. Certainly, the queen could not have mutilated the king's sister-in-law with impunity.

Finally, as noted above, Ctesias has Amestris continuing in the "queen mother" capacity long after Xerxes' death. Herodotus also claims that when Amestris was old, she had fourteen noble Persian youths buried alive as an offering to the god of the underworld (*Hist.* 7.114). It is difficult to imagine that a woman who had been dishonored and deposed could have gotten away with perpetrating such an atrocity on members of the nobility.

Esther is Amestris. This notion, advocated by Gordis, holds that the name Esther is an apoc. form of Amestris.[119] Philologically, this idea seems more likely than viewing "Amestris" as a form of "Vashti." But if Herodotus is at all accurate, there are too many flaws with this theory to grant it any credence. Herodotus tells us that Amestris was the daughter of Otanes, a general in Xerxes' army. He seems to identify her as Xerxes' wife before the beginning of the Greek campaign (*Hist.* 7.61), but she surely is his wife when he returns, when Amestris mutilated the mother of her rival. Also, Amestris is an unrelentingly cruel woman—certainly no one we would want to identify as a biblical heroine.

118. Shea, "Esther and History," 242.

119. Gordis, "Religion, Wisdom and History," 384.

Neither Vashti nor Esther is Amestris. Rather, all three were wives of Xerxes. This idea seems on the surface to make sense, for there is little reason to doubt that Xerxes had multiple wives. Nonetheless, Herodotus seems to know only of Amestris and clearly regards her as the queen. The Bible, on the other hand, seems to know only of Vashti (before her deposition). In Esth 1, Vashti is repeatedly called "the queen." There were never multiple queens in a kingdom. It is Vashti who wears the royal crown (Esth 1:11), the sign of her office. When Vashti has been deposed, the "royal crown" is placed on Esther's head, and she becomes queen (Esth 2:17). In short, while Xerxes may have possessed a harem of wives, he would not have multiple queens.

So far, there has been no satisfactory answer for this difficulty. To contend that the book of Esther is literal history, one must conclude that Herodotus and the other ancient authors were mistaken in their identification of Amestris as Xerxes' queen. If we allow that the Greek authors were correct, then we must conclude that the book of Esther is not a literal historical account of events in the reign of King Xerxes. There really seems little hope of reconciling the accounts.

Evidence for Esther's Authenticity

Several studies have undertaken to demonstrate that the book of Esther realistically reflects conditions of the ancient Persian court.[120] Clines (261), who does not regard the text as historical, has noted several of these authentic features:

> [T]he extent of the empire under Xerxes from India to Ethiopia (1:1); the counsel of seven nobles (1:14); the efficient postal system (3:13; 8:10); the keeping of official diaries including records of the king's benefactors (2:23; 6:8; the use of impalement as a form of capital punishment (2:23; 5:14; 7:10); the practice of obeisance to kings and nobles (3:2); belief in lucky days (3:7); setting crowns on the heads of royal horses (6:8); reclining on couches at meals (7:8).

In addition to these authentic features, Shea has demonstrated how the events of the book of Esther can be fit neatly into the timeline of Xerxes' history as recorded by Herodotus.[121] The demotion of Vashti would have occurred before the Greek campaign, and the selection of Esther as queen would have occurred a few months after his return. Also, the fact that the

---

120. See J. Wright, "Historicity of the Book of Esther"; W. Shea, "Esther and History," 227–46; Yamauchi, *Persia and the Bible,* 237–39.

121. Shea, "Esther and History," 237–40.

great majority of the names found in the book are Persian names has been long recognized, though there has been disagreement about their significance.[122] The name Mordecai is widely attested in the period. A cuneiform tablet from the time of Darius or Xerxes refers to an imperial financial officer who bore the name "Marduka," a variant of Mordecai.[123] The names of Haman's sons may be especially significant, since some scholars have identified them as compounds of *daiva*-names.[124] The *daiva* were worshiped as minor deities in the time of Xerxes, but later relegated to the status of demons—thus the names of the *daiva* would have been dropped as theophoric elements. The name Vaizatha (Esth 9:9) also appears authentic and may accurately reflect Persian pronunciation in the time of King Xerxes, since the "ai" diphthong shifted to "e" in the Persian language between the reigns of Xerxes and that of his successor, Artaxerxes I.[125]

Some scholars would argue that if the book of Esther demonstrates accuracy in some of its features, we are obligated to give it the benefit of the doubt in other, more dubious matters. Yamauchi writes,

> Gordis summarizes the various lines in favor of the historicity of Esther by concluding, "all in all, the case for the historical basis for the book is impressive." Moore admits, "on the face of it, the story seems to be true. ... Nothing in the book seems improbable, let alone unbelievable." If this is the case, and if the alleged historical problems are not insoluble, then it would seem preferable to take the book at face value as a historical narrative rather than to resort to subjective and highly speculative reconstructions. Scholars such as Wright, Shea, and Schedl have indeed argued for such a view.[126]

---

122. Many of these names and their proposed meanings were surveyed by Paton, 66–71.

123. Gordis, "Religion, Wisdom, and History," 384, among others, argues that the Mordecai of Esther is the same figure mentioned in the tablet, stating, "That there were two officials with the same name at the same time in the same place is scarcely likely." This position has now been largely refuted: the Marduka of the tablets was apparently in Babylon at the time of the events of Esther. See D. Clines, "In Quest of the Historical Mordecai," in *On the Way to the Postmodern: Old Testament Essays 1967–1998*, vol. 1, JSOTSup 292 (Sheffield: Sheffield Academic Press, 1998), 436–43.

124. See J. Duchesne-Guillemin, "Le noms des eunuques d'Assuérus," *Mus* 66 (1953): 108; A. Millard, "The Persian Names in Esther and the Reliability of the Hebrew Text," *JBL* 96 (1977): 481–88.

125. Yamauchi, *Persia and the Bible*, 238.

126. Ibid., 239.

The weakness of this argument is that it assumes that the default option is that the text is historical, and that the burden of proof is on those who would contend for a different genre identification. While this position may be understandable in light of the traditional identification of the text and the "surface appearance" of the Esther narrative, in light of our growing knowledge of literary genres in ANE texts, it appears somewhat naive. No one would advocate that library patrons should assume that any book they take from the shelf is nonfiction until proven otherwise. It is important to bear in mind that the vast majority of narrative literature that has come down to us from the ancient world, such as myths and epics, is not historical, even if there is a historical "kernel" at its base (as in the case of the Gilgamesh epic or the story of Ahiqar). In earlier times, works like the books of Judith and Tobit were also accepted as history, in part because their general form is very like that of historical narrative. Few today, however, would contend that these books should be taken as literal accounts of events that actually happened.

Other Issues

In addition to these issues, some narrative features of Esther suggest that the book has at least taken some literary license in telling its story.[127] Several of these are associated with the names of the main characters. The name Esther (אֶסְתֵּר, *ʾestēr*), for instance, sounds very similar to the Heb. word meaning "hidden" (סתר, *str*), an interesting coincidence in a book where the queen hides her Jewishness and God seems to be hidden entirely.[128] The name Haman (הָמָן, *hāmān*) sounds very similar to the Heb. word meaning "pomp" and "turmoil" (הָמוֹן, *hāmôn*). Haman is also identified as an Agagite, reminding the reader of Agag, the king of the Amalekites. The Amalekites were the bitter enemies of the Israelites, and Israel had been ordered by God to destroy them utterly, wiping them out from the earth (Exod 17:14–16; Deut 25:19). The perpetual war between the Israelites and the Amalekites forms the "backstory" for Haman's attempt to utterly destroy the Jews. Mordecai is identified as a Benjaminite descended from Kish, inciting reminiscences of King Saul. Saul was deposed from his kingship partly because he had spared Agag, king of the Amalekites (1 Sam 15). Through these lineages and patronymics, the book of Esther presents its story as something of a rematch between Saul and Agag.

One last point concerning the story's historicity is that it exists in several different versions. The LXX version of Esther—the version used

127. Jobes (31–32) notes the use of "poetic license" on the part of the author, while denying that the book is "entirely fiction."

128. This identification was not lost on the rabbis. See, e.g., *b. Ḥul.* 139b.

almost universally by the early church—contains several additional scenes not found in the MT version. As noted above, these include an opening prophetic vision seen by Mordecai, several prayers, the text of Xerxes' decree, the prayers of Mordecai and Esther, an expansion on Esther's appearance before the king, and a closing interpretation of the opening vision. The Greek AT version, meanwhile, exhibits some abridgements of the MT and LXX narrative. Josephus, in his version, reorders some elements of the story. While these variations do not constitute major contradictions, they do raise the somewhat uncomfortable issue of what really happened.

The Verdict: Is Esther "History"?

Does this difficulty mean that the book of Esther is not historical? Even in light of all the evidence considered, that question is not easily answered. It is quite clear that "history" of the type that most people would recognize today did not exist in the ANE world. Modern people think of history as an account of things that happened. The writers may add their own commentary or analysis, but we expect the core to remain the same from one account to another. In the ancient world, however, events were just the starting points of traditions. Stories would be augmented, reworked, and recast to serve their tellers' purposes, just as we have found the story of Esther reworked in the Greek versions. Our book of Esther may have had a starting point in events that happened, but those events are secondary to the lessons that our author(s) wished to convey.[129] The book of Esther is, above all, a work of literature. It is a carefully constructed story, full of humor, intrigue, and irony. Its structure has been determined not by chronology alone, but by a concern for drama, congruity, and remarkable reversals.

As a final note on this subject, we should remember that the truth of the narrative is independent of the issue of historicity. Just as the parables of Jesus resound with moral insight and theological significance despite their

129. I would disagree with Fox (*Character and Ideology*, 138) and others who hold the position that "to read Esther as fictional ... runs contrary to the intentions of the author, who almost certainly meant us to read the book as a precise report of actual historical events." First, it is unlikely that Fox or anyone could have such a confident ability to discern the intentions of the ancient author. Second, if the "authors" of Esther (a slippery term with a book existing in multiple recensions) believed they were creating a "precise report" of events, would they have felt so little compunction to take liberties with the story, adding, deleting, or rearranging materials to fit their purposes? Finally, the liberal use of humor and exaggeration (see commentary) in the text make it unlikely to me that the author(s) understood the material to be a literal history. As Berlin (7) notes, "Historiography is not a comic genre, and Esther is very comic."

being are "only stories," so too the message of a book like Esther need not be bound to those matters that can be historically verified. Fox writes,

> Although I doubt the historicity of the Esther story, and as a critical reader I must make that clear, every year at Purim when I hear the Scroll read in the synagogue, I know that it is *true*, whatever the historical accuracy of its details. Almost without an effort of imagination, I feel something of the anxiety that seized the Jews of Persia upon learning of Haman's threat to their lives, and I join in their exhilaration at their deliverance. Except that I do not think "their," but "my."[130]

Literary Type

However we might assess the historical accuracy of the Esther narrative, we are still obliged to ask the literary questions of the text. On its surface, it has the appearance of a historical monograph, even going so far as to invite us to look into the chronicles of the Persian kings for the "rest of the story" (10:2). It has loosely followed the pattern of Kings and Chronicles, beginning with a summary statement about the king's reign and ending with a reference to the royal archives. It begins with the *waw*-consec. introductory phrase וַיְהִי (*wayĕhî*, "and it came to pass"), as do the books of Joshua, Judges, 1 Samuel, and 2 Samuel. It reads as if it were continuing the Israelite national epic, picking up where the Chronicles left off. But a skillful storyteller might well add such elements to give his narrative an air of authenticity—not for the purpose of deception, but of literary style.

Esther as Court Tale

When comparing the book of Esther to other texts of the era, it is in some ways in a league of its own. Like most great works of literature, it cannot be easily pigeonholed. Frequently, the book is considered to belong to the genre labeled "court tale." As the name implies, these compositions are stories set in the royal court. The drama occurs when a hero uses skill, luck, or divine intervention to rise above his rivals and receives the favor of the king. Humphreys divides these stories into two basic types: the court-conflict and the court-contest.[131] In the court-contest, some kind of challenge (a riddle or crisis) occurs, and the hero uses his wits or special abilities (e.g., magical

---

130. Fox, *Character and Ideology*, 11.

131. W. Humphreys, "A Lifestyle for Diaspora: A Study of the Tales of Esther and Daniel," *JBL* 92 (1973): 217. This classification has been criticized by S. Niditch and R. Doran, "The Success Story of the Wise Courtier: A Formal Approach," *JBL* 96 (1977): 179–93, who seem to find it methodologically unsophisticated. Their own

skills or miraculous powers) to solve the problem and rise above his peers. Two biblical examples would be the story of Joseph in Egypt (Gen 41) and Daniel in Babylon (Dan 2; 4), who both attain favor through their ability to interpret dreams.[132] Outside the Bible, an example of this type of tale may be found in the Tale of Ahiqar, the Syriac version, chapters 5–7.[133] The Tale of Ahiqar is about an Assyrian courtier who uses his wits to escape trouble and to help his king respond to a challenge posed by the Pharaoh of Egypt, thus obtaining even greater honor. Though Ahiqar was Assyrian, the story was very popular among the Jews.[134] In literary tradition, Ahiqar was "adopted" as a Jew and even became Tobit's nephew in the book of Tobit (1:21–22). Talmon has explored a number of parallels between the Esther narrative and the story of Ahiqar.[135]

In the other form of court narrative, the court-conflict, the hero must overcome the schemes of another courtier in order to achieve his fame. These tales may sometimes be combined with the tales of contest: in the early chapters of Ahiqar, Ahiqar must overcome the plotting of his treacherous nephew in order to save himself from execution. Likewise, in Dan 2 and 6, the Jewish heroes must deal with the accusations and schemes of their rivals, or they will be executed. The story of Mordecai, too, falls into this category. There are some striking similarities between Mordecai and the heroes of Daniel:[136]

approach emphasizes structural elements in the identification of what would be called "court-contest" by Humphreys.

132. See Humphreys, "A Lifestyle for Diaspora," 211–23; J. Collins, "The Court-Tales in Daniel and the Development of Apocalyptic," *JBL* 94 (1975): 218–34; L. Wills, *The Jew in the Court of the Foreign King* (Minneapolis: Fortress, 1990).

133. For an English translation, see *ANET*, 427–30. Such stories may be based on historical figures, and perhaps even actual events. It now appears likely that Ahiqar, though his tale (as it has come down to us) is probably largely fiction, actually existed. J. Lindenberger, *The Aramaic Proverbs of Ahiqar* (Baltimore: Johns Hopkins University Press, 1983), 22, and J. Greenfield, "The Background and Parallel to a Proverb of Ahiqar," in *Hommages à André Dupont-Sommer*, ed. A. Caquot and M. Philonenko (Paris: Adrien-Maisonneuve, 1971), 49–59, draw attention to a late text from Uruk that lists Ahiqar as a counselor of Esarhaddon.

134. Copies of the sayings of Ahiqar and fragments of the narrative were found in the Elephantine Archives of the Jewish military colony in Egypt. See A. Cowley, *Aramaic Papyri of the Fifth Century B.C.* (Oxford: Clarendon, 1923), 204–48.

135. Talmon, "Wisdom in Esther," 438–39.

136. A list of similarities between Esther and Daniel is found in R. Stiehl, "Das Buch Esther," *WZKM* 53 (1956): 4–22, esp. 16–17.

- All are officials in the court of a foreign king.[137]
- The heroes give offense to another courtier or courtiers. (Mordecai refuses to bow to Haman [Esth 3:5]; Shadrach, Meshech, and Abednego refuse to bow to the king's image [Dan 3:8]; Daniel inspires the jealousy of other courtiers [Dan 6].)
- The evil courtiers urge the king to pass a decree condemning the good courtiers. (Haman gets Xerxes to sign the death warrant for Mordecai [Esth 3:8–13]; the courtiers accuse Shadrach, Meshach, and Abednego to the king [Dan 3:8–12]; the courtiers trick Darius into signing a law prohibiting any petition to any God or man but himself for thirty days [6:5–9].)
- The plot backfires, and the schemers suffer the fate they had planned for the good courtiers. (Haman ends up hanging on the pole he had constructed for Mordecai [Esth 7:9–10]; the men throwing Shadrach, Meshach, and Abednego into the fire are burned up [Dan 3:22]; the men who had sought to have Daniel thrown in the pit of lions are thrown in the pit [5:22].)
- The good courtiers are promoted. (Mordecai gets Haman's office [Esth 8:2]; Shadrach, Meshach, and Abednego get promoted over Babylon [Dan 3:30]; Daniel was promoted [6:28].)

These similarities are not signs of dependence, but of the "boilerplate" structure of the court-conflict tale. The sequences of events in these stories are somewhat stereotyped. But there is a major difference between the stories of Daniel and Mordecai: whereas Daniel and his friends achieve success through reliance on the power of God, Mordecai merely depends on his cousin's charms to deliver his people from crisis. Indeed, in other Jewish court tales, the theme of religious conflict is prominent.[138] Set as they are in foreign lands, these tales provide an excellent vehicle for demonstrating the superiority of the Jewish God and implicitly urging faithfulness to Yahweh. The book of Esther ostensibly departs from this theme.[139]

---

137. In Mordecai's case, his status is implied in the statement that he dwelt in the "fortress of Susa" (2:5) and "sat in the gate of the king" (2:19), translated by the NLT, "Mordecai had become a palace official."

138. J. Collins, "The Court-Tales in Daniel and the Development of Apocalyptic," *JBL* 94 (1975): 218–34, esp. 218 n. 3 and 225.

139. Gordis, "Religion, Wisdom, and History," 375–78, offers a variation on the "court tale" identification. Gordis believes that the ostensibly nonreligious nature of Esther is best accounted for by identifying the book as an artificial "royal chronicle by a Gentile scribe at the Persian court." Gordis believes that the Jewish author has tried to emulate an official chronicle, and so has avoided any religious language

Court tale is but one suggested genre identification for Esther. It has also been given the somewhat broader designation of "novella," or somewhat more precisely, "Diaspora novella."[140] This form of literature is "built around a plot that moves from the establishment of a tension through complications to its resolution."[141] Fox, while not disagreeing with the general characterization, has criticized the term *novella*, arguing that a novella would be either a short novel or a long story, while Esther is really neither.[142] He would prefer simply "Diaspora story," emphasizing how Esther and the other court tales teach lessons about life in the Diaspora. But a Diaspora setting alone seems a scant criterion for a genre identification. Surely there are Jewish stories set in the Diaspora that have little in common formally with Esther and Daniel. Susannah, for instance, or Tobit, both teach good, moral lessons for Jews living among Gentiles, but they are formally and ideologically very different from Esther, the other Daniel narratives, or even the Joseph romance.

Nonetheless, this categorization does invite interesting comparisons to other Jewish narratives of this era. Wills has noted that "novels" often feature prominent female characters.[143] This observation reminds us of the similarities between the book of Esther and its mirror image, the apocryphal book of Judith. Judith is the story of a Jewish heroine who uses her "sex appeal" to rescue her people from destruction at the hands of an Assyrian general. There are some clear similarities between the books: both Esther and Judith are beautiful, wise women. They use their beauty to beguile a Gentile leader. They both deliver their people and wreak a terrible vengeance on their enemies. Banquets and drunkenness are important plot elements in both stories.

But here the comparisons end and the contrast begins. Judith is the "anti-Esther." Whereas the book of Esther is almost secular, Judith drips

---

in his account. It is hard to imagine, however, that ancient chronicles would have been so secular, even avoiding mention of prayer or religious observance.

140. So Humphreys, "The Story of Esther and Mordecai," 97–113. L. Wills, *The Jewish Novel in the Ancient World* (Ithaca, NY: Cornell University Press, 1995), chap. 4, treats Esther under this same broad rubric, as well as J. Loader, "Esther as a Novel with Different Levels of Meaning," *ZAW* 90 (1978): 417–21. The term "diaspora novella" has been used by A. Meinhold, "Die Gattung der Josephgeschichte und des Estherbuches: Diasporanovelle I," *ZAW* 87 (1975): 306–24, and "Die Gattung der Josephgeschichte und des Estherbuches: Diasporanovelle II," *ZAW* 88 (1976): 72–93. Another term used synonymously for this style of literature is "romance." See Fox, *Character and Ideology*, 144 n. 10.

141. Humphreys, "Novella," 83.

142. Fox, *Character and Ideology*, 146.

143. Wills, *The Jewish Novel*, 96.

with piety. Fasting, prayer, sacrifices, and the sanctuary are prominent elements. Esther is a queen, while Judith is a widow. While Esther shares the bed of the king, Judith's chastity is frequently emphasized. Ironically, worldly Esther delivers her people by revealing the truth about her ethnicity and about the villainous Haman; the virtuous Judith delivers her people through lies, treachery, and the murder of a helpless man. These contrasts demonstrate graphically that the Jewish Diaspora was no monolithic entity—the cultural and literary diversity of the era was pronounced. Yet there was a unifying uncertainty about their situation: an angst that the Gentiles among whom they lived could turn antagonistic.

Esther and Wisdom

A somewhat different assessment of Esther's genre is offered by Talmon, who interpreted the book as a Wisdom tale. He writes,[144]

> The Esther-narrative is a historicized wisdom-tale. It may be described as an enactment of standard the "wisdom" motifs which are present also in other biblical narratives of a similar nature and which biblical literature has in common with ancient Near Eastern Wisdom literature, as defined by the literary-type analysis.

"Wisdom" is a widely recognized genre of ancient literature, epitomized in the Bible by such works as Job, Proverbs, and Ecclesiastes.[145] Typically, Wisdom literature is divided into two categories: lower wisdom, which gives pithy advice on how to live a successful life; and higher wisdom, which explores deep questions such as the meaning of life, the problem of evil, and the nature of God. It is notably universal in tone, addressing questions shared by people of all cultures. Talmon notes a number of similarities between Esther and the Wisdom tradition, including such features as its attribution of success or failure to human effort rather than divine intervention; a distant view of God; lack of interest in Jewish history, community, or cult; static characters; emphasis on some motifs and behaviors that are themes of Wisdom texts (e.g., adoption by a wise man, drunkenness of kings, the untimely end of the wicked). However, few seem

---

144. Talmon, "Wisdom," 427.

145. Two accessible introductions to Wisdom literature may be found in C. Bullock, *An Introduction to the Old Testament Poetic Books* (Chicago: Moody, 1979), chaps. 1–2, and R. Murphy, *The Tree of Life: An Exploration of Biblical Wisdom Literature*, 3rd ed. (Grand Rapids: Eerdmans, 2002).

to have been persuaded by Talmon's evidence.[146] The words *wise* and *wisdom* never appear in the book. It contains no proverbs, riddles, or accounts of clever deeds. It addresses none of the great questions that perplex the soul in any overt fashion (though, perhaps, in covert fashion, as will be noted below). As Fox writes, Talmon seems to have "overstretch[ed] the category of Wisdom."[147] Finally, in spite of the "secular" characterization of Wisdom, the foundational principle of the biblical Wisdom tradition is evident: "The fear of Yahweh is the beginning of wisdom" (Prov 1:7, 9:10; Job 28:28; cf. Eccl 12:2). What character in this story demonstrates such fear of Yahweh?

Esther as Comedy

A number of recent studies have seen in Esther not so much wisdom as tomfoolery. Certainly, an underappreciated aspect of the book of Esther is that it is, among other things, quite funny at times. Recognizing this fact, several scholars have argued that the book of Esther was designed primarily for entertainment.[148] Levenson (12) writes, "The book of Esther is so entertaining, so comical, and so subtle that to speak of its 'message' can be profoundly misleading." Greenstein calls it a "cartoon," with "cardboard caricatures" instead of full-blown actors.[149] Berlin (xviii) goes farthest of all, arguing not only that the book has comical elements, but rather *is* a comedy:

> The comic aspects of the book are not incidental, merely to provide comic relief; they are the essence of the book. They define the genre of the book, and thus set the parameters according to which we should read it. We cannot appreciate the story fully unless we realize that it is meant to be funny.

Given this point of view, it should be no surprise that Berlin has conducted the most thorough exploration of Esther as comedy, producing

146. An exception is Moore 1971, xxxiii–xxxiv, but many criticisms have been leveled against Talmon's position. See, e.g., J. Crenshaw, "Methods in Determining Wisdom Influences upon Historical Literature," *JBL* 88 (1969): 129–42.

147. Fox, *Character and Ideology*, 143.

148. While many scholars have noted the satirical elements of Esther, the concept of humor has been especially explored by Y. T. Radday, "Esther with Humour," in *On Humour and the Comic in the Hebrew Bible*, ed. Y. T. Radday and A. Brenner (Sheffield: Almond, 1990), 295–313; J. Levenson, *Esther: A Commentary*; J. Sasson, "Esther," in *The Literary Guide to the Bible* (Cambridge, MA: Belknap Press of Harvard University Press, 1987), 339; and A. Berlin, *JPS Bible Commentary: Esther*.

149. E. Greenstein, "A Jewish Reading of Esther," in *Judaic Perspectives on Ancient Israel*, ed. J. Neusner, B. Levine, and E. Frerichs (Philadelphia: Fortress, 1987), 231.

many enlightening comparisons to Greek and Roman comedy to bolster her case.

It is probably no accident that this aspect of the text has been especially emphasized by Jewish scholars, for in the Jewish tradition, the celebration of Purim is often a riotous affair, the most laughter-filled occasion of the Jewish year. That the Jewish scholars view the book of Esther through the lens of the Purim celebration has probably given them a somewhat different perspective on the text than others without this background might possess.[150] Without doubt, they have certainly identified some of the ironies, incongruities, and reversals in the story that can be recognized as comical by any reader. These elements include:

- that the mightiest king on earth was apparently unable to control his wife (1:10–12);
- the fear of a mass rebellion among the wives of the empire (1:16–18) and the (apparent) subsequent issuing of an official decree that all men were to be rulers over their households, and women were to respect their husbands (1:19–22);
- the use of a beauty pageant to choose the new queen (2:1–4);
- the humiliation of Haman, when he is forced to convey on Mordecai the honors he had designed for himself (chap. 6);
- the misinterpretation of Haman's imprecations of Esther as attempted rape (7:8);
- the helpful eunuch reminding the king of the ready-made gallows, and the hanging of Haman on the pole he had prepared for Mordecai (7:9);
- the destruction of the Jews' enemies on the very day they had expected to destroy the Jews (9:16–17); and
- of course, the many unlikely coincidences of the story could be further occasions for humor. How ironic—how funny—is it that Haman was waiting outside Xerxes' door, looking for permission to kill Mordecai, at the very moment when the king was pondering how to reward him (6:1–5)?

Comedy is a broad category, and there have been attempts to define Esther's humorous elements more precisely. Weisman has used the term *satire* in his efforts to define the book.[151] In his understanding, Esther is

---

150. Indeed, Berlin, ix, writes that the book of Esther and the celebration of Purim "are now inextricably bound together." This position is somewhat myopic, overlooking the fact that many Christians profitably read Esther with little thought of the celebration of Purim.

151. Z. Weisman, *Political Satire in the Bible* (Atlanta: Scholars Press, 1998), 139–63.

deliberately making fun of the self-important rulers of Persia, and the humorous elements have the serious function of making the foreigners look ridiculous. This point is well taken, and we shall return to it below. Berlin (xix), however, is critical of this identification, arguing that the satirical elements of the book are incidental, not integral to the story line. In her opinion, the book does not seek to undermine the Persian Empire. She argues, "After all, Xerxes emerges stronger at the end of the story than he was at the beginning, and Mordecai and Esther benefit handsomely from all that the Persian court has to offer and become two of its most elite members." If the text was meant to be a thoroughgoing satire of the Persian Empire, our author might well have been a little more explicit in his criticisms.

Berlin (xix) contends that the most fitting term for the book of Esther is *farce*. A farce is "a type of comedy designed to provoke the audience to simple, hearty laughter. To do so, it employs highly exaggerated or caricatured character types, puts men into impossible and ludicrous situations, and makes free use of broad verbal humor and physical horseplay."[152] But is this term really descriptive of Esther? The setting in the Persian court, for instance, is more realistic than highly exaggerated. Xerxes really *did* reign from India to Ethiopia; his palace truly *was* lavish; his parties actually did involve a great deal of wine. The characters of Mordecai, Esther, and even Xerxes do not seem either exaggerated or caricatured. Indeed, Fox demonstrates that the main actors of the book of Esther are rather full characters and somewhat realistic.[153] Even Haman, in spite of his obvious pomposity, does not seem utterly unrealistic (many of us have known someone like him). Furthermore, history has demonstrated that the circumstances that form the heart of this story are not totally ludicrous. In fact, the Jewish people have been in perilously similar situations on several occasions. There may be some farcical elements in Esther, but it seems unfair to call the book a farce.

An approach that has found a warmer response is to view the book through the lens of "carnivalesque."[154] Comedy is often related in various ways to carnival. In fact, as Berlin (xxi) notes, our English word *comedy* comes from a Greek word meaning a riotous celebration. The association of Esther with the carnival atmosphere is almost self-evident: the book begins

152. M. Abrams, *A Glossary of Literary Terms*, 8th ed. (Boston: Wadsworth, 2004), 26. Cited by Berlin, xix.

153. Fox, *Character and Ideology*, chaps. 6–10.

154. The riotous atmosphere of Purim celebrations led James Frazier to compare the holiday to saturnalia and other carnival-like celebrations. J. Frazier, *The Golden Bough: A Study in Magic and Religion*, 3rd ed. (New York: Macmillan, 1935), 9:345–415.

with a drinking party, it features several banquets, and it culminates in the institution of the feast of Purim, the ultimate Jewish carnival. In Jewish culture, at least, the story and the carnival are intrinsically intertwined.

The carnivalesque approach to Esther has been refined by the incorporation of the ideas of twentieth-century Russian literary critic Mikhail Bakhtin (1895–1975).[155] Bakhtin's starting point was carnival as a social phenomenon, a phenomenon that began in antiquity and reached its peak in the Middle Ages. Carnival was a supreme expression of folk culture and humor, involving the inversion of typical social norms and a celebration of the low and vulgar. Convention and class were overturned, as carnival allowed the "temporary suspension of all hierarchic distinctions and barriers among men and of the prohibitions of usual life."[156] Various "non-official" feasts, such as the Feast of Fools, came to embody the spirit of carnivalesque, as the common people were freed to act out their fantasies and appetites in the public square. There was an indulgence of the bodily desires, of gluttony and drunkenness, as well as an emphasis on other carnal matters (e.g., the excretory and reproductive organs): "To degrade also means to concern oneself with the lower stratum of the body, the life of the belly and the reproductive organs; it therefore relates to acts of defecation and copulation, conception, pregnancy, and birth."[157] The carnival spirit could also find literary expression: the "element of carnival in literature is subversive; it disrupts authority and introduces alternatives."[158] Bakhtin's supreme example was Rabelais, whose work *Gargantua and Pantagruel* had been largely disdained by academics because of its coarseness. From classical literature, the Socratic dialogues have been cited as examples, since they often expose supposed logic as nonsense. More frequently, the Menippean satires, which mocked various attitudes and types (rather than individuals), such as "pedants, bigots, cranks, parvenus, virtuosi, enthusiasts, rapacious and incompetent professional men of all kinds," are cited as examples of carnivalesque.[159]

---

155. The concept was primarily developed in M. Bakhtin, *Rabelais and His World*, trans. H. Iswolsky (Bloomington: Indiana University Press, 1993), and *Problems of Dostoevsky's Poetics*, ed. and trans. C. Emerson (Minneapolis: University of Minnesota Press, 1984).

156. Bakhtin, *Rabelais*, 15.

157. Bakhtin, *Rabelais*, 21.

158. J. Cuddon and C. Preston, *A Dictionary of Literary Terms and Literary Theory*, 4th ed. (Oxford: Blackwell, 1998), s.v. "carnivalization" (111).

159. N. Frye, *The Anatomy of Criticism: Four Essays* (Princeton, NJ: Princeton University Press, 1957), 308.

Esther was first systematically analyzed in terms of Bakhtian carnivalesque by K. Craig in 1995, and this work has proven quite influential.[160] Craig notes several elements in Esther that parallel those of carnival: the emphasis on feasting, the ironic reversals ("peripety"), and the satirical treatment of people in positions of power. The festival of Purim, too, seems consistent with the idea that the book of Esther is a literary manifestation of the carnival spirit. Yet this identification of Esther is not without some difficulties. The spirit of carnivalesque is one of subversion of authority. While the book takes some lighthearted jabs at King Xerxes, there seems to be a greater emphasis on his magnificence, as noted in the first and last verses of the book. Esther does not trick the king because he is foolish; she wins his favor and implores his mercy. That the Jews Mordecai and Esther can serve in the court of such a great king is celebrated, not mocked. Furthermore, it is not Haman's position that is the subject of derision here, as evidenced by Mordecai later assuming that very same post. Rather, it is the person of Haman—a hated Amalekite—that is lampooned.

There are other characteristics of carnivalesque that seem absent in Esther. For instance, the book of Esther displays little of the bawdiness or carnality characteristic of carnivalesque literature, in spite of several opportunities in the story,the line to do so. There are no overt references to bodily functions, nor to the grotesque, which also frequently characterizes carnivalesque. Even when recounting the parade of virgins into the king's chambers (Esth 2), the book of Esther veils the proceedings in modesty. Finally, the feasts of Esther are not lighthearted occasions of mirth and abandon (except for the feast anticipated in the establishment of Purim), but tense occasions filled with drama and danger. For these reasons, it seems that while we might identify some carnival-like features in the book of Esther, it is not accurate to identify the book with the carnivalesque. It is probably significant that Bakhtin, who was undoubtedly familiar with Esther, never identified the book with carnivalesque.

In spite of the impressive scholarship on Esther as comedy, there appears to be one major weakness: why does it take a modern expert in biblical studies to point out the jokes? The great majority of Bible readers do not laugh as they read the book of Esther (even though they might smile

160. K. Craig, *Reading Esther: A Case for the Literary Carnivalesque*, Literary Currents in Biblical Interpretation (Louisville: Westminster/John Knox, 1995). See also A. LaCocque, *Esther Regina: A Bakhtian Reading* (Evanston, IL: Northwestern Univ, 2008); T. Wheelock, "Drunk and Disorderly: A Bakhtinian Reading of the Banquet Scenes in the Book of Esther," unpub. Ph.D. diss., Baylor University, 2008; J. Grossman, *Esther: The Outer Narrative and the Hidden Reading*, Shiphrut 6 (Winona Lake, IN: Eisenbrauns, 2011).

on occasion). No doubt the modern sense of humor is somewhat different from that of the ancient Mediterranean world. But even so, we typically have little difficulty recognizing the comedy in the satires of Aristophanes or Juvenal. Even more significant: why did *ancient* readers seem to take the story so seriously? Would not they, at least, have recognized the presumed hilarity of what they were reading? Instead of taking it lightly, we find that the reading of Megillah was surrounded with ritual and regulation. No doubt the feasting of Purim was a riotous affair, but this was due to Jews taking the book of Esther very seriously, and literally interpreted the words of 9:22, "to make them days of feasting and rejoicing."[161] Reading Esther purely as farce or carnivalesque may have a tendency to pacify what is, in reality, a very dangerous book. It would be better, it seems, to view the book as a court tale with comedic elements.

Festival Etiology

A final genre identification shall be mentioned here, but we will leave its discussion for the next section. Often, the book of Esther is identified as a "festival etiology," an explanation for the celebration of Purim.[162] According to this approach, the genre of Esther is best understood as a story that accounts for the festival of Purim. As we will see, there is certainly this element involved in the structure and development of the book of Esther. This identification, however, has as much (or more) to do with the purpose of the narrative as its form. We will treat it in some detail in the next section.

The Purpose of the Book of Esther

Why was the book of Esther written? This issue overlaps that of its genre identification, since genre typically relates to the function of a literary work, and function typically means purpose. So, for example, on the basis of its form, someone may identify a saying as a "proverb" and conclude on that basis that its purpose was to educate in an entertaining fashion. "Communal psalms of lament" will typically contain certain stereotyped elements, and they are typically designed to aid the assembly in expressing its grief. "Judgment oracles" are typically designed for the purpose of calling their hearers to repentance.

On the other hand, the connection between literary form and function is not always so straightforward. An oracle predicting the judgment of Israel's enemies (e.g., the book of Nahum) will not be designed to get them

161. See, e.g., *b. Meg.* 5b.

162. E.g., Ringgren, 375; Gerleman, 23; Laniak, 174.

to repent of their sins, but rather to comfort Israel and perhaps seal the doom of the offenders. The books of Kings and Chronicles are both "histories" and even cover roughly the same events, but the two works have very different purposes: the books of Kings primarily explain the Babylonian exile, while Chronicles encourages the restoration of the monarchy and bolsters priestly leadership. Likewise, even if one were to identify the book of Esther as a historical chronicle, this identification alone would not tell us all we need to know about its purpose. Biblical histories are not designed merely to provide information; they have a greater rhetorical purpose that may not be immediately evident. Similarly, if we identify Esther as a comedy, we know it has a component of entertainment; but slapstick routines and political satires, while both comedies, have very different intentions. We have identified Esther as a court tale with comedic elements, but we still have some work to do to identify its purpose.[163]

The Historical Basis for Purim

Unlike the issue of genre, there is widespread consensus regarding the purpose of the book of Esther. Childs writes that there is "general agreement that the major purpose of the book of Esther is to provide the historical grounds for the celebration of the feast of Purim."[164] Indeed, one is hard-pressed to find a dissenter from this position, and with good reason.[165] About half of the book's penultimate chapter consists of a directive for celebrating Purim. The account of Purim is not an appendage; it forms the counterbalance to the feasts of the first chapter. Thus the Purim account is

---

163. Our discussion here will primarily concern the MT version of Esther. There are, after all, a Heb. version and two Greek versions, and these versions clearly have different emphases. The additions in the Greek versions have created works with different purposes than the original.

164. B. S. Childs, *Introduction to the Old Testament as Scripture* (Philadelphia: Fortress Press, 1979), 599.

165. Scholars holding that the purpose of Esther was to encourage the celebration of Purim include Paton, 56; D. Daube, "The Last Chapter of Esther," *JQR* 37 (1946): 139–47 (esp. 146); Knight, 18; Kelly, 42; Bickerman, *Four Strange Books of the Bible*, 202; Moore 1971, liii; Humphreys, "Lifestyle," 213; Keil and Delitzsch, 3:304; Murphy, 156; J. Sasson, "Esther," in *The Literary Guide to the Bible*, ed. R. Alter and F. Kermode (Cambridge, MA: Belknap Press, 1987), 335; K. Craig, *Reading Esther: A Case for the Literary Carnivalesque* (Louisville: Westminster John Knox, 1995), 26–32; Bush, 306; K. Larkin, *Ruth and Esther* (Sheffield: Sheffield Academic Press, 1996), 89; C. Dorothy, *The Books of Esther: Structure, Genre and Textual Integrity* (Sheffield: Sheffield Academic Press, 1997), 327–29; Levenson, 22; Omanson and Noss, 3; Jobes, 40; Laniak, 172; Berlin, xv; A. Lacocque, *Esther Regina: A Bakhtinian Reading* (Evanston, IL: Northwestern University Press, 2008), 14.

a structural element, integral to the story. Since Purim is never mentioned in the Law, it is argued, a rousing literary composition like the book of Esther was necessary to encourage its observance. "The book was written to explain why the feast of Purim, which does not have the authority of the Torah behind it, came to be, and must be celebrated" (Murphy, 156).

This hypothesis requires some elaboration. First, who would have both the motive and means to encourage the celebration of Purim? What would they have to gain by doing so? The feast of Hanukkah provides a good basis for comparison. Like Purim, Hanukkah was a feast that had no basis in the Torah. It originated as a commemoration of Judas Maccabeus' cleansing of the temple in 164 BC. The Hasmonean regime would surely have encouraged its celebration, since the story legitimized their claim to the throne. Likewise, Hanukkah would have been popular with the priesthood, since it reminded everyone of the centrality of the temple to Judaism. Furthermore, the story reinforced the belief in God's ability to protect His house and His faithful, so it would have been readily accepted by many of the Jewish people. The feast of Purim, on the other hand, would benefit no particular interest group or ruling faction. It would proffer no benefit to the government, since the story of Esther might actually provoke the animosity of the Jews' Gentile neighbors, as the Talmud rightly notes (*b. Meg.* 7a). The priesthood would gain no benefit, since neither priest nor sacrifice makes an appearance in Esther. Nor would a religious sect seem to benefit from the observation of Purim. The only ones who would really seem to profit from its promotion would be the winemakers and breweries.

Another fact to consider is the nature of the Purim celebration itself. According to Esth 9:22, Purim was to be celebrated as "days of feasting and rejoicing and sharing food with one another and giving gifts to the poor." As described here, there was no necessary connection between the way Purim was celebrated in the early years of its institution and the story of Esther and Mordecai. By the Mishnaic period (third century AD), the reading of the Megillah had become a central feature of the celebration, but we have no way of knowing when the custom began. Other customs linking Purim and the story of Esther, such as reenactments of the story or the designation of traditional pastries as "Hamantaschen" (Haman's Pockets), were much later additions. In its early days, Purim seems to have been a rather generic feast. Indeed, as noted above, the feast may well predate the story of Esther. The celebration of Purim and the commemoration of "Mordecai's Day" may well have become linked because they occurred about the same time in the calendar year.

In light of these facts, it seems unlikely that the book of Esther was designed to *institute* the celebration of Purim. More likely, it was designed to *bring it legitimacy* and to enhance the enjoyment of a festival that was already well established among the Jews. We might compare the book of Esther to yearly holiday specials that tell us about the meaning of Christmas (either the actual biblical story or the popular Santa Claus version). Society already celebrates the holiday; the stories enhance the celebration by providing an entertaining and perhaps educational presentation of the well-loved tale. It seems very likely that the story of Esther and Mordecai was known in some form before the book of Esther was written, though perhaps not widely recognized, and many Jews may not have made a connection between Esther and the feast of Purim. The book of Esther, as entertaining and accessible as it is, surely popularized the story and solidified its connection with Purim.

Esther and Resistance

Nonetheless, we do the book an injustice if we consider it merely the excuse for a party. When the celebration of Purim is firmly linked to the story of Esther and Mordecai, Purim is not merely about having a good time. Rather, it becomes a time for remembering that there are enemies surrounding God's people and that deliverance is not merely a matter of passive trust in God, but of human response to divinely appointed opportunity. The comedy of this book is not the delight of surprise; it is the darker humor of mockery and *Schadenfreude*. The great reversal of the story is not Mordecai's triumph over Haman, but the Jews' turning the tables on their enemies and destroying those who had been so eager to destroy them. Historically, *these* are the themes that have been emphasized in the reading of Esther, not its etiological function or its entertainment value. Indeed, it is in this light that we might say that Esther is both a powerful and dangerous book. It is a book designed to encourage resistance.

To understand how Esther functions as resistance literature, it is helpful to be familiar with the work of James C. Scott.[166] Scott argues that domination manifests itself in similar forms throughout human societies and history, and that consequently, "to the degree structures of domination can be demonstrated to operate in comparable ways, they will, other things equal, elicit reactions and patterns of resistance that are also broadly comparable."[167] One of these reactions is the appearance of compliance. The oppressed will seem to conform to the expectations placed on them by their overlords. Publicly, they act in an obsequious manner, ingratiating themselves to the overlords through word and action. They may even attempt

166. J. C. Scott, *Domination and the Arts of Resistance: Hidden Transcripts* (New Haven, CT: Yale University Press, 1990).
167. Ibid., xi.

to emulate their rulers, with varying degrees of success.[168] This pattern of behaviors Scott terms the "public transcript." But beneath the surface, there are various ways that the oppressed can demonstrate, at least among themselves, their will to resist. The methods might include gestures, rituals, stories, theater, or songs. These tactics are what Scott calls the "hidden transcript": "At its most elementary level the hidden transcript represents an acting out in fantasy—and occasionally in secretive practice—of the anger and reciprocal aggression denied by the presence of domination."[169]

In the Persian period and the early Greek era, the Jews were a people living under foreign domination. Their land, Yehud, had been humiliated, and its political clout was now practically nonexistent. The Jews' God was not honored as sole Creator and Sovereign, but merely as one of many deities of the conquered peoples. The Jews' unique customs and their cliquish ways engendered some resentment from their neighbors in the Diaspora communities. While there was no government-sponsored persecution of the Jews before the Hasmonean era, there were certainly incidents of ethnic conflict with their neighbors.[170] In spite of the relatively benign policies of the Persians, any such situations of political and cultural domination tend to engender feelings of resentment among the subjugated. These feelings increased in the Greek era, as the new overlords actively promoted the notion of their cultural and political superiority.[171] The book of Esther is a response not to physical persecution, but to the pressures of cultural domination. The story betrays an assumption that the Jews are in some sense unwelcome (thus the necessity for keeping Esther's nationality secret; Esth 2:20), and that danger lurks around every corner. In every province of the empire, the Jews have enemies who relish the prospect of destroying them.

The book of Esther responds to the conditions of cultural domination by exposing and subverting them. In the two heroes, we see the ultimate example of Jews who are outwardly conforming to the expectation placed

---

168. Ibid., 39–40.

169. Ibid., 37–38.

170. E.g., as at Elephantine in Egypt, where the priests of Khnum destroyed the Jewish temple and the governor took no action. See further B. Porten, *The Archives from Elephantine: Life of an Ancient Jewish Military Colony* (Berkeley: University of California Press, 1968). Also, Josephus reports an incident in *Ant.* 11.297–301 where a Persian general defiled the temple and imposed a tribute on the Jews. But this action was prompted not by ethnic hatred, but as retaliation against a murder in the temple.

171. See S. K. Eddy, *The King Is Dead: Near Eastern Resistance to Hellenism, 334–31 B.C.* (Lincoln: University of Nebraska Press, 1961), chaps. 8–9; M. Hengel, *Judaism and Hellenism: Studies in the Encounter in Palestine during the Early Hellenistic Period*, trans. John Bowden (Philadelphia: Fortress, 1974), 47–57.

on them by their subordinate place in Persian society. Both Mordecai and Esther bear foreign names: but they are not just foreign, they are actually the names of the chief Babylonian deities, Marduk and Ishtar.[172] Esther must conceal that she is Jewish and apparently succeeds at the subterfuge. Both she and Mordecai serve faithfully in the court of the foreign king—Mordecai as the hero who saves his life; Esther as the compliant wife, in stark contrast to the insubordinate Vashti. Esther does not resist being taken from her home and incorporated into the harem of the Gentile king. On the surface, these two characters are the epitomes of a subjugated people. At the beginning of the narrative, they are depicted as Jews who play out the "public transcript" and do it well. It is a picture that could have made the Jewish blood boil.

But the reader gradually becomes aware that the story is not simply about Jews on the brink of assimilation. The royal court is the target of numerous subtle (and not-so-subtle) gibes. In the opening chapter, we are treated to the spectacle of a king who, while demonstrating his power and magnificence to his allies and courtiers, proves unable to impose his will on his own wife. We see the king's advisers reduced to trembling anxiety at the prospect of a mass breakout of insubordination among the women of the kingdom. There is the barely disguised lampoon of bureaucracy run amok in the ridiculous edict designed to make all men rulers in their own houses. Then, there is the contest for the new queen: the world's largest empire selects its queen not on any of the typical bases, such as political expediency or family prominence. Nor is she selected on a noble basis such as wisdom or a reputation for piety. She is chosen because of her ability to "please the king" (2:4). The criteria for choosing this lucky lady include physical attractiveness, enhanced by a full year of cosmetic treatments, and the ability to make a good impression on the king during one night in his bedchamber. Undoubtedly this scenario was designed to satirize the famous hedonism of the Persian court, a characteristic that fascinated and repelled even classical Greek authors. But such mockery of the overlords is endemic in resistance literature, an expression of the resentment the subordinates feel toward the privileged classes.

Mordecai's character, too, quickly changes from subservient to subversive. His rescue of the king from the assassins is reminiscent of tales where clueless lords must be delivered by their cunning servants—like the *eiron* of classical Greek comedy.[173] But more significant is Mordecai's refusal to

172. On the significance of names and the appearance of compliance, see J. C. Scott, *Domination*, 32–33.

173. See N. Frye, *The Anatomy of Criticism: Four Essays* (Princeton, NJ: Princeton University Press, 1971), 171–72.

bow before Haman (Esth 3:2–4). Fox calls this act the "biggest puzzle" of the book of Esther, an "almost irrational" act of defiance.[174] But it is here that the true nature of the book of Esther begins to manifest itself. By this point of the narrative, the reader knows that Mordecai is associated with King Saul and that Haman is a descendant of Agag, the Amalekite king. Mordecai's refusal to bow represents a perpetuation of the ancient blood feud between the Israelites and Amalekites. This action not only demonstrates insubordination to Haman, but to the king as well, who installed Haman in his position. Scott makes the somewhat obvious observation that "any public refusal, in the teeth of power, to produce the words, gestures, and other signs of normative compliance is typically construed—and typically intended—as an act of defiance."[175] This refusal to bow to a superior constitutes "a particularly dangerous form of insubordination"—a fact borne out by Haman's response to the slight.[176]

Furthermore, Mordecai's ability to get away with such a public demonstration of defiance elevates him in the view of the audience to something like a folk hero.[177] He operates like the "trickster" of folklore, comparable to Br'er Rabbit of African American tales.[178] Typically, tricksters are characters of little power (often physically small, like the rabbit) and ostensibly naive, who use their wits or magical powers to gain the upper hand over their more potent adversaries, making them look like fools in the process. Mordecai is obviously a less powerful character than Haman or the king. He seems oblivious to social convention, hanging around the king's harem and refusing to honor the king's vizier. He uses trickery to obtain his ends, concealing Esther's Jewish identity until it is revealed at the opportune moment. He has no magical powers, but the remarkable coincidences that accomplish the Jews' deliverance are surely similar.

Esther, too, appears skilled in the "arts of resistance." She maintains the public transcript better than Mordecai can manage and uses it to her advantage. As Scott notes, rituals of subordination may be deployed "both

---

174. Fox, *Character and Ideology*, 191.

175. Scott, *Domination*, 203.

176. Ibid., 205.

177. Cf. a similar example from ibid., 39: "They say a white man hit a colored man up north and that colored man hit that white man, knocked him cold, and nobody did a damned thing."

178. Accessible overviews of the trickster figure in folklore include *The Trickster*, ed. H. Bloom and B. Hobby, Bloom's Literary Themes (repr., New York: Infobase, 2010), and S. Niditch, *A Prelude to Biblical Folklore: Underdogs and Tricksters* (Champaign: University of Illinois Press, 2000). The trickster element of Mordecai's character is noted in passing by Niditch, 137.

for purposes of manipulation and concealment."[179] This is precisely Esther's strategy.[180] She presents her initial request with all the proper qualifiers, asking, "If it please the king, let the king and Haman come today to the banquet I have prepared for the king" (5:4). She comes as a humble suppliant and asks to be allowed to act as a servant. She follows this request with yet another for the king to allow the queen to serve him. When she finally presents her real entreaty, it is couched in terms of exaggerated submissiveness: "If we had merely been sold as male and female slaves, I would have remained silent" (7:4).

Esther's fawning approach secures the survival of her people, but that is just the beginning. Xerxes makes several other concessions as well. The king gives the order for the execution of Haman, the Jews' adversary. Then, at Esther's request, his ten sons are killed as well. Esther receives permission for a massacre within the king's palace, and five hundred men are killed there. Finally, seventy-five thousand of the Jews' enemies are destroyed. Esther and Mordecai no longer hide their Jewishness. Once the rabbits, they have now become the wolves. Haman's wife and advisers warn him that he cannot stand against a Jew (6:13). The king's officers grant Mordecai whatever he desires because of their dread of him (9:3). The people of the nations convert to Judaism, because they are afraid of the Jews (8:17). In these examples, it is apparent that the Jewish author, as Scott says, is "acting his anger out in fantasy." In this scenario, the subjugated Jews who had been forced to blend in and emulate their neighbors are now dominant and dangerous; now, their neighbors are striving to emulate them.

The case that Esther should be read as resistance literature is further bolstered by it having always been read in this manner by the Jewish community. In the earliest extant commentary on Esther, embedded in the LXX, we find this notion embraced. In the additions to the text, we find the idea of conflict with the Gentiles expanded from a rivalry between Jews and Amalekites into a universal struggle for survival, as noted by Moore:

> What in the MT had been essentially a plot involving court rivalry (3:1–4), intrigue (3:8–9), and long-standing hostility between Jews and Amalekites (3:1, 10, 13; 5:13; 6:13) becomes, implicitly in Mordecai's dream and explicitly in the narrative, an antagonism between Israel and all the rest of the world. What was portrayed in the MT as a pogrom in the Persian Empire became in the Greek version a cosmic struggle between the Jews and everyone else.[181]

179. Scott, *Domination*, 34–35.
180. See Niditch, *Prelude to Biblical Folklore*, 137–45.
181. C. Moore, "Esther, Book of," *AYBD* 2:629.

Though the later rabbis read from the Heb. text, they still recognized the spirit of antagonism made explicit in the Greek version. We have already noted how the rabbis argued that the book of Esther should not be canonized, because the story would be recognized as subversive (*b. Meg.* 7a). In the early centuries AD, as Christianity became dominant and Judaism became marginalized, the feast of Purim became an outlet for Jewish resentment against their rivals. Jews had little trouble identifying the wicked Haman, enemy of the Jews, with Jesus and with Christianity in general. According to Josephus and the LXX translation of Esther, Haman and his sons were not impaled or hanged, but "crucified," just like the Christians' Lord Jesus.[182] Rome was easily associated with Haman as well. Haman was one of the Amalekites, who were associated in the Bible with Edom (Gen 36:12). By the time of the Bar Kokhba Rebellion (AD 130–135), Edom had become a Jewish epithet for the Roman Empire, and the code name is taken for granted in rabbinic literature.[183] Armed with these traditions, Purim became for many a celebration of the anticipated downfall of Christianity.

Early Christian accounts of the Purim festivities tell how the Jews would burn the hated Haman in effigy "on a cross"—an obvious taunt of their Christian neighbors.[184] Roth cites the following account from fifth-century church historian Socrates, identifying it as the earliest account of riotous Purim behavior getting out of hand and resulting in murder:

> Now a little after this the Jews paid the penalty for further lawless acts against the Christians. At Inmestar, a place so-called, which lies between Chalcis and Antioch in Syria, the Jews were in the habit of celebrating certain sports among themselves: and, whereas they habitually did many foolish actions in the course of their sports, they were put beyond themselves [on this occasion] by drunkenness, and began deriding Christians and even Christ himself in their games. They derided the Cross and those who hoped in the Crucified, and they hit upon this plan. They took a Christian child and bound him to a cross and hung him up; and to begin with they mocked and derided him for some

182. On the Jewish identification of Haman with Jesus, see E. Horowitz, *Reckless Rites: Purim and the Legacy of Jewish Violence* (Princeton, NJ: Princeton University Press, 2006), 81–106.

183. See Herr, "Edom," in *Encyclopaedia Judaica*, 6:378.

184. See C. Roth, "The Feast of Purim and the Origins of the Blood Accusation," *Speculum* 8 (1933): 520–26, esp. 520. Both Josephus and the Septuagint interpreted Haman's impalement as a crucifixion, thus giving impetus to the identification of Haman and Jesus.

> time; but after a short space they lost control of themselves, and so ill-treated the child that they killed him.[185]

The story may be an anti-Semitic fiction, but it might also be an accurate account of some zealotry run amok. In any case, the potential for violence on Purim was considered so significant that Byzantine emperor Theodosius passed a law forbidding the Jews from burning Haman in effigy during the feast. By the Middle Ages, the charges of Jewish violence during Purim were multiplying. Many of these allegations can be dismissed as anti-Jewish rhetoric, but a growing number of scholars have begun to give some of them serious consideration.[186]

Nor did this tradition end in antiquity. Recently in Israel, there has been a spate of anti-Christian incidents associated with Purim, so that in some communities, Israeli Christians refuse to go about on the night of the holiday.[187] And it has not only been Christians who have suffered. Some Israeli Jews have transferred the identification of Amalek from the Christians to the Palestinians and have taken seriously the biblical injunction to destroy the offending nation.[188] On Purim in 1994, a Jewish physician opened fire in a mosque in Hebron, Israel, killing fifty-five Palestinians and wounding more than 170 others. He committed this act of terrorism only hours after leaving synagogue and hearing the reading of the book of Esther.[189]

In light of such incidents, it is clear that Esther cannot merely be regarded as a sweet little story of a poor orphan girl who became a queen, nor as an excuse for a merry get-together. Esther is a potentially dangerous book, capable of inciting passions and resistance. It was a story designed for the private consumption (in Heb., a language known only to the Jews) of those who would "get it," to encourage them not to be totally assimilated into a culture in which they were aliens, a society that would force them to

185. Quoted in ibid., 521.

186. Much of this reconsideration has come from the realm of Jewish scholarship. In addition to Roth, see N. Doniach, *Purim or the Feast of Esther* (Philadelphia: Jewish Publication Society, 1933), 174; Horowitz, *Reckless Rites*; A. Toaff, *Pasque di sangue: Ebrei d'Europa e omicidi rituali* (Bologna: Società editrice il Mulino, 2007), chap. 8. It should be noted that Toaff's book has been heavily criticized because of its somewhat sensationalistic tone and was removed from the market shortly after its release.

187. Horowitz, *Reckless Rites*, 12.

188. Ibid., 1–5.

189. R. Walter, "Massacre in a Mosque," *Newsweek* 123 (March 7, 1994): 34–37. Jobes, 19, begins her commentary on Esther by recounting this incident, noting how it illustrates that the book of Esther is a "somewhat troubling" presence in the Heb. Bible.

change their names and their customs and abandon their God. Indeed, it might even be said to nurture resentment against the Jews' enemies. Here again, we find it reminiscent of Wiesel's *Night*: In the original Yiddish version, *Un di velt*, Wiesel wrote for Jewish readers of the events that transpired after the emancipation of the concentration camps. He writes: "Early the next day Jewish boys ran off to Weimar to steal clothing and potatoes. And to rape German girls. The historical commandment of revenge was not fulfilled" (apparently, he is referring to the Torah commandment to leave vengeance to God; Lev 19:18). In the English translation, however, the passage is rendered, "On the following morning, some of the young men went to Weimar to get some potatoes and clothes—and to sleep with girls. But of revenge, not a sign." In the privacy of the Jewish reading community, the hidden transcript could be indulged; before a broader public, the more docile version of the narrative was offered.[190]

Secondary Purposes of Esther

In addition to the principal purpose of encouraging the celebration of Purim, scholars have noted several secondary purposes of the book of Esther. We have already observed that Talmon regarded the text as a Wisdom composition and so would not find its primary purpose in the establishment of Purim but in showing the Jews how to live and prosper in their daily affairs.[191] Meinhold takes a similar position, arguing that Esther provides a model for Jews living in the Diaspora.[192] Humphreys, while not denying that the text as it appears in the MT was designed mainly to encourage the celebration of Purim, holds that in an earlier incarnation, the story of Esther demonstrated a "lifestyle for the Diaspora."[193] In one sense, we can agree with this assessment: the text surely encourages resistance, while demonstrating how one can attain one's ends while maintaining a public appearance of servility. We should note, however, that the text is a unique species of "Diaspora novella." The other Jewish narratives set in the Diaspora address themes of great importance in maintaining Jewish

190. See N. Seidman, "Elie Wiesel and the Scandal of Jewish Rage," *Jewish Social Studies* 3 (1996): 1–19, esp. 5–6.

191. Talmon, "Wisdom," 419–55.

192. Meinhold, "Gattung," 72–93.

193. Humphreys, "Lifestyle," 213. So also L. Thompson, *Introducing Biblical Literature: A More Fantastic Country* (Englewood Cliffs, NJ: Prentice-Hall, 1978), 127–30. B. Jones, "Two Misconceptions about the Book of Esther," *CBQ* 39 (1977): 171, argues that one of Esther's purposes "is to reconcile Jewish readers to their status as a minority among gentiles, whose attitudes toward Jews may vary unpredictably from honor to persecution."

distinction while living among foreigners. Thus, we find emphasized in these stories the importance of eschewing idolatry (as in Dan 2; 6; and Bel and the Dragon), of keeping kosher (as in Dan 1; Tob 1:10–12), rejecting intermarriage (as in Tob 4:12–13), or even simply showing proper respect for those of the Jewish race (as repeatedly emphasized in Tobit). In its Heb. version, Esther addresses none of these issues, except for the last, which was essential for its nationalistic purposes.

An equally significant secondary purpose has to do with the religious message of the story. As the majority of scholars agree, the book of Esther is not a story about remarkable coincidences, but about divine providence. Not only are the Jews to resist assimilation, but they are to trust in the deliverance of their God, however hidden He might be. As Levenson (21) states, "Esther's God is one who works behind the scenes, carefully arranging events so that a justice based on the principle of 'measure for measure' will triumph and the Jews will survive and flourish." In this light, the book may share an emphasis with some other Diaspora tales, though in an indirect manner: it affirms the importance of trusting in God (as in the Joseph saga and the Daniel narratives). This theme will be discussed in detail in the theology section of this introduction.

Esther and Purim

The book of Esther and the feast of Purim have been linked from time immemorial. According to Esth 9:20–32, Mordecai and Esther established Purim as a time of celebrating the Jews' conquest over their enemies. By rabbinic times, Purim was observed with the reading of the scroll of Esther. But was there a time when Purim existed apart from the story of Esther and Mordecai? Many scholars believe that Purim, a raucous festival where Jews are actually encouraged to drink to excess, has its origins in a pagan holiday. According to Esth 9:24–28, the celebration is called "Purim" because Haman cast a "lot" (*pur*) to determine which day the Jews would be exterminated. This etiology presents several difficulties. The first is that the word *pur* is an Akkadian word for "lot," not Heb., Aramaic, Median, or Persian.[194] The book of Esther is written in Heb. Why was the Heb. word for "lot" not used? Or, failing that, why not the Aramaic word, since Aramaic was the diplomatic language of the Persian Empire? Even the Persian or Median word would make sense in this context, but the use of the Akkadian word for "lot" is odd. Another difficulty is that *purim* is a pl. form, "lots" rather than "lot." According to Esth 3:7 and 9:24, Haman cast but a single lot, not "lots," to determine the day on which the Jews would be destroyed (in Heb.,

194. See J. Lewy, "Old Assyrian Puru'um and Pūrum," *RHA* 5 (1939): 117–24.

unlike English, a sg. "lot" can be cast).[195] Yet another problem is that the lot plays a very minor (and completely negative) part in the story of the Jews' deliverance.[196] For Jews to call this feast "lots" would be analogous to Christians calling Easter "The Feast of the Thirty Pieces of Silver"!

The name of the festival, however, is not the only problem. There is also the problem of the general character of the celebration. The book of Esther describes Purim as a day of feasting, rejoicing, and giving gifts to the poor. These are all rather generic holiday observances that have little to do with the deliverance chronicled in the book of Esther itself. From the Mishnah, however, it is apparent that there was one element of Purim that was not at all generic: it was the only holiday on which drunkenness was a central element of the festivities. Each description of Purim celebrations includes references to becoming "mellow" with wine, and the rabbis recommended that celebrants become so drunk that they could not tell the difference between "blessed be Mordecai" and "cursed be Haman" (*b. Meg.* 7b). While there is nothing particularly odd about people becoming drunk at parties, it does seem strange to make it a *mitzvah*.

These facts have led many scholars to conclude that Purim may have begun as a non-Jewish festival that was adopted by the Jews of the Diaspora. Later, the nature of the celebration was transformed by linking it with the story of Mordecai and Esther. We might compare this process to the development of the Christian Christmas celebration, some customs of which may have derived from pre-Christian pagan rituals. Long after the pagan foundation has been obliterated, some of the words (e.g., *yule*) and traditions (the Christmas tree) have survived.

Critical scholars have long tried to discover the pagan roots of Purim. Numerous attempts have been made to interpret the story of Esther as a historicization of a mythical confrontation between the various deities. Zimmerman saw in Mordecai and Esther the Babylonian deities Marduk and Ishtar, and the evil gods Kingu and Tiamat he identified with Haman and Vashti by associating them with the Elamite deities Humman and Mashti.[197] Purim, in this scenario, was originally a festival celebrating Marduk's victory over Tiamat. This theory, however, has numerous

195. On some recent attempts to explain the pl. form and their weaknesses, see Clines, 263–64.

196. Many scholars regard the tradition of the lots to be an intrusion or secondary addition to the narrative. See Clines, *Esther Scroll*, 53.

197. The idea originated with H. Zimmerman, "Zur Frage nach dem Ursprunge des Purimfestes," *ZAW* 11 (1891): 157–69, and P. Jensen, "Elamitische Eigennamen. Ein Beitrag zur Erklärung der elamitischen Inschriften," *WZKM* 6 (1892): 47–70, 209–26.

problems. It seems strange that the Akkadian names of the heroes would be used, while the villains were identified with Elamite names. Furthermore, there is no evidence that Ishtar had any role in the myth of Marduk's conquest over Tiamat. Humman was also apparently a rather minor god in the Elamite pantheon and not the great rival this theory would make of him. In light of these facts, scholars have sought parallels between Esther and several other myths, including the Gilgamesh Epic, the Enuma Elish, and the Tammuz-Ishtar myth (Paton, 87–94).[198] But even more to the point: what evidence is there for the "historicization" of ancient myths? There is certainly evidence for stories about mortals and their affairs becoming mythologized, as in the case of Gilgamesh or the Trojan War. But there is little reason to believe that mythological conflicts were recast as history in antiquity.

The idea that the story of Esther was derived from pagan mythology receives little credence today. On the other hand, the theory that the Purim festival has origins in the pagan world seems more probable. In light of the fact that the word *pur* is apparently Akkadian, scholars have naturally looked to Babylon for Purim's basis. Zimmerman believed that Purim could be traced to the Babylonian New Year festival of Zagmuk, the beginning of an eleven- or twelve-day festival that occurred in the spring.[199] The festival celebrated the triumph of Marduk over chaos and involved a great deal of drinking and merrymaking. At this festival, it was believed that the gods cast lots to determine the fates of humanity for the coming year. It may have involved the elevation of a condemned prisoner to a faux kingship, complete with robes, crown, and royal procession. There are clearly some similarities between Purim and Zagmuk, but numerous differences as well: Zagmuk was celebrated at the beginning of the month of Nisan, while Purim was celebrated in Adar; Zagmuk kicked off a festival that lasted nearly two weeks, while Purim was only two days; Zagmuk centered on the king and his role as divine intermediary, while Purim had little royal focus. Finally, there is no historical evidence that the Babylonians ever referred to their New Year's festival as "Purim."

Other scholars have looked to Persia, where the story is set, to discover Purim's prototype. Lagarde suggested that Purim was a Jewish transformation of Farvardigan, the Zoroastrian festival of the dead, which was celebrated at the end of the Persian year.[200] An important aspect of this

---

198. For a more recent example, see A. Silverstein, "The Book of Esther and the Enuma Elish," *BSOAS* 69 (2006): 209–23.

199. Zimmerman, "Zur Frage."

200. P. Lagarde, *Purim, ein Beitrag zur Geschichte der Religion* (Göttingen: Dietrich, 1887).

argument is the linguistic variation displayed in the word *Purim* in the LXX, where it is typically spelled Phourai, but also Phurdaia. The major weakness with the theory is that there is no similarity between the Persian festival of the dead and the celebration of Purim. The theory also attributes a good deal of significance to Septuagintal variants that may represent no more than scribal errors. Lewy similarly connected Purim with Farvardigan, but he proposed that it was a (wholly hypothetical) Babylonianized version of the festival that was celebrated among the Jews.[201] In a rather complicated scenario, Lewy argued that the story of Esther reflected the struggles between Marduk worshipers and the worshipers of the god Mithra in the days of Artaxerxes II (404–358 BC). The theory has found few supporters.

The more modest approaches of Gaster and Ringgren, on the other hand, have received a more positive response. Both contended that Purim was derived from a Persian New Year festival, noting that such festivals often include such activities as the choosing of a new queen and parading a commoner around in royal garb.[202] The theory is not without its weaknesses: their parallels to Purim often come from widely divergent sources and do not represent any single New Year festival known from antiquity. Also, there is no linguistic evidence to tie the word *Purim* to any of these festivals.

A theory sometimes found in popular writing but rarely in academic texts is that Purim is connected to the ancient Hittite *Purulli* festival ("festival of the earth"), a New Year celebration that occurred in the spring.[203] Like Babylonian New Year festivals, it involved much drinking and merriment. Central to the celebration was the recitation of the Illuyanka myth. This story tells how the storm god Teshub defeated his enemy, the serpent Illuyanka. Teshub's daughter Inara invited Illuyanka to come to a banquet with his sons. When the serpent and his sons were quite drunk, Inara's mortal lover bound them with rope, and then Teshub and the other gods killed them.[204] There are several parallels here to the story of Esther and the celebration of Purim. The festival was dedicated to the goddess Hannahannah, who corresponds to the Akkadian Ishtar, for whom Esther is likely named. The hero of the tale is a storm god, corresponding to the Babylonian Marduk, for whom Mordecai is named. The god's daughter invites the enemy to a feast, as Esther invites Haman to a feast. The enemy and his sons

---

201. J. Lewy, "The Feast of the 14th Day of Adar," *HUCA* 14 (1939): 127–51.
202. T. Gaster, *Purim and Hanukkah in Custom and Tradition* (New York: Henry Schumann, 1950), 18. H. Ringgren, "Esther and Purim," *SEA* 20 (1956): 5–24.
203. See, e.g., D. Conway, *Maiden, Mother, Crone: The Myth and Reality of the Triple Goddess* (St. Paul, MN: Llewellyn, 2004), 59.
204. For the text of the myth, see G. Beckman, "The Anatolian Myth of *Illuyanka*," *JANES* 14 (1982): 11–25.

are killed, just as in the book of Esther, where both Haman and his sons were killed. Just as the celebration of Purim involved reading the story of Esther, so the celebration of *purulli* required the recitation of the Illuyanka myth. And of course, there is also the similarity of names, *purulli* and *purim*. One could well imagine that if there had been Jews celebrating *purulli*, they might have shortened the foreign word to something more familiar (just as the name "Moses" might have been a shortened version of an originally longer Egyptian name).[205] Of course, this approach assumes that the myth of Teshub and Illuyanka somehow shaped the story of Mordecai, Esther, and Haman. As noted above, there is little evidence for the historicization of ancient myths. But the more substantial problem with the theory is that the Hittite Empire had disappeared centuries before the arrival of the Jews in Mesopotamia, having fallen to the Sea Peoples ca. 1200 BC. The Neo-Hittite kingdoms of Carchemish, Melid, and Kummuhi persisted, however, until they were conquered by the Assyrians around 700 BC.[206] Judahite exiles might well have had extensive contact with the remnants of these people in their settlements "by the River Chebar" (Ezek 1:1). It is possible that the name and some of the traditions of *purulli* could have survived long after the Hittite Empire was gone. Again, we might see an analogy in the way the name "Eostre" (Easter) and the yuletide traditions survive long after the meanings of the words and their significance have been lost to modern Christians.

Another attempt is the linking of Purim with "Nicanor's Day," a festival that celebrated Judas Maccabeus' defeat of the Syrian general Nicanor in 161 BC (cf. 1 Macc 7:26–49; 2 Macc 14:12–15:36). Haupt proposed the theory that the book of Esther was composed as a "festal legend" for the celebration of Nicanor's Day during the time of the Maccabees. Nicanor's Day was then combined with the Persian New Year celebration, and the New Year's traditions were transferred to the Jewish holiday.[207] More recently, Herst argued that John Hyrcanus I (134–104 BC) tried to replace Nicanor's Day with a festival of Babylonian-Persian origin called Purim.[208] Neither author gives an adequate explanation for the origin of the name "Purim," nor why such a festival is not attested among surviving Babylonian

---

205. See BDB, משׁה; *EDB*, "Moses"; J. G. Griffiths, "The Egyptian Derivation of the Name Moses," *JNES* 12 (1953): 225–31; V. Matthews, *Exodus: An Exegetical Commentary* (Grand Rapids: Baker, 2011), 91–92.

206. See T. Bryce, *The World of the Neo-Hittite Kingdoms: A Political and Military History* (Oxford: Oxford University Press, 2012).

207. P. Haupt, *Purim* (Baltimore: Johns Hopkins Press, 1906), 3.

208. R. Herst, "The Purim Connection," *USQR* 28 (1973): 139–45.

and Persian sources. Furthermore, the notion that the book of Esther was fully composed in the Hasmonean era is now widely rejected.[209]

With such a plethora of theories, it is obvious that there is little consensus regarding the origins of Purim. In part, it is due to the nature of holidays: they are remarkably persistent, passed on from generation to generation; but they are remarkably malleable, adapting to new situations and contexts. Nations and ethnic groups often adopt holidays foreign to their heritage, adjusting them as necessary for their tastes and circumstances. It seems reasonable to conclude that Purim was not originally a Jewish feast, but that there were Jews who celebrated it in some generic fashion. The story of Esther displaced whatever pagan story might have been originally associated with the holiday, giving it instead a more nationalistic focus. The bacchanalian elements of the celebration remained and were infused with new significance.

Literary Features

The book of Esther is a remarkable work of literature. Its author employs numerous literary devices to create an entertaining story, one that has stood the test of time and copious retelling. Its style shares many features with earlier examples of biblical storytelling. It is written in the form of narrative prose, with a rapid pace that is largely devoid of embellishments. It has been carefully crafted around significant recurring elements. As is typical of biblical prose, the author rarely gives physical descriptions of his characters, beyond assertions that Vashti was "beautiful" (Esth 1:11) and that Esther "found favor in the eyes of all who saw her" (Esth 2:15, 17).[210] Though the story is told from the point of view of a third-person omniscient narrator—a fact that led some of the rabbis to argue that the book was divinely inspired (*b. Meg.* 7a)—the author only occasionally delves into the internal monologues of his characters, typically allowing their actions to speak for themselves.

In this section, we will consider three major literary features of Esther: characterization, motifs, and structure. Other literary aspects of the text will be noted from time to time in the commentary.

209. See the section on "Composition" above.

210. On the use of description by biblical authors, see A. Berlin, *Poetics and Interpretation of Biblical Narrative* (Sheffield, UK: Almond, 1983), 136–39; R. Alter, *The Art of Biblical Narrative* (New York: Basic Books, 1983), 115–16; T. Linafelt, "Narrative and Poetic Art in the Book of Ruth," *Int* 64 (2010): 117–29.

Characterization

The book of Esther could accurately be described as plot driven as opposed to character driven. It is the turn of events, not the people involved, that truly captures and holds our interest.[211] Nonetheless, the characters certainly enhance our enjoyment of the narrative. While they appear on the surface to be somewhat "flat," seeming to change little through the course of the narrative, this impression is dispelled by a careful reading of the text. The characters are, as Sasson puts it, "deceptively static."[212] Further reflection on their acts and words reveals something of their complexity.

Though it is not character driven, the book of Esther certainly does not lack for characters. The book positively teems with names of individuals, some with greater roles, some with lesser. In Esther, it seems that a single line of dialogue or single act of significance will suffice for the recording of the character's name. There might be a note of satire in this approach, a subtle mockery of the officiousness of the Persian Empire. No doubt, too, the recurrence of so many exotic-sounding names added to readers' and listeners' pleasure. But of all these named characters, only a few are truly significant to the story line. Several important studies on the main characters of Esther have emerged recently, and these will be frequently cited in the commentary.[213] Here, we will consider briefly the portrayal of the major characters and their roles in the Esther narrative.

King Xerxes

Xerxes is the "real-world anchor" for the narrative. He is more than merely a character in a story; he was a person whose name would have evoked

---

211. See L. Ryken, *The Literature of the Bible* (Grand Rapids: Zondervan, 1974), 76–77.

212. Sasson, "Esther," 336.

213. Undoubtedly the most influential of these treatments is Fox, *Character and Ideology*. L. Day, *Three Faces of a Queen: Characterization in the Books of Esther*, JSOTSup 186 (Sheffield, UK: Sheffield Academic Press, 1995) surveys the character of Esther in the Heb. and Greek versions. A. Fountain, *Literary and Empirical Readings of the Book of Esther* (New York: Peter Lang, 2002) also compares the characterization of the major figures in Esther in the Heb. and Greek versions, employing empirical analysis to draw out the differences in the portrayals. Other studies that consider characterization in Esther include F. Weiland, "Plot Structure in the Book of Esther," *BSac* 159 (2002): 277–87; S. Crawford, "Esther and Judith: Contrasts in Character," in *The Book of Esther in Modern Research*, ed. S. Crawford and L. Greenspoon, JSOTSup 380 (London: T&T Clark, 2003), 61–76; M. Mills, "Household and Table: Diasporic Boundaries in Daniel and Esther," *CBQ* 68 (2006): 408–20.

numerous impressions.[214] For the ancient audience, he would have represented the height of Persian glory, a man of great power and wealth. His efforts to conquer Greece demonstrate the breadth of his ambition; his failure to carry through speaks poorly of his military competence. According to Herodotus, Xerxes was a passionate figure, one who held his own honor in high regard. Herodotus records an episode where Xerxes, frustrated when a storm destroyed a bridge he was building across the Hellespont, ordered that the channel itself be flogged with lashes and "fettered" with chains thrown into the water (*Hist.* 7.34–35). He was a man who did nothing on a small scale: on failing to conquer Greece, he devoted himself to the building of Susa and Persepolis, enhancing them with great, imposing edifices. He constructed a palace for himself that was nearly twice the size of that of his father, Darius. He was temperamental and sometimes ruthless, but he seems to have been unable to refuse his queen Amestris anything she requested.

While these images of Xerxes probably percolated in the mind of Esther's author, the depiction of the great king in the book of Esther is not nearly as complex as that which appears in Herodotus and other ancient literature. Here, he seems rather shallow, a "flat" figure who develops little in the course of the narrative. He apparently has no inner life, no hidden motives or agendas. He is the only major character in the story who does not change office from beginning of the narrative to the end; indeed, the book begins by extolling his magnificence and describing his reign, and it ends in the same way. Though he is prominent throughout the story (as will be discussed below), he is easily the least interesting of the main characters.

Xerxes is a figure driven by the honor of kingship. In the opening scene, he is hosting a banquet to display the wealth of his kingdom and the "honor of his great splendor" (1:4). The fateful discharge of Vashti results because she has not appropriately honored the king (1:17). The insult to the king's dignity is so important a matter that it provokes a royal inquiry drawing on the collective wisdom of all the king's closest advisers—while the decision to destroy an entire race could be undertaken on the word of a single

---

214. *Pace* Levenson, 25, who writes that "the author borrowed Xerxes's name but little else about him in order to create the novella." It would not have been possible for the author to center a story on so famous a figure as Xerxes without importing some of Xerxes' "baggage" into the character. We might compare it to someone writing a story about George Washington and assuming the reader would have no thoughts, ideas, or information about Washington. In fact, the figure of Xerxes as depicted in Esther is not incompatible with his portrayal in Herodotus and other ancient literature. It seems likely that Esther's author drew on Xerxes' reputation in laying the foundation for his story.

individual. Haman appeals to the king's dignity when he asks the king to order the Jews' destruction, stating that it is not "fitting" (שֹׁוֶה, *šāweh*) for the king to tolerate them (3:8). In one of the narrative's most entertaining scenes, the king is once again concerned with the question of honor—specifically, how to honor Mordecai for saving his life (6:3). The king's own honor, too, is at stake in this episode, for in failing to reward Mordecai, the king threatens to bring shame on himself. Xerxes can be a dangerous figure, especially when his honor is at stake. One who has the effrontery to appear before him unbidden can forfeit his life (4:11). Haman is put to death not so much because he plotted against the Jews, but for insulting the king by "assaulting" the queen in his own house (7:8).

But the most prominent feature of King Xerxes as he is depicted here is his inability to make a decision on his own. He comes across as indecisive, easily moved, and manipulated by those around him. He is, to use Fox's term, lazy.[215] It is not he, but his counselor Memucan, who determines what is to be done to Vashti (1:16–21). Once the queen is deposed, it is Xerxes' counselors who devise a plan for finding her replacement (2:2–4). Xerxes accepts Haman's charges against the Jews without investigating the matter himself (3:8–11), casually ordering the execution of an entire race before getting down to the "important" business of eating his lunch (3:15). He capitulates at once to Queen Esther's requests (5:5; 8:5–8; 9:12–14) and to the suggestion of his eunuch Harbona (7:9). Indeed, there is not one request or word of advice that the king does not answer favorably. He seems a most agreeable fellow. Ironically, though Haman exploits Xerxes' tractability in launching his plot against the Jews, it is this very aspect of his character that also leads to Haman's great humiliation in Esth 6: the king unquestioningly accepts Haman's advice regarding what should be done for a man that the king wishes to honor. His are not the actions of an indecisive man; instead, he is consistently portrayed as a man who would rather let someone else do his thinking for him.

Queen Vashti

Though a much-maligned figure in early Jewish and Christian interpretations of Esther, Vashti has emerged in modern times as something of a heroine in her own right, especially among feminist interpreters.[216] According to *The Woman's Bible*, she was "a sublime representative of self-centered

---

215. Fox, *Character and Ideology*, 173.

216. The Talmud depicts Vashti as a tyrant and an anti-Semite who was punished by God with some physical deformity. For references and discussion, see further the commentary.

womanhood."[217] Telushkin calls her "an unsuccessful heroine in an early struggle for women's dignity."[218] Queen Vashti, though she only appears in the first chapter, serves a major function in the story, both by introducing the important motif of submission versus resistance (to be discussed below) and by making the way for Esther to become queen. She speaks no lines and performs only one action (hosting a banquet for the women of Susa), but it is what she refuses to do—present herself to be ogled by the king's guests—that proves so fateful.[219]

The Bible does not say why Vashti refused the king's summons. While a modern author would probably want to tell us what Vashti was thinking, biblical narrative tends to be spare in its use of such inner monologue, often allowing the reader to fill in his or her own impressions. Most likely, as a number of commentators have observed, the issue at stake was one of propriety: it was the job of concubines, not queens, to entertain party guests.[220] But her motives aside, the act of defiance serves an important role in the Esther narrative. It contrasts sharply with Esther's submissive acceptance of Mordecai's commands, thus setting up a stark distinction between the woman whose resistance lost her the queenship and one whose submissiveness won her the office. It also foreshadows the insubordination of Mordecai, who, like Vashti, will refuse to capitulate to the demands of one who deems himself his superior.

Mordecai

Mordecai surely appears to be the hero of our narrative, since his virtues are lauded in the final verse of the book (10:2). As is typical in biblical narrative, there is no description given of him. It is possible that he represents the upper class of Judaea, since his ancestor was taken away in the first deportation with Jehoiachin (2:6)—the deportation that had consisted primarily of the "gentry" of Jerusalem. The account of his genealogy, designating him a Benjaminite of the family of Kish (2:5), is probably designed to imply still more: he is almost certainly linked here to the line of King Saul, who was also a Benjaminite and son of Kish. Thus, he is not merely noble, but royalty. His clash with Haman the Agagite is a personal one: the text implies that

217. E. Stanton, ed., *The Woman's Bible, Part II* (New York: European Publishing Co., 1895), 88.
218. J. Telushkin, *Biblical Literacy: The Most Important People, Events, and Ideas of the Hebrew Bible* (New York: William Morrow, 1997), 367.
219. Note Laniak, 6–7, who remarks that in current feminist scholarship, Vashti is more highly praised than Esther on account of what she refused to do.
220. Thus E. Bickerman, *Four Strange Books*, 185–86. Several scholars have accepted this explanation, including, e.g., Fox, *Character and Ideology*, 168. Further consideration of Vashti's refusal will be found in the commentary.

Haman is a descendant of Agag, the Amalekite king whom Saul had failed to kill, precipitating his rejection by God (1 Sam 15).[221]

Like many Jews of his day, Mordecai (מָרְדֳּכַי) bears a foreign name. But in his case, there is something more than a little disturbing about the name, since Mordecai is a barely-Hebraized form of the name Marduk, chief god of Babylon.[222] The name was not uncommon and even appears as the name of one of the Jews returning from Babylon to Jerusalem in Ezra 2:2. Nonetheless, we may well imagine that the name would not have held positive connotations for the story's audience. It is quite possible that readers or hearers of this story would have been somewhat prejudiced against Mordecai from the start: at the very least, he seems to have represented a thoroughly acculturated Jew. But on the other hand, the author of the book of Esther might have seen a rather different significance in this somewhat conspicuous name: the first letters of the name, מרד (*mrd*), form the Heb. word for "rebel." In the biblical narratives, it was not uncommon for great significance to be attached to the sound of a name, irrespective of its actual meaning.[223] With a little imagination and tongue planted firmly in cheek, "Mordecai" could have been read as "Your Rebellious One"—a not-unsuitable name for this insubordinate hero.

Most assessments of Mordecai's character are that he is a mostly or wholly positive figure. According to Fox, he is "unblemished," a man of unfailing virtue and wisdom.[224] While we will find reason to question this assessment, it cannot be denied that his character is generally good. He is introduced in 2:7 as someone who has taken in an orphan, and he also demonstrated his goodwill by exposing the plot to kill King Xerxes

---

221. For more on this aspect of the conflict, see the commentary on 3:1.

222. It might be noted that in Daniel the "three Hebrew children," Shadrach, Meshach, and Abednego, also bore foreign names. The name given to Daniel, Belteshazzar, has been vocalized in the MT to connect it with the divine name Bel. The name Abednego may derive from Abed-Nabu, "Servant of Nabu" (see further J. Collins, *Daniel,* Hermeneia [Minneapolis: Fortress, 1993], 140–41). These names, however, were imposed on the Jewish youths by their captors, an indication of their subjugation by overlords.

223. We might note the case of the name Moses: according to Exod 2:10, the name was given to the child "because I drew him out (מְשִׁיתִהוּ, *mĕšîtihû*) from the water." Most scholars are agreed, however, that the name is actually Egyptian, derived from the word *mes*, "born of," as in the names Ramses and Thutmosis. The sound of the name, however, could be connected to the seldom-used Heb. root meaning "draw."

224. Fox, *Character and Ideology*, 185–90, provides a list of Mordecai's supposed virtues, including his Jewishness, his wisdom, pride (which Fox believes the author appreciates), courage, and loyalty, among others.

(2:21–23). The last verse of the book (10:2) states that he was "well regarded" among the Jews, because he sought "the welfare of his people" (טוֹב לְעַמּוֹ, *ṭôb lĕʿammô*). In spite of his suspect name, he proved himself in the end to be a true Jew at heart.

But his character is not lacking in some ambiguity. He allows Esther to be taken into the palace of the king to become a member of Xerxes' harem; could not a good Jewish man have obtained a more "kosher" husband for his cousin? While Jewish women were not prohibited from marrying Gentiles by the Torah, the practice was certainly frowned on in the Persian era. Both Ezra and Nehemiah railed against intermarriage (Ezra 9:1–4; Neh 13:23–27), and the book of Malachi apparently decries the practice as well (Mal 2:11). Furthermore, Mordecai ordered Esther to conceal her Jewishness (2:10, 17). What had motivated this cover-up? The text does not say. There seems to be little reason for Esther to hide her ethnic background, since the women who competed for Vashti's office were drawn from all over the empire. There is no suggestion that the Jews would have been barred from the contest, or in some way subject to prejudice. While Bush (368) writes that the cover-up forebodes that disclosure of Esther's nationality would be "dangerous in the extreme," it is probably only to those who know the rest of the story that it appears ominous.[225] Based on what has been revealed thus far in the narrative, the subterfuge seems more a matter of cunning than caution, a jockeying for potential advantage that may be exploited. In any event, Mordecai's foresight will surely pay off later in the story. He will pressure Esther to act on behalf of her people, even resorting to thinly veiled threats to cow her into compliance (4:14).

Some of Mordecai's other acts are equally unsettling. No explanation is given for his refusal to bow before the king's vizier in chapter 3, in direct disobedience to the king's command (3:2–3). While modern egalitarian thinkers may find nothing wrong with refusing to prostrate oneself before a "superior," such customs were taken for granted in antiquity. Herodotus (*Hist.* 1.134) writes that the Persians were very conscious of social class and observed strict protocols: greeting equals with a kiss, but bowing and making obeisance before those of higher standing. Similar practices are attested throughout the Middle East and in the Bible.[226] Indeed, Mordecai's refus-

225. Similarly Paton, 175, who argues that Esther would have been mistreated if her nationality were known. Fox, *Character and Ideology*, 31–32, holds instead that though there was no widespread anti-Semitism, there was an ever-present threat from the "enemies of the Jews."

226. E.g., Jacob prostrated himself before Esau (Gen 33:3); Joseph's brothers bowed before him before recognizing Joseph as their brother (Gen 42:6); David prostrated himself before both Jonathan (1 Sam 20:41) and Saul (1 Sam 24:8). The possible

al to bow before Haman is so inexplicable that the rabbis felt it necessary to invent a story that Haman carried an idol around his neck, and it was to the idol that Mordecai refused to bow, not to the person of Haman.[227] Bickerman suggests that Mordecai was motivated by resentment: Haman had received a promotion that he himself, as the king's rescuer, should have rightly received.[228] But whether motivated by "pigheaded pride" (Baldwin, 76) or commitment to some unstated principle, his act of disobedience placed the entire Jewish people in great peril. Mordecai then forced Esther to risk her own life in order to save his people from a destruction that he had caused himself. And yet, he is the one who is rewarded and praised for his greatness in 10:2, while Esther receives no mention at all.

Haman

One may be tempted to identify Haman as a "round" character, given how puffed up he is with self-importance! He is, however, presented as a rather one-dimensional figure, driven almost entirely by a single motive: his own vanity. He is the very model of pretension. Indeed, his name (הָמָן) sounds very similar to the Heb. word meaning "big noise" (הָמוֹן, *hāmôn*).[229] His sense of self-importance is his most prominent quality, and the quality that will lead to his downfall.

Unlike Mordecai, whose motives are always veiled to us, Haman is utterly transparent. His emotions are often noted: he is filled with wrath (3:5); he is joyful and in good spirits (5:9a) and then angry again (5:9b); he is pleased (5:14); he mourns (6:12); he is terrified (7:6). Furthermore, the narrator often invites us into the mind of Haman to observe his thoughts and motives: he thinks it below his station to lay hands on Mordecai alone (3:6); he restrains himself from assaulting Mordecai (5:10); he waits in order to speak to the king about Mordecai's execution (6:4); he wrongly believes that that the king wishes to pay him honor (6:6). This last incident is the only scene in the book where a character uses inner dialogue. By allowing us to hear his thoughts, the author of Esther lets us enjoy Haman's mortification even more.

Through this peek into Haman's psyche, the book of Esther reveals a character who is obsessed with his own significance. Not that he is actually

---

motives for his refusal will be discussed further in the commentary.

227. See Fox, *Character and Ideology*, 43–44.

228. Bickerman, *Four Strange Books*, 178–80.

229. Most likely, his name was Persian. The most plausible explanations are that Haman is a form of the name Omanes, commonly found in Greek literature, or that it is a form of the name Humpan, an Elamite deity. R. Zadok, "On the Historical Background of the Book of Esther," *BN* 24 (1984): 18–19. Even so, the sound of the name would have been suggestive to the Heb.-speaking audience.

insignificant: he is, after all, second in command to the most powerful man on earth. But for Haman, the position alone is not enough. It is the honor that comes with the position that he truly craves. He brags to his friends of his wealth and power (5:11). He exults in having received a personal invitation to the table of the queen (5:12). He relishes the idea of being honored before the people of Susa (6:6). So important is this expected deference that the thought of even a single individual not paying him his due is intolerable. Haman is not anti-Semitic per se; he does not hate the Jews because they are Jewish. It is Mordecai whom he hates; he hates the Jews only because they are the people of Mordecai (3:6). Destroying an entire nation because of one man's insult is a vengeance that is truly worthy of so "great" a man as Haman.

Our narrator has surely had some fun at the expense of Haman. This strutting peacock goes blithely to his destruction, oblivious to the snare that is tightening around his neck. He is a hapless victim of his own ego. Yet the narrator bears Haman no personal animosity. He is not depicted as a fool; indeed, he might be said to be somewhat cunning.[230] Haman, in one sense, was a victim of his own ambition. His gravest error was choosing the wrong target for his demonstration of power. Because he clashed with the Jewish people, he was destined to fail from the start (6:13).

Esther

It is appropriate that this book bears the name of Esther, for she is the most fully developed character. So remarkable is her development through the course of events that she has been the subject of several monographs as well as numerous shorter studies.[231] Like Haman and Mordecai, her significance begins with her name. We are told only once (Esth 2:7) that she possessed a Heb. name, Hadassah, which apparently means "Myrtle." The name is not without significance, since "Myrtle is symbolic of peace and

---

230. See Fox, *Character and Ideology*, 182–93.

231. These include several that have already been mentioned, including Fox, *Character and Ideology*; Day, *Three Faces of a Queen;* Fountain, *Literary and Empirical Readings*; Weiland, "Plot Structure"; Crawford, "Esther and Judith." Esther has been the subject of several feminist critiques, including S. Niditch, "Esther: Folklore, Wisdom, Feminism, and Authority," in *Underdogs and Tricksters: A Prelude to Biblical Folklore* (San Francisco: Harper & Row, 1987), 126–45, 168–70; S. White, "Esther: A Feminist Model for Jewish Diaspora," in *Gender and Difference in Ancient Israel*, ed. P. Day (Minneapolis: Fortress, 1987), 161–77; B. Wyler, "Esther: The Incomplete Emancipation of a Queen," in *A Feminist Companion to Esther, Judith, and Susannah*, ed. A. Brenner (Sheffield: Sheffield Academic Press, 1995), 111–35. T. Beal, *Book of Hiding*, also devotes a good deal of space to the interpretation of Esther from the feminist perspective.

divine blessing."[232] The audience of the book might have taken this name as a sign of good things to come. But they might have had more mixed reactions to her other name, Esther. Several different suggestions have been proffered for the origin of this name. Zadok derives the name from the Old Iranian *stara*, meaning "star."[233] Yahuda, on the other hand, has concluded that Esther is the Persian equivalent of Hadassah.[234] But it is unlikely that the original audience could have read this name in its literary context without making another association: it appears most likely to be an adaptation of the name Ishtar, the Babylonian goddess of love and war (see Lewy, 128–30). Given that Mordecai bears the name of the chief Babylonian god, it would have been difficult not to see here a reference to the chief Babylonian goddess, given the similarity of the names. Given Esther's role in the story, Ishtar's associations with love and war might have seemed most appropriate, indeed. Once again, we seem to be presented with a Jewish figure who has capitulated to paganism.

But just as the name Mordecai might have an element of double entendre, "Esther" seems to hold some meaning that could only be appreciated by insiders. In unpointed Heb., Esther (אסתר, *'str*) could be read as "I hide" or "Let me hide." Such a name would have significance in the context of this book. Esther is a woman who hides her ethnicity, a fact that will become absolutely crucial later in the narrative. But Esther is a book where God Himself is hidden. The rabbis (*b. Ḥul.* 139b) noted the linguistic connection: "Where is Esther indicated in the Torah? 'And I will surely hide (אַסְתִּיר) my face.'" The rabbis draw a line from the book of Esther to Deut 31 based on the similarity of sounds, but it is likely that they recognized a theological aspect of the narrative as well. We will explore this very important idea in the "Theology of Esther" section of the introduction.

However significant her name may be, Esther is far more than merely a name in this story. She is a central figure, perhaps eclipsed in the end by Mordecai, but substantial nonetheless. Esther is described in only the most positive terms. Physically, she is "fair of form and lovely to look at" (2:7). Through either her appearance or her demeanor, she garners the favor of

232. *AYBD* 2:807. See also Baldwin, 66. "Myrtle" is not attested as a proper name elsewhere, and so a variety of other explanations have been proposed for the meaning of Hadassah. These will be noted in the commentary.

233. R. Zadok, "Notes on Esther," *ZAW* 98 (1986): 107.

234. A. Yahuda, "The Meaning of the Name Esther," *JRAS* (1946): 174–78; repr. in C. A. Moore, ed., *Studies in the Book of Esther: Selected with a Prolegomenon by Carey A. Moore* (New York: KTAV Publishing House, 1982), 268–72. Though the Persian word for myrtle is *as*, Yahuda argues that the name "Esther" reflects a hypothetical older and longer form, the Median *astra*, which was preserved in Old Persian.

everyone who meets her. When she was brought to the harem, she pleased its overseer Hegai and "won his lovingkindness (תִּשָּׂא חֶסֶד לְפָנָיו, *tiśśāʾ ḥesed lĕpānāyw*)," so that he gave her the best place in the harem (2:9). Without apparent effort on her part, she "obtained favor in the eyes of all who saw her (נֹשֵׂאת חֵן בְּעֵינֵי כָּל־רֹאֶיהָ, *nōśēʾt ḥēn bĕʿênê kŏl rōʾeyhā*)" (2:15). During her turn with the king, she won lovingkindness and obtained favor (וַתִּשָּׂא־חֵן וָחֶסֶד לְפָנָיו, *wattiśśāʾ ḥēn wĕḥesed lĕpānāyw*) more than any of the other virgins (2:17). Coming before the king unbidden, she again obtains favor in his eyes (5:2). She prefaces each request that she puts to Xerxes (save the last) with the words, "If I have found favor in your eyes, O King … " (5:8; 7:3; 8:5). The king's positive response indicates that Esther has, indeed, won his favor.

Of all the main characters, only Esther displays any character development through the course of the narrative. While other characters may experience a change of position or office, Esther actually develops a backbone. When first introduced, she is a totally submissive figure. Repeatedly, action is done to her, rather than by her: Mordecai raised her (2:7); he took her as his daughter (2:7); she was taken into the king's palace (2:8); she was given her cosmetic treatments (2:9); she was commanded not to reveal her ethnicity (2:11). When the young women were to be brought before the king, they could take with them anything they requested (2:13); Esther, however, was too passive even to ask for anything—she took what was given to her by the keeper of women (2:15). In chapter 4, Esther attempts to take a more active role, trying to get Mordecai to abandon his sackcloth and ashes for clothes she sends him (4:4). He rejects the offer, however, and in turn pressures her into pleading the Jews' case before the king (4:8, 13–14). But the tables are turning: in 4:17, it is Mordecai who carries out Esther's commands. By 8:2, Esther is acting as Mordecai's benefactor, bringing him before the king and bestowing on him the estates of Haman. "In the course of events she ascends from the role of Mordecai's protégée to become her mentor's guardian."[235]

Her relationship with the king undergoes a similar development. She is initially passive and timid: while the other young women went (בָּאָה, *bāʾâ*) to the king (2:13–14), she was taken (תִּלָּקַח, *tillĕqaḥ*) to the king (2:16). She is the object of the king's actions: he loves her, sets the crown on her head, and makes her queen (2:17). She is reluctant to come before him unbidden; indeed, she may well be said to display a little cowardice in her desire to protect her own life over that of her people (4:11). When she does appear before the king, she presents her requests to him with fitting obsequiousness, asking "If it please the king" and "If I have found favor in your

---

235. B. Jones, "Two Misconceptions," 177.

sight" (5:4, 8; 7:3); she weeps, pleads with him, and falls at his feet (8:3). But by 9:12, the king is coming to Esther and asking her what she would like him to do next. It is not a complete inversion of roles; he is still king, and she still must couch her request in the proper forms.[236] But Esther has grown as a character, transformed from a submissive supplicant to royal adviser.[237] In the last episode of the narrative proper, 9:23–32, Esther has risen to a status among the Jews that is essentially equal to that of the king. She possesses authority (תֹּקֶף, *tōqēp*, 9:29), just as Xerxes does (תָּקְפּוֹ, *tŏqpô*, 10:1). Other than the king himself, she is the only character in the book who "issues a decree" (מַאֲמַר אֶסְתֵּר, *maʾămar ʾestēr*, "the decree of Esther," 9:32).

The Parallels

In spite of the dramatic differences between these characters, there is clearly a sense in which they go together and need to be viewed in comparison and contrast with one another. Aside from the king, who stands in a sense above the action, the fortunes of the main characters are bound together. The two Gentile characters, Vashti and Haman, are deposed from their positions of power. The two Jewish characters, Esther and Mordecai, are exalted to these positions of power. (Of the major characters, only the king's status remains unchanged.) The two women, Vashti and Esther, change status rapidly. In the cases of the two male leads, Mordecai and Haman, the changes in their status occur incrementally.

There are also interesting parallels to be drawn between the Gentile and Jewish characters. Vashti and Mordecai represent what are essentially subjugated groups within the Persian Empire: Vashti is the exemplar of oppressed womanhood; Mordecai is the exemplar of the endangered Jews. Both act in defiance of an order of the king, inciting wrath against them (1:12; 3:5). Memucan characterizes Vashti's act as an effrontery not only to the king, but to the entire nation (1:18). All women will hear of it and become insolent toward their husbands. Disrespect will run rampant! It is not enough that Vashti alone be put in her place. Memucan persuades the king to issue a decree forcing all women to be subordinate to their husbands (1:19–20). Likewise, Mordecai's insubordination results not only in his own condemnation—that would be too small a response to his crime, in the

236. According to B. Wyler, "Esther: The Incomplete Emancipation," 130, Esther becomes "a liberated Jew but remains a discriminated-against woman."

237. Niditch, 135, sees Esther as prototype of a wise woman. Several women bring about the salvation of their people through acts of insight or cunning (Deborah in Judg 4–5; the wise woman of Abel in 2 Sam 20; Judith in the book of Judith). It is uncertain, however, how much of Esther's deliverance is the result of special wisdom on her part and how much simply arises from being in the right place at the right time. The text never praises Esther for wisdom, only for beauty.

eyes of Haman. So, Haman presents the Jews as an unruly and dangerous people, people who refuse to obey the law (3:8). He urges the king to issue a decree not to punish Mordecai only, but to punish his entire people (3:9).

A similar parallel may be drawn between Haman and Esther. Both achieve rapid promotion into a position that gives them special access to the king. Haman uses this access twice in the course of the narrative: once, to obtain the order for the destruction of the Jews; and the second time, to attempt to get an order for the death of Mordecai. Queen Esther uses her right of access to the king for the purpose of undoing Haman's acts, first by inviting the king to a banquet where Haman's plot would be revealed (5:2–4), then by securing the rights of the Jews to defend themselves (8:3–12). At the end, however, the request she brings before the king is not that different from that presented initially by Haman: the Jews are empowered to destroy their enemies, along with women and children, just as Haman had been empowered to exterminate the Jews. We might surmise that those enemies would include the people of Haman. Thus Esther's request would allow the Jews to carry out the *ḥerem* against Amalek that King Saul had so long ago failed to complete (1 Sam 15:21–23).

Motifs

The term *motif* is used to mean "a situation, element or idea which recurs in the book of Esther in such a manner that the repetition contributes to the unity of the narrative" (Berg, 16). Such motifs are found in all biblical literature, but Esther seems especially adept at weaving the motifs into the story line so that they form not mere accoutrements, but the very fabric of the narrative. This is especially apparent in the case of the first motif, the "banquet."

The Banquet

The Heb. word for "banquet" (מִשְׁתֶּה, *mišteh*) derives from the verb שׁתה (*šth*), meaning "drink." It occurs forty-six times in the OT, but nineteen of those occurrences are in the book of Esther. No other biblical book even comes close to this frequency. In addition, the verb שׁתהappears three times in the book, twice implying a banquet (3:15, 7:1). Eleven different banquets are mentioned in the book:[238]

238. Clines, "Reading Esther from Left to Right: Contemporary Strategies for Reading a Biblical Text," in *The Bible in Three Dimensions: Essays in Celebration of Forty Years of Biblical Studies in the University of Sheffield,* ed. W. E. Fowl, D. J. A. Clines, and S. E. Porter (Sheffield, UK: JSOT Press, 1990), 37–38, notes only nine banquets, omitting the Jewish banquet of 8:17 and the Purim banquet. Technically, the last banquet does not occur in the narrative, but is more an addendum to it.

- 1:3–4—Xerxes' banquet for his nobles
- 1:5–8—The king's banquet for the people of Susa
- 1:9—Vashti's banquet for the women
- 2:18—Esther's coronation banquet
- 3:15—Xerxes and Haman's banquet together
- 5:4–8—Esther's first banquet with Haman and the king
- 6:14–7:8—Esther's second banquet
- 8:17—The Jews' banquets on receiving the king's decree
- 9:17—Rural Jews' feast of the fourteenth of Adar
- 9:18—Jews of Susa feasting on the fifteenth of Adar
- 9:22–23—The establishment of Purim as a perpetual feast

The first five feasts are given by the Persians; the next two are given by the Jew Esther for the Gentiles Xerxes and Haman; the last four are Jewish celebrations. As will be seen later, the shift from Gentile to Jewish banqueting corresponds with the turning point in the story from the growing danger to the Jews to their deliverance and blessing. These banquets serve as structural elements in the narrative.

The banquet (or literally, "drinking occasion") is an appropriate image for a story set in the Persian Empire. The Persians were well known for their love of wine and strong drink. According to both Herodotus (*Hist.* 1.133) and Strabo (*Geog.* 15.3.20), the Persians decided the most important matters of state when they were drunk. (Herodotus adds that the decisions would be confirmed when they had sobered up.) Any decisions made when one was fully sober were considered suspect and had to be reconsidered when inebriated. These charges have the tone of slander, but that they were promulgated says much about the reputation of the Persians in this era. Undoubtedly the author of Esther has this reputation in mind, the banquet serving as a fitting symbol of the self-indulgence that characterized the Persian court.

Berg has noted a number of similarities, as well as ironic dissimilarities, between the characteristics of these feasts (Berg, 31–59). First, the banquets of the opening and closing chapters are both issued by royal decrees: in chapter 1 by Xerxes, but in chapter 9 by Queen Esther and Mordecai. Also, the first banquet of chapter 1 is for the residents of all the provinces, while the second is for the residents of Susa; the first Purim banquet of chapter 9 is for the Jews spread throughout the empire, while the second Purim banquet was for the Jews of Susa. The banquets are accompanied by similar events: the removal of a queen in chapter 1, the installation of a queen in chapter 2, the removal of a vizier in chapter 7. In 3:15, the king and Haman

---

This consideration will be an important one when we consider the structure of the book.

"banquet" (here, שׁתה, *šth*, is used as a verb) after the decree is issued to destroy the Jews; in 7:1–9, the order to destroy Haman is issued at a banquet. Banquets not only illustrate the self-indulgence of the Persians; they also are the framework on which the narrative hangs.

Kingship/Sovereignty

Kingship is another prominent motif. Berg notes that the root מלך (*mlk*, "rule"; root of the noun מֶלֶךְ, *melek*, "king") occurs over 250 times in the 167 verses of the book of Esther (Berg, 59). Typically, it appears in the titles "king" and "queen," referring to Xerxes (194 times), Vashti, and Esther; but it also is used in reference to Jeconiah and Nebuchadnezzar (2:6), as well as the "kings of Media and Persia" (10:2). It appears frequently in the noun מַלְכוּת (*malkût*, "kingdom" or "reign"; 21 times), with various meanings and implications. This noun is sometimes used to designate the realm of the king's power, the Persian Empire (2:3; 3:6, 8; 5:3, 6); sometimes it means the office of royalty (1:19; 4:14). More often, it is used as the second element of a const. phrase, modifying the *nomen regens** with an adj. force: the "royal throne" (1:2; 5:1); "royal glory" (1:4); "royal wine" (1:7); "royal house" (1:9; 2:16); "royal crown" (1:11; 2:17; 6:8); "royal robes" (5:1; 6:8; 9:1). Finally, the root also occurs as a verb (*qal* inf. const.) in 1:3 and 2:16.

It might not be surprising that the motif of kingship figures prominently in a book we have identified as a "court tale," but the references here deserve attention. There are several different sub-motifs associated with the notion of kingship in this book. One of these is the king's person. The king's presence pervades this narrative to such an extent that even in those few episodes where he does not appear, he is prominent: in 3:1–7, it is the king's decree that elevates Haman and incites Mordecai's insubordination; in chapter 4, the king's command that the Jews be destroyed and Esther's fear of his wrath shape the dialogue between Esther and Mordecai; in 5:9–14, Haman boasts of the honors bestowed on him by the king. The only episode where the king is not prominent is 9:18–22, where Esther has largely displaced him, at least among the Jews.

Another sub-motif is the decree of the king (דָּת, *dāt*). This Persian loanword appears twenty times in Esther (only twice elsewhere in the Bible), always of the king's commands. Several other words and phrases are also used for the king's commands, including פִּתְגָם (*pitgām*, 1:20); the verb צוה (*ṣwh*) and its nominal form מִצְוָה (*miṣwâ*, "command"; 3:2, 3); and the "proclamation" (מַאֲמָר, *ma ʾămār*; 1:15) or "word" (דָּבָר, *dābār*; 1:19; 2:8; 3:15; 4:3; 8:14; 9:1) of the king. These royal commands are not incidental to the story. The decrees of Xerxes depose Vashti (1:19–22), initiate the "beauty contest" that makes Esther queen (2:4), order the officials to prostrate themselves before Haman (3:2), initiate the annihilation of the Jews (3:9), grant the

Jews the right to defend themselves (8:11), and hang the sons of Haman (9:13). The plot is driven by the commandment of the king.[239]

When it is not the will of the king, it is "the pleasure of the king" that impels the action. This motif is first introduced in 1:19, where Memucan suggests that "if it seems good to the king" (אִם־עַל־הַמֶּלֶךְ טוֹב, *ʾim ʿal hammelek ṭôb*) he should decree that Vashti be deposed. In 1:21, it is confirmed that it did, indeed, seem good to him (וַיִּיטַב הַדָּבָר בְּעֵינֵי הַמֶּלֶךְ, *wayyîṭab haddābār bĕʿênê hammelek*). In 2:4, it is suggested that the maiden who "pleases the king" (תִּיטַב בְּעֵינֵי הַמֶּלֶךְ, *tîṭab bĕʿênê hammelek*) be made queen in place of Vashti, and this recommendation received precisely the same reaction as that in 1:21, "The word seemed good in the eyes of the king" (וַיִּיטַב הַדָּבָר בְּעֵינֵי הַמֶּלֶךְ). The phrase "if it seems good to the king" (אִם־עַל־הַמֶּלֶךְ טוֹב) occurs six times in the book (1:19; 3:9; 5:8; 7:3; 8:5; 9:13). This emphasis on the king's "pleasure" certainly reinforces the impression of the Persians as hedonists.

Submission/Assertiveness

The contrast between submissive and assertive behavior is an important motif in the book of Esther.[240] We have already touched on this issue in our consideration of the characters of Vashti and Esther, but the motif goes beyond those characters alone. It is central to the story line and organically linked to the purposes of the book.

Unlike some of the other motifs, submission/assertiveness is not necessarily identified with the use of certain *Leitworten**. Instead, we must infer from the actions of the characters whether they are being submissive or assertive. Typically, submission will involve obedience, but might also include the acknowledgment of another's superior status by symbolic or practical acts. Assertiveness can include disobedience, but here it will also include any actions where someone stands up against power, transcends their "place," or resists oppression.

The submission/assertiveness motif is introduced in the opening episode (chap. 1): Vashti, ordered to come and appear before the king, refuses. Her act of insubordination enrages the king and throws his advisers into turmoil. Memucan warns, "Word of the queen's action will go out to all

239. Only one broad commandment is not issued on the king's authority: in 9:32, the last commandment of the book is issued not by the king, but by Queen Esther (מַאֲמַר אֶסְתֵּר), establishing the perpetual observation of Purim among the Jews. The significance of this fact will be considered in the commentary.

240. Berg, 72, identifies this motif as "obedience/disobedience." The terms used here, while covering mostly the same material, are broader and allow for the inclusion of some episodes that Berg's treatment omits.

the women, and they will despise their husbands" (1:17). Unless the king takes decisive action, insubordination will become rampant. Vashti is to be deposed so that women will pay their husbands proper respect (1:20). Furthermore, the king issues a decree—not merely in the Aramaic of the realm, but in every language of the empire—that all men are to be masters of their own houses (1:22).

This incident might make it appear that the submission of women is a major focus of the book. This impression is reinforced in the introduction of Esther, a woman who appears to be the opposite of Vashti. Unlike the disobedient queen, we are told that Esther always obeyed Mordecai (2:20). Ironically, it is only by becoming assertive that Esther can deliver her people. She must break the law stating that no one is to come into the king's presence unbidden (4:11). This act of assertiveness is an important moment in the development of Esther's character, but it is more than that: as we will see below, it is a turning point in the narrative.

But Esther is not merely about the submission or assertiveness of women. Mordecai's refusal to obey the king's decree and submit to Haman (3:2) sets off the chain of events that occupies the rest of the book. He compounds his insubordination by refusing to listen to the king's servants (3:3–4). Haman then presents the Jews to the king as an insubordinate people "who refuse to obey the king's decrees" (אֶת־דָּתֵי הַמֶּלֶךְ אֵינָם עֹשִׂים, *ʾet dātê hammelek ʾênām ʿōśîm*; 3:8). But when Esther finally presents her petition to the king, she implies that her people are the most submissive: if they had merely been sold as slaves, she would not have protested (וְאִלּוּ לַעֲבָדִים וְלִשְׁפָחוֹת נִמְכַּרְנוּ הֶחֱרַשְׁתִּי, *wĕʾillû laʿăbādîm wĕlišpāḥôt nimkarnû*; 7:4). As the king storms out in anger, it is Haman's turn to be submissive: he must beg Queen Esther for his life (7:7), as she had begged for the life of her people. In a great moment of irony, as Haman falls before the queen in submission, the king interprets his act as one of aggression: "Would he even force the queen while I am in the house?" (7:8). The verb translated "force" here, כָּבַשׁ (*kābaš*), though it may imply "rape," primarily means to make someone subservient or force them into slavery (e.g., 2 Sam 8:11; 2 Chr 2:10; Neh 5:5).

There is yet one more major occurrence of the submission/assertiveness motif. In order to counter Haman's plot, the Jews are given the right to defend themselves against any who attack them (8:11). This fact raises an obvious question: what were the Jews expected to do before? Were they merely to submit to any who sought to kill them? Now, the Jews are explicitly given the right not to be submissive, but to resist. The resolution of the crisis shall be achieved by an act analogous to that performed by Vashti in chapter 1: they will refuse to be victimized by others.

Reversal/Peripety

The final motif we will consider, reversal (or "peripety," as it has come to be known), plays a very important role in the narrative.[241] Several studies of Esther have focused on the role of reversal, and rightly so: since classical times, the significance of this narrative technique has been studied and appreciated.[242] Aristotle believed reversal to be one of the most essential elements of the tragic genre.[243] For Aristotle, it was the change of the fortunes of the hero from good to bad that truly aroused the interest and passions of the audience. We might suppose, then, that the reversal of fortunes from bad to good could be one of the most powerful elements of comic literature. How much better when combined with the reversal of fortunes for the villain! In the book of Esther, reversal makes us smile; it makes us cheer; but it also makes us look for the hand at work behind the scenes.

Most of these reversals center on the character of Haman. These include:

- Haman is exalted above all the courtiers (3:10); Mordecai is later awarded his office (8:2).
- Haman hatches a plot to kill all the Jews; instead, Haman himself is executed.
- The couriers go out swiftly to take word of the king's decree against the Jews (3:15); the couriers go out swiftly to take word of the Jews' reprieve (8:14).
- Haman erects a pike for the hanging of Mordecai (5:14); instead, he is hung on it (7:9–10).
- Haman believes that the king wishes to honor him (6:6–9); instead, he ends up honoring Mordecai (6:11–12).

Other reversals centering instead on Mordecai and the Jews:

- Mordecai tears his garments and dresses in sackcloth and ashes (4:1); Mordecai is dressed in royal robes (8:15).
- The Jews mourn on receiving word of Haman's decree (4:3); the Jews rejoice on receiving word of the new decree (8:17).
- The Jews were to be slaughtered, killed, and destroyed by those who attacked them (3:13); the Jews were given permission to slaughter, kill, and destroy all who attacked them (8:11).

---

241. The term *peripety* derives from the Greek περιπέτεια, literally "fall around." Peripety is used in literature to refer to a sudden and unexpected reversal of the narrative's plot. The use of the term in studies of Esther has been popularized by Fox, *Character and Ideology*, 158, but he cites its use by earlier scholars as well.
242. Some significant treatments include Berg, 103–6; Fox, *Character and Ideology*, 158–63; Craig, 80–119; Bush, 323–26.
243. Aristotle, *Poetics*, esp. chap. 11.

Several scholars have identified reversal not merely as a motif, but a thematic element of Esther. Fox identifies it as "a major theme" of the book,[244] and Goldman writes, "Ironic reversal is a central theme of Esther."[245] While it is certainly a central motif and major rhetorical technique, it does not seem accurate to speak of it as a theme. The reversals, as entertaining and significant as they are, do not actually constitute a principal idea or message that the author wishes to communicate. Rather, it seems more accurate to say that reversal is the major technique used by the author to communicate his primary themes.

Theme

The notion of "theme" is closely related to that of "motif," but it is somewhat more expansive. According to the *The Concise Oxford Dictionary of Literary Terms*, theme is a "salient abstract idea that emerges from a literary work's treatment of its subject-matter; or a topic occurring in a number of literary works."[246] Since we are dealing with a single text, the second half of this definition will not apply. The notion of a salient abstract idea, however, is relevant to our discussion.

Two major themes are readily apparent in the book of Esther. The first theme may be associated with the book's *raison d'être*: the celebration of Purim. It is almost universally agreed that the text as it exists in the MT is designed to encourage the observance of the holiday. It should come as no surprise that Purim is an important thematic element as well. This fact is evidenced primarily by the attention devoted to Purim in the penultimate chapter of the book. Fourteen verses—about a tenth of the text—are devoted to encouraging the celebration. That Purim is prescribed to the audience as a perpetual statute (9:22–23, 26a-32) is also significant. But it is not only in the conclusion of the book that this theme is established; the author introduces this theme at the beginning and reinforces it throughout, by the use of the banquet motif. The transition from Gentile banquets to Jewish banquets foreshadows the transition from danger to triumph in the celebration of Purim.

The other significant theme is connected with the motif of peripety. The reversals of fortune arise because of a "salient idea": the invincibility of the Jews. Reversals are not merely twists of fate or entertaining story lines; they are an outworking of a principle that is twice articulated by characters in the story. In 4:13–14, it is Mordecai who expresses his confidence

244. Fox, *Character and Ideology*, 158.

245. S. Goldman, "Narrative and Ethical Ironies in Esther," *JSOT* 47 (1990): 15–31.

246. Chris Baldick, "Theme," in *The Concise Oxford Dictionary of Literary Terms* (Oxford: Oxford University Press, 1990), 333–34.

in Jewish invulnerability: "Then Mordecai told them to reply to Esther, 'Do not think to yourself that of all the Jews, you alone shall escape in the king's house. Because if you insist on remaining silent at this time, relief and deliverance will arise for the Jews from another place.'" Haman's plot against the Jews is bound to fail in one way or another. In 6:13, Haman's counselors and his wife, Zeresh, state why the plot will fail: "If Mordecai, before whom your downfall has begun, is of the Jewish race, you will not be able to overcome him. For you will surely fall." The threat against the Jews was turned into their victory not merely because it was an entertaining story twist, but because it could not happen any other way.

These two themes are not unrelated to each other. Purim is not just a celebration of a Jewish victory, like the "Nicanor's Day" holiday that it overwhelmed. In a sense, it is a celebration of Jewish invincibility. Through the celebration of Purim, the Jews are reminded that their enemies cannot prevail against them. Esther is remarkably silent on why this is so, but surely the implication is clear. Invisible though He may be, God is with His people.

Structure

The book of Esther is structured around the motif of reversal: the first half introduces and intensifies the danger to the Jews, while the second half chronicles their deliverance and exaltation. The banqueting motif also serves as a structuring element. A key to discerning the structure may be found in the opening and closing scenes. The book begins with the two banquets of King Xerxes; in the final scene, the Jews hold two banquets. These banquets form the bookends for the intrigue that transpires in the narrative. This fact suggests that the book may be arranged symmetrically, with balanced elements strategically positioned throughout the narrative.

A common form that such symmetry takes in biblical narrative (as well as poetry) is the chiasm*. Several scholars have undertaken to identify a chiastic arrangement to the book of Esther, typically basing their efforts on either the recurrent banquet motif or the reversals. Radday, Fox, Berg, and Levenson have all proposed very similar chiastic structures for Esther, though each proposal has some significant differences from the others.[247] The most important difference is that each locates the "turning point" or "hinge" at a different place in the narrative: Radday, at 6:1 ("During that night the king's sleep fled from him"); Fox, at 6:9 ("Thus it shall be done to the man whom the king desires to honor"); Berg, at 4:13–14 ("who knows

---

247. Y. Radday, "Chiasm in Joshua, Judges and Others," *LB* 3 (1973): 613; M. Fox, "The Structure of the Book of Esther," in *Isac Leo Seeligman Volume: Essays on the Bible and the Ancient World*, ed. A. Rofé and Y. Zakovitch III (Jerusalem: Rubenstein, 1983), 291–303; Berg, 103–13; Levenson, 5–12.

whether you have not attained royalty for such a time as this?"); Levenson, the whole sixth chapter.

Each of these studies makes substantial contributions to our understanding of Esther, but we would suggest a somewhat simpler structure, based not so much on motifs as on scenes. The MT version of Esther consists of thirteen scenes, along with an introduction and a conclusion. Their relationship may be illustrated in this manner:

- A) Introduction: The glory of Xerxes (1:1–2)
  - B) The two feasts of the king (1:3–22)
    - C) Esther's triumph over her rivals (2:1–18)
      - D) Mordecai foils the plot against the king (2:19–23)
        - E) Conflict between Haman and Mordecai is initiated (3:1–6)
          - F) Haman appears to request the death of the Jews (3:7–15)
            - G) Mordecai and Esther conspire against the plot (4:1–17)
              - H) Esther appears before the king unbidden (5:1–8)
            - G′) Haman and Zeresh conspire against Mordecai (5:9–14)
          - F′) Haman appears to request the death of Mordecai (6:1–14)
        - E′) Conflict between Haman and Mordecai is concluded (7:1–10)
      - D′) Mordecai foils the plot against the Jews (8:1–17)
    - C′) The Jews triumph over their rivals (9:1–17)
  - B′) The two feasts of the Jews (9:18–32)
- A′) Conclusion: The glory of Xerxes and Mordecai (10:1–3)

In this proposed structure, the "hinge" is identified as the episode where Esther sets in motion her plot to overturn Haman's plot. It is precisely at this point that the Jews' deliverance begins. Here, too, begins the transformation of our main character: Esther first appears here as an assertive character, defying both the king's command and the instructions of her uncle. Perhaps coincidentally, this scene also contains the verse identified by the Masoretes as the central verse of the book (5:7).

In this structure, the motifs of banqueting and reversal play prominent roles. We have already noted that the book begins and ends with two feasts.

In the first half of the narrative, all the feasts are given by Gentiles, and the half ends with the proclamation of a Jewish fast (4:16), the reverse of the feast. In the second half, all the feasts are given by Jews. It begins with Esther inviting Gentiles to a feast and ends with Esther "inviting" the Jews to a feast—the feast of Purim. The proclamation of the feast of Purim reverses the proclamation of the fast found at the end of the first half.

In the parallel episodes, we find numerous verbal similarities, but also ironic reversals:

- The opening (A) and conclusion (A′) both include references to the geographical extent of Xerxes' kingdom. The conclusion reiterates the idea of Xerxes' glory, while ironically referencing the glory of Mordecai as well.
- In scene B, we have the description of Xerxes' two feasts; B′ concerns the two feasts of the Jews. Both scenes share several incidental vocabulary items (e.g., *days*, *provinces*, *writing*) and both conclude with a decree being sent throughout the entire Persian Empire: the first, a declaration of the uppity queen's demotion designed to make men rulers in their houses; the other, a declaration by the queen commanding the Jews to celebrate their deliverance.
- In scene C, a young Jewish woman surpasses all her rivals to become a ruler (וַיַּמְלִיכֶהָ, *wayyamlîkehā*; 2:17) over the empire. The king's own officer aids her in her task (2:9, 15). In C′, the Jews achieve dominion (יִשְׁלְטוּ, *yišlĕṭû*; 9:1) over all their enemies, with the aid of the king's officers (9:3). Both triumphs result in feasting (2:18; 9:17). There is also a somewhat ironic parallelism between the figures of Esther and Mordecai: in C, Esther receives the grace and favor from all who see her (2:9, 15), while in C′, Mordecai inspires fear in all who hear of him (9:3–4).
- In scene D, Mordecai foils a plot against the king, through the mediation of Queen Esther. In D′, Mordecai foils the plot against the Jews, again through Esther's intervention with the king. Additionally, scene D begins with the note that Esther had not revealed her kinship with Mordecai to the king (2:20); but at the beginning of D′, their relationship is revealed (8:1). Also, in both scenes, the villains are impaled (2:23; 8:7).
- In scene E, the story line of the conflict between Haman and Mordecai is introduced with Mordecai's refusal to bow to Haman. In E′, that storyline is brought to an end with the death of Haman. Both scenes culminate in someone being sentenced to death: the Jews in E, and Haman in E′. There are reversals, as well: in E, Haman becomes furious with Mordecai (3:5); in E′, it is the king who is furious with Haman (7:7, 10). In E, Haman has been "raised

up" by the king (3:1); in E′, he has "fallen down" before the queen (7:8). In E, it was Mordecai's refusal to bow down to Haman that brought about Haman's plot to kill the Jews; in E′, it is when Haman falls down before Esther that he seals his own fate (3:8).

- In scene F, Haman comes to King Xerxes to request that the Jews be destroyed. In F′, Haman has once again come to the king, this time to request the death of a specific Jew—Mordecai. In an ironic reversal, Haman is never allowed to present his request, being ordered instead to honor Mordecai. A further irony is found in comparing the latter portions of the two scenes: in 3:13, the order is issued to utterly destroy the Jews, while in 6:13, Haman is told that he will not be able to prevail over a Jew. Finally, both scenes end with a reference to feasting (3:15; 6:14).
- Scenes G and G′ both begin with Mordecai at the king's gate (4:2; 5:9). They focus on the interchange between a male and female character. In both cases, the male presents his complaint: Mordecai, about Haman's decree to kill the Jews; Haman, about Mordecai's continued existence. In each case, the woman appears to present a solution to the problem. But there are several striking contrasts between them, as well. Scene G opens with Mordecai in mourning (4:1); G′ begins with Haman rejoicing (5:9). As we continue through scene G, the narrator describes the grief and humiliation of the Jews (4:3); in G′, we read of the pride and exaltation of Haman (5:11–12). In scene G, there are two references to the Jews fasting: the fast that preceded the dialogue between Esther and Mordecai (4:3), and that which Esther anticipates for the days to come (4:11). In G′, two banquets figure prominently: the banquet that preceded Haman's meeting with his wife and friends (5:12a), and the banquet he anticipates enjoying the next day (5:12b, 14).
- Finally, we come to the "hinge." It appears that this scene marks the true crisis of the story. Esther is about to appear before the king without an invitation. If he decides to kill her, the story is finished. If he allows her to live, there is hope for the Jews. It is here that the reversal will truly begin: Haman will no longer be the hunter, but the hunted. As in the best chiasms, this hinge has connections both to the material that precedes and that which follows. Scene H harks back in something of a parody to the beginning of the book (scene B), where Queen Vashti refused to come when bidden to the king's banquet; here, Queen Esther comes unbidden to invite the king to her own banquet. It also foreshadows the ending of the book (scene B′), where Queen Esther will establish Purim as

a perpetual Jewish feast (9:11), essentially inviting all the Jews to a banquet celebrating Haman's defeat.

There are numerous other connections, reversals, and parallels between characters and scenes in this narrative. They are certainly not confined to the scenes as they have been laid out in this suggested structure. Nonetheless, this proposal seems to account better than others for all the units of the text and their principal ideas, as well as some verbal and symbolic repetitions.

Theology of Esther

We can now return at last to the question with which we opened this introduction: Where is God in the book of Esther? What can we know about Yahweh and His relationship with humanity through this ostensibly nonreligious book? Scholars have puzzled over this question for decades. Howard seems to speak for many when he writes, "In a strict sense, there is no 'theology' (i.e., 'study of God') in Esther, since God is not mentioned in the book. In addition, there is no reference to religious institutions or practices (except fasting), making the task of adducing a 'theology' of the book doubly difficult."[248] Some scholars are even more negative in their assessments. Browne writes, "If the book fills any useful place in the Bible, it is as a picture of unredeemed humanity."[249] According to Anderson, "If a Christian minister is faithful to the context, he will not take his text from Esther; and, if the leader of a church-school class shows any Christian discernment, he will not waste time trying to show that the heroes of the book are models of character, integrity, and piety."[250] If the best we can hope for from this book is a depiction of people behaving badly, it indeed has little to offer to the devotional reader.

That point of view, however, cannot account for the lasting appeal of this book through the ages. While it has always had its detractors, it has also found a place in the hearts of many believers. Among some of the rabbis, Esther was second only to the Torah in its appeal. In Jewish tradition, it is a book about a "miracle" (נֵס, *nēs*), not about coincidences or moral failings.[251] According to *b. Yoma* 29a, the story of Esther is the "end of all miracles, as dawn is the end of the night." Somehow, people through the

248. D. Howard, "Esther, Theology of," *NIDOTTE* 4:582.

249. L. Browne, "Esther," in *Peake's Commentary on the Bible,* ed. M. Black and H. H. Rowley (New York: Thomas Nelson and Sons, 1962), 381.

250. B. Anderson, "The Place of the Book of Esther in the Christian Bible," *JR* 30 (1950): 140.

251. In postbiblical Hebew and Aramaic, the word *nēs* commonly means a miraculous sign, rather than merely a flag or standard.

ages have drawn inspiration and insight from this book, even without it ever mentioning the name of God.

Pre-Critical Interpretations

Many efforts to read Esther theologically have employed some methods that most modern interpreters would find questionable. In rabbinic Jewish exegesis, the theological messages of Esther were not so much derived from the text as interpolated into it through the insertion of sometimes-lengthy "glosses." The earliest such glosses appear in the LXX and are then reproduced in the AT. Three of the additions are explicitly religious in character, providing pious relief to the otherwise nonspiritual narrative. These additions, however, cannot be said to be consonant with the apparent worldview of the original story, or of the Judaism it seems to espouse. Indeed, they seem to try to correct the original narrative. The first and last additions—the prophetic vision of Mordecai and its interpretation in light of the events that transpired—are designed to tell the reader that the events of Esther have been divinely orchestrated and did not take place by chance. There are also explicit statements that there is no other God but the Lord, and that none can oppose His will (C 2–4, 22). The Jews are God's chosen people, and their exile is a result of their idolatry (C 16–18). Their deliverance can come only from His divine intervention (C 25).[252] We also find efforts in these glosses to reform the behavior of the protagonists: in the MT, there is no indication that Esther did not assimilate entirely into Persian court life. Indeed, it would have been difficult for her to hide her ethnicity if she did not compromise her observance of at least the traditional Jewish dietary laws, as well as observance of the Sabbath. Also, Esther's marriage to a Gentile would surely have been offensive to a large segment of Second-Temple-era Judaism. But in the additions, these infelicities, too, are addressed: Esther claims that she has not partaken in any of the king's banquets, hates the crown she wears, and abhors the bed of the uncircumcised (C 26–29). The interpolators seemed to have been stuck with a text that offended some of their beliefs about proper Jewish conduct and sought not so much to interpret the narrative as to improve it.

The "exegesis" of the Mishnah, Talmud, and the two targums of Esther may be divided into two classes. The first is the *halakhot* (sg. *halakhah*), the practical instructions regarding the reading of the Megillah and the celebration of Purim. Such comments predominate in the Mishnah, and frequently appear in the Talmud as well. The other class is the *midrashim* (sg. *midrash*). These commentaries consist of expansions and glosses on the text for the purposes of theological enlightenment, moral instruction, and,

252. On the depiction of God in the additions, see Moore 1977, 205, 213.

perhaps, entertainment. Seldom do the commentaries consist of explanations or clarifications of Esther's theology; rather, they will often read the theology of the Talmudic rabbis back on to the text of Esther. While they are interesting, sometimes insightful, and often enjoyable, their primary interest for scholars is in what they tell us about the Judaism of the early rabbinic era, rather than the theology of Esther's author. Their emphases are frequently similar to those of the LXX: the unique sovereignty of God; the dependence on Him for deliverance; the importance of observing Jewish purity and Sabbath regulations (see the Targums on Esth 2:20). There is also an emphasis on a theme that is suggested by the book of Esther itself: just retribution. According to rabbinic traditions, Vashti lost her throne (and, they contend, her life) because of sins she had committed against the Jews. She had forced Jewish girls to work in the nude on the Sabbath day, and so she was punished by being summoned to appear in the nude before King Xerxes (see *b. Meg.* 12b; *Tg. Esth I* 1:11).

By the Middle Ages, Jewish approaches to Esther had changed considerably. It remained a popular book, both because of its association with the festival of Purim and because of its unpopularity with Christians.[253] The great medieval rabbis, including Saadia Gaon (882[?]–942), Rashi (1040–1105), Rashbam (1085–1158), and Ibn Ezra (1089–1164) wrote commentaries on the book. In these scholars, there began a shift away from the midrashic commentaries of the Amoraic rabbis (rabbis of the Talmudic era, ca. AD 200–500) toward a form of exegesis based on the "plain meaning" of the text, its so-called *peshat*. According to Walfish, "Peshat exegesis first developed in Spain and North Africa in conjunction with the study of Heb. grammar which reached an advanced level in these communities."[254] Frequently, this approach was concerned with determining the meanings of obscure words.[255] Nonetheless, there was much interest in the theological meaning of the text as well. Many of these exegetes wrestled with the very questions that concern modern interpreters of the book: the absence of the divine name, the role of providence, and the ethics of the Jewish characters in the book. Some of their ideas (e.g., that the coincidences of Esther are truly works of the hidden God) are still widely held today.

In the thirteenth century, there was something of a reversion of Jewish exegesis back toward *midrash*. The influence of the earlier exegetes, however,

253. See B. Walfish, *Esther in Medieval Garb: Jewish Interpretation of the Book of Esther in the Middle Ages* (New York: SUNY Press, 1993), 75.

254. Ibid., 14. See also D. Halivni, *Peshat & Derash: Plain and Applied Meaning in Rabbinic Exegesis* (Oxford: Oxford University Press, 1998), 79–88. Halivni likewise attributes the growth in *peshat* to Arab influence.

255. Walfish, *Esther*, 13–15.

especially Ibn Ezra, continued to shape the interpretive traditions that followed. In the fifteenth and sixteenth centuries, Jewish interest in the book of Esther blossomed with the rise of preaching in the synagogues. More Jewish commentaries were produced on Esther in the sixteenth century than in all the preceding centuries combined.[256] Walfish identifies some theological themes that especially interested the rabbis of the medieval period:[257]

- The absence of the name of God. This difficulty was often explained as an effort to protect the Name from profanation by Gentiles reading the book.
- The role of divine providence. According to the medieval rabbis, the attempted extermination of the Jews was just as much a matter of providence as was their deliverance: God was punishing the Jews for worshiping Nebuchadnezzar's idol. Nonetheless, God had providentially taken action to assure the survival of His people by positioning Esther and Mordecai where they could intervene on the Jews' behalf. Furthermore, the coincidences of Esther are interpreted as miraculous interventions.
- Redemption. The defeat of the Amalekite Haman, prototype of all enemies of the Jews, was often interpreted as a type of the eschatological triumph of the Jews over all their oppressors.

Christian exegetes took a different approach to the interpretation of the book. As noted earlier, the church fathers demonstrated relatively little interest in Esther. When it was cited, it was typically used as a source for historical background information or examples of courage, not theology. There are, however, exceptions: Clement of Rome attributed the Jews' deliverance to Esther's great faith and virtue (*1 Clem.* 55:6). Origen seems especially fond of the prayers of Mordecai and Esther (from the LXX) and found in them and other passages from Esther insights regarding the nature of evil and the purpose of prayer. In his estimation, the plot against the Jews was not a political or personal vendetta, but a spiritual battle that could be won only by prayer and fasting.[258] In a somewhat different vein, Jerome anticipates later exegetes in interpreting Esther typologically: "Esther, a type of the church, frees her people from danger and, after having slain Haman

256. Ibid., 237n14.

257. Ibid., 77–94.

258. See M. Kuyama, "Origen and Esther—A Reflection on the 'Anti-Jewish' Argument in Early Christian Literature," in *Studia Patristica vol 34: Papers Presented at the Thirteenth International Conference on Patristic Studies at Oxford in 1999*, ed. M. Wiles, E. Yarnold, and P. Parvis (Leuven: Peeters, 2001), 424–35.

whose name means iniquity, hands down to posterity a memorable day and a great feast."[259]

But Jerome's typological understanding of the book soon gave way to the even more suspect technique of allegorical interpretation. More often than not, this method, like *midrash*, read a meaning into the text that was never intended by its author. Nonetheless, it did provide a way of redeeming the book from the obscurity to which it had been consigned by the early church fathers. The earliest full Christian commentary on Esther, that of Rhabanus Maurus, employed this method extensively: the virgins gathered to the palace represent the nations gathered together under the gospel; the banquet prepared for Esther represents the eucharistic banquet; Haman's plot to destroy the Jews represents the plot against Christ.[260] Rhabanus followed the reading of Jerome in seeing Esther herself as representing the church. King Xerxes, then, had to represent none other than Christ himself.

Later in the Middle Ages, however, the identification of Esther with the church was displaced by one that would become even more popular: she represented none other than the Virgin Mary. One of the earliest proponents of this identification was Anthony of Padua (AD 1196–1231). According to Jeffrey, Anthony had built on the story of Esther and Assuere a complex of prefiguration for the relationship between Christ and Mary (and between Christ and the Church) in which Esther's finding favor with Assuere (Esth 5:2) foreshadows the way in which God shows favor to Mary. Christ is the Assuere who crowns Esther in Esth 2:15–17, the Blessed Virgin.[261]

This line of interpretation became the standard Catholic teaching and continued to develop: "In the later Middle Ages, Esther's destruction of Aman became a type of the Virgin's triumph over the Devil in her Immaculate Conception, and her pleading for the Jews before Assuerus became a type of the Virgin's intercession for mankind at the Last Judgment."[262]

In the publication of the Douay version of the Bible in 1609, this understanding was incorporated into the annotations of Esth 9. Indeed, the identification of Esther with the Virgin Mary remains common among Catholics into modern times.[263]

---

259. Letter 53.8, "St. Jerome: Letters and Selected Works," in *A Select Library of Nicene and Post-Nicene Fathers of the Christian Church*, 2nd series, vol. 6, trans. P. Schaff and H. Wace (New York: Christian Literature, 1893), 110.

260. This commentary is available in English translation in Conti and Pilara, 374–99.

261. D. Jeffrey, *A Dictionary of Biblical Tradition in English Literature* (Grand Rapids: Eerdmans, 1992), 237.

262. K. Harty, "The Reputation of Queen Esther in the Middle Ages: The Merchant's Tale, IV (E). 1742–45," *Ball State University Forum* 19, no. 3 (1978): 67.

263. See Paton, 56. More recently, see J. Ratzinger, *Daughter Zion: Meditations on the Church's Marian Belief* (San Francisco: Ignatius Press, 1983), 20.

Among Protestants, the book of Esther had a somewhat chillier reception, due no doubt in part to the Protestant adoption of the overtly secular Heb. text. As mentioned above, Martin Luther famously remarked that he was so hostile to the book that he wished it had never been included in the Bible,[264] so we should not be surprised to learn that he never undertook to write a commentary on the text. There were, however, a number of Protestant commentaries written in this era, including important works by Münster (1546), Drusius (1586), and Grotius (1644; Paton, 108). These works were mostly practical or homiletic in nature. Since their authors assumed the historical nature of the text, they often addressed issues that seemed to involve contradictions or historical difficulties, such as whether Esther was justified in marrying a pagan or whether she would have indulged in the king's food. Typology, however, remained an important approach. Rhabanus' interpretation of Xerxes, Mordecai, Esther, and Haman was cited with approval by John Mayer in his "Many Commentaries in One" of 1647.[265] Jonathan Edwards, writing in the early eighteenth century, interpreted the book as a thoroughgoing typology:

> It appears to me very probable, that this book of Esther is a history that is a shadow of gospel things and times, by the agreement of it with events, and the agreeableness to the names of other typical histories of the Old Testament. The great feast that Ahasuerus made, is the gospel feast. ... Vashti, the queen, is the church, or God's people, who is called the queen in gold of Ophir. ... Ahasuerus repudiates Vashti, and gives the royal estate to another. So we find the rejection of the Jews and calling of the Gentiles compared to God's repudiating his ancient church, and taking another better than she. Esther was exceedingly fair and beautiful, and the king delighted in her. So Christ's heart is ravished with the beauty of the church. Mordecai is the gospel ministry; he nourished and brought up Esther, and was as a father to her.[266]

In this manner Edwards drew meaning from the various elements of the Esther story and made it relevant to the Christians of his day.

---

264. *Table Talk*, xxiv, Weimar Ausgabe 22, 2080.

265. J. Caruthers, *Esther through the Centuries* (Malden, MA: Blackwell, 2008), 28–29.

266. J. Edwards, *The Works of Jonathan Edwards. Volume 15: Notes on the Scripture* (New Haven, CT: Yale University Press, 1998), 60–61.

Contemporary Approaches

The typological approach to Esther continues to appear occasionally in modern studies, primarily in popular treatments.[267] There are several reasons for a lack of enthusiasm for typology among scholars. First, the method may involve a confusion of genre categories: it interprets texts that were designed to be read as one type of literature as another. There is also a general suspicion of methods that attribute to the text insights that the original authors could not have possessed. Among liberal scholars, there is a reluctance to accept the idea of a supernatural inspiration behind the text. But even among evangelicals, the typological method is often considered illegitimate. Since many evangelicals would agree that the meaning of the text is "the principle that an author consciously willed to convey by the words (shared symbols) used," typology would seem to be excluded.[268] An author of biblical narrative could not have consciously intended to insert references to Christ into his story several hundred years before Jesus' birth. Evangelicals are hardly persuaded by this method having been embraced by the church since the first century, since they tend to put little stock in the authority of tradition. But while Protestant evangelicals' rejection of church tradition may be defensible, it is difficult to ignore that typology is employed in the NT as well, being found in the teachings of Jesus (e.g., John 3:14–15) and other NT writers (e.g., Heb 9).

Perhaps the main reason why the typological approach wins few adherents today is that it tends to be a selective undertaking. Wechsler, for example, catalogues several similarities between the work of Esther and the passion of Jesus: the Jews' three days of fasting (which begins on the day the Jews would have been celebrating Passover) foreshadows the three days of Jesus' affliction; Esther putting on royal garments at the end of the fast

267. Some modern typological studies include T. Thornton, "The Crucifixion of Haman and the Shadow of the Cross," *JTS* 37 (1986): 419–26; W. McClure, *The Book of Esther: Prophetic Foreshadowings from the Book with No Divine Name in It* (Kilmarnock, UK: John Ritchie, 1990); M. Wechsler, "Shadow and Fulfillment in the Book of Esther," *BSac* 154 (1997): 275–84.

268. R. Stein, *A Basic Guide to Interpreting the Bible: Playing by the Rules*, 2nd ed. (Grand Rapids: Baker, 2011), 31. This sentiment is embraced by most evangelicals. See, e.g., W. Kaiser, "The Single Intent of Scripture," in *Evangelical Roots*, ed. K. Kantzer (Nashville: Nelson, 1978), 123–41; G. Fee and D. Stuart, *How to Read the Bible for All Its Worth*, 3rd ed. (Grand Rapids: Zondervan, 2003), 23: The purpose of exegesis is "to find out what was *the original intent of the words of the Bible*" (italics original); G. Osborne, *The Hermeneutical Spiral: A Comprehensive Introduction to Biblical Interpretation* (Downers Grove, IL: InterVarsity, 1991), 8: "the very process of interpretation builds a base for discovering the original intended meaning of the biblical text."

and appearing before the king foreshadows Jesus' ascent into Heaven; the approval of Esther that results in the salvation of her people foreshadows the salvific work of Christ.[269] He does not, however, account for the substantial differences: Esther fasts with her people and her handmaids, while Jesus suffers His passion alone; Esther's royal garments are obviously intended to catch the king's eye (and perhaps incite his desire), whereas Jesus is accepted by God because of His obedience; when Esther appears before the king, she is only beginning the task of securing the deliverance of her people, whereas Jesus appears before the Father when the work of salvation was completed. Whatever significance the superficial similarities may have, they are undercut by very significant differences that are incompatible with the Gospel story.

Instead of seeking a "coded" meaning in the text of Esther, most contemporary approaches have concentrated on what the author(s) may have actually intended to say by their words and silences. There are basically two positions that have been taken: that the book of Esther is a secular composition with no theological content, or that the book has a theological message that has been deliberately hidden by its author. Some statements on the secularity of the book were noted above. We could multiply such comments, especially from late nineteenth- and early twentieth-century commentaries, where opposition to Esther seems to have been extensive.[270] In recent decades, however, there are fewer proponents of this view. Talmon is an exception: he sees Esther as a "wisdom tale" and thus sharing the somewhat secular nature of wisdom.[271] Talmon, however, seems to blur the line between the categories of "universalistic," meaning "non-sectarian," which may well be a fair characterization of much Wisdom literature, and "secular," which certainly does *not* categorize ancient Wisdom literature. Indeed, much Wisdom literature is obsessed with the concept of God and His ways, as the book of Job and even the eminently practical book of Proverbs demonstrate (see, e.g., Prov 1:7, which proclaims "fear of Yahweh" to be the foundational principle of wisdom).

A major difficulty with the idea that Esther is a secular composition is that there was virtually no such thing as secularism in the time when Esther was created. The vast majority of the literature that has come down to us from antiquity centers on religious themes. We have a great quantity of mythic, epic, and ritual material demonstrating the pervasive piety of ancient peoples. The law codes, covenants, and marriage contracts invoke the

269. Wechsler, "Shadow and Fulfillment," 281–84.

270. For a somewhat depressing compendium of such opinions, see F. Bush, "The Book of Esther: Opus non gratum in the Christian Canon," *BBR* 8 (1998): 39–41.

271. Talmon, "Wisdom," 430.

gods as witnesses and enforcers. Royal chronicles make frequent reference to divine assistance and intervention. Even graffiti often invoked the names of gods. As Sanders observes, "Loyalty to the community was inseparable from loyalty to the deity who called it into being; group identity and devotion to God went together."[272] With such religious saturation, the notion that the book of Esther is merely a reflection of the secularism of its society is unlikely.

The far more widely accepted notion is that the book of Esther is, indeed, a religious work, and that its apparent secularism is a deliberate device of the author. God is indeed present in Esther, but He is "hidden." This venerable understanding of the book can be found already in the Talmud. In *b. Ḥul.* 139a the question is posed, "Where is Esther (אסתר) indicated in the Torah?" (because it was essential that a feast such as Purim have its justification the Law of Moses). The answer was given, "'And I will surely hide (אסתיר) my face'" (Deut 31:18). The wordplay was typical of rabbinic exegesis, but the statement is revealing: the sages recognized that God was not absent in Esther, but merely concealed. This idea has now been adopted by the majority of scholars, and it has been competently argued in many studies.

There are two principal lines of evidence for God's presence in Esther. The first is that there are subtle references to God in the text that a discerning reader would recognize. One common idea is that the name of God, YHWH, is hidden in acrostic form four different times in the text:

- At 1:20, in reverse, in the first letters of the words of the phrase הִיא וְכָל הַנָּשִׁים יִתְּנוּ (***h****î*ʾ ***w****ĕkol* ***h****annāšîm* ***y****ittĕnû*, "it, and all the women will give");
- At 5:4, in proper order, in the phrase יָבוֹא הַמֶּלֶךְ וְהָמָן הַיּוֹם (***y****ābô*ʾ ***h****ammelek* ***w****ĕhāmān* ***h****ayyôm*, "Let the king come, and Haman come today");
- At 5:13, the final letters of the words, in reverse, in the phrase זֶה אֵינֶנּוּ שֹׁוֶה לִי (*ze****h*** ʾ*ênennû(****w****)*[273] *šōwâ(****h****) lî(****y****)*, "This is not sufficient for me");
- And finally in 7:7, in the final letters of the words of the phrase כִּי־כָלְתָה אֵלָיו הָרָעָה (*kî(****y****) koltâ(****h****)* ʾ*ēlāy****w*** *hārāʿâ(****h****)*, "That evil was determined against him")

272. E. P. Sanders, *Judaism: Practice and Belief, 63 BCE–66 CE* (London: SCM Press, 1992), 144. See also Fox, *Character and Ideology*, 136.

273. Letters in parentheses represent silent Heb. consonants internal to full-letter vowels.

Walfish observes that this idea already appears in the commentary of fifteenth-century Spanish Jew Zechariah ben Saruq and theorizes that it originated among the Spanish mystics.[274] It has since spread widely: some Esther scrolls dating to the nineteenth century incorporate it by highlighting the letters believed to reveal the name, and a number of Christian writers have advocated the notion as well.[275]

But there are several difficulties with these proposed acrostics. First is the fact that only two of these occurrences are even spelled correctly, since the others depend on reading in reverse. Furthermore, the phrases in which the name supposedly appears are not in any way significant, and in fact do not even form complete thoughts. Indeed, they even break up grammatical units. Also, the sequence of the letters Y-H-W-H at the beginning of words is not at all surprising, since these letters are the most common in the Heb. Bible: *yodh*, as the prefix for the 3 m. sg. and 3 m. pl. impf. forms of the verb, and the first letter of many proper names; *he*, as the definite article; and *waw*, as the conj. "and." Quickly scanning the historical books of the OT reveals the Y-H-W-H "acrostic" also occurs in 1 Chr 5:12 and 1 Kgs 10:17–18, apparently by accident.

Other proposed hints at religious content are more convincing. The reference to the Jews' fasting (4:3, 16) implies an effort to move God to act on their behalf.[276] Indeed, what would be the point of fasting, if not to demonstrate sincerity before God? In the biblical canon, fasting is almost always accompanied by prayer (e.g., 2 Sam 12:16; 2 Chr 20:3; Ezra 8:21; Neh 9:1–3; Luke 2:37; 5:33; Acts 14:23); in this context, the absence of prayer cannot help but catch the reader's attention. Also, Mordecai's musing that "Who knows if you have come to queenship for such a time as this?" (4:14, see commentary) suggests that events have been orchestrated in such a way as to place Esther on the throne in just that moment—implying, of course, that "Someone" had done the orchestrating. Furthermore, his statement that help would come to the Jews from "another place" if Esther did not provide assistance (4:13–14) might well imply an expectation of divine assistance.[277] Several scholars have suggested that the Heb. word for "place"

---

274. Walfish, *Esther in Medieval Garb*, 68.

275. On Jewish tradition regarding the hidden Tetragrammaton, see R. Sabua, "The Hidden Hand of God," *BR* 8 (1992): 31–33. For Christian interpretations, see E. Bullinger, *The Companion Bible* (repr., Grand Rapids: Kregel, 1999), appendix 6, 85–86; J. Baxter, *Explore the Book: A Survey and Study of Each Book from Genesis through Revelation* (Grand Rapids: Zondervan, 1966), 261.

276. As noted by Loader, 418.

277. J. Wiebe, "Esther 4:14: 'Will relief and deliverance arise for the Jews from another place'?" *CBQ* 53 (1991): 409–15, suggests that this statement should be read instead as a rhetorical question. We will address this suggestion in the commentary.

(מָקוֹם, *māqôm*) in this verse has the same meaning that it sometimes has in later Heb., serving as a circumlocution for the name of God.[278] This interpretation, however, seems unlikely, since the phrase "another place" would then literally mean "a different God"! But on the other hand, the fatalistic statement of Haman's wife and friends that Haman cannot conquer Mordecai if he is a Jew (6:13) implies that there is some fate—or, better yet, a providence—that protects the Jews against their enemies.

Perhaps an even greater indication of the role of providence in Esther is the remarkable number of improbable coincidences that occur. The selection of a Jewish orphan as queen just in time for her to thwart the plan of Haman; the promotion of Mordecai the Jew and Haman the Agagite within the court of Xerxes; that Haman should be waiting outside the door to request the death of Mordecai at the moment when the king was contemplating how to show Mordecai honor. For a people who did not believe in an apathetic fate, such coincidences as these seem to demand the orchestration of a beneficent providence. This concept, as recognized by the ancient Jewish commentators, would seem to be the principal theological theme of the book of Esther: it is a book about the providence of God, even when God does not seem present.[279] Clines (154) would take this idea yet a step further, arguing that the theology of Esther involves the complementary nature of "divine action and human initiative." Clines is certainly correct: it is Esther's willingness to risk her life by coming before the king that makes the salvation of the Jews possible. But certainly, divine providence is primary, since it is providence that creates the situation where human action can make a difference.

The Absence of God

If the book of Esther truly is primarily about divine providence, then why is God never mentioned? As noted above, this question has engaged commentators from earliest times. Among those who hold that the book is religious, the question is most significant. Is this absence accidental, or deliberate? Was there a practical consideration that drove the censorship, or was it a theological statement in its own right?

---

278. So P. R. Ackroyd, "Two Hebrew Notes," *ASTI* 5 (1967): 82–86; Talmon, "Wisdom," 429n1.

279. Fox, *Character and Ideology*, 240–44, summarizes several suggestions for clues to God's presence in Esther: coincidences, especially involving the motif of anger; the casting of the *pur*; reversals; religious themes. As he notes, none of these evidences are particularly conclusive in themselves. Taken together, however, they do suggest the presence of a hidden orchestrator behind the action.

There is general agreement that the book of Esther did not begin its life as a "secular" composition, since there was essentially no such thing as an "accidentally secular" story in the ancient world. God was deliberately banished from the story at some point in its history. Unfortunately, the religious version of Esther has been lost to us. The text that underlies the MT and the separate text or texts that underlies two Greek versions shared an absence of God. The rabbinic argument that the name of God was removed to prevent the Gentiles from profaning it has no advocates today. There have been, however, alternative versions of the theory proposed by contemporary scholars. One perennially revived notion is that the feast of Purim, associated as it was with drunkenness, could become a venue for inappropriate behavior or indiscretions. The name of God was removed from the book of Esther, therefore, to protect its sanctity from accidental profanation.[280] But while this explanation could account for the lack of God's name, it does not explain the elision of the other references to religious observance or practice. Surely, there would be no dangers of blasphemy by simply mentioning prayer along with fasting.

Meinhold and Berg both make similar arguments that God is kept at the edges of the story in order to emphasize human action.[281] By making God's actions hidden, the story makes human responsibility more significant. But is the diminishing of the one really necessary for the emphasis of the other? The book of Deuteronomy, for example, puts great emphasis on human responsibility and making correct choices, and yet God holds a central, explicit place in the book. Furthermore, the message that we should put confidence in human initiative seems contrary to the spirit of the Scripture as a whole and glaringly at odds with the messages of the Joseph and exodus narratives that seem to have exerted a formative influence on the book of Esther.

A common explanation is that the absence of God in Esther is designed to draw attention to the work of God behind the scenes. According to Fox, "When we scrutinize the text of Esther for traces of God's activity, we are doing what the author made us do."[282] It is the literary equivalent of being told, "Do not think about elephants"—the result being, of course, that elephants are precisely what you contemplate. For Fox, the purpose of this reticence is not to deceive the readers, but to comfort them in their own times of questioning: "The story's indeterminacy conveys the message that

280. Paton, 95; E. Greenstein, "A Jewish Reading of Esther," in *Judaic Perspectives on Ancient Israel*, ed. J. Neusner, B. Levine, and E. Frerichs (Philadelphia: Fortress, 1987), 233.

281. A. Meinhold, "Gattung," 1:306–24; and "Gattung," 2:72–93; Berg, 178–79.

282. Fox, "Religion," 147.

the Jews should not lose faith if they, too, are uncertain about where God is in a crisis."[283] This is also Howard's conclusion, who writes:

> The best solution would seem to be that the author is intentionally vague about God's presence in events, affirming on the one hand that God indeed is involved with his people and on the other that perceiving this involvement is sometimes difficult. While the author and his readers know (rationally) that God is always present and in control, the experience of life is that the specific manifestations of his presence are not always so clear.[284]

This interpretation is appealing for its practicality and the succor it offers, but there is much in the book for which it does not account. First, the characters in Esther do not seem uncertain about where God is—indeed, they do not seem to be looking for God at all! These are not good, pious people who cry out to God but feel they are being ignored, like the long-suffering Job. Mordecai and Esther are flawed Jews who deliver themselves and their people not by cleverness or piety, but by taking advantage of the opportunities presented to them.

Beal addresses the problem in a different way.[285] In the light of the experience of exile, the Jewish people have been "ungrounded," cut free from religious and geographical moorings. In that situation, Beal seems to say that the book of Esther depicts God as distant and unavailable. In his opinion, the book represents "a fissure in the divinely ordained order established elsewhere" and "an interrogation of biblical authority from within."[286] Beal is not clear about what is going on in Esther, but he seems to have a more negative assessment of God's absence than does Fox. He seems to see God's disappearance from this narrative as an accusation against God, rather than a clever misdirection by the author.

A less-noted, but perhaps ultimately more accurate, explanation for God's absence in Esther has been proposed by Huey.[287] Huey notes that the behavior of Esther and Mordecai leaves much to be desired: Esther marries a pagan; Mordecai refuses to bow to his superior; Mordecai is willing to endanger his cousin; Esther is reluctant to save her people; Esther takes delight in vengeance. Huey asks, "If the purpose of the book is to show God's providential care for his people, as many commentaries say, could he have saved them without manipulating Mordecai and Esther to break

283. Ibid., 146.

284. D. Howard, "Esther, Theology of," *NIDOTTE*, 4:583.

285. Beal, *Book of Hiding*.

286. Ibid., 118–19.

287. F. Huey, "Irony as the Key to Understanding the Book of Esther," *SwJT* 32 (1990): 36–39.

both ceremonial and moral laws?" (37) Huey argues that the book of Esther shows that after the exile, the people of Israel have not changed, but continue to act in sinful ways. Huey argues that as a result of this sin, God has hidden Himself from His people, as He does elsewhere when Israel sins (citing Job 13:24; Psa 44:24; Isa 1:15, 45:15; 59:2; 64:7; Mic 3:4 as examples). He concludes that the book is not about God's providence, but Israel's sinfulness.

The strength of Huey's analysis is that it takes the moral flaws of Mordecai and Esther far more seriously than most other commentators have. His argument can indeed be taken even further. As noted above, the Talmud links the book of Esther to Deut 31:18, "I will surely hide my face." The connection is based primarily on the similarity of sound between the name "Esther" and the Heb. word "I will hide (אסתיר)," but there are other substantial links between the passages as well. The passage (Deut 31:16–18) reads:

> And Yahweh said to Moses, "Look, you are about to lie down with your ancestors, and this people will arise and they will play the prostitute after the foreign gods of the land to which they are going. And my anger shall flare up against them on that day, and I will forsake them, and I will hide my face from them, and they shall become as prey, and disasters and troubles shall find them, and they shall say on that day, 'Is it not because our God is not in our midst that these disasters have found us?' But I will certainly hide my face on that day, because of all of the evil that they did because they turned to other gods."

We should note first the similarity of the circumstances envisioned in this section of Deuteronomy and those of Esther. In Deut 31–32, God speaks to Moses of what will transpire after Moses has died. When the Israelites settle in among pagans, they will adopt their gods, thus breaking the exclusive covenant between God and Israel. God will be forced to hide His face from them (31:16–18). God gives Moses a song to teach to the Israelites in order to warn them of their coming judgment because of the mischief they will indulge in "in the future days" (בְּאַחֲרִית הַיָּמִים, *bĕʾaḥărît hayyāmîm*; Deut 31:29). In the book of Esther, we also see the Jews living among foreigners. Have they adopted the pagan gods? Though the story never explicitly states it, that both Mordecai and Esther bear the names of Babylonian deities is suggestive of syncretism, surely enough to have earned the ire of one of the book's redactors. Also, Esther's concealment of her Jewish identity in the harem of King Xerxes implies some compromise on her part. Might the author of proto-Esther (the version from which all our existing texts derive) have been subtly condemning the Diaspora community for apostasy similar to that which Deuteronomy envisioned?

There are several clues that the redactor might have had the greater context of Deut 31–32 in mind, perhaps incorporating some allusions to these chapters into the book of Esther. In Deut 31:17, where God first declares that He will "hide his face" from the apostate Israelites, he adds that "many evils and adversity"[288] (וּמְצָאֻהוּ רָעוֹת רַבּוֹת וְצָרוֹת, *ûmĕṣ ʾūhû rā ʿôt rabbôt wĕṣārôt*) will befall the apostate Israelites in that day. In Esth 7:6, when asked to name her persecutor, Esther says he is "an adversary and enemy, this evil one Haman" (אִישׁ צַר וְאוֹיֵב הָמָן הָרָע הַזֶּה, *ʾîš ṣar wĕ ʾôyēb hāmān hārā ʿ hazzeh*). When we come to the song in Deut 32, we discover several parallels to Esther. It repeats the idea that Yahweh will "hide his face" from the apostate Israelites (32:20). He will then provoke his people to jealousy with "a foolish nation" (32:21)—perhaps a fitting description of Persia, especially as it is depicted in the book of Esther. God will bring disasters and destruction against His people. But He will not allow them to be destroyed, lest the "enemy" (אוֹיֵב, *ʾôyēb*) and "their adversaries" (צָרֵימוֹ, *ṣārêmô*) think they have been triumphant by their own power (32:27). When He sees that their power is gone, He will render justice for them (32:36) and avenge His people with His glittering sword (32:43). The theme of this song seems apropos to the story of Esther: the apostate people, the threat of destruction, the gracious deliverance. But there are some verbal parallels to the song in Esther, as well:

- In Deut 32:20, where we read of God hiding His face from Israel, we also read that they are a "perverse" (תַּהְפֻּכֹת, *tahpūkōt*), or literally "reversed," generation. The same word is used in Esth 9:1, this time in reference to the plot against the Jews, which was also "reversed."
- In Deut 32:30, God asks, "How could ... two ... cause a myriad to flee, if their Rock had not sold them?" (אִם־לֹא כִּי־צוּרָם מְכָרָם, *ʾim lōʾ kî ṣûrām mĕkārām*). In Esth 7:4, Esther complains to the king that she and her people had been "sold for destruction, and to be slain, and to perish" (כִּי נִמְכַּרְנוּ אֲנִי וְעַמִּי לְהַשְׁמִיד לַהֲרוֹג וּלְאַבֵּד, *kî nimkarnû ʾănî wĕ ʿammî lĕhašmîd lahărôg ûlĕ ʾabbēd*).[289]

---

288. Author's translation.

289. The use of the word *sold* in Esth 7:4 may, once again, be an oblique reference to God: elsewhere, whenever there is a reference to Israel being "sold" in the Scriptures, it is Yahweh who has conducted the transaction. Though Israel is sold *to* Haman for destruction, Esther might assume that God has done the sale. The idea of being "sold" by God to enemies also occurs in Judg 2:14; 3:8; 4:2, 9; 10:7. It is always a result of wickedness.

- In Deut 32:32–33, the Jews' oppressors are described as people whose "vine is from the vine of Sodom" and whose "wine is the poison of snakes." Wine is a prominent element in the story of Esther, beginning in 1:10, where the king was drunk with wine when he gave the fateful order for Vashti to appear before his guests (1:10). The banquets are specifically described as "banquets of wine" in 5:6; 7:2, 7, 8. One of these references includes yet another verbal parallel: the phrase "poison of serpents" is חֲמַת תַּנִּינִם, *ḥămat tannînīm*; the word חֵמָה (*ḥēmâ*) appears also in Esth 7:7: וְהַמֶּלֶךְ קָם בַּחֲמָתוֹ מִמִּשְׁתֵּה הַיַּיִן, *wĕhammelek qām baḥămātô mimmištēh hayyayīn*, "The king arose in his wrath from the banquet of wine."
- In 32:41, it is stated that Yahweh will use His sword to "take vengeance on [His] adversaries and recompense [His] haters." Similar language appears in Esth 8:13, where the Jews were told to prepare to "take vengeance on their enemies" and in 9:5, where they "struck with the sword" their enemies and did as they pleased to "their haters." The words "enemy" (אוֹיֵב, *ʾôyēb*), "adversary" (צַר, *ṣar*), and "hater" (שֹׂנֵא, *śānēʾ*) appear together in key verses in both Deuteronomy and Esther.

These parallels, then, might provide a clue as to why God is absent from the book of Esther: at some point in the book's redaction, an editor was offended by the behavior of the text's Jewish protagonists. (Perhaps this editor lived during the hyper-nationalistic period following the Hasmonean Revolt, when the Jews were recovering from the martyrdoms suffered because the Greeks and their Jewish collaborators had tried to separate the people of Judaea from their religion.) The redactor was deeply troubled by the names of the main Jewish characters in Esther, seeing them as evidence of a people flirting with syncretism. Esther's concealment of her Judaism and her mixed marriage were even worse. If God chose to work with such characters, it was not because He approved of them, but rather because He loved His nation Israel. The redactor interpreted the trouble that the Jews experienced as a judgment from God. Just as Israel had been "sold" to their enemies in the days of the judges, God had sold them into the hands of Haman and the Persians. This editor likely made the same connection between Esther and Deuteronomy that the later rabbis would make and chose to illustrate the idea that God would hide Himself from His people by literally hiding God in the text, expurgating all references to the divine. Nonetheless, the Jews had obviously been saved from their ordeal—proof not of their ingenuity or worthiness, but of God's mercy. This outcome, too, had been predicted by Deuteronomy (32:36–43).

So in Esther, it is not so much human courage or virtue that is on display as divine beneficence. This beneficence must be interpreted in light of another of Esther's theological emphases: the divine election of Israel. The action that God takes on behalf of His people is certainly evidence of this idea. Why would such miraculous coincidences have occurred, if Israel were not in some way "special" to God? It is more clearly implied, however, in Zeresh's assertion that Haman must fall before Mordecai because Mordecai is a Jew (6:13). Zeresh recognizes that the turn of events that has caused her husband's embarrassment arises from the Jews having a unique relationship with the divine. Somewhat less explicit is Mordecai's observation that deliverance could arise for the Jews from another place, but Esther may have been "brought into the queenship" for such a time as this. He is not as certain as the apparently pagan Zeresh, but his assertion that there could be a greater purpose to Esther's rise in prominence seems to indicate a belief that the one who orchestrates such matters has a special consideration for the Jewish people.

It is not inaccurate to say that the book of Esther (as it now exists) is about divine providence, veiled in the guise of a "fate" that plays favorites. On the other hand, it is also about human failure—especially the failure to maintain Jewish distinctiveness while living in the context of Diaspora. By removing God from the narrative, our redactor eloquently voiced his disapproval of the compromises the characters made in their Diaspora setting.

The Ethics of Esther

If we understand the book of Esther as condemning the behavior of its protagonists, interpreting its ethics becomes a difficult undertaking. Under the best circumstances, interpreting the ethical position of biblical narrative is a challenge, since biblical authors often simply report the actions of the protagonists without comment. Of course, reporting an action does not mean that the narrator approves of it; often it is just the opposite. The book of Judges provides many examples of "men behaving badly," with only subtle textual clues that these characters are very flawed heroes, if not antiheroes. There may be an echo of Gideon in Esther: like her, he was reluctant to accept the call to deliver the people of Israel from their oppressors, but as the victories accumulated, he too seemed to develop an unwholesome taste for blood (Judg 8:4–21).[290]

With the book of Esther, we are sometimes left to wonder: what did the author/redactor of the text really think about the Jewish woman marrying a foreign king? Of Mordecai refusing to bow to Haman? Of the impaling of Haman's ten sons? Of the massacre of seventy-five thousand

290. On Gideon's personal vendetta, see R. Boling, *Judges*, AYB (New York: Doubleday, 1975), 150–58; J. Harris, C. Brown, and M. Moore, *Joshua, Judges, Ruth*, NIBC (Peabody, MA: Hendrickson, 2000), 198–201.

"enemies" of the Jews? The author tells us that the Jews rejoiced over these final victories (9:18), but our narrator might not have considered these Jews to be good people. When bad people rejoice about an event, should we not suspect that the event is not good, but evil? The nature of this book puts us in a difficult situation, uncertain how to interpret the characters' behavior.

One reliable indicator of the narrator's ethical stand might be found in the actions that he attributes to God. Of course, the author never invokes God directly, so we are required to infer the acts of God through God's apparent manifestations in this text: the remarkable coincidences. In the twists of fate that pepper the book, we discover not only that God has a sense of humor, but also that He has a powerful sense of retributive justice. Haman had built a pike for Mordecai, but it is he who is impaled upon it. The enemies of the Jews had thought they would win a victory over them; instead, that very day turns into a victory for the Jews. Such reversals are typical of the Wisdom tradition: e.g., Prov 26:27, "He who digs a pit, in it he will fall, and he who rolls a stone, on him it will come back" (see also Pss 7:15–16; 57:6).

Another aspect of Esther's ethics is the notion of vengeance. In this book, the Jews were not content to simply secure their lives against their enemies. Mordecai's decree granted them the right to kill not only men, but women and children as well (8:11)—an act that surely goes beyond mere self-defense. Throughout all the provinces, it was explicitly proclaimed that the Jews were "to avenge themselves" (לְהִנָּקֵם, *lĕhinnāqēm*) against their enemies. Furthermore, when Esther learned that the Jews had successfully killed five hundred men in Susa, she requested permission to continue the slaughter for another day (9:13). The Jews turned the carnage into an occasion of celebration (9:17–22), but it is not clear whether the narrator shared their enthusiasm for the bloodbath.

In Deut 32:35, God states, "Vengeance is mine, and recompense; their foot shall slip in due time" (NKJV). In Deut 32:41 and 32:43, as well, God announces that it is He who will take vengeance when His people are oppressed. Indeed, in most occurrences of the word "vengeance" (נָקָם, *nāqām*) in the Heb. Bible, it is typically God who exacts revenge; typically, humans are encouraged not to seek vengeance (see Lev 19:18). Vengeance, it seems, is mostly a privilege of Yahweh. According to Mendenhall, such vengeance was not a lawless revenge, like a blood feud; rather, it was a divine prerogative exercised when human justice failed.[291] It would seem, then, that the Jews' intention to take vengeance on their enemies would have likely been contrary to the will of God. Some scholars, however, would disagree.

291. G. E. Mendenhall, *The Tenth Generation: The Origins of the Biblical Tradition* (Baltimore: Johns Hopkins University Press, 1973), 69–103.

Baldwin (100) notes that the word *avenge*, like *vindicate*, comes from the Latin *vindicare*. She contends that the translation "avenge" may not do justice to the meaning of the Heb. verb נָקַם in Esth 8:13 and that it could mean rather to "inflict a just punishment" or "vindicate oneself." Indeed, such a meaning is certainly appropriate when the exacter of vengeance is Yahweh, but human vengeance often appears to be less noble. Would it have been "just" for the Jews to kill women and children? Perhaps, from the standpoint of retributive justice; after all, the enemies had intended to kill Jewish women and children. In that light, the vengeance would not have been too dissimilar from the slaying of the firstborn (Passover), which was a poetic reversal of Pharaoh's slaughter of the Heb. infants. The difference, of course, is that the enemies in Esther never had a chance to strike the first blow.

One other issue must be taken into consideration in judging the morality of these acts: who are these enemies who might seek the death of the Jews? If they are understood to be Amalekites, like Haman the Agagite, then their slaughter could be justified on the basis that it is carrying out the commands given to Moses (Exod 17:14–16), Israel (Deut 25:17–19), and Saul (1 Sam 15:3) that the Amalekites were to be utterly destroyed.[292] In Esth 3:10, Haman is identified as "the Jews' enemy." It is not difficult to take this phrase as meaning "enemy *par excellence*," the epitome of the Jews' enemies. If the book of Esther is meant to be viewed as a final struggle between Israel and Amalek, then the only fitting end would be that Amalek would be utterly destroyed. Of course, this solution only pushes the ethical problem back further into the biblical tradition, because we are still faced with the command to exterminate all the people of Amalek. But that would be an issue for another study.

In any event, it would surely be unwise to judge characters of the OT according to ethical principles that were not fully revealed until the time of Jesus Christ. But on the other hand, we would do well to note that the foundation of Jesus' ethics was the OT, and that the Law and Prophets were not far removed from His own ideas. If the people of the OT at times appear to be behaving in ways that are morally indefensible, it may well be because they frequently fail to live up to their own standards—just like us.

Conclusions

The book of Esther is a strange, complex, and wonderful work of literature. No doubt it originated in oral tradition, with stories told about a courtier named Mordecai and a Jewish queen named Esther who delivered her

292. There are other possible meanings of the term *Agagite*. These will be considered in the commentary.

people from destruction. It developed through a process that we cannot reconstruct with any certainty. The story was tailored to justify the most raucous celebration of the Jewish year, but it was far more than that: it was also designed to encourage a sense of pride in Jewish ethnic identity and thereby discourage the assimilation of the race.

Esther's approach was more nationalistic and less pietistic than, say, Daniel, or Judith, or *Jubilees*. Yet it would be a mistake to say that the book lacks theological insights. In fact, it could be said to be one of the most incisive books in the Bible. In this text, we are skillfully directed to contemplate a God who is committed to His people, even when they show little interest in Him. The characters here display little of the pervasive piety typical of biblical heroes; indeed, they are much more like modern people than we may care to admit. Just as we typically do not recognize the providence of God even as we experience it, so, too, do the characters in Esther seem mostly oblivious to the hand that is guiding their fate, making only oblique references to His purposes.

Perhaps the most remarkable thing about the book of Esther is that God is most manifest in the irony of Haman, impaled on the gallows that he had prepared for another man. In this violent act, we see the designs of a wicked and powerful man reversed and turned back by a power greater than his own. We see the culmination of a plan that was laid before the crisis ever ensued. In fact, we see a justice fulfilled that had been postponed for six hundred years—the destruction of the Amalekites, requiting them for their predation of Israel. In contrast to the experience of Eliezer in Wiesel's *Night*, this hanging does not lead one to wonder what has happened to God. Indeed, it does just the opposite: we see that God has not died and has not been absent. He is very much alive and present among His people.

Outline

I. Introduction: The Greatness of Xerxes (1:1–2)
II. The Rise of Esther and Mordecai (1:3–2:23)
    A. Queen Vashti Deposed (1:3–22)
        1. The Royal Banquets (1:3–9)
        2. The Queen's Insubordination (1:10–12)
        3. The King's Response (1:13–22)
    B. Esther Chosen as Queen (2:1–18)
        1. The Contest Is Proposed (2:1–4)
        2. Introducing Mordecai and Esther (2:5–7)
        3. Esther Wins the Contest (2:8–18)
    C. Mordecai Saves the King (2:19–23)
III. The Threat to the Jews (3:1–4:17)

- A. Mordecai Provokes Haman (3:1–7)
- B. Haman's Plot to Destroy the Jews (3:8–15)
    1. Haman Petitions the King (3:8–11)
    2. Haman Issues the Decree (3:12–15)
- C. Esther Resolves to Help (4:1–17)
    1. Mordecai and the Jews Lament the Order (4:1–3)
    2. Mordecai Appeals to Esther (4:4–17)
        - a. Mordecai Refuses Clothing from Esther (4:4)
        - b. Mordecai Orders Esther to Intercede (4:5–9)
        - c. Esther Agrees to Intercede (4:10–17)

IV. The Plot Reversed (5:1–7:10)

- A. Esther's First Banquet (5:1–8)
    1. Esther Invites the King and Haman to a Banquet (5:1–5a)
        - a. Esther Appears before the King (5:1–2)
        - b. Esther Issues an Invitation (5:3–5a)
    2. Esther Invites the King and Haman to a Second Banquet (5:5b-8)
- B. Haman Plots to Kill Mordecai (5:9–14)
- C. Mordecai Is Honored; Haman Humiliated (6:1–14)
    1. The King Discovers His Oversight (6:1–3)
    2. Haman Counsels the King on Honoring a Benefactor (6:4–10)
    3. Haman Is Forced to Honor Mordecai (6:11)
    4. Haman's End Is Foretold (6:12–14)
- D. Esther's Second Banquet (7:1–10)
    1. Esther Appeals to the King for the Jews (7:1–6a)
    2. Haman Appeals to the Queen for His Life (7:6b-8a)
    3. Haman Is Condemned (7:8b-10)

V. The Triumph of the Jews (8:1–9:32)

- A. Esther and Mordecai Arrange Deliverance for the Jews (8:1–17)
    1. The King Promotes Mordecai (8:1–2)
    2. Esther and Mordecai Are Authorized to Write an Edict (8:3–8)
    3. Mordecai Issues the Decree (8:9–17)
        - a. The Counter-Decree Is Written (8:9–14)
        - b. Mordecai Leaves with Honor, and the Jews Rejoice (8:15–17)
- B. The Jews' Victories over Their Enemies (9:1–19)
    1. The First Wave of Victories (9:1–10)
        - a. Victories in the Provinces (9:1–5)
        - b. Victories over Enemies in the Palace (9:6–10)

2. The Second Wave of Victories (9:11–15)
    a. Esther Requests a Second Day of Carnage (9:11–13)
    b. Five Hundred Killed in Susa (9:14–15)
3. The Jews Celebrate Their Victories (9:16–19)
    a. Celebrating the Victories in the Provinces (9:16–17)
    b. Celebrating the Victories in Susa (9:17–19)

C. Purim Established (9:20–32)
1. Mordecai Establishes Purim (9:20–28)
    a. Mordecai Issues the Order Establishing Purim (9:20–22)
    b. The Jews Commit to the Perpetual Observance (9:23–28)
2. Esther Confirms the Celebration of Purim (9:29–32)

VI. Conclusion: The Greatness of Xerxes and Mordecai (10:1–3)

Selected Bibliography

Anderson, B. "The Place of the Book of Esther in the Christian Bible." *JR* 30 (1950): 32–43.

Beal, T. K. *The Book of Hiding: Gender, Ethnicity, Annihilation, and Esther.* New York: Routledge, 1997.

Beckwith, R. *The Old Testament Canon of the New Testament Church.* Grand Rapids: Eerdmans, 1986.

Berg, S. B. *The Book of Esther: Motifs, Themes and Structure.* SBLDS 44. Missoula, MT: Scholars Press, 1979.

Berlin, A. "The Book of Esther and Ancient Storytelling." *JBL* 120 (2001): 3–14.

Bickerman, E. J. "The Colophon of the Greek Book of Esther." *JBL* 63 (1944): 339–62.

———. *Four Strange Books of the Bible: Jonah, Daniel, Kohelet, Esther.* New York: Schocken Books, 1967.

Bresciani, E. "The Persian Occupation of Egypt." In *The Cambridge History of Iran*, ed. I. Gershevitch, 2:502–28. Cambridge: Cambridge University Press, 1985.

Briant, P. *From Cyrus to Alexander: A History of the Persian Empire.* Winona Lake, IN: Eisenbrauns, 2002.

Broyde, M. "Defilement of the Hands, Canonization of the Bible, and the Special Status of Esther, Ecclesiastes, and Song of Songs." *Judaism* 44 (1995): 65–79.

Bush, F. W. "The Book of Esther: Opus non gratum in the Christian Canon." *BBR* 8 (1998): 39–54.

Childs, B. S. *Introduction to the Old Testament as Scripture.* Philadelphia: Fortress, 1979.

Clines, D. J. A. *The Esther Scroll: The Story of the Story*. JSOTSup 30. Sheffield, UK: JSOT Press, 1984.

———. "Reading Esther from Left to Right: Contemporary Strategies for Reading a Biblical Text." In *The Bible in Three Dimensions: Essays in Celebration of Forty Years of Biblical Studies in the University of Sheffield*, ed. W. E. Fowl, D. J. A. Clines, and S. E. Porter, 3–22. Sheffield, UK: JSOT Press, 1990.

———. *The Redaction of the Books of Esther: On Reading Composite Texts*. Atlanta: Scholars Press, 1991.

Cook, H. "The A-Text of the Greek Versions of the Book of Esther." *ZAW* 81 (1969): 369–76.

Dandamaev, M. A. *A Political History of the Achaemenid Empire*. Leiden: Brill, 1989.

De Troyer, K. *The End of the Alpha-Text of Esther: Translation and Narrative Technique in MT 8:1–17, LXX 8:1–17 and AT 7:14–41*. SBLSCS 49. Atlanta: Scholars Press, 2000.

Fox, M. V. *Character and Ideology in the Book of Esther*. Columbia: University of South Carolina Press, 1991.

———. "The Religion of the Book of Esther." *Judaism* 39 (1990): 135–47.

———. "The Structure of the Book of Esther." In *Isac Leo Seeligman Volume: Essays on the Bible and the Ancient World*, ed. A. Rofé and Y. Zakovitch III, 291–303. Jerusalem: E. Rubenstein, 1983.

Gordis, R. "Religion, Wisdom and History in the Book of Esther—a New Solution to an Ancient Crux." *JBL* 100 (1981): 359–88.

Greenstein, E. "A Jewish Reading of Esther." In *Judaic Perspectives on Ancient Israel*, ed. J. Neusner, B. Levine, and E. Frerichs, 225–43. Philadelphia: Fortress, 1987.

Huey, F. B. "Irony as the Key to Understanding Esther." *SwJT* 32 (1990): 36–39.

Humphreys, W. "A Lifestyle for Diaspora: A Study of the Tales of Esther and Daniel." *JBL* 92 (1973): 211–23.

———. "Novella." In *Saga, Novella, Legend, Tale: Narrative Forms in Old Testament Literature*, ed. G. Coats, 82–96. Sheffield, UK: JSOT Press, 1985.

———. "The Story of Esther and Mordecai: An Early Jewish Novella." In *Saga, Novella, Legend, Tale: Narrative Forms in Old Testament Literature*, ed. G. Coats, 97–113. Sheffield, UK: JSOT Press, 1985.

Jacob, B. "Das Buch Esther bei dem LXX." *ZAW* 10 (1890): 241–98.

Jobes, K. *The Alpha-Text of Esther—Its Character and Relationship to the Masoretic Text*. SBLDS 153. Atlanta: Scholars Press, 1996.

Jones, B. "Two Misconceptions about the Book of Esther." *CBQ* 39 (1977): 171–81.

Klasens, A. "Cambyses en Égypte." *Ex Oriente Lux* 10 (1946): 339–49.

Leiman, S. *The Canonization of the Hebrew Scriptures: The Talmudic and Midrashic Evidence.* Hamden, CT: Archon, 1976.

McDonald, L., and J. Sanders. *The Canon Debate.* Peabody, MA: Hendrickson, 2002.

Meinhold, A. "Die Gattung der Josephsgeschichte und des Estherbuches: Diasporanovelle, I." *ZAW* 87 (1975): 306–24.

———. "Die Gattung der Josephsgeschichte und des Estherbuches: Diasporanovelle II." *ZAW* 88 (1976): 72–93.

Merrill, E. H. *Kingdom of Priests: A History of Old Testament Israel.* Grand Rapids: Baker Book House, 1987.

———. "A Theology of Ezra-Nehemiah and Esther." In *A Biblical Theology of the Old Testament*, ed. R. Zuck, 189–205. Chicago: Moody Press, 1991.

Milik, J. "Les Modèles Araméens du Livre d'Esther dans la Grotte 4 de Qumran." *RQ* 15 (1992): 321–406.

Moore, C. A. "Esther Revisited: An Examination of Some Esther Studies over the Past Decade." In *Biblical Studies in Honor of Samuel Iwry*, ed. A. Kort and S. Morschauser, 163–74. Winona Lake, IN: Eisenbrauns, 1985.

———. "A Greek Witness to a Different Hebrew Text of Esther." *ZAW* 79 (1967): 351–58.

———. "On the Origins of the LXX Additions to the Book of Esther." *JBL* 92 (1973): 382–93.

Newman, R. "The Council of Jamnia and the Old Testament Canon." *WTJ* 38 (1976): 319–48.

Niditch, S. *A Prelude to Biblical Folklore: Underdogs and Tricksters.* Champaign: University of Illinois Press, 2000.

Olmstead, A. *History of the Persian Empire.* Chicago: University of Chicago Press, 1948.

Schildgen, B. "A Blind Promise: Mark's Retrieval of Esther." *Poetics Today* 15 (1994): 115–31.

Schürer, E. *The History of the Jewish People in the Age of Jesus Christ* (175 BC–AD 135). Rev. and ed. Geza Vermes, Fergus Millar, and Matthew Black. 4 vols. Edinburgh: T&T Clark, 1973–1987.

Scott, J. *Domination and the Arts of Resistance: Hidden Transcripts.* New Haven, CT: Yale University Press, 1990.

Shea, W. "Esther and History." *AUSS* 14 (1976): 227–46.

Talmon, S. "Was the Book of Esther Known at Qumran?" *DSD* 2 (1995): 253–56.

———. "Wisdom in the Book of Esther." *VT* 13 (1963): 422–55.

Torrey, C. C. "The Older Book of Esther." *HTR* 37 (1944): 1–40.

White-Crawford, S. "Has Esther Been Found at Qumran? 4QProto-Esther and the Esther Corpus." *RevQ* 17 (1996): 307–25.

Wright, J. S. "The Historicity of the Book of Esther." In *New Perspectives on the Old Testament,* ed. J. Barton Payne, 34–47. Waco, TX: Word, 1970.

Wyler, B. "Esther: The Incomplete Emancipation of a Queen." In *A Feminist Companion to Esther, Judith, and Susanna*, ed. A. Brenner, 111–35. Sheffield, UK: Sheffield Academic Press, 1995.

Yamauchi, E. *Persia and the Bible*. Grand Rapids: Baker, 1990.

Young, T. C. "The Early History of the Medes and Persians and the Achaemenid Empire until the Death of Cambyses." In *CAH 4: Persia, Greece, and the Western Mediterranean,* ed. J. Boardman. Cambridge: Cambridge University Press, 1988.

Commentary Bibliography

Anderson, Bernhard W. "The Book of Esther: Introduction and Exegesis." *IB* 3:823–74. New York: Abingdon, 1954.

Baldwin, Joyce G. *Esther.* TOTC. Downers Grove, IL: InterVarsity, 1984.

Bardtke, Hans. *Das Buch Esther.* KAT 17.5. Gütersloh: Gütersloh Verl.-Haus Mohn, 1963.

Beal, Timothy K. *Ruth and Esther.* Berit Olam. Collegeville, MN: Liturgical Press, 1999.

Bechtel, Carole M. *Esther.* IBC. Louisville, KY: John Knox, 2002.

Berlin, Adele. *The JPS Bible Commentary: Esther.* Philadelphia: The Jewish Publication Society, 2001.

Bjornard, Reider B. "Esther." In *The Broadman Bible Commentary*, ed. Clifton J. Allen, 4:1–21. Nashville: Broadman, 1971.

Bos, Johanna W. H. *Ruth, Esther, Jonah.* Atlanta: John Knox, 1986.

Breneman, Mervin. *Ezra, Nehemiah, Esther*. NAC 10. Nashville: Broadman and Holman, 1993.

Brockington, Leonard H. *Ezra, Nehemiah and Esther.* Greenwood, SC: Attic Press, 1969.

Bush, Frederic W. *Ruth, Esther.* WBC 9. Dallas: Word, 1996.

Cassel, Paulus. *An Explanatory Commentary on Esther*. Edinburgh: T&T Clark, 1888.

Clines, David J. A. *Ezra, Nehemiah, Esther.* NCB. Grand Rapids: Eerdmans, 1984.

Coggins, Richard J., and S. Paul Re'emi. *Israel among the Nations: Nahum, Obadiah, Esther*. ITC. Grand Rapids: Eerdmans, 1985.

Conti, Marco, and Gianluca Pilara. *1–2 Kings, 1–2 Chronicles, Ezra, Nehemiah, Esther.* ACCS 5. Downers Grove, IL: InterVarsity, 2001.

Craghan, John F. *Esther, Judith, Tobit, Jonah, Ruth.* Wilmington, DE: Michael Glazier, 1982.

Crawford, Sidnie White. "The Book of Esther." In *NIB*, vol. 3, *Kings to Judith.* Nashville: Abingdon, 1999.

Demaray, C. E. "The Book of Esther." *Beacon Bible Commentary*, vol. 2. Ed. A. F. Harper. Kansas City, MO: Beacon Hill, 1965.

Dommershausen, Werner. *Die Estherrolle: Stil und Ziel einer alttestamentliche Schrift.* Stuttgart: Verlag Katholisches Bibelwerk, 1968.

Duguid, Iain. *Esther and Ruth.* Reformed Expository Commentary. Phillipsburg, NJ: P&R, 2005.

Fuerst, Wesley J. *The Books of Ruth, Esther, Ecclesiastes, the Song of Songs, Lamentations: The Five Scrolls.* Cambridge: Cambridge University Press, 1975.

Gerleman, Gillis. *Esther.* BKAT. Neukirchen-Vluyn: Neukirchener Verlag, 1973.

Goldman, D. "The Book of Esther." In A. Cohen, ed., *The Five Megilloth: Hebrew Text & English Translation with an Introduction and Commentary*, rev. ed., 115–92. New York: Soncino Press, 1984.

Gordis, Robert. *Megillat Esther: The Masoretic Hebrew Text with Introduction, New Translation, and Commentary.* New York: Ktav, 1974.

Gunkel, Hermann. *Esther.* Tübingen: J. C. B. Mohr/P. Siebeck, 1916.

Huey, F. B., Jr. "Esther." In *The Expositor's Bible Commentary*, ed. F. E. Gaebelein, 4:775–839. Grand Rapids: Zondervan, 1988.

Jobes, Karen H. *Esther.* NIVAC. Grand Rapids: Zondervan, 1999.

Keil, Carl F., and Franz Delitzsch. *Commentary on the Old Testament: Kings-Esther.* Reprint, Grand Rapids: Eerdmans, 1978.

Kelly, Balmer H. *Ezra, Nehemiah, Esther, Job.* London: SCM Press, 1962.

Knight, George A. F. *Esther, Song of Songs, Lamentations: Introduction and Commentary.* London: SCM Press, 1955.

Kravitz, Leonard S. *Esther: A Modern Commentary.* New York: URJ Press, 2010.

LaCocque, André. *Esther Regina: A Bakhtinian Reading.* Evanston, IL: Northwestern University Press, 2008.

Laniak, Timothy S. "Esther." In L. C. Allen and T. S. Laniak, *Ezra, Nehemiah, Esther.* NIBC. Peabody, MA: Hendrickson, 2003.

Larson, Knut, and Kathy Dahlen. *Holman Old Testament Commentary—Ezra, Nehemiah, Esther,* ed. Max Anders. Nashville: B&H, 2005.

Levenson, Jon D. *Esther: A Commentary.* Louisville, KY: Westminster John Knox, 1997.

Mangano, Mark. *Esther and Daniel.* The College Press NIV Commentary. Joplin, MO: College Press, 2001.

Martin, John A. "Esther." In *The Bible Knowledge Commentary: Old Testament*, ed. John Walvoord and Roy Zuck, 699–713. Colorado Springs: Cook, 1983.

McConnville, J. G. *Ezra, Nehemiah, and Esther.* Daily Study Bible Series. Louisville, KY: Westminster John Knox, 1985.

McGee, J. V. *Exposition on the Book of Esther.* Wheaton, IL: Van Kampen Press, 1951.

Moore, Carey A. *Esther: Introduction, Translation, and Notes.* AYB 7b. Garden City, NY: Doubleday, 1971.

———. *Daniel, Esther, and Jeremiah: The Additions*. AYB 44. Garden City, NY: Doubleday, 1977.

Murphy, Roland E. *Wisdom Literature: Job, Proverbs, Ruth, Canticles, Ecclesiastes, and Esther*. FOTL. Grand Rapids: Eerdmans, 1981.

Omanson, Roger L., and P. A. Noss. *A Handbook on the Book of Esther*. New York: United Bible Societies, 1997.

Paton, Lewis B. *A Critical and Exegetical Commentary on the Book of Esther*. ICC. Edinburgh: T&T Clark, 1908.

Philips, Elaine A. "Esther." In *Expositor's Bible Commentary 4: I Chronicles-Job*, ed. Tremper Longman III and David Garland, 569–674. Grand Rapids: Zondervan, 2010.

Roop, Eugene F. *Ruth, Jonah, Esther*. BCBC. Scottdale, PA: Herald Press, 2002.

Smith, Gary. *Ezra-Nehemiah & Esther*. Cornerstone Bible Commentary. Carol Stream, IL: Tyndale, 2010.

Streane, Annesley W. *The Book of Esther: With Introduction and Notes*. Cambridge: Cambridge University Press, 1907.

Tomasino, Anthony J. "Esther." In *Zondervan Illustrated Bible Backgrounds Commentary: 1 and 2 Kings, 1 and 2 Chronicles, Ezra, Nehemiah, Esther*, ed. John H. Walton, 468–505. Grand Rapids: Zondervan, 2009.

Walton, John H., Victor H. Matthews, and Mark W. Chavalas. "Esther." In *The IVP Bible Background Commentary: Old Testament*, 483–90. Downers Grove, IL: InterVarsity, 2000.

Wells, Samuel. *Esther & Daniel*. BTC. Grand Rapids: Brazos, 2013.

Whitehead, Brady B. *Ezra, Nehemiah and Esther*. Nashville: Abingdon, 1988.

Wolfe, Lisa M. *Ruth, Esther, Song of Songs, and Judith*. Eugene, OR: Cascade Books, 2011.

Würthwein, E. "Esther." HAT. Mohr, 1964.

The Introduction (1:1–2)

Introduction

The opening verses of the book of Esther provide the context. In addition to giving us the historical and geographical settings, they introduce the character whose decrees drive the entire narrative. They also allude to the vast expanse of the great king's domain.

These verses form an inclusion* with the last verses of the book, which reiterate the idea of the great king's glory. They should therefore be regarded as a discrete unit and not as the beginning of a larger section composed of 1:1–9, as some scholars contend.[1]

Translation

1 These events transpired in the days of Xerxes—that Xerxes who ruled from India to Cush, 127 provinces **2**—in those days when King Xerxes occupied his royal throne, which was in Susa the citadel.

Textual Notes

As noted in the introduction ("The Greek Versions"), the LXX and AT versions of Esther begin with an addition, an account of a symbolic dream seen by Mordecai that left him perplexed. This dream certainly represents an expansion of the original story and should not be considered in attempting to reconstruct the "original" version of Esther.

1.a. The LXX and Josephus have Ἀρταξέρξης for the Hebrew אֲחַשְׁוֵרוֹשׁ here and throughout the book of Esther. Of the other translations, AT reads Ἀσσυῆρος; the Vg., Asuerus; the Tg., אחשורוש; and in the Syr., we have *ʾḥšyš*. These readings are all consistent with that of the MT.

1. That Mordecai is not present in these verses does not weaken this proposal (contra Bush, 343). Rather, it is the natural outcome of the "peripety" (reversal) so central to this book. At the beginning of the book, the focus is on the glory of Ahasuerus; at the end, Ahasuerus has been joined by the unlikely figure of the Jew Mordecai.

1.b. The Syr. has here 120 provinces, rather than the 127 of the MT. This emendation was probably made to harmonize with Dan 6:2 (Eng. 6:1), "It pleased Darius to set over the kingdom 120 satraps."

Commentary

1:1 The Esther narrative opens with words that could be literally translated, "And it was ... " (וַיְהִי). This particular *waw*-consec. construction is frequently used to establish a continuity between the ensuing narrative and that which preceded it, as in Judg 1:1, "And it came to pass after the death of Joshua" (ASV), or 2 Sam 2:1, "And it came to pass after the death of Saul."[2] In the case of Esther, however, it is unlikely that the text was ever part of a longer historical work. The construction more likely serves a stylistic function, imitating the historical narratives to create a sense of a march of history (Paton, 120–21). The book of Jonah, which is certainly an independent story, begins this way as well. The closest biblical parallel to the construction here, however, is Ruth 1:1, וַיְהִי בִּימֵי שְׁפֹט הַשֹּׁפְטִים "And it came to pass in the days when the judges judged" (ASV). There is no reason to conclude that either Esther or Ruth were originally part of a longer literary work. Both books form coherent, self-contained units.

Some scholars (e.g., Jobes, 57) have argued that the use of וַיְהִי (*wayĕhî*) at the beginning of this narrative indicates that the author intended the story to be taken as literal history. The basis for this assumption is uncertain. The phrase "there was" is used to open obviously nonhistorical narratives, like Nathan's parable of the man who stole his neighbor's ewe-lamb (1 Sam 12), or (in its Greek equivalent) Jesus' parables (e.g., Luke 7:41; 16:1; 18:2). But more significant still is the question of how the book would differ if its author had intended its readers to understand it as fiction. Would we expect the author to begin by stating that the following work was not to be taken literally? In ancient fiction writing, as in modern literature, there was no such convention. Typically, authors attempt to emulate the style of "historical" narrative, even in such obviously fictional works as Aesop's fables. Good storytellers strive to create the illusion of historicity, to help their audiences to suspend disbelief.

The name Xerxes is the Greek rendering of the Persian name *khšayāršа*, which in the Heb. Bible is rendered "Ahasuerus" (אֲחַשְׁוֵרוֹשׁ, *ʾăḥašwērôš*). Since the Greek version of the name is familiar to modern readers, we have chosen to retain it in this translation.[3] Josephus and the LXX mistakenly identify Ahasuerus as Artaxerxes, but this identification can be eliminated

2. See Christo H. van der Merwe et al., *A Biblical Hebrew Reference Grammar* (Sheffield, UK: Sheffield Academic Press, 1999), 331–33 (§44.5). Hereafter, *BHRG*.
3. Cf. Omanson, 14.

on linguistic grounds: the Persian name *Artaxšaça* (Artaxerxes) is attested in seven different ancient languages, and it is consistently spelled with a *t*, which Ahasuerus lacks.[4] Most scholars identify this figure with Xerxes I, who ruled Persia from 486–465 BC. (There was later a Xerxes II, but since he ruled only forty-five days in 424 BC, he could not have been the subject of this narrative.) Recently, however, some commentators have balked at identifying Ahasuerus with Xerxes I. Levenson (25) and Berlin (5) contend that Ahasuerus is merely a character in a story. Berlin, however, seems ambivalent, noting that the reputation of Xerxes I might well have informed the depiction of the character in this narrative. As noted in the introduction (under "Historical Background"), Xerxes was a very well-known ruler. It seems unlikely that the author would have created the character of Xerxes without incorporating some aspects of the historical figure.

Evidence for this notion is found in the brief description of the king. The identification of Xerxes as "the one who ruled ... from India to Ethiopia" appears to be a historically accurate depiction of the extent of his realm. On the foundation inscription of his palace in Persepolis, Xerxes describes his realm thus:

> Thus speaks King Xerxes: These are the countries—in addition to Persia—over which I am king under the "shadow" of Ahuramazda, over which I hold sway, which are bringing their tribute to me—whatever is commanded them by me, that they do and they abide by my law(s)—: Media, Elam, Arachosia, Urartu [Pers. version: Armenia], Drangiana, Parthia, (H)aria, Bactria, Sogdia, Chorasmia, Babylonia, Assyria, Sat-tagydia, Sardis, Egypt (Mi-fir), the Ionians who live on the salty sea and (those) who live beyond [lit: on the other shore of] the salty sea, Maka, Arabia, Gandara, India, Cappadocia, Da'an, the Amyrgian Cimmerians [Pers. and Elam. versions: Sakans], the Cimmerians (wearing) pointed caps, the Skudra, the Akupish, Libya, Banneshu (Carians) (and) Kush.[5]

Greek sources describe Xerxes' domain in similar terms. According to Xenophon, it reached to the south where it was too hot for human habitation, and to the north where it was too cold.[6]

---

4. See W. Shea, "Esther and History," *AUSS* 14 (1976): 228.

5. *ANET*, 316–17.

6. Xenophon, *Anabasis*, 1.7.6. On the extent of the Persian Empire, see P. Briant, *From Cyrus to Alexander: A History of the Persian Empire*, trans. P. T. Daniels (Winona Lake, IN: Eisenbrauns, 2002), 175–83; J. M. Cook, "The Rise of Achaemenids and the Establishment of Their Empire," *CHI*, 2.200–291, esp. 244–67.

The spelling of Xerxes' name in this narrative illustrates well the difficulties of rendering Persian names in Heb., but it might illustrate another tendency of the Esther narrative as well. According to Radday, the way the name is spelled would make it sound something like "King Headache" to its Heb./Aramaic-speaking audience—an appropriate epithet for a king who thoughtlessly orders the destruction of the Jews as well as one who spends much of narrative in his wine cup.[7] The book of Esther (like other biblical narratives) often uses names with some sense of double entendre.[8]

The clause beginning הוּא אֲחַשְׁוֵרוֹשׁ הַמֹּלֵךְ, "that Xerxes who ruled ...," is a relative clause modifying "Xerxes." The construction is unusual on several counts. Grammatically, it is unwieldy, since it produces a long parenthesis in the middle of a sentence. This construction is probably deliberate, forcing the reader to linger over the description of Xerxes' vast empire. Also, the repetition of Xerxes' name is unnecessary: the phrase "that Xerxes" could be replaced with the relative pronoun אֲשֶׁר (*ʾăšer*), producing a much smoother sentence. Indeed, the author uses the name "Xerxes" three times in these two verses. The redundancy is probably intentional: the name could have easily been omitted, since he is the only character mentioned to this point. But one remarkable feature of the book of Esther is its lavish use of names, recording names for even the most minor characters (e.g., Esth 1:10, 14; 2:14, etc.). This tendency will be discussed in more detail below.[9] Here, a possible explanation would be that the threefold reference increases the sense of Xerxes' importance. Or alternatively, if the Heb. transliteration of Xerxes' name did indeed sound funny to the Jewish audience, the repetition could be designed to allow the listeners to thoroughly enjoy the effect.

The purpose behind the description of the size of Xerxes' realm has been the subject of some speculation. It could not have simply been designed to distinguish Xerxes from other Persian emperors. As Clines (275) observes, the empire had already reached this extent in the days of Cambyses and retained it for several emperors to come, so this detail would have been of little help in distinguishing one emperor from another. Nor could this description of his domain be intended to distinguish this Xerxes from another king of the same name (contra Paton, 121, and many others). Only one other Persian emperor bore the name Xerxes, and his rule was far too brief to have been the subject of this narrative. Paton (121–22) suggests the author would have known of Xerxes' father, Darius the Mede (Dan 9:1),

7. Y. T. Radday, "Esther with Humour," in *On Humour and the Comic in the Hebrew Bible*, ed. Y. T. Radday and A. Brenner (Sheffield, UK: Almond, 1990), 296.

8. For a general discussion of the humorous use of names in the Bible, see Y. Radday, "Humour in Names," in *On Humour and the Comic in the Hebrew Bible*, 59–97.

9. See the commentary on 1:10.

or the Xerxes who halted the temple building in Ezra 4:6. However, the first of these figures is clearly described as a Mede, and not a Persian king, while the latter is likely the same Xerxes as the king of our narrative. More likely, the author included this note about the size of the empire merely to emphasize the king's majesty as well as to give the story an air of antiquity (thus Berlin, 5).

The name "India" designated the northwestern region of the Indus River Valley, a region that had been conquered by Xerxes' father Darius.[10] It corresponds to modern western Pakistan. The term *Cush* was used to designate the region south of Egypt. Cush was originally an Egyptian name for the expanse between the second and third cataracts of the Nile River. By the time of Xerxes, the term had come to mean southern Egypt, Sudan, and northern Ethiopia.[11]

As noted in the introduction, the 127 provinces mentioned here have been considered a historical inaccuracy, since Herodotus and ancient Persian inscriptions place the number of "satrapies," or administrative districts, in the Persian Empire at somewhere between twenty-two and thirty. But the "provinces" (Heb. מְדִינָה, *mĕdînâ*) of this verse should not be confused with satrapies. In Esth 3:12; 8:9, and elsewhere, the satraps—administrators of satrapies—are distinguished from governors (Heb. פַּחוֹת, *pāḥôt*), who administer the provinces. The "provinces" spoken of here are probably administrative districts that had their own governors, as Judah and Samaria did. The number given here, 127, cannot be verified by ancient sources. In Dan 6:2 and 9:1, it is stated that Darius the Mede ruled over 120 provinces.

1:2 The way one translates this verse depends to a great extent on how one understands the relationship between this unit and the rest of the chapter. In the NIV, NRSV, and the Complete Jewish Bible, verse 2 begins a new sentence, separated from verse 3 with a comma. The NASB, NKJV, and ESV treat the first three (in some cases, four) verses of the narrative as a single sentence. Our understanding is that the two verses form a complete unit introducing the entire narrative. See the commentary on 1:3 for the grammatical explanation for this division.

The phrase כְּשֶׁבֶת הַמֶּלֶךְ אֲחַשְׁוֵרוֹשׁ עַל כִּסֵּא מַלְכוּתוֹ translates "when King Xerxes sat on his royal throne." The reference is not to literal sitting, but to occupying the royal office. A similar expression occurs in 1 Chr 29:23, "Then Solomon sat upon the throne of Yahweh as king in place of David

10. *Hist.* 3.94–106.

11. See K. A. Kitchen, "Cush," in *NBD*, 249.

his father." In Esther, the phrase is probably meant to focus on the location where the story is set.

Many scholars, both ancient and modern (see Bush, 346, for references), have contended that the use of the ptc. in this verse (כְּשֶׁבֶת, *kĕšebet*) should be translated "sat securely," implying that Xerxes had already put down the revolts in Egypt and Babylon before the events of this narrative transpired. But as Fox notes, the verb form does not necessarily have any such connotation, and the author of our narrative shows little interest in the events preceding our story.[12] More likely, the form here is meant to define the geographical setting of the narrative: i.e., it occurred while he was dwelling in Susa, rather than one of the other Persian capitals.

Susa was one of four capitals in the Persian Empire: in the east, Babylon; in the north, Ecbatana; in the west, Persepolis; and in the south, Susa. Susa was located about two hundred miles northeast of Babylon. Darius I chose Susa as the primary capital for his empire due to its central location, and it served as his winter residence. In the summer, however, it became too hot for comfort, and affairs of state were conducted in Ecbatana.[13] The city covered about 250 hectares and was divided into two sections: the "lower city," which comprised the vast majority of the site, and a ten-acre fortified "upper city" that housed the royal palace and other residences.

The word בִּירָה (*bîrâ*) is sometimes translated "capital" (e.g., RSV, GNT, CEV). It seems rather to mean a fortified building or cluster of buildings and so here is translated "citadel." The word appears only in late biblical Heb. (e.g., 1 Chr 29:1, 19; Neh 2:8; 7:2, of the temple complex in Jerusalem; and in Neh 1:1 and Dan 8:2, as throughout Esther, of the fortified section of Susa), apparently as a loanword from the Akkadian *birtu*. In Esther, the phrase "citadel of Susa" designates the upper city, the fortified center of government. This area of the city has been well excavated, and the remains of many impressive buildings can be seen there.[14] Little remains today of the larger, unfortified lower city, which is simply designated "Susa" in Esther (e.g., 9:13–15).

---

12. *Character and Ideology*, 16.

13. According to *Geog.*, 15.3.10–11, the city was so hot in the summer that snakes or lizards attempting to cross the street at noon in the city were burnt to death before they completed the trip.

14. Further descriptions of Susa may be found in A. Olmstead, *A History of the Persian Empire* (Chicago: University of Chicago Press, 1948), 163–71; Yamauchi, *Persia and the Bible* (Grand Rapids: Baker; 1990), 298–303; P. Miroschedji, "Susa," in *AYBD*, 4:244–45.

Biblical Theology Comments

The first verses of the book of Esther introduce one of the primary themes of the book: kingship. More specifically, the book will address the relationship between the people of God and the powers of this world, a theme frequently addressed in postexilic Jewish literature and the NT. In Esther, we are introduced to the mightiest king in the world at the height of his glory. Anywhere one looked, his wealth and power were evident. Even the Greeks, who hated him more than any man, were impressed with his splendor. Yet in the book of Esther, he is only the second power. His word has authority, but there is another Word that dictates human affairs, speaks through the mouths of counselors, gives favor to Jewish maidens, robs kings of sleep, and inspires terror in the enemies of God's people. In the book of Esther, there is a Power that is hidden from human eye that manipulates events in ways that even the world's greatest monarch cannot resist.

Application and Devotional Implications

The opening verses of Esther may be considered ominous, because it is inevitable that the interests of the kingdoms of this world will come into conflict with those of the kingdom of God. In the book of Daniel, we see that these conflicts can take a variety of forms. In some cases, the assault is direct, as when Nebuchadnezzar ordered the Jewish heroes to worship his golden image (Dan 2), or when the "little horn" of the fourth beast makes war against the holy ones of God (Dan 7). At times, the attack is ideological, as when Nebuchadnezzar lays claim to building Babylon by his own power (Dan 4). And at times, the king is the unwitting dupe of powers that hate God's people, as when Darius was tricked into signing the order forbidding prayer (Dan 6), or as Xerxes will be in the book of Esther. Human governments are not in themselves bad things (see Rom 13:1–7), but their goals are not the same as those of the kingdom of God. Often, they will come into conflict. And, lest we forget, the "ruler of this world" (John 12:31; 14:30; 16:11) holds sway over these earthly powers and can twist them to his own ends. Xerxes, for all his glory, is merely a pawn in a contest that stretches far beyond the boundaries of his kingdom. Do not be misled by the pomp and majesty that will be on display here: the real struggle is occurring behind the scenes, invisible to the human eye.

Selected Bibliography

Briant, P. "Persian Empire." In *AYBD*, 5:236–44.

Cameron, G. G. "The Persian Satrapies and Related Matters." *JNES* 32 (1973): 47–56.

Cook, J. M. "The Rise of the Achaemenids and Establishment of Their Empire." In *The Cambridge History of Iran*, vol. 2, *The Median and Achaemenian*

Periods, ed. L. Gershevitch, 200–291. Cambridge: Cambridge University Press, 1985.

De Miroschedji, P. "Susa." In *AYBD*, 6:242–45.

Fox, M. V. *Character and Ideology in the Book of Esther.* Grand Rapids: Eerdmans, 2001.

Gordis, R. "Studies in the Esther Narrative." *JBL* 95 (1976): 43–58.

Haupt, P. "Critical Notes on Esther." *AJSL* 4 (1907–8): 97–106.

Heltzer, M. "'From India to Ethiopia' and 'from the Hellespont to India' (the Imperial Outlook)." In *Studies in Historical Geography and Biblical Historiography: Presented to Zechariah Kallai*, ed. G. Galil and M. Weinfeld, 42–43. VTSup 81. Leiden: Brill, 2000.

Herzfeld, E. *The Persian Empire: Studies in the Geography and Ethnography of the Ancient Near East.* Wiesbaden: Steiner, 1968.

Olmstead, A. T. A *History of the Persian Empire*. Chicago: University of Chicago Press, 1948.

Radday, Y. "Esther with Humour." In *On Humour and the Comic in the Hebrew Bible*, ed. Y. T. Radday and A. Brenner, 295–313. Sheffield, UK: Almond, 1990.

———. "Humour in Names." In *On Humour and the Comic in the Hebrew Bible,* ed. Y. T. Radday and A. Brenner, 59–97. Sheffield, UK: Almond, 1990.

Shea, W. "Esther and History." *AUSS* 14 (1976): 227–46.

Stronach, D. "Pasargadae." In *The Cambridge History of Iran*, vol. 2, *The Median and Achaemenian Periods*, ed. L. Gershevitch, 838–55. Cambridge: Cambridge University Press, 1985.

Yamauchi, E. *Persia and the Bible*. Grand Rapids: Baker; 1990.

Zadok, R. "Notes on Esther." *ZAW* 98 (1986): 105–10.

The Rise of Esther and Mordecai (1:3–2:23)

Introduction

Here we are told of the rise of our protagonists, Mordecai and Esther. The unit is composed of three main sections. Section 1, 1:3–22, tells the story of Vashti's downfall. This unit is itself composed of three units: 1:3–9 describes the royal banquets; verses 10–12 are concerned with Vashti's insubordination; and 1:13–22 tell of the king's response to the incident.

Though it forms a self-contained unit with buildup, crisis, and resolution, section 1 serves in this narrative to create the scenario described in section 2. In fact, it might even be seen to provide a rationale for the bizarre procedure for choosing the new queen. In chapter 1, Vashti felt herself justified in refusing the king's order. If Vashti had been chosen in the typical manner of Persian queens, we may assume she had an aristocratic background. Perhaps it was her own vaunted bloodline that let her think she could defy the order of the king. In any case, her presumption might have inspired the unorthodox method of selecting her replacement. Rather than choosing a queen from one of the noble families of Persia—women who might have imagined themselves somehow the equals of the king—the contest would draw together women from all over the empire and have them compete to please the king. The new queen was to be taken from obscurity and could not have helped but feel inferior in the presence of the king's majesty. Furthermore, she was chosen based on the criterion that seemed (in light of the recent scandal) to be the most salient: her willingness to satisfy the king's desire.

This unit also provides an ironic parallel to the story of Mordecai and Haman. Vashti refuses to obey the king's command to appear before his guests, and she is deposed from her office. The king then issues a decree with the effect that all women everywhere are to obey their husbands. In chapter 3, Mordecai refuses the king's order to bow before Haman. His insubordination will result in a threat to Mordecai's life, and the king will also issue an order for all the Jews to be killed.

Section 2 tells the story of how Esther became queen. The narrator first turns his attention to the Jews, whose fate will be the unwavering focus of the rest of the story. Like section 1, it is divided into three units. In 2:1–4, the king's advisers propose the contest to replace Queen Vashti. Young virgins shall be gathered from all over the empire to the city of Susa, and the woman who pleases the king will be named the new queen. In 2:5–7, we are introduced to Mordecai and Esther, the Jewish exile and his orphaned cousin. In 2:8–18, there is an account of the preparations and the contest, culminating in Esther's victory.

Section 3, the story of Mordecai's deliverance of the king, almost seems like an excursus. So far, the focus has been on the king's marriage; in this scene, it is on the threat to the king's life. This episode introduces the theme of threat and deliverance that occurs several times in the narrative:

1. The threat against the king's life initiated and resolved (2:19–23)
2. The threat against the Jews is initiated by Haman (3:5–15) and resolved by Mordecai (9:1–17)
3. The threat to Esther's life is initiated and resolved (4:10–5:2)
4. The threat to Mordecai is initiated by Haman (5:14) and resolved (8:1–2)
5. The threat to Haman from Esther—which, of course, ends in his execution (chap. 7)

The threat to the Jews is primary. But Mordecai's deliverance of the king will be revisited later in the narrative, in the ironic episode of chapter 6, and as at least a contributing factor in the execution of Haman (7:9). In this unit of the text, however, the episode is coordinated with the story of Esther's rise to royalty. Both the Jewish heroes have distinguished themselves in service to the king. Esther receives her reward, while Mordecai's satisfaction will have to wait. But the relationships they establish here will later pay dividends to the entire Jewish race.

Outline

- II. The Rise of Esther and Mordecai (1:3–2:23)
  - A. Queen Vashti Deposed (1:3–22)
    - 1. The Royal Banquets (1:3–9)
    - 2. The Queen's Insubordination (1:10–12)
    - 3. The King's Response (1:13–22)
  - B. Esther Chosen as Queen (2:1–18)
    - 1. The Contest Is Proposed (2:1–4)
    - 2. Introducing Mordecai and Esther (2:5–7)
    - 3. Esther Wins the Contest (2:8–18)
  - C. Mordecai Saves the King (2:19–23)

Queen Vashti Deposed (1:3–22)

Translation

3 In the third year of his reign, he held a banquet for all his rulers and servants, the aristocracy of Persia and Media. The nobles and the governors of the provinces were present, **4** while he displayed the glorious wealth of his kingdom, and the magnificent splendor of his greatness for a long time, 180 days. **5** When those days were completed, the king held a seven-day banquet for all the people who were found in the citadel of Susa, from great to least, in the garden court of the king's palace. **6** There were hangings of white and purple linen attached with cords of fine linen and purple cloth to silver rings and marble pillars; there were couches of gold and silver, on a mosaic floor of porphyry, marble, shell marble, and decorative stone.[1] **7** The drinks were served in vessels of gold, each one unique. The royal wine was abundant, according to the king's generosity.[2] **8** The rule regarding the drinking was that there was to be no compulsion,[3] for the king had issued a command to all the stewards of his house[4] that each man could drink as he desired. **9** Even[5] Queen Vashti gave a banquet for the women of King Xerxes' royal palace.

10 On the seventh day, when the king was in a good mood because of the wine, he told Mehuman, Biztha, Harbona, Bigtha, Abagtha, Zethar, and Karkas—the seven eunuchs who served in the presence of King Xerxes— **11** to bring Vashti the queen before the king, with her royal crown, to show the people and the officers her beauty, because she was lovely to behold. **12** But the queen, Vashti, refused to come at the king's order that

---

1. The identification of this stone is unknown. "Jewels" or "precious stones," however, seem unlikely to have been used as a paving material.
2. The phrase used here (literally, "according to the hand of the king") is uncommon, and its meaning is uncertain. In the other contexts in which it appears (1 Kgs 10:13; Neh 2:8; Esth 2:18), the implication seems to be one of generosity.
3. In this translation, we have decided that the phrase אֵין אֹנֵס (*ʾên ʾōnēs*) conveys the contents of the rule (דָּת, *dat*) that governed the drinking. Many translators have separated the two phrases, creating what seems to be a contradiction, that drinking was both "according to the law" and "without constraint."
4. Literally, "every great one of his house." In the LXX, it is οἰκονόμοις "household managers." These are not just servants, but individuals with managerial oversight.
5. The Heb. particle גַּם (*gam*) is typically translated "also," but it has an emphatic sense that is present to greater or lesser degrees. Often, it is understood to have an intensive sense, as in Prov 14:20; 17:26; Joel 3:2. This translation reflects the understanding that this phrase forms the climax of the first unit rather than the beginning of a new paragraph.

the eunuchs had delivered. The king grew very angry, and his wrath burned
in him.

13 Then the king said to the wise men who know the times (for this was
the king's practice before all who knew decree and judgment), **14** who were
near to him[6]—Carshena, Shethar, Admatha, Tarshish, Meres, Marsena,
and Memucan, the seven officials of Persia and Media, who saw the king's
face, and sat first in the kingdom— **15** "According to the law, what is to be
done with Queen Vashti, on account of her not doing according to the
word of King Xerxes that he had sent by his eunuchs?"

16 Memucan said before the king and the officials, "It is not against the
king only that Vashti has done wrong, but against every official and all the
people who are in every province of King Xerxes, **17** because the queen's
deed will get out to all women, causing them to view their husbands with
contempt as they say, 'King Xerxes said to bring Queen Vashti before him,
and she did not come!' **18** This very day the noble women of Persia and
Media, when they hear of the queen's conduct, will revolt[7] against all the
king's officials, and contempt and wrath will abound. **19** If it seems good to
the king, let a royal decree go forth from the king's presence, and let it be
written according to the laws of the Persians and the Medes so it will not
be annulled, that Vashti will no longer be allowed to come before the king,
and let the king give her royal position to another who is better than she is.
20 Then when the king's decree[8] that he will make is heard through all his
kingdom—How vast it is!—all women will give honor to their husbands,
from the greatest to the least."

21 The word seemed good in the view of Xerxes and his officials, so he
did as Memucan said. **22** He sent letters to all the king's provinces, to each
province according to its writing and to each people in its own language, so
that[9] every man would be ruling in his house, and speaking the language of
his people.

Textual Notes

3.a. For לְכָל־שָׂרָיו וַעֲבָדָיו חֵיל the LXX reads τοῖς φίλοις καὶ τοῖς λοιποῖς ἔθνεσιν, "the friends and the rest of the nations." The "princes" of the MT (שָׂרִים)

6. The word קָרֹב (*qārōb*) can imply proximity in time, place, or relationship. In this case, both location (i.e., stationed near) and relationship may be indicated.
7. This translation adapts the emendation suggested by *BHS*, reading תִּמְרֶינָה (*timreynâ*) "they will rebel," for the MT תֹּאמַרְנָה (*tō ʾmarnâ*), "they will say." The verb אָמַר (*ʾāmar*, "say") requires a complement, but there is none in this context.
8. The word here translated "decree" is פִּתְגָם (*pitgām*), a loanword from Persian. The word occurs only twice in the OT, here and in Eccl 8:11.
9. The inf. const. is translated here with a causative force. See *BHRG*, 20.1.3.iv.

could have been interpreted as the "friends" (i.e., close advisers) of the Persian king, but the balance of the phrase cannot be explained on the basis of the Heb. of the MT and must represent a different Heb. *Vorlage**.

4.a. כְּבוֹד, "glory," is absent in the Greek. This word, however, is essential to the parallelism of the verse; see the commentary below.

4.b. יָמִים רַבִּים, "a long time," is absent in the Greek; *BHS* suggests deleting because the phrase seems redundant.

5.a. LXX and AT read αἱ ἡμέραι τοῦ γάμου, "days of the wedding feast." There is, however, no suggestion earlier in the text that the feast was in celebration of the king's wedding. Moore (7) reads τοῦ γάμου as a corruption of τοῦ ποτου, "of the drinking."

5.b. לְמִגָּדוֹל וְעַד־קָטָן, "from great to least," is omitted in the Greek.

6.a. בַּהַט־וָ, "porpyry and," is absent in the Greek.

8.a. For וְהַשְּׁתִיָּה כַדָּת, LXX has ὁ δὲ πότος οὗτος οὐ κατὰ προκείμενον νόμον εγένετο, "But this drinking was not according to the designated law."

9.a. וַשְׁתִּי, "Vashti," in the LXX is Αστιν; in the AT, Ουαστιν; in Origen, Ουασθη.

10.a. The names of the eunuchs vary considerably in the LXX. Some of the names could well reflect free phonetic transliterations of the Heb., but others appear to be different names entirely.

13.a. הָעִתִּים, "the times," *BHS* suggests emending to הַדָּתִים, "the laws." There is no textual support for this suggestion. See further the commentary.

14.a. In the LXX, only three counselors are named.

16.a. *Kethib** מומכן should be emended to מְמוּכָן ("Memucan") as in the *Qere**. Compare vv. 14, 22.

17.a. לְהַבְזוֹת *BHS* suggests this hiphil form (which occurs only here) could be emended to the niphal form לְהִבָּזוֹת.

18.a. תֹּאמַרְנָה, "they will say," has no complement. *BHS*, following several scholars, suggests emending to תַּמְרֶינָה, "they will rebel."

20.a. כִּי רַבָּה הִיא, "How vast it is," is absent in the LXX.

22.a. וּמְדַבֵּר כִּלְשׁוֹן עַמּוֹ, "to each province according to its writing," is absent in the LXX.

Commentary

This section forms a complete unit in itself, while at the same time providing essential background for the events that follow. It is possible that the story may have existed in some form independent of the book of Esther, but as it now exists, the story is intricately woven into the structure of the book. As we will see, the story foreshadows several episodes to come later in the narrative. It also forms an element in the chiastic structure of the book.

As noted above, this unit consists of three sections. In the first, 1:3–9, we read of the royal banquets where the king shows off the treasures of his kingdom to his nobles. In the second, we are told of how the king summoned Queen Vashti, but she refused to appear. The third, 1:13–22, tells of the king's response to the incident. Consulting with his wise men, he is informed that the queen's insubordination could set off an empire-wide women's revolt. The wise men counsel the king to make an example of Vashti by deposing her from her position.

While the story of Vashti is often viewed today as an early example of feminism, this interpretation of the queen's actions is probably inaccurate. Nonetheless, her actions have potential ramifications for all women, just as Mordecai's act of insubordination (3:1–6) will have an effect on all the members of his group, the Jews.

1:3 The episode begins with the temporal phrase, "In the third year of his reign … " The clause is not linked to the preceding clause by the typical *waw*-consec. or *waw*-conjunctive. Often, such a construction would indicate the beginning of a new "paragraph," but in the first few verses of Esther, several such nonconjunctive clauses appear without indicating a new unit. The grammatical construction itself, therefore, is not a definitive guide for interpreting the structure of this passage.

A better guide to the significance of this phrase may be found by comparing it to similar clauses found in several passages in Kings and Chronicles. For example, in 2 Kgs 22:1–3, the first two verses of the chapter introduce King Josiah using the typical regnal formula: "Josiah was eight years old when he became king, and reigned in Jerusalem 31 years. … He did what was right in the eyes of Yahweh." After the introduction, v. 3 reads, "In the eighteenth year of his reign, King Josiah sent Shaphan the scribe … " We find an even closer parallel in 2 Chr 17:1–7. The passage begins with a general introduction to King Jehoshaphat, describing his piety. The first event of his reign comes in v. 7: "In the third year of his reign he sent his princes … " (וּבִשְׁנַת שָׁלוֹשׁ לְמָלְכוֹ שָׁלַח לְשָׂרָיו). Similar phrases appear in 2 Chr 29:1–3 (like Esth 1:3, without a conj.); 2 Chr 34:1–3; Jer 52:1–4. Each narrative begins with an introduction of the king and a general characterization of his reign, then the year formula opens the episode that follows. These parallels suggest that Esth 1:1–2 function as an introduction to the book as a whole, and v. 3 opens the first episode.

The third year of Xerxes' reign would correspond to 483 BC. According to Herodotus (*Hist.* 7.8), that was the year that Xerxes assembled his war council to plan his campaign against the Greeks. Several scholars (e.g., Jobes, 60) have suggested that the feasts described here could have been designed to raise support for the king's impending invasion of Athens. The historical background, however, is of no interest to our author. (It is also worth noting that such a motive was unknown to the Septuagint translator, who characterized the banquet as a wedding feast.) The main concerns here are to introduce the banqueting motif and to set the stage for the removal of Vashti from her royal office.

The Heb. word מִשְׁתֶּה (*mišteh*), "banquet," literally means a "drinking bout." In this case, the word is particularly appropriate, given the emphasis on the consumption of wine. Nonetheless, the party undoubtedly featured a wide variety of foods as well.[10] Such banquets were often used to demonstrate the wealth and power of the king and to elicit the goodwill of the members of the royal court and the nobility. In spite of the lavish descriptions of the banquet hall, the banquets are the real focus of this section, as evidenced by its structure: the entire passage consists of three statements of action, each containing a finite form of the verb עשׂה (*ʿśh*, "make, do"):

> 1:3b—He held a banquet for all his rulers ...
> 1:5b—The king held a banquet ... for all the people ...
> 1:9a—Queen Vashti held a banque t...

For clarity, other verbs in this passage are typically translated like finite forms (v. 3, "while he displayed"; v. 5, "when these days were fulfilled"; v. 7, "they served"), but they are actually inf. forms, indicating "concomitant circumstances." The main action is the giving of the banquets (Bush, 342). In telling of the vast wealth on display, the author is attempting to convey a sense of awe to his audience; but one suspects we are being "set up." The description of luxury and self-indulgence in these verses will make the king's humiliation by Queen Vashti even more biting.

"His rulers" (שָׂרָיו, *śārāyw*) refers not necessarily to princes or members of the aristocracy, but rather to overseers at various levels in the administration. The word used here for "servants" (עֲבָדָיו, *ʿăbādāyw*) can mean "slaves," but in this context, it clearly means "civil servants," government officials of various responsibilities. The rest of this verse and that which follows

10. See M. Heltzer, "A propos des banquets des rois achéménides et du retour d'exil sous Zorobabel," *RB* 86 (1979): 102–6, for the contents of a Babylonian text that describes the types of food offered at such banquets.

are syntactically difficult, and the relationship between the phrases is not certain. The phrase חֵיל פָּרַס וּמָדַי (*ḥêl pāras ûmāday*; literally, "the might of Persia and Media") is not attached to the preceding phrase with a conj., which could mean it begins a new sentence. The most literal translation of the phrase would be, "The army of Persia and Media" (ESV, NRSV, CJB). Many translations, however, have taken a different tack, since it seems unlikely that the entire army would be present at the feast. Moore (1971, 5–6) suggests emending the text to "officers of the army," citing a possible textual corruption in the *Vorlage* of the LXX in support. This approach has been adopted by the NASB, CEV, and NLT.[11] Gerleman (54–55), followed by Clines (276), Bush (346–47), and others, suggests that the noun חֵיל, instead of being translated "army," should here be understood to mean "nobility." The entire phrase, then, would not begin a new sentence, but rather would be in apposition with "His rulers and servants." This reading seems to account better for the syntax of the verse.

In addition, Xerxes' company included the "governors of the provinces" (שָׂרֵי הַמְּדִינוֹת, *śārê hammĕdînôt*). Contrary to the LXX translation, these are not the satraps, but regional officials.

1:4 The intention of the banquet is here revealed: the king desires to display his splendor and glory. Similar expressions are found elsewhere in Scripture, to describe the glory of the king of Israel (Psa 21:5) and King Nebuchadnezzar (Dan 4:36), and especially to describe the glory of Yahweh (1 Chr 29:11; Psa 96:6). The language here, however, is especially effluvious and almost poetic, consisting of two parallel phrases:

> the riches—of the glory—of his kingdom
> the magnificence—of the splendor—of his greatness

As Laniak observes, the first phrase refers to the king's wealth, while the second speaks of beauty.[12] The multiple flatteries, however, along with the descriptions of indulgence to follow, seem designed as a subtle mockery of a monarch whose glory is unrivaled, but whose wisdom will often appear suspect.

The statement that the feast lasted "a full 180 days" has raised many questions for interpreters. The business of governing the Persian Empire

---

11. Moore also observes, however, that Herodotus (*Hist.* 7.40–41) numbers the "core" of Xerxes' army at about fourteen thousand, and Ctesias (as reported by Athenaeus, *Deipnosophistae* 4.146e) writes that fifteen thousand nobles regularly dined at the tables of Persian kings. The idea that the entire army was present, then, is not utterly inconceivable.

12. Laniak, *Shame and Honor in the Book of Esther* (Atlanta: Scholars Press, 1998), 43–44.

could hardly be suspended for six months while the king entertained his nobles. Though such a long span certainly would seem to be an extravagant amount of time for a banquet, it is not unprecedented in Jewish literature. The book of Judith tells of an Assyrian king who threw a four-month feast (1:1), though the text is likely fantasy. One possibility is that the text is not envisioning 180 days of actual feasting, but a festival in which the participants would come and go. It is also possible to read the Heb. text as describing successive events: a feast for the nobles, followed by a six-month display of Xerxes' wealth, and finally a feast for the residents of Susa. A number of scholars (e.g., Jobes, 60) have suggested that the six-month display might be identified with Xerxes' "war council" preceding his invasion of Greece (*Hist.* 7.8). She contends that the display of wealth was designed to inspire confidence in Xerxes' ability to wage war against the Greeks. There is a sense in which the display is reminiscent of 2 Kgs 20:12–19, where Hezekiah showed all the wealth of Jerusalem to envoys from Babylon, apparently in an effort to draw them into an alliance. Clines (276), on the other hand, suggests Xerxes might have been showing off the recently completed palace complex, which had been started by his father, Darius. It should be noted, however, that the text makes no mention of any motive, tactical or otherwise, for the banquet. Rather, the author's purpose for including this detail in his account is to highlight the self-indulgence of the Persian monarch, not to provide a complete historical record of Xerxes' reign.

The description of vast riches found here is not necessarily hyperbole. The wealth of Persia was the envy of the ancient world. Herodotus reports that Darius received more than fourteen thousand talents of gold and silver as annual tribute.[13] According to Strabo, the treasures Alexander the Great gathered from Persia and Babylon totaled 180,000 talents of gold and silver, or more than 10 million pounds.[14] Olmstead reports that when Alexander captured the Persian cities of Susa and Persepolis in 331 BC, he found treasures that were the equivalent of 836 tons of gold.[15] The narrator is being somewhat indulgent in his detailed description, but he is not exaggerating.

1:5 After the feast for the nobles, Xerxes held a feast for the general populace, a true show of his magnanimity. This feast was given for all the residents of the citadel, the fortified area that served as the center for government. It included people "from great to small," that is, those of social standing and influence, and those considered insignificant (see Deut 1:17). This banquet

13. *Hist.* 3.95.

14. Strabo, *Geog.* 15.3.9.

15. Olmstead, *History of the Persian Empire* (Chicago: University of Chicago Press, 1948), 518, 520.

took place in the garden court. In ANE palaces, such courtyards were typically lavish.[16] They were often furnished with exotic plants and animals for the amusement of their visitors. The Persian gardens, however, were especially renowned in the ancient world for their refinement.[17] In Pasagardae, Cyrus the Great constructed a garden furnished with stone channels, basins, and colonnaded pavilions, situated so the king and his guests could see it from his audience hall. Susa's garden was probably similar. The Persians called these gardens *paridaida*, "beyond the wall" (i.e., an enclosed area). From this word the Greeks derived their word *paradeisos*, which came into English as "paradise."[18]

Xerxes' garden was attached to the king's palace (Heb. בִּיתַן). The word בִּיתַן is an Akkadian loanword that came into Heb. through Aramaic. In Mesopotamian documents, it refers to a covered pavilion or "summer house."[19] The garden where the banquet occurred would have been connected to the pavilion, but would have been uncovered, like a huge patio.

1:6 This verse exhibits a very unusual syntax, consisting mostly of a series of nouns and noun phrases with little coordination. The formation is certainly deliberate; it has the effect of producing what sounds like a series of exclamations, as if the author is trying to capture the wonder of the spectacle of Xerxes' garden. Some of the vocabulary is obscure as well, perhaps to enhance the exotic effect of the description (Dommershausen, 146).

The hangings were designed to provide shade on the diners, but even these utilitarian features were opulently dyed in royal blue. They were attached by silver rings to marble pillars, an architectural aspect borrowed from the Medians. Herodotus (*Hist.* 1.135) notes that the Persians were apt to adopt the customs of foreigners. The gold and silver couches were apparently solid metal rather than merely gold or silver plated. Herodotus (*Hist.* 9.82) reports that the Greeks plundered solid gold couches from the Persian camp after the Persians withdrew from Athens. The mosaic pavement consisted of colored pebbles laid in the ground in decorative patterns.[20] The stones included porphyry or malachite, a red stone; marble, which varied in color from white, to yellow, to blue-black; and possibly shell marble.

16. See A. L. Oppenheim, "On Royal Gardens in Mesopotamia," *JNES* 24 (1965): 328–33; K. L. Gleason, "Gardens in Preclassical Times," *OEANE* 2:382–85.

17. See the descriptions in Xenophon, *Anabasis* 1.4.10; 2.4.14; *Oeconomicus* 4:20–24.

18. For more on Persian gardens, see Yamauchi, *Persia and the Bible* (Grand Rapids: Baker, 1997), 332–34; P. Briant, *From Cyrus to Alexander: A History of the Persian Empire* (Winona Lake, IN: Eisenbrauns, 2002), 201–2; 442–44.

19. Oppenheim, "Royal Gardens," 330–31.

20. C. Kondoleon and L. A. Roussin, "Mosaics," *OEANE* 4.50–55.

The Heb. word used here (דַּר, *dar*) is often translated "mother of pearl," but as Haupt observes, this stone would have been too fragile to serve as flooring material.[21] Following his suggestion, I have adopted the reading "shell marble"— translucent stone containing fossilized pieces of shells.

There are several other words in this verse of uncertain meaning, including some that occur only in the book of Esther. The word שֵׁשׁ (*šēš*) is apparently an Egyptian loanword, and seems to designate a "true marble," as opposed to Italian or English gypsum-based marble (Clines, 277). Likewise, בַּהַט (*bahaṭ*) could be from the Egyptian word meaning "porphyry."[22] The word סֹחָרֶת (*sōḥeret*) presents a unique challenge. It has been translated in a variety of ways, most often something like "jewels" or "costly stones" (e.g., JB, NIV, NASB). The word may be related to the Heb. root סחר (*sḥr*) "surround," or to its derivative סֹחֵרָה (*sōḥērâ*), "shield." One possibility might be fossilized coral, which can display a circular shield-like pattern.

1:7 Given the variety of foods that could be served at a royal banquet, it is somewhat surprising that drinks are the focus of the narrative. One reason behind this emphasis is the role that drunkenness will play a little later. Another is that alcohol played an important role in Persian society. Clines (277) cites several sources demonstrating that the Persians were famous in the ancient world for their drinking. Classical sources also report that the Persians took pride in having large collections of drinking vessels.[23] In Esther, the vessels—the generic term probably means both serving vessels and cups—were made of gold, each one unique, a work of individual artistry. The wine was provided by the king himself: in Achaemenid Persia, grape wine was primarily a drink for the wealthy. The masses typically could enjoy only "strong drink," which included beer and date wines. By emphasizing the abundance of wine, the narrator is again highlighting the opulence of Xerxes' banquet.

1:8 This verse is somewhat difficult and has been handled in a variety of ways by translators. It begins with the assertion that "Drinking was according to the law." The word translated "law" (דָּת, *dat*) occurs frequently in Esther, but elsewhere only in Ezra 8:36. It can mean "law" in the sense of an established code of conduct (as apparently in Esth 1:15, 19), but more often in the sense of a decree (as in Esth 2:8; 3:14, 15), or even, apparently, as a custom (Esth 2:12). Several scholars (e.g., Moore 1971, 7–8) interpret this law to be an existing custom, especially the law mentioned by Herodotus (*Hist.* 1.33) that all the king's guests were required to drink whenever the king himself

21. P. Haupt, "Critical Notes on Esther," *AJSL* 24 (1907–1908): 105–6.
22. Haupt, "Critical Notes," 106.
23. Xenophon, *Cyropaedia* 8.8, 18; Strabo, *Geog.* 15.3.19.

drank. But that interpretation would seem to contradict the next phrase, which says that the drinking was "without compulsion." We understand the "law" to be an order issued to the servants concerning how the guests were to drink (as in the NJB, NLT, and others).

It seems odd that a decree would have to be issued permitting guests to drink as they desired, rather than being compelled to drink. Josephus (*Ant.* 11.188) explains that it was the custom of the Persians to force the guests to drink nonstop, with the servants bringing wine continually to the table. This explanation, however, sounds somewhat contrived. It may be more likely that the stewards were being ordered not to stop anyone from drinking, but to allow everyone to drink as much as they pleased. The Heb. word אֹנֵס (*ʾōnēs*, here translated "compulsion," as in the NASB) occurs only once in the Bible, but is frequently attested in postbiblical Heb. and Aramaic. It has the sense of forcing someone to act in some manner. The implications here are dual: that no one was forced to drink, but also that no one was restrained from drinking.[24] The stewards were charged to bring the guests all the wine they desired. Once again, the implication is that the king was an exceedingly generous man. There also may well be some irony here, as Clines (278) observes: a law is even required to allow people to do as they please.

1:9 The name "Vashti" is unattested in any ancient sources. As noted in the introduction, Herodotus identifies Xerxes' queen as Amestris, daughter of his general Otanes. Moore 1971 (8), Clines (278), and others suggest that "Vashti" may have been a title applicable to any Persian queen, derived from Avestan words meaning "the best" or "the beloved." The name "Vashti," then, could actually refer to Amestris or another queen and should not be used as a criterion for determining the historicity of the story.[25]

There may also be a poetic purpose to the use of the name: verse 8 begins with the phrase וְהַשְּׁתִיָּה, *wᵉhaššᵉtiyya;* "And the drinking ... " The name Vashti וַשְׁתִּי (*waštî*) is a homonym for this word. The similarity of sound is not only pleasing to the ear, but also somewhat significant, since the fate of Vashti is precipitated by the unbridled drinking at Xerxes' banquet.[26]

There was no custom in ancient Persia requiring men and women to dine separately. Typically, wives accompanied their husbands to dinner

---

24. Haupt, "Critical Notes," 106.

25. On other historical problems regarding the identity of Xerxes' queen, see the introduction, "The External Evidence."

26. B. Jones, "Two Misconceptions about the Book of Esther," *CBQ* 39 (1977): 174.

banquets (*Hist.* 5.18).[27] There is no reason to doubt, however, that segregated events could occur. According to one of the Persepolis Fortification Tablets, Artystone, one of the wives of Darius I, had 1,940 liters of wine delivered to one of her houses for some occasion, perhaps indicating that she was hosting a banquet similar to that given by Vashti.[28] Greek historian Plutarch claims that Persian monarchs would dine with their wives unless the party became "wild." Then the wives would be sent away to shield them from the debauchery that would follow, and the concubines and dancing girls would take their place.[29] But while this scenario might account for Vashti's absence, it does not explain the purpose of her own banquet. In the book of Esther, Vashti's banquet serves two functions. First, it emphasizes yet again the royal generosity, in that even the women are being treated liked privileged guests. Second, it sets up the scenario where the king and queen are in separate locations, so that the king may issue his fateful summons to the queen.

1:10 The phrase "good mood" is literally "good of heart." The heart, according to ancient Israelite anthropology, was the seat of reason and will. To be "good of heart" often meant to be cheerful or pleased (e.g., Deut 28:47; Judg 18:20; Prov 15:15), but that the king's mirth is inspired by wine implies that the king was intoxicated. The wording, however, seems euphemistic, since the author has avoided the common Heb. word for "drunk" (שִׁכֹּר). The author may be trying to appear artificially deferential, "sparing" the king's dignity while at the same time implying his inebriation.

It is worth noting that Herodotus (*Hist.* 1.133) and Strabo (*Geog.* 15.3.20) report that the Persians decided the most important matters when they were drunk (but this report is probably a slanderous rumor rather than historical truth). Herodotus adds that their decisions would be confirmed when they had sobered up. On this basis, Jobes (67–68) argues that the king was engaged in planning with his war council and that the drinking was part of the deliberations. The text, however, knows nothing of any planning taking place; it states only that the king was showing off all his glorious possessions and wished to include the queen in the display. But regardless of Persian custom, the Jewish author of this text would probably not have approved of the king becoming drunk. Proverbs 31:4 states explicitly that kings should not drink wine or strong drink, and in the Bible,

27. Cf. J. Grossman, *Esther: The Outer Narrative and the Hidden Reading* (Winona Lake, IN: Eisenbrauns, 2011), 45, who contends that the women and men were separated at Persian banquets so the men could participate in uninhibited immorality.
28. The order for wine is recorded in R. T. Hallock, *Persepolis Fortification Tablets* (Chicago: University of Chicago Press, 1969), no. 1795.
29. *Moralia* 140B 16.

drunkenness is frequently associated with foolishness and senseless behavior (e.g., 1 Kgs 20:16; Job 12:25; Psa 107:25; Jer 51:7).[30] We can be fairly sure that the author considered the king's command, issued while he was drunk, to be an example of such foolishness.

The sending of seven eunuchs to fetch Queen Vashti is surely excessive. One person could have delivered the message, as when Hatach acts as the go-between for Mordecai and Esther in chapter 4. There could not have been any expectation that force would be needed, nor would it be used; but some resistance may have been anticipated. The dispatch of seven officers gives the messengers the appearance of an official envoy. It seems to anticipate that the queen would not view the request favorably. Perhaps the expectation was that the envoy would intimidate the queen into obedience.

Eunuchs, or castrated male servants, were typically used to oversee the royal harems. But since eunuchs were deemed more trustworthy than other men (because they could not start their own family lines or dynasties), their duties often extended beyond just caring for the royal wives and concubines and included administrative and even military tasks.[31] These eunuchs may have been present at the king's dinner, since they were officials of the realm, but they were likely among those charged with care of the royal harem. The task of fetching the queen from a banquet of noblewomen could not be entrusted to any men but eunuchs.

The names of the eunuchs all appear to be Persian, and some have been associated with various Persian roots, but their meaning is dubious.[32] None of these individuals are known from other classical literature. As in vv. 1–2, the use of names here seems excessive, since these eunuchs play a very minor role in the story. Fox suggests the list of names gives the story "historical verisimilitude";[33] Clines (279) and Bush (349) contend that the list of names contributes to an atmosphere of pompous solemnity. It is also possible that they were intended to sound funny.[34] Some of the names would

---

30. For a further consideration of drunkenness in biblical narrative, see C. E. Walsh, "Under the Influence: Trust and Risk in Biblical Family Drinking," *JSOT* 90 (2000): 13–29.

31. For an extensive discussion of eunuchs' responsibilities, see Briant, *Cyrus to Alexander*, 268–77.

32. See H. S. Gehman, "Notes on the Persian Words in Esther," *JBL* 43 (1924): 321–28; J. Duchesne-Guillemin, "Les noms des eunuques d'Assuérus," *Le Muséon* 66 (1953): 105–8; A. R. Millard, "The Persian Names in Esther and the Reliability of the Hebrew Text," *JBL* 96 (1977): 481–88.

33. Fox, *Character and Ideology*, 19–20.

34. On the use of funny names in the Bible, see Y. Radday, "Humour in Names," in *On Humour and Comic in the Hebrew Bible*, ed. Y. Radday and A. Brenner (Sheffield: Sheffield Academic Press, 1990), 59–98.

certainly have had humorous connotations to Heb. speakers: Mehuman sounds like the word הָמוֹן (*hāmôn*), "be in an uproar"; Biztha could have been derived from the Heb. root בָּזָה (*bāzâ*), "despise"; Harbona sounds like the word חָרֵב (*ḥārēb*), "be desolate" (perhaps an appropriate name for a eunuch); and other names might have created similar associations for the Jewish audience. The authors of the Targumim demonstrate their awareness of this aspect of the text, making puns off the names of the eunuchs.[35]

1:11 The eunuchs were ordered to bring Queen Vashti to be displayed before the drunken revelers. The king was displaying his wealth, and the queen was essentially being treated as if she were one more of his possessions. The reference to the royal crown is ironic: while the king may have thought of it as a beautiful piece of adornment, to Vashti and the readers it would symbolize her station. It has been suggested that the royal crown was actually more like a turban or braided cloth.[36] At Persepolis, however, a bust of a Persian noblewoman—perhaps Queen Atossa (mother of Xerxes)—has been found, wearing a traditional metal conical crown rather than a turban.[37] Women depicted on an Achaemenid Persian cylinder seal wear similar headgear.[38] On the other hand, no depictions of women in turbans have been discovered.

There is no reason to assume that Xerxes' command meant that Vashti was to appear wearing *only* her crown. This common assumption derives from rabbinic lore. According to the rabbinic commentaries, Queen Vashti, the granddaughter of King Nebuchadnezzar of Babylon (a pure fiction), was commanded to appear naked as a poetic judgment for her forcing Jewish girls to work on the Sabbath day in the nude. She was allowed to wear the crown, however, because Nebuchadnezzar had clothed Daniel in royal purple (*b. Meg.* 12b; *Tg. Esth. I*, 1:11). The scenario is designed to demonize Vashti and add to the enjoyment of the audience; there is no support for such a scenario in the text.

---

35. See *Tg. Esth I* 1:10, which provides an interpretive gloss for the names based on their sounds.

36. See A. Salvesen, "Keter–Something to Do with a Camel?" *JSS* 44 (1999): 35–46. Salvesen's understanding of the כתר (*ktr*, "crown") as a cloth diadem depends on rabbinic texts and Hellenistic texts, composed in a time when the royal crown had been replaced by the Graeco-Roman diadem. More significant, it seems, is the likely relationship between the word כתר and כתרת (*ktrt*, "capital"), the head of a column. In 1 Kgs 7:16 and Jer 52:22, these capitals are described as being made of cast brass.

37. The bust is on display in the Archaeological Museum of Tehran.

38. The seal is in the Louvre; see http://commons.wikimedia.org/wiki/File:Cylinder_seal_harem_Louvre_AO22359.jpg.

1:12 While the king's motives in summoning Vashti are transparent, the reasons behind the queen's refusal are not so obvious. Josephus stated that Vashti was acting in obedience to Persian law, which forbade a wife from being seen by strangers (*Ant.* 11.6). There is, however, no evidence for such a law in ancient Persia and much evidence that contraindicates it.[39] Indeed, numerous ancient sources depict Persian wives appearing in public. Jewish tradition holds that Vashti refused to come because she was suffering from a physical affliction: according to some, God had struck her with leprosy, while others contend that God had punished her by sending the angel Gabriel to attach a tail to her (*b. Meg.* 12b). Again, these explanations are designed primarily to heap more humiliation on the insubordinate queen. In early Christian interpretation, Vashti was a type of the Jews who would refuse the summons of Jesus Christ: she "undoubtedly signifies the sentence our Savior passes against the arrogance of the Jewish people."[40] But this interpretation seems even more forced than the rabbinic approaches and cannot be reconciled with the context of the passage: one can hardly imagine Jesus calling the Gentiles to Himself in order to show them off to His drunken friends. In some modern interpretations, Vashti refused to answer the summons because she was standing up for the rights of women. She was, sadly, "an unsuccessful heroine in an early struggle for women's dignity."[41] This explanation, too, seems to misrepresent the situation. There is no evidence that Vashti was campaigning for the rights of all women, though there could be implications in her actions for other women who might feel put upon by their husbands.

Perhaps the most plausible explanation for the refusal is that suggested by Bickerman.[42] Bickerman notes that in Persian feasts, once the drinking became serious, the queen would leave. The concubines and courtesans would then be summoned to entertain the guests (cf. Dan 5:2, 10, which indicate that the queen was not present at Belshazzar's feast, though his concubines were). Concubines were the lowest level of royal wives, and these women were specially trained to entertain the king and his guests with music and dance. Vashti probably felt that being put on display before

39. Josephus may have been familiar with ancient Greek sources that implied the queen was cloistered away from the public (Plutarch, *Artaxerxes* 5.6; *Themistocles* 26.5), but see M. Brosius, *Women in Ancient Persia, 539–331 B.C.* (Oxford: Clarendon, 1996), 83–93, for evidence to the contrary.

40. Rabanus Maurus, *Explanation on the Book of Esther 2*. Translation Conti and Pilara, 377.

41. J. Telushkin, *Biblical Literacy: The Most Important People, Events, and Ideas of the Hebrew Bible* (New York: William Morrow, 1997), 367.

42. E. Bickerman, *Four Strange Books of the Bible: Jonah, Daniel, Kohelet, Esther* (New York: Schocken Books, 1967), 185–86.

the king's guests reduced her to the status of a concubine. That she was told to wear the royal crown added insult to injury: the royal crown was a sign of her status, while the king's summons seemed to deny that status. Vashti's refusal was not a blow for women's rights, but for the dignity of the royal office. It might be significant that the word order in Vashti's title is reversed here: when summoned, she is called "Vashti, the queen"; when she refuses, she is called "the queen, Vashti."[43]

Some scholars have also speculated on why the king became so angry. Jobes (68), appealing once again to the theory that this banquet was to garner support for his coming invasion of Greece, contends that Xerxes was afraid the queen's refusal would undermine the allies' confidence in Xerxes as a leader. It seems unnecessary, however, to resort to a hypothetical historical setting to explain the king's response. He believes himself to be the greatest power on the planet (and humanly speaking, he was). His will was publicly flouted by someone he regarded as his inferior. It should not be surprising that he would become angry. We would see the same reaction from a modern male chauvinist if his wife humiliated him in front of his friends. No logical explanation for the anger is needed.

1:13 The phrase "Thus was the manner of the king" indicates that the king's practice was to seek the advice of his counselors in matters of law. This notion is borne out in the narrative, where the king never makes a decision without consulting his advisers. Here, the advisers are called "those who know the times." The phrase was understood by rabbinic interpreters to imply astrological knowledge (Paton, 151–52). The presence of astrologers in the king's court would not be unusual, as Herodotus attests to their presence there (*Hist.* 1.107; 7.19). The answer the king seeks, however, has nothing to do with astrology, but with law. The phrase "decree and judgment" (דָּת וָדִין, *dāt wādîn*) probably refers to statutes enacted by the king or other officials and legal decisions rendered by judges. Thus some scholars (e.g., Moore 1971, 9) have argued that the manuscripts are in error, and the word "times" (עִתִּים, *ʿittîm*) should be corrected to "statutes" (דָּתִים, *datîm*). The suggestion is not impossible, since the *daleth* in many ancient manuscripts could easily be mistaken for an *ʿayin*. In fact, the reconstruction has been adopted by the NJB, NAV, and NRSV. But though scribal error is possible here, there is no textual support for this emendation. Furthermore, changing the word "times" to "decrees" would make the two clauses unnecessarily redundant. Instead, it seems that the phrase "those who knew

43. See B. Wyler, "Esther: The Incomplete Emancipation of a Queen," in *A Feminist Companion to Esther, Judith, and Susanna,* ed. A. Brenner (Sheffield: Sheffield Academic Press, 1995), 117.

the times" should be allowed to stand as it is. The same phrase occurs in 1 Chr 12:33, where it may mean people of general expertise (though it might also imply some kind of supernatural insight). In this case, "those who knew decree and judgment" could be viewed as a subset of "those who knew the times" (cf. Gerleman, 64–65).

The phrase דָּת וָדִין ("statute and judgment") has both an alliterative and rhythmic quality to it, similar to the English "this and that." The phrase is not only designed to be phonetically pleasing, however, since it embodies the entire corpus of legal tradition, implying the vast knowledge of these counselors.

1:14 Many scholars have seen this council of seven princes to be the continuation of a group established in the time of Darius. According to Herodotus, *Hist.* book 3, when Cambyses was assassinated, seven noble Persians formed a pack to overthrow the man who had usurped his throne and appoint a new king in his place. After they exposed the tyrant, Darius was chosen king, and the others served as his advisers. These advisers were granted access to the king at all times, except when he was with a woman. This act, however, only established a group of six advisers, since Darius himself had been one of the conspirators. The number was apparently expanded, since a group of seven advisers is mentioned in Ezra 7:14, and again by Xenophon, *Anabasis* 1.6.4. They were "near to him," perhaps physically, in that they were granted access to the king; but they were also near him socially in that they were of the most noble families, as close to the king's peers as anyone in Persia.

As with the eunuchs, names are given for all seven advisers, even though only one actually responds to the king. Several of these names have been given reasonable Persian derivations.[44] Their significance, however, does not reside in their philological accuracy, since most Jewish readers would have had little interest in such matters. Rather, the listing of the names was certainly designed to enhance the readers' pleasure, perhaps with the air of the exotic, or perhaps with their humorous sounds.[45]

1:15 The verse begins, "According to the law … " The placement of this phrase at the beginning of the verse is clearly designed for emphasis. As Clines (281) observes, it is somewhat ironic that the response from the

44. See H. S. Gehman, "Notes on the Persian Words in Esther," *JBL* 43 (1924): 321–28; J. Duchesne-Guillemin, "Les noms des eunuques d'Assuérus," *Le Muséon* 66 (1953): 105–8; A. R. Millard, "The Persian Names in Esther and the Reliability of the Hebrew Text," *JBL* 96 (1977): 481–88.

45. See Radday, "Humor in Names," 70–71. It has also been observed by Guillemin, "Les noms des eunuques d'Assuérus," that if the names are read in reverse order, this list sounds quite similar to the list of the eunuchs' names.

wise men has nothing to do with the law: they give no legal precedent for the advice they offer. Rather, their response is based on a fearful anticipation of the possible social repercussions of Vashti's actions.

1:16–18 In addition to failing to address the question of legal precedent, Memucan diverts the issue from the matter of royal authority in a couple of ways. First, he seems to identify the core issue not as a matter of a subject who disobeys an order from the king, but of a wife disobeying her husband. Furthermore, he diverts the question from the personal insult to the king to one of the general good of the empire. The officials will suffer first, because their wives were probably dining with the queen when the order was given, and they actually witnessed Vashti's insubordination. But the matter will certainly not stop there, because word of the deed will spread throughout the entire empire. If women hear that the queen could refuse the king with impunity, then they, too, will believe that they can disobey their husbands. Contempt will abound—from the women toward their husbands. Wrath, too, will multiply— the response of the men toward their insubordinate wives.

Memucan's anxiety seems excessive. It may be another example of hyperbole in this narrative, a device that allows the narrator to subtly mock his characters. At the very least, as Levenson (51) says, Memucan's distress represents "an extreme lack of proportion." He elevates the king's marital problem into a national crisis. Perhaps it is his own insecurity that comes into play: according to rabbinic tradition (*Tg. Esth II*), Memucan had been having problems with a disobedient wife at home and saw this episode as an opportunity to bring her in line! But this problem is not Memucan's alone, since his words are pleasing to all the king's counselors (v. 21). Berlin (17) suggests that there is some subtle sexual anxiety at work and that there was fear that Vashti's refusal to come before the king could set off a "sexual strike" among the women, similar to the one featured in the Greek play *Lysistrata* (cf. Jobes, 80). While there is little direct evidence in the text for this reading, it may be significant that Vashti's replacement will be chosen based on her ability to please the king in his bedchamber (Esth 2:13–14).

There also seems to be something wrong with Memucan's reasoning. Why should other women disrespect *their* husbands, just because the queen had disrespected *her* husband? It seems that respect, in this context, is not earned by fulfilling important duties or by any meritorious conduct. Rather, it is assigned to the husband simply by virtue of his position. In other words, men do not have to gain their wives' respect; it is to be theirs by virtue of their gender. One can see how Vashti's conduct could be dangerous to such a situation. A sufficiently influential person such as Queen Vashti could certainly influence a societal norm. It is troubling, however, that Memucan assumed that all women would follow Vashti's lead. Were the men of the Persian Empire so undeserving of respect that if it were not required of the wives, the wives would not give it? It is ironic that Memucan believed that a sense of respect could be imposed from above by a decree.

In this verse, the word used for "husband" is בַּעַל (*ba ʿal*) rather than the far more common Heb. אִישׁ (*ʾîš*). Though both words could be used in Heb. to mean "husband" (e.g., Exod 21:22), the word *ba ʿal* implies lordship and mastery (it is also used for a slave owner). The use of the term here might subtly reveal the narrator's opinion of Persian marriage.

1:19 The recommendation begins with the appeal, "If it seems good in the eyes of the king." This is the first time this phrase will occur in the book of Esther, but it is hardly the last. It will occur five more times (1:21; 2:4, 9; 8:5, 8), and the similar "If it seems good to the king" will appear six times (3:9; 5:4, 8; 7:3; 8:5; 9:13). The king's pleasure is a major theme in the book of Esther. There may well be some irony in this motif, since he rarely seems to be able to decide what is pleasing to him without assistance from his counselors.

The idea that the laws of the Persians and Medes cannot be annulled will later prove important to the story, but it is historically difficult to fathom. A similar idea is found in Dan 6:8, 12, but it is not clearly attested in any classical literature outside the OT. Indeed, the kings of Persia are frequently depicted changing their decrees (e.g., as when King Darius changed a decree he had given that the entire family of Intaphrenes was to be executed, instead sparing his brother-in-law and eldest son; *Hist.* 3.118–19). It also would seem to be very poor governmental policy to bind the king by a decision made while perhaps angry or ill-informed. Some have suggested that it would have been considered shameful for the king to admit to having made an error, and so once the laws were written down they would be unchangeable. Often, it is noted (e.g., Huey, 802) that the advisers would want to make sure that once Vashti was deposed, she could not return to power to exact revenge on them—further evidence of their insecurity and fear of a woman. Berlin (18) takes a different approach, noting that the word עָבַר (*ʿābar*) often means "transgress," as in Esth 3:3. In her understanding, the idea is that the law, once enacted, could not be broken—even by the king himself, if he should wish to do so. Though grammatically her approach is different, the effect would be the same: the king is being urged to make a law that will not be changed.

Ironically, the decree bars Vashti from coming before the king, which was the very thing that she had refused to do. Contrary to rabbinic tradition, which holds that Vashti was executed, the text requires only that she was deposed from office and "put away," like David's wife Michal, daughter of Saul (2 Sam 6:20–23). Levenson (52) notes that the wording of the advice, "Let the king give her royal position to one who is better than she," is reminiscent of Samuel's words to Saul (1 Sam 15:28): "Yahweh this day has torn kingship over Israel away from you and given it to someone better than you." Given the other allusions to Saul that will arise later in the text, the possibility that this similarity is intentional seems likely. In Saul's case, "better" meant "more obedient to Yahweh"; in Vashti's case, her replacement will be more obedient to the king. It is also possible, as Clines (282) observes, that "better" can imply "more beautiful." We should not rule out the possibility that the narrator had both implications in mind.

1:20 Here, there is yet another of the ironies of the story. Memucan counsels that the words of the king's decree should be spread throughout the empire. Indeed, to assure that all people can read the decree, it will be published in every language of the empire (v. 22). But this action will result in precisely the effect they feared in the first place: the queen's action will become widely known to the women of the empire. Memucan, however, is trying to do some damage control. He expects women to be so intimidated when they hear of Vashti's fate that they will fear being disobedient to their husbands. Instead, they will give "honor" (יְקָר, *yĕqār*). This word, which occurs only seventeen times in the OT, typically means "riches." In its seven occurrences in Esther, however, it always has the sense of "honor," a recognition of value or importance. The word does not necessarily imply submission or obedience (see esp. Esth 6:6, 7, 9, where the king wishes to "honor" Mordecai), although that idea may be implied in this context.

The decree accords well with the understanding of women's status in ancient Persian society. Persia was patriarchal, and women in general were expected to honor and obey their husbands.[46] But this fact does not mean that women were always held in lower esteem than men. The Persepolis Fortification Tablets reveal that women often worked as managers or directors of various businesses and sometimes supervised men.[47] Pay levels seem to have been the same for men and women. Thus, while men might have been expected to rule in their homes, women were not generally oppressed in the workplace.

The parenthetical statement "How vast it is!" has little syntactical connection to the rest of the verse. The above translation incorporates Fox's observation that the particle כִּי (*kî*) can have an emphatic force (as in

46. On the general status of aristocratic women in ancient Persia, see M. Brosius, *Women in Ancient Persia*, 83–182.

47. Ibid., 180–82; R. T. Hallock, *Persepolis Fortification Tablets, passim.*

Gen 18:20).[48] The insertion of this exclamation reveals the narrator's opinion of these counselors: they are fawning sycophants, desperate to stay in the king's good graces.

1:21–22 The king sends forth a decree to all his empire that the men are to do the very thing he was incapable of doing: rule their own houses. We might well suspect that this decree would be about as effective as the king's order for Vashti to appear before his banquet.

There are a several difficulties in this verse. The first is the statement that the dispatch was sent out in the languages of all the provinces. Given the ethnic diversity of the empire, this feat would have been very difficult, as Paton (160–61) observes. It would also have been completely unnecessary. Since the time of Nebuchadnezzar the Great (634–562 BC), the Aramaic language had been used for administration and trade throughout the entire Near East. It was widely understood, even by common folk.[49] The Achaemenid rulers continued to use the *lingua franca* of the Babylonian Empire in the western half of their empire, typically publishing laws and decrees in Aramaic.[50] The account of the decree being issued in every language is probably conscious hyperbole, designed to parody the anxiety and officiousness of an empire that would go to such vast extremes to keep the women of the kingdom in their proper place.

The second difficulty is with the content of the decree. Memucan's suggestion was merely that Queen Vashti be deposed and that her punishment be published throughout the empire. The decree, as typically understood, seems to have gone well beyond that recommendation, requiring that all men rule in their own households. It seems to say, "The message of Vashti's demotion was not obvious enough. Let us make it explicit!" One possibility is that Memucan was anticipating this pronouncement when he referred to "the king's decree that he will make" (v. 20), rather than the decree to depose Vashti. In that case, the decree that all men rule their homes would be reinforced by the example of the king, who demonstrated how a man should rule. A wife who did not obey her husband would similarly be put away.

48. Fox, *Character and Ideology*, 275.

49. The extensive use of Aramaic in this period is apparent in the Elephantine Papyri from Egypt. These texts, written by Jewish soldiers living in Egypt during the Persian era, are mostly composed in Aramaic. See B. Porten, *Archives from Elephantine: The Life of an Ancient Jewish Military Colony* (Berkeley: University of California Press, 1968).

50. See J. C. Greenfield, "Aramaic in the Achaemenian Empire," in *The Cambridge History of Iran*, ed. I. Gershevitch (Cambridge: Cambridge University Press, 1985), 2:698–713.

In the above translation, I have adopted Berlin's (20) suggestion that the king did *not* issue a decree that men were to rule in their houses. Rather, Berlin reads the inf. const. לִהְיוֹת (*lihĕyôt*, "be") to have a causative force in this context: the king's decree was issued *so that* men would be rulers in their houses. The decree, then, was precisely the report about Vashti's removal, and its expected outcome would be that women would be so intimidated by the queen's fate that they would be cowed into obeying their husbands.

This reading of the inf. const. also helps clarify the last difficulty in the verse. The final line of the decree reads, "and speaking the language of his people." Ostensibly, this phrase has little to do with the rest of the decree and has been the subject of much speculation. It is omitted in the LXX, and several modern translations have followed this precedent (e.g., JB, NAB, NRSV). (It is easy to understand, however, why someone translating the Bible into Greek would have been uncomfortable with what appears to be a command requiring the Jews to speak their ancestral tongue only.) One popular suggestion is to emend the text to read "and speak whatever suited him" (וּמְדַבֵּר כָּל־שָׁוֶה עִמּוֹ, *ûmĕdabbēr kol-šāwēh ʿimmô*), adopted by Meinhold (22), Moore (11–12), and others. The idea here would be that the men could say whatever they wanted, if they were truly ruling their households. Another suggestion, adopted by Bardtke (284) and the NEB, requires even more emendation, reading the phrase, "and keep all his wives in subjection" (וּמַדְבִּיר כָּל־נָשָׁיו עִמּוֹ, *ûmdbîr kol-nāšāyw ʿimmô*). Besides both suggestions lacking any textual support, neither suggestion is proper Heb. (see Bush, 352, for discussion). The rabbinic understanding of the phrase was that it was addressing the problem of mixed marriages: according to Neh 13:23–28, in the households where Jewish men had married foreign women, the children did not know how to speak Heb. Nehemiah considered this cultural drift to be a grave problem. A command requiring the men to speak their native language would have been appropriate in the context of Diaspora Judaism, but it seems out of place at this point in this narrative, considering that the issue of ancestral tongue has not surfaced at all.

In this translation, I have adopted Gerleman's (70) suggestion that the phrase refers to the actual reading of the decree in the households. Grammatically, this proposal makes good sense. The inf. const. לִהְיוֹת apparently governs the two ptcs., "ruling" (שֹׂרֵר, *šōrēd*) and "speaking" (מְדַבֵּר), so that both are to be understood as part of the purpose clause. The decree would be issued in all the languages of the empire, *so that* all men would be rulers in their houses, and *so that* they would be speaking in the language of their people. In that way, the people—especially the women—would be able to understand what had happened, and take it to heart (see also Berlin, 21). There was no second decree for people to speak their own languages; it would be the natural outcome of the decree having been issued in so many different tongues.

Biblical Theology Comments

1:4–8 There is sometimes a sense of ambiguity regarding wealth in the Heb. Bible. On the one hand, wealth is usually depicted as a sign of divine favor.[51] Figures like Abraham (Gen 13:2), Isaac (Gen 26:12–14), and Job (Job 1:10) became wealthy because of God's abundant provision. King Solomon, too, was rewarded with riches because he pleased Yahweh (1 Kgs 3:13; 10:23). Physical prosperity is one of the blessings promised to Israel when the people are true to God's covenant (Deut 28:1–13). The book of Psalms promises that "wealth and riches" will be in the house of the man who fears Yahweh (Psa 112:1, 3).

But there is another side to the coin: wealth brings many temptations, and the rich are often subject to unflattering portrayals. In Nathan's parable in 1 Sam 12:1–4, it is a rich man who steals and kills his poor neighbor's lamb. In the Prophets, the rich are often equated with the wicked, typically because they have obtained their wealth through oppression of the poor (Isa 10:1–4; Jer 5:26–29; Amos 4:1). Those who have become rich are also tempted to trust in their wealth instead of trusting in God (Prov 11:28; Jer 9:23–24; 48:7; 49:4). But perhaps the sternest warning in the Heb. Bible comes from Psa 49, which could have been talking about King Xerxes when it tells us not to be impressed by people who grow rich, for "a rich man who lacks understanding is like the beasts that perish" (49:20).

Xerxes' vast wealth was no doubt impressive to his guests, but there is an edge of sarcasm in this description of his indulgences. He is a man who controls immense wealth and power, and yet he will prove unable to control the will of his own wife. The scene foreshadows one that will come later in the book of Esther, when Haman will brag about his own great wealth and influence and yet admit that it is all unfulfilling, because Mordecai refuses to bow to his will (5:11–13). The great wealth of Xerxes and Haman proves meaningless, just as stated in Eccl 5:10: "He who loves money will not be satisfied with money, nor he who loves wealth with its income. This is also vanity."

1:10–12 These three verses raise two significant ethical questions: first, was the king justified in summoning Vashti to appear before his banquet? Second, was Vashti justified to refuse? The first question concerns the limits of the king's authority. The frequent references in this chapter to the king's presence, his favor, and other uses of the root מלך (*mlk*, "rule") demonstrate

51. See D. B. Knox, "Wealth," *NBD* 1233.

that the person of the king and the general notion of dominion are of deep concern to our author. We may leave aside for now the question of whether it would be proper for a man to invite other men to leer at his wife. As appalling as that behavior seems to us, it was not really at issue in our narrative. The more important issue here has to do with the question of honor and dishonor. The king was attempting to use his authority in a way that would dishonor the queen. The queen's response resulted in some dishonor for the king, but it might well have been deserved.

The lesson of this episode is quite similar in a way to that of Dan 5. There, King Belshazzar was hosting a banquet and decided to impress his guests by bringing forth his greatest prize, the vessels taken from the temple in Jerusalem, so they could be used for drinking. God responded by publicly humiliating the king and pronouncing judgment on Babylon. In Esth 1, King Xerxes tries to demonstrate his authority over the queen by summoning her to appear at his banquet. The king is publicly humiliated when she refuses to appear. In both cases, the kings failed to show the proper respect to the "treasure" they sought to display. Also in both cases, the main issue can be boiled down to pride: the king becomes so impressed with himself that he believes there is nothing he cannot do. In Dan 5, God demonstrates to Belshazzar that he is not as sovereign as he might believe; in Esth 1, the queen shows Xerxes that he is not sovereign over her will. Both stories serve as reminders that human power, even the greatest human power on earth, has limitations. This point will become more explicit in later chapters of Esther, as circumstances arise that will be beyond the control of a human monarch—orchestrated by a hidden, sovereign power.

We might also note the great contrast between King Xerxes and his exercise of power and the way the King of Kings exercises power. For Xerxes, kingship meant that his word was to be obeyed without question. People—even the queen—could be used for his entertainment. How very different was his attitude from that of Jesus Christ,

> Who, being in very nature God, did not consider equality with God something to be used to his own advantage; rather, he made himself nothing by taking the very nature of a servant, being made in human likeness. And being found in appearance as a man, he humbled himself by becoming obedient to death—even death on a cross! (Phil 2:6–8 NIV)

King Xerxes is not the model for Christian conduct. Our model is Jesus Christ, who embodied the spirit of humility and who sought to serve, rather than be served (Mark 10:45).[52] Authority as modeled by Jesus and taught by Paul calls us to be servants of those who are below us. As Sittser observes, Paul's ethical teaching "requires that those who occupy dominant positions in social order be subject to their subordinates; they are to order their lives *under* the very people *over* whom they exercise authority."[53]

The other issue raised by this episode is the appropriateness of Vashti's response. As noted above, Jews and Gentiles alike in antiquity regarded Vashti to be a malefactor. How dare she refuse the command of her husband! At this point of the narrative, however, the question is not so much about a wife disobeying her husband, but of a subject disobeying the king. Are we required to accept the dictates of those in power, even if they violate our sense of right and wrong? While the NT requires us to submit to human institutions and those in power (Rom 13:1–7), it also requires us to give our ultimate allegiance to God (Matt 21:22 par.; Acts 5:29). Thus, submission to authority is not absolute. Vashti, however, was not disobeying the king because of her religious conviction, but only because of her honor.

Vashti may not have been attempting to strike a blow for women's rights, human dignity, or godly modesty, but her refusal to appear before the banquet was both courageous and just. The king's efforts to force her to obey in a matter that violated her dignity constituted an abuse of power. The ethics involved can be compared to those of a very different biblical story: that of Judah and Tamar (Gen 38). When Judah refused to fulfill his obligations to provide Tamar with a husband who could give her a son, she deceived him in order to procure a son for herself. Her actions were not good in any traditional sense, but Judah proclaimed, "She is more righteous than I"—more "in the right" than her father-in-law, who failed to act in a manner appropriate for their relationship. Cremer's observation regarding "righteousness" has been widely accepted by scholars: people may be deemed righteous when they meet the claims that others have on them by virtue of their relationship.[54] Vashti may have been prideful in her refusal to appear before Xerxes' guests, but she was more "in the right" than the king, who violated the normal expectations for how a queen was to be treated.

---

52. On Christ's submission to the Father as a model for submission in the church, see S. M. Park, *Submission within the Godhead and the Church in the Epistle to the Philippians: An Exegetical and Theological Examination of the Concept of Submission in Philippians 2 and 3* (Edinburgh: T&T Clark, 2007).

53. See G. L. Sittser, *Love One Another: Become the Church Jesus Longs For* (Downers Grove, IL: InterVarsity, 2008), 42.

54. H. Cremer, *Die paulinische Rechtfertigungslehre im Zusammenhange ihrer geschichtlichen Voraussetzungen, von Hermann Cremer* (Gütersloh: Bertelsmann, 1899), 34–38. See also E. Achtemeier, "Righteousness in the Old Testament," *IDB*, 4:80–85; J. D. G. Dunn, *Romans 1–8* (Dallas: Word Books, 1988), 40–42.

1:15–22 The main issue raised by Memucan's counsel is one of perennial debate: what is the proper relationship between husband and wife? Apparently, Vashti's refusal to obey Xerxes was primarily due to her position as queen. Memucan, however, persuaded the king that the principal issue at stake was the relationship between men and their wives. Vashti did not respect her husband, or else she would have obeyed him. Other women, if they were to see Vashti get away with such disrespect, would believe for some reason that they should disrespect their own husbands. Memucan's counsel was designed not only to correct Vashti's behavior, but to head off a potential wife-rebellion throughout the empire.

We cannot properly engage the thorny issues of male-female relationships in the Bible in the context of this study.[55] We may note, however, that Memucan's idea of male headship is consistent with the Persian cultural context. It is also consistent with the description of male-female relations resulting from the curse in Gen 3:16 (Day, 42). The NT also affirms the idea that wives are to respect their husbands (e.g., Eph 5:33), though never apart from the command for husbands to treasure and care for their wives (Eph 5:25–33). A few passages even imply that wives should be obedient to their husbands (e.g., Titus 2:5). But as Marshall observes, the NT authors never order husbands to take authority over their wives, as Xerxes implies. The husband's authority is assumed as a reality of life in the ancient Graeco-Roman (and Persian) cultural context.[56] Thus, we might best understand the commands for wives to submit to their husbands in the light of several NT injunctions to submit to the emperor and other established authorities in society (Rom 13:1–7; Heb 13:7; 1 Pet 2:13–14), since patriarchy was a fact of life in biblical times. Yet, just as there are limits to the authority of kings and governors, there must also be limits to the authority of the husband over his wife. The apostles' statement that they must obey God rather than men (Acts 5:29) applies to women just as to men: our ultimate obedience must belong to God and the principles of His kingdom. If Christians had

---

55. Among the many studies available on this topic, see (from a traditionalist/complementarian perspective) W. Grudem, ed., *Biblical Foundations for Manhood and Womanhood* (Wheaton, IL: Crossway, 2002); J. Piper and W. Grudem, eds., *Recovering Biblical Manhood and Womanhood: A Response to Evangelical Feminism* (Wheaton, IL: Crossway, 2006); and (from an egalitarian perspective) C. S. Keener, *Paul, Women, and Wives: Marriage and Women's Ministry in the Letters of Paul* (Peabody, MA: Hendrickson, 1992); R. W. Pierce and R. M. Groothuis, eds., *Discovering Biblical Equality: Complementarity without Hierarchy* (Downers Grove, IL: InterVarsity, 2004); G. Bilezikian, *Beyond Sex Roles: What the Bible Says about a Woman's Place in Church and Family*, 3rd ed. (Grand Rapids: Baker, 2006).

56. See I. H. Marshall, "Mutual Love and Submission in Marriage: Colossians 3:18–19 and Ephesians 5:21–33," in *Discovering Biblical Equality*, 187.

merely accepted the dictates of the existing social order, we would never have abandoned the practice of slavery.

Selected Bibliography

Bickerman, E. *Four Strange Books of the Bible: Jonah, Daniel, Koheleth, Esther.* New York: Schocken Books, 1967.

Briant, P. *From Cyrus to Alexander: A History of the Persian Empire.* Winona Lake, IN: Eisenbrauns, 2002.

Brosius, M. *Women in Ancient Persia, 539–331 B.C.* Oxford Classical Monographs. Oxford: Clarendon, 1996.

Duchesne-Guillemin, J. "Les noms des eunuques d'Assuérus." *Le Muséon* 66 (1953): 105–8.

Fox, M. V. *Character and Ideology in the Book of Esther.* 2nd ed. Grand Rapids: Eerdmans, 1991.

Gehman, H. S. "Notes on the Persian Words in Esther." *JBL* 43 (1924): 321–28.

Greenfield, J. C. "Aramaic in the Achaemenian Empire." In *The Cambridge History of Iran*, ed. I. Gershevitch, 2:698–713. Cambridge: Cambridge University Press, 1985.

Grossman, J. *Esther: The Outer Narrative and the Hidden Reading.* Winona Lake, IN: Eisenbrauns, 2011.

Hallock, R. T. *Persepolis Fortification Tablets.* Chicago: University of Chicago Press, 1969.

Haupt, P. "Critical Notes on Esther." *AJSL* 24 (1907–1908): 97–186.

Heltzer, M. "A Propos des Banquets des Rois Achéménides et du Retour D'Exil sous Zorobabel." *RB* 86 (1979): 102–6.

Herzfeld, E. *The Persian Empire: Studies in Geography and Ethnography of the Ancient Near East.* Weisbaden: Steiner, 1968.

Hubbard, R. L. "Vashti, Amestris, and Esther 1, 9." *ZAW* 119 (2007): 259–71.

Jones, B. W. "Two Misconceptions about the Book of Esther." *CBQ* 39 (1977): 171–81.

Laniak, T. S. *Shame and Honor in the Book of Esther.* Atlanta: Scholars Press, 1998.

Marshall, I. H. "Mutual Love and Submission in Marriage: Colossians 3:18–19 and Ephesians 5:21–33." In *Discovering Biblical Equality: Complementarity Without Hierarchy*, ed. R. W. Pierce and R. M. Groothuis, 186–204. Downers Grove, IL: InterVarsity, 2005.

Millard, A. R. "The Persian Names in Esther and the Reliability of the Hebrew Text." *JBL* 96 (1977): 481–88.

Olmstead, A. T. *History of the Persian Empire.* Chicago: University of Chicago Press, 1959.

Oppenheim, A. L. "On Royal Gardens in Mesopotamia." *JNES* 24 (1965): 328–33.

Porten, B. *Archives from Elephantine: The Life of an Ancient Jewish Military Colony.* Berkeley: University of California Press, 1968.

Radday, Y. "Esther with Humour." In *On Humour and the Comic in the Hebrew Bible*, ed. Y. T. Radday and A. Brenner, 295–313. Sheffield: Sheffield Academic, 1990.

———. "Humour in Names." In *On Humour and the Comic in the Hebrew Bible*, ed. Y. T. Radday and A. Brenner, 59–97. Sheffield: Almond, 1990.

Wyler, B. "Esther: The Incomplete Emancipation of a Queen." In *A Feminist Companion to Esther, Judith, and Susanna*, ed. A. Brenner, 111–35. Sheffield: Sheffield Academic Press, 1995.

Yamauchi, E. *Persia and the Bible*. Grand Rapids: Baker, 1997.

Esther Chosen as Queen (2:1–18)

Translation

1 After these things, when King Xerxes' anger had subsided, he remembered Vashti and what she had done, and what had been decreed against her. 2 The servants[57] of the king who ministered to him said, "Let a search be made[58] for the king for young women, maidens,[59] good-looking ones. 3 And may the king appoint overseers in every province of his kingdom, and let each of those[60] good-looking young maidens be gathered to Susa the Citadel, to the House of Women,[61] to the care of Hegai the king's eunuch, keeper of the women, and given their cosmetic treatments. 4 Then the

57. The word translated "servants" here is נַעַר (*naʿar*), the basic meaning of which is "youth," or even "child" (Gen 43:8; Exod 2:6; Judg 13:5, 7; 1 Sam 4:21). It is often used, however, of a servant, irrespective of age (Gen 37:2; 1 Sam 9:5; 2 Sam 16:1), like the Greek παῖς (*pais*) or the French *garçon*.

58. The Heb. 3 m. pl. verb form, when used without an antecedent, has the force of a pass. formation.

59. Often, the word בְּתוּלָה (*bĕtûlâ*) is translated "virgin." The basic meaning of the word, however, is simply a girl who is old enough to be married. See G. J. Wenham, "*Bᵉtûlâ:* A Girl of Marriageable Age," *VT* 22 (1972): 326–48.

60. The phrase refers to the women mentioned in the previous verse. Some translations (e.g., NASB) are ambiguous and give the impression that every beautiful, unmarried woman in the empire was to be taken to Susa! See Bush, 361, for the grammatical explanation.

61. Typically, this phrase is translated "harem." The word "harem," however, implies wives who are sequestered. There is no evidence that wives in Achaemenid Persia were sequestered in the way typically associated with harems. I have translated it literally.

young woman who is best in the opinion of the king[62] will rule in place of
Vashti." This word seemed good in the opinion of the king,[63] and he did so.
5 There was a Jewish man[64] in Susa the Citadel, and his name was
Mordecai, son of Yair, son of Shimei, son of Kish, a Benjaminite, **6** who was
taken into exile from Jerusalem, with the exile that was taken into exile with
Jeconiah the king of Judah, whom Nebuchadnezzar the king of Babylon ex-
iled. **7** He was raising Hadassah—that is, Esther—the daughter of his uncle,
because she had neither a father nor a mother. The young lady was fair of
form and good-looking. At the death of her father and mother, Mordecai
had taken her for his daughter.

8 When the word of the king and his decree were heard, and when
he was gathering many young women into Susa the Citadel, to the care of
Hegai, Esther also was taken to the house of the king, to the care of Hegai,
the keeper of women. **9** The young woman was pleasing in his view, and
she gained[65] kindness[66] before him. He hastened to give her cosmetic treat-
ments and her food ration[67] to her, and to assign seven choice maidens from
the king's palace to her, and moved her and her maidens to the best place
in the house of women. **10** Esther had not made known her people or kin-
dred, because Mordecai had commanded her that she was not to make it
known. **11** Every day, Mordecai walked about in front of the court of the
house of women to learn about Esther's well-being, and what was happen-
ing to her. **12** When the time approached for each maiden to come to King
Xerxes, at the end of twelve months being under the prescribed regimen[68]
for women—since this was how the period of their cosmetic treatments
were fulfilled: six months with oil of myrrh and six months with spices and

---

62. Lit., "in the eyes of the king." This figure of speech would seem to imply in English that the king would judge the women on their appearance. It is clear, however, from the following verse, where the same idiom is used, that "eyes" in this context means more broadly "view" or "opinion." See C. Shultz, עַיִן I, *TWOT*.

63. Lit., "This word seemed good in the eyes of the king." "Opinion" is meant here as well, since one cannot see a word.

64. Lit., "a man, a Judahite." The term "Judahite" as it is used here is typically rendered in English as "Jewish."

65. Lit., "she lifted up kindness."

66. Heb. חֶסֶד (*ḥesed*), typically translated "lovingkindness," "mercy," etc. In many modern translations (ESV, NIV, NKJV), this word is translated "favor," which has English connotations that are somewhat different from the Heb. word. See the commentary below for further discussion.

67. Lit., "portion."

68. Heb. דָּת (*dāt*), typically rendered "decree" or "practice."

cosmetics for women— **13** then in this manner[69] the maiden came before the king: whatever she said would be given to her to take with her from the dwelling of women to the dwelling of the king.[70] **14** In the evening, she would enter, and in the morning she would return again[71] to the dwelling of women, to the care of Shaashgaz, the king's eunuch, overseer of the concubines. She did not come again to the king unless he was pleased with her and she was summoned by name. **15** When the time arrived for Esther—daughter of Abihail, the uncle of Mordecai, who had adopted her as a daughter—to go in to the king, she did not ask for anything except what Hegai, the king's eunuch who was in charge of the women, said. And Esther was gaining favor in the eyes of all who saw her. **16** Then Esther was taken to King Xerxes, to his royal dwelling,[72] in the tenth month (that is, the month of Tebeth), in the seventh year of his reign. **17** The king loved Esther more than any of the women, and she found favor and kindness[73] before him more than any of the virgins. He placed the royal crown on her head, and made her queen in place of Vashti. **18** Then the king threw a great banquet for all his nobles and servants—Esther's banquet. He made a holiday[74] for the provinces and gave gifts according to the king's generosity.[75]

Textual Notes

1.a. For זָכַר אֶת־וַשְׁתִּי, "he remembered Vashti," the LXX reads, "he no longer remembered Vashti."

3.a. The name of the king's eunuch, here spelled הֵגֶא (*Hēge*), is spelled הֵגַי (*Hēgay*) in vv. 8, 15.

6.a. Jeconiah is an alternate form of the name Jehoiachin.

---

69. Lit., "in this." It is unclear what "this" refers to. I have understood it to refer to the clause that follows, as in the NIV and NASB. See further Bush, 365.
70. This sentence is difficult to render in English. In v. 12, there is a complex temporal clause, employing a series of inf. const. constructions. The description of the beauty treatments is a parenthetical expansion on the twelve-month regimen. The main thought is resumed in v. 13.
71. The word שֵׁנִי (*šēnî*) is interpreted here as an adv. modifying "return," rather than an adj. modifying "house." Either reading is somewhat problematic. See below for discussion.
72. Lit., "the house of his kingship."
73. חֶסֶד, as in v. 9.
74. Lit., "he gave rest."
75. Lit., "according to the king's hand," as in 1:7.

7.a. The name Hadassah is omitted from the ancient versions, with the exception of the Vulgate.

7.b. For "daughter of his uncle," LXX reads, "the daughter of his uncle Aminadab." The same name is given for Esther's father in the LXX in 2:15 and 9:29 instead of the Abihail of the MT. According to Josephus (*Ant.* 11.195), the OL, and the Vg., Mordecai was Esther's uncle. The weight of tradition, including the LXX, AT, and rabbinic tradition, favors the MT reading.

7.c. For the last clause, "Mordecai had taken her for a daughter," the LXX reads ἐπαίδευσεν αὐτὴν ἑαυτῷ εἰς γυναῖκα, "He had raised her as a wife for himself," i.e., intending to marry her. A similar tradition is found in the Talmud, which holds that Esther was simultaneously wife of both Mordecai and Xerxes.

8.a. In the LXX, the eunuch is called Gai, rather than Hegai. In the AT, he is called Bougaios.

10.a. 10–13 are absent in the AT.

12.a. The phrase "being under the prescribed regimen for women" (כְּדָת הַנָּשִׁים הֱיוֹת לָהּ) is absent in the LXX, apparently regarded as a redundancy. The LXX is a fairly free translation of the Heb., and this deletion and the others that follow likely represent a simplified rendering of the original Heb., rather than an alternate textual tradition.

12.b. For "twelve-month period," the Syr. reads, "twelve-day period." Apparently, this reading represents an attempt to make the time period sound more reasonable.

14.a. "He was pleased with her" (חָפֵץ בָּהּ) is absent in the LXX.

15.a. 15–16 are absent in the AT.

15.b. The phrase "who had adopted her as a daughter" (אֲשֶׁר לָקַח־לוֹ לְבַת) is absent in the LXX.

16.a. The phrase "to his royal palace" (אֶל־בֵּית מַלְכוּתוֹ) is absent in the LXX.

16.b. For "in the tenth month (that is, the month of Tebeth)" (בַּחֹדֶשׁ הָעֲשִׂירִי הוּא־חֹדֶשׁ טֵבֵת) the LXX reads, "in the twelfth month, which is the month of Adar" (τῷ δωδεκάτῳ μηνί, ὅς ἐστιν Αδαρ).

17.a. "In place of Vashti" (תַּחַת וַשְׁתִּי) is absent in the LXX.

18.a. The phrase "according to the king's generosity" (כְּיַד הַמֶּלֶךְ) is absent in the LXX.

Commentary

In this section of the book of Esther, the story takes a turn in a familiar direction. In the first chapter, there was no mention of Israel or its place in salvation history. The effect was somewhat disconcerting, since the vast majority of the OT focuses on God's relationship with His people. Here, we first meet our Jewish protagonists, Mordecai and Esther. The real focus of the story will soon become apparent: it is not the intrigues of the Persian court that are primary, but the fortunes of Israel.

The unit falls into three sections. In the first, the servants of the king propose that he should replace Queen Vashti with someone who will be more tractable. The servants propose that beautiful young virgins from all over the kingdom be gathered to Susa to compete for the position of queen. Each girl will spend one night with the king, and the one who pleases him the most will become queen in place of Vashti. As Fox bluntly states, it is not so much a beauty contest as a "sex contest."[76] This method of selecting a queen is unorthodox, to say the least: typically, a queen would be chosen only from an aristocratic family, in order to create or reaffirm political alliances. Xerxes' own mother, Atossa, was daughter of none other than Cyrus the Great (*Hist.* 3.88). But under the circumstances, this method might have been considered appropriate. Vashti had lost her position because she had not shown proper submission to the king. Her replacement would not be apt to do likewise.

In the second section, we meet the heroes Mordecai and Esther. Mordecai, the elder and Esther's adoptive father, is introduced first. He is a Jew of some standing, apparently descended from the family of King Saul. His cousin, first introduced as Hadassah, is a figure of tragedy. Being an orphan, she is utterly dependent on the goodwill of others. But when taken in by Mordecai, she becomes the epitome of the perfect daughter: beautiful, shapely, and extremely obedient. She will win the favor of all who see her.

The third and largest section has a pleasant literary quality about it. In this section, we are told in detail about the gathering of the virgins and their preparations for the night with the king. The focus is on Esther and the special favors she received from the chief eunuch, as well as the king. The narrator describes the preparations of the virgins in remarkable detail, including their twelve months of treatments with perfumes and cosmetics. But as for the actual night when the maiden was taken to the king, he tells

---

76. M. V. Fox, *Character and Ideology in the Book of Esther*, 2nd ed. (Grand Rapids: Eerdmans, 2001), 28.

us nothing. We are left to guess at what it was that Esther did that the king found so pleasing.

As a whole, the unit is self-contained and characterized by a good deal of symmetry (Bush, 359–60). It is partially demarcated by an inclusion* near the beginning in 2:4, "Let her be made queen in place of Vashti," and near the end in v. 17, "And she was made queen in place of Vashti." In between, there are numerous repeated phrases and words that create a sense of cohesiveness.

2:1 The opening line of the episode, "After these things," is identified by Berlin (22) as an "archaizing phrase." It is frequently found in historical texts to introduce a new scene. Some time has passed since Vashti's demotion, but the text does not say how long. It seems unlikely that it would have been a protracted period, since a kingdom would not go long without a queen. It had only been long enough for the king's anger to "subside."[77] It is possible that his cooling-off period consisted of several years: the fateful banquet where Vashti was deposed took place in the third year of Xerxes' reign (1:3), whereas Esther was crowned queen in the seventh year (2:16). Since the cosmetic treatments took a whole year, Esther would have been taken in to the "house of women" in the sixth year. However, we cannot say how long it took to gather the candidates.

Typically, to "remember" someone in the Bible is a good thing, meaning that someone (usually God) has taken notice of them and will act on their behalf: e.g., God remembered Noah (Gen 8:1) and delivered him from the flood; He remembered Rachel (Gen 30:22) and opened her womb. In this case, however, it is difficult to interpret the phrase in this manner. Xerxes has already demoted Vashti, and he will not be restoring her to the queenship. Rather, he will now move on to find a new wife. The LXX attempts to resolve the problem by inserting a negative, "He *no longer* remembered Vashti, what he said and how he condemned her." It makes little sense, however, that Xerxes would have such a complete lapse of memory. Josephus (*Ant.* 11.194) seems to understand the text to mean that the king was pining for his lost queen, an interpretation followed by a number of medieval commentators (Paton, 164). It was his lovesickness that motivated his servants to suggest finding a replacement through the contest, reminding him that "There are plenty of fish in the sea," and he could have his pick.

---

77. T. S. Laniak, *Shame and Honor in the Book of Esther* (Atlanta: Scholars Press, 1998), 204, sees a connection between the imagery here and that in the story of the flood (Gen 8:1), which speaks of the flood waters "subsiding" and God remembering Noah.

The phrase "what had been decreed concerning her" likewise reflects the king's mindset. The use of the pass. construction implies that the king does not take responsibility for the queen's fate. The rabbinic commentators recognized this implication as well: according to the Targums, when the king had sobered up and realized what had been decreed, he ordered the wise men who had advised him to be executed.

The phrase נִגְזַר עַל (*nigzar ʿal*, "decreed concerning") occurs only here in the Heb. Bible. The typical biblical expression would be נִצְוָה עַל (*niṣwâ ʿal*). The expression is, however, common in MH, perhaps attesting to the lateness of Esther's Heb.[78]

2:2 In his typical fashion, King Xerxes does not formulate a response on his own; he receives advice from his attendants. It is interesting that in this verse, Xerxes is advised by his servants (נְעָרִים, *nĕʿārîm*), rather than his wise men (חֲכָמִים, *ḥăkāmîm*).[79] This is the only place in the book where servants give advice (they answer some brief questions in 6:3–5, but do not advise), and their advice is wholly unsolicited. The word נַעַר (*naʿar*), while it may mean a servant of any age, primarily means a youth or a young man. The fem. form of this word is used in the same verse to designate the "young women" who will be gathered into the king's harem. There may be an implication here that the "young men" will better understand the king's needs than would the more senior advisers or eunuchs.

As noted earlier, this method of procuring a queen is unprecedented in the ancient world. Typically, the queen was of noble rank, chosen for family or political connections. While she might be comparatively attractive, given the fact that she would have access to the best clothes, cosmetics, and hairstylists, beauty was not a qualification for queenship. Persian society was fiercely hierarchical, and people rarely crossed class lines in marriage. Among the later Achaemenid rulers, the purity of the royal line was so protected that there were even marriages of brothers and sisters, and even fathers with daughters.[80] The procedure described here sounds more like the way one would choose a concubine, as when King David's servants

78. See further R. Bergey, "The Book of Esther: Its Place in the Linguistic Milieu of Post-exilic Biblical Hebrew: A Study in Late Biblical Hebrew" (diss., Dropsie College, 1983), 109–10.

79. The Targums conclude that the wise men had been put to death because of their recommendation that Vashti be put away, and that is why they are not mentioned here or later in the book.

80. M. Brosius, *Women in Ancient Persia, 539–331 B.C.* (Oxford: Clarendon, 1996), 64–68.

conducted a search in Israel to find a young woman to share his bed and keep him warm (1 Kgs 1:2–3).[81]

The word translated "maiden" (בְּתוּלָה, *bětûlâ*) in this verse is typically translated "virgin" (e.g., NIV, NLT, NASB, ESV, CJB). The word, however, does not necessarily mean one who has never had sexual intercourse, but only a young woman of marriageable age.[82] Nonetheless, in the ANE, it would have been unlikely that the king would have taken married or sexually active women as wives or concubines. While there were cases where a king might take another man's wife, such cases were usually politically motivated (as when David took Michal, daughter of the former king Saul, from her current husband in order to solidify his association with the royal house; 2 Sam 3:13–15), or they were regarded as examples of tyranny (as with David and Bathsheba; 2 Sam 11). It is unlikely that any married women were taken from their husbands to be brought into Xerxes' "house of women."

Nor is there any reason to assume that they would have to force women to participate in this event. In general, marriage in the ancient world was not so much a romantic affair as a business arrangement. A man needed a wife to bear his children and take care of the home; a woman needed a husband to provide for her and to give her a child who would care her for when she was a widow.[83] "Love" in these relationships was more a recognition of value than an emotional bond.[84] Most women probably did not look to their husbands as a source of emotional support, so Baldwin's (67–68) lament that the women of the harem were "virtually widows" is probably a misplaced concern. Families might well arrange marriages for their children without the children ever having met each other. Almost all fathers, especially of less-noble families, would probably have been thrilled to provide their daughters with such a comfortable and secure life as that which Xerxes was offering. Overseers were not necessary to enforce compliance, but more likely to manage the vast numbers of candidates who would be vying for the title of "Miss Persia."

---

81. The Talmud (*b. Meg.* 12b) contrasts the two accounts. The rabbis claimed that men brought their daughters gladly to share the bed of the aged King David, so no overseers were necessary; but in the case of Xerxes, men hid their daughters from him.

82. G. J. Wenham, "*Betûlâ:* A Girl of Marriageable Age," *VT* 22 (1972): 326–48.

83. See further L. Perdue et al., eds., *Families in Ancient Israel*, The Family, Religion, and Culture (Louisville, KY: Westminster John Knox, 1997), 182–85.

84. There were, of course, exceptions to this rule: lovers might be attracted to one another by sexual desire, like the Shulammite and the shepherd of the Song of Solomon, or David and Bathsheba.

2:3 The candidates for queen were to be taken from "every province in his kingdom," so all the different ethnic groups in the empire were represented in this group. While it would not have been unusual for the king's harem to include women of various nationalities, it would have been exceptional for the queen to be a non-Persian.[85] Even if we discount Herodotus' claim (*Hist.* 3.84) that the queen was only taken from one of the seven noble Persian families, there is some evidence that Persian policy typically required the queen to be native born.[86] The method used by the king in this narrative to secure his new queen virtually assured that she would be an anonymous person, fully dependent on the king's good graces.

The women will be triply secured for the king's pleasure: They will be brought into the citadel, locked up in the "house of women," and placed under the watchful eye of the eunuch, a man who would have no interest in them. It is to be the king's own private playground: the world's most beautiful women, for him and him alone! The "house of women" mentioned here was probably a special quarters of the palace complex reserved for the king's wives and concubines.[87] The original excavators of Susa believed they had located these quarters in the northwestern corner of the complex, but many modern scholars believe the identification is dubious at best, and that the location of these quarters is still unknown.[88]

The word נָתוֹן (*nātôn*), "given," is an inf. abs. form, here acting as a finite verb. According to Waltke and O'Connor, this construction typically continues the sense of the preceding finite verb.[89] It is more common in late BH than earlier forms of the language, occurring nine times in the book of Esther.

The word translated "cosmetic treatments" comes from a root meaning "scrape" or "rub." The nature of these treatments will be described in more detail later in the narrative.

2:4 The king will select the young woman "who is best in his opinion" (literally, "his eyes"). The phrase may mean "best looking," although the text was more explicit in saying the women would be "good of appearance" when

---

85. On the Persian tradition and its exceptions, see Brosius, *Women in Ancient Persia*, 32–33.
86. There were documented exceptions to the tradition, including Artaxerxes I and Darius II, both of whom had Babylonian queens. See further Brosius, *Women in Ancient Persia*, 32–33.
87. The difference between these two classes of wives will be discussed in the commentary on 2:14 below.
88. The "women's quarters" were identified by M. Dieulafoy, *Revue des Etudes Juives* (1888): 255–56; but see, e.g., Moore 1971, 18.
89. *IBHS*, 582 (§35.2.2b).

referring specifically to their looks. It is obvious the contest will involve more than merely the looks of the young women, given the procedure that shall follow. The king, thrilled by the plan, sets it in motion immediately. The terse phrase, "And he did it," conveys something of the enthusiasm the servants had elicited from the king.

2:5 The transition from the preceding scene to this one seems rather abrupt in our English translations, but there are connections between the scenes that give some unity to the passage. We have just heard how the young maidens from around the kingdom would be carried off to Susa, separated from homes and families to be placed in the service of the king. In these verses, we meet the Jews who are themselves exiles. Indeed, one can hardly miss the point, since the narrator uses a form of the word גָּלָה (*gālâ*), "exile," four times in v. 6. The historical displacement they have suffered as a people may soon be mirrored in personal displacement, as Esther faces a further deportment into the king's bevy of beauties (Levenson, 54–56).

Yet another obvious connection is the fact that we have been told in 2:2–3 that the king's officers will be on the lookout for maidens who are טוֹבַת מַרְאֶה (*ṭôbat mar'eh*), "good of appearance." In 2:7, Esther is described with precisely the same phrase: טוֹבַת מַרְאֶה. It takes no prophetic giftedness to see where this is going.

Mordecai is introduced as a "Judahite" man. Technically, this term means "a man of Judah." The predicate, "a man, a Judahite," is placed here at the front of the sentence, before the verb. The purpose of reversing the typical Heb. word order is probably emphatic. Later in this verse, however, he is identified as a Benjaminite, a man of the tribe of Benjamin. How could he be both a Judahite and a Benjaminite?

The term "Judahite" rarely occurs in the OT with the restricted sense of someone from the tribe of Judah (see, e.g., 2 Kgs 16:6). Typically, the designation for someone from the tribe is "son of Judah" (e.g., Num 1:26; Josh 7:14). After the destruction of the northern kingdom Israel, in 722 BC, the tribe of Judah (the largest of the remaining tribes) loaned its name to the entire southern kingdom. As a designation for the ethnic group, the word "Judahite" occurs only once in the book of Kings (2 Kgs 25:25); eight times in Nehemiah; but forty-six times in Esther, both as a general designation of the Jewish people and a frequent appellation of Mordecai. (It also occurs eleven times in Jeremiah and once in Zechariah.) The frequent reference to "the Jews" (as it is typically translated) reinforces the impression that the book of Esther has a primarily nationalistic focus, or, as Anderson put it, "made nationalism a religion."[90]

---

90. B. Anderson, "The Place of the Book of Esther in the Christian Bible," *JR* 30 (January 1950): 40.

The name Mordecai almost certainly derives from Marduk, who was a storm god and chief god of the Babylonian pantheon. The name was common in that era and widely attested in ancient Babylonian records (Bush, 361–62). It was even borne by one of the Jewish leaders who returned from Babylon to rebuild the temple in 520 BC (Ezra 2:2), and has recently been found in Greek form on a Jewish funerary inscription in Alexandria, Egypt.[91] The primary question here is not the existence or meaning of the name, but the significance of the fact that it was borne by a Jew.

Historically, there is little doubt that it was fairly common for Jews to bear foreign names, even those of obviously pagan origin. In papyri documents discovered in Elephantine, Egypt, there are many examples of Jewish children bearing pagan names.[92] In some cases, these names clearly reflect the syncretistic tendencies of Jews in that era (there are also examples of people with Jewish names invoking pagan gods in their prayers). In other cases, the pagan names may have just sounded appealing, like when a modern American names a child "Thor." Mordecai's parents may have simply given their son a name that was familiar in the land where he was growing up. It was also common for Jews in this era to possess two names: a Heb. name that was used in the Jewish community and a Gentile name that was used in business or "official" settings. Daniel and his comrades, whose religious fidelity is beyond question, all possessed pagan names that were given to them by their Babylonian overseer (Dan 1:7). That these names may have pagan origins reveals little about the faithfulness (or lack thereof) of those who bore them.[93]

But the historical background behind such names does not rule out the probability that the name "Mordecai" could have been perceived negatively, especially in the Hellenistic era, when the book of Esther was being edited. When paired with Esther (Ishtar), Esther's audience would likely have concluded that the Jewish heroes of the book of Esther were (to some degree at least) assimilated to the pagan culture surrounding them.

The genealogy given here may be a list of Mordecai's immediate ancestors, or it may be selective, going back to his more illustrious ancestors.[94]

---

91. See W. Horbury, "The Name Mardochaeus in a Ptolemaic Inscription," *VT* 41 (1991): 220–26.

92. See B. Porten, *Archives from Elephantine: The Life of an Ancient Jewish Military Colony* (Berkeley: University of California Press, 1968).

93. On the possible significance of Daniel's companions' names, see J. J. Collins, *Daniel,* Hermeneia (Minneapolis: Fortress Press, 1993), 140–41.

94. In the Targums, there is a tradition that David spared Saul's relative Shimei from his purges until after he had had children, because he had prophetically discerned that Shimei would be the ancestor of the man who would save the Jewish

In Heb., the phrase "son of" may mean either direct biological offspring or a more distant descendant (as in Jesus being called "Son of David"). If Kish and Shimei are more distant ancestors, then they likely tie in Mordecai with the line of Saul, the first king of Israel. Saul was also a Bejaminite, son of a man named Kish (1 Sam 9:1). The name Shimei, too, is associated with the house of Saul (2 Sam 16:5). Mordecai's forebears who are named in the text might not be the same people mentioned in the books of Samuel, but it is not impossible. There can be no question, however, that the allusion to Saul is deliberate. See the commentary on 3:1 for further discussion.

According to Jewish tradition, Esth 2:5 is the first of the four "verses of redemption" in the book of Esther (the others being 8:15, 16; 10:3). These verses all chronicle the rise of Mordecai, who is regarded as the hero of the tale. At the reading of Esther on Purim, these verses are recited aloud by the entire congregation before being recited by the reader.

2:6 As discussed in the introduction ("The External Evidence"), 2:5–6 are among the most controversial in the book of Esther. If read in the most natural way, they would seem to imply that Mordecai had been one of the exiles taken from Jerusalem with King Jeconiah. Jeconiah (also called Jehoiachin) was deported by Nebuchadnezzar in 597 BC, a full 114 years before the beginning of Xerxes' reign (see 2 Kgs 24:10–16). While it is conceivable that Mordecai could have been alive and active at more than 120 years of age, it seems unlikely that his cousin would have been a desirable virgin at the time, even if she were several decades his junior. One possibility is that the narrator was not aware of the actual chronology (so Moore 1971, 27).[95] Though some scholars (Bardtke, 299; Bush, 363) argue that it would be improbable for a narrator so well versed in various aspects of Persian culture to be ignorant of its basic chronology, this possibility should not be rejected out of hand. From the evidence of traditional rabbinic texts like the *Seder ʿOlam*, it is apparent that the Jews of the first century and later had a wildly inaccurate concept of how long the Persian period actually lasted.[96] The same could well be true of the era when the book of Esther was written. If the narrator understood the Persian era to have lasted only a few decades, then the idea that Mordecai had been carried off in the exile would have made perfect sense. It is even more likely, however, that the narrator was not

---

race. The rabbis who composed this story clearly understood the genealogy to be selective.

95. Also, Fox, *Character and Ideology*, 29.

96. See, e.g., *S. ʿOlam Rab.* 30 and *b. AbZar* 9a, both of which claim (based on Dan 9:24–27) that Persian rule lasted thirty-four years after the rebuilding of the temple. The actual number was more than 180 years.

so much ignorant as simply uninterested in chronological accuracy. It was not essential to his purpose.

Other commentators argue that the problem lies in the translators, rather than the narrator. It has been proposed that the Jew who went into exile with Jeconiah was not Mordecai, but Kish, the last man named in the genealogy.[97] While not the most natural reading of the Heb., this interpretation is entirely possible and certainly makes much better sense chronologically. The main problem with the reading is that it precludes the possibility that the Kish spoken of here is the father of King Saul. (It would not, however, eliminate the mental connections that the audience would make between these names and the house of Saul.)

In any event, the association of Mordecai with the first deportation under Jeconiah reveals something of his social class. According to 2 Kgs 24:14–17, this deportation consisted of leading men, officers, artisans, and soldiers of Jerusalem. The implication is that Mordecai or his ancestors were of the upper classes. They were not necessarily rich or aristocratic, but they were not commoners.

2:7 Like Mordecai, Esther had a Babylonian name, but her Heb. name is also recorded. It was typical in this era for Jews to have an ethnic name of Heb. origin, as well as a name that reflected their cultural surroundings (cf. Dan 1:6–7). The Heb. name, Hadassah, evidently is a fem. form of the word הֲדַס (*hădas*), meaning "myrtle." An older theory that her name derived from the Akkadian title for the goddess Ishtar (see Paton, 88) has now been largely abandoned.[98] "Hadassah" is not attested anywhere else in the OT or in any ancient records or literature as a personal name.

The most common explanation for the name "Esther" is that it is a form of the name "Ishtar," one of the most widely honored pagan goddesses. Since Ishtar was the goddess of love and war, the name would seem especially fitting for the woman who was destined to win the heart of the Persian king and later lead the Jews in taking bloody vengeance against their enemies. This identification has been challenged by Zadok, who argues that graphic and onomastic evidence militate against it.[99] He suggests instead that it comes from the Persian word *stara*, meaning "star." Yahuda has suggested that it is from a (hypothetical) Persian word meaning "myrtle," but this idea

97. So J. S. Wright, "The Historicity of the Book of Esther," in *New Perspectives on the Old Testament*, ed. J. B. Payne (Waco, TX: Word, 1970), 38; E. Yamauchi, "The Archaeological Background of Esther," *BSac* 137 (1980): 99–117; D. Edelman, "Kish," *AYBD*, 4:86.

98. See further Fox, *Character and Ideology*, 275.

99. R. Zadok, "Notes on Esther," *ZAW* 98 (1986): 107.

has found little support.[100] Her name sounds very much like the Heb. word meaning "Let me hide" (אַסְתֵּר, *ʾastēr*), a coincidence(?) that could not have escaped the notice of the book's Heb. audience, especially when the maiden is counseled to conceal her Jewish identity.

Mordecai is raising his cousin Esther, who is an orphan. In the world of the OT, orphans were common, given that there was a high rate of death in childbirth, and the average life expectancy (due to disease, war, etc.) was much lower than today. It is somewhat surprising, then, that there is no official provision for adoption. Indeed, biblical Heb. has no technical term for the idea. Nonetheless, it seems virtually certain that adoption was practiced in ancient Israel. Not only did adoption figure prominently in other ANE cultures (e.g., in the Code of Hammurabi, LH 185–93); the notion of adoption occurs as a biblical metaphor (see, e.g., 2 Sam 7:14; Psa 2:7).[101] Living in Babylon, where adoption was regulated by the legal codes, it is possible that Mordecai would have had a more formal legal relationship with Esther than they might have had in Israel.

The notion found in the rabbinic tradition (e.g., *b. Meg.* 13a) that Esther was raised by Mordecai to be his wife is based on a wordplay on the word בַּת (*bat*), "daughter," and a postbiblical meaning associated with the Heb. word בַּיִת (*bayit*), "house." Speculation along these lines, however, is rather natural: Mordecai was an unmarried man without children, who had taken in a beautiful young woman. There was no law in Israel forbidding cousins from marrying. Even the LXX suggests that Mordecai had been raising her for the purpose of one day marrying her. This theory might well be more tasteful than the one proposed by Wright that Mordecai was a eunuch.[102] No doubt there were Jewish eunuchs, but the practice was probably not widespread, since manmade eunuchs were considered in some sense "second class" Jews and barred from the assembly (Deut 23:1).

The name Abihail, given in 2:15 in the MT (also here in the LXX) as the name of Esther's father, is borne by five people in the OT. Three are male (a Levite in Num 3:35; a Gadite in 1 Chr 5:14; and Esther's father), and two are female (a wife of a Judahite in 1 Chr 2:29; and cousin and wife of King Rehoboam in 1 Chr 11:18).

2:8 As anticipated, Esther was gathered with the other young women. She is "taken" into the house of women, but there is no implication she was forced to go against her will. As Fox observes,[103] Mordecai will later state

100. A. Yahuda, "The Meaning of the Name Esther," *JRAS* (1946): 174–78.
101. A good summary may be found in F. W. Knobloch, "Adoption," *AYBD*, 1:76–79.
102. Wright, "Historicity," 45.
103. Fox, *Character and Ideology*, 34.

that Esther "attained" the royal station (4:14), perhaps implying that she had actively pursued the position. Nonetheless, there is a sense at this point of the narrative that she is being "acted upon," rather than acting: orphaned through (we assume) no fault of her own; "taken" in by her cousin; raised up *by* him to be a daughter. Esther's later emergence from passive character to aggressive is one of the delightful aspects of the narrative.

There is little basis for stating, as some do, that Esther was committing fornication. All the women gathered were now, essentially, either wives or concubines of the king. They might have sexual relations with him only once—on the night when they were brought into his presence—but they were not to have sexual relations with any other man. The arrangement might well offend our modern sense of morality, but it was legal under ancient custom.

On the other hand, there can be little doubt that most readers would have found the procedure rather offensive. The fact was, the king was taking all the most beautiful women from the entire empire, spending only a single night with most of them, and then sequestering them away from the company of men. What a waste! While many women might have found the life of luxury that these young ladies would receive to be enviable, the male audience would surely have found this arrangement distasteful. The king was taking all the best women for himself, leaving only those women who were not deemed "beautiful" for the rest of the men in the empire to fight over. We can assume that the author is satirizing the self-indulgence of the Persian Empire.

Another troubling issue here for the Jewish readers is the fact that Esther has now become the wife of a foreigner and a pagan. In the OT, mixed marriages are discouraged, but not completely prohibited. In Deut 7:1–4, the Israelites are forbidden to give their daughters in marriage to the Canaanites, but nothing is said about intermarriage in general. Intermarriage was certainly practiced among the Jews of the Diaspora, as the Elephantine archives clearly demonstrate.[104] Nonetheless, among the traditional Jews, intermarriage was highly discouraged in the Persian and Hellenistic eras. The books of Ezra (chaps. 9–10) and Nehemiah (13:23–31) both end with accounts of how these Persian-era governors attempted to stop the Jews of Judah from marrying foreigners of any nationality. (Ironically, in the LXX and English Bible translations, Ezra and Nehemiah immediately precede the book of Esther.) Roughly contemporary, the book

104. See, e.g., A. Cowley, *Aramaic Papyri of the Fifth Century B.C.* (Oxford: Clarendon, 1923), 41.

of Malachi also seems to condemn marriage to foreigners (Mal 2:11–12).[105] During the Hellenistic period, condemnations of mixed marriages multiply, especially in works like Judith, Jubilees, and the Dead Sea Scrolls (esp. 4QMMT).[106] The Jewish audience of the book of Esther could not have approved of Esther's conduct.

2:9 Not surprisingly, Esther quickly distinguishes herself among the women. She "lifts up kindness" (תִּשָּׂא חֶסֶד, *tiśśāʾ ḥesed*) from the head eunuch. The use of the word חֶסֶד (*ḥesed*) in this context is rather different from its typical usage. The current understanding of this word is that it typically has the sense of "loyalty" or "covenant faithfulness."[107] This meaning fits well in the context of Gen 39:21, where God demonstrates His "loyalty" (חֶסֶד) to Joseph by giving him favor (חֵן, *ḥēn*) in the eyes of the prison warden. In Dan 1:9, God gives Daniel חֶסֶד and affection before the head of the eunuchs. In those cases, it is God who is the ultimate source of favor. In this context, "loyalty" does not seem an accurate translation. The word חֶסֶד here apparently has the meaning that will become common in Tannaitic Heb., where it will be regarded as a cardinal virtue (see, e.g., *m. ʾAbot* 1.2).

Esther apparently wins the favor on her own. As noted by Bardtke (303) and Moore 1971 (21), the idiom used here is more active than the alternative expression, "find favor/grace" (מָצָא חֵן, *māṣāʾ ḥēn*). It implies that Esther was not so passive as some interpreters have suggested. She has been "taken" into the king's palace, but she will make the best of her situation.

Because of the favor she receives, the chief eunuch moves Esther to the "front of the line." He expedites her assignments of food, personal attendants, and housing. It is apparent from this verse that unlike Daniel, Esther does not request a kosher diet: to do so would make it impossible for her to conceal her Jewish identity, as she is said to do in the very next verse. Indeed, the juxtaposition of these two statements may well imply that the narrator

---

105. Due to the difficult syntax of the passage, its meaning has been disputed. See, e.g., D. Petersen, *Zechariah 9–14 and Malachi*, OTL (Louisville, KY: Westminster, 1995), 198–201, who reads the passage as an indictment of idolatry.

106. Studies on the problem of mixed marriage in Judaism include M. Himmelfarb, "Sexual Relations and Purity in the Temple Scroll and the Book of Jubilees," *DSD* 6, no. 1 (1999): 11–36; M. Himmelfarb, "Levi, Phinehas, and the Problem of Intermarriage at the Time of the Maccabean Revolt," *Jewish Studies Quarterly* 6 (1999): 1–24; J. Klawans, *Impurity and Sin in Ancient Judaism* (Oxford: Oxford University Press, 2000); C. Hayes, *Gentile Impurities and Jewish Identities: Intermarriage and Conversion from the Bible to the Talmud* (Oxford/New York: Oxford University Press, 2002).

107. For a thorough discussion see N. Glueck, *Hesed in the Bible*; also, *TDOT*, 5:44–64; *TLOT*, 449–64.

is anticipating his audience's response to Esther's situation. This issue troubled ancient commentators, who insisted that she had not defiled herself with Gentile food.[108] But also note that some Jews felt it was acceptable to suspend some of the Mosaic dictates in times of crisis. In 167 BC, when the Jews were fighting for independence from the Greeks, the Hasmoneans deemed that it was acceptable to fight on the Sabbath day rather than perish (1 Macc 2:39–41).

There is some debate regarding whether Esther was the only maiden to receive maids (see Bush, 364, for discussion). In my opinion, the text's use of the word "choice" implies that all the maidens received attendants, but Hegai assured that the best of these attendants were assigned to Esther.

2:10 It is not difficult to imagine that Esther could have kept her identity secret (*pace* Berlin, 27): with women coming to Persia from all over the Middle East, Esther would not have been visibly different from many of them. What is difficult here is *why* Mordecai ordered Esther to keep her ethnicity a secret. Fox assumes the issue is anti-Semitism, and that there was some lurking danger that Mordecai feared.[109] (The term *anti-Semitism,* while sufficiently precise for modern usage, is not technically correct for this era. There were many other Semites in the ANE besides the Jews.) That may well be the case, since later in the story many enemies appear to challenge the Jews (seventy-five thousand, according to Esth 9:16). The hostility, however, was not an official government policy and is not even assumed to be widespread. Xerxes appears to have no problem with the Jews, and he is not informed that it is the Jews whose annihilation he orders (3:8–9). Furthermore, when Mordecai is promoted into Haman's office, the entire city of Susa celebrates (8:15). Apparently, it is not general anti-Semitism, but the hatred of a *certain* people—Haman's people—that inspires Mordecai's caution.

2:11 That Mordecai could walk about near the royal women's quarters has led some commentators to speculate that Mordecai may have been a eunuch. On the other hand, that he seems to have kept his distance from the women's quarters and sent messages to Esther through intermediaries militates against this idea. For that matter, it is not likely that only eunuchs had access to the women's chambers. While Greek author Plutarch and others reported that the Persian nobles were very jealous of their harems, killing any man who approached them, other sources disagree.[110] Herodotus writes

108. See, e.g, the LXX, which has Esther state that she has not eaten the king's food (14:17).

109. Fox, *Character and Ideology*, 32.

110. *Life of Artaxerxes* 27.1; *Themistocles* 26.5.

that the eunuchs admitted men to the harems (*Hist.* 3.130), and a nobleman named Otanes spoke regularly with his daughter Phaidyme, who was one of the royal wives (3.68). In addition, there are Persian sources indicating that the royal women traveled freely and participated in public events.[111] It would probably not have been difficult for Mordecai to see his cousin and even speak to her, so long as he had the permission of the chief eunuch. Yet he apparently preferred to speak to her through an intermediary, in order to preserve the secret of their relationship.

2:12 As many scholars have noted, the language here becomes somewhat suggestive. The phrase "to come to" (בּוֹא אֶל, *bôʾ ʾel*), used four times in this section, is often used in the OT as a euphemism for sexual intercourse (e.g., Gen 16:2; 29:21, 23; 2 Sam 11:4; 16:21, 22; Ruth 4:13). Myrrh, the precious spice derived from the resin of the commiphora bush, was frequently associated with lovemaking in the Song of Solomon (e.g., Song 1:13; 3:6; 4:6, 14; 5:5, 13; see also Prov 7:17). The text discreetly avoids any overt references to sex, but the implications of the scenario are clear, and the language is charged with innuendo.

The idea of six months of cosmetic treatments to prepare for a single night with the king is ridiculously indulgent. Myrrh was an expensive spice with many different applications and was not typically wasted.[112] (Among other uses, oil of myrrh was the principal ingredient in the oil used for anointing the Israelite tabernacle and priests [Exod 30:23].) The "perfumes" mentioned here might have included frankincense, cassia, or aloe. They might have been applied in a number of fashions, most commonly as a liquid, or worn as a sachet. There is no logical reason, however, for these perfumes to be applied for a full six months. Albright suggested that the perfumes were burned as incense, and the fumes allowed to pervade the skin and hair.[113] In any case, the treatments seem like a classic case of excess. Matthew Henry commented, "Even those who were the masterpieces of

111. See P. Briant, *Cyrus to Alexander: A History of the Persian Empire* (Winona Lake, IN: Eisenbrauns, 2002), 284–86, and Brosius, *Women in Ancient Persia,* 83–97, for discussion.

112. See M. Zohary, *Plants of the Bible* (Cambridge: Cambridge University Press, 1982), 200.

113. W. F. Albright, "The Lachish Cosmetic Burner and Esther 2:12," in *A Light unto My Path: Old Testament Essays in Honor of Jacob M. Myers*, ed. H. N. Bream (Philadelphia: Temple University Press, 1974), 25–32, argues that the incense burners excavated at Lachish were used in this fashion, but many commentators have pointed out that there is no evidence that ancient peoples actually used this method to perfume themselves.

nature must yet have all this help from art to recommend them to a vain and carnal mind."

2:13 Each young woman was to be supplied with whatever she deemed would be necessary in order to appeal to the king's desires. Once again, the text is delightfully elusive, leaving it to our imaginations to fill in the details. Most commentators conclude, rather blandly, that the women were given clothing or jewelry (e.g., Paton, 179; Mangano, 56; Huey, 808). According to *Tg. Esth. I*, she could ask any noble or prince she desired to accompany her—a strange request, it seems, but they presumably would recommend her to the king. Yet another possibility is that they brought items intended to entertain the king. Concubines often used musical instruments (harps and flutes), musicians to accompany their singing, or other tools to gain the king's favor.[114] Laniak (208) is more daring. Recognizing that this contest is primarily about sex, he suggests that the women took something for "erotic entertainment." On the other hand, in v. 15, the narrator seems to draw a connection between the accoutrements that Esther takes with her and that she gains the favor of all who see her. If that is the case, then the items she had taken would surely be some kind of beauty enhancements, not some personal item for use in the bedchamber.

In most modern translations, the "house of the women" is translated "harem," while the "house of the king" is translated "palace," so the women leave the harem and go to the palace. This translation gives the impression that the concubines were housed in a separate building from the king, which is highly unlikely. The "house of the king" is the palace complex, and the concubines would have dwelt in a section to which the king alone had access.[115]

2:14 After her night with the king, the maiden would leave the care of Hegai and go to "the-house-of-women second." There has been some debate over the meaning of the word "second" in this phrase: is it an adj. meaning a "second" dwelling place, separate from the quarters where they made their preparations (so Paton, 180; Moore, 23–24; and others), or is it an adv., meaning a return to the same dwelling "a second time" (thus Gordis, 54; Bush, 365–66)?[116] The fact that this area is under the watch of a different eunuch could indicate that the text refers to a separate quarters where royal concubines were housed, as opposed to the area where preparations were made.

---

114. See Briant, *Cyrus to Alexander*, 277–79; Brosius, *Women in Ancient Persia*, 31–34.

115. Fox, *Character and Ideology*, 276.

116. Also ibid., 276.

Grammatically, the phrase הִיא שָׁבָה אֶל־בֵּית הַנָּשִׁים שֵׁנִי (*hîʾ šābâ ʾel-bêt hannāšîm šēnî*) is difficult. If intended to be an adj. modifying the word "house," the word שֵׁנִי (*šēnî*), "second," should be prefixed with the definite article; thus, הַשֵּׁנִי (*haššēnî*). The phrase "the house of women" is definite, and the Heb. attributive adj. must agree with the noun it modifies in definiteness. On the other hand, if the word is an adv. modifying the word שָׁבָה (*šābâ*), "she returned," it should be spelled with a final *taw*, thus: שֵׁנִית (*šēnît*). This second possibility, though difficult, seems to make better sense in the context. We are left then trying to explain the unusual form of the adv. Gordis suggests it may be a deliberate abbreviation;[117] Fox suggests a textual error.[118]

The women who failed in their bid to become queen did not return home; they became royal concubines. Concubinage was widely practiced throughout the ANE; but in Israel after the age of the judges, only the king is depicted with concubines.[119] In Persia, as elsewhere, a man could have both several wives and numerous concubines.[120] Essentially, a concubine was a second-class wife. The husband had exclusive sexual rights to her, but she did not entail the same responsibilities from him as an "actual" wife would demand. They usually came into their marriage without ceremony and might be drawn from the poor, slaves, or prisoners of war. They could be divorced without penalty, and their children could be cast out without support. But it was not an entirely dreary existence. Given that they received a roof over their heads, meals, and whatever amenities the household might provide, life as the concubine of a wealthy man would have been far more comfortable than that of the wife of a pauper.

Given how many women were being brought into the king's harem (according to Josephus, *Ant.* 11.200, they numbered four hundred), he would hardly have been expected to maintain a close relationship—or any relationship at all—with most of them. The losers in the king's contest would likely never see his bed again. They might well be confined to "practical widowhood" (Paton, 180), but it would be a comfortable retirement, surrounded by all the luxuries that the Persian palace could provide.

2:15 In the middle of the story, we are suddenly given a "formal introduction" to Esther, including the name of her father, which had not previously been revealed. Berlin (28) takes the statement as Esther's formal introduction

117. "Studies," 54.
118. *Character and Ideology*, 276.
119. Further information and references may be found in J. A. Thompson, "Concubine," *NBD*, 216.
120. *Hist.* 1.135.

when she is presented before the king. The phrase is somewhat out of sequence for her introduction to the king. Rather, we might imagine it as her summons to come before Hegai, before she enters the king's chambers—the calling of her name from a roll. When asked what she would like to take with her into the king's presence, her response is, "What would you recommend?" Fox sees here evidence of passivity: "So devoid is she of individual will that she does not ask for further aids on her big night—a request that might at least show active participation in the process."[121] But Esther does not fail to ask for *anything*; she asks what Hegai thought she should take. It might be said that she was humble, not presupposing to know what would please the king. Rather than being passive, this move appears shrewd and calculating: Hegai, keeper of the royal women, would have known all the royal gossip and would have heard from the wives and concubines about the king's preferences. Equipped with whatever Hegai had deemed best, Esther pleased all her admirers. Her strategy was working.

2:16 It seems remarkable that the text gives us some detail on *when* Esther won the king's heart, but it gives us little insight into *how* she did so. The text designates the time as "the tenth month." Typically in the Bible, months are designated by an ordinal number: "the first month," "the second month," etc. In ancient Heb., they did have names for the months, but they were seldom used in the biblical narrative, and only a few were preserved. During the Babylonian exile, the Jews adopted the Babylonian calendar and continue to use it as their ceremonial calendar to this day. The month of Tebeth corresponds to December–January of the Gregorian calendar (which would have been winter in Susa).[122] Frieberg attempted to demonstrate that the method of dating used in the book of Esther proves that the book is older than typically believed, but the argument has not proven persuasive.[123] The seventh year of Xerxes' reign would correspond to 479 BC. According to Herodotus, he returned from his campaign against Greece in September

121. Fox, *Character and Ideology*, 198.
122. See further F. Rochberg-Halton and J. Vanderkam, "Calendars," *AYBD*, 1:810–20.
123. A. Friedberg, "A New Clue in the Dating of the Composition of the Book of Esther," *VT* 50 (2000): 561–65. Friedberg claims that the author's use of both ordinals and Babylonian names for the months indicates that the author was unfamiliar with the Babylonian system, meaning it was a novelty when the book was written. The argument was adequately rebutted by G. Larsson, "Is the Book of Esther Older than Has Been Believed?" *VT* 52 (2002): 130–31, and again by D. Talshir and Z. Talshir, "The Double Month Naming in Late Biblical Books: A New Clue for Dating Esther?" *VT* 54 (2004): 549–55.

of his seventh year (479 BC), just a few months before Esther was installed as queen.[124]

2:17 While all those who have seen Esther have had a favorable impression, the king "loves" her more than the other women. The word "love" here is likely meant to contrast the word "delight" (חָפֵץ, *ḥāpēṣ*) of v. 14: the other women might be pleasing, but Xerxes' feelings for Esther go a step beyond. The Heb. word translated "love" (אָהַב, *ʾāhab*) can signify a wide variety of emotions or attitudes, from lust to appreciation to genuine love (see 1 Sam 1:4–8, which seems to depict true, committed love)—*pace* Bush (366), who claims the word "expresses neither the deep emotional bonds nor the romantic feelings that are usually associated with the English term." In Xerxes' case, he could surely not have had a mature emotional commitment to Esther after only a single night.[125] But we need not be completely cynical about his feelings, either. Obviously, this was a woman who could make quite an impression—so much so that he is later willing to give her half his kingdom.

In addition to his love, Esther won "favor and kindness" from the king, just as she had from everyone else whom she encountered. In 2:9, she had won "kindness" from Hegai; in 2:15, "favor" from those who saw her; from the king, she receives both, signifying the great impression she had made on him.

2:18 As noted in the introduction ("The Banquet"), every major event of the Esther narrative is punctuated with a feast. Here is no exception. Esther's selection and coronation is punctuated by one of the feasts thrown by the Persians. Like the feast in 1:3, this one includes all his "nobles and servants"—the upper classes in the citadel. But the king's generosity was extended to the common people, as well. The Heb. reads, "He caused a rest to take place." Most likely, this phrase refers to a release from taxes and other obligations, like the one proclaimed by "Pseudo-Smerdis" in 522 BC, when he usurped the throne of Persia and proclaimed a release from taxation and military service for three years (*Hist.* 3.67).

Biblical Theology Comments

2:1–4 The contents of this unit, and this entire chapter, raise considerable issues regarding the model of marriage endorsed by the Bible. King Xerxes, one of the main characters of our story, is married to many, many women.

---

124. On the circumstances surrounding his return, see further Briant, *Cyrus to Alexander,* 539–42.

125. Cf. Fox, *Character and Ideology*, 38.

With most of them, he spends only one night. How many does he know by name? Women are taken to his palace by the droves, where they will compete to please him sexually, for the chance to become the queen of Persia. They are officially his wives, but these marriages almost constitute a kind of prostitution: if they do their job well and make the king happy, they might be rewarded handsomely. All in all, the scenario looks very unsavory. And yet, God uses this contest and its winner to rescue the Jewish people from destruction.

Are we to conclude that God approves of the morality displayed here? Certainly, we must bear in mind that to describe behavior is not to prescribe behavior. The Bible frequently records people behaving badly without explicitly condemning their actions. We must also note that God frequently uses sinful human actions to achieve His greater good, as in the case of Joseph (Gen 50:20). We might well say that if it were not for God using human misbehavior, He would have precious little to work with. So the Bible's recording of Xerxes' behavior, and even God's use of his behavior, do not constitute an endorsement of polygamy or immorality.

The biblical ideal for marriage is portrayed in the story of Adam and Eve: one man, one woman, working in partnership with each other. Of course, polygamy became a fact of life in the ANE, and the ability to support multiple wives was seen as a sign of prosperity and blessing (e.g., 2 Sam 5:6–15). But while the Bible never actually forbids polygamy, it never endorses the practice, either.[126] In fact, there are a number of clues that polygamy is not considered normal or good: the first polygamist of the Bible is Lamech, a descendant of the wicked Cain, and himself a murderer (Gen 4:19–24). Stories of polygamy are typically characterized by tension and rivalry, as in the case of Sarah and Hagar (Gen 16:1–6; 21:8–14), Rachel and Leah (Gen 30–31), and Hannah and Penninah (1 Sam 1:1–8). Deuteronomic regulations assume the troubles these relationships can cause (Deut 21:15–17), and kings are warned not to take many wives, because they will draw their hearts away from Yahweh (Deut 17:17)— as happened in the case of Solomon (1 Kgs 11:1–8). The NT, also, expresses a distaste for polygamy, as the Pastoral Epistles require that overseers and deacons are to be husbands of but one wife (1 Tim 3:2, 12; Titus 1:6). The procedure recommended by Xerxes' servants did not directly violate any biblical law (after all, the women he took into his house became wives and concubines), but it certainly flew in the face of the true, biblical ideal for marriage.

---

126. For further discussion on the issue of polygamy, see C. J. H. Wright, *Old Testament Ethics for the People of God* (Downers Grove, IL: InterVarsity, 2011), 330–31; B. Waltke, *An Old Testament Theology: An Exegetical, Canonical, and Thematic Approach* (Grand Rapids: Zondervan, 2011), 429–30.

2:6 The repeated emphasis on "exile" in this verse hammers home the reality of the Jews' situation in this era. Exile is a situation with political, social, and spiritual aspects. The political aspect is the reality of foreign domination. The Jews are in exile because they have been overwhelmed by another nation so thoroughly that they were deprived of their home country. The experience is shattering to national pride and personal identity. It also means that they are no longer autonomous. Even under the relatively benign rule of the Persians, they are not their own masters. Their existence as a people is dependent on the hospitality of others. The social aspects of exile were equally unpleasant and challenging. Separated from the homeland, no longer surrounded by the familiar sights of home and the institutions and landmarks that reminded them of their heritage, the Jewish exiles were easy prey to assimilation by the dominant cultures in which they dwelt. Frequently, they would find refuge in ghettos, where they could preserve their language and traditions. But this was only a temporary fix, for people in exile had to interact with their overlords in order to survive. They were forced to learn a new language and new customs, and even adopt new names so they could fit in among the natives.

But it is the spiritual aspect of exile that is our greatest concern here. For Israel, the land was a gift of God. They had not earned it; He had given it to them, just as He had promised to Abraham (Gen 12:6; 13:14–17; 15:7, 17–21). Yet in another sense, the land was not actually theirs: God still retained possession of it and allowed the Israelites to live there (Lev 25:23). If Israel should fail to keep their covenant with God, He could dispossess them, just as He had dispossessed the Canaanites before them (Deut 8:20; 28:63–64). Indeed, God promises Israel that if they abandon Him or turn to other gods, He will drive them from the land, so that they will become vagrants among the nations (Deut 4:25–28; 28:36; 29:25–28).

The idea of exile as punishment is one of the most significant OT themes.[127] Adam and Eve failed to keep the commandment of God and were punished with exile from the garden of Eden (Gen 3:23). Cain slew his brother, Abel, and was punished by being "exiled" from the face of the ground, so that he became a vagrant and a wanderer (Gen 4:14). In the days of Noah, God exiled all living creatures from the face of the land on account of the sinfulness of humanity (Gen 6:7). Being driven from the land was a devastating tragedy, for the land was the channel of God's blessings for His people. But there was a spiritual element of the tragedy as well: as Cain observed, being driven from the face of the land entailed being "hidden" from

---

127. On the pervasiveness of this theme, see P. Akroyd, *Exile and Restoration: A Study of Hebrew Thought in the Sixth Century* (Philadelphia: Westminster, 1968), 237–47; L. Ryken, J. Wilhoit, and T. Longman III, "Exile," in *DBI*, 250–51.

the face of God (Gen 4:14). Likewise, God promised His people that when they have sinned against Him and turned to other gods, He will hide His face from them (Deut 31:16–18; 32:19–20) as they are sent into exile.

But even in exile, there is hope. Just as God acted with compassion toward Adam and Eve (Gen 3:21), and as He placed a sign on Cain to protect him in his exile (Gen 4:15), and as He saved a remnant in the ark during the flood, so, too, God promised to preserve His people in the midst of exile (Deut 4:30–31; 32:28–43). Mordecai and Esther are in exile, hidden from the face of God; but as events will demonstrate, God is still working on behalf of His people.

2:7 Esther is introduced not merely as an exile, but as an orphan as well. Unlike being in exile, being an orphan is not typically regarded in the Bible as a divine judgment. Nonetheless, the condition had its own theological implications.[128] In the Bible, and in the ANE in general, orphans (along with widows) are often cited as the epitome of the poor and oppressed.[129] The first mention of orphans in the Bible is found in Israel's earliest law code, the so-called Covenant Code (Exod 21–24). In this text, God expressed His special concern for the orphan: "You will not afflict any widow or orphan. If you indeed afflict him, yes, if he cries out at all to me, I will certainly hear his cry of distress. And I will become angry, and I will kill you with the sword, and your wives will be widows and your children orphans" (Exod 22:22–24 LEB). Thus God promises "poetic justice" to those who oppress the fatherless. Frequently, the prophets condemned Israel for its mistreatment of the orphan, who was a prime example of the "least of these" in ancient Israel (Isa 1:23; 10:2; Jer 5:28; Ezek 22:7; Mal 3:5). God Himself is described as "the helper of the fatherless" (Psa 10:14). In Jas 1:27, we are advised that true religion will entail the care of orphans. Again, Jesus sets the example, as He promised at the last supper that He would not leave His disciples as orphans, but come to them in the presence of the Holy Spirit to bring them comfort (John 14:18).

In the book of Ezekiel, the orphan was used as a metaphor for Israel (Ezek 16). In this passage, Israel was depicted as a baby who had been cast out by her parents, left to die of exposure. God cared for the infant and raised her to adulthood. Then, when she was grown, she became His bride. The situation might be somewhat parallel to Esther's own, if Mordecai had indeed intended her to become his wife, as the rabbis claimed.

---

128. See further H. Ringgren, יָתוֹם, *TDOT*, 6:477–81.

129. See D. E. Gowan, "Wealth and Poverty in the OT," *Int* 41 (1987): 341–53.

Adoption, too, had theological significance.[130] Although, as noted above, the Bible records no formal adoption procedures, the concept recurs frequently. Moses was the most famous biblical adoptee, having been taken in by Pharaoh's daughter (Exod 2:10). But it is in the realm of metaphor that adoption is most significant. God speaks of making Solomon His son (2 Sam 7:14) and proclaims His adoption of the Davidic monarch in Psa 2:7. The nation Israel, too, is described as God's son, adopted and made God's heir (His "firstborn," not genetically but legally; see Jer 3:19 and Exod 4:22–23). Paul reiterates this notion in the NT, stating that to Israel belonged "the adoption as sons" (Rom 9:4). But in the NT, this notion is expanded to include the Gentiles and all those who place faith in Jesus Christ (Eph 1:5). Because we have been adopted by God, we can cry out, "*Abba*, Father" (Rom 8:15; Gal 4:4–6).

2:10 Mordecai and Esther are people of two worlds. Mordecai is introduced as a Jewish man before we are even told his name (2:5), intimating that this aspect of his character will be crucial to the story. Esther, his cousin, is (as we would expect) Jewish as well, and will later embrace her people as she pleads for their lives (7:3–4). On the other hand, they are people of the Persian court, trying to function in the midst of a powerful pagan society. How, then, do they live? How are they to fulfill their calling to be a "kingdom of priests" (Exod 19:6) in a foreign land? Mordecai ordered Esther to conceal her Jewishness, to blend into the world around her. It is a counsel that will contribute later to her success and the Jews' triumph over their enemies. But is concealment a righteous response to a potentially hostile environment?

Mordecai and Esther present a striking contrast to two other biblical examples of Jews in similar settings: Joseph and Daniel. Joseph, taken to Egypt against his will, maintains his faithfulness to God and His principles. He refuses the advances of his master's wife, knowing that such a betrayal would be a sin against God (Gen 39:9). Through his steadfast obedience, he becomes a blessing to the Egyptian nation and saves its people and his own from famine, and he carefully gives God credit for his success (Gen 41:16, 51–52; 45:5–8). Daniel manages to rescue the wise men and leaders of Babylon (Dan 2:12–16), while continually maintaining his fidelity to the laws of Moses (Dan 1:8). He refuses to compromise his Jewish distinctives, even at the risk of his life. As a result, he serves as a witness to the pagan kings of the sovereignty of Israel's God (Dan 2:47; 6:25–27). Shadrach, Meshach, and Abednego, too, stand firm for their principles, even when they are threatened with a horrible death (Dan 2). Compared

130. See further "Adoption," in *DBI*, 14–15.

to such figures as these, Mordecai and Esther seem hardly worthy of praise or emulation.[131]

Jobes (115) writes at length about some of the "moral ambiguities" in this episode from the story of Esther, where "every choice is an odd mix of right and wrong." She celebrates that God is able to redeem even wrong choices in such situations. But not every choice is fraught with ambiguity. Perhaps it was not clear-cut, in that time and social setting, whether Esther should marry the foreign king—after all, many biblical heroes, such as Joseph, Moses, and Boaz, had foreign wives. But there could be little question about whether or not Esther should have eaten non-kosher food or observed the Sabbath day. These were not matters of uncertain ethics, but of clear violation of the Mosaic law. Esther's and Mordecai's actions in these instances are not "ambiguous"; they are simply wrong. The wonder of God is that He can take even a sinful action and redeem it to bring about salvation, as in the crime of Joseph's brothers selling him into slavery (Gen 50:20), or humanity's ultimate act of wickedness in betraying and crucifying the Son of God.

2:12 It is tempting to draw a parallel between the maidens' preparation for their night with the king and Christians' spiritual purification for their union with Christ. (A similar application was drawn by Rhabanus Maurus, the earliest Christian commentator on the book of Esther.)[132] Such an application of the text would be incorrect and offensive on several levels. First, it employs an allegorical method that most Christian scholars today consider illegitimate. The story of Esther is not a symbolic account of Christ's union with the church; it is a narrative account of events set in ancient Persia. Furthermore, it misunderstands the purpose of this episode, which is not to model proper Christian behavior, but to satirize the excess and self-indulgence of the Persian Empire. Finally, it casts the Lord into the role of the lusty and profligate king and characterizes the church's relationship with Him in a manner that might bring a blush to the face of a Baal worshiper.

Application and Devotional Implications

Jobes (113) raises the question of the lessons that Esther's victory might have for the modern Christian. She asks, "How would you use this episode from Esther's life to teach virtue to your teenage daughter as she stands on the

131. R. Pierce, "The Politics of Esther and Mordecai: Courage or Compromise?" *BBR* 2 (1992): 75–89, generally concludes that neither figure is praiseworthy, and both capitulate entirely to secularism.

132. For the text, see Conti and Pilara, 374–99.

threshold of womanhood? What message would she get? Make yourself as attractive as possible to powerful men? Use your body to advance God's kingdom? The ends justify the means?" These are all legitimate and challenging questions. Esther is often used as a role model to girls and young women, but what message does she send? She spends a whole year undergoing expensive cosmetic procedures in order to be beautiful enough to win the king's heart. Eventually, she would use her sex appeal to save her people, but that is not what she is doing in this episode. Rather, she is using her enhanced attractiveness to win the position of queen, without any virtuous goal in sight. At this point in the story, there is no crisis looming on the horizon. There appears to be no principle in play but ambition. We need not even debate the question of whether "the end justifies the means": there is no praiseworthy end here.

However, it would be unfair to Esther to depict her as a woman without virtue. Her courage and her willingness to sacrifice herself for the sake of her people that we will later observe are admirable and can be cited as qualities to be emulated. But we should be selective about the qualities that we laud in her. Christian women are urged to adopt the standard of modesty (1 Tim 2:9–10), adorning themselves with good works instead of external embellishments. Our society is increasingly driven by vanity, and physical beauty is often embraced as the measure of a person's worth. Given the obscene amounts of money that are spent in the pursuit of perfect teeth, flawless skin, and a fabulous figure, we should be cautious about how we cite Esther's example.

Selected Bibliography

Ackroyd, P. *Exile and Restoration: A Study of Hebrew Thought in the Sixth Century.* Philadelphia: Westminster, 1968.

Albright, W. F. "The Lachish Cosmetic Burner and Esther 2:12." In *A Light unto My Path: Old Testament Essays in Honor of Jacob M. Myers*, ed. H. N. Bream, 25–32. Philadelphia: Temple University Press, 1974.

Anderson, B. W. "The Place of the Book Esther in the Christian Bible." *JR* 30 (1950): 32–43.

Briant, P. *From Cyrus to Alexander: A History of the Persian Empire.* Winona Lake, IN: Eisenbrauns, 2002.

Brosius, M. *Women in Ancient Persia, 539–331 B.C.* Oxford Classical Monographs. Oxford: Clarendon, 1996.

Fox, M. V. *Character and Ideology in the Book of Esther.* 2nd ed. Grand Rapids: Eerdmans, 2001.

Friedberg, A. D. "A New Clue in the Dating of the Composition of the Book of Esther." *VT* 50 (2000): 561–65.

Glueck, N. *Hesed in the Bible.* Cincinnati: Hebrew Union College Press, 1967.

Gordis, R. "Studies in the Esther Narrative." *JBL* 95 (1976): 43–58.
Gowan, D. E. "Wealth and Poverty in the OT." *Int* 41 (1987): 341–53.
Hayes, C. *Gentile Impurities and Jewish Identities: Intermarriage and Conversion from the Bible to the Talmud*. New York: Oxford University Press, 2002.
Laniak, T. S. *Shame and Honor in the Book of Esther*. Atlanta: Scholars Press, 1998.
Larsson, G. "Is the Book of Esther Older than Has Been Believed?" *VT* 52 (2002): 130–31.
Perdue, L. G., et. al. *Families in Ancient Israel*. The Family, Religion, and Culture. Louisville, KY: Westminster John Knox, 1997.
Pierce, R. W. "The Politics of Esther and Mordecai: Courage or Compromise?" *BBR* 2 (1992): 75–89.
Porten, B. *The Archives of Elephantine: The Life of an Ancient Jewish Military Colony*. Berkeley: University of California Press, 1968.
Talshir, D., and Z. Talshir. "The Double Month Naming in Late Biblical Books: A New Clue for Dating Esther?" *VT* 54 (2004): 549–55.
Wenham, G. J. "Bᵉtûlâ: A Girl of Marriageable Age." *VT* 22 (1972): 326–48.
Wright, J. S. "The Historicity of the Book of Esther." In *New Perspectives on the Old Testament*, ed. J. Barton Payne, 37–47. Waco, TX: Word Books, 1970.
Yahuda, A. S. "The Meaning of the Name Esther." *JRAS* 78 (1946): 174–78.
Yamauchi, E. "The Archaeological Background of Esther." *BSac* 137 (1980): 99–117.
———. *Persia and the Bible*. Grand Rapids: Baker, 1997.
Zadok, R. "Notes on Esther." *ZAW* 98 (1986): 105–10.

Mordecai Rescues the King (2:19–23)

Translation

19 When the virgins were re-gathered,[133] Mordecai would sit in the gate of the king. **20** Esther was not making her family or her people known, just as Mordecai had commanded her. Esther did as Mordecai said, just as she had[134] when he was raising her. **21** In those days, when Mordecai was sitting in the gate of the king, Bigthan and Teresh, two of the king's eunuchs who were keepers of the threshold, became angry, and sought to stretch out their hand against King Xerxes. **22** The matter became known to Mordecai, and he reported it to Esther the queen. Esther told it to the king in the name of Mordecai. **23** The matter was investigated and uncovered, and the two

133. The word שֵׁנִית (*šēnît*) can mean "second," "again," or "another." On this translation, see the commentary on 2:19.
134. Lit., "just as she was."

of them were hung on wooden pikes.[135] It was recorded in the book of daily events in the presence of the king.

Textual Notes

19.a. In the AT, 19–22 are found near the beginning of the narrative, after Mordecai's dream in chapter 1. The LXX actually contains two versions of the conspiracy, one after the dream account in chapter 1 and another here.

19.b. The clause וּבְהִקָּבֵץ בְּתוּלוֹת שֵׁנִית ("and when the virgins were gathered a second time") is absent in the LXX.

20.a. After כַּאֲשֶׁר צִוָּה עָלֶיהָ מָרְדֳּכָי ("as Mordecai had commanded her"), LXX inserts φοβεῖσθαι τὸν θεὸν, "to fear God."

21.a. וּמָרְדֳּכַי יֹשֵׁב בְּשַׁעַר־הַמֶּלֶךְ, "and Mordecai was sitting in the gate of the king," duplicates the end of v. 19. Possibly a dittogr.?

21.b. According to the LXX, the eunuchs were angry ὅτι προήχθη Μαρδοχαῖος, "because Mordecai was promoted."

21.c. בִּגְתָן וָתֶרֶשׁ ("Bigthan and Teresh"). Different names are recorded in both Greek versions.

22.a. LXX adds at the end, τὰ τῆς ἐπιβουλῆς, "about the plot."

Commentary

2:19 This second appearance of the word *second* (after 2:14) has generated extensive discussion. In this case, the problem is not the meaning of the word, but its significance in the context. Its most straightforward meaning is that the virgins were gathered "a second time." The question that arises is, why should there be a second gathering of virgins, when the new queen has already been chosen? A variety of explanations have been offered: the LXX, perhaps finding the notion inexplicable, omitted the phrase. *Tg. Esth. II* added an explanatory gloss to the effect that more virgins were gathered in order to provoke Esther to jealousy. Among modern commentators, there are four major positions:

135. Typically translated "gallows." The Heb. word refers only to a wooden object. Since the most common method of "hanging" in ancient Persia was impalement, we have translated the word accordingly.

1. The phrase is a mistake, and the word should be omitted or emended to שָׁנוֹת (*šānôt*), "various."[136]
2. The text is referring to a continued or different gathering of new virgins (Cassel, 77–78; Levenson, 67; Bush, 372).[137]
3. The text is referring to a second gathering of the virgins who had been previously gathered.[138]
4. The text refers to the same gathering of virgins that was mentioned earlier in the text (Gerleman, 83).

It is generally acknowledged that the function of this entire clause is temporal, that it establishes the time in which Mordecai is sitting in the king's gate. There is a contrast being drawn between the earlier time, when he was walking about near the women's quarters, and now, when he has taken his place at the gate. Mordecai's return to the gate occurs once the contest has been completed and all the virgins have been gathered together under the care of Shaashgaz. Thus the most logical understanding would seem to be that the text refers here to the gathering of the new wives into the women's dwelling.

There are two main objections to this interpretation. The first is that these women are now concubines and cannot accurately be described as "virgins." But while calling these women "virgins" at this point in the narrative is not entirely accurate, it is not inexplicable: there is really no better way to refer to the women who had recently competed for the king's favor. If the text had called them "the concubines," they would not be distinguished from the members of the king's harem who were not part of the competition, so it would not be clear who was meant. On the other hand, since the contestants have already been introduced as "virgins," the identity of the group should be clear. To offer a modern analogy: after the conclusion of an election, it might be reported that "All the candidates congratulated the new president." Technically, it would not be correct, since the people offering congratulations would no longer be candidates. Nonetheless, the readers would know precisely who was meant, and specifying "the former

---

136. W. Rudolph, "Textkritisches zum Estherbuch," *VT* 4 (1954): 89–90, says it should be omitted. Ehrlich, *Randglossen zur hebräischen Bibel; Textkritisches, Sprachliches und Sachliches* (Leipzig: J. C. Hinrichs, 1914), 7:114, and Moore 1971, 30, say it should be emended.

137. Cf. also E. Groves, "Double Take: Another Look at the Second Gathering of the Virgins in Esther 2.19a," in *The Book of Esther in Modern Research*, ed. L. J. Greenspoon and S. W. Crawford (London: T&T Clark, 2003), 108–10.

138. Gordis, "Studies in the Esther Narrative," *JBL* 95 (1976): 47; Fox, *Character and Ideology in the Book of Esther*, 2nd ed. (Grand Rapids: Eerdmans, 2001), 277.

candidates" would be unnecessary. Likewise, if the narrator here had said, "the gathering of the former virgins," it would have struck readers as odd.

The second objection is more substantial. Typically, when referring to something mentioned previously in the text, biblical Heb. would use the definite article. So if these virgins are those who were gathered earlier, then the word בְּתוּלוֹת (*bětûlôt*, "virgins") should have the definite article: "*the* virgins." While this omission is a real problem, it need not be disqualifying. Biblical Heb. can be inconsistent in its use of the definite article (in poetry, e.g., it is regularly omitted). Since the Heb. of the book of Esther is frequently irregular, we should not exclude the most logical interpretation of the text because of a small grammatical difficulty.

Once the new wives have been settled into the "second house of women," Mordecai took his post in the city gate.[139] Most likely this means that he was a city official, thus giving him the "connections" that allowed him to uncover the plot of the eunuchs (2:22).[140] Business of the state was often conducted within the city gates, as when Absalom offered judgment at the gates of Jerusalem (2 Sam 15:2). According to Xenophon (*Cyropaedia* 8.1.6), all the officials of the Persian king resided within the king's gate. Though it is grammatically possible, it seems unlikely that Mordecai is being depicted here only as a "man of leisure," spending his time where he could keep up on the latest gossip (*contra* Paton, 188).

2:20 As Berlin (30) notes, the grammatical construction implies "synchronicity," that Esther was concealing her identity the whole time Mordecai dwelt in the gate. On the reasons why Mordecai insisted that Esther conceal her ethnicity, see the comments on 2:10 above. The verse also reiterates the idea of Esther's obedience. While fathers had near absolute authority over their daughters in ancient Israel (cf. Exod 21:15, 17; Deut 21:18–21), that authority was limited when they married and the husband assumed legal liability for his wife. To our narrator, that Esther continued to be obedient to her stepfather, even when such obedience was technically unnecessary, is an important aspect of the story, further demonstrating Esther's submissiveness. Her character is the antithesis of the disobedient Vashti, which of course made her an ideal candidate for Vashti's replacement. There is a somewhat ominous note to the description, as well, since Esther's

139. For a description of the gate, see E. Yamauchi, *Persia and the Bible* (Grand Rapids: Baker, 1997), 298–300.

140. Cf. Dan 2:49, where Daniel is said to have "remained in the king's gate," meaning that he served in the king's court. The LXX translation of this verse states explicitly that Mordecai resided in "the king's court."

submissiveness will be put to the test in the next chapter: will she obey her cousin, even if it could cost her life?

The word אָמְנָה (*ʾomnâ*) is something of a puzzle. According to *HALOT*, the word is a noun derived from the root אמן (*ʾmn*), to be firm or secure. But if treated as a noun, the syntax of the passage would be very difficult to decipher. Driver[141] analyzes it instead as an inf. const. form of the verb, with the 3 f. sg. pronominal suf.: "when [he] was raising her."

2:21 This incident should strike us as a little odd. Two eunuchs become angry with the king and plan to kill him. We are told their names—as is typical of the Esther narrative—but we are not told why they are angry. Eunuchs are typically associated with tractability and trustworthiness, which is why they were often given sensitive jobs in government.[142] What could have moved them to such drastic measures?[143] It is possible that there is some connection between this episode and one recorded by the Greek historian Diodorus Siculus, in which a eunuch named Bagoas assassinated Artaxerxes III (d. 336 BC) in order to replace him with his son Arses.[144] Indeed, there is even some similarity between the name "Bigthan" and that of "Bagoas." But that incident, if it occurred at all, took place long after the setting of Esther. More likely, it is not history that interests our narrator, but irony: two figures who should by nature be submissive have conspired to rise up against the king. It is similar to the Vashti incident, but here the insubordination is taken a step further.

Short as it is, this incident serves a strategic function in our book. First, it demonstrates Mordecai's loyalty to the king, belying the claim that Haman will later level against the Jews and emphasizing the role of the Diaspora Jews as model citizens in their adopted lands. As Levenson (64) puts it, "A courtier who takes action to save the king's life cannot fairly be accused of contempt for the king's laws." It is probably no coincidence that the episode appears just before the scene in which Mordecai refuses to obey the king's command: this story places that incident in a very different light. Furthermore, this story serves the very important function of providing the

141. Driver, "Problems," 235.

142. On the other hand, Greek sources delighted in stories of conspiratorial eunuchs. See P. Briant, *From Cyrus to Alexander: A History of the Persian Empire* (Winona Lake, IN: Eisenbrauns, 2002), 268–70.

143. The LXX implies that the eunuchs were part of a conspiracy to overthrow the king and replace him with Haman, thus explaining both the eunuchs' plot and Mordecai's refusal to bow before Haman: he knew that the man was disloyal to the king.

144. See M. Dandamayev, *Iranians in Achaemenid Babylonia*, Columbia Lectures on Iranian Studies 6 (Costa Mesa, CA: Mazda, 1992), 64–65.

basis for the later incident where Haman will be forced to honor Mordecai (chap. 6). Mordecai's service to the king, recorded but not rewarded, will become the reason behind the first visible evidence that the tables have begun to turn in favor of the Jews. Furthermore, this act of loyalty will be fresh in the king's mind when Esther reveals Haman's plot against the Jews and against Mordecai personally (chap. 7).

One other interesting aspect of this episode is that it foreshadows the events that will come to dominate the rest of the book. Here, Mordecai enlists Esther's aid to thwart a plot against the king's life. Soon, Mordecai will be enlisting Esther to foil a larger plot against the entire Jewish race. Haman's role parallels that of the eunuchs, and his fate will also parallel theirs.

2:22 According to *Tg. Esth. I*, Mordecai was able to learn of the plot because he could understand seventy different languages, a fact unknown to the eunuchs, who spoke in their own obscure tongue. The narrator of the book of Esther, on the other hand, does not explain how Mordecai came to know of the plot, the detail being irrelevant to his story and (unlike the record of the eunuch's names) of little stylistic value. But that he did learn of the plot is evidence of some divine orchestration at work: Mordecai was in the right place at the right time to overhear the would-be assassins making their plans.

Esther is careful to give her cousin credit for the discovery of the plot. This fact makes sense, since it would have been unlikely that the queen herself would have access to the conversations of assassins. A number of scholars, however, find it remarkable that the king did not "put two and two together" and conclude that Esther was related to Mordecai and therefore a Jew (e.g., Clines, 105; Levenson, 64). Levenson (64) even sees it as a comic touch, a lampoon of Persian bureaucratic inefficiency. This conclusion is unwarranted. As Fox remarks, queens were not sequestered away from human contact and may have had their own networks of connections and acquaintances.[145] There is no reason to assume that a queen could not have received information from a subordinate official in the royal court.

2:23 The execution of the eunuchs is an instance of foreshadowing in this narrative. Rarely mentioned elsewhere in the OT, hanging was a particularly abhorrent form of punishment to the Jews, since Deut 21:23 states that anyone hanged on a tree is under a curse. The image of hanging will recur later in the story, as the threat of impalement will hang over Mordecai's head from the end of chapter 5 to the end of chapter 7. That threat will be

---

145. Fox, *Character and Ideology*, 40.

reversed when Haman ends up on the pike instead (7:9–10). His execution will be followed by the hanging of his ten sons (9:13–14). But it is not only the eunuchs' hanging that foreshadows Haman's fate: like the eunuchs, he, too, will be deprived of progeny. The execution of Haman's sons will bring his family line to an end. While this detail may seem incidental to modern readers, it was of great concern to the ancient audience.

The Heb. word typically translated "gallows" here literally means "tree," or simply "wooden object." There is no evidence in antiquity for execution by hanging someone with a noose around their neck and allowing them to strangle. More likely, the text refers to the common practice of impaling victims on wooden stakes. This barbaric practice could be used either as an actual method of execution, or—more often—it could be used to display the bodies of people who were executed by other means. As a method of execution, impalement would have been very painful; the real purpose of the practice, however, was not so much torture as to make a public display of the malefactors.[146] Another possibility, though less likely, is that the text was referring to crucifixion, which the Persians also practiced (*Hist.* 7.33, 194; see also Clines, 292–93).[147]

2:23 The recording of the incident will prove to be an important detail. As Laniak (212) observes, writing is a significant motif in this book. There are two main instances: the writing of laws, used to empower or (more often) disenfranchise individuals or groups, and the writing of records, used to remember certain persons and their deeds. The evil deeds of the eunuchs are thus forever preserved, as are the good deeds of Mordecai.

What is truly remarkable is that the incident would be recorded in the very presence of the king, but no reward would be given. The Persian monarchs were very diligent about rewarding their benefactors, as both Herodotus (e.g., *Hist.* 3.139–41; 5.11; 9.107) and Thucydides (*History of the Peloponnesian War* 1.129) observed. Fox notes that Mordecai could have reminded Xerxes of the oversight.[148] He sees it as a sign of faith that Mordecai was willing to wait to see whether and when he would have his reward. On the other hand, how could he have pointed out the king's oversight without embarrassing the monarch? As we will see later, Esther is very careful not to suggest that the king may have been in any way responsible for the plot against the Jews (Esth 7:3–6). When dealing with the powerful

146. For further information, see R. Westbrook, "Punishments and Crimes," *AYBD*, 5:546–556; *ANET*, 276.

147. T. Thornton, "The Crucifixion of Haman and the Scandal of the Cross," *JTS* 37 (1986): 419–26.

148. Fox, *Character and Ideology*, 40.

and capricious, it is best to pretend not to notice their mistakes. Perhaps the best comment that can be made regarding the lack of reward is that divine providence was at work, anticipating the moment when the reward would be needed.

Biblical Theology Comments

2:21–22 There is a sense in which the book of Esther's depiction of King Xerxes mirrors the Bible's general attitude toward the Jews' foreign overlords. On the one hand, Xerxes is depicted as something of a fool, an indecisive monarch whose only interest seems to be in his own pleasure. On the other hand, he is the king, and the preservation of his life and honor are worthy goals. This depiction is reminiscent of the way foreign monarchs appear in the book of Daniel: in Dan 2 and 3, Nebuchadnezzar is a rash figure, threatening to kill his wise men for failing to interpret his dream and sentencing the Jews to death for refusing to worship his golden image. At the end of each episode, however, he becomes an admirer of Israel's God and passes laws protecting the Jews. In Dan 4, the king is full of hubris and pays the penalty for his sin, but once he recognizes that his authority comes from God, his majesty is restored. In Dan 6, Darius is duped into signing an order that will result in Daniel's death in the lions' den. However, as with Nebuchadnezzar, he ultimately acknowledges the greatness of Israel's God and signs a decree enforcing His worship.

Nor is this ambivalence merely a literary motif. The prophet Jeremiah calls down fierce curses on the land of Babylon for its treatment of Judah (Jer 50; 51), and the king is not spared in the diatribe (e.g., 50:43; 51:34–35). On the other hand, during the days after the first Babylonian deportation, Jeremiah admonished the exiles to pray for the city of their captivity and to seek its welfare (Jer 29:7–9).

Many centuries later, when the Jews were living under the harsh yoke of the Roman Empire, this ambivalent attitude persisted. The animosity that the church felt toward Rome is abundantly evident in the depiction of Roman authority in the Gospels, and even more so in the symbolism of Revelation. Yet Peter urges Christians to be subject to every human institution, including kings and governing authorities, because those authorities are established by God Himself (1 Pet 2:13–17). Paul, too, admonishes the Christians in Rome to submit to governmental authorities (Rom 13:1–7), both to avoid wrath and to have a clear conscience before God. Barrett comments,

> Honour and respect are due to earthly rulers not because they are powerful and influential *men,* but because they have been appointed by God. It follows that to treat them with less than their due of honour is to dishonour God; and honour without

> its practical corollary of the due payment of taxes for the maintenance of the authority would be a mockery.[149]

The circumstances surrounding the composition of the book of Esther were likely quite different from those that existed when Daniel and Revelation were written, though they might not be too dissimilar from the time when the book of Romans was composed.[150] When the government is not actively hostile to the people of God, we might well hope to win the favor of the powers that be by respectful submission to their authority. But that rationale is not what lies behind Paul's and Peter's instructions to Christians: these are not so much pragmatic responses to a potentially dangerous government, but an obligation to God.

The text does not tell us what motivated Mordecai's loyalty to Xerxes. It may have been enlightened self-interest or some sense of justice. His actions, though, are consistent with the biblical injunctions regarding the relationship between the people of God and the earthly powers that be. It is obvious that Esther's storyteller does not like King Xerxes, but he does not deny him the authority and deference his office is due.

Application and Devotional Implications

It is sometimes difficult for us to wish well government leaders whose policies we oppose. Indeed, it is not uncommon to hear Christians make disparaging or even hateful comments about people who have been elected to high office. The examples of a number of biblical heroes, however, could well put us to shame. King Xerxes was no paragon of virtue: he was a pagan, and as depicted here, not especially competent. Yet Mordecai rescued the king from danger and even worked as his close adviser. Daniel, too, worked within the administrations of Nebuchadnezzar, the despoiler of Jerusalem, and his equally tyrannical successors. Paul admonished the Christians of Rome to submit to emperors who were among the most self-indulgent, cruel, and immoral people the world has known (Rom 13:1–7). They were basically following the instructions that God had given the exiles in Babylon, according to the prophet Jeremiah: "Seek the prosperity of the city where I have deported you, and pray on behalf of it to Yahweh, for in its prosperity you will have prosperity" (29:7).

---

149. C. K. Barrett, *A Commentary on the Epistle to the Romans* (London: Harper & Row, 1957), 248.

150. There is a diversity of opinions on when these books were composed, though most commentators would put Daniel (in its final form) in the period of the Antiochan persecution (164–167 BC), Romans in the early part of Nero's reign, and Revelation near the end of the first century AD.

Through the ages, Christians have disagreed and even fought over the relationship between believers and civil authorities. Many of the faithful live under the rule of tyrants, infidels, or incompetents. When we hear of the hardships of our brothers and sisters, we might well think our only recourse is legal or even military intervention. The church has often been tempted, in one way or another, to force civil authorities to bow to its authority. The Scriptures, however, are unambiguous in their counsel that the responsibility to bow is ours. Bow, and pray, and eschew the temptation to seize civil power. Our weapons are spiritual, not political.

Selected Bibliography

Dandamayev, M. *Iranians in Achaemenid Babylonia.* Columbia Lectures on Iranian Studies 6. Costa Mesa, CA: Mazda, 1992.

Driver, G. R. "Problems and Solutions." *VT* 4 (1954): 224–45.

Ehrlich, A. *Randglossen zur hebräischen Bibel; Textkritisches, Sprachliches und Sachliches.* Vol. 7. Leipzig: J. C. Hinrichs, 1914.

Fox, M. V. *Character and ideology in the Book of Esther.* 2nd ed. Grand Rapids: Eerdmans, 2001.

Frolov, S. "Two Eunuchs, Two Conspiracies, and One Loyal Jew: The Narrative of Botched Regicide in Esther as Text- and Redaction-Critical Test Case." *VT* 52 (2002): 304–25.

Gordis, R. "Studies in the Esther Narrative." *JBL* 95 (1976): 43–58.

Groves, E. "Double Take: Another Look at the Second Gathering of the Virgins in Esther 2.19a." In *The Book of Esther in Modern Research*, ed. L. J. Greenspoon and S. W. Crawford, 91–110. London: T&T Clark, 2003.

Rudolph, W. "Textkritisches zum Estherbuch." *VT* 4 (1954): 89–90.

Thornton, T. "The Crucifixion of Haman and the Scandal of the Cross." *JTS* 37 (1986): 419–26.

Yamauchi, E. *Persia and the Bible.* Grand Rapids: Baker, 1997.

The Threat to the Jews (3:1–4:17)

Introduction

In this section of Esther, we enter the focus of the narrative. The final main character, Haman, is introduced as the newly appointed vizier of Xerxes' kingdom. Haman is identified as an Agagite, a designation that would raise red flags for the Jewish readers of this text. The name "Agag" is associated with the Amalekites, bitter enemies of the Jews. The king orders all people to bow before Haman, but Mordecai the Jew refuses. This act of defiance sets off the main crisis of the narrative: Haman becomes so enraged at Mordecai that he has the king pass a decree to destroy all the Jews. When Mordecai learns of the edict, he goes to his cousin Queen Esther and pleads for her to intercede with the king. Overcoming her initial reluctance, she agrees to do so.

This unit falls into three main sections. In the first section, the crisis is initiated when Mordecai refuses to bow to Haman, and Haman decides to kill all the Jews. In the second scene, Haman appeals to the king for the destruction of the Jews. The third scene is the encounter between Mordecai and Esther.

These first two scenes form a parallel to the episode of Queen Vashti:

Table 2: Parallels between Esth 1:10–22 and 3:1–15

Xerxes and Vashti	Haman and Mordecai
• Xerxes, apparently full of pride, orders Vashti to appear before his guests (1:10–11)	• Haman, apparently full of pride, expects all people to follow the king's order to bow before him (3:2)
• Vashti refuses to obey the king's order (1:12)	• Mordecai refuses to obey the king's order (3:3)
• Xerxes is publicly humiliated (implied)	• Haman is publicly humiliated (implied)
• Xerxes is filled with wrath (1:12)	• Haman is filled with wrath (3:5)
• Memucan warns Xerxes that all women will become insubordinate (1:17–18)	• Haman warns Xerxes that the Jews are insubordinate (3:8)
• Xerxes issues a decree attempting to subjugate all women (1:20–22)	• Xerxes issues a decree attempting to exterminate all Jews (3:12–15)

In both cases, the defiance of one representative of a marginalized group precipitates action against the entire group. But while the decree in the first case was mostly designed to send a message, the second decree has upped the stakes considerably. Memucan's decree directly affected only Vashti, but it was intended to cause a reaction among all the women of the Persian Empire; Haman's decree, though designed as a response to Mordecai, would destroy all the Jews of Persia.

Memucan's decree left Vashti with little recourse. She had no advocate, and her story was ended. In the case of the Jews, however, the story was only beginning. Ironically, Vashti's defiance had created the way for the Jews to be delivered from the consequences of Mordecai's defiance, since her replacement, Queen Esther, would arise as the Jews' deliverer.

The third scene of this unit (chap. 4) is quite different from the others. The air of frivolity and indulgence that marked the earlier sections of the book evaporates, replaced by tension and uncertainty. Instead of feasting, there is fasting. Instead of gold and precious stones and perfumes, there is dust and ashes. The action moves outdoors, away from the splendor of the palace and its pomp. The women's quarters, formerly a place for indulgence, seems now more like a cloister, a place where Esther is sheltered from the affairs of the kingdom. But in this chapter, too, Esther speaks her first words and begins to emerge as the strong and cunning character she will become by the end of the book.

Outline

- III. The Threat to the Jews (3:1–4:17)
  - A. Mordecai Provokes Haman (3:1–7)
  - B. Haman's Plot to Destroy the Jews (3:8–15)
    - 1. Haman Petitions the King (3:8–11)
    - 2. Haman Issues the Decree (3:12–15)
  - C. Esther Resolves to Help (4:1–17)
    - 1. Mordecai and the Jews Lament the Order (4:1–3)
    - 2. Mordecai Appeals to Esther (4:4–17)
      - a. Mordecai Refuses Clothing from Esther (4:4)
      - b. Mordecai Orders Esther to Intercede (4:5–9)
      - c. Esther Agrees to Intercede (4:10–17)

Mordecai Provokes Haman (3:1–7)

Translation

1 After these things, King Xerxes promoted[1] Haman, son of Hammedatha, the Agagite. He elevated him and placed his office[2] above all his noble companions.[3] **2** All of the king's servants who were in the king's gate would do obeisance and bow down before Haman, because thus had the king commanded concerning him. But Mordecai did not do obeisance or bow down.
3 The king's servants who were in the king's gate said to Mordecai, "Why do you transgress the king's command?" **4** While they were speaking to him daily, he did not listen to them. So they told Haman, to see whether Mordecai's deeds would be tolerated,[4] because he had told them he was a Jew. **5** When Haman saw that Mordecai was not doing obeisance or bowing to him, Haman was filled with fury. **6** He considered it contemptible to stretch out his hand against Mordecai only, because Mordecai's race had been reported to him; so Haman sought to destroy all the Jews who were

1. Lit., "magnified."
2. Lit., "his seat."
3. Lit., "all the nobles who were with him."
4. Lit., "to see whether Mordecai's deeds would stand."

in the entire kingdom of Xerxes—Mordecai's race. **7** In the first month, the month of Nisan, in the twelfth year of King Xerxes, a "pur"—that is, the lot—was cast[5] before Haman, day by day and month by month for twelve months. *The lot fell on the thirteenth day of*[6] the twelfth month, the month of Adar.

Textual Notes

1.a. Instead of הָאֲגָגִי, "the Agagite," the LXX and AT read Βουγαῖον.

4.a. Instead of בְּאָמְרָם the *Qere** reads כְּאָמְרָם.

5.a. A few Syr. manuscripts add "against Mordecai" at the end of the verse.

6.a. The phrase וַיִּבֶז בְּעֵינָיו לִשְׁלֹחַ יָד בְּמָרְדֳּכַי לְבַדּוֹ כִּי־הִגִּידוּ לוֹ אֶת־עַם מָרְדֳּכָי ("He considered it contemptible to stretch out his hand against Mordecai only, because Mordecai's race had been reported to him") is absent in the LXX.

7.a. The final section of this verse, מִיּוֹם לְיוֹם וּמֵחֹדֶשׁ לְחֹדֶשׁ שְׁנֵים־עָשָׂר הוּא־חֹדֶשׁ אֲדָר ("from day to day and from month to the twelfth month, the month of Adar"), makes little sense in the context. Clearly, some words have been dropped in transmission. Based on the LXX and later passages from the book, we can reconstruct the meaning of the verse (if not necessarily the precise words): "from day to day and from month to month. The lot fell on the thirteenth day of the twelfth month, the month of Adar." See further Bush, 380–81.

Commentary

3:1 The events that now occur come "sometime afterward," without specification of when. Since Haman launches his plot against the Jews in the first month of the twelfth year, we can probably assume that Haman's promotion came in the eleventh year, since he would have been unlikely to have endured Mordecai's insubordination for a very long time.

Our introduction to Haman comes without warning. He is not mentioned among the king's previously named advisers, seeming to make his appearance out of nowhere. Nor does the book of Esther give an explanation for his meteoric rise to prominence. His name, "Haman," as well as that of his father, Hammedatha, appear to be Persian, though their meanings are disputed. Haman's name is most likely a Hebraized form of the name that

---

5. Lit., "he cast." Used without a subject, the verb form is the equivalent of an English pass. formation. Usually, however, the verb form would be pl. (cf. English, "They cannot take away my dignity" = "My dignity cannot be taken away").

6. Not present in the Heb. See the textual notes for explanation.

appears in classical sources as Omanes. Omanes is probably a form of the name "Humpan," an Elamite deity.[7]

More important to the audience, however, would have been how the name sounded to their ears. It is impossible to imagine that this name would not have brought a smile to an ancient Jew's face, since it sounds so similar to the Heb. word הָמוֹן (*hāmôn*), "tumult, confusion."[8] The term "Agagite" is rendered as a gentilic noun likely indicating ethnic origin, though a few interpreters have taken it to refer to a geographical location.[9] Most interpreters through the ages have understood the text to mean that Haman was a descendant of Agag, king of the Amalekites (a summary of these sources can be found in Moore 1971, 35). Given the apparent connection of Mordecai with the line of Saul, the connection between Haman and the line of Agag seems poetic and darkly foreboding.

The Amalekites, a nomadic people descended from Esau (Gen 36:12, 16), were one of Israel's archenemies in the days of Moses (Exod 17:8–13; Deut 25:17–18). Indeed, it could be said that they *were* the archenemy, since they are the only people against whom God Himself proclaimed war ("A war will be for Yahweh with Amalek from generation to generation," Exod 17:16). During the reign of King Saul, however, the conflict came to a fateful head. God had ordered Saul to utterly destroy the Amalekites and to take no plunder from them. Saul, however, spared some of the loot and took the Amalekite king Agag back to camp as a captive. When the prophet Samuel came into camp, he was outraged and hacked Agag to pieces. He then proclaimed to Saul that his disobedience would cost him his throne (1 Sam 15). Because Saul had failed to annihilate the Amalekites, his reign was brought to an end. In the story of Mordecai and Haman, we see the reversal of that fateful event: now, it is the Amalekite who attempts the destruction of Israel. The affair appears to be a rematch of Saul and Agag—but this time, it is Agag who appears to have the upper hand.

In the LXX and AT versions, Haman's appellation is rendered Βουγαῖος. Though various explanations have been offered for this term, the most

---

7. See R. Zadok, "On the Historical Background of the Book of Esther," *BN* 24 (1984): 18–19.

8. *Pace* Bush, 379, who argues that the names have no significance since the author makes no pun on them. The author is sophisticated enough to assume that his readers would get the joke without having it pointed out to them.

9. See M. Weschler, "Two Para-Biblical Novellae from Qumran Cave 4: A Reevaluation of 4Q550," *DSD* 7 (2000): 135n31. Jobes, 120–21, suggests that the name might be a general term for an anti-Semite, but there is no evidence for the term being used in this manner in biblical or postbiblical times.

likely is that it is related to the common Greek noun Βουγαῖος, "braggart."[10] Though the syntactical formation would suggest instead that Βουγαῖος should be an ethnic designation, the nearly identical form of the name with the word for a braggart cannot be ignored. If a modern novelist described a loudmouthed character as "Bill, of the Blowhardians," the audience would hardly be puzzling over the identity of a people known as the "Blowhardians." Making Haman a braggart rather than an Amalekite is another illustration of the LXX tendency to universalize the story of Esther, transforming the struggle from an ethnic conflict into a cosmic conflict between Jews and the rest of the world.

Haman's promotion also offers a set of problems. The first is his office: what position did Haman occupy? Modern writers frequently call him Xerxes' "vizier" or "prime minister," but there is no evidence that the Achaemenid court had such a position.[11] Some scholars suggest that he held the position of *hazarpatish*, or "Commander of the Thousand" (called the "chiliarch" by the Greeks). This officer was the head of the king's personal bodyguard, and no one could enter the king's presence without his permission. But while the Greeks believed the chiliarch was the second great power of the Persian Empire, the Persian sources do not seem to attribute much authority to the position.[12] Furthermore, the book of Esther never depicts Haman acting in this capacity. Instead, he has to wait to be admitted to the king's presence, like everyone else (cf. Esth 6:4–5). It has also been suggested that Haman held the office that Greek sources call the "King's Eye," an inspector who had charge over the satraps.[13] Such a position would have been very powerful, but there is little evidence from Persian sources that such an office even existed.[14] It appears that our narrator is not interested

10. P. Haupt, "Critical Notes on Esther," *AJSL* 24 (1907–1908): 141. For other explanations, see M. Weschler, "The Appellation Βουγαῖος and Ethnic Contextualization in the Greek Text of Esther," *VT* 51 (2001): 109–14, who associates it with the Beja of the Sudan region; and K. Jobes, "How an Assassination Changed the Greek Text of Esther," *ZAW* 110 (1998): 75–78, who connects it with the Bagoas who was involved in a plot to assassinate Artexerxes II.

11. Some Persian officials seemed to function as the king's second-in-command, but there was no specific office associated with such authority. He might be the chiliarch under one king and cupbearer under another. Cf. Cook, *CHI*, 2:232–33.

12. On various officers in the Achaemenid court, see Cook, *CHI*, 2:232–38; on the limitation of the power of the chiliarch, see Briant, *From Cyrus to Alexander: A History of the Persian Empire* (Winona Lake, IN: Eisenbrauns, 2002), 222–23, 258–59.

13. See Olmstead, *A History of the Persian Empire* (Chicago: University of Chicago Press, 1948), 59.

14. So Briant, *Cyrus to Alexander*, 343–44.

in defining Haman's office: he is "second in command," like Joseph was in Pharaoh's court (Gen 41:37–45). Indeed, like Joseph, all people will be commanded to bow before him (Gen 41:43; cf. Esth 3:2). The irony here is that Joseph used his position to secure the preservation of the Israelites; Haman would use his position to attempt their destruction.

The other mystery is why Haman rose to prominence so quickly. Classical authors note that the Persian kings greatly honored those who did them a service.[15] That Haman's promotion comes so quickly after the assassination attempt had been foiled might well make the reader wonder whether there is some connection between the two events: did Haman receive a reward that should have been Mordecai's? The suggestion is even more intriguing in light of Mordecai's later receiving a reward that Haman thought should be his (chap. 6), perhaps a case of dramatic reversal. If such is the case, it might well give credence to the theory that Mordecai's refusal to honor Haman was a case of "sour grapes," as we will consider below.

3:2–4 The order for all the people to bow before Haman would not have been unusual. According to Herodotus, the Persians were very conscious of social class and observed strict protocols regarding rank.[16] They would greet equals with a kiss, but would always bow and make obeisance before those of higher standing. The practice was also common among the Jews, who had no problems kneeling before those whom they respected or whose favor they wished to garner (see, e.g., Gen 33:3; 42:6; 1 Sam 20:41; 24:8).

Why, then, does Mordecai refuse to bow? The common assumption among Christians seems to be that Mordecai considered such prostration to be akin to idolatry.[17] This idea was also found in ancient times: in the LXX, Mordecai contends that the reason he would not bow is that he refused to put any man's glory over that of God and would worship no one but Him (Add Esth C.5–7). The notion clearly rests on an understanding that bowing before someone implies worship, an idea that was not known in the ANE. The LXX also implies that Haman had been in on the plot to kill the king and that Mordecai was aware of the fact (Add Esth A.17). The translators apparently inserted this detail into the narrative to clarify the ambiguity regarding Mordecai's motives, and it is not helpful for

15. Xenophon, *Cyr.* 8.4.5; Herodotus, *Hist.* 3.154.

16. *Hist.* 1.134.

17. This idea appears in many popular depictions of the Esther story and in many Sunday school curricula. It is apparently illustrated by the cover art on Keith Green's 1978 album, "No Compromise." The picture shows a man standing upright in the midst of a group of people prostrating themselves before a ruler. The picture (by artist Joe Zucker) implies that bowing would be a compromise of religious principle.

understanding the MT version. Some of the traditional Jewish texts (e.g., *Tg. Esth. I*; *Esth. Rab.*) explained Mordecai's actions by claiming that Haman carried an idol with him, and it was before this image that Mordecai refused to bow.[18]

Paton (197) finds Mordecai's conduct inexplicable and attributes it to arrogance. Likewise, Baldwin (76) sees Mordecai's act as one of "pigheaded pride." They offer no reason, however, for why Mordecai felt he should be above Haman. Bickerman, however, suggests that Mordecai might have been suffering from "sour grapes": Mordecai was jealous because Haman received a promotion that he thought was his due.[19] There is much to commend this theory. First, there is the placement of the episode immediately after the story of Mordecai's intervention on behalf of the king. It is fresh in the reader's mind that Mordecai had received no reward for his heroic act. It might be considered a biblical trope that when Jews do favors for foreign kings, they are rewarded with a promotion, as in the case of Joseph (Gen 41) and Daniel (Dan 2 and 5). The parallel to Joseph is especially striking, since Esther's narrator has used language that clearly alludes to the Joseph story (Levenson, 68; Laniak, 221).[20] The narrator and audience might have known not only these stories, but others of similar vein, conditioning them to expect that Mordecai's actions would have been rewarded with a similar promotion—but instead the promotion goes to Haman. Of course Mordecai would have been offended. Also, that Mordecai refuses to explain his behavior gives the impression that he is pouting over a perceived injury. Finally, there is—typically overlooked—that even before the Jews are empowered to defend themselves, Mordecai receives the office vacated by Haman (Esth 8:2). His promotion appears to be part of the reversal motif, representing the righting of a wrong. If this narrative is truly "balanced," this act could be the correction of an earlier injustice and implies that Mordecai should have received the office that had been given to Haman. It should also be noted that Mordecai receives Haman's office right after a eunuch reminds the king of Mordecai's aid to the king (Esth 7:9).

---

18. For sources of this story and similar rabbinic explanations, see Fox, *Character and Ideology*, 43–44.

19. E. Bickerman, *Four Strange Books of the Bible: Jonah, Daniel, Kohelet, Esther* (New York: Schocken Books, 1967), 178–80.

20. E.g., Potiphar's wife attempts to seduce Joseph "day after day," but he "would not listen" (Gen 39:10); precisely the same phrases are used in this episode of Mordecai's refusal to listen to the daily entreaties from the king's servants. Both heroes will be sentenced to death, but will be delivered and receive promotions to second-in-command.

Most scholars, however, have not been persuaded by Bickerman's proposal. Rather, the most widely accepted interpretation (by Ehrlich, Meinhold, Moore, Fox, Bush, Laniak, and others) is that Mordecai refused to bow to Haman because of the ethnic antagonism between Jews and the Amalekites. Many have argued that Mordecai's revelation that he was a Jew (3:4) was his explanation for refusing to bow. The text, however, implies that Mordecai did not answer when the other officials asked why he would not bow, so there is little reason to conclude that "he had told them he was a Jew" was his explanation for his obduracy—it was background information that he had already given them. Nor would his being Jewish have served as an explanation for his behavior, since his coworkers would have had no reason to know of the enmity between Jews and Amalekites. Rather, what the text states is that they were curious whether Mordecai's behavior would be tolerated "because he was a Jew." The implication is that Jews were somehow treated differently from other people. We have already seen that Mordecai believed it would be detrimental to Esther's bid to become queen if it were known that she was a Jew. Perhaps Mordecai felt he had been passed over for the promotion and his service overlooked because he was a Jew. Perhaps the narrator assumed that his audience, who may have experienced some prejudice living in the Gentile world, would draw that conclusion. On the other hand, the text also implies that the Jews *were* different from other people, as Haman's wife, Zeresh, will later acknowledge (6:13). Mordecai's colleagues were interested in seeing whether Mordecai could get away with insubordination because he was a member of an ethnic group that was subject to prejudice and yet apparently lived a "charmed life."

It is also worth noting that Mordecai's refusal to bow was not only an insult to Haman, but to the king as well. After having just saved the king's life, he is now deliberately insubordinate. This fact further supports the theory that Mordecai is responding to an apparent snub. Mordecai is not just stubborn; he is angry at the king.

The phrase לִרְאוֹת הֲיַעַמְדוּ דִּבְרֵי מָרְדֳּכַי (*lirĕʾôt hăya ʿamdû dibrê mordŏkay*; translated here "to see whether Mordecai's deeds would be tolerated") is a crux in this passage. Fox, followed by Bush (379–80), Berlin (37), and others, argues that this phrase means something like, "to see if his explanation would hold up."[21] They then argue that the following phrase, "for he had told them he was a Jew," was Mordecai's explanation for his behavior. This understanding seems to have been adopted by several translations (e.g., NASB, NRSV). Other translations have understood the phrase in a way similar to that offered here, such as the NIV's "to see whether Mordecai's behavior would be tolerated" (so, too, the NLT).

21. Fox, *Character and Ideology*, 45–46.

The phrase יַעַמְדוּ הַדְּבָרִים (*ya'amdû haddĕbārîm*; lit., "the words/deeds would stand") occurs nowhere else in the Heb. Bible. The words, however, are very common. The first, דבר (*dbr*), basically means "word," but it very frequently means "thing," "issue," or "deed" (cf. Esth 2:23 and 6:1, "the book of the deeds of the days"; 1 Kgs 11:41, "the deeds of Solomon"). The word עמד (*'md*) typically means "stand," though it can also have the sense of "endure." In late-biblical and postbiblical Heb., it begins to appear in some of the idioms where previously the word קום (*qwm*; "arise," "endure") had been used. On that basis, Fox compares the expression in Esth 3:4 with Deut 19:15, "By the mouth of two or three witnesses will the charge be confirmed (יָקוּם דָּבָר, *yāqûm dābār*)," paraphrasing the words as meaning "a claim being accepted as valid."[22] The analogy is far from perfect. In Deut 19:5, the meaning of דבר is clearly dictated by the context. The expression seems to be a technical phrase quite similar to the English phrase "the charges will stand." In Esth 3:4, it is unlikely that the other courtiers would consider Mordecai's declaration that he was a Jew to be a sufficient excuse for refusing the order of the king. Surely, they would not have thought that Haman would have considered it a sufficient excuse!

My understanding is that the word עמד in Esth 3:4 is based on one of its common meanings, "continue, endure." The phrase could literally be translated, "to see whether Mordecai's words/deeds would be allowed to continue" (understanding the verb form to have a juss. force). The phrase "for he had told them he was a Jew," in this interpretation, is not the content of Mordecai's "words," but the reason why the courtiers suspected his actions would not be tolerated. Fox's argument that the text would then have simply said, "Because he was a Jew," does not take full account of the context: Mordecai had earlier told Esther not to *tell* anyone that she is Jewish.[23] The other courtiers would not have known Mordecai was Jewish unless he had told them. The narrator is drawing a contrast between Esther, who was concealing her Jewish identity, and Mordecai, who had revealed his Jewishness.

3:5 Haman is now informed that Mordecai is not bowing before him. Previously, he had been unaware that he was being publicly insulted; now, the insult is known to him. We might well imagine that part of his anger comes from the humiliation of knowing he was being treated disrespectfully for days without ever knowing it.

3:6 Haman felt it would be beneath him to strike out against one man. If he punished only Mordecai, it would mean that Mordecai had accomplished

---

22. Ibid., 277–78.

23. Ibid.

precisely what he had intended, which was to insult Haman. Executing Mordecai would have made the insult appear significant, which Haman could not allow. But his pride would not allow him to overlook it, either. His decision to kill an entire nation because he felt insulted was, to say the least, excessive. It would sound almost comedic, if not for it having eerie reverberations in later history: it is often argued that Adolf Hitler's hatred of the Jews was inspired partly by his rejection by a Jewish director when he had applied to art school in Vienna. The real irony of this response, however, is in its connections to other episodes in the Esther narrative and beyond. On the one hand, it is similar to the story of Vashti: when one woman had refused to submit to the will of the king, he chose to pass an edict that would order the submission of the entire sex (we might suspect this edict was generally ineffective). Now, when Haman feels insulted by one Jew, he responds with an edict that will punish the entire race. On the other hand, there is a kind of twisted symmetry in Haman's plan: Israel had been commanded to utterly exterminate the Amalekites (Deut 25:17–19; 1 Sam 15:3), and now an Amalekite would attempt to exterminate Israel.

3:7 Haman, confident that his plan will be approved, selects a day for the deed. Haman could have come before the king and asked that all the Jews be destroyed as quickly as possible, but he apparently believes that this undertaking will require divine sanction—evidence, perhaps, of a notion that the Jews were considered a particularly lucky people (Esth 6:13). He chose the month of Nisan (March–April) for his undertaking. It makes sense that Haman would have cast his lots in the first month of the year: in Babylonian thought, the opening days of the new year were the time when the gods determined mortal destinies. Since they did so by casting lots, it was appropriate that Haman used the same method to decide the fate of the Jews. In a sense, he was attempting to control the fate of the Jews and likely appealing to pagan deities to help him fulfill his designs against them.[24]

For the Jewish audience of this text, however, the thirteenth day of Nisan would have sounded a significant note for another reason. It was only two days before the Jews celebrated the Passover. On the eve of the day when the Jews celebrated their greatest deliverance, Haman was determining when the Jews were to die. This link between the story of Purim and that of Passover was only one of many recognized by the rabbis. The Jerusalem Talmud states that the two acts of deliverance are linked to each other (*y. Meg.* 1:5), and the *Megillath Ta'anith* draws several comparisons between

24. See further J. Rosenheim, "Fate and Freedom in the Scroll of Esther," *Prooftexts* 12 (1992): 127–29.

the two events.[25] Many scholars and expositors have drawn links between the two festivals of deliverance, which form bookends on the Jewish year: Nisan in the first month of the year, and Purim in the last month.[26]

Throughout the ANE, the casting of lots was considered a reliable method of seeking divine guidance, and both Herodotus and Xenophon attest to the use of lots in Persia.[27] Various prayers and rituals were used to insure that the lot was true.[28] Typically, the method involved placing pebbles or potsherds in a jug or jar and shaking it until one popped out.[29] In the case of Haman's lot, the apparent corruption of the text has caused questions about how the lot was cast and what its purpose was. The wording "from day to day and month to month" reads on the surface like the lot was continually cast for several months. More likely, it means that the lot was cast to determine, first, the proper day of the month for the prosecution of the pogrom, and then the proper month. The other question concerns what the lot was determining. Paton (201–2) argues that the lot was intended to choose the day for Haman to approach the king, but that notion cannot be readily reconciled with the context (as Fox observes, it would mean that two years elapsed between the time Haman decided to annihilate the Jews and the time of the pogrom).[30]

Because of the selection of the lot, eleven months would pass between the issuing of the proclamation and the time of its enactment. This month would have been the latest possible date that the lot could have chosen, since they were casting to select months, not years. The thirteenth day was considered an unlucky one to the Babylonians and Persians (Clines, 297). It is almost as if "fate" itself were balking at the notion of the Jewish genocide.

The classical issue regarding this verse concerned the meaning of the word *pur*. Once thought to be a mistake or corruption of a foreign word, since the publication of Lewy's study there has been little question that

---

25. See H. Lichtenstein, "Die Fastenrolle, eine Untersuchung zur jüdisch-hellenistischen Geschichte; מגלת תענית," *HUCA* 8–9 (1931–1932): 347.
26. See further A. Cohen "'Hu Ha-goral': The Religious Significance of Esther," *Judaism* 23 (1974): 87–94.
27. *Hist.* 3.128; *Cyr.* 1.6.46; 4.5.55.
28. See A. Oppenheim, *Ancient Mesopotamia: Portrait of a Dead Civilization* (Chicago & London: University of Chicago Press, 1964), 208–9; A. M. Kitz, "The Hebrew Terminology of Lot Casting and Its Ancient Near Eastern Context," *CBQ* 62 (2000): 207–14.
29. For a survey of methods and terminology, see C. Van Dam, *The Urim and Thummim: A Means of Revelation in Ancient Israel* (Winona Lake, IN: Eisenbrauns, 1997), 40–44.
30. Fox, *Character and Ideology*, 47.

the text is correct in identifying the meaning of *pur* as "lot."[31] It is not the Heb. word, however, but the Akkadian word, attested in Assyrian and Neo-Babylonian sources. Esther's author provides the Heb. translation for his readers who would have been unfamiliar with the term.[32] The more interesting question concerns why a Heb. text set in ancient Persia would use an Akkadian word (and not even the primary Akkadian word) for the lot.[33] There is no use of this word attested in Persian literature. While it cannot be proven that the word *pur* was *not* used in Persia at this time, the evidence suggests that the Akkadian word was given in order to provide an explanation for the name of the holiday "Purim."[34]

Biblical Theology Comments

3:2 As Mordecai refuses to bow before Haman in direct defiance of the king's order, we are once again confronted with the issue of obedience to those in power. What is our Christian obligation to the powers that be? This question is discussed in some detail in the "Biblical Theology Comments" on 1:10–12 and 2:21–22.

The specific question of Mordecai's justification has been addressed differently by various Christian scholars. For Baldwin (76), Mordecai's refusal to bow was a display of pride. Jobes (126), on the other hand, sees the action as heroic: "Although Mordecai did not refuse to pay homage to Haman for explicitly religious reasons, in the Esther story, he (and Vashti?) stands on the side of those who refuse to bow to the beast and who, as a result, suffer the crushing force of earthly powers driven by Satan." (Jobes' understanding may have been influenced by Fox's characterization of Mordecai as an "unblemished" figure, a characterization that makes him unwilling to attribute any bad motives to Mordecai.[35]) One's evaluation of the refusal depends on what one understands to be the motivation behind his act. If we believe, as argued here, that Mordecai was motivated by bitterness, there would seem to be no possible excuse for his action. We may find the practice of prostration before superiors to be distasteful, but in the ancient world, it was the normal way of showing respect to those of higher standing.

---

31. J. Lewy, "Old Assyrian *puru'um* and *pûrum*," *RHA* 5 (1939): 116–24. For a survey of classical (pre-Lewy) opinions, see Paton, 77–94.
32. See W. Hallo, "The First Purim," *BA* 46 (1983): 19–26.
33. An interesting discussion of terminology may be found in A. Taggar-Cohen, "The Casting of Lots among the Hittites in Light of Ancient Near Eastern Parallels," *JANES* 29 (2007): 97–103.
34. See further the discussion "Esther and Purim" in the introduction.
35. Fox, *Character and Ideology*, 185.

Mordecai's refusal to comply was no less than a direct insult to Haman. How could such an act have been a good thing?

If we accept, like most scholars, that Mordecai's action resulted from longstanding ethnic hatred, as Jobes (119–20) argues, does it make it less objectionable? He still is refusing to give Haman the respect his office was due. Again, Paul instructs the Romans, "Give to everyone what you owe them: If you owe taxes, pay taxes; if revenue, then revenue; if respect, then respect; if honor, then honor" (Rom 13:7 NIV). Paul did not qualify the statement by saying, "Give respect to those whom you like."

3:6 Haman's response to Mordecai's disrespect is excessive, but not surprising. One should not be surprised by any evils perpetrated by the unregenerate. Mordecai provoked a wicked man, and the man acted wickedly. That is not to exonerate him; the book of Esther will hold Haman responsible for his actions, and he will pay a price proportional to the wickedness he had intended to do. But we should not excuse Mordecai, either. What did he expect his show of defiance to accomplish? It was a rash and ineffectual display. His pride provoked the crisis that Haman has initiated, because he failed to account for Haman's evil. Well should we heed the advice that Jesus gave His disciples: "I am sending you out like sheep in the midst of wolves. Therefore be wise as serpents and innocent as doves" (Matt 10:16).

3:7 Does God have a role in the casting of lots? The use of lots is typically discouraged in Christian circles. The casting of lots, however, is never forbidden in the Bible. It was not considered a form of divination (which was strictly forbidden; Lev 19:26; Deut 18:10), which used magic to implore spirits to answer inquiries. In the Heb. Bible, lots had both secular and cultic uses. They could be used for gambling (Psa 22:18) or to settle a dispute, just as we might flip a coin today (Prov 18:18). Apparently lots were cast at slave auctions as well (Joel 3:3; Job 6:27; Nah 3:10), a sign of callous disregard for human dignity. In the religious context, lots had a variety of roles. They were cast to determine which goat would be slaughtered and which would be driven away on the Day of Atonement (Lev 16:8); to divide up the promised land among the tribes (Josh 18:6–10); and to publicly verify the choice of Saul as king of Israel (1 Sam 10:20–21). Lots were used to determine guilty parties (Josh 7:14–18; 1 Sam 14:42) and to assign responsibilities for the singers in the temple (1 Chr 25:8).[36]

Lots continued to have an important role in intertestamental and NT times. The Dead Sea Scrolls community apparently believed that the destinies of every individual was determined by "lots"—people were born into

36. J. Lindlom, "Lot-casting in the OT," *VT* 12 (1962): 164–78.

either the lot of Sons of Light or the lot of Sons of Darkness, and they received their measure of goodness or wickedness according to their place in the lot (see, e.g., 1QS 1:10; 7:15–16; 11:7–8; CD-A 13:11–12; 11QMelch 2:8).[37] No such idea is found in the NT, but the practice of casting lots continued, with both negative and positive connotations. Lots were cast to determine who would get Jesus' robe (Matt 27:35) and to determine which of the disciples would replace Judas Iscariot among the apostles (Acts 1:24–26). The prayer offered by the disciples when the lot was cast demonstrates the principle behind the casting of lots in Israel and among the Jews: it was God who determined how the lot would fall. "The lot will be cast into the lap, but all of its decisions are from Yahweh" (Prov 16:33).

Selected Bibliography

Bickerman, E. *Four Strange Books of the Bible: Jonah, Daniel, Kohelet, Esther*. New York: Schocken Books, 1967.

Briant, P. *From Cyrus to Alexander: A History of the Persian Empire.* Winona Lake, IN: Eisenbrauns, 2002.

Fox, M. V. *Character and Ideology in the Book of Esther*. 2nd ed. Grand Rapids: Eerdmans, 2001.

Hallo, W. "The First Purim." *BA* 46 (1983): 19–26.

Haupt, P. "Critical Notes on Esther." *AJSL* 24 (1907–1908): 97–186.

Kitz, A. M. "The Hebrew Terminology of Lot Casting and Its Ancient Near Eastern Context." *CBQ* 62 (2000): 207–14.

Lewy, J. "Old Assyrian puru'um and pûrum." *RHA* 5 (1939): 116–24.

Lichtenstein, H. "Die Fastenrolle, eine Untersuchung zur jüdisch-hellenistischen Geschichte; מגלת תענית." *HUCA* 8–9 (1931–1932): 257–351.

Olmstead, A. T. *History of the Persian Empire*. Chicago: University of Chicago Press, 1959.

Oppenheim, A. *Ancient Mesopotamia: Portrait of a Dead Civilization*. Chicago: University of Chicago Press, 1964.

Taggar-Cohen, A. "The Casting of Lots among the Hittites in Light of Ancient Near Eastern Parallels." *JANES* 29 (2007): 97–103.

Weschler, M. "Two Para-Biblical Novellae from Qumran Cave 4: A Reevaluation of 4Q550." *DSD* 7 (2000): 140–72.

37. See further A. Lange, "The Determination of Fate by the Oracle of the Lot in the Dead Sea Scrolls, the Hebrew Bible and Ancient Mesopotamian Literature," in *Sapiential, Liturgical and Poetical Texts from Qumran: Proceedings of the Third Meeting of the International Organization for Qumran Studies, Oslo, 1998: Published in Memory of Maurice Baillet,* ed. D. Falk, F. Garcia Martinez, and E. Schuller (Leiden: Brill, 2000), 39–48.

Zadok, R. "On the Historical Background of the Book of Esther." *Bible Notes* 24 (1984): 18–23.

Haman's Plot to Destroy the Jews (3:8–15)

Translation

8 Then Haman said to King Xerxes, "There is one people scattered and sep-
arated among the peoples of your provinces of your kingdom, and their
laws differ from those of all the peoples, and the laws of the king they do
not do. It is not worth it for the king to put up with them. **9** If it seems good
to the king, let it be written to destroy them. Ten thousand talents of silver I
will pay to those who do the work to deposit in the royal treasury."

10 So the king took off his signet ring from his hand and gave it to
Haman son of Hammedatha, the Agagite, enemy of the Jews. **11** The king
said to Haman, "The silver is given to you, and so are the people, to do with
as you see fit." **12** The scribes of the king were summoned in the first month
on the thirteenth day, and it was written according to all that Haman com-
manded, to the king's satraps and to the governors over each province, and
to the officials of all the peoples, to each province in its own script and to
each people in its own language. In the name of King Xerxes it was written,
and it was sealed with the king's signet ring. **13** Letters were sent by couriers
to all the king's provinces to destroy, to kill, and to annihilate all Jews, from
young to old, children and women, in one day—the thirteenth day of the
twelfth month, which is the month of Adar—and to plunder their goods.
14 The copy of the writing was to be issued[38] as a decree in each province to
be published to all the peoples so they will be ready for this day. **15** The cou-
riers went out hastily by order of the king, and the decree was published in
Susa the Citadel. Then the king and Haman sat down to banquet,[39] but the
city of Susa was thrown into confusion.

Textual Notes

8.a. Vv. 8–12 are absent in the AT, essentially making Haman completely responsible for the plot against the Jews.

10.a. The LXX adds *σφραγίσαι κατὰ τῶν γεγραμμένων κατὰ τῶν* Ιουδαίων ("to seal what had been written concerning the Jews") after "to Haman" (לְהָמָ֑ן).

38. The use of the inf. const. here implies a "modal" construction (*IBHS*, 609 [§36.2.3.f]), indicating this verse is part of the proclamation.

39. Lit., "to drink."

10.b. The phrase בֶּן־הַמְּדָתָא הָאֲגָגִי צֹרֵר הַיְּהוּדִים ("son of Hammedatha, the Agagite, enemy of the Jews") is absent in the LXX.

11.a. For הַכֶּסֶף נָתוּן לָךְ (lit., "the silver is given to you") the LXX reads Τὸ μὲν ἀργύριον ἔχε, "Keep the silver."

13.a. "On the thirteenth day" is absent in the LXX.

13.b. After v. 13, the LXX and AT insert the text of Xerxes' decree, which is composed of seven verses.

Commentary

3:8 Haman's charge against the Jews is a masterful mix of truth and manipulation. He refers to the Jews as עַם־אֶחָד (*ʿam-ʾeḥād*), literally, "one people." Since Heb. has no indefinite article, the word "one" is used where the sense of indeterminacy must be made explicit: "There is a people ... "; or, as often translated, "There is a certain people ... " But in this context, Haman seems to have deliberately chosen the word to point out how unique the Jews are. Of all the peoples in his realm, there is *one* (and only one?) that is causing trouble.[40]

Haman's description of the Jews as "dispersed and separated" likewise has powerful connotations. The Jews were indeed dispersed, but they were also concentrated in Judah. By failing to mention that point, Haman made it sound like the Jews had no land of their own, and were little more than insignificant vagabonds. The verb מְפֹרָד (*mĕpōrād*) is problematic. It appears here in the pual stem, the only time it is used in this stem in the Heb. Bible. In the niphal stem, it means "separated," with the connotation of being at enmity or aloof (2 Sam 1:23; Prov 18:1). Logically, we might imagine that the pual could be an intensive form of the niphal, so giving the idea of a people who are violently at odds with others. Haman is implying the Jews are misanthropic. It is similar to the charge that the Jews' enemies leveled against the Jews in the days of Artaxerxes (Ezra 4:15), claiming that the Jews were seditious by nature. Similar charges were leveled against the Jews throughout the Greek and Roman eras.[41]

---

40. Cf. M. Fox, *Character and Ideology in the Book of Esther*, 2nd ed. (Grand Rapids: Eerdmans, 2001), 48.

41. See J. Sevenster, *The Roots of Pagan Anti-Semitism in the Ancient World* (Leiden: Brill, 1975), chap. 3; J. Daniel, "Anti-Semitism in the Hellenistic-Roman Period," *JBL* 98 (1979): 45–65.

The charge that the Jews had their own unique laws (the Persian word *dāt* is used here, instead of the Heb. word *torah*) is also true.[42] The Jews did have unique customs, such as keeping the Sabbath and eating kosher foods. (*Targum Sheni* inserts here a long and detailed list of the distinctive Jewish practices, presenting them with a falsified sense of outrage. The author, of course, was actually proud of the distinctive Jewish practices. The narrator and original audience of Esther might well have felt similar pride in Haman's contention that the Jews had their own peculiar laws, unlike those of any other people in the world.) This fact presented no problem for Xerxes, since the Persians allowed subject peoples to follow their own laws and customs, so long as these did not interfere with the well-being of the empire.[43] More troubling, however, was the charge that the Jews would not obey the king—i.e., that they were rebellious. This notion would surely have been cogent to Xerxes, since the king was known for his ruthless suppression of revolts (Egypt in 485 BC and Babylon in 484 and 482 BC). There was also a grain of truth in the charge, since Mordecai had deliberately disobeyed the king's command. But of course, Haman is overgeneralizing. He expands one instance of insubordination into a general tendency to ignore all the king's laws and attributes the actions of one man to an entire race. We have seen this tendency once before in the book of Esther, when Memucan expressed fear that the insubordination of one woman could spread to the entire sex.

The phrase שֹׁנוֹת מִכָּל־עָם (*šōnôt mikkol-ʿām*) "differing from all people" is unique in the OT. The use of the phrase שנה מן (*šnh mn*) to mean "differing from" is standard in MH, but not in SBH, which typically uses the word אחר (*ʾḥr*) to express the concept.[44]

The phrase וְלַמֶּלֶךְ אֵין־שֹׁוֶה לְהַנִּיחָם (*wĕlammelek ʾên-šōweh lĕhannîḥām*; lit., "And to the king it is not worth it to leave them alone") is noteworthy. The word שוה (*šwh*; "equal, like, worth") occurs only in one other passage from the OT historical books (2 Sam 22:34), and there it is in a poetic passage. Elsewhere in the OT, it always appears in poetic contexts. In the book of Esther, however, the word שוה appears three times: here in 3:8, where Haman requests the death of the Jews (3:8); second, where Haman

42. The word דָּת (*dāt*) is frequently translated "custom" in its first usage this passage, referring to the "customs" of the Jews. It certainly can have that meaning; but in the phrase דָּתֵי הַמֶּלֶךְ (*dātê hammelek*), "laws of the king," it must mean "laws" or "commands." The king would not be disturbed that a people have their own customs or traditions, only that they put their own laws above those of the empire.

43. See H. Sancisi-Weerdenberg, "Darius I and the Persian Empire," *CANE*, 2:1035–50.

44. See Bergey, "Book of Esther," 115.

contemplates the execution of Mordecai (5:13); third, where Esther requests that the Jews be spared (7:4). While it is unclear whether any significance should be attached to these usages, at the very least, the odd vocabulary draws special attention to these passages. It should be noted, however, that the word is common in Aramaic (cf. Dan 5:21), and its use here might reflect the lateness of Esther's dialect. In the LXX, the word is translated συμφέρει, "profitable." What Haman seems to be referring to here is the financial loss that the king would suffer if the Jews were allowed to live. The revenue they generate is not sufficient to justify their continued existence.

The last word in the phrase, לְהַנִּיחָם ("to let them be"), is also interesting: as Fox observes, it is a homophone and (in unpointed Heb.) a virtual homograph for the word meaning "give rest" (הניח, *hnyḥ*).[45] The word choice is hardly an accident. It foreshadows the outcome of this entire affair, when the Jews will receive "rest" (נוח, *nwḥ*) from all their enemies (Esth 9:22; the same root occurs in 9:17, 18).

3:9 Haman begins his petition with the obligatory, "If it seems good to the king ... " This form of address is not evidence of fawning obsequiousness; it is just good court protocol (cf. Ezra 5:17; Neh 2:5, 7). His suggestion, however, is remarkable: this certain race is insubordinate, so let us destroy it. Was no less radical solution considered? Could not a decree have been issued, ordering all Jews to be subordinate to their overlords? In chapter 1, the example of Vashti was deemed sufficient to bring all women in line. Could an example have been made of Mordecai? No thought is given to such possibilities; the only solution entertained for the Jewish problem was the "final solution."[46] It seems abhorrent to the modern mind, but genocide was considered an acceptable way to deal with insubordination in ancient times. The Egyptian Pharaoh Merneptah (1234?–1214 BC) bragged that to put down rebellion in Canaan, he had to utterly destroy the Israelites

45. Fox, *Character and Ideology*, 51.

46. S. Berg, *The Book of Esther: Motifs, Themes and Structure,* SBLDS 44 (Missoula, MT: Scholars, 1979), 101–2, suggests that Haman's words may have been deliberately misleading. Berg argues that the Heb. word for "destroy" used here (אבד, *ʾbd*) is a homophone for the word meaning to "enslave" (עבד, *ʿbd*). Thus Xerxes might have thought that Haman was recommending that the Jews be enslaved, not destroyed. Indeed, the sounds of the initial *ʾaleph* and *ʿayin* in this period may have been very similar. One problem with this theory is that the Heb. word for "destroy" is in the piel stem, while the Heb. word for "enslave" would be in the qal or hiphil stem (e.g., Exod 1:13; Jer 17:4). In the piel stem, the vowel sounds and the sound of the middle consonant would be quite different from what they would be in the qal or hiphil stems.

(among others), leaving them no descendants.[47] Among the Persians, too, there is evidence of such excessiveness. In 522 BC, when Darius overthrew a Magian who had seized the throne of Persia, the Persians went on a rampage, slaughtering all the Magians they could find. Herodotus (*Hist.* 3.79) reports that only nightfall prevented their extinction.

To be sure that Xerxes would not balk at the thought of the lost tax revenue that such a slaughter might entail, Haman was quick to add that he would personally provide the funds for this undertaking. Clearly, this offer constitutes a bribe, promising to provide the royal treasury with a sum far above what was needed to carry out the work of eradication.[48] The money is to be given to the "doers of the work"—not the work of execution; their pay would be the spoils they took from the slaughtered Jews. Rather, the "workers" here refers to fiscal workers, the people responsible for the oversight of the royal treasury. They would have a large task to complete: the size of the bribe that Haman was offering was fantastic. According to the standard weight of the talent that was established by King Darius, ten thousand talents equaled about 333 tons of silver. According to Herodotus (*Hist.* 3.95), Persia's annual income from taxes and tribute equaled 14,560 "Eobic" (probably meaning standard Athenian) talents, which would be equivalent to about 10,920 Babylonian talents. Haman's bribe was almost equal to Persia's annual revenue (see further Moore, 39; Bush, 381–82)! It is difficult to take such a figure literally: it would be akin to the vice president offering to donate a trillion dollars to the president of the United States in exchange for a favor.[49] There is nothing indicating here where those funds would come from, whether from Haman's personal wealth or from the funds of his office. It could not have been from anticipated plunder of the Jews (*pace* Bardtke, 322), since the Jews' executioners were given permission to take the spoils themselves (Esth 3:13). Bechtel (40) suggests that possibly Haman was bluffing—that he had no intention of paying such funds. If that were the case, however, we might have expected him to come up with a more realistic-sounding sum. Most likely, our narrator is taking another opportunity to lampoon the excesses of the Persian Empire and

47. Thus according to his Merneptah Stele, *ANET*, 376–78.

48. Alternatively, Haman's offer has been explained as an example of the ancient, revered custom of *bakshish:* offering a gift in exchange for a favor. See M. Vogelstein, "Bakshish for Bagoas?," *JQR* 33 (1943): 89–92.

49. Jobes (121) believes that the offer was particularly attractive because Xerxes needed to replenish the state coffers after the "disastrous" war with Greece. The war, however, was not really that disastrous, and the treasury surely had not been depleted: Xerxes engaged in numerous construction projects on a vast scale after his return from Greece.

Haman's hatred of the Jews, which—in spite of his vast resources—will prove impotent.

3:10 The vizier had made the king an offer that he could not refuse. Without investigation or even question, the king approved the plan. Such is Xerxes' typical *modus operandi* in this book: act rashly and deal with the consequences later. He gives Haman his signet ring, essentially a *carte blanche* to do anything he saw fit. The king turns the entire matter over to Haman (just as he will later turn the matter of the Jews' deliverance over to Mordecai and Esther), exhibiting once again the quality that Fox finds so important to his character: laziness.[50] He does not even bother to find out the identity of the people he has just consigned to destruction.

In case we might have forgotten, the text reminds us of the baleful implications of this act: unlimited power has been placed in the hands the Jews' enemy. He is not merely the enemy of Mordecai; indeed, it is likely that his response to Mordecai has been at least partly inspired by his hatred of the Jewish race.

3:11 The phrase "The money is given to you" is unclear. In the LXX and the NIV it is translated, "Keep the money" (so also Bechtel, 40), as if the king were so concerned at Haman's description of the Jews that he thought the government should pay for their eradication. But in Esth 4:7, Mordecai states that Haman's money would go into the royal treasury, and in 7:4, Esther declares that her people had been "sold." These statements imply that the king accepted Haman's bribe. Indeed, it would be in keeping with his character to do so, since in the book of Esther Xerxes never responds negatively to any suggestion put before him. Some scholars have suggested, then, that the phrase be translated something like, "Well, it's your money." But that reading is difficult as well. The king links the money and the Jews with a single verb: "The money *and the people* are given to you." While we can see why the king might say, "It's your money," it would make no sense for him to say, "They're your people." The precise point of Haman's request and his offer of remuneration is that the Jews are the king's people, and their destruction would represent a significant loss to the king.

BHS suggests changing "the silver is given to you, and the people" to read simply, "the people are given to you." There is no textual basis for this suggestion. While it would make the passage easier to understand, it would eliminate the likely implication that Xerxes is driven primarily by mercenary inclinations.

50. Fox, *Character and Ideology*, 173.

A different possibility is that "the money" is not referring to Haman's bribe at all. In linking the money and the people with a single verb, it is possible that Xerxes is regarding them as a single entity, so that Xerxes is granting Haman the power to deprive him of both people and the income they represented. "The money," then, does not refer to the ten thousand talents that Haman would deposit, but rather to the financial liability that would be entailed in the destruction of the Jews. Haman had alluded to that liability in his request in 3:8, when stating that it was not "profitable" to the king to allow the Jews to live. With this statement, Xerxes might be acknowledging that loss of revenue and accepting Haman's offer to replace it.

It is worth noting that Xerxes' decree would have violated a Persian policy noted by Herodotus (*Hist.* 1.137) forbidding anyone to be executed on the testimony of a single witness. Given the typical bias against the Persians in Greek literature, we should be inclined to accept this testimony as accurate. It also seems to be corroborated by the so-called harem inscription found at Persepolis, where Xerxes proclaims that he would not render a judgment in a case without hearing the testimony of both parties.[51]

3:12 The thirteenth day of the first month, the month of Nisan, would be the day before the Jews were to celebrate Passover; see comment on 3:7 above. The language of the edict (like this entire narrative) parallels that of the edict against Vashti in Esth 1. The big difference between the two, of course, is the consequences involved: while that decree would have had only a little effect outside its consequences for Vashti, this decree will affect all the Jews of the empire. Memucan's decree might have cowed women into submission; Haman's decree would render the Jews extinct.

The edict was issued to the "satraps," "governors," and "officials," a phrase designed to include all the governing bodies from global to local. On the edict being written in the languages of all the different peoples of the empire, see the comment on 1:22 above.

Haman wrote the letter in the name of King Xerxes and sealed it with Xerxes' signet ring, making it as if the king himself issued the decree. The king, of course, was mostly ignorant of its consequences. The text never divulges what pressing business so occupied Xerxes' time that he could not give attention to the annihilation of an entire people from his realm.

The form of calendrical reference used here, which uses a prep. and resumptive pronominal suf. (lit., "the first month, the thirteenth day in it"), is found nowhere else in biblical Heb.. It does appear in the DSS, however,

---

51. Published by W. Hinz, *Altiranische Funde und Forschungen* (Berlin: DeGruyter, 1969), 48–49.

and is the typical form found in MH. Once again, the idiom of Esther is characteristic of a very late form of biblical Heb.

3:13 A series of three words is used in Haman's decree. The first word, "destroy" (שׁמד, *šmd*), is the word used when Haman first decided that the Jews would be executed (3:6). The last verb in the series, "annihilate" (האביד, *hʾbyd*), is the one Haman used when presenting his petition to the king (3:9). These two words are used together in Deut 28:20, 51, 63 for the judgment God will bring on Israel when they abandon His covenant. Between these is the word "kill" (הרג, *hrg*), a fairly common verb meaning "slay" in various contexts, including the execution of lawbreakers and killing in battle. Given that this decree is issued on the day before Passover, however, it might be significant that this verb is used in Exod 4:23; 13:15 for the killing of the firstborn in Egypt.

The use of the three words together seems redundant, but it has a powerful rhetorical purpose. Using a trio of related terms frequently conveys a sense of completion, as in the combination of "satraps," "governors," and "officials" in 3:12.[52] The combination of three words of destruction is certainly designed to convey a sense of utter annihilation (cf. Dommerhausen, 52).[53] The same method is used in Deut 28:20, "Yahweh will send on you curses and confusion and rebuke," in Deut 28:28, "Yahweh will smite you with madness, and blindness, and stupefaction," and yet again in Deut 28:65, "Yahweh will give you a trembling heart, failing eyes, and a troubled soul." Jeremiah uses the combination "sword, and famine, and plague" numerous times to characterize the judgment Yahweh would bring on Judah (Jer 14:12; 21:7, 9; 24:10; 27:8, 13; 29:17, 18; 32:36; 34:17; 42:17, 22; 44:13); the prophet Ezekiel envisions the same trio of terrors (Ezek 5:17; 6:11, 12; 7:15; 12:6). The narrator has probably used this phrase to conjure images of the judgments that Deuteronomy, Jeremiah, and Ezekiel foretold would come upon Israel in exile.

The inclusion of women and children in the destruction demonstrates that this action was designed to be genocide and not merely a punitive action. Women and children would typically be taken as spoils and/or sold into slavery, making the military action more profitable. The slaughter of the women and children would have represented a financial loss to those

52. The most famous example is Paul's "faith, hope, and love" in 1 Cor 13. Other examples include the three righteous men of Ezek 14:14; the three counselors of Job 2:11 and *passim*; the three mighty warriors of King David, 2 Sam 23:8; the three yearly assemblies of the Israelites in Exod 23:14 and elsewhere.

53. Moore 1971, 41, believes this structure is designed to represent the "legal device of being as specific and precise as possible." Such repetition is unnecessary for clarity, however, since each of these terms alone implies utter destruction.

taking part in the slaying. On the other hand, it also represents an ironic reversal of the conquest narratives (cf. Deut 2:34), and of God's instructions to King Saul regarding the Amalekites: "You must not spare [them], but kill both man and woman, both child and nursing infant, both ox and sheep, both camel and donkey" (1 Sam 15:3b).

The text says nothing about who would be responsible for the Jews' destruction. Since this pogrom was to be an official action, we should suspect that the Persian army would be involved. The army, however, consisted mostly of conscripts, volunteers, and mercenaries. It might have been felt unnecessary to designate the executioners, since they would be the same people whether this operation was "formal" or "informal." The Jews would be slaughtered by their neighbors, in whatever community wherein they resided. The promise of plunder was used as an incentive for wide participation. This notion may be implied in 3:14, which states that the message was sent out to the "peoples."

3:14 The verb translated here "published" גלה (*glh*) means "uncover, reveal." It implies both visual and audible revelation. The decree was to be both posted and read aloud, for the many people who would not have been able to read.

3:15 Here, four different scenes are cleverly woven together: the couriers hastening to deliver their message; the decree being published in the Citadel of Susa; the king and Haman sitting down to banquet; and the lower city (probably where a larger population of Jews resided) in a state of confusion. The hastening has nothing to do with a need for alacrity, since the decree is not to be enacted for nearly a year; rather, haste is due to the fact that the couriers are doing the king's business, and must carry it out with their best ability (cf. 1 Sam 21:8). The decree was formally proclaimed in the citadel, where the more prominent and connected people lived. In the rest of the city, there were apparently rumors that left people with questions and uncertainties. Surely this was no groundswell of sympathy for the Jews, but the response of the populace to rumors that seemed nearly unbelievable. In stark contrast with the commotion all around, the king and Haman have settled down for another banquet. Once again, the cluelessness of the monarch is highlighted without a word being explicitly said about it.

The verb used here for Xerxes' and Haman's "banquet," לִשְׁתּוֹת (*lištôt*), literally means "drink." In this context, however, scholars are agreed with Paton (211) that the verb is a metonymy for both eating and drinking. It should be remembered that the standard noun for "banquet" (מִשְׁתֶּה, *mišteh*) derives from this same verb. In the book of Esther, however, the emphasis is not on the food, but on the drinking of wine.

Biblical Theology Comments

3:8 Haman avers that the Jews are a danger because their laws set them apart from all the peoples of the world. This is precisely what they were intended to do. The Holiness Code (Lev 17–26) frequently asserts that Israel's laws will set them apart from the peoples of the world, who practice various "abominations":

> You must not carry out the practices of the land of Egypt, in which you lived, and you must not carry out the practices of the land of Canaan, to which I am bringing you; and you must not follow their statutes. You must carry out my regulations, and you must observe my statutes by following them; I am Yahweh your God. (Lev 18:3–4)

These unique practices arise from the special relationship that Israel had with God. God told Moses to tell Israel, "Now if you will carefully listen to my voice and keep my covenant, you will be a treasured possession for me out of all the peoples, for all the earth is mine, but you, you will belong to me as a kingdom of priests and a holy nation" (Exod 19:5–6). The covenant between God and Israel set Israel apart and above other peoples, making them (in a sense) intermediaries between God and humanity (see Gen 18:18). It was not so much their laws that made them unique as their covenant relationship with God. The laws and practices arose out of the special relationship.

In the book of Esther, we see the notion that the unique customs of Israel could incite the enmity of their neighbors. Typically, the tendency is in the other direction: the OT frequently expresses disgust and rejection of the customs of Israel's neighbors (e.g., Lev 18:24; 20:23), but rarely do we see evidence of the sentiment being returned in kind. It is not until the Greek era that this becomes common. Indeed, it seems that this form of anti-Semitic rhetoric began in Alexandria, Egypt, with the writings of Manetho (ca. 270 BC).[54] From there, it rapidly spread throughout the Hellenistic world, to be inherited by the Romans.[55]

In the NT, the idea of the people of God as a separate, unique race is transferred to the church:

> But you are a chosen people, a royal priesthood, a holy nation, God's special possession, that you may declare the praises of him

---

54. E. Flannery, *The Anguish of the Jews: Twenty-Three Centuries of Antisemitism*, rev. ed. (Mahwah, NJ: Paulist Press, 2004), 11–12; P. Schäfer, *Judeophobia* (Cambridge, MA: Harvard University Press, 1997), 208.

55. J. Daniel, "Anti-Semitism in the Hellenistic-Roman Period," *JBL* 98 (1979): 45–65.

> who called you out of darkness into his wonderful light. Once you were not a people, but now you are the people of God; once you had not received mercy, but now you have received mercy. (1 Pet 2:9–10 NIV)

Called into a relationship with God, the people of God respond by living a life set apart from other people. But this relationship has its price. "I have given them your word, and the world has hated them, because they are not of the world just as I am not of the world" (John 17:14). Just as Haman expresses suspicion of the Jews for their differences, the people of God continue to experience resentment in the present age. Perhaps Peter had the story of Esther in mind when he wrote, "Live such good lives among the pagans that, though they accuse you of doing wrong, they may see your good deeds and glorify God on the day he visits us" (1 Pet 2:12 NIV).

3:13 That the language employed in Haman's decree echoes that of Deut 28 might well imply that the people of God are facing judgment because of apostasy from Yahweh. Indeed, the very setting of the book and the names of the Jewish heroes imply that those curses are coming to pass: "Yahweh will bring you and your king whom you set up over you to a nation that you or your ancestors have not known, and there you will serve other gods of wood and stone" (Deut 28:36). Just as God had warned in Deut 28:64, they are scattered among the people (Esth 3:8). A foreigner has been exalted over them, just as foretold in Deut 28:43–44.

But the message is not all baleful. In Deut 30, God promises that if the people return to Him, He will reverse their captivity and reassemble His people. Indeed, the curses that He had previously brought on the Israelites will fall on their enemies instead (Deut 30:7). God's commitment to His covenant people is a recurring theme of Scripture, and the prophets frequently temper their predictions of judgment with promises that God will return and have mercy on His people. Perhaps the most poignant example is found in the book of Hosea, where the prophet's prediction of exile for Israel is suddenly punctuated with the exclamation, "How can I give you up, O Ephraim? How can I hand you over, O Israel? … My heart is disturbed within me; all my compassions are aroused" (Hos 11:8).

Selected Bibliography

Berg, S. B. *The Book of Esther: Motifs, Themes and Structure*. SBLDS 44. Missoula, MT: Scholars Press, 1979.

Bergey, R. L. "The Book of Esther: Its Place in the Linguistic Milieu of Post-exilic Biblical Hebrew: A Study in Late Biblical Hebrew." Diss., Dropsie College, 1983.

Daniel, J. "Anti-Semitism in the Hellenistic-Roman Period." *JBL* 98 (1979): 45–65.

Flannery, E. *The Anguish of the Jews: Twenty-Three Centuries of Antisemitism*. Rev. ed. Mahwah, NJ: Paulist Press, 2004.
Fox, M. V. *Character and Ideology in the Book of Esther*. 2nd ed. Grand Rapids: Eerdmans, 2001.
Sancisi-Weerdenberg, H. "Darius I and the Persian Empire." *CANE*, 2:1035–50.
Schäfer, P. *Judeophobia: Attitudes toward the Jews in the Ancient World*. Cambridge, MA: Harvard University Press, 1997.
Sevenster, J. *The Roots of Pagan Anti-Semitism in the Ancient World*. Leiden: Brill, 1975.
Vogelstein, M. "Bakshish for Bagoas?" *JQR* 33 (1942–1943): 89–92.

Esther Resolves to Help (4:1–17)

Translation

1 When Mordecai learned of everything that had been done, Mordecai tore
his clothes and put on sackcloth. Then he went out into the midst of the
city and cried out with a loud and bitter cry. **2** He went as far as the king's
gate, because no one is allowed to enter the king's gate while wearing sack-
cloth. **3** In each province and place that the king's word and decree reached,
there was great mourning among the Jews, and fasting, and weeping, and
wailing. Many put on sackcloth and ashes. **4** When Esther's maidservants
and eunuchs came and reported it to her, the queen was very upset. She sent
garments to Mordecai to clothe him and to remove the sackcloth from him,
but he would not accept them.

5 Then Esther called to Hatach, one of the king's eunuchs who waited
upon her, and she commanded him concerning Mordecai to find out what
was going on. **6** So Hatach went out to Mordecai, to the city square that
was in front of the king's gate. **7** Mordecai reported to Hatach what had
happened to him, and the exact amount of silver that Haman had said he
would pay into the king's treasuries so that the Jews would be destroyed.
8 A copy of the written decree issued in Susa for their destruction Mordecai
gave to him, that he might show it to Esther and explain it to her and com-
mand her to go to the king to implore his favor and appeal before him on
behalf of her people. **9** Then Hathach went and reported Mordecai's words
to Esther. **10** But Esther spoke to Hathach and commanded him *to say*[56] to
Mordecai, **11** "All the king's servants and the people of the king's provinces
know that for any man or woman who goes to the king, to the inner court,
without being called, there is but one law—to be put to death. Only the
one to whom the king holds out the golden scepter may live. But as for me,

56. Not present in the Heb., but required by context.

I have not been called to come unto the king these thirty days." **12** And Esther's words were reported[57] to Mordecai.

13 Then Mordecai said to reply to Esther, "Do not think to yourself that you will escape in the king's palace out of all the Jews. **14** For if you indeed keep silent at this time, relief and deliverance will arise for the Jews from another place, but you and your father's house will perish. And who knows if for such a time as this you have not come to the kingdom?"

15 Then Esther said to reply to Mordecai, **16** "Go, gather all the Jews found in Susa, and fast on my behalf, and do not eat or drink for three days, night or day, and I and my maidens will also fast so. Thus I will go to the king, though it is against the law. And if I perish, I perish." **17** Mordecai then went away and did everything as Esther had commanded him.

Textual Notes

1.a. The LXX adds at the end of the verse that Mordecai cried out, "An innocent nation is being destroyed!"

2.a. For MT בִּלְבוּשׁ שָׂק, "while wearing sackcloth," the LXX reads, "while wearing sackcloth and ashes."

3.a. Verse 3 is omitted in the AT.

4.a. *BHS* suggests deleting סָרִיסֶיהָ ("her eunuchs"), as in the Syr.

5.a. For Hatach (הֲתָךְ), the LXX has "Hachrathaios" (Αχραθαῖος); the AT does not record his name.

7.a. 7–8 are omitted in the AT.

9.a. For "the words of Mordecai," LXX reads "all these things." AT reads "the tribulation of Israel."

11.a. The AT, OL, and Vg. add, "And how can I go without being summoned?"

12.a. For וַיַּגִּידוּ לְמָרְדֳּכָי ("And when they had told Mordecai … ") the LXX and OL read, "And when Hatach had told Mordecai … " The pl. form of the MT is inexplicable, since only Hatach had been involved as the intermediary. The MT form may, however, be read as a pass., "And when Mordecai was told … "

17.a. After v. 17, the Greek versions add prayers of Mordecai and Esther.

---

57. 3 m. pl. act. verb form, apparently used here with the pass. sense, since the context implies that only Hatach carried the messages between the queen and Mordecai.

Commentary

4:1 The previous episode focused on Haman and his negotiation with the king; this one focuses on Mordecai and his negotiation with the queen. He "learns" of everything that had been done, including the words that had passed between Haman and Xerxes (cf. 3:7), undoubtedly through his own contacts in the palace. Perhaps he is still receiving intelligence from the same source that informed him of the eunuchs' plot. His response would have been typical of an ANE person receiving such troubling news: he tore his clothes. Such a demonstration could be a formalized show of grief, a social convention expected in very bad circumstances (e.g., the death of a great person, as in 2 Sam 1:11–12; or the witnessing of words or acts perceived to be blasphemous, as in Matt 26:65).[58] Thus it was a symbolic action, but it might also be a spontaneous expression of shock.[59]

The custom of wearing sackcloth is widely attested. Sackcloth was sometimes worn under the garments (2 Kgs 6:30) in times of grief or as a belt or girdle (Isa 32:11), but Mordecai apparently wore an entire garment of the coarse cloth. He also covered himself in ashes, another typical way that people might make an external demonstration of their internal pain.[60] Mordecai was making a public demonstration of his distress. He went into the midst of the city, where he could gather an audience. His cry was not a wail of repentance for having brought down this injustice on the Jews. Rather, it was a cry for justice, a public statement that a wrong had been committed, and that Mordecai sought for it to be made right.

Gerleman (104) has argued that Mordecai's outcry at the king's gate constituted a formal legal protest intended to move the king to intervene. Similarly, Clines (299) interprets the cry as a gesture of protest against the king. Bush (394) rejects both ideas, claiming instead that the action was meant only to get the attention of Queen Esther. But it is impossible to imagine that someone wearing sackcloth and ashes, crying out before the king's doors, would not be trying to get the attention of the king. Indeed, this behavior was typical of those who sought the king's intervention on their behalf (2 Sam 15:1–6; 2 Kgs 6:26–28; *Hist.* 3.117). While perhaps not a formal complaint *against* the king, Mordecai's actions surely amounted to a formal complaint *to* the king.

---

58. See *m. Sanh.* 7.5 for rabbinic requirements that a judge rend his garments on hearing blasphemy uttered in his presence.

59. D. R. Hillers, "A Convention in Hebrew Literature: The Reaction to Bad News," *ZAW* 77 (1965): 86–90.

60. See J. A. Thompson, "Sackcloth" *NBD*, 1034; P. J. King and L. E. Stager, *Life in Biblical Israel*, 372–73; Hillers, "A Convention in Hebrew Literature."

4:2 The text states that Mordecai was only allowed to go as far as the king's gate in his mourning clothes. The "king's gate" likely refers to the entrance of the palace, not to a city gate named after the king. Bush (372–73) argues that "the king's gate" should be understood "in a figurative sense" as referring to Mordecai's office. While it is true that the phrase "sitting in the king's gate" probably implies holding an administrative position, it is obvious from this verse that the king's gate is also a geographical location, beyond which Mordecai could not pass.

The prohibition against entering the palace dressed in sackcloth is unattested in classical sources, but it is consonant with the spirit of the court as described in the book of Esther. The palace is a place of unbridled indulgence and pleasure, and the presence of someone in mourning garb would dampen the spirits of the place. Note that Nehemiah, cupbearer of King Artaxerxes, was "very afraid" when the king observed his sad countenance (Neh 2:2), so there may be some factual basis to the undoubtedly satirical picture painted by our narrator.

It is clear that Mordecai's object is to get the attention of the royal palace, but to whom is his appeal addressed? Is he hoping to get the attention of the king, to get him to right the wrong that has been perpetrated? Appealing to the king is a practice with much precedence in the Bible and the ANE. In the OT, it was considered the king's duty to hear the complaints of the people and provide them justice (2 Sam 14; 15:1–6; 1 Kgs 3:28; 2 Kgs 6:26; 2 Chr 9:8). Herodotus (*Hist.* 3.117), too, describes people coming to the king's gates with weeping and wailing, in order to gain royal at tention to their grievances. Mordecai's wailing, however, apparently cannot reach the ears of the king. Xerxes is too insulated from the concerns of his people to hear their cries at his doors. Mordecai was forced to turn to someone who had more direct access—his cousin, Queen Esther.

Many scholars argue that Mordecai was not appealing to the king; his intention was to get Esther's attention from the start (e.g., Laniak, 225).[61] But with his obvious palace connections, could not Mordecai have sent a message to the queen immediately if he had wanted to do so? The more likely scenario seems to be that his wailing at the gate caught the queen's attention, rather than that of its intended target, the king. Because she knew and cared about Mordecai, Esther wanted to know why he had been reduced to wailing at the gate. The use of the queen to deliver a message to Xerxes to seems to have been Mordecai's "plan B."

---

61. See also M. Fox, *Character and Ideology in the Book of Esther,* 2nd ed. (Grand Rapids: Eerdmans, 2001), 57.

4:3 The Jews as a group make their first appearance in this verse. Like Mordecai, they are weeping and wailing. Unlike Mordecai, they are also fasting. Mordecai's weeping and wailing was designed to get the attention of the king, the human authority that he believed could remedy the situation. The Jews outside Persia, however, cannot go to the king's palace to make their appeal. Their entreaties are undoubtedly directed to a higher power—Yahweh. Even though the text makes no mention of prayer per se, it is almost certain that the intention of this demonstration is to move heaven on their behalf.

According to the Law, the Jews were required to fast only on the Day of Atonement (Lev 16:29, 31; 23:26–32; Num 29:7–11), but both corporate and individual fasts occurred at other times. Corporate fasts could occur when Israel was in mourning after the loss of a king or great figure (1 Sam 31:13), during seasons of repentance (1 Kgs 21:27; Neh 9:1), or in situations where the people desired to demonstrate their sincerity to God (2 Chr 20:1–4, Dan 9:3). In this case, both of the latter cases may have applied: perhaps the Jews were demonstrating their repentance, as well as their desire for God to intervene on their behalf.

It is interesting how often in this book the fortunes of the Jews seem to mirror those of Mordecai. Fox observes that Mordecai's mourning precedes that of the rest of the Jews, so that he is cast in the role of their leader, before even they recognize it.[62] In 8:16–17, after Mordecai has been honored by the king and promoted to vizier, the Jews are to have "honor," in addition to rejoicing. In 8:17 and 9:2, we are told that fear of the Jews had seized the Gentiles, and in 9:3, we are told that the Gentiles were afraid of Mordecai. Finally, in 9:20–22 we are told that Mordecai wrote an edict establishing the perpetual observance of Purim, and in 9:27 the Jews established and took it upon themselves to observe Purim as a perpetual ordinance. Mordecai is not only the leader of the Jews; he is also their epitome.

4:4 The phrase וַיַּגִּידוּ לָהּ (*wayyagîdû lāh*), "And they reported (it) to her," has no obj. Frequently in biblical Heb. the obj. is omitted when it can be easily inferred from the context. Here, the obj. is Mordecai's actions.

Did Esther's servants know of her relationship to Mordecai? Most scholars assume that the reason they reported to Esther that Mordecai was wailing at the gate was because they knew she was his daughter. But if all of Esther's servants knew about the relationship, how did Esther keep her Jewishness secret? Another possibility is that the servants were not bringing news specifically because they knew of the relationship, but were merely reporting the latest court gossip. It could have been quite an object of

62. Fox, *Character and Ideology*, 213.

interest that one of the court officials was at the king's gate dressed in sackcloth, weeping and wailing.

At this time, Esther does not know of the king's decree, so she is puzzled by Mordecai's behavior. He has no family to mourn, so his state could not be due to bereavement. Perhaps she concluded that he had been reduced to poverty and was mourning his own misfortune. Esther wants to know what is wrong, but she cannot ask Mordecai directly: she cannot go to him, because it would reveal their relationship and uncover her as a Jew, and he cannot come to her, because he cannot enter the king's gate dressed in mourning garb. Esther sends Mordecai clothes so that he can come into the palace complex. In the narrative, the act is not only pragmatic: in the book of Esther, changes of clothing typically reflect a change in circumstances. For example, the Jews are clothed in sackcloth to signify their mourning (4:3); Esther puts on her royal robes before going to Xerxes, reminding him of her status as queen (5:1); Haman seeks to be clothed in royal robes as a sign of his own desire for honor (6:8–9); Mordecai is clothed in royal robes because the king wishes to honor him (6:10–11); Mordecai is clothed in royal robes to signify his promotion to vizier (8:10).

Josephus is probably correct in his understanding that Mordecai refused the clothes because "the situation that had compelled him to put it on had not yet ceased" (*Ant.* 11.223). Anderson (868) and Moore (1971, 48) contend that Mordecai's refusal reflects the Talmudic injunction that public displays of grief should be reserved for communal, not personal, sorrow, and his refusal to put off the sackcloth was a signal to Esther that a public crisis was afoot. This explanation is probably anachronistic; no such injunction against mourning private calamity is found in the OT (cf. Job 1–2; Joel 1:8; Psa 35:13), intertestamental literature, or the NT.

The hithpalpel form of the verb חול/חיל (*ḥwl/ḥyl*) occurs only here. The basic meaning of the verb is "writhe." A closely related hithpolel form of this verb occurs in Jer 23:19, where it means "twirl about" or "spin," referring to the action of a whirlwind. Perhaps the verb is designed to suggest an image of Esther turning back and forth, perplexed about how to respond to Mordecai's actions.

4:5 Mordecai's refusal to change his clothes necessitates Esther sending an intermediary to find out what has happened. The confidence Esther places in him casts Hatach in a generally positive light. In Esther, eunuchs are depicted in a variety of ways: they can be depicted favorably, like Hatach here, as well as Hegai (2:8–9, 15) and Harbona (7:9). Two of them, Bigthan and Teresh (2:21), are wicked characters, and several more are neutral, merely appearing as men with access to the royal wives (the seven eunuchs of 1:10; Shaashgaz, overseer of the harem in 2:14; the eunuch who brings Haman to the queen's feast in 6:14). The book of Esther is not unequivocally on the side of the marginalized; its depiction is more nuanced and individualized than that.

While Mordecai had managed to learn of the king's decree and even the negotiations involved, Esther is ignorant of the proceedings. It is obvious that she is living a sequestered life in the palace, insulated from the troubles of life outside the women's quarters. The contrast between the informed and uninformed is important in this scene, as indicated by the repeated use of the word "know" (ידע, *yd'*). It was used in v. 1, "When Mordecai knew all that had been done"; in this verse; in v. 11, "All the king's servants and the people of the king's provinces know that any man or woman who goes to the king ... "; and in v. 14, "And who knows if for such a time as this ... " In each case, "knowledge" is a life-and-death matter: Mordecai knows that the Jews have been condemned to death (v. 1); Esther does not know that the Jews are to die (v. 5); Mordecai does not know that Esther may be executed (v. 11); who knows whether Esther's ascension was so that the Jews could live (v. 14). It is somewhat reminiscent of Hos 4:6a, "My people are destroyed for lack of knowledge," though the context here is quite different.

4:6 The city square of Susa has been excavated by archaeologists.[63] These locations often served as markets and public meeting places in ancient times. It would have been a very crowded, bustling location. Mordecai and Hatach could meet in such a place without drawing attention to themselves.

4:7 Interestingly, Hatach seems to have been as ignorant about the affairs of Susa as Esther appeared to be. While this detail seems to reinforce the impression of the women's quarters as a cloister, isolated from the affairs of the state, such was not the historical reality of the time. The king's wives, and especially the queen, were fully engaged in their communities.[64]

The reference here to the silver being deposited in the treasury should dispel the notion that Xerxes had told Haman to "keep the money" in 3:11. Whatever the meaning of the phrase "The money is given to you," it does not mean that Haman's bribe was refused (see comment on 3:11 above).

4:8–9 The obj. of the sentence, the "copy of the decree," has been moved to the front of this sentence. There are a number of reasons why a Heb. writer might do this, but the most common and likely here is for emphasis. In an age where paper was still not a common commodity and writing not

63. See further E. Yamauchi, *Persia and the Bible* (Grand Rapids: Baker, 1997), 298–300.

64. See M. Brosius, *Women in Ancient Persia, 539–331 B.C.* (Oxford: Clarendon, 1996), 83–93, for evidence of royal women's public presence.

a widely acquired skill, a physical copy of the decree would lend a sense of gravity to the situation. As earlier, the narrator has used a series of three verbs: "show," "explain," "command." In this case, however, the verbs are not synonymous, as in 3:13, "destroy, slay, and annihilate." The sense is not one of completeness, but urgency. Three terse phrases are used, designed to convey the idea of rapid response that Mordecai seeks from Esther.

There has been some speculation about why the decree must be shown and explained to Esther. Paton (218) and Clines (301) suggest that perhaps the edict was written in Persian and had to be translated into Aramaic for Esther's benefit. Another possibility is that Esther was illiterate and could not read the edict for herself. The extent of literacy in ancient Israel is uncertain, but some scholars argue that less than 5 percent of ancient Israelites could read.[65] While epigraphic evidence from the Dead Sea Scrolls and the Babatha archives seem to militate against such a low percentage, it is certain that reading was not a common skill and was even less common among Jewish women, who enjoyed few rights and little social status in this era.

But what of the queen of Persia? Greek sources report that Persian royal women were trained in horsemanship, martial arts, and other skills, but make no mention of literary training.[66] Some women apparently possessed the literary skills necessary for their occupations (Persian tablets demonstrate that women were employed as record keepers), but they were barred from the role of scribe.[67] There is no reason to believe that the Persians considered general literacy important, or that Esther would have been expected to read the decree for herself. Fox's argument that there would have been no point of showing Esther the decree if she were illiterate is not especially compelling: even if illiterate, she would have recognized an official document with a royal seal, and its existence would have added weight to Mordecai's appeal.[68]

4:10 In English, it is necessary to provide a complement to the verb "commanded him" (commanded him to do what?). In Heb., the verb צוה (*ṣwh*) can have the sense of "commission" and be used without a complementary

65. See, e.g., A. Demsky and M. Bar-Ilan, "Writing in Ancient Israel and Early Judaism," *Compendia Rerum Iudicarum ad Novum Testamentum*, sec. II, vol. I, *MIKRA*, ed. M. J. Mulder (Assen: van Gorcum and Fortress, 1988), 1–38. For a more recent treatment of literacy in the biblical period, see C. Rollston, *Writing and Literacy in the World of Ancient Israel: Epigraphic Evidence from the Iron Age* (Atlanta: Society of Biblical Literature, 2010).

66. Ctesias, §54; see further P. Briant, *From Cyrus to Alexander: A History of the Persian Empire* (Winona Lake, IN: Eisenbrauns, 2002), 285.

67. Brosius, *Women in Ancient Persia*, 146–63.

68. Fox, *Character and Ideology*, 213.

verb, as in Gen 50:16, וַיְצַוּוּ אֶל־יוֹסֵף לֵאמֹר (*wayĕṣawwû ʾel-yôsēp lēʾmōr*), "And they commissioned (messengers to speak) unto Joseph, saying ... "

4:11 Esther finally speaks with her own voice. Until this point, she has been silent and passive, obeying Mordecai's orders, going where she was sent, doing what she was told to do. When finally she opens her mouth, we discover that there is some defiance in her soul. Esther's response to Mordecai is, in fact, somewhat condescending: "Every servant of the king, and even the common people, know this is the rule." The implication, of course, is that Mordecai knows the rule as well. He should be aware that he is demanding that his daughter place her life in the hands of a king who has proven willing to dispose of queens who seem to him to be insubordinate.

I would agree with those scholars who interpret Esther's statement as a rebuff and that Esther is unwilling to risk her life to do as Mordecai has commanded. Berlin (47–48), on the other hand, believes that Esther is "introducing a new piece of information" in preparation for a subtle plan to do what Mordecai requested. That explanation might be plausible, if, first of all, this were a new piece of information. But as Esther herself states, everyone knows this fact. Second of all, if it were her intention to give only background information, why would she mislead Mordecai by sending him only this statement—one that implies not compliance, but refusal? This information is, indeed, new, but the narrator is introducing it for the readers' benefit, not for Mordecai's.

As for the law itself, historical evidence for such a policy is scant. Josephus (*Ant.* 11.205) gives a colorful description of executioners standing around the throne with axes, quick to dispatch anyone who entered the king's presence uninvited. Yamauchi notes a Persepolis relief that depicts the king guarded by a Median soldier with an axe in hand.[69] We should note, however, that most Persian throne room scenes do not depict any such guards surrounding the king. More often, they are surrounded by servants bearing fans, cups, or parasols. Josephus' account was probably inspired by his imaginative reading of Esther, not by any intimate knowledge of the Persian court. Jobes (132) cites the case of Deioces, a Median king who established a policy that no one was permitted to enter his presence or petition him directly (see *Hist.* 1.99), but that ruler was regarded as an idiosyncratic tyrant, not the norm for Persian practice. Herodotus does state that access to the king was limited (*Hist.* 3.118) and claims that it was Darius' policy that only the seven nobles of Persia were allowed free passage into his presence. Other ancient authors write that no one could enter the king's presence without the permission of the chiliarch, who would demand to

69. *Persia and the Bible*, 360.

know their business.[70] But as noted above, there is little evidence that such a figure actually existed as the Greeks envisioned.

Whatever the policy, the more intriguing question is why Esther did not simply request an audience with the king, especially since Haman's edict would not be carried out for another eleven months. (For that matter, Mordecai himself, as a hero who had saved the king's life, could certainly have requested an audience.) We have already seen that the queen has access to the king, because she was able to pass on Mordecai's report about the assassination plot (Esth 2:22). Has her access to the king been curtailed over the passing years? Or has the narrator simply changed the rules of the game, without bothering to explain why? Walton et al. (188) suggest that if Haman were, indeed, Xerxes' chiliarch, Esther would have had to make an appeal to Haman in order to be admitted into the throne room (so, too, Laniak, 229). Revealing her plans to Haman would have put her in a difficult position, to say the least. But surely she could have given him some other reason for seeking an audience besides Haman's plot to murder the Jews. Perhaps the best explanation is that suggested by Moore: that Esther could not simply request an audience makes for a more exciting story (Moore 1971, 50).

The custom of the king extending his scepter in this manner is unattested outside the book of Esther. There are many Persian reliefs, however, that depict the king holding a scepter, a thin staff about the length of his body, with a knob on one end. It apparently had some function when he was holding court, since the scepter is prominent in scenes of royal audiences.[71] It should be noted, however, that some scenes seem to show other people with similar staffs in hand. There was apparently no royal privilege needed to carry a stick in Persia.

The final revelation offered by Esther, that she had not been called to the king's chamber for thirty days, may be the most intriguing comment made here. The phrase "come unto the king" surely implies sexual concourse.[72] In one night of passion, Esther had made such an impression on the king that he had chosen her to be queen over all others. But now, the king and Esther have been married for several years. The passion is waning. Has the king grown tired of his queen? Certainly, the king had other wives, and Esther could not expect to share his bed every night. Also, she had her own living quarters in the palace, and queens did not regularly dine with the king. But a full month without sexual relations, or even friendly

70. See comment above on 3:1; Nepos, *Conon* 3.2–3; Plutarch, *Themistocles* 27.2–7.
71. See the illustrations in Briant, *Cyrus to Alexander*, 209, 210, 218, 219; *ANEP*, 463.
72. See the comment on 2:12.

conversation? It may imply that Esther had fallen out of the king's favor, which could explain her reluctance to appear before him unannounced.

4:12 The use of the 3 m. pl. form of the verb in the phrase וַיַּגִּידוּ לְמָרְדֳּכָי (*wayyagîdû lĕmordŏkāy*), lit., "They reported to Mordecai," should be taken as the functional equivalent of a pass. form, as often occurs in English ("They say you can't keep a good man down" = "It is said that you can't keep a good man down"). There is only one intermediary between Esther and Mordecai, the eunuch Hatach, so a literal rendering of the pl. would not be appropriate for the context.

4:13–14 Mordecai begins his response to Esther with a warning. He assumes that she is contemplating taking no action, allowing her people to perish while she enjoys the seclusion of the palace. In order to persuade her to act, he will resort to what sounds like a threat.

Before issuing the threat, however, apparently Mordecai expresses his confidence that the Jews will find deliverance. Most scholars, along with the ancient translations (LXX, AT, Vg.) and Josephus, understand Mordecai to be speaking almost prophetically in this passage: the Jews will be delivered, but Esther, because of her disregard for her people, will perish. Wiebe's 1991 study has caused several scholars (e.g., Bush, 396–97) to question this understanding.[73] Wiebe notes some problems with the traditional understanding:

1. Where was the "other place" from which Mordecai expected help? According to Wiebe, there were no other human agents who could provide the relief, and Mordecai does not appear to be a man of faith who would trust God's ability to rescue His people.
2. Why would Esther and her "father's house" perish? Would it be by human agents, or divine retribution? The text does not say. Wiebe assumes that the "father's house" refers to Mordecai himself, rendering the statement difficult. Why should Mordecai perish because of Esther's disobedience, if the rest of the Jews will be delivered?
3. Wiebe observes that the particle כִּי (*kî*) at the beginning of v. 14 must have a causal force, meaning "because." It should explain the reason for Mordecai's warning in v. 13, that Esther should not think she will escape. The reason appears to be that she will not escape because she and "her father's house" will perish. Wiebe

73. J. M. Wiebe, "Esther 4:14: 'Will Relief and Deliverance Arise for the Jews from Another Place?'" *CBQ* 53 (1991): 409–15.

argues that it makes no sense that Esther's silence would result in the destruction of Mordecai.

Based on these supposed difficulties, Wiebe renders the sentence not as a statement, but as a rhetorical question: "Will relief and deliverance come to the Jews from another place? For you and your father's house will perish." Wiebe's reading would change our understanding of Mordecai's words from an expression of trust to one of despair. The Heb. certainly *can* be read that way; but is that truly the best understanding of this verse?

In fact, each of Wiebe's difficulties can be resolved. The first issue, regarding the "other place" from which help would come, has traditionally been understood to refer to divine intervention. It is also possible that Mordecai expected some kind of human deliverance. There were still eleven months before the pogrom, and appeals could be made to the king by other high-ranking Jews. Perhaps Mordecai believed that he could be that deliverer. In any case, is it so difficult to believe that Mordecai would expect that *somehow*, the Jews would be delivered, no matter how secular he might seem to be? Haman's pagan wife, Zeresh, will express precisely the same sentiment, that the Jews are indestructible, in 6:13. Mordecai did not have to be explicit about where the help would come from; he was simply confident that it would come.

The second objection, that Mordecai would be punished for Esther's transgression, is easily dismissed if we understand that her father's house refers not to Mordecai, but to her biological father and his descendants. If Esther were to die, her father's line would be cut off, since she would have no children. As for the question of how Esther would die, divine retribution—perhaps through human agents—seems most likely.[74] We have observed that poetic justice is an important theme in Esther. If Esther had attempted to save only her own life, we might well expect that she would end up losing it (cf. Luke 17:33).

The last problem is not really a problem at all, if one recognizes that Esther's "father's house" refers to her biological father. The particle כִּי is indeed causative: if Esther remains silent, it will cause the relief and deliverance to arise from another place and not from her. It will also result in her death and eliminate the possibility of her having children.

There is thus no compelling reason to depart from the understanding of this verse that has been shared by translators and interpreters through the centuries, as not a question but a statement. However secularized Mordecai may have been, he was confident that his people would overcome

74. R. Pierce, "The Politics of Esther and Mordecai: Courage or Compromise?" *BBR* 2 (1992): 87, argues that Mordecai is threatening to kill Esther personally. That theory misses the element of poetic justice that is implied in Mordecai's statement.

their current crisis. Perhaps he was merely superstitious, or perhaps he possessed some deep conviction that God would remain faithful to His covenant people. The text allows us only to speculate.

Esther, however, would enjoy no such protection. Mordecai's words sound like a threat, but more than that, they constitute a curse. In the ancient world, pronouncing doom on someone's future was not considered merely bad behavior; it was understood to have the power to bring such things to pass. "For the Hebrew, just as a word was not a mere sound on the lips but an agent sent forth, so the spoken curse was an active agent for hurt."[75] Mordecai's prediction of Esther's death would have been more ominous to the Jews of Esther's day than it is to modern people.

Mordecai's final appeal, on the other hand, softens the tone somewhat. The question that Esther might have come to the queenship for the purpose of saving the Jews assumes, at the very least, a divine providence at work. It is not a statement of great faith—after all, he does couch it as a question. It is, nonetheless, an expression of belief in a guiding power. It is also a challenge to Esther: do you believe circumstances have allowed you to become queen merely so that you can live in luxury, or will you accept the responsibility that your elevation might entail?

Many interpreters through the years have argued that the phrase "another place" in this verse is an allusion to divine intervention, since "The Place" was one of God's titles in rabbinic literature.[76] The possibility that such an allusion is intended, however, is unlikely. The use of the expression "The Place" as a divine epithet is only attested in literature composed long after the time of the book of Esther. Furthermore, if we read the word *Place* as an epithet for God, the phrase "another place" would literally mean "another god." The equivalent of this phrase, אֱלֹהִים אֲחֵרִים (*ʾĕlōhîm ʾăḥērîm*, "other gods"), is used in Deut 6:14; 7:4; Jer 1:16; 7:18, and elsewhere to mean pagan gods or idols.

4:15–16 Esther now calls on Mordecai to join in the fasting that the rest of the Jewish community had begun spontaneously (4:3). She also will fast and include her maids as well. We can probably assume the maids knew that Esther was Jewish, since it would have been difficult for her to ask them to abstain from food and water without knowing why. Apparently, Mordecai's instructions for Esther not to reveal her Jewishness did not extend to her close associates in the women's quarters, who could be counted on to keep confidences.

75. J. A. Motyer, "Curse," *NBD*, 249.

76. So, e.g., Talmon, "Wisdom in the Book of Esther," *VT* 13 (1963): 429n1; Moore 1971, 50.

Fasting often accompanied prayer, to demonstrate the deep concern of those making petitions to Yahweh (2 Sam 7:6; 12:16–22; Ezra 8:21, 23; Jonah 3:3–8).[77] In Esther's case, prayer is never mentioned, but the imprecatory quality of the fast seems clear: what other reason would there be for her to abstain from food or drink before going before the king, other than to persuade God to give her favor? The only other possibility might be as a show of repentance, which we can assume would also have included prayer.

The three days of preparation before going into the presence of the king is reminiscent of several biblical scenarios. I have noted previously the parallels between the story of Esther and that of Joseph in Genesis, and this detail provides yet another point of comparison: the baker and cupbearer dwelt in prison with Joseph for three days before they were summoned to appear before Pharaoh (Gen 40:12–13, 18–19). The cupbearer, in fact, was presented before Pharaoh for pardon, while the baker was presented for execution. Both possibilities lie before Esther. Some interpreters have seen Esther's three days of preparation as a type of Jesus' days in the tomb before his ascent to heaven. But as noted in the introduction ("Theology of Esther: Contemporary Approaches"), Esther's work of deliverance was only beginning when she came before the king, while Jesus' work was finished on the cross (John 19:30).

Esther's final words have often been taken as a sign of resolve or courage, but may be better understood as sarcasm. She states once again that the action she is about to take is illegal. Mordecai (and the audience) knows this fact already; it has been the point of the whole exchange. The repetition can only be intended to drive home the fact to Mordecai that he is forcing Esther to become a lawbreaker just as Mordecai was, in his refusal to obey the king's command regarding Haman.

Her comment "If I perish, I perish" is also a truism. Esther already has the threat of death hanging over her head: if she does nothing, Mordecai has cursed her with destruction. If she goes to the king, she may perish; if she does not go, she may still perish. Caught between a rock and a hard place, all she can do is accept the fate that Mordecai has thrust upon her. The grammatical construction here is very similar to that found in Gen 43:14, where Jacob is forced to send his son Benjamin to Egypt. Not knowing that it is Joseph who has demanded Benjamin's presence, Jacob assumes that he will probably lose his youngest son. Knowing he has no choice but to comply, he says with resignation, "If I am bereaved, I am bereaved."

4:17 The development of Esther's character is evident in this verse: Mordecai did what Esther ordered. In Esth 2:20, Esther did everything

---

77. A. G. Belben, "Fasting," *NBD*, 364.

that Mordecai commanded her to do. Now, it is Esther who gives the orders, and Mordecai who obeys. It is important to notice the language here: Esther did not "instruct" Mordecai (as in the NIV) or simply "tell" him what to do (CEB; NCV). The verb צָוָה (*ṣāwâ*) is the same word used in Esth 2:10 for Mordecai's commands of Esther, in 3:2 of the king's commandment regarding Haman, and in 3:12 of Haman's commandment. The vocabulary here clearly demonstrates a reversal is taking place: Esther is growing into her role as queen, and even her uncle is subject to her will.

Biblical Theology Comments

4:3 The first reference to fasting in this text avoids references to prayer, as does the rest of the book. There are typically two purposes for fasting in the Bible: it can be a sign of mourning (e.g., 2 Sam 1:12; 3:35), or it can be an act of serious devotion to God.[78] As an act of devotion, fasting could be an accompaniment to prayer (1 Kgs 12:27–29; Jonah 3:5), a preparation for receiving a vision or revelation (Exod 34:28), or a means of dedication before engaging in holy war (1 Sam 7:6; 14:24). The purpose of the Jews' fast in this verse is ambivalent: out of context, there is no way of knowing whether it was a sign of mourning their announced destruction or an effort to invoke God's mercy on their behalf. Later in the scene, however, when Esther asks Mordecai to have the people fast for her before she goes before the king, it is clearly intended as a way of entreating (divine) favor. It is probably in this same light that we should read the Jews' fasting in 4:3—as an appeal for divine mercy. We might find a good analogy in 1 Kgs 21:27–29, where King Ahab fasted and wore sackcloth and ashes to beseech God's forgiveness for his hand in the death of Naboth.

4:13 Mordecai's threat against Esther implies an idea that appears repeatedly in the book of Esther: retributive justice. Mordecai assumes that if Esther sacrifices her people in order to save herself, she will bring about her own ruin. Indeed, Mordecai's words might well reinforce that notion, since the words themselves essentially constitute a curse. There is no reason to interpret his words as a personal threat, suggesting that Mordecai himself will kill his adopted daughter. Ultimately, it is God who is responsible for the judgment of malefactors (Deut 32:35, 36).

Typically, however, He does use human instruments to execute His vengeance. Israel was His tool for the destruction of Amalek, and of all the wicked peoples of Canaan (Deut 9:4). Babylon was used for the judgment of Judah (Jer 1:14–16; Hab 1:6). Individuals, too, could be used as tools of judgment, as when a woman was used to destroy Gideon's rogue

---

78. See D. L. Smith-Christopher, "Fasting," *EDB*, 456.

son Abimelech, fulfilling the curse pronounced by his half-brother Jotham (Judg 9:53–56). It is not impossible, however, for God to undertake His judgment personally, as when He dispatched an angel to destroy the forces of the boastful king Sennacherib (2 Kgs 19:35). Mordecai does not specify how Esther would meet her ruin; no explanation was necessary. The options were many.

The question to ask, however, is whether Mordecai had the right to pronounce such a judgment. Typically, these proclamations come through prophetic channels. Could Mordecai really say with authority that Esther would die if she did not act on behalf of the Jews? While Moses, Jeremiah, or Nathan might seem to have better credentials than Mordecai for invoking judgment, the example of Jotham (Judg 9) would seem a close parallel to Mordecai's. Jotham seemed to have made no claims to prophetic insight, and yet he pronounced the doom of both Abimelech and the men of Shechem if they had not acted in good faith (Judg 9:20). After Abimelech's downfall, the text states explicitly that events had fulfilled the curse of Jotham (Judg 9:57).

4:14 Mordecai's prediction that Esther's father's house would perish highlights the importance that the Jews placed on the survival of the family line. It is not only Esther's own life that is at stake: should she perish, her father's lineage would cease as well. Typically in Israel, a man's lineage continued through his sons; but if he had no sons, his "name" was preserved through his daughters (Num 27:4), and they would receive his inheritance (Num 27:8). If the daughters died without children, the inheritance would pass to their husbands' families.

Another important concept Mordecai introduces in this speech is the indestructibility of the Jews. Deuteronomy hints at this notion: God promises that after He has scattered and destroyed the nation of Israel, He will regather and bless them, if they repent of their evils (Deut 30:1–10). The idea that Israel will never be utterly forsaken is developed as a theme by the prophets, beginning with Amos 9:8: "'Look, the eyes of my Lord Yahweh are on the kingdom of sin, and I will destroy it from the surface of the earth. However, I will not utterly destroy the house of Jacob,' declares Yahweh." The idea that God will preserve a remnant—not necessarily because of their righteousness, but because of His faithfulness—recurs frequently in the prophetic corpus (Isa 10:20–23; Jer 50:18–20; Ezek 11:13–21; Mic 5:7–15; 7:8–20).

There is, however, danger in this notion. During the days of the prophet Jeremiah, the Judaeans took solace in the notion of the "inviolability of Jerusalem," the belief that Jerusalem could not be destroyed because of the presence there of the temple (Jer 7:1–15). As the people learned, God was willing to reduce the nation to a small remnant in order to correct their sinful ways. Jesus warned the Jewish people that they should take no comfort in being descendants of Abraham, for "God is able to raise up children for Abraham from these stones" (Matt 3:9). God does, indeed, have a covenant relationship with His people, but Jesus implies that the basis of the relationship is not so much genetic as spiritual.

Selected Bibliography

Briant, P. *From Cyrus to Alexander: A History of the Persian Empire.* Winona Lake, IN: Eisenbrauns, 2002.

Brosius, M. *Women in Ancient Persia, 539–331 B.C.* Oxford: Clarendon, 1996.

Fox, M. V. *Character and Ideology in the Book of Esther*. 2nd ed. Grand Rapids: Eerdmans, 2001.

Hillers, D. R. "A Convention in Hebrew Literature: The Reaction to Bad News." *ZAW* 77 (1965): 86–90.

Pierce, R. "The Politics of Esther and Mordecai: Courage or Compromise?" *BBR* 2 (1992): 75–89.

Smith-Christopher, D. L. "Fasting." In *EDB*, 456.

Stager, L. E. *Life in Biblical Israel.* Louisville, KY: Westminster John Knox, 2001.

Talmon, S. "Wisdom in the Book of Esther." *VT* 13 (1963): 419–55.

Wiebe, J. M. "Esther 4:14: 'Will Relief and Deliverance Arise for the Jews from Another Place?'" *CBQ* 53 (1991): 409–15.

Yamauchi, E. *Persia and the Bible.* Grand Rapids: Baker, 1997.

The Plot Reversed (5:1–7:10)

Introduction

This section partially resolves the major crisis of the story. The focus of the narrative will shift from Mordecai (who literally says nothing in this section) to Esther, who will bring about the deliverance of her people in her own way. Disregarding the order given her by Mordecai, and disobeying the rule of the king that no one could come into his presence uninvited, Esther enters the court of the king's throne room in order to invite him and his vizier to a banquet. This invitation leads to yet another, for the following day. In the intervening time, Haman, on the counsel of his wife, decides to have Mordecai impaled on a spike.

While Haman waits for an audience with the king to obtain his permission to kill Mordecai, the king has discovered that Mordecai was never rewarded for his rescue of the king. Summoning Haman into his presence, Xerxes asks him what should be done for someone the king wishes to hon or. Haman assumes the king is referring to himself and prescribes that the honoree should be led in elaborate procession through Susa, led by a noble prince. Xerxes orders Haman to do as he had said—for Mordecai the Jew.

After the procession, the humiliated vizier is summoned to the queen's banquet. As they are drinking, the king asks Esther what she really desires. She begs him to save her people, the Jews, and implicates Haman as the one who hatched the plot against them. As the king storms out of the room, Haman throws himself down before the queen to beg for mercy. The king enters and finds Haman throwing himself on the queen and accuses him of rape. He orders him impaled on the pike he had built for Mordecai.

Reversal is the key theme of this section. Like the book as a whole, it is constructed chiastically, but several of the elements are the antithesis of their antecedents, rather than synonyms:

(A) The king spares Esther (5:1–2)

(B) Esther requests the king and Haman come to a banquet (5:3–5a)

(C) Esther requests that the king and Haman come to a second banquet (5:5b–8)

(D) Zeresh counsels Haman to kill Mordecai (5:9–14)

(E) The king observes that Mordecai was not honored (6:1–3)

(F) Haman counsels the king on how to honor a benefactor (6:4–9)

(E′) The king orders Haman to honor Mordecai (6:10–11)

(D′) Zeresh counsels Haman that he cannot defeat Mordecai (6:12–14)

(C′) Esther requests that the king spare her people (7:1–6a)

(B′) Haman requests that the queen spare his life (7:6b–8a)

(A′) The king condemns Haman (7:8b–10)

The section begins with the threat to Esther's life, which is averted when the king extends to her the golden staff (5:2). It ends with Haman on the end of a different shaft—the pike on which he is impaled (7:10). Each request for the king to attend a banquet (5:4, 8) is balanced with a request for mercy: one from Esther (7:3) and one from Haman (7:7). Haman's wife, Zeresh, reverses her advice that Haman should execute Mordecai (5:9–14) with counsel that he cannot overcome Mordecai (6:12–14). Even in the "hinge" (section F), there is a sense of reversal. While Haman thinks he is describing honors he will receive, he is actually describing honors that will be bestowed on Mordecai.

Outline

IV. The Plot Reversed (5:1–7:10)
- A. Esther's First Banquet (5:1–8)
  - 1. Esther Invites the King and Haman to a Banquet (5:1–5a)
    - a. Esther Appears before the King (5:1–2)
    - b. Esther Issues an Invitation (5:3–5a)
  - 2. Esther Invites the King and Haman to a Second Banquet (5:5b–8)
- B. Haman Plots to Kill Mordecai (5:9–14)
- C. Mordecai Is Honored; Haman Humiliated (6:1–14)
  - 1. The King Discovers His Oversight (6:1–3)
  - 2. Haman Counsels the King on Honoring a Benefactor (6:4–10)

3. Haman Is Forced to Honor Mordecai (6:11)
4. Haman's End Is Foretold (6:12–14)

D. Esther's Second Banquet (7:1–10)
1. Esther Appeals to the King for the Jews (7:1–6a)
2. Haman Appeals to the Queen for His Life (7:6b–8a)
3. Haman Is Condemned (7:8b–10)

Esther's First Banquet (5:1–8)

Translation

1 And it came to pass on the third day that Esther clothed herself in royalty, and she stood in the inner court of the throne room,[1] in view of the throne room, while the king was sitting on his royal throne in front of the doorway
of the room. **2** When the king saw Queen Esther standing in the court, she won favor in his eyes. The king stretched out to Esther the golden scepter that was in his hand. Then Esther approached, and she touched the head of
the scepter. **3** Then the king said to her, "What is it, Queen Esther?[2] What is your request? Up to half the kingdom, and it will be given to you."

4 Esther said, "If the king approves,[3] let the king come, and Haman, today to the banquet that I have prepared for him."

5 And the king said, "Bring quickly Haman to do as Esther said."[4]

Then the king and Haman went to the banquet that Esther had pre-
pared. **6** And the king said to Esther during the wine course,[5] "What is your petition, that it might be given to you? And what is your request? Up to half my kingdom, and it will be done."

7 And Esther replied and said, "My petition and my request … **8** If I have found favor in the eyes of the king, and if it seems good to the king to grant my petition and to do as I request, let the king come with Haman to the banquet which I will make for them tomorrow.[6] Tomorrow, I will do as the king says."

---

1. Lit., "the house of the king." Here, the phrase בֵּית הַמֶּלֶךְ (*bayit hammelek*) refers not to the entire palace, but only to the room where the king held his royal audiences.
2. Lit., "What (is) to you, Queen Esther?" Cf. Josh 15:18; Judg 18:24.
3. Lit., "If it is good to the king."
4. Lit., "to do the word of Esther."
5. Lit., "the banquet of wine." The phrase means after the food had been eaten, and the guests were enjoying wine.
6. The word "tomorrow" is not present here in the MT. It is supplied on the basis of the LXX and AT.

Textual Notes

1.a. The LXX and AT expand on the scene in vv. 1–2: Esther is accompanied by two attendants and leans on them as she enters the chamber. The king is furious as Esther enters, and Esther becomes so terrified that she faints. Xerxes' anger quickly evaporates, and he has compassion on her and speaks to her consolingly.

1.b. *BHS* and several scholars suggest that a word has dropped out of the text between אֶסְתֵּר ("Esther") and מַלְכוּת ("royalty"). Typically, it is suggested that the text originally read something like "the clothing of the kingdom." The extant construction, however, is grammatically acceptable in biblical Heb.

4.a. In the LXX, Esther prefaces her request by saying, "Today is my special day." In the AT, she says, "Tomorrow is my special day."

4.b. In the AT, Haman is called the "friend" of Xerxes.

6.a. The LXX omits the phrase, "up to half my kingdom" (עַד־חֲצִי הַמַּלְכוּת), but it is retained in the AT.

8.a. The LXX and AT read, "… which I will prepare for them tomorrow. And tomorrow, I will do according to the word of the king." The reading of the Greek here is preferable to the Heb. of the MT, which does not say when the banquet will occur. It is likely that the first מָחָר was omitted by haplogr.

Commentary

In the structure of the book of Esther, this scene represents the turning point of the entire narrative. Once Esther comes into the king's court, the die is cast. It is her initiative that will start the process whereby the crisis will be reversed.

This section is well defined, distinguished from those that precede and follow by setting and characters. The preceding section (4:1–17) focused on the interaction between Mordecai and Esther and took place mostly outside the palace. This section (5:1–8) focuses on the interaction between the queen and the king and is set entirely in the palace. The section that follows (5:9–14) moves outside the palace and focuses on Haman.

The section is divided into two scenes. The first scene takes place in the king's audience chamber, when Esther shows up uninvited and presents her petition for the king and Haman to attend her banquet. In this act of courage, human initiative takes its place beside divine providence as a driving force of the narrative. This scene ends in the middle of v. 5: Xerxes issues the command for Haman to be brought while still in his throne room. The second half of the verse is set in the banquet room, where the remainder of the section transpires. There, the king again inquires about Esther's request, and she issues the second invitation to a banquet for the following day.

5:1 In this passage, Esther's identity has come front and center. She has chosen to identify with the Jewish people privately, by joining with them in her fast. Publicly, however, she still conceals her Jewishness. Unlike Mordecai, who clothes himself in sackcloth and ashes, she clothes herself in the trappings of her office. She comes before the king in all her splendor, a sight not so much intended to stir his passions but to inspire his respect (Berlin, 52). The preparations for seduction are fairly well defined in passages such as Esth 2; Ruth 3:3; or Jdt 10:3–4. They include washing, anointing, and dressing, and often mention jewelry or other special apparel. Esther's procedure is simple and dignified: she means business, not romance. If her formal dress were not enough to get the point across, this single verse employs forms of the root מָלַךְ (*mālak*), "rule," six times.

The contrast is stark with her first encounter with Xerxes. The first time, she had spent a whole year in beautification; every possible action was taken to make her as attractive as she could be. This time, she comes in exhausted from a fast of three days.[7] Previously, she was brought passively before the king, accepting the role into which she had been cast. This time, she initiates the encounter, hoping to change her fate and that of her people. In the first case, she was segregated from her people and hiding her identification with them. This time she goes—secretly, at first—as their representative. Before, she was the passive recipient of the ministrations of eunuchs and the favor of the king. This time, she clothes herself in her royal office before making her appearance. As we have already seen, in the book of Esther, clothing is a signifier of condition. Esther does not merely wrap herself in royal robes; she dons the office itself: "And Esther clothed herself in royalty" (וַתִּלְבַּשׁ אֶסְתֵּר מַלְכוּת, *wattilbaš ʾestēr malkût*).[8] She appears now as the queen.

---

7. The explanation for how Esther could fast three days and yet still enter into the king's presence on the third day may be due to different calendrical terminology used by Esther and the narrator. See N. L. Collins, "Did Esther Fast on the 15th Nisan? An Extended Comment on Esther 3:12," *RB* 100 (1993): 533–61.

8. Some scholars have felt the construction ungrammatical and have suggested inserting a word like לְבוּשׁ (*lābûš*), "clothing of." There are, however, similar expressions elsewhere in the Bible. We might compare this expression to those found in verses such as Psa 104:1, "You clothe yourself with splendor and majesty"; Ezek 7:27, "The prince will be dressed with despair"; or Ezek 26:16, "With terror they will be clothed."

There is also a strong contrast drawn between this episode and the story of Vashti in chapter 1. Both queens have violated the law, but the circumstances are oddly inverted. Vashti had risked her life by refusing to come before the king when she was summoned. Esther now risks her life by coming before the king without being summoned. Vashti's failure to appear incited the king's wrath; Esther's unexpected appearance elicits his favor. Vashti's insubordination will result in an attempt to put all women in their place; Esther's insubordination, if successful, will result in the deliverance of all the Jews. There is more danger in what she is doing than that of the typical uninvited supplicant. Vashti had been deposed from office because she had not shown the king his proper respect, and Esther had been made queen because she seemed like someone who would "know her place." Her actions now might shatter that carefully constructed persona. She will no longer be seen as the utterly submissive wife.

Esther stands in the court outside the throne room, where she waited to see what the king would do. From here, she and the king can see one another, but she does not actually approach him in a way that could be perceived as a threat. Nonetheless, her actions are in violation of the law (4:11), and unless the king orders otherwise, her life is already forfeit.

5:2 The phrase "She found favor in his eyes" is similar to the expression used in 2:15, "And Esther found favor in the eyes of all who saw her." It is more than merely being found attractive. The word translated "favor" (חֵן, *ḥēn*) typically means "pleasing," due to character or good works. It is the word used in Gen 6:8 ("But Noah found favor in the eyes of Yahweh") and of Joseph, who gained the favor of Potiphar (Gen 39:4) and of the warden of his prison (Gen 39:21). Typically, this word is used by people who make a request of someone they deem to be in a position of power over them (Gen 18:13; Num 32:5), or of someone to whom a favor or forbearance is granted (Ruth 2:2). In this passage, Esther is clearly dependent on the mercy of Xerxes for her life. The LXX makes it explicit that Esther received "grace" from the king because "God changed the spirit of the king to gentleness."

The imagery that follows might well be designed to contain sexual innuendo, as several scholars have observed.[9] It is somewhat reminiscent of the story of Ruth and Boaz, where Ruth comes unbidden to the threshing floor to seek out Boaz's favor and to offer herself to him as wife (Ruth 3). But while that scene is chaste and sweet, in its way, this one is fraught with danger and sexual tension. We should bear in mind that in the mind of this king, the queen has but one purpose: to entertain him. Vashti was deposed

9. E.g., T. K. Beal, *The Book of Hiding: Gender, Ethnicity, Annihilation, and Esther* (London: Routledge, 1997), 76–77.

because she failed in that role; Esther was chosen precisely because she succeeded beyond all others. The first and only time the king and Esther have been seen together in this book was for their night of passion. Though it has been thirty days since he has seen the queen, the narrator might well want us to infer that the king's feelings were inflamed. If so, his expectations and hers are very different. She has come in the garb of office and means business. He, distracted from the affairs of state by the queen's appearance, may be thinking pleasure (compare the reaction of Herod Antipas to the dance of Herodias' daughter in Mark 6:14–28).[10]

5:3 The first part of Xerxes' question ("What [is it] to you, Queen Esther?") comes across almost as an expostulation, a short colloquial interrogation. The phrase מַה־לָּךְ (*mah-lĕkā*) is a colloquialism, used with a variety of implications. Fox argues that the phrase always implies that the listener is disturbed or troubled, but that is not necessarily the case.[11] Several examples militate against this idea. See further Bush, 404.

The second part ("What is your request?") is more formal. He addresses her as "Queen Esther," recognizing the royal station that she had sought to demonstrate through her dress. The most remarkable part of the verse, however, is Xerxes' promise, "Up to half the kingdom, and it will be given to you." The Persian monarchs were renowned for such extravagant oaths and their sometimes fateful outcome. According to Herodotus (*Hist.* 5.24), Darius used similar hyperbole in his effort to lure Histiaeus, tyrant of Miletus, to accept a position as his advisor in Susa: "All I have will be yours." Herodotus also depicts Xerxes as a man who made ill-considered promises to the women in his life. In *Hist.* 9.109–113, Herodotus reports that Xerxes, who had been having an affair with his niece, vowed to give her anything she requested. She foolishly demanded that he give her the robe that he was wearing, which had been hand-made by Xerxes' wife, Amestris. Though he tried to persuade her to take another gift, she would have none of it. So Xerxes gave her the robe, which she decided to wear in public. When Amestris was told that the robe she had made for Xerxes was being worn by the niece, her suspicions of the king's infidelity were confirmed. Rather than take vengeance on the mistress, Amestris decided that it was the woman's mother, the wife of Xerxes' brother, who was really behind the affair. At the king's birthday banquet, Amestris asked that Xerxes place the

---

10. On the literary dependence of Mark's story on Esther, see B. D. Schildgen, "A Blind Promise: Mark's Retrieval of Esther," *Poetics Today* 15 (1994): 115–31, and other sources cited in the introduction, "Esther in the Christian Canon: the New Testament."

11. Fox, *Character and Ideology*, 281; see also Berlin, 53.

mother in her power. Xerxes felt compelled to honor the request, because "it is impossible among them that one who makes request when a royal feast is spread before the king should not receive it" (*Hist.* 9.111). Amestris had the woman horribly mutilated and sent back to her home and husband.

While many scholars note the similarities between Xerxes' promise here and those found in Herodotus or on the lips of other rash rulers, they fail to observe how unique Xerxes' promise of up to half the kingdom truly is. This is no "stock phrase" used by monarchs to express their favor: its equivalent is found nowhere else in the Bible or in ancient literature, except in Mark 6:23, which is certainly dependent on Esther.[12] It has been chosen very deliberately by the narrator because of what it implies about Esther's changing status. If Xerxes literally gave Esther "half his kingdom," they would each have half—and the queen would become the equal of the king.

5:4 The question provoked by this verse is why Esther did not simply request that Xerxes deliver the Jews from Haman's pogrom, as Mordecai had apparently expected. Several solutions have been offered. The most obvious is that she was afraid. Fearing to reveal her connection with the Jews, she temporized by asking for this small favor so she could work up her nerve. This notion can be easily dismissed: Esther had already proven her courage by going into the king's presence uninvited; and she had already prepared a banquet for the king and Haman, which means that she had not made a spur-of-the-moment decision to put off her request for the Jews' lives. Her actions must be recognized as considered, not spontaneous.

The rabbis argued that Esther intended to make Xerxes jealous by inviting Haman to the party, thinking that perhaps Esther was sexually interested in his courtier. Being jealous of Haman, the king would be more agreeable to the prospect of executing him (*b. Meg.* 15b). This fantasy has little to recommend it: if Xerxes suspected Haman, why would he be so enthusiastic about having him brought to the banquet (v. 5, "Bring Haman quickly ... ")?

It has also been suggested that Esther wanted to get Xerxes drunk before making her request. Most scholars, however, emphasize the literary purposes of this banquet and the second to follow. The typical arguments are that by delaying Esther's request, the narrator increases the dramatic tension in the story (so Moore 1971, 56; Levenson, 90; Berlin, 54), or allows time for the episode of Haman's humiliation to transpire (so, e.g., Paton, 234; Bardtke, 339).

---

12. Herod's promise would have been especially outrageous, since he was only a governor and had no kingdom to give.

There surely is a literary component for this aspect of the episode. One underappreciated point is that by having Esther invite the king and Haman to a banquet, the narrator can place the most critical event of the story at a banquet. The banqueting motif is thus interwoven with every significant episode of the story: Vashti's removal from office (Esth 1:3–12); Esther's installation as queen (Esth 2:18); the issuing of Haman's edict (Esth 3:15); the revelation of the plot (Esth 7:3–6); and the victory celebration of the Jews (Esth 9:17–23). Also, the narrator's reticence here is an important literary device. By withholding an explanation, the author allows us to wonder about Esther's motives, or perhaps even conclude that she has lost her nerve.[13] The banquets also retard the denouement of the story, increasing the sense of expectancy and urgency. Dramatic pacing alone, however, cannot account for Esther's stratagem. It will be seen as the story continues that Esther has carefully orchestrated her actions to produce the ruin of Haman and the deliverance of her people.

The initial consonants of the words, "Let the king and Haman come today," form an acronym of the Tetragrammaton, יהוה (*yhwh*). While many interpreters through the ages have considered this collocation intentional, I contend that it is a coincidence, since these three are among the most common consonants in the Heb. Bible, especially at the beginnings and ends of words.[14]

5:5a The king does not even pause to answer Esther in the affirmative; he merely issues the order that Haman be brought to the banquet. The wording of his command implies urgency. The verb מָהַר (*māhar*) can be used in hendiadys with another verb meaning to do something hastily, or it can be used alone to mean "bring quickly," as in Gen 18:6 and 1 Kgs 22:9. Esther has intimated that the banquet is already prepared, and for some reason, Xerxes clearly relishes the prospect of dining with the queen. Perhaps, knowing that this dinner is only the preliminary to her real request, he is impatient to discover what matter would have caused the queen to risk her life.

There is some ambiguity in the wording of the last phrase. As Levenson (90) observes, it is uncertain from the Heb. text whether these are words spoken by the king or are the narrator's explanation ("And the king said, 'Bring Haman quickly,' to do the word of Esther"). I have understood the phrase as part of the king's instructions, and in that light, it has an

13. It is similar to the method used by the narrator of Jonah, who allows us to assume that Jonah fled to Tarshish because he was afraid of the Assyrians, only to reveal near the end of the narrative that he really fled because he wanted them to be destroyed (Jonah 4:2).

14. See further in the introduction, "Theology of Esther: Contemporary Approaches."

interesting implication. The phrase "the word of the king" occurs in Esth 2:8; 3:15; 4:3; and 8:14, with the meaning "commandment." A similar implication seems to be attached to Esther's request here. Haman is being forced to act according to the will of the queen. There has indeed been a turnaround in the queen's status. In Esth 1, the queen had been ordered to come before the king; here, the vizier is forced to appear at the summons of the queen. But it is not the vizier only who is experiencing the reversal. In chapter 1, Vashti's refusal to obey the king's summons left Xerxes trembling at the prospect that men might be losing control of their households; here, he eagerly obeys the word of the queen, answering her summons to a banquet that she has already prepared in anticipation of his compliance.

5:5b–6 The setting changes from the king's throne room to the place of the banquet, presumably in the queen's quarters. Unlike the huge parties of chapter 1, designed to demonstrate the king's splendor, this banquet is a private affair. The Greek author Plutarch, in contrast to other sources, indicates that the king often dined with the queen and queen mother, the mother sitting above him and the queen seated below. He notes that Artaxerxes also invited his brothers to dine with him (*Artaxerxes* 5).

The wine course (lit., "banquet of wine") apparently means that after the food had been eaten, the guests would linger at table and drink wine. It would have been an appropriate time for Xerxes to solicit the queen's request, since as noted in the commentary on 1:10, Persian kings apparently liked to deliberate their decisions while drunk. The king essentially reiterates the words he had spoken earlier, along with the oath: "What is your request? Up to half my kingdom, and it will be done." The king recognized the banquet as the prelude, the setup for the real request. He acknowledged that Esther was employing a form of negotiation. Before getting to the matter at hand, she began with a small request, easily granted. She also put the king in a more comfortable mood for deliberating the true matter.

5:7–8 Most translations supply a verb and treat this verse as if it were a complete sentence. "My petition and my request is" (NIV); "This is my petition and request" (NRSV); "This is my request and deepest wish" (NLT); "My petition and request *is this*" (NKJV). While it is quite common for biblical Heb. to omit words that may be inferred from the context, in this case, the translators seem to have misunderstood the narrator's intent. As these translations are worded, they imply that Esther's request was that the king and Haman would join her for another banquet. But that is *not* her request: she goes on to state that at that next banquet, she will make her request known. The king, too, will ask again at the next banquet for her to present her request, clearly indicating that he knew, also, that the dinner invitation was not the request. Therefore Esther's words in 5:7 are probably best understood as an anacoluthon, an incomplete thought. Esther begins to respond to the king, but breaks off her answer. It is certain that her "petition and [her] request" is not that the king and Haman attend another banquet. The king knows that the invitations to dine are but the prelude to the true request, which he asks to know at the end of each banquet (cf. Bush, 404). Instead, she states that it will be then, at the second banquet, that she will make her petition and request known.

Why does Esther begin this way, then suddenly break off? That is precisely the question the narrator wants us to ask. Is Esther afraid? Does she have second thoughts? Is the old Esther, the timid wallflower, reasserting herself? The reader cannot help but have such thoughts. Esther then strings together a series of obsequies, making it appear as if she is about to gather her nerve and confront the king about the decree against the Jews: "If I have found favor in the eyes of the king, and if it seems good to the king to grant my petition and to do as I request ... " Then, instead of stating the real matter, she invites the king to another banquet that she will prepare for the next day. The narrator has tricked us, building up our expectations, then disappointing us.

From a narrative standpoint, the storyteller has skillfully misdirected his audience. Nonetheless, there is more happening here than just the frustration of the reader's expectations. A variety of explanations have been proposed for Esther's evasiveness. Most scholars (e.g., Paton, 234; Bardtke, 339; Moore 1971, 57–58) have argued that the primary reason for the two banquets is literary: the two banquets build suspense, and delay the resolution of the crisis long enough for the humiliation of Mordecai in chapter 6. Clines (305), Bush (405–6), and Fox[15] argue instead for a "strategic" explanation. Esther has piqued the king's curiosity by the way she has worded this second request, making him even more eager to learn the matter at hand. Furthermore, since Esther phrases her invitation as a conditional sentence, she has called on the king to commit himself in advance, without ever hearing the actual petition. "If it pleases the king to grant my petition, then come to my banquet!" If the king shows up at the banquet, he is essentially saying that he *is* pleased to do as she says.

She has also cleverly included Haman explicitly in this second invitation: in the invitation to the first banquet, she says, "Let the king and Haman come to the banquet I have prepared for *him*." This time, she asks, "Let the king and Haman come to the banquet I will prepare for *them*." Haman will surely show up for a banquet prepared especially for him. Then, the queen can confront him directly, in the presence of the king. This queen

15. M. Fox, *Character and Ideology in the Book of Esther*, 2nd ed. (Grand Rapids: Eerdmans, 2001), 71–73.

is no coward. Indeed, her refusal to answer at this time is not a sign of diffidence, but of courage, since she risks the king's anger with her noncompliance (cf. Berg, 80). Esther is also no fool. She has carefully planned to sit down at a table prepared in the presence of her enemy and reveal both him and herself to the king in a single stroke.

There is certainly, then, a calculated element in Esther's actions. But we need not rule out the literary aspects. It is probably significant that Esther's banquets will occur in a pair, just like the other strategic banquets of the narrative: the two banquets of Xerxes in Esth 1, the two banquets of the Jews in Esth 9, and these two banquets given by Esther in Esth 5 and 7. The Jews celebrated their deliverance with two banquets, so it is only fitting that their deliverance is brought about in the course of two banquets.

Biblical Theology Comments

5:1–2 As in the case of the story of Esther's purification, premodern Christians tended to read these verses typologically. According to Rabanus Marus,

> The fact that Esther put on all her royal robes on the third day undoubtedly signifies that the church of the nations, in the third time of the world, that is, after the incarnation, passion and resurrection of Christ, clothed herself through the sacrament of baptism and the confession of the Holy Trinity with faith, hope, and charity, and the ornament of every virtue so that she might become worthy of the royal marriage while the love of (the Lord) remained constantly fervent.[16]

Thomas Aquinas believed that Esther's entrance foreshadowed the work of the Virgin Mary:

> Through Queen Esther, that is, through the Blessed Virgin the sentence of damnation passed against us was revoked; namely through her intercession, through the extension of the King's golden sceptre to Mary and through her kiss on the top of that sceptre we are saved from hell and damnation.[17]

Martin Luther engaged in similar speculation, comparing the golden staff of Xerxes to the gospel of Jesus Christ in his commentary on Psa 2. A little later, John Preston (1587–1628) alluded to the episode in the title to

---

16. Conti and Pilara, 386.

17. Thomas Aquinas, *The Three Greatest Prayers: Commentaries on the Our Father, the Hail Mary, and the Apostles' Creed*, trans. Laurence Shapcote (Westminster, MD: Newman Press, 1956), 24. There was a common understanding, based on the Vulgate translation, that Esther not only touched the scepter, but kissed it as well.

his tract, "The Golden Sceptre Held Forth to the Humble" (a collection of six sermons on 2 Chr 7:14 preached at Cambridge). Such comparisons continue to this day: Wechsler sees the three days that Esther spent in fasting as a type of Christ's days in the tomb before His ascension to the Father.[18] Jobes (147), too, insists that the scene should be read as an image of divine grace: "This scene pictures a gracious act of a king who holds life-and-death power. Had God not extended the cross of Jesus Christ to the world, all would die in his presence."

As cautioned earlier, the interpreter who resorts to typologies not explicitly spelled out in the NT is on treacherous ground. We may draw comparisons of the king's mercy and God's mercy, but Xerxes will always pale in that light. Xerxes spared a queen who pushed the limits of the law in a righteous cause. God spares the sinners who rebel against His commandments for their own selfish ends. Matthew Henry's observations seem more apropos than seeing Xerxes' clemency as a type of God's mercy:

> Esther came to a proud imperious man; we come to the God of love and grace. She was not called; we are: the Spirit says, *Come*, and the bride says, *Come.* She had a law against her; we have a promise, many a promise, in favour of us: *Ask, and it shall be given you.* She had no friend to introduce her, or intercede for her, while on the contrary he that was then the king's favourite was her enemy; but we have an advocate with the Father, in whom he is well pleased. *Let us therefore come boldly to the throne of grace.*[19]

Henry illustrates a better approach to discerning theological meaning in this text. It is not comparison, but contrast, that truly illuminates this episode. King Xerxes was a fearful man who isolated himself from others and used the threat of violence to keep them at a distance. God, on the other hand, longs to have fellowship with humanity. He was willing to enter into our world, live among us, and even become vulnerable for our sakes. King Xerxes regarded Esther as an object of sensual pleasure. God's love for humanity is pure and selfless. The golden staff of the king was a symbol of his absolute power and majesty; the cross of Christ was a symbol of humiliation and suffering. As Henry notes, we need not come fearfully into the presence of God. Our Intercessor shields us from His wrath.

---

18. M. G. Wechsler, "Shadow and Fulfillment in the Book of Esther," *BSac* 154 (1997): 281–83.

19. M. Henry, *An Exposition of the Old and New Testament*, ed. George Burder and John Hughes (Philadelphia: Barrington and Haswell, 1811), 2:905.

5:3–5 Xerxes' oath here and the situation surrounding it is cleverly twisted in Mark's Gospel. Here, Esther is setting in motion a plot to destroy her enemy Haman and deliver her people. She goes unbidden to intercede for her people, and her appearance so delights the king that he grants her an audience. She presents then her request: merely that the king and Haman attend her banquet. The ultimate outcome, however, will be the destruction of the Jews' enemy. In Mark 6, Herodias, wife of Herod, is hatching a plot against John the Baptist. When the king is holding a banquet for himself and his nobles, she senses her opportunity. Herodias' daughter dances and entertains the governor in what can be seen as a turnaround of Vashti's refusal to entertain King Xerxes' guests. The governor is so thrilled that he offers the young woman "up to half [his] kingdom" (Mark 6:23). Herodias seizes the opportunity to destroy her enemy, John the Baptist. In a gruesome parody of Esther's banquet, Herodias' daughter presents her mother the head of John the Baptist on a platter.

Mark's allusions to the Esther narrative were likely inspired by the similar elements occurring in the circumstances, but they also serve as an important reminder that the antagonism between the powers of this world and the kingdom of God continues to exist. Though the names and faces change, the story remains the same: the proud potentates of the earth refuse to recognize their true Master and despise His servants. Esther will win her battle, but John the Baptist will lose. In the continuing conflict, there are sometimes reversals where the kingdom of God seems to suffer setbacks. In the War Scroll of the Dead Sea sect (1QM 1), the children of light win the first three engagements against the armies of the earth, but the children of darkness win the next three. It may seem at times that the kingdom of God is in retreat, but the end of the conflict is not in doubt: "In this world you have affliction, but have courage! I have conquered the world" (John 16:33).

Application and Devotional Implications

When one thinks about Esther's character, very likely the first quality to come to mind is "courage." That characterization may or may not be accurate; after all, Esther was basically bullied into approaching the king. Yet Esther is certainly not the only person who has ever been forced to take action that they feared and discovered courage in the process. Many a pundit and celebrity through the ages has quipped that courage is not the absence of fear, but the ability to overcome fear and do what needs to be done. We should not fault the quality of Esther's courage because of the circumstances under which she finds it.

The virtue of courage is not often lauded in the Bible. It is not listed as a "fruit of the Spirit" in Gal 5:22–23, nor is it listed as a gift of the Spirit in

1 Cor 12:8–12. Often, it seems as if courage is a human capacity that needs only to be strengthened. And yet there are clearly examples in the Bible of divinely inspired courage. In 1 Sam 11:6, the Holy Spirit seems to inspire courage in King Saul, and perhaps in Gideon in Judg 6:34. In Acts 4:23–31, the believers were filled with courage that came from the Holy Spirit. So even if the Bible does not often laud courage, it values it highly.

It is fairly certain that little of importance is accomplished in the Bible—or the world—without courage. On about sixty-five occasions in the Bible, God or His spokesmen command people, "Fear not," and on about thirty more, God commands them to be courageous.[20] Rarely, however, are these words designed merely to give comfort. More often, they are meant to empower. Biblical courage is not the "courage to *be*," but the courage to *do*. It gives people the ability to take action in a wide variety of forms. In Josh 1, Joshua is told four times to be courageous, and to go forth and conquer the promised land. In 1 Chr 22:13, David counsels Solomon to be courageous and build the temple. The disciples pray for courage so that they can evangelize (Acts 4:23–31). Courage will not enable all of us to be fighters. Some of us it will make into builders. Some will become petitioners. But whatever its purpose, courage is as vital to the kingdom of God as is prophecy or patience.

Selected Bibliography

Beal, T. K. *The Book of Hiding: Gender, Ethnicity, Annihilation, and Esther.* London: Routledge, 1997.

Berg, S. B. *The Book of Esther: Motifs, Themes and Structure.* SBLDS 44. Missoula, MT: Scholars Press, 1979.

Clines, D. J. A. *The Esther Scroll: The Story of the Story.* JSOTSup 30. Sheffield, UK: JSOT Press, 1984.

Collins, N. L. "Did Esther Fast on the 15th Nisan? An Extended Comment on Esther 3:12." *RB* 100 (1993): 533–61.

Fox, M. V. *Character and Ideology in the Book of Esther.* 2nd ed. Grand Rapids: Eerdmans, 2001.

Rudolph, W. "Textkritisches zum Estherbuch." *VT* 4 (1954): 89–90.

Schildgen, B. D. "A Blind Promise: Mark's Retrieval of Esther." *Poetics Today* 15 (1994): 115–31.

Wechsler, M. G. "Shadow and Fulfillment in the Book of Esther." *BSac* 154 (1997): 275–84.

20. The count varies, of course, according to the translation.

Haman Plots to Kill Mordecai (5:9–14)

Translation

9 Haman went out that day joyful and in a good mood.[21] But when Haman saw Mordecai in the king's gate, and he neither rose nor trembled before him, Haman was filled with rage against Mordecai. **10** But he restrained himself and went home. Then he sent and gathered his friends and his wife, Zeresh. **11** Haman told them about his glorious wealth, his many sons, and all the ways[22] the king had magnified him and exalted him over the officials and servants of the king. **12** Haman said, "Even Esther the queen did not bring anyone to the banquet with the king that she prepared but me. Even tomorrow I am summoned to her, along with the king. **13** But all this means nothing to me, so long as I see Mordecai the Jew sitting in the king's gate."

14 Then Zeresh his wife and all his friends said to him, "Make a pike[23] fifty cubits high, and in the morning, talk to the king, then hang Mordecai on it. Then go with the king to the banquet happy." The suggestion pleased Haman, so he made the pike.

Textual Notes

9.a. LXX omits the phrase וְלֹא־קָם וְלֹא־זָע מִמֶּנּוּ, "and how he did not rise or tremble before him." It is present in the Vg.

11.a. *BHS* suggests deleting the relative pronoun אֲשֶׁר in וְאֵת כָּל־אֲשֶׁר. This deletion is not grammatically necessary.

11.b. A few Heb. MSS insert כָּל ("all") before הַשָּׂרִים. These texts have likely been influenced by the wording in 3:1–2.

14.a. For וַיִּיטַב הַדָּבָר לִפְנֵי הָמָן ("the word seemed good before Haman"), a few Heb. MSS and the Syr. have the more common וַיִּיטַב הַדָּבָר בְּעֵינֵי הָמָן ("the word seemed good in the eyes of Haman"). The MT is not ungrammatical and should be retained.

Commentary

This short section appears almost as an addendum to the account of the feast, but it serves a crucial function in the narrative. It seems on the surface as if the threat to the heroes has become even more immediate. Haman, on the advice of his wife and friends, decides that the execution of Mordecai

21. Lit., "good of heart."
22. Lit., "all which the king had magnified him."
23. Lit., "a tree" or "wooden object."

cannot wait for a year and decides to seek the king's permission to kill him at once. The readers know that the reversal has already been set in motion, but this episode adds some extra tension. Will Esther's delay in presenting her request cost Mordecai his life?

The episode also highlights the two levels of animosity in the Esther narrative. On one level is the general threat against the Jewish people. It is epitomized by Haman's decree, but it is also revealed in that many enemies will later rise up against the Jews in an effort to destroy them. On the other level is the personal struggle between Haman and Mordecai that set off the crisis to begin with. With the threat of genocide hanging over the nation, it is easy for the audience to lose sight of the interpersonal dynamics that incited the narrative. This episode brings the personal issues back to the forefront.

In this section, there is an inclusio* of sorts: it begins by telling us that Haman left the palace "rejoicing" and "good of heart" (5:9). In 5:14, Zeresh tells Haman how he will go to the queen's banquet "rejoicing," and the word was "good before him." Bush (412–14) argues that this section forms the opening scene of a new section, based on its parallels with 6:12–14, which is clearly a closing section. Bush fails to note, however, that these parallel units are part of a larger chiastic structure, as outlined in the introduction to 5:1–7:10 above.

5:9 Having felt honored by the invitation to dine with the queen, Haman is in high spirits. He is receiving, he believes, the one thing that he craves above all else: recognition. But his mood changes abruptly at the appearance of Mordecai. Mordecai has returned to his place at the gate, apparently aware that Esther has begun her machinations. He is conducting his business again as if nothing had happened. He also continues in his insolent refusal to show deference to Haman. Even the decree for the Jews' destruction could not humble this insolent man. Haman is furious. The queen had honored Haman, but this Jew does not!

Previously, Haman had expected Mordecai to fall before him, but Mordecai will not even rise to his feet in a show of respect. Haman had issued a decree ordering Mordecai's death. Should not the man at least tremble (עוז, *ʿwz*) in his presence, showing fear of Haman's awesomeness? The bright day of Haman's conquest was totally ruined by the single dark cloud on his horizon. Or was his rage incited by the fear of what that dark cloud might signify?

5:10 Why does Haman restrain himself? Paton (238) writes that "this delay in taking vengeance upon Mordecai is just as unnatural as is Esther's delay in taking vengeance upon Haman." But what Paton overlooks is the very issue that brought about the order for the pogrom in the first place: Haman was too proud to respond to Mordecai only. He believed that striking out at a single man was beneath his dignity. It will take the urging of his friends, and the idea of a very public display, to encourage Haman to change his policy. It is also implied that Haman cannot execute Mordecai without the king's consent, since in chapter 6 he will visit the king to obtain permission to impale Mordecai on the pole he has made.

Haman "sent" to gather his friends, almost certainly meaning that he sent his servants to fetch them. These "friends" are apparently his advisers: in 6:13, they are called "his wise ones" (חֲכָמָיו, *ḥăkāmāyw*). Haman has to summon professional friends to hear his boasting. He also summons his wife, which is somewhat ominous in the context of this book. Our drama began when a wife refused to come to her husband's summons, and just a few verses ago, Esther risked her life when she came to her husband without being summoned. What will be the effect of this summons?

5:11–12 Haman's ten sons would surely have given him some "bragging rights" in the eyes of the Persians. According to Herodotus (*Hist.* 1.136), the Persians regarded it as the "greatest proof of manly excellence" to father many sons. In fact, Herodotus reports that each year the man with the most sons would be sent a special gift by the king. We can assume that Haman's wife and advisors knew all about his wealth and how many sons he had. They would not have known, however, about his dinner with the queen. Furthermore, the queen has obviously been so taken with his company that she wants him back the next day, as the royal couple's exclusive guest. With this detail, Haman associates himself with the most exclusive company of the Persian Empire. He is seeing only the social and political aspects of the affair. He fails to note that Esther has summoned the king and the vizier because she intends to present a request. He only cares that he is now invited to the very best parties. Once again, Haman's words expose him as a posturing buffoon.

More remarkable still is that in this quote Haman apparently assumes that the queen's invitation represents an honor for him, just as he will assume that the king's request in 6:7–9 is designed to honor him. In both cases, he is mistaken, much to his discomfiture. In this case, he apparently assumes he is to be honored at a banquet, when in fact he will be exposed as a plotter. In 6:7–9, he assumes he is to be honored by the king, when actually he will be honoring Mordecai.

5:13 The only thing that mars Haman's mood is Mordecai's continued obstinacy. The phrase "All of this means nothing to me" (וְכָל־זֶה אֵינֶנּוּ שֹׁוֶה לִי, *wĕkol-zeh ʾênennû šōweh lî*) is reminiscent of Haman's words to the king in 3:8, "And for the king, it is not worth it (וְלַמֶּלֶךְ אֵין־שֹׁוֶה, *wĕlammelek ʾên-šōweh*) to let them remain." Haman's argument in 3:8 was that since the Jews were not "worth it," they should be destroyed and annihilated. The words here foreshadow the fact that Haman's wealth, his sons, and his position will all suffer the fate that he had intended for the Jews. His words almost seal their doom.

The choice of words, "As long as I see Mordecai the Jew sitting in the king's gate," could refer literally to Mordecai refusing to rise in 5:9. He remains in his seated posture when the vizier passes. But the phrase is ambiguous: it could also refer to Mordecai's office and that he continues to serve in some royal capacity for the king.[24] Perhaps his words were deliberately chosen for their ambiguity, so Haman would not have to admit even to his wife and advisers how defiant this Jewish underling continued to be, even after Haman had apparently done his worst (cf. Berlin, 55).

5:14 Haman was previously unwilling to attack Mordecai only, feeling it beneath his dignity to do so (3:6). Now, at the urging of his wife and advisers, he feels compelled to take action. It is significant that the narrator reverses the order from "his friends and his wife" (5:10) to "Zeresh his wife and all his friends," indicating that Zeresh is now taking the lead (Berlin, 55). Perhaps Haman was unaware that the king's decree in Esth 1:22 was supposed to result in all men being rulers over their own houses. Or perhaps he is following the model of ruling embraced by King Xerxes, who never seemed to make a decision without the urging of numerous counselors. In this case, it is ironic that Haman's wife gives advice that will surely help seal Haman's doom and help determine its form: after Haman's villainy is exposed in chapter 7, the eunuch Harbona points out to the king that Haman has already prepared a pike for Mordecai, the benefactor who had saved the king's life. Two women, one wittingly (Esther) and the other unwittingly (Zeresh), bring about Haman's destruction and determine its form.

On the probability that the "wooden object" (עֵץ, *ʿēṣ*) spoken of here refers to an impaling spike rather than a gallows for hanging, see the comments on 2:23. The huge pike was designed to make Mordecai's ignoble end visible to all the residents of Susa. The height of this pike, however, might have defeated that purpose. At anywhere from seventy-five to eighty-five feet tall, no one could have made out Mordecai's body at the top of the pike.[25] For that matter, how would they have mounted his body on it? The height seems quite improbable. As Berlin (55) observes, this pike would tower over every building in the city of Susa: even the palaces might have

24. So M. Fox, *Character and Ideology in the Book of Esther*, 2nd ed. (Grand Rapids: Eerdmans, 2001), 74.

25. The standard equivalence given for the cubit is about 1.5 feet, although the Achaemenid Persian cubit may have been a little longer. See Bush, 414.

stood only forty or fifty feet high. How would someone raise such a pike? Its weight alone would seem unmanageable. Some commentators have suggested that perhaps the height of this pike included a platform on which the pole stood, but even the platform would have to be colossal, larger than many buildings. Could Haman have assembled such a structure in a single night? It seems more likely that the monstrous pike should be considered a gross hyperbole, illustrating once again the size of Haman's ego and the pomposity of the entire Persian administration.[26]

Biblical Theology Comments

5:11 Haman's behavior could serve as a textbook illustration of foolishness, as described by the book of Proverbs. Proverbs 27:2 reads, "May another praise you and not your own mouth, a stranger and not your own lips." The implication is that such talk will expose the braggart for the fool that he is. Proverbs 18:12 (NIV) warns, "Before a downfall the heart is haughty, but humility comes before honor." Haman's haughtiness is evident in his boasting and his assumptions that he is to be honored. His downfall has already been set in motion, though he is ignorant of the fact.

5:14 The idea that Mordecai's execution would have constituted the "crucifixion" of an innocent man was not lost on the early Christian commentators, who saw in Mordecai a type of Christ. It is not likely, however, that the narrator considered Mordecai to be innocent in this matter. Mordecai has once again deliberately provoked Haman, and could probably have expected little different than the outcome he almost received. He is not rescued from his impending execution because of his innocence, but only because of the merciful intervention of God.

Application and Devotional Implications

It may be hard for us to feel sympathy for a man like Haman. He seems to have possessed everything a man of his day could have desired, and yet he was unsatisfied. There was only one small cloud on his horizon, one imperfection, and that imperfection became his obsession. He is like a beautiful teenager who feels she cannot show her face in public because of a blemish on her chin. When she looks in the mirror, all she can see is the flaw. Her efforts to cover or eliminate the offensive spot typically end up doing more harm than good. So, too, Haman's efforts to remove this one troublesome aspect of his life will lead to his disaster.

---

26. Bush, 414, is one of the few modern commentators to argue that the height should be taken literally.

According to Prov 27:20, the "eyes of a person" are never satisfied. For Haman, the presence of even a single person who did not treat him with the respect he thought he deserved was intolerable. But the problem is not his alone: it seems an unerring truism that the more we have, the more we desire. Often, human efforts to secure the perfect life result in embarrassment or even disaster. Some people will work so many hours that they alienate their families. Others might quit a fine job to "be their own boss," only to find that self-employment was not the gravy train they had imagined. Still others will leave a faithful, long-suffering spouse to pursue someone they find more attractive. "The eye is never satisfied with seeing, and the ear is never filled with hearing" (Eccl 1:8). In our efforts to chase that lone cloud from the horizon, we could completely miss the beauty of the sunset.

Selected Bibliography

Dorothy, C. V. *The Books of Esther: Structure, Genre and Textual Integrity*. Sheffield: Sheffield Academic Press, 1997.

Fox, M. V. *Character and Ideology in the Book of Esther*. 2nd ed. Grand Rapids: Eerdmans, 2001.

Thornton, T. C. G. "The Crucifixion of Haman and the Scandal of the Cross." *JTS* 37 (1986): 419–26.

Mordecai Is Honored; Haman Humiliated (6:1–14)

Translation

1 That night, sleep eluded the king, so he said to bring the book of chronicles, the daily records.[27] They were being read before the king, **2** and it was found written that Mordecai had reported concerning Bigthana and Teresh, the two royal eunuchs who guarded the threshold, who had sought to stretch out their hand against King Xerxes. **3** The king said, "What honor or advancement has been done for Mordecai on behalf of this matter?"

The king's young men who attended him said, "Not a thing has been done for him."

4 The king said, "Who is in the court?" Now Haman had entered the outer court of the king's dwelling to speak to the king about hanging Mordecai on the pike[28] that he had prepared for him.

27. Lit., "the words of the days."

28. Here, as throughout, the Heb. reads, "wooden object."

5 And the king's young men told him, "See,[29] Haman is standing in the court."

The king said, "Let him enter." **6** Haman entered, and the king said to him, "What should be done to the man whom the king delights to honor?"

And Haman said to himself,[30] "For whom could the king be more delighted to do honor than for me?" **7** Then Haman said to the king, "The man whom the king delights to honor ... [31] **8** Let a royal robe be brought, which the king himself has worn, and a horse that the king himself has ridden, and on whose head a royal crown is set. **9** And let the robe and the horse be entrusted to a man who is one of the king's most noble officials. Let them clothe the man whom the king delights to honor, and let them cause him to ride on the horse in the city square, and let them proclaim before him, 'Thus shall be done for the man whom the king delights to honor.'"

10 Then the king said to Haman, "Quickly—take the robe and the horse, just as you said, and do so for Mordecai the Jew, who sits at the king's gate. Do not neglect[32] one thing from all that you have spoken." **11** So Haman took the clothes and the horse, and he clothed Mordecai. He made him ride in the city square, and cried out before him, "Thus shall be done for the man whom the king delights to honor!"

12 Mordecai then returned to the king's gate, but Haman hurried to his house in mourning, with his head covered. **13** Haman told Zeresh his wife and all his friends everything that had happened. His counselors[33] and Zeresh his wife said to him, "If Mordecai, before whom you have begun to fall, is of Jewish lineage, you will not prevail over him, but you will surely fall before him." **14** While they were still speaking with him, the king's eunuchs arrived and hurried to bring Haman to the banquet that Esther had prepared.

Textual Notes

1.a. In the LXX, AT, Vg., and the two Targums, God deprived the king of sleep.

2.a. In 2:21, the name of the conspirator is Bigthan, not Bigthana, as here.

29. The Heb. particle הִנֵּה (*hinnēh*), traditionally translated "Behold," is frequently left untranslated in modern versions. The particle is used with verbs of perception to indicate point of view. It gives the impression of the servants looking out into the court and seeing Haman standing there.
30. Lit., "in his heart."
31. Haman appears to begin a sentence, then breaks off, as if considering what to say.
32. Lit., "Do not let fall."
33. Lit., "his wise ones."

2.b. In the LXX, the names of the conspirators are omitted.

8.a. The phrase "on whose head a royal crown is set" is not present in the Greek versions.

9.a. The LXX omits the phrase "Let them clothe the man."

10.a. The AT expands on this scene considerably, inserting between 6:10 and 6:11 a section telling us that Haman was deeply heartbroken and that Mordecai believed he saw a sign from God and went with Haman in reverent silence. The addition is not supported by any other versions.

13.a. For חֲכָמָיו, "his wise ones," the LXX reads οἱ φιλοί, "friends."

Commentary

The section now before us is surely the most entertaining of the entire Esther narrative. As a humorous anecdote, it could almost stand alone, an illustration of the follies of pride and presumption. In the context of the book of Esther, however, it is even more striking and enjoyable. The pompous vizier, at the urging of his wife and friends, has constructed a pike for the impaling of his enemy, the Jew Mordecai. (*Tg. Esth I* adds to the merriment by describing how Haman hired carpenters and metalworkers to do the construction, while Zeresh accompanied their work on her harp.) In his presumptuousness, he assumes that requesting the king's permission is a mere formality. The king, however, has recently been reminded of Mordecai's heroic service to the crown. Haman marches into the palace expecting to emerge with the permission he seeks to remove the only remaining impediment to his happiness. Instead, he will be forced to heap on Mordecai the honors that he craves for himself. The section will end as did the last: with the words of Zeresh, Haman's wife. This time, however, she sees no chance that Haman will be able to do away with the offending Jew. Indeed, she predicts Haman's downfall before Mordecai.

Though the crisis is still in full swing, this episode gives us a foretaste of the joy to come. Here, we are allowed to anticipate our delight at Haman's downfall and the deliverance of the Jews. It also foreshadows the rise of Mordecai, who will receive all the promotion and honor that Haman longed for himself.

6:1 The king's sleeplessness might be considered the first "proximate" coincidence of the Esther narrative. Vashti's disobedience and Esther's selection as queen occurred years before their importance would become known. The rivalry between Mordecai and Haman was established generations before their birth. In this incident, however, Xerxes' insomnia has a direct effect on the course of events. On the very night when Haman would seek an audience with the king to discuss Mordecai's execution, the king is reminded that Mordecai had saved his life. It seems a small thing, and yet its implications will be great.

The ancient translators were not shy about stating the reason for Xerxes' sleeplessness. In their opinions, it reflected the direct intervention of God. No doubt similar statements could be made, however, about Vashti's impertinence or Esther's attractiveness. In each case, events that might have been normal under other circumstances (who has not had a sleepless night from time to time?) conspire to bring about the deliverance of the Jews.

Paton (244) thinks it unusual that the restless king would want to hear a reading of the royal chronicles, but the request seems ordinary under the circumstances. Every parent knows that there is nothing more soporific for children than reading to them from a monotonous tome, and adults seem to differ little from children in this regard. What could have been more monotonous than the royal archives?

There is another possibility: perhaps the narrator wants us to conclude that Xerxes' sleeplessness was the result of a nagging feeling that some deed had been left undone. Indeed, Esther's impending request could have fueled such thoughts, as some rabbinic commentators suggest (Levenson, 95): what could the queen want? Was there something he should have done that he had neglected? (A modern man might be wondering whether he had forgotten his anniversary!) Intrigued and puzzled, he might well have sought out the royal archives for clues.

In any event, the reading did not put the king to sleep, as he might have hoped. The use of the ptc. form of the verb here ("and they were reading") implies continuous reading rather than a short recitation.[34] There is some disagreement among commentators as to whether Haman came to the palace in the middle of the night (so, e.g., Huey, 822; Berlin, 58; Bush, 419) or early in the morning (so Paton, 244, and Fox).[35] Given that Haman was instructed by his wife to go "in the morning" to see Xerxes (5:14), and that the king sent him forth immediately to carry out his instructions (6:10), it seems likely that Xerxes listened to the royal chronicles all through the night, until Haman arrived early the next day to present his request (6:4).

6:2 The readers come to the place in the chronicles that records Mordecai's rescue of the king. As Fox observes, the use of words that are nearly identical

34. Paton, 244; Arnold and Choi, 80–82 (§3.4.3b.b.2).

35. M. Fox, *Character and Ideology in the Book of Esther,* 2nd ed. (Grand Rapids: Eerdmans, 2001), 76.

to those found in the original account of the assassination plot (2:21) reinforces the impression of an account being read aloud.[36]

We can be fairly sure that the events were listed chronologically, so the reading might have covered several years, as Xerxes struggled to uncover some forgotten incident. We cannot know how the chronicles were read—from the beginning of Xerxes' reign to the present, or from the present backwards—but in either case, it would seem that the reading must have been going on for some time.

6:3 The king inquires about "honor or advancement," a notion that occurs several times in the book of Esther. The word "honor" (יְקָר, *yākār*) first appears in 1:4, referring to the glory of the king. In 1:20, all husbands are to receive honor from their wives. Haman craves honor, but the word has not yet been applied to him in this narrative. As it will turn out, he will never receive that which he longs for: first, the king will bestow it on Mordecai, and later on all the Jews (8:16). Advancement (גְּדוּלָּה, *gĕdûllâ*), on the other hand, has already been granted to Haman, in 3:1. Mordecai will receive no advancement from this incident, since the king will fail to mention "advancement" when he asks Haman's advice in 6:6. When Haman answers the king, he will not recommend any advancement, since he believes the king is asking about Haman himself, and he has already advanced as far as he can in the kingdom.

The Heb. syntax used in the king's question, "What has been done for Mordecai?" and the servants' answer, "Not a thing," may be telling. The syntax of the king's request is somewhat clumsy: "What has been done—honor or promotion—for Mordecai on behalf of this?" (A more natural expression would have used an inf. const. as the complement for the verb נַעֲשָׂה [*na'ăśeh*] instead of the nouns.) Grammatically, the nouns are gens., dependent on מָה (*mâ*), i.e., "What of advancement or honor ... "[37] The servants' answer is literally, "Not has been done with him a thing." The use of the prep. "with" (עִם, *'im*) instead of "for" (לְ, *lĕ*) is probably a deliberate variation suggestive of expressions such as "Do kindness with ... " (עָשָׂה חֶסֶד עִם, *'āśâ ḥesed 'im*; e.g., Gen 24:12; 40:14, etc.).

As noted earlier, Persian kings were lavish and meticulous when it came to rewarding their benefactors (see comments on 2:23). For Xerxes to discover in such a manner that a great boon had been ignored for years would have been disturbing. Indeed, his failure to reward Mordecai could have been a source of dishonor for the king himself. Perhaps in the reading

36. Ibid.
37. Haupt, "Critical Notes," 143.

he had discovered the source of his agitation and could take immediate steps to remedy the oversight.

6:4–5 King Xerxes seeks some official of whom he could ask advice on how to proceed. In his typical fashion, the king will not proffer a decision without plucking it from the mouth of one of his counselors. That Xerxes assumes that some official will be present is further evidence that it is morning, not the middle of the night. Haman has stationed himself in the outer court of the throne room to present his petition, just as Esther had done earlier in the narrative. His arrival at this very moment is most fortuitous indeed. (It is also another humorous element in the story, since Haman is so eager to present his request that he arrives at the palace before the king is out of bed.)[38] The two men are eager to put their respective problems to rest: Haman must kill and humiliate Mordecai, or he can have no peace of mind; and King Xerxes must honor Mordecai, or his sleepless nights will continue.

6:6 The king gives Haman no opportunity to present his request before launching into his own problem. In fact, Haman will be dismissed before he can present his business (6:10). The business of remedying the king's dishonor takes precedence over any business of the state that Haman might wish to bring forward. As noted above (6:3), Xerxes fails to mention "advancement" in his question of Haman. As Levenson (96) observes, this omission will prove fateful. If the king had mentioned "advancement," Haman would not have assumed the question was about himself, since Haman had already advanced as far as he could, to second in the kingdom. Without reference to advancement, Haman naturally assumed that he was the one to be honored.

Levenson (96) cogently notes that the narrative here ironically reverses a scene that occurs several times in the Heb. Bible: someone presents a question or parable to a king or other authority, and after the answer is given, it is revealed that the parable is about the person to whom the question was placed. The best example of this technique in the OT is 2 Sam 12:1–12, where Nathan the prophet traps King David with the parable of the ewe lamb. It should be noted that Jesus often used this technique as well, presenting parables to the scribes and Pharisees that obliquely condemned them (see, e.g., Matt 21:33–45). In Esther, however, it is the king who is questioning his "adviser," not the adviser who questions the king. It is not actually the king or adviser who is the subject of the inquiry, but another party entirely. Unlike those stories where the prophet or wise man is

38. See Y. T. Radday, "Esther with Humour," in *On Humour and the Comic in the Hebrew Bible*, ed. Y. T. Radday and A. Brenner (Sheffield: Almond, 1990), 306.

deliberately trapping the subject, both Xerxes and Haman are unaware that a trap is being set. It is a case of the blind leading the blind.

Haman's thoughts are revealed here for the first and only time. Indeed, the Bible does not often divulge what people are thinking, allowing readers to infer thoughts from actions (and sometimes deliberately allowing us to form the wrong impression, as in the book of Jonah).[39] It can also be observed, however, that in the majority of cases where the Bible tells us what someone was thinking "in his heart," it was something bad: Esau deciding to kill Jacob (Gen 27:41); Saul obsessing about David (1 Sam 20:26); Naaman thinking he is too good to dip in the Jordan River (1 Kgs 5:11); Jeroboam plotting to make golden calves (1 Kgs 12:26); proud people defying God (Psa 10:6, 11, 13; Isa 14:13; 47:10; Zeph 2:15); and fools who say there is no God (Psa 14:1; 53:1). Consistent with these examples, the peek into Haman's heart gives us yet another example of a proud fool, unable to imagine anyone more deserving of honor than himself.

6:7 Typically, modern translations of this verse have inserted the prep. *for* at the beginning of Haman's answer, interpreting the Heb.'s lack of a prep. as a "proleptic dative of advantage" (Bush, 414–15). They smooth out the Heb. syntax by joining the phrase to the following verse with a comma, as in the NIV: "For the man the king delights to honor, … " But in every other case in this passage where the phrase appears, an explicit prep. is prefixed to the word "man," as in v. 9: כָּכָה יֵעָשֶׂה לָאִישׁ אֲשֶׁר הַמֶּלֶךְ חָפֵץ בִּיקָרוֹ (*kākâ yēʿāśeh lāʾîš ʾăšer hammelek ḥāpēṣ bayqārô*, "thus shall be done for the man whom the king wishes to honor"). In v. 7, Haman does not use a prep.; he merely repeats the phrase "The man whom the king wishes to honor," as if he is simply enjoying the sound of those words. The phrase appears to be an anacoluthon, a thought that trails off before he gets into the substance of his counsel (Bush, 414–15).[40] As we shall see, he will repeat the phrase several times in the course of his answer, savoring each opportunity to speak of "the man whom the king delights to honor."

Schötz has noted that Haman does not even bother with the usual court formality, "If it please the king."[41] He is so caught up in the daydreams of his anticipated exaltation that he launches into his description without remembering whom he is addressing.

6:8 Haman does not ask for money, power, or promotion, all of which he already possesses. Instead, he asks for the opportunity to be "king for

---

39. On the use of reticence in Jonah, see A. Berlin, "A Rejoinder to J. A. Miles, Jr. with Some Observations on the Nature of Prophecy," *JQR* 66 (1976): 227–35.
40. Fox, *Character and Ideology*, 76.
41. D. Schötz, "Das Hebraïsche Buch Esther," *BZ* 21 (1933): 276.

a day." Jobes (153) notes that there is some evidence that it was believed that wearing the royal robes or sleeping in the royal bed could confer magic power, but it is not magic that Haman is seeking: it is honor. In the ancient world, clothing was closely associated with the people who wore it. People who were in grief could tear their clothes to externalize their pain (Gen 37:34; 2 Sam 1:11; 3:31; 2 Chr 34:19), though they could not cut their skin (Deut 14:1–2). In Num 20:25–28, Aaron's robes are placed on his son Eleazar as a sign of the transfer of the priestly office; likewise, when Elijah's robe was given to Elisha, it symbolized a transfer of the prophetic office (1 Kgs 19:19; 2 Kgs 2:13). For Haman, wearing the king's robe meant identifying in some sense with the king himself.

There is also good Persian precedent for the transfer of robes. Robes were frequently given by the Persian kings as signs of royal favor (Plutarch, *Artaxerxes* 15.2; Xenophon, *Anabasis* 1.8.29).[42] The king's own robes were distinctive enough to have been easily recognized by the people of Susa. Xenophon (*Cyropaedia* 8.3.13) describes Cyrus' dress as "a purple robe shot with white (which none but the king may wear), trousers of scarlet dye about his legs, and a mantle all of purple." According to Plutarch (*Artaxerxes* 5), a friend of Artaxerxes II had once requested that the king give him one of his torn robes. Artaxerxes agreed to the request, but he forbade him from actually wearing the garment. The man put on the garment anyway, prompting the king to laugh at him and call him mad. It was not typical of the king to allow anyone to wear the royal garment. Haman's request was ambitious; indeed, it might even hint at foppery.

Riding on one of the king's horses was universally a sign of royal favor. King David had Solomon brought to Gihon riding the king's own mule, as a sign that Solomon would succeed David to the throne (1 Kgs 1:33). Joseph, too, was allowed to ride in the royal chariot, next to Pharaoh (Gen 41:43). A similar practice was known in Persia: Cyrus demonstrated his favor for an officer by giving him a horse that had been led in a royal procession, raising the man's status considerably among his colleagues (Plutarch, *Cyropaedia* 8.3.23).

More puzzling is the reference to the royal crown placed on the horse's head. Why should a horse need a crown? The NIV and NLT avoid the problem by rendering the phrase "royal crest" or "royal emblem," respectively. Most other versions, however, face the difficulty head-on, recognizing that there is really no basis for translating כֶּתֶר (*keter*) as anything but "crown." Several scholars have noted that Assyrian horses are depicted in reliefs with crown-like ornaments on their heads (see Paton, 249). But the point

42. See further P. Briant, *From Cyrus to Alexander: A History of the Persian Empire* (Winona Lake, IN: Eisenbrauns, 2002), 305–6.

of whether the practice is attested elsewhere is largely irrelevant. It clearly signifies Haman's obsession with kingship. (Indeed, forms of the root מָלַךְ, *mālak*, "rule," appear six times in Haman's counsel.) He could not himself wear a royal crown, but crowning the royal horse could be the next best thing.[43]

The idea that Haman coveted the royal crown is also reflected in Jewish tradition. According to the LXX, Addition A, Haman was angry with Mordecai because he had been conspiring with the assassins that Mordecai exposed. Esther *Targum Sheni*, in a long haggadic gloss on 6:1, explicitly states that Haman sought to kill and replace King Xerxes with himself, and that was the reason he sought the royal honors. It is doubtful, however, that the narrator intended us to view Haman as a potential assassin. He certainly fantasized about the throne, but he never would have dared to take any action to attain it.

6:9 Having the man led about by one of the king's most noble officials would essentially—for a time, at least—place the official beneath the man being honored. Haman wished to be served by one of the most noble officials, demonstrating his superiority in the king's esteem to even his greatest officials.

The scenario envisioned here is inspired by the account of Joseph in Egypt, who was clothed in fine linen, placed in the king's chariot, and led about through the streets of Egypt with an officer announcing his coming before him. Josephus recognized the parallel and even added a detail that Esther omitted, a gold chain around the neck of the honoree (*Ant.* 11.254).

A second and third time, Haman manages to work in the phrase "the man whom the king delights to honor." We can imagine several different ways that Haman might have said the words: knowingly, as if intimating to the king that he knew the honors were really for him; haughtily, as if such a person were the most important person in the world; or perhaps lovingly, as if he merely enjoyed the sound of the phrase on his lips. The story could be read many times, and each interpretation could bring new enjoyment.

6:10 The narrator springs his trap. Haman is told once again to "make haste," just as he was hastily summoned to Esther's first banquet. He is told to take the robe and horse and do as he has said—and then, he is told to do it for "Mordecai the Jew, who sits in the king's gate." Xerxes does not know that the Jews are the very people that he had sentenced to extermination: he had

---

43. Plutarch tells of a Spartan named Demaratus, who, when asked by Xerxes what gift he would like to receive from the king, responded that he wished to ride through Sardis wearing a crown like that of the Persian kings. The king, however, was unwilling to grant that request (*Themistocles* 29.5).

never bothered to ask Haman the identity of the people whose destruction he had authorized. The use of the gentilic identification "the Jew," however, adds insult to the injury dealt to Haman. Not only is it *not* Haman who will be honored, it is Mordecai. Mordecai *the Jew*, a member of the hated race. The one who *sits* in the king's gate, refusing to rise before Haman. By the king's order, Haman cannot neglect any of the honors that he imagined himself enjoying. In fact, Xerxes reminds Haman twice that these are his words, his instructions, rather than those of the king. Haman's silence is more articulate than any response he could have formulated.

Many commentators have noted that the king's identification of Mordecai as a Jew implies knowledge that has not been revealed to him at this point in the narrative. While some scholars believe that this mention of Mordecai's ethnic background reveals a "redactional seam" or sloppy editing, there is no reason to assume that the narrator has told us everything that the king had heard about Mordecai. All that is essential, for the narrative, is that Xerxes did not know that Mordecai and Esther were related. Readers may assume that such incidental information could have been relayed to the king by other characters in the story.

6:11 After the long buildup, the actual procession takes but a single verse. Each of the elements in the preceding section are repeated, allowing us to feel Haman's humiliation, as each honor that he had dreamed of possessing is bestowed on Mordecai instead. Haman causes Mordecai to ride on a horse "in the city square." This phrase apparently refers not to the citadel, but to the larger city below. The king's intention is that the honoree is to be seen by as many people as possible. Of course, it also makes Haman's humiliation extremely public.

The Heb. word וַיַּרְכִּיבֵהוּ (*wayyarkîbēhû*) can be translated either "and he caused to ride" or "and he caused to mount." Several scholars (e.g., Berlin, 61) have argued that Haman did not lead Mordecai around the square, but merely sat him on a horse on display. While that understanding is certainly grammatically possible, it would not give the honoree as much exposure as leading him through the city would provide. Also, this scene was apparently inspired by the Joseph narrative, which seems to imply that Joseph was preceded by criers as his chariot made its way through the throngs (Gen 41:43). Josephus (*Ant.* 11.258), too, interprets the scene as a procession through the city.

In the Hebrew and Greek versions of the narrative, no words are exchanged between Mordecai and Haman. Indeed, none are needed. The situation itself speaks volumes without dialogue. Later Jewish tradition, however, could not help but heap more ignominy on Haman: according to *Tg. Esth. I* and *b. Meg.* 16a, as Haman led Mordecai through the streets, Haman's daughter looked out a balcony window and thought that the splendidly accoutered man on the horse must be her father, and the inglorious figure leading him about must be Mordecai. To further abuse the Jew, she dumped a chamber pot on his head. When Haman looked up and reproached her, she was so shocked that she fell from the balcony and died.

6:12 Haman has come back home in a very different mood and state from when he left in the early morning. He had gone with the intention of removing the one blot from his otherwise perfect life. He returns feeling as if his life has collapsed around him. He hastened to his house, not wishing to be seen, probably fearing mockery for his part in honoring a man who was known by the officials to be his dread enemy (Esth 3:4). Haman had been forced by the king's order to honor Mordecai, the man whom he had not been able to make honor him, in spite of the king's command.

Haman returns home in "mourning" (אָבֵל, *ʾābal*) a term that is usually associated with grief over the dead. The Heb. word, however, can indicate feelings of distress over any great loss or calamity (Exod 33:4; Num 14:39; Ezra 10:6; Dan 10:2). Covering the head seems to have been a common practice accompanying mourning in the OT (2 Sam 15:30; Jer 14:4) and might have been practiced by the Persians as well.[44] Of course, Haman might well have been covering his head to avoid being recognized by any of his acquaintances or colleagues who had heard the story of his shame.

In *b. Meg.* 16a and *Est. Tg. I*, which include the story of Haman's daughter falling from the balcony (see commentary on 6:11), it is explained here that Haman was in mourning because of the loss of his daughter.

6:13 This verse serves a wonderful literary function in the narrative. Structurally, it reverses the counsel that Zeresh and the friends gave in 5:9–14. There, they had told Haman that by killing Mordecai, Haman could makes his life happy and fulfilling; here, they tell him that he cannot kill Mordecai and that he is heading for a downfall. It also foreshadows the events to come—not only for Mordecai but for the entire Jewish race. It implies that Haman's plot against all the Jews will fail as surely as his plot against Mordecai. Finally, it is once again significant that the voice of insight in the text comes from a woman, the wife of Haman. Xerxes has repeatedly shown himself to be clueless. Haman, too, is frequently oblivious to the significance of the acts transpiring around him. Even Mordecai fails to impress with his wits, unable to foresee that his disrespect of Haman would have dire repercussions. But here Zeresh, like Esther herself, proves to be a person of insight.

---

44. See Quintus Curtius Rufus, *Historiae Alexandri Magni* 4.10; 10.5.

The "if" of the first clause ("If Mordecai is of Jewish lineage ... ") is not a "real condition"; i.e., it is not meant to imply that Zeresh was questioning Mordecai's background. That Mordecai is Jewish has been well established by this point and was acknowledged before the wife and friends in 5:13. It means, instead, that Zeresh and the friends are considering the implications of Mordecai being Jewish.

Nonetheless, the jarring contrast between this statement and the advice that Zeresh and the other counselors gave earlier raises some questions. Has Zeresh received some kind of divine revelation? Has she studied the Heb. Scriptures and learned about the animosity between the Israelites and Amalekites, and the biblical promises that God would destroy Amalek (Num 24:7, 20)? A number of commentators (Moore, 66; Bush, 417)[45] find it unlikely that Zeresh or Haman's counselors could have held the opinion they express here. Rather, they believe the text is merely placing the opinion of the author and his audience, who would have been familiar with the biblical prophecies of Israel's victory over Amelek (Num 24:20), in the mouths of the Jews' enemies, who would not have known the prophecies. Undoubtedly we have here a reflection of Jewish theology, not Persian thought, but our skillful narrator should not be so quickly accused of clumsy improvisation. Haman's counselors are here called "his wise (ones)" (חֲכָמָיו, *ḥăkāmāyw*). The word "wise" is used in the Bible with a variety of connotations: it can describe someone with skills in technical work, a good administrator, or someone who is shrewd and crafty.[46] But in the Joseph narrative (Gen 41:8) and in the Daniel narrative (e.g., Dan 2:12–14; 4:6; 5:7, and others), the "wise ones" are people with the ability to interpret dreams, signs, and omens. (This same idea might be implied in the phrase "wise ones who know the times"; see the commentary on 1:13.) Haman's counselors might have concluded that the strange coincidence of Haman's humiliation was an omen of things to come.

6:14 The pace of the narration is accelerating now, as events are happening so quickly that they begin to overlap. The sense of pace is also reinforced by the use of the words "hurried" and "hastened." There is no indication here that Haman has forgotten his appointment or that he is reluctant to go, as *b. Meg.* 16a claims. Sending messengers to summon guests to the dinner was common practice; although at this point, Haman might be wondering what could go wrong next.

---

45. See also D. J. A. Clines, *The Esther Scroll: The Story of the Story*, JSOTSup 30 (Sheffield, UK: JSOT Press, 1984), 43.

46. BDB, s.v. חָכָם.

Biblical Theology Comments

6:1–3 This episode and the Esther narrative in general serve as important reminders that divine sovereignty can take a variety of forms. The remarkable chain of events—the king's inability to sleep, his decision to read from the royal chronicles, and the choice of the passage recording Mordecai's rescue of the king occurring at the very time that Haman was seeking permission to kill Mordecai—seems like far more than mere coincidence. It is difficult not to believe (with the ancient translators) that the narrator is invoking providence, though in his typical fashion, he does not mention God directly. It is in such episodes as this that we will often acknowledge that the hand of God is at work and perhaps refer to the circumstances as "miraculous." But there are far more remarkable coincidences in play in this narrative. It is one thing for God to "head Haman off at the pass" and intervene just before Haman can present his petition. But it is even more amazing that God could prepare for that fateful night years in advance by placing Mordecai where he could overhear the assassins' plot; putting Esther in the position where she could deliver a message on Mordecai's behalf to the king; and having the king conveniently forget to reward his benefactor. It is in such an overarching command of history, not just in instantaneous interventions in mortal affairs, where God's power is truly revealed.

6:4–10 "Before destruction comes pride, and before a fall, a haughty spirit" (Prov 16:18). This scene well illustrates the proverb. Haman's predicament is not merely a blow to his pride; it is directly *because* he is proud that he suffers the embarrassment. He is like the man in Jesus' parable who assumes that he should have the place at the head of the table, only to be told to step down and make room for someone more important (Luke 14:7–11). Pride—an overwhelming sense of one's importance—is condemned throughout the Bible as a sin. It is one of the character traits that, according to Jesus, can defile a person from within (Mark 7:22). There are essentially two reasons for the Bible's disapproval of pride. One is that pride causes people to exalt themselves over God, as in the case of Nebuchadnezzar in Dan 4:30, 37; and even more so in the prince of Tyre, who says to himself, "I am a god; I sit in the seat of the gods" (Ezek 28:2). But another problem with pride is that it causes people to look down on others and treat them with contempt and abuse (Isa 3:13–24; Pss 73:6; 94:4–7). Haman epitomizes such behavior, believing it acceptable to slay an entire nation to respond to a personal insult. The Scriptures repeatedly promise that the proud will receive their just reward: "For all those who exalt themselves will be humbled, and those who humble themselves will be exalted" (Luke 14:11 NIV).

6:13 Scholars have been quick to associate this prediction with the prophecies of Israel's triumph over Amalek, but the narrator's confidence has a broader base than that single prophecy (Num 24:20; the other frequently cited references [Exod 17:16; Deut 25:17–19; 1 Sam 15] speak only of Israel's continued warfare against Amalek; they do not prophesy absolute victory).

Throughout the OT, God's special care for Israel and His wrath at her oppressors are repeatedly proclaimed and demonstrated. The first effort to destroy the people occurred when Pharaoh ordered the Israelite infants killed (Exod 1:15–16). The midwives who "feared God" rescued the babies, and Israel continued to thrive (Exod 1:17). The plan to throw all the male children into the Nile (Exod 1:22) proved an equal failure. The outcome of Egypt's efforts was the death of all their firstborn (Exod 12:29–30) and the annihilation of Egypt's army (Exod 14). At the end of Israel's trek through the wilderness, Moses proclaimed the concept of Israel's indestructibility. In Deut 32, as Moses prophesies about the future apostasy of Israel, he foretells the dire consequences that Israel will suffer: God will hide His face from them (32:20) and bring calamities on them, famine and plague and vipers (32:24). Enemies will attack them and overwhelm them, and Israel will be decimated and scattered (32:25–26). But in the end, God will relent, and His anger will turn against Israel's oppressors instead (32:36–43). Similar prophecies are uttered by the prophet Jeremiah after the destruction of Jerusalem: "I am with you, declares Yahweh, to save you. For I will make a complete destruction of all the nations to which I scattered you, but you I will not make a complete destruction. And I will chastise you to the measure, and I will not leave you entirely unpunished" (Jer 30:11). God's promise to preserve Israel is as certain as the sun and stars (Jer 31:35). Israel's unfaithfulness cannot invalidate God's commitment to His people:

> Thus says Yahweh: "If the heavens above can be measured, and the foundations of the earth below can be explored, also I will reject all the offspring of Israel because of all that they have done," declares Yahweh. (Jer 31:37)

The idea that this promise remains in force even in our day might be implied in the words of the Apostle Paul in Rom 11:29, "For the gifts and the calling of God are irrevocable." Paul's main purpose here is to tell us that God has not cast off His people Israel, but He has included them in His plan of salvation. Nonetheless, in view of two thousand years of anti-Semitism, of persecutions, inquisitions, pogroms, and the Holocaust, it is difficult to escape the sense that God has preserved Israel, even when Israel has rejected His Son, Israel's Messiah.

Application and Devotional Implications

For most modern readers, this scene is the most comical moment of the Esther narrative. Our merriment is inspired by a situation that figures frequently in both ancient and modern tales: the humiliation of a self-important windbag. Haman has obviously brought his trouble on himself, in his assuming that no one could be more deserving of honor than he. Furthermore, we get to see the hero receive the recognition he is due. And finally, Haman's comeuppance, in this scene, is relatively harmless. He is not killed or imprisoned, or even publicly flogged. The only thing that is truly injured is his pride. If this narrative were not part of a larger narrative, we could even imagine that Haman could have learned his lesson and gone on to become a more humble person and a better administrator, perhaps like Nebuchadnezzar in Dan 4.

But there is much more to the story. Haman is not a harmless blowhard; he is a man who is plotting the extermination of the entire Jewish race. The man he is forced to honor is not just some insignificant rival; he is a person whom Haman plans to execute. The story does not end with a wise moral, but with a dire warning: this is only the beginning of the downfall. This little excursus is amusing, but it should not divert us from the seriousness of the situation. Indeed, it may be seen as a brisk zephyr that presages a coming storm. One man shall rise, and another shall fall. We may laugh, but let us remember that God is not merely playing a joke—He is setting a trap. The book of Esther may be wickedly funny at times, but it is also deadly serious.

Selected Bibliography

Barrick, W. B. "The Meaning and Use of *RKB* in Biblical Hebrew." *JBL* 101 (1982): 481–503.

Briant, P. *From Cyrus to Alexander: A History of the Persian Empire.* Winona Lake, IN: Eisenbrauns, 2002.

Clines, D. J. A. *The Esther Scroll: The Story of the Story.* JSOTSup 30. Sheffield, UK: JSOT Press, 1984.

Fox, M. V. *Character and Ideology in the Book of Esther.* 2nd ed. Grand Rapids: Eerdmans, 2001.

Harrelson, W. "Textual and Translation Problems in the Book of Esther." *Perspectives in Religious Studies* 17 (1990): 105–12.

Haupt, P. "Critical Notes on Esther." *AJSL* 24 (1907–1908): 97–186.

Pokorny, D. "What Should Be Done for the Man Whom the King Wishes to Honor?" *Concordia Journal* 13 (1987): 249–51.

Radday, Y. T. "Esther with Humour." In *On Humour and the Comic in the Hebrew Bible*, ed. Y. T. Radday and A. Brenner, 295–313. Sheffield: Almond, 1990.

Ryken, L., J. Wilhoit, and T. Longman III. "Pride." In *DBI*, 661–62.

Salvesen, A. "כֶּתֶר (Esther 1:11; 2:17; 6:8): 'Something to Do with a Camel'?" *JSS* 44 (1999): 35–46.

Schötz, D. "Das Hebraïsche Buch Esther." *BZ* 21 (1933): 255–76.

Stefanovich, Z. "'Go at Once!': Thematic Reversals in the Book of Esther." *AJT* 8 (1994) 163–71.

Esther's Second Banquet (7:1–10)

Translation

1 Then the king and Haman went to drink with Esther the queen. **2** And the king said to Esther also on the second day during the wine course, "What is your request, Queen Esther? It shall be granted you. And what are you seeking? Even to the half of my kingdom, it shall be fulfilled."

3 Then Esther the queen answered and said, "If I have found favor in your sight, O king, and if it please the king, let my life be granted me for my request, and my people for what I seek. **4** For we have been sold, I and my people, to be destroyed, to be killed, and to be annihilated. If we had been sold as male and female slaves, I would have kept silent; but *the money of*[47] the oppressor is not equal to the financial loss of the king."

5 Then King Xerxes said to Esther the queen, "Who is he, and where is he, who has dared[48] to do this?"

6 And Esther said, "The man who is the oppressor and enemy is this wicked Haman!"

Then Haman trembled before the king and queen. **7** And the king arose in his wrath from the wine course [to go] to the garden of the house. Haman stood[49] to plead for his life from Esther the queen, because he saw that the king was determined to bring trouble on him.[50] **8** Then the king returned from the house garden to the room of the wine course, and Haman had fallen upon the couch where Esther was.

The king said, "Would he even assault[51] the queen, with me in the house?" As the word left the king's mouth, they covered Haman's face.

---

47. Not present in the Heb. text. See the discussion in the commentary.
48. Lit., "who has filled his heart." The idiom implies that someone is consumed with a desire.
49. I have read the verb literally to mean "stood." Many interpreters understand the verb to be a figure of speech meaning "to remain."
50. Lit., "He saw that trouble was determined for him from with the king."
51. The meaning of this word in its context is disputed. See the commentary.

9 Harbona, one of the eunuchs who served[52] before the king, said, "Look,[53] the pike that Haman made for Mordecai, who spoke beneficially on behalf of the king, stands at Haman's house, fifty cubits high."

The king said, "Hang him on it." **10** So they hung Haman on the pike he had set up for Mordecai, and the king's wrath abated.

Textual Notes

4.a. There is a good deal of difficulty in this verse, but it is unclear whether it is a textual problem or a grammatical issue. The LXX does not translate the Heb. particle וְאִלּוּ, "if," and identifies the idea of the Jews' destruction with their enslavement.

4.b. In the very difficult final clause, the Heb. word נֵזֶק, "damage," is rendered in the LXX τῆς αὐλῆς, "the courtyard," thus: "The adversary is not worthy of the courtyard of the king."

6.a. For the Heb. אִישׁ צַר וְאוֹיֵב, "a man (who is) an adversary and an enemy," the LXX reads merely Ἄνθρωπος ἐχθρὸς, "A man, an enemy."

8.a. For MT וּפְנֵי הָמָן חָפוּ "they covered Haman's face," the LXX reads διετράπη τῷ προσώπῳ, "he covered (or "changed") [his] face."

9.a. For the MT תְּלֻהוּ עָלָיו, "Hang him on it," the LXX reads Σταυρωθήτω ἐπ' αὐτοῦ, "crucify him on it."

Commentary

This section resolves the second crisis of the narrative, the threat to Mordecai (the threat to the Jews being the first, and still unresolved, crisis). The second crisis, too, is largely defused, given that the king is now made aware of the problem and that his queen is Jewish. While complications will remain, it is apparent after this point of the narrative that all will turn out well.

The queen has been plotting patiently for this moment. In her first appearance before the king, she incited his desire and his curiosity. A matter for which the queen would risk her life must be grave indeed. At the first banquet, she made it clear that her request was, indeed, grave—so much so that it had to wait for another banquet to be revealed. The king was consumed with interest by the time the second banquet arrived. Now, her trap would be sprung with Haman present. The villain would be confronted with his crime and discover to his shock that his ignorance has once

52. "Who served" is not present in the Heb., but it is implied.
53. Heb. הִנֵּה (*hinnēh*), traditionally translated "behold." The particle directs the reader's attention to the point of view of the character in the narrative.

again been his undoing. In chapter 6, he did not know that the king actually wanted to honor a Jew, and he suffered the consequences. This time, he does not know that the one who has honored him with an invitation to the banquet is also a Jew. When the truth is revealed, he must have been flabbergasted. But the worst was yet to come. Haman has no opportunity to appeal his case. His fate is sealed before he can even attempt to defend himself.

Reversal continues to be a major theme. In the last scene (Esth 6), Mordecai received the honor that Haman had intended for himself. In this scene, Haman will receive the punishment that he had intended for Mordecai. As in the last scene, the reversal will hinge on a misunderstanding: there, Haman misunderstood the reason behind the king's request for advice on honoring a deserving person; here, the king misunderstands Haman's motives in falling upon the queen's couch. As Berlin (66) notes, it is in keeping with the comedy of this story that that the villain is condemned for crimes that he did not commit (swindle and rape). Indeed, Haman has committed no crime worthy of death, in terms of the law: his decree was approved by the king.

7:1 In a rather different turn of phrase, this verse does not say that the king and Haman went "to banquet" with Esther, but literally "to drink" with her. Though the verb שָׁתָה (*šātâ*, "drink") is, in fact, the root of the noun "banquet" (מִשְׁתֶּה, *mišteh*), the verb is never used elsewhere in the Heb. Bible with the meaning of "feasting," but only of drinking. Paton (257) suggests the verb here may be denominative from the noun. While it is certain that Esther's banquet involved both food and drink, the verb used here certainly highlights the activity of imbibing (cf. Bechtel, 62).

7:2 "The second day" refers to the day after the first banquet. It does not mean that the banquet lasted two days.

Each time the king has placed his question to Esther, the wording has become somewhat more formal. In the first request, he asked almost colloquially, "What is it to you, Queen Esther, and what are you seeking?" (Esth 5:4). The second time, at the first banquet, he asks, "What is your request? It will be given to you. And what are you seeking?" (Esth 5:6). This time, he combines the unique elements of the earlier requests into a nicely balanced poetic distich (two-line poem):

> (A) What is your request, Queen Esther? (B) It shall be granted you.
> (A′) And what are you seeking? (B′) Even to the half of my kingdom, it shall be fulfilled.

Each phrase in the first line is in synonymous parallelism with the second line, thus the structure of the verse is A-B//A′-B′.

One difference in the formulation of the king's request from the previous times is that the verb form in the phrase "It shall be given to you" implies a fem. subject. In 5:6, the masc. form was used, which would be more natural when the subject was unknown (as it would be, since the king did not know what Esther was seeking). Levenson (101) speculates that the form anticipates Esther's answer, "my life" (נַפְשִׁי, *napšî*), since the noun "life" in Heb. is fem. in gender.

7:3 Esther's prelude includes the requisite formalities, but it is nonetheless shorter than the preamble she gave to her request that the king and Haman attend a second banquet. Like the king's inquiry, Esther's request is poetic, in the form of two couplets:

> (A) If I have found favor in your sight, O king,
> (A′) And if it please the king,
> (B) Let my life be granted me for my request,
> (B′) And my people for what I seek.

Like the king's poem, this one also uses synonymous parallelism, but in this case, each clause is followed immediately by its synonym. This fact is significant for the interpretation of the verse, because it means that Esther has drawn a parallel between "my life" and "my people." Thus in her request, Esther explicitly identifies herself with the Jews for the first time. She also emphasizes the threat to herself: it is *her* life that is on the line. The king had not been concerned about the destruction of a people, but the destruction of his queen would be a personal matter.

7:4 Esther's statement "We have been sold" is certainly a reference to the money that Haman paid to the king for the Jews' destruction (Esth 3:9; 4:7), though it is also reminiscent of the language used in Deut 32:30, which states that Israel could not be put to flight by a single individual unless their "Rock" had sold them. Esther is making ready to implicate Haman in the conspiracy against the Jews, but the narrator may be taking an opportunity to remind his readers of the real reason Israel finds itself in this predicament: it is not only Haman who has "sold" them, but Yahweh. Berlin (66) also sees here an echo of the story of Joseph, who was sold by his brothers. It should also be noted that it was often the fate of adulteresses to be sold into slavery (Isa 50:1; Hos 3:1–2). Esther announcing that she had been sold would have mortified the king, since the imagery would have cast him in the role of a cuckold.

The ingenuity of Esther's tactics becomes evident here. By using the pass. form of the verb, Esther cleverly avoids casting any blame on the king in this matter. Indeed, it would be possible for the king to imagine that Esther's distress has nothing to do with him at all. She also uses the personal pronoun *I*, striking home that this queen, who (by the king's own admission) has pleased him and found favor in his sight, is now slated for execution. The decree is, in fact, an indirect attack on the king. But the real genius of Esther's appeal is that she will couch the affair in terms of the king's self-interest—just as Haman had done in 3:8–9 when proposing the pogrom. There, Haman appealed to the king's greed: "It is not profitable to the king to let them be" (3:8). Esther does the same here. With exaggerated obsequy, she volunteers, "If we had been sold as slaves … I would have kept silent." Presumably, such a sale would have brought revenue to the king. This destruction, however, will not prove profitable.

This is likely the thrust of the last clause of the verse—Esther wants to point out that the king will not benefit from the destruction of the Jews. These words, כִּי אֵין הַצָּר שֹׁוֶה בְּנֵזֶק הַמֶּלֶךְ (*kî ʾên haṣṣār šōweh bĕnēzeq hammelek*), comprise the most difficult line in this section and the most controversial of the entire book of Esther. The difficulty arises from several factors:

- The conj. כִּי (*kî*), typically rendered "because," can have several different meanings, including "that" or "but."
- The noun הַצָּר (*haṣṣār*) can mean "the enemy," or it can mean "the trouble, distress."
- The verbal phrase שֹׁוֶה בְּ (*šōweh bĕ*) generally has the sense of comparison, but it can be rendered "equal to," "worth," "fitting" or "sufficient for," depending on context.
- The noun נֵזֶק (*nēzeq*), though common in postbiblical Heb., occurs only here in the OT. Its meaning, too, is disputed.

These problems have led to the line being translated and interpreted in a variety of ways. The Greek translations might actually reveal a different textual basis from the MT: the LXX reads, "For the adversary who has done this is not worthy of the king's court"; the AT translates, "For the man who did evil against us has changed his behavior." The KJV says, "although the enemy could not countervail the king's damage." The NIV reads, "because no such distress would justify disturbing the king." The NRSV has, "but no enemy can compensate for this damage to the king." The commentators, too, differ significantly on the meaning of the text. It would be difficult to summarize all the various opinions here (several major opinions are considered by Bush, 427–28, though I disagree with his conclusions). Instead, I will lay out the evidence for my own understanding of this verse, "but *the money of* the oppressor is not equal to the financial loss of the king."

The first issue to consider is the meaning of the noun הַצָּר (*haṣṣār*), translated either "distress" or "oppressor." In Esth 7:6, a mere two verses later, this same noun is used with the meaning of "oppressor" or "enemy." It seems likely that if a relatively rare word is used twice in the same context, it would be used with the same meaning. This impression is reinforced by the king's question in Esth 7:5. He asks *who* the person is who has done this thing. It would be a natural response if Esther had just stated that an enemy was attempting to swindle the king. If Esther had not mentioned an oppressor, but merely "distress," the natural response to her appeal would have been, "*How* have you been sold?" rather than "*Who* has done this?"

The noun נֵזֶק (*nēzeq*) occurs only once in the OT. In the Mishnah, however, this noun typically means financial damage. In light of Esther portraying the edict against the Jews as a financial transaction, a similar meaning would make sense here. The financial loss would represent the lost income from taxation, as well as services that the Jews might provide. Haman had argued that the king should not put up with the Jews because they were not "profitable" (see the commentary on 3:8, 9); Esther argues here that the loss of the Jews will represent a financial blow to the king that Haman has not adequately compensated.

Bush (427) and others appeal to the use of the Aramaic verb נְזַק (*nězaq*) as evidence that the Heb. noun can also mean "harm, damage" in a broader sense, citing Ezra 4:13, 15, 22; and Dan 6:3 in support. The analogy would not be conclusive in any case, since the meaning of a Heb. noun in one context cannot be ascertained on the basis of a cognate Aramaic verb in a different context. But even in the verses Bush cites, it is equally likely that the verb should be understood to mean financial loss. In Ezra 4:13, it is obvious: Rehum and Shimshai are arguing that if the Jews are allowed to rebuild the wall of Jerusalem, they will withhold their taxes, and the king will suffer "damage." The same meaning seems to fit in the other instances, as well. Ezra 4:15 is a continuation of the same argument, that because Jerusalem is rebellious, it is damaging to kings (that is, the city withholds its tribute and causes the king to expend resources putting down trouble). In Ezra 4:22, the king replies that, indeed, the city has withheld tribute in the past, and it should not be allowed to rebuild its wall so he will not suffer "damage." Finally, in Dan 6:3 (Eng. 6:2), Daniel is appointed over the satraps so that King Darius will suffer no "damage." The other officers, jealous of Daniel, attempt to find some "corruption" in him regarding the business of the kingdom, but he is faultless (Dan 6:5; Eng. 6:4). In this context as well, the verb נְזַק (*nězaq*) probably means financial loss, not general trouble. There is little basis for interpreting the Heb. noun otherwise in Esther.

Finally, the verb phrase שֹׁוֶה בְּ (*šōweh bě*) is also an uncommon construction. As noted in the commentary on Esth 3:8, outside the book of Esther, the verb שָׁוָה (*šāwâ*) occurs only in poetic contexts. It is used, however, two other times in Esther: in 3:8, where Haman advises the king that it would not be "worth it" for him to put up with the Jews; and in Esth 5:13, where Haman states that all his riches and honors are "worth nothing" to him, so long as Mordecai sits in the king's gate. With the prep. בְּ (*bĕ*), the verb typically means "equal to," "comparable to," or "worth," as in Prov 3:15 NIV, "Nothing you desire can compare with her." Literally, then, this clause could be translated, "The oppressor is not worth the financial loss of the king." These words could mean that Xerxes should not endure Haman, in light of the financial damage he is bringing to the king. Given how much the book of Esther loves reversals, that reading would seem appropriate: in 3:8–9, Haman told Xerxes that it was not profitable for the king to tolerate the Jews; now, Esther tells the king it is not profitable for him to endure Haman. However, in light of Esther's point seeming to be that the king is suffering financial loss because of the impending execution of the Jews, it is likely that "the oppressor" here is a circumlocution for "the oppressor's bribe." It might have been considered indelicate to explicitly mention the remuneration that Haman had promised the king, since that detail would draw attention to the king's responsibility in the affair. Alternatively, a word could have been omitted due to a scribal error. If the phrase had originally been "but the oppressor's talents," ככרי הצר כי (*kkry hṣr ky*), the series of *kaphs* might well have confused the scribe, leading him to omit the word that seemed redundant. (That, in some scribal hands, the letters *kaph* and *tsade* look very similar might also have contributed to the confusion.)

In short, then, we should understand the bulk of Esther's appeal here to be a request for her people to be spared, but couched in terms of the king's financial interests. The Jews have been sold, but not as slaves. Presumably they would have brought market value in the slave trade, and the king would have benefited handsomely. But they have been sold simply to be destroyed, and the compensation the king received (grand though it was) was not sufficient to offset the loss of revenue from tribute, gifts, and labor that the king would receive from allowing the Jews to live.

There is certainly some merit to Esther's argument. If every Jew in the Persian Empire were indeed sold as a slave, the revenue would have been vast. While we do not know how many Jews lived in the Persian Empire, it could have numbered more than a million: according to the census taken by Emperor Claudius in AD 48, there were about seven million Jews in the Roman Empire in the first century; the Jewish[54] population in the time of Augustus has been estimated to be 4.5 million. If there were a million Jews in the Persian Empire (or if the narrator thought there were), their value on the slave market would have far exceeded Haman's bribe. Haman offered the king 36 million shekels of silver for the destruction of the Jews. Slaves

54. E. Lohse, *The New Testament Environment* (Nashville: Abingdon, 1976), 122. See also M. Avi-Yonah, *The Holy Land: A Historical Geography from the Persian to the Arab Conquest 536 B.C. to A.D. 640* (Jerusalem: Carta, 2002), 219–21.

in the Persian era sold for about sixty to ninety shekels, so the Jews' "market value" would have far exceeded the value of the bribe.[55] As Esther presents the issue, Haman appeared to be swindling King Xerxes out of a huge sum of money.

Another cunning aspect of Esther's plea is that it invites the king to consider the question of whether the Jews really deserved to be enslaved. According to Herodotus (*Hist.* 6.32), rebellious vassals could indeed be sold as slaves. But how could Xerxes brand the Jews as rebels on the very day when he had ordered Mordecai to be honored for saving the king's life? If the Jews could not reasonably be painted as insurrectionists and sold as slaves, then they would surely not be deserving of the much harsher penalty of genocide.

7:5 Once again, the book of Esther puts an ironic twist on a beloved biblical trope: the self-incriminator. In Gen 38, Judah is confronted with his pregnant daughter-in-law, and when he demands to know who the father is, she announces that it is he himself. In 2 Sam 12:1–10, David is confronted with the story of a man who killed his neighbor's pet lamb; when he demands to know who has done such a thing, he is told, "You are the man." In 2 Sam 14:1–22, a woman presents David with a grievance. When he rules that her case is just, she reveals that the story is really about David and his son Absalom. Here in the story of Esther, the king was, in fact, responsible for selling the Jews into destruction. When the king expresses his outrage over the act, the stage is set for Esther to reveal that it is, in fact, Xerxes himself who is guilty. She builds the suspense by not revealing Haman's name until the end of the clause: "A man, the oppressor and enemy—this wicked Haman!" It is not an entirely truthful response to the first part of the question. After all, it was Xerxes who sold the Jews, not Haman.[56] But Haman was the instigator of the plot, and he is the only one whom Esther dares accuse of malfeasance.

As Berlin (68) notes, the phrase "Where is he?" can be ironic, considering that Haman is in Xerxes' very presence. It could, however, also

---

55. 10,000 talents = 36 million shekels. See A. D. H. Bivar, "Achaemenid Coins, Weights and Measures," *CHI*, 2:610–39. On the cost of slaves in this era, see M. A. Dandamayev, *Slavery in Babylonia from Nabopolassar to Alexander the Great (626–331 B.C.)* (DeKalb: Northern Illinois University Press, 1984), 181–206; M. Stolper, "Fifth Century Nippur: Texts of the Murasus and from Their Surroundings," *JCS* 53 (2001): 83–132; R. De Vaux, *Ancient Israel: Its Life and Institutions* (Grand Rapids: Eerdmans, 1997), 84.

56. M. Fox, *Character and Ideology in the Book of Esther*, 2nd ed. (Grand Rapids: Eerdmans, 2001), 85–86.

be understood to mean, "Which one is he?" If that is the case here, then Xerxes is being redundant, perhaps even sputtering in his outrage.

The phrase אֲשֶׁר־מְלָאוֹ לִבּוֹ לַעֲשׂוֹת כֵּן (*ʾăšer-mĕlāʾô libbô laʿăśôt kēn*) is a little ambiguous. Literally, it can mean, "who is he-filled-it his heart to do this" (so Bush, 423) or "whose his-heart has filled him to do this" (so Bardtke, 355; Berlin, 69). Both are grammatically possible, since Heb. often uses a proleptic suf. on verbs in anticipation of the obj. (GKC, §131m). In my opinion, the first option makes better sense conceptually: in Heb. anthropology, the heart is typically "filled" with thought or emotion; it does not "fill" the person with intention.

The language in this scene is reminiscent of another story of an exposed conspiracy: in Acts 5, a couple named Ananias and Sapphira attempted to defraud the apostles by selling a piece of property and retaining a portion of the proceeds, while pretending to give the entire sale price to the apostles. When Ananias appeared before Peter with the money, Peter asked him, "Why has Satan filled your heart to lie to the Holy Spirit?" As a result of their attempt to cheat God, Ananias (and later his wife) fell down dead before the apostles. Several elements of the story parallel that of Haman:

- Both are stories of ambition gone awry: Haman was attempting to exalt himself in Persia; Ananias and Sapphira were attempting to look good before the church (Acts 4:32–37)
- A couple (Haman and Zeresh vs. Ananias and Sapphira) linked in conspiracy
- Both conspiracies involve selling (Esth 7:4; Acts 5:1)
- An attempt to financially cheat those in power
- A heart filled with an evil plan
- The crooks fall down before their accuser (Esth 7:8; Acts 5:5, 10)
- The conspirator is covered (Esth 7:8; Acts 5:6)

The author of Acts has apparently subtly crafted his account of Ananias and Sapphira with an eye on the story of Haman's downfall. Given the atmosphere of threat that permeates this portion of Acts, it is no wonder that the author would have had the story of Esther in the back of his mind.

7:6 The syntax of this entire passage is unique. In typical Heb. narrative, each sequential action is introduced with the *waw*-consec. construction followed by the preterite form of the verb. In this passage, however, each clause begins with the conjunctive *waw* followed by the subject. Typically this construction is used for a "disjunction," indicating a parenthesis, a new scene, or simultaneous actions, but no such disjunction can be intended here. The acts are certainly sequential: Haman trembles before king and queen; then the king leaves; then Haman falls on the queen's couch; then the king returns. Most likely, the "disjunctive" construction here is used to convey a sense of rapid action, as if everything is happening at once.

The change in circumstances is signaled by the king and queen being mentioned together, implying how her status has risen, even as she must beg the king's mercy. Haman trembles before both the king and the queen, recognizing that she is as dangerous as her husband. Yet another reversal has occurred: Haman was enraged when Mordecai did not shake (זוּעַ, *zûa'*) before him (5:9); now it is the king who is enraged, and Haman who is trembling in terror (בָּעַת, *bā'at*) before the queen.

Haupt argues that the phrase וְהָמָן נִבְעַת מִלִּפְנֵי הַמֶּלֶךְ וְהַמַּלְכָּה (*wĕhāmān nib'at millipnê hammelek wĕhammalkâ*) means that Haman was surprised by the king and queen, rather than terrified.[57] Haupt's case is philologically weak, since it depends on an Arabic cognate, but it also makes little sense in the context: while Esther's revelation may have surprised Haman, why should he be surprised by the king, who has been just as unaware of Esther's purpose as he is?

7:7 Surely, the king has had adequate cause to be enraged. Earlier, his anger flared when Queen Vashti refused to appear before him. Now, it appears that someone is trying to deprive him of his current queen—and that someone is his trusted adviser, Haman. Torn between loyalty to his wife and the vizier that he himself appointed, the king feels a need to retreat before investigating the matter further.[58] Clines notes that the king's first instinct when faced with the dilemma is to flee.[59] He is not a decisive man and does not commit himself to a course of action without input from his advisers. But now, it is his chief adviser who stands accused. From whom can he seek counsel?

Bush (423–24) asserts that the verb עָמַד (*'āmad*) in this verse should be rendered "remained" or "stayed behind" rather than "stood" (so also NIV, NRSV, NLT). The verb can certainly mean "remain" and would fit well in the context with that meaning. However, it makes more sense to see the phrase "Haman stood to plead for his life" as yet another ironic reversal (cf. Berlin, 69). Haman had been outraged when Mordecai refused to rise before him (5:9); now, Haman must stand before the queen to plead for his life. It is possible that a double entendre is intended.

---

57. P. Haupt, "Critical Notes on Esther," *AJSL* 24 (1907–1908): 150; cf. also Moore 1971, 71.

58. On the "house garden," see the comment on 1:5.

59. D. J. A. Clines, *The Esther Scroll: The Story of the Story*, JSOTSup 30 (Sheffield, UK: JSOT Press, 1984), 15.

The phrase, “Because he saw that the king was determined to bring trouble on him” (כִּי רָאָה כִּי־כָלְתָה אֵלָיו הָרָעָה, *kî rāʾâ kî-koltâ ʾēlāyw hārāʿâ*) has been interpreted as another example of the “hidden name of God” in this book. This time, it is supposedly the last letters of the words that form the Tetragrammaton, along with the shortened version of the name: *YH-YHWH*. I would argue that this sequence of letters is simply a coincidence, and not designed by the author, who could surely have placed the name in a more significant place in the text. The same sequence appears in Gen 12:15: וַיִּרְאוּ אֹתָהּ שָׂרֵי פַרְעֹה וַיְהַלְלוּ אֹתָהּ אֶל־פַּרְעֹה (*wayyirʾû ʾōtāh śārê*[***y***] *parʿō**h** wayĕhallû*[***w***] *ʾōtā**h** ʾel-parʿōh*,“And the officers of Pharaoh saw her, and they praised her to Pharaoh”). No one seems inclined to argue that the name of Yahweh was deliberately “hidden” in this verse.

7:8 Now, Haman’s humiliation is complete. When the king returns from the garden, the vizier has fallen before Esther, prostrating himself in a manner that Mordecai had refused to do before him. Mordecai would not bow (3:2), nor would he stand (5:9), nor would he tremble (5:9); Haman is forced to tremble (7:6), then to stand (7:7), then to bow (7:8). The Jew could not be forced to humiliate himself before the Amalekite, even by the order of the king; but the Amalekite humiliates himself before a Jew without compulsion.

It was the custom of Persian nobles to recline on couches when they dined.[60] Haman had risen from his couch, but Esther remained recumbent, seemingly unmoved by the vizier’s plight. In a severe breach of protocol, Haman throws himself on the queen. According to Plutarch (*Artaxerxes* 27.1), touching the Persian king’s wife was a capital offense. In Assyrian law, no man was allowed to draw within more than seven paces of a member of the king’s harem (see Clines, 312). Haman must surely have been out of his mind to have made such an error.

Levenson (104) considers this scene to be the funniest in the book of Esther. It is likely that his images of the scene have been shaped by Purim plays that he has seen, but anyone can appreciate its irony. The king has returned from his walk to find Haman sprawled atop the queen. The vizier is begging for his life; the king accuses him instead of trying to force the queen. But the attack is not the real issue for the king: it is that it occurs in his presence, “with me in the house.” It is not the insult to the queen, but the insult to the king that really matters here.

The meaning of the verb כָּבַשׁ (*kābaš*) in this context has been disputed. Its basic meaning is “subdue” or “subjugate.” In this verse, it is usually

---

60. See P. Briant, *From Cyrus to Alexander: A History of the Persian Empire* (Winona Lake, IN: Eisenbrauns, 2002), 297.

understood to mean "rape." It has been argued, however, that Haman certainly had no intention of attacking the queen, so perhaps the word here refers rather to the violation of court protocol, of simply coming too close to the queen (Bardtke, 359). But though Haman had no intention of violating Esther, that Xerxes emphasizes that the offense was occurring in his presence implies that he interpreted the scene as more than a mere proximity breach. One might even wonder whether Xerxes deliberately misinterpreted the scene, in order to simplify his decision regarding Haman's fate (Bush, 433).[61] While it would have been difficult for Xerxes to condemn Haman for attempting to execute a decree issued in the king's name, he could certainly execute him for attempted rape of the queen.

Some scholars (e.g., Paton, 264) argue that Esther should have interceded for Haman, telling the king that he was not attacking her. Her silence at this point, it is argued, reveals that she is a callous woman and unsuitable role model. Undoubtedly, Esther's conduct here does not seem to be up to the standards of NT morality (i.e., forgiving enemies; Matt 5:43–48; Rom 12:19–20). In fact, it even falls short of OT ethical behavior, which commands Israelites to speak up if their testimony could vindicate their neighbor (Deut 5:1). Nonetheless, Esther's conduct does seem pragmatic. Had Haman lived, he might have persuaded the king to go through with his plot against the Jews. He could certainly have brought forward evidence that Mordecai was insubordinate. Haman's execution takes care of what could have been a troublesome loose end in the storyline.

The covering of Haman's face is a troubling detail, historically speaking. While it may have been customary in ancient Greece and Rome to cover the head of condemned prisoners (Moore 1971, 72), there is no evidence for such a practice among the Persians. Several emendations of the text have been suggested: Rudolph would change the verb חָפוּ (*ḥāpû*, "they covered") to חוּרוּ (*ḥûrû*, "grew pale").[62] Fox would adopt the suggested emendation of the verb to חָפְרוּ (*ḥāprû*,"he was shamed").[63] Gerleman (123–24) argues on the basis of an Arabic expression that the phrase means "he fainted." None of these emendations seems necessary. It is possible that the act was designed to keep the king from having to see Haman's direful countenance, given how sensitive the Persian kings seem to have been to people appearing before them in distress (note Neh 2:2). Whatever the historical significance of the act, it is certain that it is linked literarily to Esth 6:12, where Haman rushed home with his head covered after his humiliation before Mordecai.

---

61. Thus Fox, *Character and Ideology*, 87.

62. W. Rudolph, "Textkritisches zum Estherbuch," *VT* 4 (1954): 90.

63. Fox, *Character and Ideology*, 283–84.

Haman's attempt to hide his shame foreshadowed this scene, where the servants covered his face for him.

7:9 An obliging eunuch (probably the same Harbona mentioned in 1:10) points out that there is a ready-made pike that can be used for eliminating the troubling vizier. As is typical of the unimaginative monarch, Xerxes needs help to decide how to respond to the problem of Haman's treachery. Once the suggestion is made, Xerxes agrees to it readily.

It is not surprising that the eunuch knew of the pike and its purpose. It was not the kind of thing that Haman would have kept secret. The reason the eunuch brings up the matter is apparently that he has little love for Haman. Such self-important figures are often unpopular with servants. This Harbona not only suggests the means for the execution, but he provides further justification for why it should be done. He points out to the king that Haman intended to kill the man whom he had just honored for saving his life. Haman thus appears to be a traitor to the king's interests. He would murder the king's rescuer and attack the king's wife on the same day.

Once again, the narrator gives us ironic twists. First, and most obvious, is that Haman's death occurs on the instrument of doom that he had created for Mordecai. The pike that was going to show everyone what happens to those who oppose Haman becomes the place for demonstrating what happens to those who oppose the Jews. But there is another level of irony here, too. In the Esther narrative, the only persons to be impaled besides Haman and his sons are the two eunuchs who had plotted to assassinate the king. Now, Haman is to be impaled at the instigation of a eunuch. It seems as though the Esther narrative is deliberately seeking to rehabilitate the image of eunuchs. As noted earlier, in Greek literature, eunuchs often appear near the center of Persian court intrigues.[64] The conspirators Bigthan and Teresh, then, were acting as eunuchs were typically expected to act in that day (at least by the Greeks). Other eunuchs in Esther, however, are depicted in a more favorable light. Hegai assists Esther in her preparations to meet the king (Esth 2:8–15); Hatach served as the go-between for Esther and Mordecai (Esth 4:5–9); Harbona is yet another who helps make up for the failings of Bigthan and Teresh by revealing Haman's duplicity. It was noted earlier (see commentary on 4:5) that marginalized members of society were not always positively portrayed in the book of Esther. But perhaps there has been a rehabilitation of the image of eunuchs here, similar to the transformation of Esther herself.

Yet another irony in this episode is that when Haman is finally executed, it is for a crime that he did not commit. Though Haman had instigated the

64. Briant, *Cyus to Alexander*, 268–70.

destruction of the Jews, it was the king's order that set the plot in motion. Haman is not legally culpable in the affair (though he most certainly was morally culpable). And of course, he was not actually attempting to rape the queen. We can almost hear Haman muttering, "But ... but ... but ... " as he is dragged away to the pike.

7:10 With the vizier executed, the king's anger abates. The wording is reminiscent of 2:1, where the king's wrath against Vashti abated. In chapter 1, the flaring of the king's anger led to the removal of the queen; when it abated, he chose a new queen. In this chapter, his wrath meant the removal of Haman. The abating of Xerxes' wrath signals the coming of Haman's replacement, which will occur in the next chapter.

Biblical Theology Comments

7:1–5 The most interesting theological issue in this section concerns the interaction of divine and human initiative. We have observed already how the hidden hand of providence created the reversals that the Jews have experienced in this narrative. Esther's elevation to queenship, Mordecai's overhearing the plot against the king, the king's sleepless night and the reading of Mordecai's loyalty in the royal chronicles—all these acts appear to be the machinations of a secret providence. In this section, however, Esther's intellect and people skills come to the fore. Like Joseph, she has been placed in a situation where she has access to a foreign king, and she will use that access to bring deliverance to her people. Like Moses, she is in a remarkable position to save the children of Israel from a dark fate. But unlike either Joseph or Moses, Esther has no miraculous powers or divine insights. There is no indication in the text that she received any supernatural guidance in her planning. Instead, she relies wholly on her own cleverness to achieve her ends. In this regard, she is no different from the wise woman of Abel (2 Sam 20), from Judith, or even from the midwives Shiphrah and Puah, who rescued the Israelite infants from Pharaoh. There is a well-established tradition of Israelite women using their wits to overcome power.

It has long been recognized that such human-divine interaction is a main theme of Esther: God creates opportunities, but Esther must act on them (see, e.g., Burrows, 140; Clines, 268–71).[65] It is a pattern that God repeats throughout Scripture and throughout history. While Yahweh initiates the work of deliverance, there is also the human response required. God will part the Red Sea, but Moses must raise the staff. God will destroy the walls of Jericho, but the Israelites must blow the horns. God sends Jesus

65. See also S. Berg, *The Book of Esther: Motifs, Themes and Structure*, SBLDS 44 (Missoula, MT: Scholars Press, 1979), 182–83.

Christ to make the way of salvation, but humanity must still respond by placing faith in Him.

7:8b The queen's plot for the removal of Haman, while effective, is ethically troublesome. She uses her sex appeal to win an audience with the king. She does not address, much less refute, Haman's charge that the Jews are rebellious. Instead, she suggests that Haman is attempting to swindle Xerxes. She allows the king to form the misapprehension that Haman is trying to rape the queen, and then does nothing to correct that misunderstanding (a fact that Paton, 264, finds offensive). While her methods were effective and her goal was just, we are prompted to consider the question, "Does the end justify the means?"

This book is not the only one that raises this question. Judges is teeming with such questionable incidents: Ehud lies to Eglon to gain a private audience, then assassinates the unarmed king (Judg 3:12–29); Jael deceives and murders a sleeping general (Judg 4:17–22); Samson kills thirty men in order to steal their cloaks (Judg 14:19–20). In Judg 14:1–4, God uses Samson's lust for a Philistine woman to stir up trouble between Israel and its overlords. The text does not necessarily endorse or excuse such actions. In fact, the final words of the book, "In those days there was no king in Israel; everyone did whatever they thought was right" (Judg 21:25), could be seen as an indictment of the behavior of the whole lot of them.

But it is not beyond God to use evil actions to accomplish his goals. This principle is stated explicitly in the Joseph narrative, where God used the abduction and enslavement of Joseph to bring about the preservation of Egypt and the Israelites during a famine: "You meant it for evil, but God meant it for good" (Gen 50:20). The supreme example of such serendipity is the crucifixion of Christ: an unambiguously evil act was used by God to accomplish the greatest of all possible goods, the salvation of humanity (Acts 2:22–24). It is not an endorsement of bad behavior, but an acknowledgment that there is precious little else to work with in this world. Indeed, if God refused to use evil people, He would have no one to work with at all.

Application and Devotional Implications

How should we feel about Haman's fate? Should a Christian have dealt with this villain differently, seeking his pardon and restoration, rather than his destruction? Or would such an outcome have left the demands of justice unsatisfied?

One of the primary ethical drives of humanity is the feeling that justice must be served. From seemingly as soon as we learn to talk, we are obsessed with the notion of fairness. When a wrong has been done, a penalty must be paid. In the book of Esther, the wrong is mostly potential: Haman does not actually kill anyone, though his intentions were clear and he had already set the process in motion. Does the murder not occuring absolve Haman from responsibility? If someone were planning to bomb a public building, they would be treated under the law as if they had committed the crime. What Haman had planned to do would have been one of the most monstrous crimes imaginable, on par with anything accomplished by Hitler or Stalin. One should only contemplate pardoning Haman if one could justify pardoning Hitler. Only an individual total bereft of moral outrage, it seems, could possibly imagine such a thing.

It is perhaps a weakness of evangelical Christianity that we put such an emphasis on God's mercy that we underappreciate His justice. We seem to enjoy bragging about our sinfulness and claim to be just as bad as mass murderers and other criminals. While it is indeed true that any sin separates us from God, there is no biblical basis for arguing that all sin is equal in God's eyes. Some sins clearly merit a "greater condemnation" (Mark 12:40), or the concept of a final judgment becomes nonsense.

Haman had opportunity to repent of his deed and make a decree rescuing the Jews himself. Eventually, however, he ran out of chances for repentance. We must reconcile ourselves to justice being served, in this world or the next. Indeed, we should comfort ourselves with that truth (cf. Rev 6:9–11). Compassion for Haman would have been as ill-placed as compassion on cancer cells.

Selected Bibliography

Berg, S. B. *The Book of Esther: Motifs, Themes and Structure*. SBLDS 44. Missoula, MT: Scholars Press, 1979.

Briant, P. *From Cyrus to Alexander: A History of the Persian Empire*. Winona Lake, IN: Eisenbrauns, 2002.

Clines, D. J. A. *The Esther Scroll: The Story of the Story*. JSOTSup 30. Sheffield, UK: JSOT Press, 1984.

Dandamayev, M. A. *Slavery in Babylonia from Nabopolassar to Alexander the Great (626–331 B.C.)*. DeKalb: Northern Illinois University Press, 1984.

De Vaux, R. *Ancient Israel: Its Life and Institutions*. Grand Rapids: Eerdmans, 1997.

Fox, M. V. *Character and Ideology in the Book of Esther*. 2nd ed. Grand Rapids: Eerdmans, 2001.

Haupt, P. "Critical Notes on Esther." *AJSL* 24 (1907–1908): 97–186.

Rudolph, W. "Textkritisches zum Estherbuch." *VT* 4 (1954): 89–90.

Thornton, T. "The Crucifixion of Haman and the Scandal of the Cross." *JTS* 37 (1986): 419–26.

Wilcock, M. *The Message of Judges: Grace Abounding*. Leicester, UK: Inter-Varsity, 1992.

The Triumph of the Jews (8:1–9:32)

Introduction

The final section of the narrative deals with the problem of Haman's decree. Even though the villain himself is dead, the threat of imminent destruction still hangs over the heads of the Jews, because "an edict written in the king's name ... cannot be revoked" (8:8). Esther and Mordecai, working together openly for the first time, now seek to spare the Jews from the destruction that looms ahead. This section divides into three major units: in the first, Esther and Mordecai devise a plan to overturn Haman's decree. In the second, the Jews fight against their enemies and win a stunning victory. In the third, the Jews celebrate their victory over their oppressors by establishing the observance of Purim.

Throughout this section, the theme of reversal that has been so prevalent throughout the narrative is brought to a satisfying conclusion. This occurs most explicitly in chapter 8, where even the choice of words makes the reversals apparent. The office that had been bestowed on Haman is now awarded to his archnemesis, Mordecai. The decree that had been issued in chapter 3 is now echoed in 8:11–12, using many of the same phrases and images, but its intent is reversed so that the Jews will be the killers rather than the victims. The royal couriers are dispatched in haste as in 3:15, but this time, they bring good tidings for the Jews. Instead of grief and mourning in each province where the edict arrives (4:3), there is joy and gladness (8:17). In chapter 9, reversal is not as obvious, but the theme continues. The Jews, threatened with destruction, are now destroyers. The sons that had inspired so much pride in Haman are now shamefully impaled. The fasting of the Jews has been changed into feasting. The theme of banqueting also reaches its culmination here. The two days of feasting that celebrate the Jews' victory over their enemies balance the two feasts of King Xerxes that opened the narrative (1:2–12) and culminate the feasts of Esther's inauguration (2:18), Haman and Xerxes' celebration of Haman's decree (3:15), and Esther's two banquets (5:5b–8; 7:1–7).

With the establishment of Purim, the Esther narrative achieves its climax and its ultimate purpose: to provide the etiology for the only festival of the Jews (to that time) that had no basis in the Pentateuch. Mordecai, often depicted in this narrative as a new Joseph, is now something of a "poor man's Moses"—someone who can deliver his people from oppression and become a new "lawgiver" capable of winning favor with both the Jews and the Gentiles.

Outline

V. The Triumph of the Jews (8:1–9:32)
- A. Esther and Mordecai Arrange Deliverance for the Jews (8:1–17)
  - 1. The King Promotes Mordecai (8:1–2)
  - 2. Esther and Mordecai Are Authorized to Write an Edict (8:3–8)
  - 3. Mordecai Issues the Decree (8:9–17)
    - a. The Counter-Decree Is Written (8:9–14)
    - b. Mordecai Leaves with Honor, and the Jews Rejoice (8:15–17)
- B. The Jews' Victories over Their Enemies (9:1–19)
  - 1. The First Wave of Victories (9:1–10)
    - a. Victories in the Provinces (9:1–5)
    - b. Victories over Enemies in the Palace (9:6–10)
  - 2. The Second Wave of Victories (9:11–15)
    - a. Esther Requests a Second Day of Carnage (9:11–13)
    - b. Five Hundred Killed in Susa (9:14–15)
  - 3. The Jews Celebrate Their Victories (9:16–19)
    - a. Celebrating the Victories in the Provinces (9:16–17)
    - b. Celebrating the Victories in Susa (9:17–19)
- C. Purim Established (9:20–32)
  - 1. Mordecai Establishes Purim (9:20–28)
    - a. Mordecai Issues the Order Establishing Purim (9:20–22)
    - b. The Jews Commit to the Perpetual Observance (9:23–28)
  - 2. Esther Confirms the Celebration of Purim (9:29–32)

Esther and Mordecai Arrange Deliverance for the Jews (8:1–17)

Translation

1 On that day, King Xerxes gave to Queen Esther the household of Haman, the Jews' enemy. Also, Mordecai came before the king, because Esther had told what he was to her. **2** And the king took off his signet ring that he had taken away[1] from Haman and gave it to Mordecai. Then Esther set Mordecai over the household of Haman.

3 Then Esther spoke again before the king. She fell at his feet and she wept and entreated him to annul[2] the evil of Haman the Agagite and the plot that he had plotted against the Jews. **4** The king held out the golden scepter to Esther, and Esther rose and stood before the king. **5** Then she said, "If it is pleasing to the king, and if I have found favor before him, and if the thing seems proper before the king, and I am pleasing in his opinion,[3] let it be written to recall[4] the letters devised by Haman the Agagite, the son of Hammedatha, that he wrote to destroy the Jews who are in all the king's provinces. **6** For how can I bear to look on the evil that will find my people? Or how can I bear to look on the destruction of my kindred?"

7 King Xerxes said to Queen Esther and to Mordecai the Jew, "See, the estate of Haman I have given Esther, and him they have hanged on the pike, because he stretched out his hand against the Jews. **8** But (both of) you,[5] write whatever seems good to you about the Jews in the name of the king, and seal it with the king's signet, for a document written in the name of the king and sealed with the king's signet cannot be recalled." **9** The king's scribes were called at that time, in the third month (that is, the month of Sivan), on the twenty-third day. And it was written according to all that Mordecai commanded concerning the Jews, to the satraps and the governors and the nobles of the provinces from India to Ethiopia, 127 provinces, to each province according to its own script and to each people according to its own language, and to the Jews according to their script and according to their language. **10** He wrote in the name of King Xerxes and sealed it with the king's signet ring. Then he sent the letters by means of mounted couriers riding on royal postal horses, bred from the royal stud, **11** that the king allowed the Jews who were in all of the cities to gather and to take a stand for their lives; to destroy, kill, and annihilate any army of any people or province that might oppress them, (along with) children and women, and plunder their goods, **12** on one day in all King Xerxes' provinces, on the thirteenth day of the twelfth month, which is the month of Adar. **13** A copy of the writing was to be issued as a decree in all the provinces, publicly

1. Lit., "that he had caused to pass from Haman."
2. Lit., "cause to pass away."
3. Lit., "in his eyes." The expression here, however, does not seem to imply physical appearance, but general acceptance.
4. Typically translated "to overrule" (NIV), "to reverse" (NLT) or "revoke" (NASB; NRSV). In my opinion, the more common meaning of this verb form, "cause to return," is preferable here. See commentary.
5. The Heb. pronoun here is pl.

displayed to all peoples, that the Jews were to be ready for that day to take vengeance on their enemies. **14** So the couriers, riding on the royal postal horses, rode out hastily, being urged on by the king's word. The decree was also issued in Susa the citadel.

15 Then Mordecai went out from the presence of the king in royal garments of blue and white, with a great golden headdress and a mantle of fine linen and purple. The city of Susa shouted and rejoiced. **16** For the Jews, there was light and gladness and joy and honor, **17** and in all the provinces and all the cities where the king's command and his decree reached, there was gladness and rejoicing among the Jews, a feast and a holiday.[6] Many of the peoples of the land became Jews, because fear of the Jews had fallen on them.

Textual Notes

1.a. The appellative הַמַּלְכָּה, "the queen," is absent in the LXX.

2.a. In the AT, the king himself (not Esther) grants Haman's property to Mordecai.

3.a. In the AT, this portion of the text through to the end of the narrative is greatly abbreviated and somewhat reordered, representing either a separate tradition or a different recension of the text.

5.a. Instead of הָמָן בֶּן־הַמְּדָתָא הָאֲגָגִי ("Haman, son of Hammedatha, the Agagite"), the LXX and AT have simply "Haman."

7.a. "And to Mordecai the Jew" is absent in the LXX, AT, and other translations.

9.a. For בַּחֹדֶשׁ הַשְּׁלִישִׁי הוּא־חֹדֶשׁ סִיוָן ("in the third month, that is, Sivan"), the LXX reads ἐν τῷ πρώτῳ μηνί, ὅς ἐστι Νισα ("in the first month, that is, Nisan").

12.a. Following v. 12, the LXX and AT insert Addition E, which includes the text of the decree.

17.a. After וְרַבִּים מֵעַמֵּי הָאָרֶץ ("and many of the peoples of the land"), the LXX inserts περιετέμοντο ("were circumcised").

Commentary

This section of the unit can be divided into three scenes. In the first scene, 8:1–2, the Jewish heroes receive their rewards from the king. Esther is given

6. Lit., "a good day," also in Esth 9:19, 22, as well as 1 Sam 25:8.

the property of Haman, which she entrusts to Mordecai. Mordecai, now revealed as Esther's kin, is promoted to the position vacated by Haman.

The second scene, 8:3–8, relates the dialogue between Esther and Xerxes, as Esther seeks to get the king to revoke Haman's decree. The king will not revoke the decree, which would be considered a breach of Persian law. Instead, he gives Esther and Mordecai permission to write an edict that will countervail Haman's plot. It is still unclear how that end will be accomplished.

In the third scene, 8:9–17, Esther does not appear. Instead, the focus is entirely on Mordecai. Mordecai calls the royal scribes and has a decree written that grants the Jews a right to assemble and defend themselves against anyone who attacks them. The decree is sent out, carried by swift couriers to all the provinces of the empire. Mordecai then goes forth from the king's presence dressed in royal attire, and the Jews rejoice at his promotion. Everywhere the decree arrives, it inspires celebration among the Jews. The language and imagery of this section closely parallel that of Esth 3:12–15, where Haman issues his decree for the Jews' destruction. However, it reverses the intent of Haman's decree. It also exhibits some other subtle differences that tend to highlight the narrator's purpose. These differences will be noted in the commentary.

8:1 In ancient Persia, betrayal of the king meant not only loss of life, but loss of property. According to Herodotus (*Hist.* 3.128–129), the property of a certain traitor named Oroetes became the property of the state. In a similar vein, Josephus wrote that Cyrus decreed that anyone who did not obey his laws concerning the Jews would be crucified, and their estates would be confiscated by the government (*Ant.* 1.17). While it is doubtful that Cyrus was really so concerned about the Jews, there is no reason to question the authenticity of the penalty Josephus describes for refusal of the king's orders. So with Haman dead, the ownership of his estate would have been transferred to Xerxes, who could dispose of it however he saw fit. In a rare case of personal initiative, the king decides to bestow it on Esther, either to compensate her for her grief or to demonstrate his royal favor.

Mordecai now appears before the king for the first time in the narrative. Paton (267–68) and other commentators find it ridiculous that Xerxes would not have known about the relationship between Mordecai and Esther, but it hardly seems impossible that they could have kept their secret. In the narrative, the only time Mordecai and Esther were publicly in the same context was when Esther had relayed word of the eunuchs' plot to the king. If the king had ever wondered why the queen was receiving messages from minor officials, he probably would not have given it much thought—curiosity does not seem to have been a character trait of this king.

Also, since Esther became queen, Mordecai and Esther have conducted all their correspondence through a loyal eunuch, a person whose job was to be trustworthy. He would have gained nothing by revealing their confidence. It does not strain the reader's credulity to see here a grand revelation.

8:2 In another coup for the Jews, Mordecai receives the office vacated by Haman, making him second-in-command in Persia. The transfer of the signet ring is somewhat different in this episode than in the case of Haman. Haman had not received the ring when installed in office, but only when the king commissioned him to write the edict concerning the Jews (Esth 3:10). Here, however, the signet ring is transferred as a sign of office. Haman, it seems, came into his authority more incrementally than Mordecai. All the power granted to Haman with the signet is immediately placed at Mordecai's disposal, empowering him to do what is necessary to overturn Haman's edict.

The act also draws another parallel between Mordecai and Joseph, a parallel noted earlier in the honors granted Mordecai in chapter 6 (see commentary on 6:9). In Gen 41, when Pharaoh named Joseph second-in-command over Egypt, he immediately "took the signet ring from his hand, and put it on the hand of Joseph" (Gen 41:42). The narrator of Esther, by placing the transfer of the signet immediately upon Mordecai's investiture, is likely making another allusion to Joseph. The audience has been somewhat primed to recognize this allusion by the previous allusions that appeared in chapter 6. The broader parallels between the two figures are obvious: both are Israelites residing in a foreign land as "exiles"; both are threatened by the authorities; both are promoted to second-in-command; both use their authority to secure the salvation of their people (Joseph by saving his father and brothers from the famine in Canaan; Gen 45:4–11). We might note, however, that Mordecai's character pales in comparison to Joseph: Joseph was imprisoned because of his refusal to compromise his high morals; he achieved his office because of the supernatural gifts bestowed on him by God; and he carefully gave credit to God for his abilities (Gen 41:16). Mordecai will indeed rescue his people, but it was through Esther's beauty and cleverness that the deliverance was made possible.

Why is Mordecai promoted to Haman's vacant office? Surely, there were other princes who would have been in line for the post. One possibility is that Mordecai's advancement is meant to compensate Esther for the grief she suffered because of Haman's decree. In that case, it is Esther who is being compensated, not Mordecai. But another possibility is that Mordecai's promotion represents a further reward for his deliverance of the king from the assassination plot. If so, it might seem a very generous boon. Overhearing a conversation would not necessarily make one qualified to be a chief administrator. But on the other hand, professional qualifications seem to have played little part in promotions in this narrative, as in the case of Esther's promotion to queenship. Furthermore, according to Herodotus, *Hist.* 9.107, a certain Xenagoras, apparently not a particularly illustrious man, was made governor of all Cilicia as a reward for saving the life of the king's brother during a brawl. Perhaps becoming the vizier for saving the king's life would not be out of proportion.

In that light, Mordecai's promotion here might support the theory presented above regarding Mordecai's refusal to bow before Haman (see commentary on 3:1)—that Mordecai refused to bow because he felt Haman had received the promotion unjustly and that it should have been his. In that case, Xerxes' elevation of Mordecai would simply be righting the wrong that had led to all the unpleasantness in the first place.

In yet another interesting reversal, Esther bestows mastery of Haman's property on Mordecai. The act demonstrates her growth as a character: when she is introduced to the audience, she is an orphan, taken in by Mordecai. Now, she serves as his benefactor. There is, however, a somewhat unsavory aspect to this exchange. If the conflict between Mordecai and Haman is indeed a "rematch" of the Saul-Agag affair, then Mordecai has once again failed to carry out God's instructions regarding the Amalekites. God had given King Saul explicit instructions not to take any spoil from the Amalekites: all their property was placed under the ban (1 Sam 15:3). Mordecai fails to carry out God's orders concerning the Amalekites by receiving the property of Haman as spoil.

8:3 Though Haman has been executed, the threat to the Jews remains. Esther speaks again to the king, in order that Haman's decree should be revoked. Some commentators have puzzled over why Esther should have to risk her life in another appearance before the king, when Mordecai could have easily presented the matter as the king's vizier. Apparently, however, Esther is not actually seeking another audience; she never left the king's presence in the first place. The text does not say that she "came before" the king, but merely "spoke before" the king.[7] The plea she presents here occurs on the same day as her banquet with the king and Haman. Very likely, there has been a change of location back to the throne room; it seems unlikely that the king would have taken his golden scepter to the queen's banquet. But there is no reason not to assume this episode is a continuation of the appeal made at the banquet.

---

7. M. Fox, *Character and Ideology in the Book of Esther*, 2nd ed. (Grand Rapids: Eerdmans, 2001), 92.

The verb translated "entreated" (הִתְחַנֵּן, *hitḥannēn*) literally means "implore favor for oneself." She is finally fulfilling Mordecai's command in 4:8, where he told Esther to "entreat" the king on behalf of the Jews. It may seem to be a foregone conclusion that Esther would receive the favor she seeks, since she has found "favor" (חֵן, *ḥēn*, from the same root, חנן, *ḥnn*, as the verb used here) in the eyes of all who have seen her (Esth 2:15), and especially with the king (Esth 5:2, 8). She will need that favor now, since she is about to ask the king to do what, according to Esth 1:15, cannot be done: to "cause to pass away" (לְהַעֲבִיר, *lĕhaʿăbîr*) a law of the Medes and Persians.

This is the first time since 3:10 that Haman has specifically been identified as "the Agagite." Haman is mentioned by name forty-four times in the book, but only identified as "the Agagite" four times. There is surely some significance here. After the introduction of Haman in 3:1, each time Haman is called "the Agagite," it is associated with an explicit mention of Haman's plot against the Jews: in 3:10, when he first receives approval to destroy the Jews; here in 8:3 and again in 8:5, when Esther asks the king to overturn the wicked plot of Haman; and in 9:24, which summarizes Haman's plot. It appears that the narrator is reminding us that Haman's hatred is not just personal, but racial.

8:4 The extending of the scepter in this case is obviously not a sign that Esther's life is spared; her danger is surely past. Nor is it sufficient to state that it is merely a sign of "royal favor," as several commentaries suggest (e.g., Laniak, 248).[8] Instead, the meaning of the gesture seems to be that permission has been granted to present a petition before the king, as in Esth 5:2. Esther seems to realize that the king believes he has done all that is necessary to right the wrongs committed by Haman, and that the matter of Haman's decree is closed. But of course, that would be a tragic mistake, since the scheduled pogrom has not been canceled. Esther's new petition will reopen the matter for Xerxes.

8:5 Esther strings together blandishments here as nowhere else in the book. Two of these obsequies appeared in 7:3 ("If I have found favor with you" and "If it is pleasing to the king"), though their order is reversed here. The other two, "If the thing seems right before the king, and I am pleasing in his opinion," are new. The statements are mostly synonymous, adding little real substance to her appeal, except perhaps the admission that such a reversal might appear improper.[9] Nonetheless, the new formulation cer-

8. Also Fox, *Character and Ideology*, 92.

9. D. J. A. Clines, *The Esther Scroll: The Story of the Story*, JSOTSup 30 (Sheffield, UK: JSOT Press, 1984), 101.

tainly adds weight and even some dignity to her request by couching it in something of a poetic distich:

> (A) If it is pleasing to the king, and (B) if I have found favor before him
> (A′) And if the thing seems proper before the king, and (B′) I am pleasing in his opinion

Apparently, Esther feels the need for stronger appeal here, because there is a different issue at stake. In chapter 7, Esther could present the matter as one of personal insult to the king and an attempt to swindle him. Here, however, the king's honor is no longer at issue. Indeed, it might be seen as dishonorable for the king to rescind an order he had already signed into law. Esther must proceed carefully, but passionately.

As in 7:2, the king's approval of the queen is linked with his acceptance of her appeal. The king must essentially say that he is not pleased with her if he is to refuse her request. This is no empty rhetorical ploy; theoretically, Haman's edict of extermination would include Esther as well. If the king desires to keep his queen, he should respond favorably to her request.

Esther's request is carefully worded, perhaps to find some "legal loophole" that she may exploit. She does not use the word "decree" (דָּת, *dat*), but instead speaks of the "letters" (סְפָרִים, *sĕpārîm*) sent out by Haman. She does not ask the king to "overturn" (עָבַר, *ʿābar*, hiphil) the decree, which (according to Esth 1:15) cannot be done, but only that he "recall" (שׁוּב, *šûb*, hiphil) the letters that were sent out instead. The verb הָשִׁיב (*hāšîb*) has the literal meaning "cause to return." This meaning is by far its most common in the OT (cf. Num 22:8; Ruth 4:15; Jer 32:44) and makes sense in this context.

She is careful to lay responsibility for the decree wholly on Haman, rather than the king (Bardtke, 365). Perhaps the king could find it acceptable to rescind the decree, if it were not actually the king's doing? As Clines observes, Esther tells the truth, but not the whole truth.[10] She probably is not trying to mislead the king, but rather to provide him an "out," a way he can spare the Jews without violating his own law.

8:6 Should the legal appeal fail, Esther adds a personal appeal. The destruction of her people would be an unbearable tragedy for the queen herself. If the king truly loves her, would he not desire to spare her such heartache? He has already stated by his actions that she has "found favor in his eyes." Even if he cares nothing for the Jews, he cannot deny that he cares for her.

10. Clines, *Esther Scroll*, 101.

Esther uses a form of the exclamation, "How?" (אֵיכָכָה, *ʾêkākâ*) that occurs only here and in Song of Songs 5:3 (twice). The word seems to be a form used when a female character expresses a rhetorical question (Berlin, 74). A similar phrase, using the more conventional form of the interrogative, אֵיךְ (*ʾêk*), is used in Gen 44:34, "For how can I go up to my father if the boy is not with me?" The usage once again demonstrates that the Joseph story exerted a strong influence on the narrator of Esther.

Does Esther's statement that she does not want to "see" the destruction of her people imply that she expects to escape the destruction herself? Not necessarily. First, the phrase "to see" or "look upon" can be synonymous for "experience," typically of something thought too wonderful or too evil to occur in one's own lifetime: e.g., Psa 69:33 (Eng. 69:32), "The humble will see, and rejoice"; Jer 17:6, "He will not see when prosperity comes"; or Job 21:20, "Let his own eyes see his destruction." Also, unless Esther expected to be the first person executed, she would surely be forced to witness the destruction of her people if the decree were to go into effect. In Esth 7:3–4, she surely speaks as if she expected to be included in the destruction, and Haman's death has not changed the situation. No explicit decree has been issued exempting Esther from the slaughter. As unlikely as it might seem that she would be slain, it is still a legal possibility and one that Esther can use to her advantage.

8:7 The king includes Mordecai in his response, acknowledging his new role and authority. Paton (270) suggests the reference to Mordecai is a scribal insertion, but in his instructions (v. 8), Xerxes uses the pl. pronoun, clearly indicating he is addressing multiple parties.

Fox argues that at this point in the narrative, the phrase "Mordecai the Jew" becomes a fixed epithet, parallel to the title "Xerxes the king" and "Esther the queen." He contends it is a title of "high dignity."[11] Both assertions are questionable: Mordecai is referred to by name eleven more times in the book, and only four times is he called "Mordecai the Jew." The epithet is not honorific, but is rather like "Haman the Agagite." It highlights the ethnic dimension to the persecution and celebrates the exaltation of one of the narrator's own race to a position of power and honor. It is important to remember the resistance element of this story: just as Haman delighted to think of himself as "the man whom the king delights to honor," so the narrator and his audience relish the idea that it is a *Jew* who exercises such power in the kingdom.

The king reminds the pair of the benefits he has already granted them. The king's claim that he had Haman impaled because he "stretched out his

---

11. Fox, *Character and Ideology*, 94.

hand against the Jews" is not technically correct: in fact, it was because he attempted to "violate" the queen that he was impaled. But the king here presents Haman's execution as a favor to the Jews in an effort to show his goodwill, and probably to imply that he has already done *his* part.

The phrase "stretched his hand out against the Jews" implies not necessarily an actual attack (as in the NIV), but a plot or scheme.[12] Levenson (108–9) contends that the phrase is an allusion to Esth 2:21, where the two eunuchs sought to "stretch out their hands" against King Xerxes, thus casting Haman in the role of a co-conspirator against the king. It should be noted, however, that the phrase "he stretched out his hand against" is quite common in the OT (e.g., Gen 22:12; 37:22; Exod 3:20; 9:15; 1 Kgs 13:4; Psa 55:21 [Eng. 20]; Job 1:12; Dan 11:42, and more), so it is not necessary to assume an allusion here to the eunuchs' conspiracy. It is possible Levenson has been influenced by the Jewish tradition, found as early as the LXX, that the eunuchs were conspiring with Haman against the king.

8:8 King Xerxes, as usual, is unwilling to take any action personally. The use of the personal pronoun "you" (אַתֶּם, *'attem*) here is redundant and certainly emphatic. The king is definitively washing his hands of the matter, delegating it to his queen and new prime minister. One frequently suggested explanation for his reluctance to be involved is that he does not want to be forced into a situation where he will be required to override his own orders. This explanation seems unlikely, however, since the king allows the decree to be written in his own name. A more likely scenario, it seems, is that he simply does not want to be bothered with the problem of reversing an irrevocable decree. I have noted several times that this Xerxes is unable to make a decision on his own, depending on his counselors and even his attendants (as in 7:9) to help determine his course of action. Berlin (75) further observes that Esther and Mordecai are cast fully in the role of the heroes. It is they who deliver the Jews, not the Persian king.

The king explains that they are to write the decree in his name and seal it with his own signet, because a document so authorized cannot be recalled (הָשִׁיב, *hāšîb*). His wording here is in direct response to what Esther has asked: she requested that the king recall the letters; he answers here that any document sealed with the royal signet cannot be recalled. The answer may be designed to serve either of two purposes: (1) it might explain why the king cannot simply recall the letters that Haman had written without his having to admit culpability in the matter; or (2) it might be meant to

12. See H. Tawil, "Two Notes on the Treaty Terminology of the Sefire Inscriptions," *CBQ* 42 (1980): 36.

assure Esther and Mordecai that whatever action they take at this time will be irrevocable. It is also possible that both implications were intended.

On the historical and logical difficulties involved in the idea of the immutability of Persian law, see the commentary on Esth 1:19. Clines and the many commentators who accept his thesis argue that the idea of the irrevocability of Persian law is a secondary addition to the narrative.[13] The original Esther tale, they believe, is more accurately reflected in the AT version, in which the king simply agrees to rescind Haman's decree. It should be noted, however, that the AT version has a major difficulty of its own: in the AT, after the king has revoked the decree, Esther merely asks the king for permission to kill her enemies, which he freely grants. After killing Haman's sons and seven hundred men in Susa, the king then grants her permission to kill whoever she wants. The Jews then go on a rampage, killing seventy thousand men. Without the problem of Haman's decree still being in effect and the threat to the Jews remaining, this wholesale slaughter makes no sense. It seems one would be forced to argue that the whole scenario of the Jews' slaughter of their enemies was an addition to the AT based on either the LXX or the MT versions of the story, which would make the idea that the AT represents an independent narrative tradition suspect.

8:9 The counter-decree is issued two months and ten days after Haman's decree had been issued (3:12–14). The month of Sivan is mentioned only here in the OT. The Babylonian month names were adopted by the Jews during the Babylonian exile.

As many scholars have noted, the time span could itself be significant: two months and ten days is the equivalent of seventy days. Seventy is a significant biblical number, being the product of two numbers that represent completion, seven and ten. The importance of the number is illustrated in numerous Bible passages: Jacob took seventy Israelites to Egypt (Gen 46:27); the Egyptians mourned Jacob seventy days (Gen 50:3); seventy elders presided over Israel (Exod 24:1; Num 11:16–25); seventy years was considered a full life span (Psa 90:10). Clines (316) sees a reference here to the seventy years of the Babylonian exile: in his understanding, the time between the threat of annihilation and the issuance of reprieve represents the time between Judah's downfall and its return. It is difficult, however, to see much similarity between the joy the Jews felt at the death of Haman and promotion of Mordecai and the despair they would have felt at the destruction of Jerusalem. Nor is it altogether obvious that the return from the Babylonian exile figured prominently in this narrator's thinking. As a Jew of the Diaspora, Cyrus' decree may have meant little to him.

13. Clines, *Esther Scroll*, 151.

The narrative makes a significant shift at this point. From the time where Mordecai first approached Esther about petitioning the king in chapter 4, the focus has been on Queen Esther and her scheme to get the king to reverse his decree. But from this point on, there will be greater emphasis on Mordecai's actions. As Berlin (76) observes, that Mordecai writes the decree overturning Haman's edict serves to emphasize the sense of reversal: since Mordecai's actions brought about the crisis, it should be Mordecai who undoes it. In fact, Esther is not mentioned at all from 8:9 to 9:12, where the king asks her what more she desires. While it is apparent that Mordecai has become the figure of power and prestige before the people, Esther continues to have greater influence before the throne.

The account of Mordecai's decree echoes elements from the accounts of the two earlier decrees: in v. 9, the description of the decree being issued in every language and script of the empire reiterates the description of King Xerxes' decree in 1:22 and Haman's decree in 3:12. Here, however, it is added explicitly that the decree is also issued to the Jews in their language (presumably Heb., since Aramaic was the *lingua franca* of the western Persian Empire and would not have been unique to the Jews). In chapter 1, there was a sense of universality to the story, as if this narrative would not involve Israel at all. Here, however, it is clear that the Jews are not merely another aspect of the story; they *are* the story. The narrative has cleverly moved from a universal story to a nationalistic one. It is a pattern familiar to Bible readers, since the biblical historical narrative similarly moves from the universalistic focus of the primeval history (Gen 1–11) to the particularistic narratives of Israel's origins, when God chose one man (Abram/Abraham) to be the patriarch of a unique people.

8:10 Once again, there is an allusion to Haman's decree. The decree is sealed with the king's signet ring, just as Haman's had been (3:12). In Esth 3:13 and 3:15, we read that the couriers (הָרָצִים, *hārāṣîm*) were dispatched to carry the letters (סְפָרִים, *sĕpārîm*) proclaiming the decree; the same terms are used here.

There are, however, several details added in the account of Mordecai's edict related to the horses. The term אֲחַשְׁתְּרָנִים (*ʾăḥaštĕrānîm*) is apparently a loanword, derived from the Persian word meaning "rule," with a Persian adj. suf. attached.[14] It seems to refer, then, to royal steeds, horses reserved for the king's business. The other equine terms, however, are more obscure. The term הָרֶכֶשׁ (*hārekeš*) occurs here, in v. 14, and in 1 Kgs 5:8 as a synonym for "horse," but it certainly refers to a special kind of horse. The term is also

14. P. Haupt, "Critical Notes on Esther," *AJSL* 24 (1907–1908): 157.

attested in Aramaic and Syriac.[15] In spite of all this attestation, however, the nuance of the word remains uncertain. Klingbeil has argued on the basis of an Aramaic ostracon from Arad that the term refers to "the team of horses used for the royal postal system."[16] The suggestion seems reasonable, since that is precisely what they are being used for here. The final equine term, הָרַמָּכִים (*hārammākîm*), is often rendered "(swift) mares," on the basis of late Aramaic and Arabic cognates (Bardtke, 366; Moore 1971, 80). Other scholars, however, believe the Syriac *ramkâ*, "herd," is a more appropriate cognate from which to derive its meaning.[17] The phrase "*the* herd" would likely mean a special herd, the king's royal horses. On this basis, it is argued that the phrase בְּנֵי הָרַמָּכִים (*bĕnê hārammākîm*) should be rendered something like "offspring of the king's herd" (so NRSV, NIV, NLT). In any event, it is apparent that the emphasis is on the special nature of the horses. It is uncertain whether the terms here would have been familiar to the readers of the narrative. They might well have been used because of their exotic sound.

8:11 While Haman's decree is not revoked, the Jews are given permission to form armies to defend themselves against anyone who dares to attack them. There is something of a letdown in this outcome: after more than two months of deliberation, is this solution the best they could come up with? One could hardly imagine that the Jews would not have defended themselves, even without such an edict.

But the decree is not so empty as it might first appear. Its chief provision is to give the Jews the right to "assemble" (לְהִקָּהֵל, *lĕhiqqāhēl*). The Heb. term used here often means to muster an army (e.g., 2 Sam 20:2; 21:5, 8; Ezek 16:40, and elsewhere). Without such official sanction, the process of assembling an army would have been viewed as an act of rebellion. It also appears that the Persian army will not take part in the action against the Jews, but it is not obvious that they were ever expected to participate. Perhaps the major effect of the edict is that it would provide a warning to anyone who was considering taking part in the slaughter of the Jews: the victims would not go meekly, as lambs to the slaughter.

The stipulations of Mordecai's decree parallel those of Haman's edict:

---

15. G. R. Driver, *Aramaic Documents of the Fifth Century B. C.* (Oxford: Oxford University Press, 1954), 61.
16. G. Klingbeil, "רכש and Esther 8,10.14 : A Semantic Note," *ZAW* 107 (1995): 302.
17. Haupt, "Critical Notes," 157–58.

3:13 Letters were sent by means of couriers to all the king's provinces to destroy, kill, and annihilate all Jews, from young to old, children and women, in one day, the thirteenth day of the twelfth month, which is the month of Adar, and plunder their goods.	8:11 The king allowed the Jews who were in all of the cities to gather and to take a stand for their lives; to destroy, kill, and annihilate any army of any people or province that might oppress them, (along with) children and women, and plunder their goods.

Both decrees use the triple formula of "destroy, kill, and annihilate." They also grant the victors a right to the spoils. Most troubling of all, however, is that both decrees provide for the destruction of women and children.

There have been a number of attempts to circumvent the moral difficulty that this decree presents. Most widely cited is that of Gordis,[18] who argued that "women and children" should be read in connection with the word "them," as part of those covered under Haman's original decree: "to destroy ... any who oppress 'them, their women and children, and their goods to plunder'" (cf. also Baldwin, 97–98; Bechtel, 75; and the NIV, which translates the verse similarly; Mangano [109] seems favorably disposed to this position, but states that the question is moot, since the text later speaks only of killing men. This point will be addressed in the commentary on 9:6). Thus, according to Gordis, the decree was not granting the Jews the right to kill women or children or take plunder, but merely reporting the kind of behavior that would be subject to reprisal.

While it is easy to understand why Gordis and those who have accepted this interpretation would want to distance the Jewish heroes from such barbarism, the interpretation is not very persuasive, based on contextual and grammatical difficulties. First, there is the matter of the parallelism between Haman's decree and Mordecai's decree. Haman had given the Jews' enemies permission to kill men, women, and children, and to plunder their goods. Mordecai's reversal would logically include the same provisions (see further Bush, 447). Furthermore, if the narrator meant for us to understand the children and women as those of the Jews, we should find a pronominal suf. attached to the nouns (*their* women and children), as well as the direct obj. marker indicating that they are objs. of the verb "attack." Finally, if the Jews had not been granted permission to plunder the oppressors, the narrator would not have found it noteworthy that the Jews

18. R. Gordis, "Studies in the Esther Narrative," *JBL* 95 (1976): 49–53.

refrained from taking plunder (9:10, 15). As repellent as it appears, the most straightforward interpretation of the decree is that the Jews were given the right to wreak wholesale slaughter on their attackers.

In the ANE context, however, such a provision would not be considered immoral or unjust. Given that these people frequently passed on grudges from generation to generation as a matter of "honor," the destruction of children assured that the conquerors would not have to fight the same wars over and over again. In the Esther narrative, it may be an especially fitting provision. I have argued that this story is presented as a "rematch" between Saul (Mordecai) and Agag (Haman). The Jews had been ordered to utterly annihilate the Amalekites, including their men, women, and children (Exod 17:14; Deut 25:19; 1 Sam 15:3). Now, they would have their chance to fulfill that command.

Finally, the provision to "plunder" the goods of the attackers is also mandated by Haman's decree being included this provision. Nonetheless, it is somewhat troubling, because it makes the enterprise seem somewhat mercenary. When the day of the action arrives, the Jews actually do not take any of the plunder (Esth 9:10, 15), eliminating any appearance of impropriety.

8:12 For the significance of the thirteenth day of the twelfth month, see the commentary on Esth 3:7.

8:13 In Esth 3:14, "all people" were told to be ready for the day when the Jews were to be destroyed. They were to make preparations to attack and plunder the Jewish people. In this decree, it is the Jews who are to "be ready." They are to assemble armies and make provisions to defend themselves against any who would still dare to attack them.

The word "vengeance" (נָקָם, *nāqam*) is very significant in this context. For Baldwin (98), this word provides the moral imperative for the slaughter: "This was justice, not revenge." As Fox notes, "*NQM* never refers to a simple defense or rescue, but everywhere designates a punitive action and presupposes a prior wrong, that is, some offense to which the avenging party is responding."[19] In this initial decree, at least, the Jews are not simply given carte blanche to do away with anyone they do not like. It is possible that the decree could be understood broadly to refer to anyone who has afflicted the Jews in the past. It is apparent throughout the narrative that there is some stigma attached to being Jewish, since Mordecai wished to conceal Esther's Jewishness. The Jews might well have been subject to prejudice, and this vengeance might have included anyone who had insulted or abused the Jews in the past. More likely, however, it specifically empowered

19. Fox, *Character and Ideology*, 101.

the Jews to respond to anyone who followed Haman's decree and attacked them on the thirteenth of Adar.

8:14 Though the day of attack is still nine months away, Mordecai's decree (like Haman's edict; 3:14) goes forth in great haste. Indeed, there is even more urgency attached to this edict than Haman's. Some commentators have expressed puzzlement over the need for speed: as Berlin (78) notes, Herodotus claimed that due to the great efficiency of the Persian postal system, it took only three months for a message to circulate through the entire empire (*Hist.* 5.52–3). Nonetheless, it would take some time to assemble, equip, and train the Jews into an army, so the haste is understandable on purely pragmatic grounds.

There are also literary considerations at play. Each detail shows how Mordecai and his decree do not merely parallel Haman and his decree, but go it one better: Xerxes gives Haman the signet ring only when he needs to authorize a decree (3:10), but Mordecai receives it from the start; Haman's decree goes forth by couriers (3:13), while Mordecai's goes forth by couriers mounted on special royal steeds; Haman's decree goes out in "haste" (3:15), but Mordecai's decree goes out with "urgent haste." Mordecai has triumphed over Haman in every particular.

8:15 Mordecai's new clothes illustrate his new status. As noted earlier, a change of clothing in this narrative typically indicates a change of position. This motif is not unique to the book of Esther: both Joseph (Gen 41:42) and Daniel (Dan 5:7, 29) also received stately robes to accompany their promotion to high status by foreign monarchs. What is more, Xerxes' command to clothe Mordecai in Xerxes' own robe in 6:11 now seems almost prophetic. The honor he received at that time foreshadowed the honor he now receives from the king.

Though Mordecai undoubtedly received new garments when he was promoted to vizier, the narrative withholds the description until this point. There is a reason for the delay: once again, reversal is at work. When Mordecai had heard of Haman's decree, he had taken off his garments and clothed himself in sackcloth (4:1). So attired, he could not enter into the king's gate (4:2). Now, when he issues his own decree, he is clothed in splendor. He can stand in the very presence of the king.

Upon Mordecai's head is a golden headdress (עֲטֶרֶת, *ʿăṭeret,* typically translated "crown"). The noun comes from a root meaning "surround" and may refer to any ornament that is worn on the head. The term is used to designate the royal crown in 2 Sam 12:30, but merely some kind of jewelry in Ezek 23:42. It is uncertain what Mordecai was wearing, but it is somewhat misleading to refer to it as a "crown," which in English usually implies kingship.

The word translated "mantle" (תַּכְרִיךְ, *takrîk*), like the word for "headdress" (עֲטֶרֶת, *ʿăṭeret*), derives from a verb meaning "encircle." In later Heb., it denotes a burial shroud. Here, it could refer to a garment, or it might refer to some other kind of headdress, as suggested by the LXX, which has Mordecai wearing both a "crown" and a "diadem."[20]

The entire city of Susa celebrates Mordecai's elevation. This detail does not necessarily imply that Mordecai was especially popular, since such festivities would naturally accompany the appointment of a new vizier (especially if his predecessor had been a fop). On the other hand, however, it is apparent that Mordecai was known in the city, since Harbona had observed that Haman had erected a pike for the Jewish hero (Esth 7:9). The situation of this underdog might have struck a chord with the Persian masses. In any case, the celebration continues the trend of reversals: at Haman's decree, the city of Susa was thrown into confusion (3:15); but at Mordecai's decree, it rejoices.

8:16 The pattern of reversal continues. The Jews, who had responded to Haman's decree with mourning, weeping, lamentation, and fasting (4:3), respond to Mordecai's decree with light (that is, happiness; cf. Psa 97:11), joy, gladness, and feasting. Like every other major event of the narrative, the proclamation of Mordecai's decree is celebrated with banqueting (מִשְׁתֶּה, *mišteh*).

8:17 The phrase "peoples of the land" here clearly means Gentiles, those who are natives of the countries where the Jews dwell. The phrase "people of the land," using the sg. noun, is used to refer both to Canaanites (e.g., Gen 23:7; Ezra 4:4) and Israelites (e.g., Exod 5:5; Lev 4:27). The pl. form, however, always refers to Israel's pagan neighbors (e.g., Deut 28:10; Josh 4:24; 2 Chr 6:33). In the Mishnah, the phrase "people of the land" becomes a pejorative appellation for Jews who are not careful about keeping the oral law.

The meaning of the verb translated "became Jews" (מִתְיַהֲדִים, *mityahădîm*) is controversial. It occurs nowhere else in the OT, but it appears to be the Heb. equivalent of the verb Ἑλληνίζω, which literally means "Hellenize" (that is, act like a Greek). "To Hellenize" could simply mean "to speak Greek," or it could mean a deeper adoption of Greek customs and values. The same ambiguity applies to the term "became Jews." Could the word here merely mean that the Gentiles tried to "act Jewish," in order to avert Jewish wrath? This interpretation does not seem likely because, in general, the lives of the Gentiles were not endangered. The Jews had not been

20. See further K. De Troyer, "On Crowns and Diadems from Kings, Queens, Horses and Men," *IOSCS Congress* 9 (1997): 360–61.

authorized to kill all Gentiles, but only those who attacked them. Another possibility is that the word refers to a sincere attempt by the Gentiles to convert to Judaism as both a faith and a culture. The LXX certainly understood the word in this manner, adding that the Gentiles circumcised themselves—certainly a sign of sincere conversion and not mere disguise. We might then compare their actions to those of other famous biblical proselytes, like the harlot Rahab, whose fear of the Israelites caused her to worship their God (Josh 2:11). The apocryphal book of Judith also features such a conversion, an Ammonite who became a believer in Yahweh when he saw how the Jews had conquered the Assyrians (Jdt 14:10). The later rabbis compared these converts to the "lion proselytes" of Samaria, those who adopted the Jewish faith because of their fear of the lions that God sent to punish idolaters in the land (2 Kgs 17:24–28).[21] They looked on such conversions with disdain.

While the nature of the "conversion" is uncertain, the significance for the narrator and his audience is clear. First, it represents yet another example of the "reversal" motif. Early in the story, Esther had to conceal her Jewishness. Though we are not told why, we might infer that there was some kind of danger to or prejudice against Jews. Now, it is the Gentiles who are afraid, and they try to hide their non-Jewishness. But this reversal is not merely a literary device. It is, in fact, connected to one of the main purposes of the Esther narrative: to encourage Jewish resistance to foreign cultural domination. The scenario envisioned here is part of a "hidden transcript" similar to the folklore of African American slaves and other oppressed peoples.[22] In such tales, the oppressed show their resentment of dominant groups by subtle insults or mockery expressed in forms or venues that would be accessible only to members of the oppressed group. A book like Esther, written in Heb., is clearly designed for exclusively Jewish consumption. This report of Gentiles converting to Judaism is included because of the boost it gives to Jewish esteem by demonstrating the fear the Jews inspire in their enemies and the desire of the nations to identify with the Jewish people. (Actually, the Jews of this era were not especially interested in winning proselytes to their race.[23]) This story is designed for Jewish consumption, and its nationalistic spirit will become increasingly evident in these last two chapters.

21. *b. Qidd.* 75b–76a.

22. See "Esther and Resistance" in the introduction.

23. Studies of Jewish proselytism almost invariably focus on the later Second Temple period, for which sources are more plentiful and evidence more easily interpreted. See, e.g., S. J. D. Cohen, "Crossing the Boundary and Becoming Jewish," *HTR* 82 (1989): 13–33; S. McKnight, *A Light among the Gentiles: Jewish Missionary Activity in the Second Temple Period* (Minneapolis: Fortress, 1991).

What is the "fear" that so moves the Gentiles that they want to become Jewish? The term used here (פַּחַד, *paḥad*) refers to a nearly debilitating fear, one that induces trembling. The word is used often for fear of Yahweh (e.g., Isa 2:10; 2 Chr 17:10), but also of the fear of the military might of Israel (Deut 2:25; 11:25). In this case, the most obvious reading would be that the Gentiles feared annihilation—that they would be intimidated by the Jews' new political and military power and so would want to switch to what looks to be the winning team (so Dommerhausen, 110; Bush, 449).[24] That obvious answer, however, is not altogether satisfying. The Gentiles who did not attack the Jews would have nothing to fear from the Jews, since Mordecai's decree only permitted the Jews to destroy those who attacked them. Is it, then, a fear of the Jews' God—an awe of the numinous power that protects the Jewish people—that prompts these conversions, as Clines maintains?[25] There are certainly examples in the Heb. Bible of Gentiles who fear the God of Israel (Josh 2:9; Exod 15:16; Psa 105:38), though these episodes do not appear to result in conversions, or even in Gentiles trying to emulate the Jews. Since this scenario is a reversal of the earlier relationship between Jews and Gentiles, the most likely explanation is that the narrator is projecting onto the Gentiles the fear that the Jews had of their Gentile overlords—a fear of their power, influence, and disdain. Since the Jews now have the upper hand, the threat exists that they will become as insensitive as the Gentile overlords had been. The Jews now pose such a threat that the Gentiles must hide from them by becoming Jewish themselves.

Biblical Theology Comments

8:2 There is a measure of moral ambivalence in Esther's transfer of Haman's property to Mordecai. On the one hand, there is the matter of the "ban." If we can understand the clash between Mordecai and Haman as a rematch of Saul-Agag, then the same rules should apply in this case as in the first. Saul lost his kingdom because he thought to spare some of the Amalekites' property: not for his own personal gain, but to offer as a sacrifice to Yahweh (1 Sam 15). Mordecai, on the other hand, will be directly benefitting from Haman's wealth. There is not even a pretense of piety about his newfound prosperity.

On the other hand, there is certainly some poetic irony in this development. The material resources that Haman would have used to destroy the Jews are now in the hands of a Jew. The scenario is somewhat reminiscent of the "plundering of the Egyptians." When the Israelites came out of Egypt, they were instructed to ask their Egyptian neighbors for articles of

24. See also Fox, *Character and Ideology*, 106.

25. Clines, *Esther Scroll*, 41.

silver and gold. When they left Egypt, they took these items with them and thus "plundered the Egyptians" (Exod 12:36).[26] The loot they took can be viewed as compensation to the Israelites for the labor they performed as slaves in Egypt. Similarly, it is possible to view Mordecai's windfall as compensation for the distress he suffered because of Haman. Also, it is obvious that Haman is a wicked man, and his possession of wealth could be viewed as an injustice. According to Prov 13:22, "He who is good will leave an inheritance to his grandchildren, and stored up for the righteous is the wealth of a sinner." It is altogether fitting that Haman should lose everything; the more questionable aspect is whether Mordecai should have benefitted in the process.

8:11 One of the more distressing aspects of the book of Esther is the provision of Mordecai's edict allowing the Jews to kill women and children. There are basically two ways we can approach this aspect of the text: we can argue that Mordecai's decree did not actually grant such a right, or that it did. I have argued above in the commentary that it is highly likely that Mordecai did, in fact, grant the Jews the right to massacre women and children. The question, then, is how such a position can be morally justified.

It must be admitted at the outset that this problem is not merely one found in the book of Esther. There are several occasions in the OT where Israelites were commanded by God to kill women and children (along with the Amalekites [1 Sam 15:3], we can include Heshbon [Deut 3:6], Bashan [Num 21:35], Jericho [Josh 6:17–21], Ai [Josh 8:24–26], and other cities of Canaan). The case of Mordecai's edict is somewhat different, because it is not altogether certain that Mordecai is acting under divine direction. But even so, the problem of Mordecai's edict cannot be considered in isolation: it must be viewed in light of the general OT ethics of war.

It is impossible to give adequate treatment in a few paragraphs to a subject that has filled several academic tomes, but I can briefly summarize some of the positions commentators have taken on this issue in Esther:

1. Berlin (77) notes that similar, and far worse, atrocities were routinely committed in ancient warfare. This statement is undoubtedly true, but it does not provide a theological rationale for the Jews' slaughter of defenseless noncombatants, since God's standards of justice should not be based on human conventions.

26. Since the days of Augustine, this passage has been employed metaphorically to refer to the use of secular wisdom/arts for Christian enrichment (see Augustine, *On Christian Doctrine* 2.60), which is a more comfortable interpretation than the literal understanding that the people of God have permission to rob their neighbors.

2. Levenson (110–11) notes the repugnance of the possibility of slaughtering women and children, but contends that "the symmetry of the two decrees" issued by Haman and Mordecai required that a provision for such barbarity be included in both. In this case, the rationale is literary rather than historical/cultural (cf. also Bush, 453). Once again, however, it does not address the moral problems raised by the slaughter of innocents.
3. A number of commentators (e.g., Mangano, 109) argue that the question of whether women and children were included in the decree is moot, since chapter 9 only speaks about the killing of men. But this point is itself moot; women and children were rarely included among casualty counts from ancient (or even modern) battles. Nor does it address the morality of the decree itself.
4. Several scholars (e.g., Jobes, 184; Laniak, 253; Levenson, 110–11) see the slaughter of the women and children as a completion of the destruction of the Amalekites. In that case, the issue of morality is shifted back from Mordecai's decree to God's decree for the destruction of the Amalekites (Exod 17:14; 1 Sam 15:3). Since the extermination of the Amalekites is treated as a matter of divine judgment, the destruction of the Jews' enemies in Esther—women and children included—must then be viewed in the same light. While this explanation is appealing because of its literary symmetry, it is difficult to imagine that all the Jews' enemies were considered to be Amalekites.

One consideration that has received little attention is that the destruction of women and children prescribed by Mordecai's decree—and Yahweh's earlier decrees—must be understood in light of the corporate responsibility characteristic of OT thought. The idea of "corporate personality," once prominent in biblical studies, has been largely abandoned in current scholarship, but the notion of "corporate responsibility" is well recognized. Essentially, it means that an entire family or ethnic group could be held responsible for the actions of an individual or individuals within the group. When Achan stole some of the plunder of Jericho, God proclaimed, "Israel has sinned; they have transgressed my covenant" (Josh 7:11). All Israel suffered because of his guilt when Israel was defeated at Ai (7:1–5), and Achan's entire family was executed for the sins of this one man (7:24–25). Similarly, when David sinned by conducting a census of Israel, God sent a plague that destroyed seventy thousand men (2 Sam 24:1–25). The entire nation was punished for one man's transgression. In a similar manner, in the book of Esther the women and children of Israel's enemies bore the same guilt as the men. While this concept may be repugnant to us—indeed, the OT itself seems at times to repudiate it (Jer 31:29–30; Ezek 18:1–3)—there are positive elements to the idea of corporate responsibility, because it goes hand-in-hand with corporate election. Kaminsky notes,

> Before utterly rejecting all corporate notions as primitive one should note the centrality of such corporate ideas in Israelite theology. In many respects the concept of divine mercy is predicated on being treated as a favored member of a group rather than being judged exactly according to one's own merits. … The OT's message is not directed to a loose configuration of individuals but to a living community called the people of Israel.[27]

Application and Devotional Implications

What can be made of the "conversions" of the Gentiles in this section? In modern times, the power of fear as a motivator is often underappreciated or even despised. But in the Bible, fear often plays an important role. Humanity's dominion over creation is ensured by the fear the lower creatures have of us (Gen 9:2). The Israelites conquered Canaan because fear had gripped the inhabitants of the land (Num 22:3; Deut 2:25; Josh 2:9). But fear is not merely a force of domination and destruction. The OT makes frequent reference to the fear of Yahweh and its power to influence human behavior for the better (Deut 4:10; 5:29; 6:2; 10:12; 13:4, 11, etc.). Fear of Yahweh is the "beginning of wisdom" (Psa 11:10; Prov 1:7) and motivates us to turn away from evil (Prov 16:6). In Deuteronomy, loving God and fearing God stand side by side in a complementary relationship (Deut 6:1–5; 10:12). They may do so in the life of the Christian as well. While perfect love might indeed cast out all fear (1 John 4:18), most Christians' relationship with God will involve elements of both love and fear from time to time (2 Cor 5:11; 1 Pet 2:17). Such fear is not a paralyzing terror or anxiousness that drives us away from God, but a healthy respect for God's power and a recognition of His sovereignty.

We may not be certain that it was fear of the Jews' God that led to the Gentile conversions, but there can be little question that these conversions were a positive outcome. Pagans became followers of the true God. In modern Western society, unfortunately, the trend is the opposite: Christianity is in decline, while paganism, humanism, and atheism are on the rise. Perhaps part of the reason is that we Christians have deemphasized the power and judgment of God and overemphasized the love and forgiveness of God. The idea of a God who judges sin and holds people accountable for their actions has become passé, and "There is no fear of God in this place" (Gen 20:11). Perhaps our ineffectiveness in evangelizing the modern West

27. J. Kaminsky, "Corporate Personality," in *EDB*, 286–87.

can be attributed in part to our seeming to have embraced a God who does not scare anyone.

Selected Bibliography

Clines, D. J. A. *The Esther Scroll: The Story of the Story*. JSOTSup 30. Sheffield, UK: JSOT Press, 1984.

De Troyer, K. *The End of the Alpha Text of Esther: Translation and Narrative Technique in MT 8:1–17, LXX 8:1–17, and AT 7:14–41*. SBLSCS 48. Atlanta: Society of Biblical Literature, 2000.

———. "On Crowns and Diadems from Kings, Queens, Horses and Men." *IOSCS Congress* 9 (1997): 355–67.

Dorothy, C. V. *The Books of Esther: Structure, Genre and Textual Integrity*. Sheffield, UK: Sheffield Academic Press, 1997.

Driver, G. R. *Aramaic Documents of the Fifth Century B. C.* Oxford: Oxford University Press, 1954.

Fox, M. V. *Character and Ideology in the Book of Esther*. 2nd ed. Grand Rapids: Eerdmans, 2001.

Gordis, R. "Studies in the Esther Narrative." *JBL* 95 (1976): 43–58.

Haupt, P. "Critical Notes on Esther." *AJSL* 24 (1907–1908): 97–186.

Kaminsky, J. "Corporate Personality." In *EDB*, 285–87.

Klingbeil, G. "רכש and Esther 8,10.14 : A Semantic Note." *ZAW* 107 (1995): 301–3.

Tawil, H. "Two Notes on the Treaty Terminology of the Sefire Inscriptions." *CBQ* 42 (1980): 30–37.

The Jews' Victories over their Enemies (9:1–19)

Translation

1 Now in the twelfth month—that is, the month of Adar—on its thirteenth
day, when the command of the king and his decree were about to be done,
on the very day when the enemies of the Jews hoped to have power over
them, it was reversed, as the Jews received power over those who hated
them. **2** The Jews mustered in their cities in all the provinces of King Xerxes
to stretch out their hand against those who sought their harm. Not a man
could stand against them, because fear of them had fallen on all peoples.
3 All the nobles of the provinces and the satraps and the governors and
those who conduct the king's business were assisting the Jews, because fear
of Mordecai had fallen upon them. **4** For Mordecai was important in the
king's house, and his fame was spreading throughout all the provinces, so
that the man Mordecai was becoming more and more important.

5 The Jews struck down all their enemies with the stroke of the sword,
and with killing and destruction, and doing whatever they pleased to those

who hated them. **6** In Susa the citadel itself the Jews killed and destroyed five hundred men, **7** and also Parshandatha and Dalphon and Aspatha **8** and Poratha and Adalia and Aridatha **9** and Parmashta and Arisai and Aridai and Vaizatha, **10** the ten sons of Haman the son of Hammedatha, the enemy of the Jews, they killed, but they laid no hand on the plunder. **11** On that very day, the number of those killed in Susa the citadel came before the king.

12 Then the king said to Esther the queen, "In Susa the citadel alone[28] the Jews have killed and destroyed five hundred men, and the ten sons of Haman—what must they have done in the rest of the king's provinces![29] Now what is your request? It shall be given to you. And what more do you seek? It shall be done." **13** And Esther said, "If it seems good to the king, let it be granted for the Jews who are in Susa to be allowed to do tomorrow also according to this day's edict, and the ten sons of Haman let them hang on pikes." **14** So the king ordered it[30] to be made so, and a decree was issued in Susa, and the ten sons of Haman were hanged. **15** The Jews who were in Susa were gathered also on the fourteenth day of the month of Adar, and they killed in Susa three hundred men. But they did not stretch out their hands for the plunder.

16 Now the remainder of the Jews who were in the king's provinces had mustered, and defended their lives, and got rest from their enemies, and killed seventy-five thousand of those who hated them, but they laid no hands on the plunder. **17** It was on the thirteenth day of the month of Adar, and they rested on the fourteenth day of that month[31] and made it a day of feasting and rejoicing. **18** The Jews who were in Susa, however, mustered on the thirteenth day and on the fourteenth and rested on its fifteenth day, making it a day of feasting and rejoicing. **19** Therefore the Jews of the villages, who live in the open towns, hold the fourteenth day of the month of Adar as a day for rejoicing and feasting, as a holiday,[32] and as a day on which they send portions of food[33] to one another.

---

28. As in v. 6, "Susa the citadel" is in the emphatic position, and so the translation "In Susa the citadel alone."

29. The question here is surely rhetorical rather than an actual inquiry, since the king does not wait for an answer before posing his next inquiry.

30. Lit., "said."

31. Lit., "the fourteenth day in it."

32. Lit., "a good day."

33. Lit., "portions." Food is implied.

Textual Notes

3.a. In the LXX, "those who conduct the king's business" is translated "the royal scribes."

5.a. The LXX omits this entire verse.

7.a. The AT lists five names of people who were killed, then "the ten sons of Haman" without names. The LXX lists the names of Haman's sons, though they vary considerably from the MT versions.

7.b. LXX has Φαρσαννεσταιν for MT פַּרְשַׁנְדָּתָא.

7.c. LXX has Δελφων for MT דַּלְפוֹן.

7.d. LXX has Φασγα for MT אַסְפָּתָא.

8.a. LXX has Φαρδαθα for MT פּוֹרָתָא.

8.b. LXX has Βαρεα for MT אֲדַלְיָא.

8.c. LXX has Σαρβαχα for MT אֲרִידָתָא.

9.a. LXX has Μαρμασιμα for MT פַּרְמַשְׁתָּא.

9.b. LXX has Αρουφαιον for MT אֲרִיסַי.

9.c. LXX has Αρσαιον for MT אֲרִדַי.

9.d. LXX has Ζαβουθαιθαν for MT וַיְזָתָא.

10.a. LXX and AT insert "the Bougean" (Βουγαίος) after "son of Hammedatha" (בֶּן־הַמְּדָתָא).

11.a. LXX omits "the citadel" (הַבִּירָה).

13.a. According to the AT, Esther requests, "Let it be granted to the Jews to kill and plunder whoever they want."

16.a. According to the LXX, fifteen thousand were killed in the provinces. According to the AT, the total was seventy thousand. The reading of seventy-five thousand is supported by Josephus and the Syr.

19.a. The noun הַפְּרְוזִים differs in the *Kethib** and the *Qere**. Comparison to the noun הַפְּרָזִי ("open country"; Deut 3:5; 1 Sam 6:18) indicates that the *Qere* is correct.

19.b. The LXX adds that the Jews of large walled cities celebrate on the fifteenth of Adar, apparently trying to clarify the question of when Jews outside Susa celebrated the victory.

Commentary

Esther 9:1–19 is concerned with the actual battles and their aftermath. It is composed of three main divisions, each of which consists of two units. The first division (9:1–10) tells of the first day of victories throughout the provinces of the Persian Empire. It can be further divided into two units: vv. 1–5 tell of the general Jewish successes throughout the empire, and vv. 6–10 focus on the victories that occur in the citadel of Susa, including the destruction of Haman's ten sons. The second division of the section, vv. 11–15, focuses on the second day of fighting. It begins with Esther requesting of the king that the Jews may do for yet another day as they had done on the first day; then it reports the death of five hundred in the city. The third section consists of the reports of celebration. It consists of vv. 16–17, which tell of the Jews' victory in the province and the rejoicing that followed, and vv. 18–19, which tell of the victory in Susa and the resulting celebration.

9:1 The month of Adar would correspond to February or March, 473 BC. The first verse of this chapter consists of a single long, complex sentence, very similar to the syntactic constructions found in Esth 1. This kind of construction is not especially unusual in biblical Heb., but it does have a tendency to slow the pace of the narrative down and focus the reader's attention. In this case, it is likely that the focus here is intentional, since this verse essentially summarizes the message of the book of Esther: "it was reversed." The verb used in this phrase (נַהֲפוֹךְ, *nahăpôk*) can literally mean "flip over" (2 Kgs 21:13; Hos 7:8). The plot has been flipped over, like all the attempted actions against the Jews in this narrative. Now it is the Jews who are on top, and their enemies who are on the receiving end of grief.

The root of the same word occurs also in Deut 32:20, "And he said, 'I shall hide my face from them; I shall see what their end will be, for they are a twisted (תַּהְפֻּכֹות, *tahpukôt*) generation, sons in whom there is no faithfulness.'" This verse echoes the language of Deut 31:19, which is cited in the Talmud (*b. Hul.* 139b) as the place where Esther can be found in the Torah ("I will hide" in Heb. sounds like the name "Esther"). It is possible that the author/editor of Esther is making a deliberate allusion to Deut 32 to emphasize the idea that Yahweh has "hidden his face" in the Esther narrative.[34]

34. See further the discussion in the introduction, "The Absence of God."

The verb "have power" or "rule" (שָׁלַט, *šālaṭ*) is not used of royal power, and often has the sense of "domineering" (cf. Neh 5:15). As Fox notes, the ability to exert one's will over others is one of the central themes of Esther.[35] In chapter 1, the issue was Xerxes' ability to exert his will over Vashti, culminating in the broader issue of men being able to exert authority over their wives. In chapter 2, it is a matter of Esther gaining dominion over the other women taken in to Xerxes' harem. In chapter 3, the matter of Haman's ability to exert authority over Mordecai comes to the forefront when Mordecai refuses to bow before the vizier. At the end of that chapter and through chapter 7, the issue at stake is Haman's ability to exert control over the Jews, forcing them to capitulate to his will by exterminating them. Here, it is the matter of the Jews taking mastery over those who had sought to have mastery over them.

The use of the word "haters" (שֹׂנְאִים, *śōnʾîm*) as a synonym for "enemies" here, in 9:5, and in 9:16, is illustrative of "hatred" in biblical Heb. being more than merely an emotion. "Hatred" is frequently associated with rejection and the intention of doing physical harm.[36] The words "enemies" and "haters" occur as synonyms in Deut 30:7, which also speaks of a reversal, where God reassembles the scattered Israelites and places on their enemies the curses that he had formerly laid on them.

9:2 The Jews assembled and formed armies in every city where there was a substantial Jewish population. We should suspect that in most cities, Jews formed a distinct minority and could have been overwhelmed if the entire populace had decided to attack. Most people, however, did not attack them because of their fear of the Jews' power and influence. The language here shows a clear parallel to that of the conquest narratives: "No one can take a stand against you; your dread and your fear Yahweh your God will put on the surface of all the land where you tread, just as he promised to you" (Deut 11:25). As in the case of the Israel's conquest of the Canaanites, terror of the Jews rendered the attacks ineffective. We might also see here an echo of the Israel-Amalek animosity: according to Deut 25:17–19, the Amalekites would attack the weak and stragglers among the Israelites because Amalek "did not fear God." Now, their fear made them powerless to stand against Israel.

Once again, it is stated that the Jews destroyed only those who sought to destroy them. Apparently, that means those who physically attacked

35. M. Fox, *Character and Ideology in the Book of Esther*, 2nd ed. (Grand Rapids: Eerdmans, 2001), 108.

36. See T. S. Laniak, *Shame and Honor in the Book of Esther* (Atlanta: Scholars Press, 1998), 140n38.

them, and not merely those who wished them harm. The narrative seems clear that the Jews' intention is not simply to go on a murderous rampage, but to wreak vengeance on their attackers.

9:3 The officials are no longer compelled to assist in the destruction of the Jews, and they choose not to do so. Indeed, instead of attacking them, the local officials are aiding the Jews in preparing their defenses. Recognizing that Mordecai is now a man of great influence, they do not want to get on his bad side by aiding the Jews' enemies.

The verb here translated "assisting" (נָשָׂא, *nāśāʾ*) is literally "lift, bear, carry." The same verb is used in Esth 3:1 for the promotion of Haman. Once again, we see an illustration of the reversal of circumstances: previously it was Haman who was lifted up, but now it is the Jews.

It is interesting to note that in this verse, the order in which the officials are named is different from the way they are presented in 3:12 and 8:9. There, they are listed in descending order of influence. Here, it is possible that the "nobles of the provinces," being the most local officials, would have provided the most direct assistance, but there is little to be said about the order of the governors and satraps. The people who "conduct the king's business" were not named in 8:9. In light of 3:9, it appears that these people are financial administrators. They would not have had the authority to enact the king's decree, but they would have been able to assist the Jews in mustering their forces by providing loans or other resources, and perhaps by placing Jews in government jobs. Very likely, the narrator wants us to understand that some kind of affirmative action program has been adopted where the Jews are receiving preferential treatment from government officials.

9:4 The adj. "great" (גָּדוֹל, *gādôl*) can be used with a variety of meanings in biblical Heb., as in English. Here, it apparently refers to Mordecai's political influence, and so I have translated it "important." Dommerhausen (113) argues that the phrase "the man Mordecai" is designed to indicate that Mordecai is a significant individual, but the argument seems based on impression rather than evidence: in most other occurrences of this construction (Judg 17:5, "the man Micah"; 1 Sam 1:21,"the man Elkanah"; 1 Kgs 11:28, "the man Jeroboam"; Dan 9:21, "the man Gabriel"), there is no special importance or influence attached to the figure designated in this way. On the other hand, Gerleman (132) is almost certainly correct in drawing attention to the similarities between this phrase and Exod 11:3, "The man Moses was very great in the land of Egypt." The narrator has certainly made a deliberate allusion to Exod 11, drawing yet another parallel between the deliverers Moses and Mordecai. Also, it implies a parallel between the commemoration of Purim and that of Passover, which is the subject of Exod 11. The narrator draws a connection between the two great acts of national deliverance, just as the later rabbis would do (see *y. Meg.* 1.5).[37]

9:5 As a clear indicator of how complete the reversal of fates has been, the text states that the Jews wrought "killing" (הֶרֶג, *hereg*) and "destruction" (אַבְדָן, *ʾabdān*) on those who hated them, using nouns that are cognates of the verbs that appeared in Haman's decree (Esth 3:13). There, the Gentiles were ordered "to kill and to destroy" (לַהֲרֹג וּלְאַבֵּד, *lahărōg ûlʾabbēd*) the Jews.

The phrase, "killed all their enemies" sounds somewhat ambiguous, since it does not explicitly state that the Jews killed only those who attacked them. Paton (283) interprets it to refer to a wholesale slaughter of any who were hostile toward the Jews. But while it is conceivable that some of the Jews' enemies would choose not to attack them, that does not seem to be the implication of the narrative. According to Mordecai's edict, the Jews were given permission to kill only those who initiated violence against them. On this first day, at least, it is apparent that the casualties fall into this group only.

The phrase "doing whatever they pleased" sounds rather more sinister. Given the kind of atrocities that normally accompanied war in the ancient world, it is possible to imagine a great deal of cruelty reflected in that phrase. A similar phrase, however, occurs in Dan 11:16, where the "king of the north" will do as he pleases to all his enemies, and in Neh 9:24, which recalls the way the Israelites did whatever they pleased to the Canaanites during the conquest.[38] This second parallel is especially significant, since it is virtually certain that the book of Esther is linking the Jews' battle against their enemies to the "holy war" motif of the Pentateuch, Joshua, and Judges, fulfilling the command to destroy the Amalekites and other peoples of the land of Canaan as they had failed to do so long before.

9:6 The placing of the prepositional phrase "in Susa the citadel" at the front of the sentence places emphasis on it. The narrator is acknowledging the unusual circumstances that would allow the killing of so many people right outside the king's palace.

There must have been a substantial Jewish population in the citadel of Susa, if they were able to kill five hundred men there. Given the relatively small size of the fortified section (it covered only ten acres), five hundred men would constitute a substantial segment of the citadel's population. Fox,

37. See M. Wechsler, "The Purim-Passover Connection: A Reflection of Jewish Exegetical Tradition in the Peshitta Book of Esther," *JBL* 117 (1998): 321–27, for further discussion of the link between these feasts in rabbinic tradition.

38. Fox, *Character and Ideology*, 109.

Jones, and others see here a gross hyperbole.[39] Philips (661), on the other hand, believes it is likely that there was widespread "long-festering hatred" against the Jews that took this opportunity to surface. This explanation seems strained in light of the reports of joyous celebration throughout the city that accompanied Mordecai's promotion (Esth 8:15). In *Tg. Esth. I*, the glossators add that these men represent "all the chiefs of the house of Amalek." Later Jewish tradition wants to make explicit a point that might be implicit in the MT: it is not only Haman who represents the Amalekites in this struggle, but all those whom the Jews slay are representative of that hated race.

9:7–9 The destruction of Haman's ten sons would have been a prudent political action, in order to prevent Haman's descendants from taking vengeance against the Jews (so Jobes, 198). Nonetheless, it serves here as an important literary device, demonstrating Haman's total defeat. In Esth 5:11, Haman bragged to his wife and friends about "his riches, his many sons, and all the ways the king had promoted him." Each of these sources of pride has now been stripped away and given over to the Jews: his riches were given to Esther in 8:1; his promotions given to Mordecai in 8:2; and now his sons, too, have fallen into the hands of his enemies. With the death of his sons, Haman's downfall is complete.

The names of Haman's sons are controversial. Paton (70–71) lists a number of possible derivations, and more conjecture has been added in the last century. None have been definitely identified in any ancient texts—which may not be surprising, given the difficulty of transcribing Persian names into Heb. (witness the confusion regarding the identification of "Ahasuerus," who was identified in the LXX as Artaxerxes). Yet in spite of the uncertainties, these names have been cited frequently as evidence of the book's authenticity. In ancient times, it was common practice in many lands for parents to give their children names that incorporated the name of a deity: i.e., "Nathaniel" means "gift of God"; "Joshua" means "Yah(weh) saves." According to Yamauchi, Haman's sons bear names that incorporate names of Persian *daiva*, or spirits.[40] The *daiva* were still worshiped as gods by some Persians in the time of Xerxes, but as Zoroastrianism took hold in the realm (during the days of Xerxes' successor Artaxerxes I), the *daiva* came to be regarded as demons. Yamauchi notes especially that the name

39. Ibid., 109; B. W. Jones, "Two Misconceptions about the Book of Esther," *CBQ* 39 (1977): 180.
40. E. Yamauchi, *Persia and the Bible* (Grand Rapids: Baker, 1997), 237–38. See also J. Duchesne-Guillemin, "Le noms des eunuques d'Assuérus," *Le Muséon* 66 (1953): 108.

Vaizatha (9:9) appears authentic, since the *ai* diphthong shifted to *e* in the Persian language between the reigns of Xerxes and Artaxerxes. Thus, he argues, these names reflect the language of the era of Xerxes rather than that of his successors. It must be borne in mind, however, that these interpretations are conjectural, given the imprecision of transliteration into Heb.

A different possible explanation for these names is that they were not meant to be historically accurate, but entertaining. Radday argues that these names would have sounded funny to the hearers, but they might have also suggested humorous imagery.[41] I have noted earlier that the names of Xerxes (Ahashuerus; see commentary on Esth 1:1) and Haman (see commentary on Esth 3:1) may be designed to sound humorous. At least some of the names listed here also sound very similar to Heb. words that would have elicited smiles from the audience. The first name, Parshandatha (פַּרְשַׁנְדָּתָא, *paršandātā*ʾ), sets the tone: it looks and sounds very similar to the noun פַּרְשְׁדֹנָה (*paršĕdōnâ*), which occurs only in Judg 3:22, where it apparently means "excrement." The name Dalphon looks similar to the Heb. word דֶּלֶף (*delep*), which means an annoying dripping (Prov 19:13; 27:15). פּוֹרָתָא (*pôrātā*ʾ) sounds very similar to the Aramaic word פַּרְתָּא (*partā*ʾ), "dung." Aridatha and Aridai could both be plays on אֲרוֹד (ʾ*arôd*), "mule." The name Parmashta (פַּרְמַשְׁתָּא, *parmaštā*ʾ) might well be a play on the Aramaic פַּרְמַשְׁתַּק (*parmaštaq*, a Persian loanword), "penis." There may be a number of "inside jokes" in these names that the original audience would have recognized far better than we can, with our limited knowledge of the ancient vocabulary and our inability to hear the tone of voice that was used when the names were pronounced.

In all Heb. manuscripts of the book of Esther, the names of Haman's sons are written in a column, one on top of the next, with the direct-obj. marker in a second column. This orthographic tradition is found elsewhere in the Heb. Bible, especially in poetry, but sometimes also in lists. Berlin (84) suggests that this arrangement is patterned after Josh 12:9–24, where the thirty-one kings defeated by Joshua are arranged in similar fashion. According to rabbinic tradition, however, the "stacking" of these names forms a graphic illustration of the way the ten bodies were impaled, all in a line (see Paton, 284). At the reading of the Esther scroll on Purim, the names are recited in a single breath, to illustrate the contempt in which Haman and his lineage was held among the Jews (*b. Meg.* 16b). Also, the empty space between the names and the direct-obj. marker was said to remind the Jews that there would be no resurrection for Haman's sons (Moore 1971, 87).

---

41. Y. T. Radday, "Humour in Names," in *On Humour and the Comic in the Hebrew Bible*, ed. Y. T. Radday and A. Brenner (Sheffield, UK: Almond, 1990), 71–72.

9:10 That the Jews had been given permission to take plunder but refused to do so has two important effects. First, it eliminates any appearance that the Jews were driven by greed. Thus, it makes it look like they have the moral high ground. But even more important, it demonstrates that they are carrying out the requirements of *ḥerem*, the ban. When Saul was given orders to destroy the Amalekites utterly, he was also forbidden to take any of their property as spoil (1 Sam 15:3). All their goods were to be placed under the ban, destroyed completely. Saul failed to carry out those instructions, and as a result, God declared that He would deprive him of his throne (1 Sam 15:26). Mordecai had nearly repeated Saul's mistake by issuing a decree that allowed the Jews to take the spoils of their enemies. The Jewish people, however, resisted the temptation to prosper from the treasures of the wicked. Apparently, everything was destroyed, or it became the property of the state.

Though the text says nothing here about the killing of women and children, Mordecai's edict gave the Jews the right to do so (Esth 8:11). The text makes special note that the Jews departed from the express words of the decree by taking no spoils, but it says nothing about them not killing women and children. We should assume, then, that they did. Indeed, we might well assume that some of Haman's ten sons were still children when they were killed. There is no indication in the text that Haman is an old man, and in those days, a man would continue to father children as long as he was able.

9:11–12 The text says nothing about who brought the news to the king. It is simply reported to the king as part of the day's business. The slaughter of five hundred men—presumably, along with women and children (see the comments on Esth 8:10)—in the very shadow of the king's palace would seem to be a cause for distress, but the king seems to be unconcerned. The king's exclamation, "Look at all the people the Jews have killed!" has elicited a variety of interpretations from commentators. Paton (286) believes the king to be angry, while Levenson (122) sees here a demonstration of the king's insensitivity over the death toll. Clines believes the king is merely expressing his astonishment at the extent of the slaughter.[42] Several interpreters (e.g., Berlin, 86, and Bush, 476) have followed Fox[43] in seeing here an expression of admiration for the Jews' victory.

A detail that seems to have escaped commentators is why Esther is with the king in the first place. The queen was not in the habit of lingering in the king's presence, and the king was not in the habit of summoning her.

---

42. D. J. A. Clines, *The Esther Scroll: The Story of the Story*, JSOTSup 30 (Sheffield, UK: JSOT Press, 1984), 47.

43. Fox, *Character and Ideology*, 112.

Evidently, the reason Esther is with the king now is because she has come before him once again as a supplicant. Certainly, that is how Xerxes interprets her presence, because he asks her to present a request. But as a prelude to her request, the king told her what had already been accomplished—information he would have known, but she may not have received. Nonetheless, Xerxes assures Esther that he is willing to grant her whatever else she desires. The wording here parallels that of his promises at Esther's two banquets (Esth 5:6; 7:2), but it is somewhat more restrained, since he does not promise her up to half his kingdom. Is the king beginning to have some misgivings about his generous accommodation of the queen's desires?

9:13 Esther's request of the king is that she be allowed another day of taking vengeance on the Jews' enemies. This request, too, has puzzled commentators. Haman's decree ordered the Gentiles to attack and destroy the Jews on the thirteenth of Adar. Mordecai's counter-decree allowed the Jews to form armies and defend themselves on that day against anyone who attacked them. No one, however, would have had legal permission to attack the Jews on the fourteenth. Many scholars, therefore, have seen this second day of violence as totally gratuitous: "For this horrible request no justification can be found" (Paton, 287). "Perhaps Esther's request for a second day of killing shows that she herself had begun to feel the heady intoxication of the power she has so remarkably attained" (Jobes, 202). Fox, though he gives a more positive slant to the episode, nevertheless states that "Esther seems harder, blunter, even cruel."[44]

The wording of Esther's request, however, is of utmost importance here. Esther asks that the Jews be allowed to do as they had done on the first day for a second day. Presumably, the same rules would apply on this day as had applied on the first: the Jews would be permitted to kill anyone who attacked them. Given the carnage that the Jews had just visited on their enemies, it seems reasonable that survivors might well seek revenge, whatever the law would normally allow. Indeed, in an honor-driven culture, it would be their responsibility to do so. A royal edict allowing a second day of violent self-defense would serve as a deterrent against any such reprisals.

Another factor that may play into the request for the second day of killing is the backdrop of the Israelite-Amalekite struggle. In 1 Sam 15, the Israelites had failed to carry out God's instructions to utterly annihilate the Amalekites. Now, that failure had come back to haunt them in the person of Haman and his evil decree. This time, they were going to make sure that their enemies were destroyed utterly. As Jobes (198) puts it, "The Jews of Persia succeeded where Saul failed." Fox recognizes the difficulty with

44. Ibid., 115.

viewing this struggle as a continuation of the conflict between the Jews and Amalekites: "To be sure the reversal is not perfect: the enemies are not Amalekites and the author does not say that the Jews destroyed the spoil."[45] On the other hand, Haman, the Amalekite, was the enemy *par excellence* of the Jews in this narrative. It is quite possible that his nature in some sense characterizes all the Jews' enemies.

There is yet another explanation for the second day of slaughter, and particularly that this decree applies only to the city of Susa: it explains why the Jews of Susa celebrated Purim a day later than Jews outside the city (Esth 9:18–19). The request for a second day provides an etiology for an aspect of the festival that probably puzzled some Jewish celebrants. In any event, the two days of slaughter bring this event in alignment with another significant motif of the Esther narrative: significant events happen in pairs. It begins with the two feasts of Xerxes in chapter 1; it continues with the two gatherings of virgins in chapter 2; it figures significantly in the two feasts Esther held for the king and Haman; it is manifested in the two decrees regarding the Jews (that of Haman and that of Mordecai) and the two feasts of Purim.

Haman's sons had already been executed (9:7–10), so Esther's request for them to be hanged can only mean that the sons' carcasses were to be impaled on pikes in public display. This act, too, might represent a bit of poetic justice, another chapter in the rematch between Saul and Agag. According to 2 Sam 21:9, seven of Saul's descendants were hanged by Gibeonites (people of Canaan) to appease their anger at Saul's attempt to annihilate them. Now, ten of the Amalekite's sons were hanged by a descendant of King Saul. Though Gibeonites were not Amalekites, it does appear as if Saul is getting some satisfaction for the wrong suffered so many generations earlier (cf. Berlin, 86).

This ignominious treatment of the dead, so barbaric to our sensibilities, was common in the ancient world. The Assyrian kings gloried in such treatment of their enemies. The inscription of Ashurnasirpal II is typical, where he is described as the one who "defeated all his enemies and hung the corpses of his enemies on posts."[46] But impalement was not just an Assyrian practice. Xerxes' father, Darius, bragged of having impaled the rebel Babylonians when he reconquered the city (Behistun inscription 3.50). Impalement was a particularly graphic public spectacle, designed to sap the will to resist from any enemies. One could say that Esther's request, cruel as it seemed, could be designed to quell further violence. It should be noted, however, that biblical law pronounced a curse on anyone who

45. Ibid.

46. Grayson, *Inscriptions*, 120.

was displayed in this manner (Deut 21:22–23). The impalement of Haman's sons fulfilled the tradition of curses pronounced on Amalek, starting in the days of Balaam son of Beor (Num 24:20).

9:14 The request is granted without hesitation. Haman's ten sons, killed the day before, are impaled in a public demonstration. To any who might have doubted, it is now graphically obvious that Haman's ambitions have come to utter futility. His lineage has been cut off; his "house" has been made destitute. The fate that Mordecai had warned would come on Esther (Esth 4:14) has befallen the enemy instead. Such is the fate of any who rise up against the Jews.

9:15 The additional three hundred men now killed are residents of Susa, but not the citadel itself. Presumably, these deaths would be in addition to however many had been killed in the lower city on the previous day, whose numbers have not yet been announced.

9:16 This verse is not a continuation of vv. 6–15, but of vv. 1–2. The previous reports were about the casualties inflicted in the city of Susa and its citadel. These reports, however, refer to those killed in the provinces. It apparently includes not only men, as specified in the other reports, but women and children as well.

Clines (324) observes that the emphasis in this verse is not on wanton violence but on the Jews getting "rest" (נוּחַ, *nôaḥ*) from their enemies. He writes,

> "Rest" has been envisaged since the time of Deuteronomy as an ideal state of affairs (Dt. 3:20; 12:9; cf. *NIDNTT*, I, pp. 254ff.), and this is the ultimate dream of diaspora Judaism—to be allowed to live in peace. Its literature shows it not to crave confrontation but to negotiate for co-operation without undue compromise.

According to Clines, this verse indicates that the ultimate goal of Esther's entire operation was to secure peace for the Jews, not to prosper ("they laid no hands on the plunder") or to destroy all of the Jews' rivals. Such "rest" was the goal of the conquest of Canaan: the warfare took place so that the Israelites could drive out the inhabitants of the land and so they could know peace (Deut 3:20; 12:9–10; Josh 1:13, 15). It is possible that the narrator is specifically alluding to Deut 25:19. In this section, Moses tells the Israelites that when Yahweh has given them rest from their enemies "in the land that Yahweh your God is giving you as an inheritance," Israel is to blot out the memory of Amalek. We can recognize the accomplishment of this mission in the slaughter of Haman's ten sons.

Fox[47] and Berlin (87), among others, argue that the phrase "getting rest" is out of sequence in this verse, since it occurs before the report of the extensive killing. (The Heb. uses a series of inf. abs., which seem to be the functional equivalent of *waw*-consecs. here, indicating consecutive acts.[48]) "Rest," they argue, occurs only after the fighting is done. Fox suggests emending the text to read נָחוֹם (*nāḥôm*, "got relief") instead of נוֹחַ (*nôaḥ*, "got rest"), but this emendation still seems out of sequence. Berlin recommends eliding the phrase entirely. Possibly, however, the unusual sequence here is based on an allusion to Deut 25:19. According to that verse, it is after the Israelites have defeated their enemies and have "rest" that they are to blot out the memory of Amalek. In that case, the slaughter of the seventy-five thousand here is being identified with the destruction of the Amalekites that Yahweh had commanded through Moses.

It is difficult to deny that the narrator seems to take a certain pleasure in reporting these victories. The death toll reported here—seventy-five thousand—is huge: the size of a very large city in those days.[49] It is regarded by almost all commentators as fantastic, or at least "inflated" significantly. Bechtel (80) states that the number is representative of the book's "tendency toward exaggeration"; Berlin (87) argues that it comes from the realm of "carnivalesque fantasy," while at the same time admitting that such numbers are also found in the (decidedly non-carnivalesque) Assyrian royal annals. It would be good to consider the purposes of such numbers in the Assyrian accounts: they are meant to glorify the king and his gods, to strike fear into his rivals, and demonstrate to posterity his overwhelming might. The casualty report in Esther does not bring glory to a particular king, but it is designed to bring glory to the Jewish people—not before their enemies (who would not read this text anyway), but among themselves. This report reassures the Diaspora Jews of their power and their invulnerability, in spite of evidence to the contrary. The hearers of this text, though they seemed weak and oppressed in their "real" lives, were reassured of their hidden might. They were capable of decisively defeating their enemies and of wreaking vengeance on a grand scale. Should another Haman arise, the Jews would show their true natures.

The LXX uses here a word for "enemies" (πολέμιος) that implies combatants engaged in warfare, rather than merely those who hold hostile feelings.

---

47. Fox, *Character and Ideology*, 285.

48. See A. Rubinstein, "Finite Verb Continued by an Infinitive Absolute In Biblical Hebrew," *VT* 2 (1952): 365.

49. According to G. Roux, *Ancient Iraq* (London: George Allen & Unwin, 1964), 326, Babylon—the world's largest city in this period—had a normal population of one hundred thousand, though the city could have housed twice that number.

It illustrates the LXX translator's understanding that the Jews were engaged only in killing those who attacked them, not in general slaughter of everyone whom they disliked.

9:17–18 In these verses, we have our first account of the celebration that is the basis for the observation of the feast of Purim. The text continues in its somewhat confusing organization, due to the divergent practices of the rural Jews and the Jews of Susa. Verse 17 follows up on the action of v. 16, explaining the celebrations of the rural Jews on the fourteenth of Adar. Verse 18 follows up on the events of v. 15. Purim is a day later in Susa than it is outside the city, since the fighting continued in the city for two days.

The word translated here "feasting" (מִשְׁתֶּה, *mišteh*) is the same word translated "banquet" elsewhere in the narrative. The banquet motif, so prominent throughout, is here finally linked to the triumph of the Jews over their enemies.

9:19 The Jews of the villages (cities too small for walls) had their rest on the fourteenth of Adar, and so they set aside that day for their festivities. It is interesting that this verse only draws a distinction between the Jews of Susa and Jews in villages. It makes no mention of Jews living in other walled cities like Babylon or Jerusalem. Presumably, however, the readers of the text would have known when they celebrated Purim. This text is not designed to prescribe the proper way to celebrate, but to describe the rationale behind a well-established practice. According to later Jewish tradition, towns and villages read the scroll of Esther on 14 Adar, but cities surrounded by a wall since the days of Joshua read it on 15 Adar (*m. Meg.* 1.1).

The notion of giving gifts of food seems somewhat incongruous: what does giving food to others have to do with celebrating deliverance from destruction? The practice should be read, however, in light of Neh 8:10–12 and Esth 9:22. In Neh 8:10–12, the people were instructed to celebrate the reading of the Law by feasting and sending portions of food to anyone who did not have anything available with which to celebrate. In 8:12, it states simply that they "sent portions." Likewise, the instructions here probably mean that the Jews were to send gifts of food to the poor so that they, too, could rejoice. Indeed, the word used here, "portions" (מָנוֹת, *mānôt*) refers to a section apportioned for a specific purpose—a "share." The text seems to mean that the Jews were sharing with people who did not have resources. This interpretation seems to be confirmed by Esth 9:22, which specifically adds that the Jews were to send gifts to the poor.

Moore (1971, 89) and others identify this verse as a gloss because they believe it contradicts Esth 9:20–21, which they argue prescribes two days of celebration for all Jews. It is not necessary, however, to read these verses as contradictory. See the comments below on v. 21.

Biblical Theology Comments

9:1 The "summary statement" of this narrative ("it was reversed") reminds us of a major motif of the book of Esther: the concept of peripety.[50] In this verse, the danger that has pervaded this entire narrative has been dissipated. The scheme that had been hatched against the Jews has been turned against its perpetrators. This fact is, perhaps, one of the most compelling aspects of the book of Esther. It is not simply the idea that the plot was canceled. The plot was reversed, so that the evil that had been launched was turned back again. What had appeared to be a victory for evil was not merely averted; it became instead a victory for good.

This may perhaps be part of the reason that Esther has found such an enduring place in the Jewish and Christian tradition. Essentially, it epitomizes a pattern that is significant throughout the Bible, especially in the major acts of salvation history. The classic example of Joseph, to which the book of Esther frequently alludes, contains the first explicit statement of this pattern: "You planned evil against me; but God planned it for good" (Gen 50:20). The exodus, to which Esther also alludes, is certainly another case of this process at work. Once again, Israel was in apparently dire circumstances. Pharaoh was doling out oppression and violence against the people of God, attempting to exterminate them (Exod 1:15–22). But God reversed the situation, so that not only did the Israelites come forth from Egypt as a great nation, but they came forth materially blessed, as they plundered the Egyptians and carried away some of the gold and silver of the land with them (Exod 12:35–36). But even more important, God reversed the oppression by elevating Moses in the eyes of the Egyptians (Exod 11:3), instilling in Israel a respect for Moses (Exod 19:9) and inculcating in Egypt and Israel the truth that Yahweh is the greatest of the gods (Exod 7:5; 10:1–2).

This pattern of reversal, however, is only the foreshadowing of a much greater reversal: the crucifixion of Jesus was engineered by the devil and by evil people to do away with the threat posed by the Son of God. But that act of violence was turned into a victory, both through God accepting the death of Christ as atonement for our sins and through the resurrection, which demonstrated his victory over the power of death. In this sense, then, the book of Esther only demonstrates the continuation of a pattern wherein God uses enemies' devices against them. Of course, it pales in comparison to the coup that God pulled off in Jesus Christ.

Another point to observe in these reversal narratives is that in no case was God taken by surprise and forced to resort to His "plan B." Long before Israel was enslaved, God had foretold that the bondage and the deliverance

---

50. See introduction, "Motifs: Reversal/Peripety."

would occur and that Israel would prosper through it (Gen 15:13–14). God's divine forethought is also apparent in the Esther narrative, as the elevation of Esther to the office of queen occurred long before the crisis. God had anticipated the coming threat and had made preparation "for such a time as this" (Esth 4:14). The atonement was not God's effort to make the best of the unanticipated death of Jesus: it was God's plan from the beginning that Jesus, "the Lamb slain from the foundation of the world" (Rev 13:8 KJV), should suffer and die to take away our guilt (Isa 53:6, 10).

Application and Devotional Implications

The idea of reversal is more than a literary motif, and it is more than a recurrent biblical theme. Indeed, it is even more than a theological proposition. For the Christian, it is an existential reality, the foundation of our identity in Christ. Like the Jews in the book of Esther, we were under the decree of destruction: "We were by nature children of wrath, like the rest" (Eph 2:3). But as in the case of Jews in the book of Esther, "it was reversed": "But God … even when we were dead in our trespasses, made us alive together with Christ" (Eph 2:4–5 ESV). The decree of death was overturned, not because of the will of a mortal sovereign, but because of the merciful intervention of God.

Selected Bibliography

Belibtreu, E. "Grisly Assyrian Record of Torture and Death." *BAR* 17 (1991): 51–61.

Clines, D. J. A. *The Esther Scroll: The Story of the Story*. JSOTSup 30. Sheffield, UK: JSOT Press, 1984.

Duchesne-Guillemin, J. "Le noms des eunuques d'Assuérus." *Le Muséon* 66 (1953): 105–8.

Fox, M. V. *Character and Ideology in the Book of Esther*. 2nd ed. Grand Rapids: Eerdmans, 2001.

———. "The Structure of the Book of Esther." In *Isac Leo Seeligmann Volume: Essays of the Bible and the Ancient World*, ed. A. Rofe and Y. Zakovitch, 3:291–303. Jerusalem: E. Rubinstein.

Grayson, A. K. *Assyrian Royal Inscriptions, Part 2: From Tiglath-pileser I to Ashurnasir-apli II*. Wiesbaden: Otto Harrassowitz, 1976.

Jones, B. W. "Two Misconceptions about the Book of Esther." *CBQ* 39 (1977): 171–81.

Radday, Y. T. "Humour in Names." In *On Humour and the Comic in the Hebrew Bible*, ed. Y. T. Radday and A. Brenner, 59–97. Sheffield, UK: Almond, 1990.

Roux, G. *Ancient Iraq*. London: George Allen & Unwin, 1964.

Rubinstein, A. "Finite Verb Continued by an Infinitive Absolute In Biblical Hebrew." *VT* 2 (1952): 362–67.

Wechsler, M. "The Purim-Passover Connection: A Reflection of Jewish Exegetical Tradition in the Peshitta Book of Esther." *JBL* 117 (1998): 321–27.

Yamauchi, E. *Persia and the Bible.* Grand Rapids: Baker, 1997.

Purim Established (9:20–32)

Translation

20 Then Mordecai wrote down these things and sent letters to all the Jews who were in all the provinces of King Xerxes, near and far, **21** to take it upon themselves to keep the fourteenth day of the month of Adar and its fifteenth day, year by year, **22** as the days on which the Jews had rest from their enemies and as the month when it had been turned for them from sorrow into rejoicing and from mourning into a holiday, to make them days of banqueting and gladness, days for sending portions of food to one another and gifts to the poor.

23 So the Jews obligated themselves regarding what they had begun to do, and what Mordecai had written to them, **24** that Haman the Agagite, the son of Hammedatha, the oppressor of all the Jews, had plotted against the Jews to destroy them, and had cast *pur* (that is, lots), to exterminate and to destroy them. **25** But when it[51] came before the king, he ordered[52] in a written document that his evil plot that he had plotted against the Jews should return on his own head, and they impaled[53] him and his sons on pikes. **26** Therefore they called these days Purim, on account of the term *pur*.

Therefore, on account of all the words of this missive, and what they had witnessed concerning this matter, and what had happened to them, **27** the Jews firmly obligated themselves and their descendants and all who might join them, that the keeping of these two days would not pass away, according to what was written and at the proper time every year, **28** that these days should be remembered and observed throughout every generation, in every clan, province, and city, and that these days of Purim should never pass away among the Jews, nor should the memory of these days fade among their descendants.

29 Then Queen Esther, the daughter of Abihail, along with Mordecai the Jew, wrote again[54] with all their authority this missive, confirming the

---

51. Or, "she."
52. Lit., "said."
53. Lit., "hung."
54. Reading שֵׁנִית (*šēnît*), "again," for הַשֵּׁנִית (*haššēnît*), "second." See the commentary.

observance of[55] Purim. **30** He sent letters to all the Jews, to the 127 provinces of Xerxes' kingdom, in words of well-being and security, **31** to establish these days of Purim at their proper times, just as Mordecai the Jew had imposed upon them, along with Queen Esther, and just as they had established concerning themselves and their descendants the matter of their fasts and their lamentations. **32** The decree of Queen Esther established these practices of Purim, and it was recorded in a scroll.

Textual Notes

20.a. LXX reads, "And Mordecai wrote these things in a book."

21.a. The phrase לְקַיֵּם עֲלֵיהֶם ("to take it upon themselves") is not reflected in the LXX translation.

23.a. Vv. 23–26 are omitted in the AT.

23.b. Several MSS have the pl. קִבְּלוּ ("received") instead of the sg. קִבֵּל.

24.a. The LXX has "the Macedonian" (ὁ Μακεδὼν) instead of "the Agagite" (הָאֲגָגִי).

28.a. The AT omits vv. 28–32.

29.a. Instead of "daughter of Abihail," LXX has "daughter of Aminadab" (Αμιναδαβ).

29.b. LXX and Syr. omit "second" (הַשֵּׁנִית).

30.a. The OL leaves out vv. 30–32.

Commentary

This section records the official procedures that were followed to establish Purim as a Jewish holiday. It is somewhat convoluted, and scholars disagree about which letters are being written by Mordecai and which by Esther. My understanding, however, is that Mordecai writes the first letter, then Esther writes a letter confirming that of Mordecai with Mordecai's assistance. The idea seems to be that the letters would have been written shortly after the victory, when the effects of the deliverance are still fresh in the Jews' minds, but before the spontaneous celebration has become a formal annual observance.

This section can be divided into three sub-units:

a. Mordecai Issues the Order Establishing Purim (9:20–22)

55. "Observance of" is not present in the Heb., but the context seems to require it.

b. The Jews Commit to the Perpetual Observance (9:23–28)

c. Esther Confirms Mordecai's Order (9:29–32)

Clines' view (325) that this section forms a secondary addition to the book has been widely adopted by scholars. According to Clines, 9:1–19 is an addition as well, but vv. 20–32 form an addition subsequent to the first. Given the generally recognized chiastic structure of the book of Esther, it is difficult to imagine that this section was tacked on to the end of the narrative. In the current form of the book, it plays an important role of balancing the banquet scenes (chap. 1) and Esther's triumph over her Gentile rivals (chap. 2) that begin the story (see further "Composition" in the introduction).

9:20 Once again, the Esther narrative emphasizes the role of written documents. Perhaps in a mockery of the officiousness of the Persian Empire, almost everything that occurs is solemnized with writing, for example Vashti's removal (1:19–22) and Mordecai's rescue of the king (2:23). Mordecai, having earlier written a decree to the Jews to muster and defend themselves, now writes a decree that they are to celebrate their victory. The statement that Mordecai wrote "these things" has led many interpreters of earlier generations (e.g., Rashi) to conclude that Mordecai was the author of the book of Esther. That conclusion is not warranted by the language. It is apparent from the following account that the reference here is to the contents of the letters Mordecai wrote to the Jews about the observation of Purim, not to the book of Esther itself. The narrator probably wants us to recognize the very brief overview of the affair found in vv. 24–26 as a summary of the account that Mordecai sent to the Jews.

9:21 At first glance, it appears as if Mordecai has taken on an unprecedented task: ordering the Jews to celebrate a holiday that has no precedent in the Law of Moses. In actuality, however, the verb translated "take it upon themselves" in v. 21 (קַיֵּם, *qayyēm*) has the sense of "confirm, ratify," rather than "command" or "impose."[56] Mordecai was calling upon the people to accept the responsibility of celebrating Purim annually, rather than forcing them to do so against their will. In this light, Mordecai is not so much establishing a new holiday as formalizing that which the people are already doing.

A number of authors (e.g., Paton, 293; Moore 1971, 93) have argued that the text states that all Jews were to observe two days of Purim, contradicting v. 19, which states that some Jews observed the fourteenth of Adar as Purim and some the fifteenth of Adar. This conclusion is unnecessary.

---

56. M. Fox, *Character and Ideology in the Book of Esther*, 2nd ed. (Grand Rapids: Eerdmans, 2001), 118.

To state that Purim was celebrated on two days, as this text does, is not the same as saying that everyone was required to celebrate for two days. In contrast, Exod 12:15–20 is quite clear in dictating that for seven days all the Israelites are to eat unleavened bread, and for those seven days no yeast is to be found in any of their houses. Had the author of Esther wanted to prescribe that all Jews were to celebrate for two days, he could have been similarly explicit. Furthermore, the narrator of this section would certainly have known that Purim was not a two-day holiday. According to 2 Macc 15:36, "Mordecai's Day" was observed on 14 Adar; there is no mention of a two day celebration. If we were to argue that this section is a later addition to the text (as most scholars do), we must presume that Purim began as a one-day festival celebrated on two different days, then became a two-day festival, then became a one-day festival again. It seems more likely that the narrator was merely presenting a summary in his account of how Purim was observed, just as he will summarize the events of the book of Esther in vv. 24–25.

The use of the verb קִיֵּם (*kayyēm*) in the piel stem is characteristic of late biblical Heb.; in standard biblical Heb., this verb is typically used in the hiphil stem.

9:22 In a somewhat poetic formulation, the Jews are enjoined to remember the "day" of their rest and the "month" of their rejoicing. The phrases are broadly synonymous: both refer to the time period in which the victory occurred. Both, too, emphasize that it is not the killing or the violence that the Jews celebrate, but the joyous rest that follows—the security of knowing that the danger is passed and that the unnamed Power that preserves them remains trustworthy.

Most scholars see the reference to the giving of gifts to the poor to be an addition to the description of the spontaneous celebration in v. 19. I have argued, however, that the reference in v. 19 to giving "portions" refers specifically to sharing food with those who did not have resources with which to celebrate. The addition here is the reference to gifts, a further blessing for those who might otherwise find little joy in this festive day.

9:23 That which the Jews had begun to do spontaneously, they now commit to do formally because of the instructions of Mordecai. The verb translated "obligated themselves" (קִבֵּל, *qibbēl*) basically means "receive." The use reflected here is typical of later biblical Heb. In postbiblical Heb., the word comes to be used idiomatically of the notion of receiving a tradition. There may be a hint of that meaning present here.

The verb קִבֵּל (*qibbēl*) is sg., but the noun that follows (יְהוּדִים, *yĕhûdîm*) is pl. A number of Heb. manuscripts fix the problem by making the verb pl.

as well. It is not totally impossible, however, for a Heb. pl. noun to take a sg. verb if the group subject is taken as a single entity.

9:24–25 These verses most certainly are intended to provide a synopsis of the account that Mordecai put in his letter to the Jews, as suggested by the conj. כִּי (*kî*, "that") at the beginning of v. 24. There are obvious differences between this synopsis and the narrative found in the book of Esther: most notable are the omission of the roles of Esther and Mordecai, the reference to the king issuing a written order to reverse Haman's plot, and the failure to mention the battles between the Jews and their enemies. While some scholars have seen these differences as a sign that vv. 24–25 represent an earlier version, a later addition, or simply a different tradition from that found in the rest of the book,[57] the differences can be accounted for by these verses being a brief synopsis, leaving out most of the details found in the narrative (Bardtke, 393).

Even more significant, it should be noted that this account is ostensibly a summary of what Mordecai had written in his letter to the Jews. Seen in that light, the points brought up here are very understandable. First of all, Mordecai would not have had to describe the fighting; the Jews would have been familiar with that aspect of the story, since they had experienced it. Furthermore, the emphasis on the king's role is a well-designed bit of sycophancy. Just as Esther had carefully avoided implying that the king might have been responsible for the Jews' predicament (Esth 7:3–6), Mordecai will go her one better and give the king more credit for the Jews' deliverance than he actually deserves.[58] Finally, it would have sounded vain and self-serving for Mordecai to draw attention to his own role, or that of his cousin, in the matter. Mordecai's official account is propaganda, but the Jews knew the *real* story.

9:24 The word *pur* is an Akkadian word for "lot."[59] It is evident that the narrator did not expect his audience to know this word, since he gives its Heb. equivalent. The use of the Akkadian word in this text is odd, since the story is written in Heb. and set in Persia, where the official languages were Aramaic and Persian. It is possible the word was chosen to provide a folk etymology for the name of the holiday the Jews were already celebrating: perhaps no one knew the actual origin of the name "Purim," so our narrator connected it with a minor aspect of the story. We see a similar process at work with Moses' name, which was given a folk etymology connecting it

57. See M. Fox, *The Redaction of the Books of Esther: On Reading Composite Texts* (Atlanta: Scholars Press, 1991), 123–24.
58. Fox, *Character and Ideology*, 120.
59. See commentary on 3:7.

to the story of his rescue from the Nile ("draws")—even though it is now widely acknowledged that his name actually derives from the Egyptian word *mesu*, meaning "son" (found in names like Ramses ["son of Ra"] and Thutmosis [son of Thut]).[60]

Yet another possible wordplay in this verse is found in the statement that Haman threw lots to "exterminate" (הֻמָּם; *hummām*) the Jews. A relatively rare verb that occurs only thirteen times in the OT, it may have been chosen specifically because it sounds similar to the name "Haman." Fox suggests this wordplay might have been used to reinforce the pun on the words pur and Purim.[61]

9:25 The referent for the pronoun "it" in this verse is ambiguous. Heb. pronouns can be either masc. or fem. and typically match the gender of the noun they replace. The pronoun here is fem., and can be translated either "she" or "it." Most modern translations have understood the pronoun to mean "she" (so KJ21; NKJV; AMP; CEV; GNT; NLT; NRSV) and insert the name "Esther," who came before the king to expose Haman's plot. The main problem with this interpretation is that Esther is nowhere mentioned in the paragraph preceding this verse, essentially leading readers to supply the antecedent from their own knowledge of the story. If the pronoun is understood as "it," the question is what "it" is intended. A few translations simply translate the pronoun "it" (ESV; LEB; NASB), but the NIV goes further, translating, "But when the plot came to the king's attention." In this case, I believe the NIV's interpretation is correct. Most likely, the pronoun refers to the fem. noun מַחֲשַׁבְתּוֹ (*maḥăšabtô*), "his plot," which appears a little later in the verse.

The phrase "with a written document" (עִם־הַסֵּפֶר, *ʿim-hassēper*) is grammatically difficult. The prep. עִם (*ʿim*) is not typically used with the sense of instrumentality; typically, it means "accompanied by." The sense here could be that the king attended to the proper paperwork to reverse Haman's plot. The narrative, however, has no reference to any such written orders.

9:26 This verse describes two outcomes of Mordecai's letter, each introduced with the word *therefore*. The first observes that the holiday was called Purim ("lots") because of Haman's cast of the *pur*. The casting of the *pur* seems a rather minor element of the story for Mordecai to have included in his synopsis, but the reason for its inclusion becomes clear here: Mordecai's report of this detail was the basis for the Jews calling their celebration "Purim." As noted above, the historical accuracy of this etiology is dubious.

---

60. See, e.g., BDB, משה; W. F. Albright, "From the Patriarchs to Moses II. Moses out of Egypt," *BA* 36, no. 2 (1973): 51–52.

61. Fox, *Character and Ideology*, 120.

Not only is it unlikely that the Persian official Haman would have called his lot by the Akkadian name *pur*, but it is also noteworthy that Haman cast only a single "lot," not "lots" (Esth 3:7). Clines (328) suggests that the reason for the pl. "lots" is that the narrator is implying there were actually two lots cast: Haman's and God's. As winsome as this explanation might be, it seems to require that the narrator came up with this name for the holiday himself, which is unlikely. More likely, the name of the holiday was already fixed, and the narrator merely attempted to provide an explanation for it. See further "Esther and Purim" in the introduction.

The second *therefore* refers more broadly to the observation of Purim. This phrase begins with a list of three reasons that Purim became an established holiday. The first is Mordecai's letter, which provided the official basis for the festivities. But Mordecai's official letter, as observed above, did not tell the whole story, since it was crafted for "official" consumption. The Jews themselves had been witnesses to the whole affair. They had seen the roles Esther and Mordecai had played in the deliverance and the rise of Mordecai in the esteem of the Gentiles. The second and third reasons are that they had personally experienced the despair of Haman's decree and the rest that had been procured through the defeat of their enemies. Though Mordecai's decree made the holiday "official," the emphasis here is clearly on the experience of the Jews that had elicited their spontaneous celebration.

There seems to be some confusion in the Greek versions of Esther regarding the name of the holiday. In the LXX, it is spelled Φρουραι. In the AT, however, it is called Φουρδαια. The translators apparently did not know the Akkadian word from which the narrator draws his etiology for the word "Purim." It might also indicate that the festival was not widely known by this name in the time when the Greek versions were being translated. The word "Purim" does not appear in the Dead Sea Scrolls, the NT, the Apocrypha (in 2 Macc 15:36, the holiday is called "Mordecai's Day"), or the Mishnah.

9:27 The phrase "all who might join them" has been seen as a reference to those who converted to Judaism out of fear of the Jews in 8:17.[62] The word used here (הַנִּלְוִים, *hannilwîm*), however, is different from the word designating the "converts" in 8:17 (מִתְיַהֲדִים, *mithyahădîm*). It seems more likely that this phrase is referring to all future converts to Judaism, who will be expected to celebrate the Jews' deliverance from Haman along with those who had actually experienced the event. The ordinance is similar to that regarding the Passover. Along with the Israelites and their descendants, provisions were made for any aliens or foreigners who wished to participate: they had to be circumcised and become like native Israelites (Exod 12:43–49).

62. So Fox, *Character and Ideology*, 121–22.

The narrator is careful, it appears, not to refer to this observation as a "law," "commandment," or even a "statute" (cf. Exod 12:14). It is merely what they are to be "doing" (עֹשִׂים, *ʿōśîm*). Mordecai is not Moses. He is not creating a new holiday, but merely formalizing an existing time of celebration.

9:27–28 The emphasis here is on the universal celebration of Purim. No Jews were exempt from this holiday, from any region or family. The narrator is quite verbose in his injunction, and many scholars assume it is because he is attempting to overcome resistance to the celebration of a holiday that has no scriptural basis at the time of writing. It is also possible, however, that the narrator's words reflect the reality of his day and that Purim was already widely observed. In keeping with the "etiological" nature of the book of Esther (see "Genre: Festival Etiology" in the introduction), the narrator could be explaining the universal acceptance of the holiday by citing Mordecai's passionate insistence in the matter.

In an ironic turn, the concept of a law that "cannot pass away" arises once again in the narrative. It first appears in Esth 1:19 regarding the decree that removed Vashti from her office. It is invoked again in Esth 8:8, where it has a double meaning, implying both that Haman's decree cannot simply be revoked and also that whatever decree Mordecai writes will be unchangeable. Now, the concept has been co-opted by the Jews and applied to their own decree concerning Purim: like the laws of the Persians, this observance is to become a permanent statute among all generations. In addition to the irony, there is structural balance in the appearance of this "unchangeable decree" at this point in the narrative. The decree concerning Vashti came after the two feasts of the king and confirmed as a perpetual rule the very thing she had refused to do—appear before the king (henceforth, she was banished from his presence). The missive of Mordecai comes on the heels of the two feasts of the Jews and likewise confirms the practice they had already begun.

Moore (1971, 95) sees in the use of the distributive nouns here ("generation by generation, clan by clan," etc.) as evidence that the two days of Purim were to be celebrated by all Jews. There is no specific mention in this verse, however, of *two* days, so it seems unlikely that the narrator was trying to make such an emphasis. Rather, the narrator seeks to emphasize the universality of the feast among the Jews, perhaps to provide official basis for the widespread custom.

9:29–32 In the third paragraph of this section, Esther formalizes Mordecai's letter with one of her own, adding the cachet of her own position to the considerable authority of Mordecai. Most scholars believe that vv. 29–32 is a later addition to the book of Esther, apparently designed to bring Esther back into the picture.[63] These verses seem, at the least, redundant. The Jews have already committed to doing all the Mordecai had said (9:27). What is the purpose of yet another letter? But even more difficult would seem to be the inconsistency in the section itself, specifically regarding who actually wrote this second letter. Was it Esther, Mordecai, or both? The passage is somewhat obscure and may be the product of a complex editorial process.[64]

9:29 This verse states that Esther wrote a "second letter." The verb is fem. sg., which would agree with the subject "Esther." The text, however, adds "Mordecai the Jew," as well, which would typically require a pl. verb form in Heb. Many scholars, therefore, believe that the reference to Mordecai is a gloss, a scribal addition to the narrative. In the next verse, however, the verb form is 3 m. sg., "he sent." Perhaps the best sense that can be made of the section is that Esther wrote the letters with the assistance of Mordecai. But why would Mordecai need to send yet another letter, when his first letter seems to have been so effective?

It might be significant that Esther's patronymic, Abihail, is given here, while Mordecai's is not. The name Abihail means "father of might." There is surely a sense in which Esther's father was a "father of might," since Esther now possesses great power in Persia. She will exercise that power here, since she (and apparently Mordecai) will confirm "with full authority" the words of Mordecai. The word translated "authority" (תֹּקֶף, *tōqēp*) is very rare, occurring here, Esth 10:2, and Dan 9:17. Its Nabatean cognate seems to suggest the idea of legitimacy or validity (Moore 1971, 95).

The rest of this verse is grammatically difficult. Read literally, it would seem to say that Esther and Mordecai wrote "to confirm this second letter of Purim." But that statement makes little sense: how could this second letter confirm itself? Furthermore, the syntax of the verse is very unusual. Almost always in Heb. noun phrases, if there is a demonstrative pronoun such as "this" (זֹאת, *zʾōt*), it comes at the end of the phrase. Instead, the word "second" comes at the end of this phrase. The text almost certainly is corrupt, but how is it to be emended? From the context, we can infer that the verse seems to mean that Esther wrote a second letter to confirm Mordecai's letter that had just been described. Unfortunately, the extant Heb. text cannot be read that way. Several scholars (e.g., Gerleman, 141; Bush, 470)[65] have recognized that without the word "second" (הַשֵּׁנִית, *haššēnît*) at the end, the

63. While there is much speculation that all of chap. 9 is an addition to the narrative, the consensus is stronger with regard to vv. 29–32.

64. See S. E. Loewenstamm, "Esther 9:29–32: The Genesis of a Late Addition," *HUCA* 42 (1971): 117–24.

65. Also W. Rudolph, "Textkritisches zum Estherbuch," *VT* 4 (1954): 90.

verse makes much better sense. If one proposes that this word is a scribal addition, however, one should be able to explain how this addition came about. So far, this explanation has eluded scholars.

I would propose a less radical emendation of the text. Instead of deleting the entire word, it would be better to delete only the definite article. It is easy to imagine a scribe, after writing the noun "Purim" and the demonstrative pronoun "this" with the definite articles, simply adding the article to שֵׁנִית (*šēnît*; which he took as a fem. adj.) in order to harmonize it with the preceding words. But his addition would have made a significant grammatical difference: the form הַשֵּׁנִית is an adj., but the form שֵׁנִית is an adv., meaning "a second time, again." If the article is omitted, the verse would read, "Then Queen Esther, the daughter of Abihail, along with Mordecai the Jew, wrote with all their authority, to confirm a second time this missive about Purim." This is certainly what the narrator had intended to say. "This missive about Purim" refers to the letter that Mordecai had written. Esther is now joining with the vizier to write a second letter that reconfirms the first.

9:30 The Heb. text reads "And he sent letters," using the 3 m. sg. form of the verb. If we do not delete the reference to Mordecai in v. 29, then it is obviously Mordecai who is sending out the letters composed by Esther and him. Scholars who favor deleting the reference to Mordecai in v. 29 read the construction as the equivalent of a pass.: "And letters were sent." In Heb., as in English, a third-person verbal construction can be the functional equivalent of a pass. construction, as in, "They can't take away my dignity" = "My dignity can't be taken away." But as in English, this construction typically uses a pl. form, not sg. Fox[66] and Bush (485) suggest repointing the verb as a niphal pass. form. Once again, however, there is the problem with number: "letters" is pl., while the verb form would be sg., even if repointed. The simplest explanation is that we should understand the "he" here to be Mordecai. Even if his mention in v. 29 was merely a scribal addition, he has figured prominently in this section, and has already appeared sending letters to all the Jews (9:20).

The phrase "peace and security" has been variously interpreted by scholars. Gordis identifies it as an introductory formula,[67] but most commentators reject this possibility, since it would be odd to simply cite an introductory formula without relating any of the contents of the letter. Most interpreters believe the phrase is in apposition to "letters"; that is, it characterizes the contents of the letters. The same phrase appears in Isa 39:8 and Jer 33:6, where it is used to contrast a state of hostility and violence. It may

66. Fox, *Character and Ideology*, 286.

67. R. Gordis, "Studies in the Esther Narrative," *JBL* 95 (1976): 57–58.

be a stock phrase used to characterize a time after hostilities have ended and peaceful relations restored. Levenson (130) and Berlin (92) link it also to Zech 8:19, where the terms are reversed.

9:31 *BHS* suggests that "Esther the Queen" in this verse should be deleted as a late addition. Fox[68] and Bush (471) argue that the reference to Esther was added to associate both Jewish heroes with the issuance of this second letter. There is no textual basis, however, for viewing Esther here as a late addition.

The reference to times of fasting and lamentation has prompted much speculation. Traditionally, interpreters have viewed these fasts as those established by Mordecai and Esther in conjunction with the days of Purim. Many modern commentators (e.g., Berlin, 93; Levenson, 130–31),[69] however, have been persuaded by the interpretation of medieval rabbi Abraham ibn Ezra, who saw here an allusion to Zech 8:19:

> Thus says Yahweh of hosts: The fast of the fourth month and the fast of the fifth and the fast of the seventh and the fast of the tenth shall be to the house of Judah seasons of happiness and rejoicing and happy observances. So value security and peace.[70]

The fasts referred to in Zechariah are those established after the destruction of Jerusalem by the Babylonians. According to ibn Ezra, Mordecai and Esther were establishing a holiday after the model of Zechariah's fasts—fasts that had no precedent in the law of Moses. The reference is probably more broadly to all the public fasts that the Jews observed at the time, rituals they had firmly adopted without biblical basis.

9:32 The word translated "decree" (מַאֲמַר, *maʾămar*) is rare, occurring only in the book of Esther. Its first occurrence is in Esth 1:15, referring to Xerxes' order for Vashti to appear before him. The second occurrence, in Esth 2:20, designates the commands of Mordecai to Esther before she became queen. Both the previous occurrences, then, reflect not only the authority of those who give the orders, but authority that is derived from patriarchy. Xerxes' command is an extension of a man's authority over his wife; Mordecai's command arises from the authority a father exercises over his grown daughter. Now, however, there is a reversal: the decree of a woman is binding on all the Jews. Esther has come very far, indeed, from submissive daughter and passive wife to commander of all the Jews! In the opening episode, a decree was issued that would make all women obey their husbands; now, a woman issues a decree that all Jewish men will obey.

---

68. Fox, *Character and Ideology*, 125.
69. Also ibid., 125–26.
70. Author's translation.

Once again, there is an explicit reference to affairs being written in a book. Once, this detail proved significant, when Mordecai's deliverance of Xerxes was recorded in the royal annals (Esth 2:23). But this record of Esther's decree, like several other instances of recording, will have no impact on the story line. There are several reasons, however, why this reference to the writing is significant. Perhaps its main purpose is to lend a sense of gravity and formality to the observance of Purim. This celebration is not merely a spontaneous party; it is also a remembrance of a great chapter in the story of the Jews. Another reason is that it links the Esther narrative once again to the account of Joshua's defeat of Amalek: in Exod 17:14, God orders Moses, "Write this as a memorial in the scroll and recite it in the hearing of Joshua, because I will utterly blot out the remembrance of Amalek from under the heavens." On the completion of Israel's first victory over Amalek, an account was written on a scroll; after this final defeat, another record was made on a scroll. Finally, the detail about the writing also underscores the parallelism between Esther's decree and Xerxes' decree of Esth 1:19, which was also written in the official records. Thus, the book of Esther begins and ends with two feasts, a focus on the actions of the queen, and a reference to a decree written in the royal records. The structural balance of the narrative is truly remarkable.

Biblical Theology Comments

9:22 The image of mourning turned into rejoicing is a recurrent one in biblical narrative. In the books of Isaiah (35:10; 51:11) and Jeremiah (31:12–13), it is associated with the return from exile. Those whom God had judged in His wrath would now rejoice and dance, as Yahweh restores their fortunes and brings them back to their homeland.

But it is not only the release of the captives that can inspire such mirth. In Psa 30, the poet rejoices because he has been delivered from a threat of death. It is unclear what form the threat had taken, but it is apparent that the psalmist believed it was a judgment from God (30:4). Now, with the shadow of destruction lifted, the psalmist could sing and celebrate the mercy of Yahweh. But perhaps the most dramatic example of such a turnaround is that described by Jesus in John 16:20–24. Jesus tells the disciples that they will have sorrow, but that their sorrow will be transformed into joy. Certainly He is speaking here of His own impending death, and the grief the disciples will feel as their hopes and expectations are shattered. But the grief will transform into happiness when what was imagined to be a tragedy turns into a triumph in the hands of God. Though Esther makes no mention of God, it is clear that the complete reversal of the Jews' mood and fortunes has been divinely orchestrated. What had looked like a debacle became an occasion for feasting and sharing gifts. They could say with the psalmist, "I will not die but live, and tell of the works of Yah" (Psa 118:17).

9:23 The practice of turning spontaneous or traditional observances into formal laws was not without precedent in the Bible. It is known, for instance, that many people of the ANE practiced circumcision. But God's covenant with Abraham (Gen 17:9–14) made the practice obligatory on him and all his descendants. The same might be true of certain food laws or regulations concerning marriage or inheritance. Some practices were created by humanity and sanctified by divine decree; others were created by humanity and tolerated by God for a time (e.g., divorce; see Deut 24:1 and Matt 5:31–32; 19:1–9). It is impossible to know whether the festival of Purim was ever actually sanctioned by God.

9:28 The emphasis on remembrance here is reminiscent of the story of Passover (Exod 12–13). There, too, the Israelites were sojourners in a land where they were surrounded by animosity. In that story, too, they were delivered from an impending doom. There, too, their deliverance was to be celebrated with a special meal, first observed on the very night of the deliverance. In each case, the annual celebrations would include meals that reenacted the first celebrations and in some sense recaptured their joy. In both cases, a written record provided an account of the deliverance and instructions for future observation of the event. The story, along with the charge to "remember," assured that the festivities would always be linked with the deliverance in the hearts of the subsequent generations. No one can mistake the revelry for simple frivolity or, even worse, for magic.

This same pattern recurs in the NT, in the story of Jesus' Last Supper. As in the case of the Passover and Purim, the great act of deliverance brought about by the death and resurrection of Jesus was first marked with a meal. Jesus commanded His followers to "remember" His act of salvation and commemorate it with a reenactment of that meal. The celebration of the Lord's Supper cannot degenerate into a meaningless ritual or be transformed into a magic act. It is insolubly bound to the great act of deliverance wrought by Jesus Christ.

Application and Devotional Implications

The emphasis in this section is clearly on writing the story. Writing has a practical purpose here: it binds the celebration of Purim to the story of the Jews' deliverance from destruction. It is as if Mordecai and Esther are saying to the people, "You have been celebrating. Be certain you understand why." For a holiday like Purim, characterized as it was by drunkenness and irreverence, the narrative of deliverance provided essential perspective. The writing of the story, along with the reading of the scroll at the Purim festival, transformed what could have been a depraved bacchanalia into an opportunity for contemplating the providence of God.

If ritual becomes separated from narrative, there is a very real danger that the participants will infuse it with their own meaning. I observed in the introduction that in the early centuries AD, some Jews apparently erected Haman on a cross and abused him as a surrogate of Jesus. They infused the symbol with a meaning that was not part of the original narrative. On a little less serious note, Terry Fullam tells the story of a church where a new minister was informed by some members of his congregation that he was doing communion wrong. The previous minister, they explained, had always touched the radiator before he consecrated the communion elements. The new minister, apparently somewhat insecure, decided to call the former pastor to find out what this peculiar ritual signified. The old minister explained that he had touched the radiator before picking up the chalice to discharge static electricity, so he wouldn't shock people when they drank from the cup.[71] Without the "story," the people of the congregation ascribed their own meaning to the little ritual.

We, too, must be sure that we do not allow the forms of our faith to become separated from the story. There are typically reasons for the things we do in our churches and the ways we do them, but these reasons can be lost with the passing of time. Our activities can become empty rituals, or they can devolve into dangerous parodies of their original intent. When we gather to worship, when we perform baptisms or share the Lord's Supper, or even serve in a soup kitchen, the ceremony must not displace the story. We already see the sad effects of such etiological amnesia in our society, as modern Christmas observances often seem to glorify greed instead of Jesus. We have allowed the celebration to become separated from the story, and it has been perverted into a sinful exercise of overindulgence.

Selected Bibliography

Fox, M. V. *Character and Ideology in the Book of Esther.* 2nd ed. Grand Rapids: Eerdmans, 2001.

———. *The Redaction of the Books of Esther: On Reading Composite Texts.* Atlanta: Scholars Press, 1991.

Gordis, R. "Studies in the Esther Narrative." *JBL* 95 (1976): 43–58.

Loewenstamm, S. E. "Esther 9:29–32: The Genesis of a Late Addition." *HUCA* 42 (1971): 117–24.

Rudolph, W. "Textkritisches zum Estherbuch." *VT* 4 (1954): 89–90.

71. T. Fullam, "Worship: What We're Doing and Why," *Preaching Today*, tape no. 102.

The Greatness of Xerxes and Mordecai (10:1–3)

Introduction

In the preceding section, the focus of the narrative was on the celebration of Purim. It was like a parenthesis in the story, addressing the audience with the implications of Esther and Mordecai's decrees. This closing episode, however, returns to the flow of the narrative, showing the ultimate outcome of all that has preceded it. The narrator assumes the vantage point of a historian looking back on the accomplishments of Xerxes and Mordecai from some time in the future. The king continues to become more powerful than ever, as demonstrated by his ability to impose taxes far and wide. But standing at his side was the Jew Mordecai. Unlike the wicked Haman, who sought evil against the Jews, Mordecai only sought their good. He was a true hero of the Diaspora, a Jew who did well while doing good.

Some scholars have seen this section as a superfluous addition to the book of Esther. While it does seem somewhat terse, the section forms the counterpoint for the opening scene, where readers were first introduced to King Xerxes in all his splendor. It completes the chiastic structure that has so carefully been woven into the narrative. But unlike the opening scene, these verses focus on Mordecai the Jew. It is perhaps the ultimate example of peripety in the narrative: in the opening chapter, we were dazzled by the description of King Xerxes and the glories of Persia. In these closing verses, Xerxes' glory is overshadowed by that of the Jew Mordecai.

Translation

1 King Xerxes imposed forced labor[1] on the land and on the coastlands of
the sea. **2** And his every deed of authority and might, and the account of
the advancement of Mordecai, to which the king advanced him, are they
not written in the book of the annals of the Kings of Media and Persia?
3 For Mordecai the Jew was second in rank to King Xerxes, and he was great

1. Or, "tribute."

among the Jews and pleasing to the multitude of his brothers, for he would seek the benefit of his people and would speak for the welfare of all his kindred.[2]

Textual Notes

1.a. LXX: "The king ruled the land and sea." AT: "The king recorded the dues of land and sea."

2.a. LXX and AT add that the account was written "as a memorial."

3.a. Instead of the MT, "And Mordecai the Jew was second to King Xerxes," the LXX and AT say, "For Mordecai the Jew succeeded King Xerxes."

3.b. After v. 3, both the LXX and AT add "Addition F," which recounts the interpretation of Mordecai's vision given in Addition A.

Commentary

10:1 This verse seems "incomplete," as if part of a larger story, and some scholars suggest it has been displaced here from some other document (Levenson, 132).[3] But the brevity of this description of Xerxes is significant, because it indicates that the real focus of the narrative is not on the king of Persia, but on the Jew Mordecai. In 1–2 Kings, accounts of kings' reigns often end with a terse line about some significant aspect of their administration (e.g., 1 Kgs 14:30; 15:23, 32; 22:39, and others), so the brief line here is by no means without precedent.

The more interesting question is the significance of this particular detail. Daube has argued that the statement demonstrates Xerxes did not suffer great financial loss in the matter of the Jews (reading מַס, *mas*, as "tribute" rather than "forced labor"),[4] because Mordecai had counseled him to impose taxation as an alternative source of income.[5] This interpretation seems to read too much into the statement; the text makes no allusion to Xerxes' lost income or to Mordecai giving counsel. On the other hand, Bush's interpretation (495) that the statement is designed to demonstrate Xerxes' power and prosperity might read too little into it. The statement must be viewed in light of its immediate context. We have just read how Mordecai and Esther formalized a policy among the Jews that they were to observe a yearly celebration with feasting, giving gifts to the poor, and remembering

2. Lit., "his seed."

3. So also, e.g., D. J. A. Clines, *The Esther Scroll: The Story of the Story,* JSOTSup 30 (Sheffield, UK: JSOT Press, 1984), 57.

4. This meaning is typical of Mishnaic Heb., but is not attested in any biblical texts.

5. D. Daube, "The Last Chapter of Esther," *JQR* 37 (1946): 139–47, esp. 140–46.

their deliverance. Now, we read—as a summary of Xerxes' reign—that he imposed forced labor on all the people of his vast realm. The contrast is striking, and there can be no doubt who comes out looking superior, in the eyes of Esther's audience.

The phrase "coastlands of the sea" (אִיֵּי הַיָּם, *ʾiyyê hayyām*) refers to both coasts and islands of the Mediterranean, which represented to the Jews the westernmost reaches of the world.

10:2 The closing formula found here, "And all the acts of King Xerxes, etc.," is identical to those in the biblical books of the Kings (e.g., 1 Kgs 14:29; 15:31, etc.):

> Esth 10:2: הֲלוֹא־הֵם כְּתוּבִים עַל־סֵפֶר דִּבְרֵי הַיָּמִים לְמַלְכֵי מָדַי וּפָרָס (*hălôʾ-hēm kĕtûbîm ʿal-sēper dibrê hayyāmîm lĕmalkê māday ûpārās*), lit., "Are they not written on the scroll of the matters of the days of the kings of Media and Persia?"
>
> 1 Kgs 14:29: הֲלֹא־הֵמָּה כְתוּבִים עַל־סֵפֶר דִּבְרֵי הַיָּמִים לְמַלְכֵי יְהוּדָה(*hălōʾ-hēmmâ kĕtûbîm ʿal-sēper dibrê hayyāmîm lĕmalkê yĕhûdâ*), lit., "Are they not written on the scroll of the matters of the days of the kings of Judah?"

There can be little doubt this verse is intentionally patterned after Kings. The imitation is almost certainly intended to give this narrative a sense of continuity with the chronicle of Israelite history. It does not mean, however, that we are required to take the story as a literal account of things that actually happened. All that can be said with certainty is that the statement gives the book of Esther the *appearance* of a historical narrative, like those in the books of Kings. A skilled storyteller who wants us to "suspend disbelief" and enter the world of the narrative (as the author of Esther undoubtedly did) would be expected to include such details in his account.[6]

"His every deed" refers to the acts of Xerxes, who was also responsible for the promotion of Mordecai. It is a brief and not necessarily flattering summary of the king's work. In the narrator's view, Xerxes' actions are not important, except in that they led to the promotion of Mordecai. The king exercised authority and power, but Mordecai pleased his people and prospered them.

Different words are used to designate the "book of the annals" here than what we find in Esth 2:23 (סֵפֶר דִּבְרֵי הַיָּמִים, *sēper dibrê hayyāmîm*, "book of the matters of the days") or in 6:1 (סֵפֶר הַזִּכְרֹנוֹת דִּבְרֵי הַיָּמִים, *sēper hazzikrōnôt dibrê hayyāmîm*, "book of the remembrances of the matters of the days"). Probably the same book is meant in all three cases—certainly in

6. See introduction, "Genre."

2:23 and 6:1, since the account of Mordecai's good deed was written in the "book of deeds" (2:23) and read from the "the book of remembrances" (6:1). The terminology is fluid, adjusting to the needs of context. In this verse, the term is shaped by the allusion to the book of Kings.

It is interesting to note that the narrator reverses the order of "Media and Persia" here. In chapter 1, the order was "Persia and Media" (1:3, 14, 18, 19), apparently reflecting the political preeminence of Persia. In royal chronicles, however, Media would precede Persia, having possessed the sovereignty over the empire before Cyrus the Great conquered Ecbatana in 549 BC.

10:3 The phrase "second to the king" may reflect accurately the terminology in use in the Persian Empire.[7] That fact, however, is probably not the main point here. More important for the audience would be the use of the phrase in biblical tradition. In Gen 41:43, Joseph is made to ride in the "second chariot" of Pharaoh, and Jonathan is David's "second" in 1 Sam 17:23. We might also compare the phrase to Dan 5:29, where Daniel is made "third ruler" in Babylon after demonstrating his competence. The interesting contrast between Joseph, Daniel, and Mordecai is that the other figures earned their offices by their supernatural wisdom. It is unclear what the basis was for Mordecai's promotion, outside his being Esther's stepfather. On the possible identification of Mordecai's office, see the commentary on 3:1.

The focus of the narrator's praise of Mordecai is his benefit to the Jews. We do not know whether he was a good and just administrator; it is apparently irrelevant. The narrator highlights how Mordecai was perceived in the Jewish community. It is not only his high station that gains their admiration; it is how he uses it to benefit his own people. In some contexts, this approach might seem less than praiseworthy. Should a good administrator not be impartial, seeking the good of all people in the realm? But we must keep the context in mind: the narrator sees the Jews as a persecuted minority, a people threatened by hostile forces that would deprive them of opportunities and even their very lives. Mordecai is their champion. The role he is assigned here is the wish fulfillment of a people who see themselves as the powerless victims of an oppressive society. His role is not to be fair any more so than Robin Hood was supposed to be fair to the rich.

The last phrase, "and speaking peace to all his kindred," is odd. "Speaking peace" is most likely inspired by Esth 9:30, which likewise states that Mordecai spoke "words of peace" to the Jews. The idea here could be a little different. In this verse, "speaking peace" seems to be connected with

---

7. H. Volkmann, "Der Zweite nach dem König," *Phil* 92 (1937): 285–316.

"seeking welfare" for the Jews; thus, Mordecai is speaking on their behalf, rather than addressing them with kind words.

The more unusual usage is in the final word, "his seed" (זַרְעוֹ, *zar'ô*). Elsewhere in the Bible, "his seed" is not used to designate someone's ethnic group, but his descendants (cf. Esth 9:31, where the phrase "their seed" means the Jews' descendants). The text gives us no reason to suppose Mordecai had descendants; and besides, the phrase here seems to be used synonymously with "his people." Possibly, the choice of the word *seed* was inspired by its use in Esth 6:13: "If of the seed of the Jews is Mordecai ... you shall not prevail over him." The word *seed* there is used with the sense of "nation," as it is used in 10:3. There might also be a distant allusion here to Num 24:7, Balaam's prophecy concerning Israel: "His seed will be in many waters, and his ruler will be exalted above Agag." Israel, though spread throughout many lands, finally achieved its victory over the Amalekites—not through a king, but through a queen and vizier.

In this last section of the book, Esther is conspicuously absent. That fact may be only indirectly due to sexism. After her intercessions with the king, Esther's role was mostly over. Generally, it was not the job of queens in the ancient world to administer the government (though they could wield considerable clout under some circumstances). Rather, the queen's role was to produce royal offspring. The narrator had little interest in Xerxes' offspring, since they were irrelevant to his story. The failure to mention Esther here may be taken as further evidence that the book of Esther was not a historical chronicle of Xerxes' reign or Mordecai's administration, but only an account of the origins of Purim.

Biblical Theology Comments

The ending of the book of Esther is typical of Jewish "Diaspora tales." Like Joseph, Daniel, or even Ahiqar, Mordecai overcomes his adversity and ultimately becomes prosperous in the land of his sojourn. Joseph and Daniel rise to their positions of power because of their piety and special skills. These two figures epitomize the ideal of Diaspora Judaism, that one could do well while still doing good. We see in their stories a reflection of the principles taught in Proverbs and other Wisdom texts: fear God, work hard, be virtuous, and ultimately you will prosper (Psa 1:1–3; Prov 3:5–6; 12:21). Mordecai, perhaps in keeping more with the role of the "trickster" of folkloric literature (see the introduction, "Esther and Resistance"), seems to come into his high office through luck—or divine providence. He is no Joseph, blessed with divine insight and high moral principles. He is surely no Daniel, holding fast to the law of Moses and invoking the power of God at every turn.

But perhaps that very fact might have made him a more endearing character to his audience. It took a special person to be a Daniel, but any moderately decent Jew could become a Mordecai. The common person could identify with this hero. He illustrates not the wisdom of Proverbs, but that of Ecclesiastes:

> I looked again and saw under the sun that the race does not belong to the swift, the battle does not belong to the mighty, food does not belong to the wise, wealth does not belong to the intelligent, and success does not belong to the skillful, for time and chance befalls all of them. (Eccl 9:11)

This man Mordecai was used to deliver the Jews from oppression and secure their rights not because he was the most noble or pious or wise man in the land. He was used because he was available. He was in the right place at the right time, and providence did the rest.

Application and Devotional Implications

The book of Esther has frequently been criticized for what is seen as a "nationalistic" spirit. According to its critics, the book's attitude toward Gentiles is petty and un-Christian. But the critics forget that what might seem like unbecoming pride in one setting can be noble, or even virtuous, in another. An Aryan male in Nazi Germany who brags about his country's might and glory is likely guilty of jingoism, or worse. But a Jew in that same situation talking about the proud history and accomplishments of his people is not a braggart; he is a hero. His words may help his fellow Jews to recover hope and remember that somehow, in their darkest hour, help has always seemed to come, whether they deserve it or not.

In this light, Mordecai's lack of obvious virtues should not be seen as a weakness of the book. That he does not possess supernatural strength, divine insight, or charismatic leadership skills should be an encouragement to us. Often, we are very like Mordecai. We, too, have conformed in many ways to the values and mores of our society. Our own diaspora has (to greater or lesser extents) forced us into its mold (cf. Rom 12:2). Like Mordecai, when times of crisis come, we might seek to come up with our own solutions instead of looking to the Lord. We might pressure our friends or loved ones to rescue us from problems we have created by our own pride or stubbornness. We can relate to Mordecai's fallibility, and we can be encouraged by this depiction of an ordinary man in the hands of an extraordinary providence. If God can do His work with Mordecai, He can surely work with us as well.

But are we assuming without cause that the happy outcome of the book of Esther is truly the work of God? The crisis is resolved, Purim has been instituted, and events are now looked back on from some distant vantage point, and yet even here there is no reference to God. Nothing overtly miraculous has transpired. There have been no glorious conversions or great moral insights conveyed. Our entire story has been told without one reference to miracle, to prayer, to righteousness, or to Torah. Is it possible that we are trying to force God into a text where He is, in fact, simply absent?

In the introduction, I argued that the book of Esther is not a secular document—that it deliberately avoids references to God in order to make a theological statement. This proposal has been suggested by a number of commentators, though there is some difference of opinion regarding the nature of the theological statement that is intended. My position is that God has deliberately "hidden His face" in the book of Esther, in fulfillment of the threat made in Deut 31:18 (and 32:20): "I will certainly hide my face on that day, because of all the evil that they did because they turned to other gods." The book of Esther subtly illustrates that God's word was fulfilled. Just as He promised, His people were spread among the nations, and God hid His face from them in that foreign land. But just because God was hidden, we must not assume that He was absent. God promised in Deut 32:36–43 that He would avenge His people, even after He had hidden His face from them. Even though God takes no obvious part in the Esther narrative, He is certainly at work in the numerous unlikely coincidences that lead to the deliverance of the Jews and their conquest of their enemies.

In this way, too, the book of Esther should feel real to us. In our crises, there will undoubtedly be times that we, too, will feel as if God has hidden His face from us. Indeed, when we consider the iniquity of society, the compromise and hypocrisy of the church, and the sin that taints even the seemingly noble and good acts that we perform, we might well wonder whether God could bear to show His face among His people. Yet we experience His providence daily—not, typically, in miraculous works that defy scientific explanation, but in unlikely coincidences, improbable victories, or words that leap from the page in the middle of a sleepless night. Viewed separately, these serendipities may not seem to be part of any great master plan. We may be like people with our noses pressed against a wall and trying to make sense of a mural. We must step back and look at the big picture: the intersecting lines, the blending colors, the places where no paint has been applied. It is when we look at the whole that we can recognize that the hand of a master has been at work. In similar ways, any one coincidence may look like chance or luck. But when we consider the ways that so many chances have come together to bring us where we are, we realize that no simple roll of the dice has shaped our destiny. It is not that God is nowhere, but that He is *everywhere*, hidden in plain view in the grand design of our everyday lives.

Selected Bibliography

Clines, D. J. A. *The Esther Scroll: The Story of the Story*. JSOTSup 30. Sheffield, UK: JSOT Press, 1984.

Daube, D. "The Last Chapter of Esther." *JQR* 37 (1946): 139–47.

Fox, M. V. *Character and Ideology in the Book of Esther*. 2nd ed. Grand Rapids: Eerdmans, 2001.

Volkmann, H. "Der Zweite nach dem König." *Phil* 92 (1937): 285–316.

List of Foreign and Technical Words

chiasm: A literary structure where parallel elements correspond in an inverted order.

inclusio: A literary framing device in which the same word or phrase occurs at both the beginning and the end of a linguistic unit.

***Kethiv*:** Aramaic for "what is written." The written text of the MT, as opposed to what the Masoretic scribes read. See also *Qere*.

***Leitwort*:** A motto or catchphrase used to unify a narrative and point to a theme.

nomen regens: The first of two nouns in a gen. construction, which occurs in a phonetically abbreviated state.

***Qere*:** Aramaic for "what is read." A marginal notation in the MT made by scribes when the written text was confusing or unclear. See also *Kethiv*.

terminus ad quem: "limit until which." The latest time an event could have happened.

terminus post quem: "limit after which." The earliest time an event could have happened.

Vorlage: The manuscript from which a scribe copied a text.

General Bibliography

Technical Monographs

Beal, Timothy K. *The Book of Hiding: Gender, Ethnicity, Annihilation, and Esther.* London: Routledge, 1997.

Berg, Sandra B. *The Book of Esther: Motifs, Themes and Structure.* SBLDS 44. Missoula, MT: Scholars Press, 1979.

Bergey, Ronald L. "The Book of Esther: Its Place in the Linguistic Milieu of Post-exilic Biblical Hebrew: A Study in Late Biblical Hebrew." Dissertation, Dropsie College, 1983.

Bickerman, Elias J. *Four Strange Books of the Bible: Jonah, Daniel, Kohelet, Esther.* New York: Schocken Books, 1967.

Brenner, Athalya, ed. *Ruth and Esther: A Feminist Companion to the Bible.* Sheffield: Sheffield Academic Press, 1999.

Clines, David J. A. *The Esther Scroll: The Story of the Story.* JSOTSup 30. Sheffield, UK: JSOT Press, 1984.

Craig, Kenneth M. *Reading Esther: A Case for the Literary Carnivalesque.* Louisville, KY: Westminster John Knox, 1995.

Day, Linda. *Three Faces of a Queen: Characterization in the Books of Esther.* Sheffield: Sheffield Academic Press, 1995.

De Troyer, Kristin. *The End of the Alpha-Text of Esther: Translation and Narrative Technique in MT 8:1–17, LXX 8:1–17 and AT 7:14–41.* SBLSCS 48. Atlanta: Society of Biblical Literature, 2000.

———. "Esther in Text- and Literary-critical Paradise." In L. J. Greenspoon and S. W. Crawford, eds., *The Book of Esther in Modern Research*, 31–49. New York: T&T Clark, 2003.

Dorothy, Charles V. *The Books of Esther: Structure, Genre and Textual Integrity.* Sheffield: Sheffield Academic Press, 1997.

Fountain, Allison K. *Literary and Empirical Readings of the Books of Esther.* Oxford: Peter Lang, 2002.

Fox, Michael V. *Character and Ideology in the Book of Esther.* 2nd ed. Grand Rapids: Eerdmans, 2001.

———. *The Redaction of the Books of Esther: On Reading Composite Texts.* Atlanta: Scholars Press, 1991.

Greenspoon, Leonard, and Sidnie White-Crawford, eds. *The Book of Esther in Modern Research*. London/New York: T&T Clark, 2003.

Harvey, Charles D. *Finding Morality in the Diaspora?: Moral Ambiguity and Transformed Morality in the Books of Esther*. Berlin: Walter de Gruyter, 2003.

Heimerdinger, Jean-Marc. *Topic, Focus and Foreground in Ancient Hebrew Narratives*. Sheffield: Sheffield Academic Press, 1999.

Hoschander, Jacob. *The Book of Esther in the Light of History*. Oxford: Oxford University Press, 1923.

Jobes, Karen H. *The Alpha-Text of Esther—Its Character and Relationship to the Masoretic Text*. SBLDS 153. Atlanta: Scholars Press, 1996.

Kahana, Hannah. *Esther: Juxtaposition of the Septuagint Translation with the Hebrew Text*. Leuven: Peeters, 2005.

Laniak, Timothy S. *Shame and Honor in the Book of Esther*. Atlanta: Scholars Press, 1998.

Larkin, Katrina A. *Ruth and Esther.* Old Testament Guides. Sheffield: Sheffield Academic Press, 1996.

Longacre, Robert E. *Joseph, a Story of Divine Providence: A Text Theoretical and Textlinguistic Analysis of Genesis 37 and 39–48*. Winona Lake, IN: Eisenbrauns, 1989.

Moore, Carey A., ed. *Studies in the Book of Esther: Selected with a Prolegomenon by Carey A. Moore*. New York: KTAV Publishing House, 1982.

Rodriguez, Angel M. *Esther: A Theological Approach*. Berrien Springs, MI: Andrews University Press, 1995.

Schenker, Adrian, ed. *The Earliest Text of the Hebrew Bible: The Relationship between the Masoretic Text and the Hebrew Base of the Septuagint Reconsidered*. Atlanta: Scholars Press, 2003.

Tawil, H. "Two Notes on the Treaty Terminology of the Sefire Inscriptions." *CBQ* 42 (1980): 30–37.

von Herrmann, J. R. "Narratological Aspects of the Masoretic Text of Esther." Unpublished doctoral dissertation. Catholic University of America, 2004.

Walfish, B. *Esther in Medieval Garb: Jewish Interpretation of the Book of Esther in the Middle Ages.* New York: SUNY Press, 1993.

Weiland, Forrest S. "The Contribution of Literary Analysis to the Understanding of Genre, Unity, and Message in the Book of Esther." Unpublished doctoral dissertation. Dallas Theological Seminary, 2001.

Articles

Albright, W. F. "The Lachish Cosmetic Burner and Esther 2:12." In *A Light unto My Path: Old Testament Essays in Honor of Jacob M. Myers*, ed. H. N. Bream, 25–32. Philadelphia: Temple University Press, 1974.

Anderson, Bernhard W. "The Place of the Book of Esther in the Christian Bible." *JR* 30 (January 1950): 32-43.

Barrick, William B. "The Meaning and Use of *RKB* in Biblical Hebrew." *JBL* 101 (1982): 481–503.

Beckman, Gary. "The Anatolian Myth of *Illuyanka*." *JANES* 14 (1982): 11–25.

Beller, David. "A Theology of the Book of Esther." *ResQ* 39 (1997): 1–15.

Benjamin, Chaya. "An Illustrated Venetian Esther Scroll and the Commedia dell'Arte." *The Stieglitz Collection: Masterpieces of Jewish Art* (1987): 259–83.

Bergey, Ronald L. "Late Linguistic Features in Esther." *JQR* 75 (1984): 66–78.

———. "Post-Exilic Hebrew Linguistic Developments in Esther: A Diachronic Approach." *JETS* 31 (1988): 161–68.

Berlin, Adele. "The Book of Esther and Ancient Storytelling." *JBL* 120 (2001): 3–14.

Bickerman, Elias J. "The Colophon of the Greek Book of Esther." *JBL* 63 (1944): 339–62.

Boyd-Taylor, Cameron. "Esther's Great Adventure: Reading the LXX Version of the Book of Esther in Light of Its Assimilation to the Conventions of the Greek Romantic Novel." *BIOSCS* 30 (1997): 81–113.

Bresciani, E. "The Persian Occupation of Egypt." In *The Cambridge History of Iran*, ed. I. Gershevitch, 2:502–28. Cambridge: Cambridge University Press, 1985.

Broyde, Michael J. "Defilement of the Hands, Canonization of the Bible, and the Special Status of Esther, Ecclesiastes, and Song of Songs." *Judaism* 44 (1995): 65–79.

Bush, Frederick W. "The Book of Esther: Opus non gratum in the Christian Canon." *BBR* 8 (1998): 39–54.

Cameron, G. G. "The Persian Satrapies and Related Matters." *JNES* 32 (1973): 47–56.

Clines, David J. A. "The Esther Scroll: The Story of the Story." JSOTSup 30. Sheffield: JSOT Press, 1984.

———. "In Quest of the Historical Mordecai." *VT* 41 (1991): 129–136.

———. "Reading Esther from Left to Right: Contemporary Strategies for Reading a Biblical Text." In *The Bible in Three Dimensions: Essays in Celebration of Forty Years of Biblical Studies in the University of Sheffield*, ed. W. E. Fowl, D. J. A. Clines, and S. E. Porter, 3–22. Sheffield, UK: JSOT Press, 1990.

Cook, H. J. "The A-Text of the Greek Versions of the Book of Esther." *ZAW* 81 (1969): 369–76.

Crawford, Sidnie White. "Esther." In *Women in Scripture*, ed. Carol Meyers, 74–77. Grand Rapids: Eerdmans, 2001.

———. "Esther Not Judith: Why One Made It and the Other Didn't." *BR* 18 (2002): 22–31, 45.

———. "Has Every Book of the Bible Been Found among the Dead Sea Scrolls?" *BR* 12 (1996): 28–33, 56.

Daniel, J. "Anti-Semitism in the Hellenistic-Roman Period." *JBL* 98 (1979): 45–65.

Daube, David. "The Last Chapter of Esther." *JQR* 37 (1946): 139–47.

De Troyer, Kristin. "On Crowns and Diadems from Kings, Queens, Horses and Men." *IOSCS Congress* 9 (1997): 355–67.

Duchesne-Guillemin, J. "Les noms des eunuques d'Assuérus." *Le Muséon* 46 (1953): 105–8.

Evans, T. V. "Approaches to the Language of the Septuagint." *JJS* 56 (2005): 25–33.

Fox, M. V. "The Religion of the Book of Esther." *Judaism* 39 (1990): 135–47.

———. "The Structure of the Book of Esther." In *Isac Leo Seeligman Volume: Essays on the Bible and the Ancient World*, ed. A. Rofé and Y. Zakovitch III, 291–303. Jerusalem: E. Rubenstein, 1983.

Friedberg, Albert D. "A New Clue in the Dating of the Composition of the Book of Esther." *VT* 50 (2000): 561–65.

Frojmovic, Eva. "The Perfect Scribe and an Early Engraved Esther Scroll." *British Library Journal* 23, no. 1 (1997): 68–80.

Frolov, Serge. "Two Eunuchs, Two Conspiracies, and One Loyal Jew: The Narrative of Botched Regicide in Esther as Text- and Redaction-Critical Test Case." *VT* 52 (2002): 304–25.

Gan, M. "מגילת אסתר באספקלריית יוסף במצרים." *Tarbiz* 31 (1961–1962): 144–49.

Gehman, H. S. "Notes on the Persian Words in the Book of Esther." *JBL* 43 (1924): 321–28.

Goldman, Stan. "Narrative and Ethical Ironies in Esther." *JSOT* 47 (1990): 15–31.

Gordis, Robert. "Religion, Wisdom and History in the Book of Esther—a New Solution to an Ancient Crux." *JBL* 100 (1981): 359–88.

———. "Studies in the Esther Narrative." *JBL* 95 (1976): 43–58.

Goswell, Gregory R. "Keeping God out of the Book of Esther." *EvQ* 82 (2010): 99–110.

Grasham, William W. "The Theology of the Book of Esther." *ResQ* 16 (1973): 99–111.

Greenfield, J. C. "Aramaic in the Achaemenian Empire." In *The Cambridge History of Iran,* ed. I. Gershevitch, 2:698–713. Cambridge: Cambridge University Press, 1985.

Greenstein, E. "A Jewish Reading of Esther." In *Judaic Perspectives on Ancient Israel*, ed. J. Neusner, B. Levine, and E. Frerichs, 225–43. Philadelphia: Fortress, 1987.

Gutmann, Joseph. "Estherrolle." *Reallexicon zur Deutschen Kunstgeschichte* (1969), vol. 6, cols. 88–103.

Haelewyck, Jean-Claude. "The Relevance of the Old Latin Version for the Septuagint, with Special Emphasis on the Book of Esther." *JTS* 57 (2006): 439–73.

Hallo, William W. "The First Purim." *BA* 46 (Winter 1983): 19–26.

Haupt, Paul. "Critical Notes on Esther." *AJSL* 24 (1907–1908): 97–186.

Heltzer, Michael. "A Propos des Banquets des Rois Achéménides et du Retour D'Exil sous Zorobabel." *RB* 86 (1979): 102–6.

———. "The Book of Esther: Where Does Fiction Start and History End?" *BRev* 8 (February 1992): 24–30, 41.

———. "'From India to Ethiopia' and 'from the Hellespont to India' (the Imperial Outlook)." In *Studies in Historical Geography and Biblical Historiography: Presented to Zechariah Kallai*, ed. G. Galil and M. Weinfeld, 42–43. VTSup 81. Leiden: Brill, 2000.

Herst, Roger E. "The Purim Connection." *USQR* 28 (1973): 139–45.

Hubbard, Robert L. "Vashti, Amestris, and Esther 1, 9." *ZAW* 119 (2007): 259–71.

Huey, F. B., Jr. "Irony as the Key to Understanding the Book of Esther." *SwJT* 32 (1990): 36–39.

Humphreys, W. "A Lifestyle for Diaspora: A Study of the Tales of Esther and Daniel." *JBL* 92 (1973): 211–23.

———. "Novella." In *Saga, Novella, Legend, Tale: Narrative Forms in Old Testament Literature*, ed. G. W. Coats, 82–96. Sheffield: JSOT Press, 1985.

———. "The Story of Esther and Mordecai: An Early Jewish Novella." In *Saga, Novella, Legend, Tale: Narrative Forms in Old Testament Literature*, ed. G. W. Coats, 97–113. Sheffield: JSOT Press, 1985.

Jackowski, Karol. "Holy Disobedience in Esther." *ThTo* 45 (January 1989): 403–14.

Jacob, Benno. "Das Buch Esther bei dem LXX." *ZAW* 10 (1890): 241–98.

Johnson, Sara R. "Novelistic Elements in Esther: Persian or Hellenistic, Jewish or Greek?" *CBQ* 67 (2005): 571–89.

Jones, Bruce W. "Two Misconceptions about the Book of Esther." *CBQ* 39 (1977): 171–81.

Klasens, A. "Cambyses en Égypte." *Ex Oriente Lux* 10 (1946): 339–49.

Larsson, Gerhard. "Is the Book of Esther Older than Has Been Believed?" *VT* 52 (2002): 130–31.

Lewy, Julius. "The Feast of the 14th Day of Adar." *HUCA* 14 (1939): 127–51.

———. "Old Assyrian *puru'um* and *pûrum*." *RHA* 5 (1939): 116–24.

Liberman Mintz, Sharon. "A Persian Tale in Turkish Garb: Exotic Imagery in Eighteenth-Century Illustrated Esther Scroll." In *For Every Thing a Season: Proceedings of the Symposium on Jewish Ritual Art*, ed. Joseph Gutmann, 76–101. Cleveland: Cleveland State University Press, 2002.

Lichtenstein, H. "Die Fastenrolle, eine Untersuchung zur jüdisch-hellenistischen Geschichte; מגלת תענית." *HUCA* 8–9 (1931–1932): 257–351.

Littman, Robert J. "The Religious Policy of Xerxes and the Book of Esther." *JQR* 65 (1975): 145–55.

Loader, James A. "Esther as a Novel with Different Levels of Meaning." *ZAW* 90 (1978): 417–21.

Loewenstamm, Samuel E. "Esther 9:29–32: The Genesis of a Late Addition." *HUCA* 42 (1971): 117–24.

Longacre, Robert E. "Interpreting Biblical Stories." In T. A. van Dijk, ed., *Discourse and Literature*, 169–87. Amsterdam: John Benjamins, 1985.

Meinhold, A. "Die Gattung der Josephsgeschichte und des Estherbuches: Diasporanovelle, I." *ZAW* 87 (1975): 306–24.

———. "Die Gattung der Josephsgeschichte und des Estherbuches: Diasporanovelle II." *ZAW* 88 (1976): 72–93.

Merrill, Eugene H. "A Theology of Ezra-Nehemiah and Esther." In *A Biblical Theology of the Old Testament*, ed. R. Zuck, 189–205. Chicago: Moody Press, 1991.

Metzger, Mendel. "The Earliest Engraved Italian Megilloth." *BJRL* 48 (1966): 381–432.

———. "The John Rylands Megillah and Some Other Illustrated Megilloth of the XVth to XVIIth Centuries." *BJRL* 45 (1962): 148–84.

———. "A Study of Some Unknown Hand-Painted Megilloth of the Seventeenth and Eighteenth Centuries." *BJRL* 46 (1963): 84–126.

Milik, Jozef T. "Les Modèles Araméens du Livre d'Esther dans la Grotte 4 de Qumran." *RQ* 15 (1992): 321–406.

Millard, Alan R. "The Persian Names in Esther and the Reliability of the Hebrew Text." *JBL* 96 (1977): 481–88.

Miller, Charles H. "Esther's Levels of Meaning." *ZAW* 92 (1980): 145–48.

Mills, Mary E. "Household and Table: Diasporic Boundaries in Daniel and Esther." *CBQ* 68 (2006): 408–20.

Moore, Carey A. "Archaeology and the Book of Esther." *BA* 38 (September–December 1975): 62–79.

———. "Eight Questions Most Frequently Asked about the Book of Esther." *BRev* 3 (Spring 1987): 16–21, 28–31.

———. "Esther Revisited: An Examination of Some Esther Studies over the Past Decade." In *Biblical Studies in Honor of Samuel Iwry*, ed. A. Kort and S. Morschauser, 163–74. Winona Lake, IN: Eisenbrauns, 1985.

———. "A Greek Witness to a Different Hebrew Text of Esther." *ZAW* 79 (1967): 351–58.

———. "On the Origins of the LXX Additions to the Book of Esther." *JBL* 92 (1973): 382–93.

Newman, R. "The Council of Jamnia and the Old Testament Canon." *WTJ* 38 (1976): 319–48.

Niditch, Susan, and Robert Doran. "The Success Story of the Wise Courtier: A Formal Approach." *JBL* 96 (1977): 179–93.

Noss, Philip A. "A Footnote on Time: The Book of Esther." *BT* 44 (July 1993): 309–20.

Oppenheim, A. L. "On Royal Gardens in Mesopotamia." *JNES* 24 (1965): 328–33.

Paddock, C. L. "Lessons from Bible Characters—2: Esther." *RH* 134 (January 31, 1957): 7.

Pierce, Ronald W. "The Politics of Esther and Mordecai: Courage or Compromise?" *BBR* 2 (1992): 75–89.

Rabin, Chaim. "The Translation Process and the Character of the Septuagint." *Textus* 6 (1968): 1–26.

Radday, Yehudah T. "Chiasm in Joshua, Judges and others." *LB* 3 (1973): 6–13.

———. "Esther with Humour." In *On Humour and the Comic in the Hebrew Bible,* ed. Y. T. Radday and A. Brenner, 295–313. Sheffield: Almond, 1990.

———. "Humour in Names." In *On Humour and the Comic in the Hebrew Bible,* ed. Y. T. Radday and A. Brenner, 59–97. Sheffield: Almond, 1990.

Ringgren, H. "Esther and Purim." *SEA* 20 (1956): 5–24.

Rosenthal, Ludwig. "Die *Josephsgeschichte* mit den Buchern Esther und Daniel verglichen." *ZAW* 15 (1895): 278–84.

Roth, Cecil. "The Feast of Purim and the Origins of the Blood Accusation." *Speculum* 8 (1933): 520–26.

Rubinstein, Arie. "Finite Verb Continued by an Infinitive Absolute in Biblical Hebrew." *VT* 2 (1952): 362–67.

Rudolph, Wilhelm. "Textkritisches zum Estherbuch." *VT* 4 (1954): 89–90.

Running, Leona Glidden. "She Saved a Nation." *RH* 152 (March 13, 1975): 6–7.

Sabua, Rachel B. K. "The Hidden Hand of God." *BRev* 8 (February 1992): 31–33.

Salvesen, Alison. "כֶּתֶר (Esther 1:11; 2:17; 6:8): 'Something to Do with a Camel'?" *JSS* 44 (1999): 35–46.

Sasson, Jack M. " Esther." In *The Literary Guide to the Bible,* ed. Robert Alter and Frank Kermode, 335–42. Cambridge, MA: Belknap Press, 1987.

Schildgen, B. "A Blind Promise: Mark's Retrieval of Esther." *Poetics Today* 15 (1994): 115–31.

Shea, W. "Esther and History." *AUSS* 14 (1976): 227–46.

———. "Esther and History—1." *Ministry* 55 (July 1982): 26–27.

———. "Esther and History—2." *Ministry* 55 (September 1982): 26–27.

Sigal, L. "The Feminine Divine in the Book of Esther: A Psychoanalytic Study." In *Bible in Light of Cuneiform Literature,* Scripture in Context III, ed. W. Hallo, 381–411. Lewiston, ME: Edwin Mellen, 1986.

———. "Models of Love and Hate [Esther, Deborah, Ruth, Beruriah]." *Daughters of Sarah* 16 (1990): 8–10.

Simon, Moshe D. "'Many Thoughts in the Heart of Man ... ': Irony and Theology in the Book of Esther." *Tradition* 31 (1997): 5–27.

Snyman, Gerrie. "Race in South Africa: A Hidden Transcript Turned Public? The Problem of Identifying with Esther/Mordecai or Haman in the Book of Esther." *Scriptura* 84 (2003): 438–52.

Stefanovic, Z. "'Go at Once!': Thematic Reversals in the Book of Esther." *AJT* 8 (1994): 163–71.

Sterk, J. P. "How Many Books of Esther Are There?" *BT* 36, no. 4 (1985): 440–42.

Taggar-Cohen, A. "The Casting of Lots among the Hittites in Light of Ancient Near Eastern Parallels." *JANES* 29 (2007): 97–103.

Talmon, Shemayahu. "Was the Book of Esther Known at Qumran?" *DSD* 2 (1995): 253–56.

———. "Wisdom in the Book of Esther." *VT* 13 (1963): 422–55.

Talshir, David, and Zipora Talshir. "The Double Month Naming in Late Biblical Books: A New Clue for Dating Esther?" *VT* 54 (2004): 549–55.

Thornton, Timothy C. G. "The Crucifixion of Haman and the Scandal of the Cross." *JTS* 37 (1986): 419–26.

Torrey, Charles C. "The Older Book of Esther." *HTR* 37 (1944): 1–40.

Tov, Emanuel. "The 'Lucianic Text' of the Canonical and the Apocryphal Section of Esther: A Rewritten Biblical Book." *Textus* 10 (1982): 1–25.

Vogelstein, M. "Bakshish for Bagoas?" *JQR* 33 (1942–1943): 89–92.

Volkmann, H. "Der Zweite nach dem König." *Phil* 92 (1937): 285–316.

Wechsler, Michael G. "The Appellation Bougaios and Ethnic Contextualization in the Greek Text of Esther." *VT* 51 (2001): 109–14.

———. "The Purim-Passover Connection: A Reflection of Jewish Exegetical Tradition in the Peshitta Book of Esther." *JBL* 117 (1998): 321–27.

———. "Shadow and Fulfillment in the Book of Esther." *BSac* 154 (July–September 1997): 275–84.

———. "Two Para-Biblical Novellae from Qumran Cave 4: A Reevaluation of 4Q550." *DSD* 7 (2000): 140–72.

Weiland, Forrest S. "Historicity, Genre, and Narrative Design in the Book of Esther." *BSac* 159 (2002): 151–65.

———. "Literary Clues to God's Providence in the Book of Esther." *BSac* 160 (2003): 34–47.

———. "Plot Structure in the Book of Esther." *BSac* 159 (2002): 277–87.

Wenham, Gordon J. "Beᶜtûlâ: A Girl of Marriageable Age." *VT* 22 (1972): 326–48.

White-Crawford, S. "Has Esther Been Found at Qumran? 4QProto-Esther and the Esther Corpus." *RevQ* 17 (1996): 307–25.

Wiebe, John M. "Esther 4:14: 'Will Relief and Deliverance Arise for the Jews from Another Place?'" *CBQ* 53 (1991): 409–15.

Wischnitzer, Rachel. "The Esther Story in Art." In *The Purim Anthology*, ed. P. Goodman, 222–49. Philadelphia: Jewish Publication Society, 1973.

Wright, J. Stafford. "Esther, Book of." In *The Zondervan Pictorial Encyclopedia of the Bible*, 2:376–80. Grand Rapids: Zondervan, 1975.

———. "The Historicity of the Book of Esther." In *New Perspectives on the Old Testament*, ed. J. Barton Payne, 34–47. Waco, TX: Word, 1970.

Wyler, Bea. "Esther: The Incomplete Emancipation of a Queen." In *A Feminist Companion to Esther, Judith, and Susanna*, ed. A. Brenner, 111–35. Sheffield: Sheffield Academic Press, 1995.

Yahuda, A. S. "The Meaning of the Name Esther." *JRAS* 78 (1946): 174–78.

Yamauchi, Edwin M. "The Archaeological Background of Esther." *BSac* 137 (1980): 99–117.

———. "Mordecai, the Persepolis Tablets, and the Susa Excavations." *VT* 42 (1992): 272–74.

Young, T. C. "The Early History of the Medes and Persians and the Achaemenid Empire until the Death of Cambyses." In *CAH 4: Persia, Greece, and the Western Mediterranean*, ed. J. Boardman. Cambridge: Cambridge University Press, 1988.

Youngblood, Ronald. "The Name of God Concealed in the Book of Esther." *BRev* 3 (Fall 1987): 6–7.

Zadok, R. "Notes on Esther." *ZAW* 98 (1986): 105–10.

———. "On the Historical Background of the Book of Esther." *BN* 24 (1984): 18–23.

General Books

Ackroyd, Peter. *Exile and Restoration: A Study of Hebrew Thought in the Sixth Century*. Philadelphia: Westminster, 1968.

Aejmelaeus, Anneli. *On the Trail of the Septuagint Translators: Collected Essays*. Kampen, Netherlands: Kok Pharos, 1993.

Avi-Yonah, Michael. *The Holy Land: A Historical Geography from the Persian to the Arab Conquest 536 B.C. to A.D. 640*. Jerusalem: Carta, 2002.

Beck, John A. *Translators as Storytellers: A Study in Septuagint Translation Technique*. Oxford: Peter Lang, 2000.

Beckwith, Roger T. *The Old Testament Canon of the New Testament Church*. Grand Rapids: Eerdmans, 1986.

Biblia Hebraica Stuttgartensia (BHS). Stuttgart: Deutsche Bibelgesellschaft, 1997.

Briant, Pierre. *From Cyrus to Alexander: A History of the Persian Empire*. Winona Lake, IN: Eisenbrauns, 2002.

Brooke, George J., and Barnabas Lindars, eds. *International Symposium on the Septuagint and Its Relations to the Dead Sea Scrolls and Other Writings: Septuagint, Scrolls, and Cognate Writings* (Manchester, 1990). Atlanta: Scholars Press, 1992.

Brosius, Maria. *Women in Ancient Persia, 539–331 B.C.* Oxford: Clarendon, 1996.

Bryce, Trevor. *The World of the Neo-Hittite Kingdoms: A Political and Military History*. Oxford: Oxford University Press, 2012.

Childs, Brevard S. *Introduction to the Old Testament as Scripture.* Philadelphia: Fortress, 1979.

Conybeare, Frederick C., and George A. Stock. *Grammar of Septuagint Greek: With Selected Readings, Vocabularies, and Updated Indexes*. Peabody, MA: Hendrickson, 1995.

Dandamayev, Muhammad A. *Iranians in Achaemenid Babylonia*. Columbia Lectures on Iranian Studies 6. Costa Mesa, CA: Mazda, 1992.

———. *A Political History of the Achaemenid Empire*. Leiden: Brill, 1989.

De Vaux, Roland. *Ancient Israel: Its Life and Institutions.* Grand Rapids: Eerdmans, 1997.

deSilva, David A. *Introducing the Apocrypha: Message, Context, and Significance.* Grand Rapids: Baker Academic, 2002.

Eddy, Samuel K. *The King Is Dead: Near Eastern Resistance to Hellenism, 334–31 B.C.* Lincoln: University of Nebraska Press, 1961.

Flint, Peter, W. E. Tov, and James C. VanderKam, eds. *Studies in the Hebrew Bible, Qumran, and the Septuagint Presented to Eugene Ulrich*. Leiden: Brill, 2006.

Geisler, Norman, and Thomas Howe. *When Critics Ask: A Popular Handbook on Bible Difficulties.* Grand Rapids: Baker Books, 1992.

Ginsberg, Harold L. *The Five Megilloth and Jonah*. Philadelphia: Jewish Publication Society, 1969.

Glueck, Nelson. *Hesed in the Bible.* Cincinnati: Hebrew Union College Press, 1967.

Hamilton, Victor P. *Handbook on the Historical Books.* Grand Rapids: Baker, 2001.

Harrington, Daniel J. *Invitation to the Apocrypha*. Grand Rapids: Eerdmans, 1999.

Harrison, Roland K. *Introduction to the Old Testament.* Grand Rapids: Eerdmans, 1969.

Hengel, Martin. *The Septuagint as Christian Scripture: Its Prehistory and the Problem of Its Canon*. Edinburgh: T&T Clark, 2002.

Herzfeld, E. *The Persian Empire: Studies in the Geography and Ethnography of the Ancient Near East.* Wiesbaden: Steiner, 1968.

Hill, Andrew E., and John H. Walton. *A Survey of the Old Testament*. 2nd ed. Grand Rapids: Zondervan, 2000.

Howard, David, Jr. *An Introduction to the Old Testament Historical Books*. Chicago: Moody Press, 1993.

James, Carolyn Custis. *Lost Women of the Bible*. Grand Rapids: Zondervan, 2005.

Jellicoe, Sidney. *The Septuagint and Modern Study*. Winona Lake, IN: Eisenbrauns, 1989.

Jobes, Karen H., and Moisés Silva. *Invitation to the Septuagint*. Carlisle, UK: Paternoster, 2000.

Kaufmann, Yehezkel. תולדות האמונה הישראלית (*The Religion of Israel, from Its Beginnings to the Babylonian Exile*). Tel Aviv: Dvir, 1964.

Klein, Lilliam R. *From Deborah to Esther: Sexual Politics in the Hebrew Bible*. Minneapolis: Fortress, 2003.

Leiman, S. *The Canonization of the Hebrew Scriptures: The Talmudic and Midrashic Evidence*. Hamden, CT: Archon, 1976.

McDonald, Lee M., and James A. Sanders. *The Canon Debate*. Peabody, MA: Hendrickson, 2002.

Merrill, Eugene H. *Kingdom of Priests: A History of Old Testament Israel*. Grand Rapids: Baker Book House, 1987.

Niditch, Susan. *A Prelude to Biblical Folklore: Underdogs and Tricksters*. Champaign: University of Illinois Press, 2000.

Olmstead, Albert Ten Eyck. *A History of the Persian Empire*. Chicago: University of Chicago Press, 1948.

Perdue, Leo G., Joseph Blenkinsopp, John J. Collins, and Carol Meyers, eds. *Families in Ancient Israel*. The Family, Religion, and Culture. Louisville, KY: Westminster John Knox, 1997.

Pfeiffer, Robert H. *Introduction to the Old Testament*. New York/London: Harper & Brothers, 1941.

Porten, Bezalel. *The Archives of Elephantine: The Life of an Ancient Jewish Military Colony*. Berkeley: University of California Press, 1968.

Rahlfs, A., and R. Hanhart, eds. *Septuaginta: id est Vetus Testamentum graece iuxta LXX interpretes*. Stuttgart: Deutsche Bibelstiftung, 2006.

Schäfer, Peter. *Judeophobia: Attitudes toward the Jews in the Ancient World*. Cambridge, MA: Harvard University Press, 1997.

Schürer, E. *The History of the Jewish People in the Age of Jesus Christ (175 BC–AD135)*. Rev. and ed. Geza Vermes, Fergus Millar, and Matthew Black. 4 vols. Edinburgh: T&T Clark, 1973–1987.

Scott, J. *Domination and the Arts of Resistance: Hidden Transcripts*. New Haven, CT: Yale University Press, 1990.

Stein, R. *A Basic Guide to Interpreting the Bible: Playing by the Rules*. 2nd ed. Grand Rapids: Baker, 2011.

Stuart, Moses. *Critical History and Defense of the Old Testament Canon*. Andover, MA: Allen, Morrill, and Wardwell, 1845.

Tov, Emanuel. *Textual Criticism of the Hebrew Bible*. Rev. 2nd ed. Assen: Van Gorcum, 2001.

Wills, Lawrence M. *The Jew in the Court of the Foreign King*. Minneapolis: Fortress Press, 1990.

———. *The Jewish Novel in the Ancient World*. Ithaca, NY: Cornell University Press, 1995.

Yamauchi, Edwin M. *Persia and the Bible.* Grand Rapids: Baker, 1997.

Young, Ian, Robert Rezetko, and M. Ehrensvärd. *Linguistic Dating of Biblical Texts*. 2 vols. London: Equinox, 2008.

Zohary, Michael. *Plants of the Bible.* Cambridge: Cambridge University Press, 1982.

Index of Biblical Verses

Old Testament

Genesis

1–11 ... 316
3:16 ... 170
3:21 ... 196
3:23 ... 195
4:14 ... 195
4:15 ... 196
4:19–24 ... 194
6:7 ... 195
6:8 ... 258
8:1 ... 177
9:2 ... 326
12:6 ... 195
12:15 ... 298
13:2 ... 167
13:14–17 ... 195
15:7 ... 195
15:13–14 ... 343
15:17–21 ... 195
16:1–6 ... 194
16:2 ... 189
17:9–14 ... 356
18:6 ... 261
18:13 ... 258
18:18 ... 234
18:20 ... 165
20:11 ... 326
21:8–14 ... 194
22:12 ... 314
23:7 ... 321
24:12 ... 277
26:12–14 ... 167
27:41 ... 279
29:21 ... 189
29:23 ... 189
30:22 ... 177
30–31 ... 194
33:3 ... 216
36:12 ... 78, 214
36:16 ... 214
37:2 ... 172
37:22 ... 314
37:34 ... 280
38 ... 169, 295
39:1 ... 258
39:9 ... 197
39:10 ... 217
39:21 ... 187, 258
40:12–13 ... 249
40:14 ... 277
40:18–19 ... 249
41 ... 61, 217, 309
41:8 ... 284
41:16 ... 197, 309
41:37–45 ... 216
41:42 ... 309, 320
41:43 ... 216, 280, 282, 361
41:51–52 ... 197
42:6 ... 92, 216
43:8 ... 172
43:14 ... 249
44:34 ... 313
45:4–11 ... 309
45:5–8 ... 197
46:27 ... 315
50:3 ... 315
50:16 ... 244
50:20 ... 194, 198, 302, 342

Exodus

1:13 ... 228
1:15–16 ... 286
1:15–22 ... 342
1:17 ... 286
1:22 ... 286
2:6 ... 172
2:10 ... 91, 197
3:20 ... 314
4:22–23 ... 197
4:23 ... 232
5:5 ... 321
7:5 ... 342
9:15 ... 314
10:1–2 ... 342
11 ... 332
11:3 ... 332, 342
12:14 ... 351
12:15–20 ... 347
12:29–30 ... 286
12:35–36 ... 342
12:36 ... 324
12:43–49 ... 350
12–13 ... 356
13:15 ... 232
14 ... 286

15:16 323
17:8–13 214
17:8–16 41
17:14 .... 319, 325, 355
17:14–16 .... 58, 127
17:16 .... 214, 286
19:5–6 234
19:6 197
19:9 342
21:15 203
21:17 203
21:22 163
21–24 196
22:22–24 196
23:14 232
24:1 315
30:23 189
33:4 283
34:28 250

Leviticus

4:27 321
16:8 223
16:29 240
16:31 240
17–26 234
18:3–4 234
18:24 234
19:18 .... 80, 126
19:26 223
20:23 234
23:26–32 240
25:23 195

Numbers

1:26 181
3:35 185
11:16–25 315
14:39 283
20:25–28 280
21:35 324
22:3 326
22:8 312
24:7 .... 284, 362
24:20 .... 284, 286, 339
27:4 251
27:8 251
29:7–11 240
32:5 258

Deuteronomy

1:17 152
2:25 .... 323, 326
2:34 233
3:5 329
3:6 324
3:20 339
4:10 326
4:25–28 195
4:30–31 196
5:1 299
5:29 326
6:1–5 326
6:2 326
6:14 248
7:1–4 186
7:4 248
8:20 195
9:4 250
10:12 326
11:25 .... 323, 331
12:9 339
12:9–10 339
13:4 326
13:11 326
14:1–2 280
17:17 194
18:10 223
19:5 219
19:15 219
21:15–17 194
21:18–21 203
21:22–23 339
21:23 205
23:1 185
24:1 356
25:17–18 214
25:17–19 .... 41, 127, 220, 286, 331
25:19 .... 58, 319, 339, 340
28 235
28:1–13 167
28:10 321
28:20 232
28:28 232
28:36 .... 195, 235
28:43–44 235
28:47 156
28:51 232
28:63 232
28:63–64 195
28:64 235
28:65 232
29:25–28 195
30 235
30:1–10 251
30:7 .... 235, 331
31 95
31:16–18 .... 122, 196
31:17 123
31:18 .... 117, 122, 364
31:19 330
31:29 122
31–32 .... 122, 123
32 .... 123, 286, 330
32:19–20 196
32:20 .... 123, 286, 330, 364
32:21 123
32:24 286
32:25–26 286
32:27 123
32:28–43 196
32:30 .... 123, 291
32:32–33 124
32:35 .... 126, 250
32:36 .... 123, 250

32:36–43 .... 124, 286, 364
32:41 .... 124, 126
32:43 .... 123, 126

Joshua

1 267
1:13 339
1:15 339
2:9 .... 323, 326
2:11 322
4:24 321
6:17–21 324
7:1–5 325
7:11 325
7:14 181
7:14–18 223
7:24–25 325
8:24–26 324
12:9–24 335
15:18 255
18:6–10 223

Judges

1:1 137
2:14 123
3:8 123
3:12–29 302
3:22 335
4:2 123
4:9 123
4:17–22 302
4–5 97
6:34 267
8:4–21 125
9 251
9:20 251
9:53–56 251
9:57 251
10:7 123
13:5 172
13:7 172
14:1–4 302
14:19–20 302
17:5 332
18:20 156
18:24 255
21:25 302

Ruth

1:1 137
2:2 258
3 258
3:3 257
4:13 189
4:15 312

1 Samuel

1:1–8 194
1:4–8 193
1:21 332
4:21 172
6:18 329
7:6 250
9:1 183
9:5 172
10:20–21 223
11:6 267
12 137
12:1–4 167
14:24 250
14:42 223
15 .... 41, 58, 91, 214, 286, 323, 337
15:3 .... 127, 220, 310, 319, 324, 325, 336
15:21–23 98
15:26 336
15:28 164
17:23 361
20:26 279
20:41 .... 92, 216
21:8 233
24:8 .... 92, 216
25:8 307
31:13 240

2 Samuel

1:11 280
1:11–12 238
1:12 250
1:23 226
2:1 137
3:13–15 179
3:31 280
3:35 250
5:6–15 194
6:20–23 164
7:6 249
7:14 .... 185, 197
8:11 102
11 179
11:4 189
12:1–10 295
12:1–12 278
12:16 118
12:16–22 249
12:30 320
14 239
14:1–22 295
15:1–6 238
15:2 203
15:30 283
16:1 172
16:5 183
16:21 189
16:22 189
20 .... 97, 301
20:2 317
21:5 317
21:8 317
21:9 338
22:34 227
23:8 232
24:1–25 325

1 Kings

1:2–3 179
1:33 280

3:13 ... 167
3:28 ... 239
5:8 ... 316
5:11 ... 279
7:16 ... 158
10:13 ... 146
10:17–18 ... 118
10:23 ... 167
11:1–8 ... 194
11:28 ... 332
11:41 ... 24, 219
12:26 ... 279
12:27–29 ... 250
13:4 ... 314
14:29 ... 24, 360
14:30 ... 359
15:23 ... 359
15:31 ... 360
15:32 ... 359
19:19 ... 280
20:16 ... 157
21:27 ... 240
21:27–29 ... 250
22:9 ... 261
22:39 ... 359

2 Kings

2:13 ... 280
6:26 ... 239
6:26–28 ... 238
6:30 ... 238
16:6 ... 181
17:24–28 ... 322
19:35 ... 251
20:12–19 ... 152
21:13 ... 330
22:1–3 ... 149
22:3 ... 149
24:10–16 ... 183
24:14–17 ... 184
25:25 ... 181

1 Chronicles

2:29 ... 185
5:12 ... 118
5:14 ... 185
11:18 ... 185
12:33 ... 161
22:13 ... 267
25:8 ... 223
29:1 ... 141
29:11 ... 151
29:19 ... 141
29:23 ... 140

2 Chronicles

2:10 ... 102
6:33 ... 321
7:14 ... 265
9:8 ... 239
17:1–7 ... 149
17:7 ... 149
17:10 ... 323
20:1–4 ... 240
20:3 ... 118
29:1–3 ... 149
34:1–3 ... 149
34:19 ... 280

Ezra

2:2 ... 91, 182
4:4 ... 321
4:6 ... 140
4:13 ... 293
4:15 ... 226, 293
4:22 ... 293
5:17 ... 228
7:14 ... 161
8:21 ... 118, 249
8:23 ... 249
8:36 ... 154
9 ... 19
9:1–4 ... 92
9–10 ... 186
10:6 ... 283

Nehemiah

1:1 ... 141
1:3 ... 54
2:2 ... 239, 299
2:5 ... 228
2:7 ... 228
2:8 ... 141, 146
5:5 ... 102
5:15 ... 331
7:2 ... 141
7:6 ... 54
8:10–12 ... 341
8:12 ... 341
9:1 ... 240
9:1–3 ... 118
9:24 ... 333
10:10 ... 19
13:23–27 ... 92
13:23–28 ... 166
13:23–30 ... 19
13:23–31 ... 186

Esther

1 ... 11, 56, 99, 101, 102, 144, 168, 201, 228, 231, 258, 262, 264, 301, 316, 330, 338, 346, 361
1:1 ... 25, 52, 56, 136, 137, 152
1:1–2 ... 128, 136, 150, 157
1:1–3 ... 50
1:1–9 ... 136
1:2 ... 54, 100, 140
1:2–12 ... 304
1:3 ... 11, 100, 140, 147, 149, 150, 177, 193, 361
1:3–2:23 ... 128, 144, 145
1:3–4 ... 51, 99
1:3–9 ... 128, 144, 145, 149
1:3–12 ... 261

1:3–22 .... 128, 144, 145
1:4 .... 88, 100, 148, 151, 277
1:4–8 167
1:5 .... 148, 150, 152
1:5–8 99
1:6 .... 13, 148, 153
1:7 .... 100, 150, 154, 174
1:8 .... 36, 148, 154, 155
1:9 .... 99, 100, 148, 155
1:9–12 53
1:10 .... 124, 139, 148, 156, 241, 300
1:10–11 .... 44, 211
1:10–12 .... 66, 128, 144, 145, 167
1:10–22 211
1:11 .... 17, 56, 86, 100, 158
1:12 .... 97, 159, 211
1:13 .... 26, 148, 160
1:13–22 .... 128, 144, 145, 149
1:14 .... 56, 139, 148, 161, 361
1:15 ...... 100, 154, 161, 311, 312, 354
1:15–22 170
1:16 148
1:16–18 .... 66, 162
1:16–21 89
1:17 .... 88, 102, 148
1:17–18 211
1:18 .... 97, 148, 361
1:19 .... 53, 100, 101, 154, 163, 351, 355, 361
1:19–20 97
1:19–22 .... 66, 100, 346
1:20 .... 100, 102, 117, 148, 164, 165, 277
1:20–22 211
1:21 .... 101, 162, 163
1:21–22 165
1:22 .... 50, 102, 148, 164, 271, 316
1–8 .... 20, 20, 24, 24
2 .... 69, 99, 257, 331, 338, 346
2:1 .... 174, 177, 301
2:1–4 .... 51, 66, 128, 145, 193
2:1–18 .... 128, 145, 172
2:2 178
2:2–3 181
2:2–4 89
2:3 .... 100, 174, 180
2:4 .... 44, 75, 100, 101, 163, 177, 180
2:5 .... 62, 90, 181, 183, 197
2:5–6 .... 53, 183
2:5–7 .... 128, 145,
2:6 .... 54, 90, 100, 174, 181, 183, 195
2:7 .... 91, 94, 95, 175, 181, 184, 196
2:8 .... 96, 100, 154, 174, 175, 185, 262
2:8–9 241
2:8–15 300
2:8–18 .... 128, 145,
2:9 .... 96, 107, 163, 174, 187, 193
2:10 .... 92, 175, 188, 197, 250
2:10–13 175
2:11 .... 96, 188
2:12 .... 51, 154, 175, 174, 189, 198
2:13 .... 96, 174, 190
2:13–14 .... 96, 162
2:14 .... 139, 175, 190, 193, 201, 241
2:15 .... 42, 86, 96, 107, 174, 175, 190, 191, 193, 241, 258, 311
2:15–16 175
2:15–17 113
2:16 .... 11, 96, 100, 175, 177, 192
2:17 .... 56, 86, 92, 96, 100, 107, 175, 177, 193
2:18 ..... 99, 107, 146, 176, 193, 261, 304
2:19 .... 62, 201,
2:19–22 201
2:19–23 ...... 128, 145, 200
2:20 .... 74, 102, 107, 201, 203, 249, 354
2:21 .... 201, 204, 241, 274, 277, 314
2:21–22 207
2:21–23 92
2:22 .... 201, 203, 205, 245
2:23 .... 56, 107, 205, 206, 219, 346, 355, 360
3 .... 92, 144, 304, 331
3:1 .... 77, 108, 213, 213, 277, 311, 332
3:1–2 268
3:1–4 77
3:1–4:17 ...... 128, 210, 212
3:1–6 149
3:1–7 .... 100, 129, 212
3:1–15 211
3:2 .... 56, 100, 102, 211, 216, 222, 250, 298
3:2–3 92
3:2–4 .... 76, 216
3:3 .... 100, 163, 211
3:3–4 102

3:4........ 213, 218, 219, 283
3:5............62, 93, 97, 107, 211, 213, 219
3:5–15.......................... 145
3:6 ....93, 94, 100, 213, 219, 223, 232, 271
3:7 .... 56, 81, 213, 220, 223, 238, 350
3:7–15.........................106
3:8 ....89, 98, 100, 102, 108, 211, 225, 226, 227, 231, 234, 235, 270, 292, 293
3:8–9 ...77, 188, 292, 294
3:8–11 .... 89, 129, 212
3:8–12......................... 225
3:8–13...........................62
3:8–15 .... 51, 129, 212, 225
3:9 ....98, 100, 101, 163, 228, 232, 291, 332
3:10 ...... 77, 103, 127, 226, 230, 309, 311, 320
3:11 ....226, 230, 242
3:12.......50, 140, 231, 232, 250, 316, 316, 332
3:12–14........................315
3:12–15................ 129, 211, 212, 308
3:13.........56, 77, 103, 108, 226, 229, 232, 235, 243, 316, 318, 320, 333
3:14 ....154, 233, 319
3:15 ....89, 98, 99, 100, 103, 108, 154, 233, 261, 262, 304, 316, 320, 321
3–7...............................22
4.....96, 100, 157, 211, 316
4:1 ...... 103, 108, 236, 237, 242, 320
4:1–3 ....129, 212
4:1–17 ....129, 129, 212, 236, 256
4:2.......108, 237, 239, 320
4:3...... 100, 103, 108, 118, 237, 240, 241, 248, 250, 262, 304, 321
4:4 .... 96, 129, 212, 237, 240
4:4–17 ....129, 212
4:5.............. 237, 241, 242
4:5–9..........129, 212, 300
4:6 242
4:7 .... 230, 237, 242, 291
4:7–8 237
4:8 96
4:8–9 242
4:9 237
4:10.............................243
4:10–5:2..................... 145
4:10–17...............129, 212
4:11 ....89, 96, 102, 108, 237, 242, 244, 258
4:12.................... 237, 246
4:13 ....246, 250
4:13–14 ....96, 104, 105, 118, 246
4:14 ....92, 100, 118, 186, 242, 246, 251, 339, 343
4:15–16...................... 248
4:16......................107, 118
4:17.............96, 237, 249
5..........................205, 264
5:1............... 100, 241, 256
5:1–2..................129, 253, 256, 264
5:1–5 ....129, 254
5:1–7:10 ....129, 253, 254, 269
5:1–8......... 106, 129, 254, 255, 256
5:2 .... 96, 113, 254, 258, 311
5:2–4 98
5:3........................100, 259
5:3–5 .... 129, 254, 266
5:4...................77, 97, 117, 163, 254, 256, 260, 290
5:4–8............................99
5:5.........89, 256, 260, 261
5:5–6...........................262
5:5–8.......... 129, 254, 304
5:6 .... 44, 100, 124, 256, 290, 337
5:7 ....13, 106, 262
5:7–8 262
5:8 .... 96, 97, 101, 163, 254, 256, 311
5:9 ....108, 268, 269, 271, 297, 298
5:9–14 ....100, 106, 129, 254, 256, 268, 283
5:10 ....93, 269, 271
5:11 ...... 94, 268, 272, 334
5:11–12............... 108, 270
5:11–13........................167
5:12........................ 94, 108
5:13....... 77, 117, 228, 270, 284, 293
5:14 ....51, 56, 93, 103, 108, 145, 268, 269, 271, 272, 276
5–7................................ 61
6 ....66, 89, 145, 205, 216, 263, 270, 290, 309
6:1 .... 105, 219, 274, 275, 360

6:1–3 .... 129, 254, 285
6:1–5 66
6:1–14 .... 106, 129, 254, 273
6:2 .... 274, 276
6:3 .... 89, 277, 278
6:3–5 178
6:4 .... 93, 276
6:4–5 .... 215, 278
6:4–9 254
6:4–10 .... 129, 254, 285
6:5–9 62
6:6 .... 42, 93, 94, 164, 277, 278
6:6–9 103
6:7 .... 164, 279
6:7–9 .... 4, 270
6:8 .... 56, 100, 275, 279
6:8–9 241
6:9 .... 105, 164, 275, 279, 281
6:10 .... 275, 276, 278, 281
6:10–11 .... 241, 254
6:11 .... 129, 255, 275, 282, 320
6:11–12 103
6:12 .... 93, 283, 299
6:12–14 .... 129, 254, 254, 269
6:13 .... 77, 94, 105, 108, 119, 125, 218, 220, 247, 270, 275, 283, 285, 362
6:14 .... 108, 242, 284
6:14–7:8 99
7 .... 23, 99, 145, 205, 264, 271, 312, 331
7:1 .... 98, 290
7:1–5 301
7:1–6 .... 129, 254, 255
7:1–7 304
7:1–9 100
7:1–10 .... 106, 129, 255, 288
7:2 .... 44, 124, 290, 312, 337
7:3 .... 96, 97, 101, 163, 254, 291, 311
7:3–4 .... 197, 313
7:3–6 .... 206, 261, 348
7:4 .... 77, 102, 123, 228, 230, 289, 291, 296
7:5 .... 293, 295
7:6 .... 93, 123, 289, 292, 296, 298
7:6–8 .... 129, 254, 255
7:7 .... 102, 107, 117, 124, 254, 297, 298
7:8 .... 56, 66, 89, 102, 108, 124, 289, 296, 298, 302
7:8–10 .... 129, 254, 255
7:9 .... 66, 89, 145, 217, 241, 289, 300, 314, 321
7:9–10 .... 62, 103, 206
7:10 .... 24, 56, 107, 254, 301
8 304
8:1 .... 107, 307, 308, 334
8:1–2 .... 129, 145, 305, 307
8:1–9:32 .... 129, 304, 305
8:1–17 .... 106, 129, 305
8:2 .... 62, 96, 103, 217, 307, 309, 323, 334
8:3 .... 97, 307, 310, 311
8:3–8 .... 129, 305, 308
8:3–12 98
8:4 311
8:5 .... 96, 101, 163, 307, 311
8:5–8 89
8:6 312
8:7 .... 107, 307, 313
8:8 .... 26, 163, 304, 313, 314, 351
8:9 .... 50, 140, 307, 315, 316, 332
8:9–14 .... 129, 305
8:9–17 .... 129, 305, 308
8:10 .... 56, 241, 316
8:11 .... 101, 102, 103, 126, 317, 318, 324, 336
8:11–12 304
8:12 .... 307, 319
8:13 .... 22, 24, 124, 127, 319
8:14 .... 45, 100, 103, 261, 316, 320
8:15 .... 103, 183, 188, 320, 334
8:15–17 .... 129, 305
8:16 .... 183, 277, 321
8:16–17 240
8:17 .... 22, 23, 77, 99, 98, 103, 240, 304, 307, 321, 350
9 .... 24, 99, 113, 264, 304
9:1 .... 100, 107, 123, 330, 342
9:1–2 339
9:1–5 .... 129, 305, 330
9:1–10 .... 129, 305, 330
9:1–17 .... 106, 145
9:1–19 .... 25, 129, 305, 327, 330, 346
9:2 .... 240, 331
9:3 .... 22, 77, 107, 240, 329, 332
9:3–4 107
9:4 332
9:5 .... 124, 329, 331, 333
9:6 .... 328, 333
9:6–10 .... 129, 305, 330

9:6–15 339
9:7 329
9:7–8 13
9:7–9 334
9:7–10 338
9:8 329
9:9 .... 57, 329, 335
9:10 .... 319, 329, 336
9:11 .... 109, 329
9:11–12 336
9:11–13 .... 130, 305
9:11–15 .... 51, 130, 305, 330
9:11–16 51
9:12 .... 97, 316
9:12–14 89
9:13 .... 101, 126, 163, 329, 337
9:13–14 .... 22, 206
9:13–15 141
9:14 339
9:14–15 .... 130, 305
9:15 .... 319, 339, 341
9:16 .... 188, 329, 331, 339, 341
9:16–17 .... 66, 130, 305, 330
9:16–19 .... 130, 305
9:17 .... 22, 99, 107, 228, 341
9:17–18 341
9:17–19 .... 130, 305
9:17–22 126
9:17–23 .... 22, 261
9:18 .... 99, 126, 228, 341
9:18–19 .... 330, 338
9:18–22 100
9:18–32 106
9:19 .... 307, 329, 341, 346, 347
9:20 .... 18, 345, 346, 353
9:20–10:3 21
9:20–21 341
9:20–22 .... 130, 240, 305, 345
9:20–28 .... 130, 305
9:20–32 .... 25, 81, 130, 305, 344, 346
9:21 .... 345, 346
9:22 .... 70, 72, 228, 307, 341, 347, 355
9:22–23 .... 99, 104
9:23 .... 345, 347, 356
9:23–26 345
9:23–28 .... 130, 305, 346
9:23–32 97
9:24 .... 81, 311, 345, 348, 348
9:24–25 .... 22, 347, 348
9:24–26 346
9:24–28 81
9:25 .... 22, 349
9:26 349
9:26–32 104
9:27 .... 240, 350, 352
9:27–28 351
9:28 .... 43, 345, 356
9:28–32 345
9:29 .... 97, 175, 345, 352, 353, 353
9:29–32 .... 130, 305, 346, 351, 352
9:30 .... 345, 353, 361
9:30–32 345
9:31 .... 354, 362
9:32 .... 97, 101, 354
9–10 .... 20, 21, 22, 23, 25
10 24
10:1 .... 97, 359
10:1–2 25
10:1–3 .... 25, 106, 130, 358
10:2 .... 18, 22, 24, 60, 90, 92, 93, 100, 352, 360
10:3 .... 18, 183, 359, 361, 362

Job

1:10 167
1:12 314
1–2 241
2:11 232
6:27 223
12:25 157
13:24 122
21:20 313
28:28 65

Psalms

1:1–3 362
2:7 .... 185, 197
7:15–16 126
10:6 279
10:11 279
10:13 279
10:14 196
14:1 279
21:5 151
22:18 223
30 355
30:4 355
35:13 241
44:24 122
49 167
49:20 167
53:1 279
55:20 314
55:21 314
57:6 126
69:32 313
69:33 313
73:6 285
90:10 315
94:4–7 285

96:6 ... 151
97:11 ... 321
104:1 ... 257
105:38 ... 323
107:25 ... 157
111:10 ... 326
112:1 ... 167
112:3 ... 167
115:2–3 ... 2
118:17 ... 356

Proverbs

1:7 ... 65, 116, 326
3:5–6 ... 362
3:15 ... 294
7:17 ... 189
9:10 ... 65
11:28 ... 167
12:21 ... 362
13:22 ... 324
14:20 ... 146
15:15 ... 156
16:6 ... 326
16:18 ... 285
16:33 ... 224
17:26 ... 146
18:1 ... 226
18:12 ... 272
18:18 ... 223
19:13 ... 335
22:20 ... 41
26:27 ... 126
27:2 ... 272
27:15 ... 335
27:20 ... 273
31:4 ... 156

Ecclesiastes

1:8 ... 273
5:10 ... 167
8:11 ... 147
9:11 ... 363
12:2 ... 65

Song of Solomon

1:13 ... 189
3:6 ... 189
4:6 ... 189
4:14 ... 189
5:3 ... 313
5:5 ... 189
5:13 ... 189
8:6 ... 42

Isaiah

1:15 ... 122
1:23 ... 196
2:10 ... 323
3:13–24 ... 285
8:14 ... 39
10:1–4 ... 167
10:2 ... 196
10:20–23 ... 251
14:13 ... 279
32:11 ... 238
35:10 ... 355
39:8 ... 353
45:15 ... 122
47:10 ... 279
50:1 ... 291
51:11 ... 355
53:6 ... 343
53:10 ... 343
59:2 ... 122
64:7 ... 122
65:16 ... 43

Jeremiah

1:14–16 ... 250
1:16 ... 248
3:19 ... 197
5:26–29 ... 167
5:28 ... 196
7:1–15 ... 251
7:18 ... 248
9:23–24 ... 167
14:4 ... 283
14:12 ... 232
17:4 ... 228
17:6 ... 313
21:7 ... 232
21:9 ... 232
23:19 ... 241
24:10 ... 232
27:8 ... 232
27:13 ... 232
29:7 ... 208
29:7–9 ... 207
29:17 ... 232
29:18 ... 232
30:11 ... 286
31:12–13 ... 355
31:29–30 ... 325
31:35 ... 286
31:37 ... 286
32:36 ... 232
32:44 ... 312
33:6 ... 353
34:17 ... 232
42:17 ... 232
42:22 ... 232
44:13 ... 232
48:7 ... 167
49:4 ... 167
50 ... 207
50:18–20 ... 251
50:43 ... 207
51 ... 207
51:7 ... 157
51:34–35 ... 207
52:1–4 ... 149
52:22 ... 158

Ezekiel

1:1 ... 85
5:17 ... 232
6:11 ... 232
6:12 ... 232
7:15 ... 232
7:27 ... 257

11:13–21 ... 251
12:6 ... 232
14:14 ... 232
16 ... 196
16:40 ... 317
18:1–3 ... 325
22:7 ... 196
23:42 ... 320
26:16 ... 257
28:2 ... 285

Daniel

1 ... 81
1:6–7 ... 184
1:7 ... 182
1:8 ... 197
1:9 ... 187
2 ... 61, 81, 142, 197, 207, 217
2:12–14 ... 284
2:12–16 ... 197
2:47 ... 197
2:49 ... 203
3 ... 207
3:8 ... 62
3:8–12 ... 62
3:22 ... 62
3:30 ... 62
4 ... 61, 142, 207, 287
4:6 ... 284
4:30 ... 285
4:36 ... 151
4:37 ... 285
5 ... 168, 217
5:2 ... 159
5:7 ... 284, 320
5:10 ... 159
5:21 ... 228
5:22 ... 62
5:29 ... 320, 361
6 ... 61, 62, 81, 142, 207
6:1 ... 137
6:2 ... 140, 140, 293
6:3 ... 293
6:4 ... 293
6:5 ... 293
6:8 ... 53, 163
6:11 ... 53
6:12 ... 163
6:15 ... 53
6:25–27 ... 197
6:28 ... 62
7 ... 142
8:2 ... 141
9:1 ... 139, 140
9:3 ... 240
9:17 ... 352
9:21 ... 332
9:24–27 ... 183
10:2 ... 283
11:16 ... 333
11:42 ... 314

Hosea

3:1–2 ... 291
4:6 ... 242
7:8 ... 330
11:8 ... 235

Joel

1:8 ... 241
3:2 ... 146
3:3 ... 223

Amos

4:1 ... 167
9:8 ... 251

Jonah

3:3–8 ... 249
3:5 ... 250
4:2 ... 261

Micah

3:4 ... 122
5:7–15 ... 251
7:8–20 ... 251

Nahum

3:10 ... 223

Habakkuk

1:6 ... 250

Zephaniah

2:15 ... 279

Zechariah

8:19 ... 354

Malachi

2:11 ... 92
2:11–12 ... 187
3:5 ... 196

Apocrypha

Tobit

1:10–12 ... 81
1:21–22 ... 61
4:12–13 ... 81

Judith

10:3–4 ... 257
14:10 ... 322

Greek Esther

10:4–11:1 ... 14, 359
11:2–12:6 ... 14, 359
12:6 ... 216
13:1–7 ... 14
13:8–14:19 ... 14, 44
13:9–11 ... 110
13:12–14 ... 216
14:5–7 ... 110
14:11 ... 110
14:14 ... 110
14:15–18 ... 110
14:17 ... 188
15:1–16 ... 14

16:1–24 14

Sirach

1:1–2 31
44–50 32
44–51 26

49:10 32
49:11–13 32

1 Maccabees

1:15 23
2:39–41 188

7 33
7:26–49 85

2 Maccabees

14:12–15:36 85
15:36 .... 33, 347, 350

New Testament

Matthew

3:9 252
5:31–32 356
5:43–48 299
10:16 223
19:1–9 356
21:22 169
21:33–45 278
26:65 238
27:35 224

Mark

6 .... 43, 266
6:14–28 259
6:22 44
6:23 .... 44, 260, 266
6:28 44
7:22 285
10:45 169
12:40 303

Luke

2:37 118
5:33 118
7:41 137
14:7–11 285
14:11 285
16:1 137
17:33 247
18:2 137

John

3:14–15 115
12:31 142
14:18 196
14:30 142
16:11 142
16:20–24 355
16:30 44
16:33 266
17:14 235
19:30 249
21 45
21:15–17 44

Acts

1:24–26 224
2:22–24 302
4:23–31 267
4:32–37 296
5 296
5:1 296
5:5 296
5:6 296
5:10 296
5:29 .... 169, 170
14:23 118

Romans

3:1 23
8:15 197
9:4 197
11:29 286
11:36 xii
12:2 363
12:19–20 299
13:1–7 .... 142, 169, 170, 207, 208
13:7 223

1 Corinthians

12:8–12 267
13 232

2 Corinthians

5:11 326

Galatians

4:4–6 197
5:11 23
5:22–23 266

Ephesians

1:5 197
2:3 343
2:4–5 343
2:11 23
5:25–33 170
5:33 170

Philippians

2:6–8 168
3:3 23

1 Timothy

2:9–10 199
3:2 194
3:12 194

2 Timothy

3:16 .... xi, 40

Titus

1:6 194
2:5 170

Hebrews

9 115
13:7 170

James

1:27 196

1 Peter

2:9–10 235

2:12 235

2:13–14 170

2:13–17 207

2:17 326

1 John

4:18 326

Revelation

6:9–11 303

13:8 343